# Workfare States

# WORKFARE STATES

Jamie Peck

*Foreword by*
FRANCES FOX PIVEN AND RICHARD CLOWARD

THE GUILFORD PRESS
New York    London

**Library of Congress Cataloging-in-Publication Data**
Peck, Jamie.
    Workfare states / Jamie Peck.
      p. cm.
    Includes bibliographical references and index.
    ISBN 1-57230-635-1 (cloth) — ISBN 1-57230-636-X (pbk.)
    1. Public welfare—United States.  2. Public welfare—Canada.
3. Public welfare—Great Britain.  4. Welfare recipients—
Employment—United States.  5. Welfare recipients—
Employment—Canada.  6. Welfare recipients—Employment—
Great Britain.  7. United States—Social policy—1993–
8. Canada—Social policy.  9. Great Britain—Social policy—1979–
I. Title.

HV95 .P43 2001
362.5—dc21
                                                00-067764

*This is for Hannah*

# Contents

Foreword      ix

List of Figures and Tables      xiii

List of Abbreviations      xv

Acknowledgments      xvii

CHAPTER ONE    **INTRODUCTION**      1
     *States of Workfare*

     Defining Workfare    9
     Transnationalizing Workfare    16
     Workfarist Labor Regulation    21
     Plan of the Book    24

**PART I**      **ROOTS OF WORKFARE**

CHAPTER TWO    **REGULATION**      31
     *Workhouse/Welfare/Workfare*

     Relief and Regulation    34
     Regulating Labor    39
     Spaces of Regulation    58
     Situating Workfare    77

CHAPTER THREE    *WORKFARE*      83
     *What Does It Mean?*

     Words of Workfare    84
     (Re)defining Workfare    90
     Reading Clinton's Lips    97
     Costly Rhetoric    103
     The Quiet Revolution    111
     The Politics of "Disentitlementarianism"    117

## Part II    SPACES OF WORKFARE

CHAPTER FOUR    POSTWELFARE STATES?                                    129
*Geopolitics of "Reform"*

Locating Massachusetts    131
Making New-Style Workfare    133
Massachusetts's After-Welfare Settlement    143
Making Space for the Workfare State?    161


CHAPTER FIVE    LOCAL DISCIPLINE                                       168
*Workfare at Work*

The Method and the Message    172
Work-First Labor Regulation    182
Selling Riverside: Discourse and Practice    190
Workfare versus the Cities    197
Go to Work, or Else: Toward "True" Workfare    201


## Part III    ECHOES OF WORKFARE

CHAPTER SIX    CANADA'S PATH                                           213
*Permeable Welfare/Fragile Workfare*

Toward Continental Workfare?    215
Permeable Fordism and Permeable Welfare    222
In and Against Ontario's Workfare State    236
Beyond the Safety Net    253


CHAPTER SEVEN    ANOTHER NEW DEAL                                      261
*Workfare, United Kingdom Style*

Creeping Compulsion: Conservative Incrementalism    264
Radical Consensus: Ending Beveridge    274
Exploring Local Workfare    292
Making a New Deal: The New Labour Program    299
Britain's Winding Path to Workfare    326


CHAPTER EIGHT    CONCLUSION                                            341
*Workfare States?*

Functions of Workfare    350
Geopolitics of Workfare    358


References                                                            369
Index                                                                 399
About the Author                                                      414

# Foreword

In New York City, some 45,000 people, mainly women, sweep the streets and clean the subways and the parks. They do the work once done by unionized municipal employees. But instead of a paycheck and a living wage, they get a welfare check that leaves them far below the poverty level, and they have none of the benefits and protections of unionized workers. Perhaps just as bad, they have become public spectacles of abject and degraded labor—of slave labor, many of them say. How could this be happening in New York City, the immigrant capital of the country and the seedbed of its social democratic and welfarist traditions?

In this book, Jamie Peck goes a long way toward answering this question. He places American-style workfare in international perspective, showing that while the United States is the indisputable pioneer, the campaign to supplant or transform the rights-based income support programs of the industrial-era welfare state is occurring on a wide scale. That campaign is directed not only at cash assistance for families headed by mothers—the main focus in the United States—but at unemployment and disability benefits, and even housing, medical, and food assistance. Making work a condition of social assistance has become an international project.

Moreover, it is a project that is gaining momentum as it spreads. In the United Kingdom, the Blair government has leaped ahead of the Conservatives in a campaign to attach work requirements to benefit programs for the unemployed and single mothers. In Canada, especially Ontario where a right wing provincial government has taken the lead, workfare has become the new paradigm for welfare state reform. Peck provides us with detailed and careful comparative case studies of the programs in each of these countries, but he also makes clear that what he calls the workfare juggernaut is unfolding elsewhere—in New Zealand and Australia, for example—and even penetrating the strong and entrenched welfare states of continental Europe.

As Peck is at pains to point out, each of these workfare projects is different, inevitably shaped not only by the workfare campaign, but by distinctive national histories and institutions. Peck explains that the workfare project takes shape in ways that are path dependent and institutionally mediated, just as the rights-based welfare state was influenced by the distinctive national context in which it developed.

Nevertheless, and notwithstanding these national (and subnational) variations, a common direction is evident, and it is in explaining the broad direction of the workfare project that Peck's work is both theoretically illuminating and politically important. The workfare offensive against the traditional welfare state and its rights-based benefits is an effort to construct a new system of labor regulation, to enforce work under the new conditions of casualization, falling wages and underemployment that characterize postindustrial labor markets in the mother countries. As Peck says, in the new international labor market, "McJobs" is being complemented by "McWelfare." The principles are evident everywhere, despite specific national differences. Where older welfare programs are ambiguous about the causes of poverty, the workfare projects stridently assert that the causes lie in the individual and the failure of individual effort. Accordingly, workfare projects deter or even refuse claims based on needs, and deliver whatever assistance they provide only on condition that people work or engage in work-like behaviors intended to move them into the labor force. Meanwhile, the projects focus on the individual's failings and insist on the exercise of program authority to demand correction of those failings, mainly by requiring work.

Of course, we should not overstate the contrast between the old welfare and the new workfare, especially in the United States. American programs for the poor have always been riddled with a tangle of multiple and contradictory rules that had the effect of according program staff a great deal of discretion in handling presumably rights-based claims. American programs were always shaped by a preoccupation with work enforcement, which is the main reason benefits were kept low in accord with the longstanding principle of "less eligibility," a principle demanding that recipients be worse off than even the lowest-paid independent laborer. Just as important, material disincentives to "dependence" were reinforced by the degrading treatment accorded recipients, thus adding a social principle of less eligibility to the market principle.

Over time, of course, the American programs improved, especially in response to the urban protests and riots of the 1960s. Benefits became more rights-based and meager cash assistance was supplemented by new medical and nutritional programs. Continuing low benefits and degrading treatment notwithstanding, this was a gain, especially for poor women. For one thing, the availability of non-wage income meant that even poor women were able to do the mothering and family care work that women have always done, and which is surely not less valuable than the jobs flipping burgers or cleaning offices that were their alternative. The availability of welfare also meant that poor women gained a small measure of independence from men, also surely not a bad thing. And many women used a spell on welfare to gain the educational credentials that would help them to escape from the low wage trap. To be sure, the work-enforcing features of welfare had not been eliminated; rather, they were reflected in the persistence of low grant levels, in the continuing rituals of public degradation of recipients, and in periodic efforts to "reform" welfare by introducing new work requirements, for example, for the mothers of very young children. Ironically, these features, as well as political efforts to amplify them, contributed to the cultural marginalization of the recipient poor which made it easier for workfare reformers to mobilize widespread public support for their project. Thus, the rhetoric of the campaign to replace welfare with workfare in the United States was popular because it told a story that invoked the themes in American culture that demonized the poor, and especially poor women, using ancient images of the slothful and licentious poor. Still, all this notwithstanding, on balance and despite its deep flaws, public assistance did in fact help the poor, particularly women, while it lasted.

The workfare offensive is aimed at just these modest achievements of the old welfare state. Peck's description of that offensive is invaluable, in part because he refuses to consider the success of the campaign inevitable. True, workfare meshes with the requirements of the new contingent labor market. However, the propelling force behind the workfare campaign arises not from some quasi-mystical postindustrial economic imperative but from neoliberal politics, from political ideas and political strategies conceived by political actors. And politics is the realm of voluntarism, of the struggle of human actors to realize advantage and resist predation. After all, even the Malthusian-inspired "poor law," promoted by the rising English manufacturing class, was ultimately defeated. Jamie Peck has written this book as a contribution to the rise of a politics of resistance that could defeat the workfare juggernaut.

FRANCES FOX PIVEN
RICHARD A. CLOWARD

# List of Figures and Tables

TABLES

**TABLE 1.1.** Generic Welfare Structures and Workfare Strategies                                    13

**TABLE 2.1.** Modes of Labor-Market Regulation                                    51

**TABLE 2.2.** The Geography of the U.S. "Welfare Explosion"                                    67

**TABLE 2.3.** Three Worlds of Welfare and Three Paths to Workfare                                    75

**TABLE 2.4.** Local Forms of Workfare                                    78

**TABLE 3.1.** The Opportunity Society as a Discursive Project                                    109

**TABLE 3.2.** Constructing Choices, Constructing Dependents                                    121

**TABLE 4.1.** OBRA Work-Welfare Demonstrations                                    136

**TABLE 4.2.** Summary of Massachusetts's Welfare Reform, 1995                                    150

**TABLE 4.3.** Summary of Federal Welfare Reform, 1996                                    154

**TABLE 4.4.** Selected Features of State Welfare Reforms (for 30 States in November 1996)                                    155

**TABLE 7.1.** Programs for the Unemployed, 1994–1995                                    270

**TABLE 7.2.** Conditions Attached to Receipt of Unemployment Benefits, 1982—1996                                    294

**TABLE 7.3.** Labour's New Deal Program                                    304

FIGURES

**FIGURE 3.1.** Incidence of references to "workfare" in major U.S. newspapers, 1971–1999.    85

**FIGURE 3.2.** Excerpts from Newt Gingrich's *Language: A Key Mechanism of Control*.    86

**FIGURE 3.3.** A discursive map of "welfare dependency."    112

**FIGURE 3.4.** A discursive map of "workfare."    113

**FIGURE 5.1.** Riverside GAIN dress code.    176

**FIGURE 7.1.** Jobseeker's Agreement.    287

# List of Abbreviations

| | |
|---|---|
| AFDC | Aid to Families with Dependent Children (United States) |
| CAP | Canada Assistance Plan |
| CHST | Canada Health and Social Transfer |
| CLFDB | Canadian Labour Force Development Board |
| CWEP | Community Work Experience Program (United States) |
| DfEE | Department for Education and Employment (United Kingdom) |
| DTA | Department of Transitional Assistance (Massachusetts) |
| EI | Employment Insurance (Canada) |
| EITC | Earned Income Tax Credit (United States) |
| ES | Employment Service (United Kingdom) |
| ET | Employment and Training Choices (Massachusetts) |
| FSA | Family Support Act of 1988 (United States) |
| GA | General Assistance (United States) |
| GAIN | Greater Avenues for Independence (California) |
| HCD | Human capital development |
| HRD | Human Resources Development Canada |
| JOBS | Job Opportunities and Basic Skills Program (United States) |

| JSA | Jobseeker's Allowance (United Kingdom) |
|-----|---------------------------------------|
| LFA | Labor force attachment |
| MDRC | Manpower Demonstration Research Corporation (United States) |
| MSC | Manpower Services Commission (United Kingdom) |
| NGA | National Governors' Association (United States) |
| OBRA | Omnibus Budget Reconciliation Act of 1981 (United States) |
| OTAB | Ontario Training and Adjustment Board (Canada) |
| OW | Ontario Works (Canada) |
| PRWORA | Personal Responsibility and Work Reconciliation Act of 1996 (United States) |
| SWD | Supported Work Demonstrations (United States) |
| TANF | Temporary Assistance for Needy Families (United States) |
| TECs | Training and Enterprise Councils (United Kingdom) |
| UI | Unemployment Insurance (Canada) |
| WFTC | Working Families Tax Credit (United Kingdom) |
| WIN | Work Incentives Program (United States) |
| WPA | Works Progress Administration (United States) |
| WTP | Work and Training Program (Massachusetts) |
| YT | Youth Training Scheme (United Kingdom) |

# Acknowledgments

This has been a long project and I have accumulated a lot of debts. Peter Wissoker at The Guilford Press has been understanding and insightful, as ever. In a more formal sense, the Harkness Fellowships program of the Commonwealth Fund (New York), along with Johns Hopkins University, created the time and space for the book to happen by providing support during my initial period in the United States. Special thanks are due to Keith Kirby, Robert Kostrzewa, and William Plowden—and my fellow participants in the Harkness program—for all their help, advice, and timely skepticism. The later stages of the research were generously supported by the Economic and Social Research Council (Research Grant R000222543), the Leverhulme Trust (Research Fellowship 10896), the Canadian High Commission, and the Social Sciences and Humanities Research Council of Canada.

Thanks to all those who helped along the way, including Greg Clark, Paul Convery, Dan Finn, Meric Gertler, Mark Greenberg, David Harvey, Andy Herod, John Holmes, Margit Mayer, Laurie Miller, Andy Mitchell, John Rodgers, Bill Sheppard, Erica Schoenberger, Alan Deacon, Eddie Webster, Jane Wills, Dana Wise, David Wolfe, Erik Wright, and especially Bennett Harrison, who set the standard—in all kinds of ways—for work in this field. I have also benefited enormously from long-standing discussions and debates with my collaborators and cowriters over recent years, especially Mike Emmerich, Graham Haughton, Bob Jessop, Martin Jones, Tod Rutherford, Nik Theodore, and Adam Tickell. Bernard Hill set me straight on a few things, too. Michael Bradford, Huw Beynon, David Coates, Peter Dicken, Diane Elson, Mark Harvey, Dean Herd, Adam Holden, Dan Mansfield, David Purdy, Steve Quilley, Mike Savage, Hilary

xvii

Wainwright, Kevin Ward, Karel Williams, and the late Peter Baker all helped to make Manchester a stimulating place in which to research, write, and rewrite this book.

Closer to home, Bryony, Holly, and Hannah cheerfully put up with my frequent absences and absent-minded presences. At last, I can now answer the perennial question, which had started to get me seriously wondering in the final stages, "When will you be finished, Dad?" Now!

# CHAPTER ONE

# Introduction

## *States of Workfare*

This book takes aim at a moving target, *"workfare."* Taken here as a provocative regulatory signifier, workfare has come to acquire a broad and quite elastic meaning, both as a pithy, generic label for work-enforcing welfare reform and as a rather vague umbrella term for a wide range of welfare-to-work policies, job-training and employability programs, and active-benefit systems. Workfare represents a moving target because, from its first stirrings in the early 1970s, through the bold experiments of the 1980s, to the ostensibly seismic shifts of the 1990s, it denotes a policy field of immense—and in many ways growing—dynamism. The pace of reform is visibly accelerating, while the geographic reach of "workfarist" regulatory frameworks and workfare-style programming continues to expand. *Workfare States* offers a series of snapshots of this fast-moving phenomenon, focusing primarily on developments since the mid-1990s, with a view to assessing the scale and scope of what is sometimes called—quite appropriately in my view—the "workfare offensive."

This book is also something of a personal journey, which began in the summer of 1995 with a year's research leave from Manchester University in the United Kingdom. The opportunity to spend a year at Johns Hopkins University in Baltimore, and to travel extensively across the United States on the Harkness Fellowships program, presented me with a chance to discover what "workfare" was really about at the sharp end of delivery and to explore participant experience in states as diverse as Massachusetts, Mississippi, Texas, and California. Hardly innocent, these inquiries were motivated by a personal (and political) antipathy toward mandatory work programs for unemployed people, which had for many years been a shadowy presence in British debates. Here, the politically loaded and manifestly pejorative term *workfare* had been used by critics on the left—to some effect—to brand as irredeemably regressive almost any movement toward work enforcement, benefit curtailment, or compulsory programming in welfare policy. The image that this slogan conjured up was of degrading, demeaning, forced labor; in policy terms, it signified a spiteful conservative victimization of the poor. But more candidly, the other thing that most participants in British (and European) debates around poverty and unemployment also knew was that these programs, and their political patrons, usually barked much louder than they bit. Even in the United States, "real" workfare programs—those requiring welfare recipients literally to work for their dole checks—were relatively thin on the ground, and they were usually expensive, bureaucratic, and ineffective. This was a case, it seemed, of symbolic policy-making, in which the interests of both reformers and critics were served by exaggerating the scale, scope, and significance of workfare.

Given this context, and as a researcher critical of the principles of workfare, I was prepared at the beginning of this initial year in the United States to be deeply *under*whelmed by the reality of workfare on the ground, in its domestic setting. Big claims, small and symbolic policy, even smaller program—that sort of thing. But this state of knowing complacency could hardly have been less appropriate in the context of the realpolitik of U.S. welfare reform in 1995–1996. True, the real achievements of workfare programs were exceptionally modest, and in their purest, public-work-for-the-dole form they remained quite rare. Yet the *threat* of workfare was almost palpable, in part because in the United States it had come to represent much more than simply a "program" pushed into place by the zealous governors of a few right-wing states. Workfare, in its many guises and permutations, had come to serve as a vent for a whole range of anti-welfare sentiments and reform efforts. OK, so it was flawed, but it did provide some kind of alternative to welfare, and after all, what is so wrong with asking people to go to work? The burden of proof had apparently shifted: the emphasis had moved toward giving reformers their head, the welfare status quo having become practically indefensible.

The newly empowered House Republicans, in particular, were taking advantage of this situation by alternately denigrating welfare and talking up workfare experiments. The messages from the Clinton White House, still smarting from the administration's failure to steer through its version of federal welfare reform, were more mixed and muddled. On the one hand, they too took it as axiomatic that employment-oriented, root-

and-branch reform was both inevitable and overdue. On the other hand, the constituencies that have traditionally defended welfarist principles and welfare recipients found themselves variously weakened, preoccupied, and divided. Their power base systematically eroded, their interests marginalized, their case discredited, the supporters of welfare rights found themselves left behind, or shut out of, the debate. The sense of crisis around the "welfare mess"—itself partly a political creation—was such around this time that social advocates seemed to be fighting a lost cause when it came to the workfare debate. So, the workfare juggernaut rolled on; the debate, in turn, shifted away from principles and philosophy, and toward pragmatics and programs. Substantively, this narrow and truncated reform debate seemed only to be concerned with which *kind* of workfare-style settlement to move toward—hard or soft, locally managed or centrally steered, public or private, employability-oriented or training based, and so forth. Antipoverty advocates found themselves confronting this reform juggernaut in a tactically impossible situation: defending the poor and defending entitlements could easily be portrayed as conservative apologism, special pleading, or the defense of turf and vested institutional interests. Never mind that advocates themselves had been calling for reform for decades, now they were being portrayed as the opponents of change.

The tumultuous year 1995–1996, which ended in the presidential capitulation that was the 1996 federal reform, demonstrated to me at least that whatever it was, "workfare" was more than a figment of the conservative imagination. Understood as a broadly based, complex, and often contradictory "regulatory project," it represented a potent force. But only in the United States? Returning to the United Kingdom in the autumn of 1996, it seemed so. While John Major's Conservative government had pushed through significant reforms of the benefit system, and had recently authorized some small-scale workfare trials, this was a government in disarray. Tony Blair's "modernized" Labour Party seemed poised finally to take control in the following year's General Election. And while this would not initiate a socialist nirvana, new life would be breathed into the political process. Not least, Labour had pledged to tackle head-on the problems of unemployment and poverty, reversing years of denial, tokenism, and malign neglect. There would be a new welfare-to-work program for unemployed young people, the subject of an explicit preelection promise, and concerted attempts to tackle social exclusion. There would, for the first time, be a national minimum wage. Progress.

Following its comprehensive General Election victory, the party that won as New Labour set about governing as New Labour. Among the first announcements of the new administration came details of the welfare-to-work program-somewhat ironically called the "New Deal"—which would be strictly mandatory, more so in fact than previous Conservative schemes. Participants would be presented with a range of "options," including subsidized employment and full-time education, but in the oft-repeated language of ministers there would be "no fifth option" . . . of nonparticipation. The tough talking on welfare during the General Election campaign was more than a gesture toward middle-class taxpayers, it was real.

Subsequent proposals to restructure disability benefits and to cut allowances for lone parents would confirm that New Labour did indeed mean business. In the language of the new administration, these were the "hard choices" that had to be confronted. And while the Blair government has repeatedly struggled to articulate a coherent vision of what a "reformed" welfare system would look like, its handling of the reform process itself bears all the hallmarks of the kind of "conviction politics" that has become all too familiar in Britain. With more than a hint of a U.S. accent, the Blair government portrays welfare expenditures as the "bills of social failure," as burdens on an otherwise productive economy; the case for reform is presented as an inevitable and self-evident one, bolstered where necessary with scare stories about fraud, abuse, and escalating costs; opposition is dismissed as "Old Labour" instinctivism, vested interest, or flat-earth denial; and for all the talk of "Third Way" pluralism, there is in fact just one-best-way for reform: work is the solution, to be encouraged wherever possible and enforced if necessary.

The U.S. undertones in this reform offensive have been there for all to see—in the adoption of "welfare dependency" accounts of unemployment and poverty, in the deference shown to reforming states such as Wisconsin, in the macroeconomic alignment between flexible job markets and active/minimalist welfare, in the "Americanized" language of the reform process itself. This does not mean, of course, that a sudden and total "Americanization" has taken place, but it does mean that the key coordinates of the reform process, its guiding ideology, its mode of political and media management, and its tactical instincts all derive strongly from the U.S. experience.

So much, perhaps, is to be expected of political rhetoric. Once off the drawing board, Britain's New Deal has been inevitably shaped by institutional, political, and economic forces that are distinctly homegrown. If nothing else, this "embedding" process reveals how complex the policy-transfer process really is, that policies are rarely—if ever—transported in toto from one jurisdiction to another, but instead evolve through path-dependent mutual adjustment. This goes both for countries such as the United Kingdom, which are actively monitoring and learning from the U.S. experience, and for countries like France, Germany, and Denmark, which perceive workfare, at least in part, as an external threat to be resisted or ameliorated. Underpinning as it does the "Washington consensus" on social policy, where it has come to symbolize a combination of active/minimalist welfare and flexible job markets, workfare has become a powerful political icon in the international policy community. Whether embracing or resisting it, national states are beginning to define their policy posture in relation to workfare.

In few places is this specter of workfare as an external threat more vividly felt than in Canada, the third leg of the comparative analysis that follows. Here, most forms of "Americanization" are likely to generate political and cultural unease, if not active resistance, and nowhere more so than in the case of the Canadian welfare state, a distinctly un-American institution in important respects. But here, too, workfare dynamics are at work. In some provinces—Ontario is the clearest example—the pace of change has been dramatic: working from a script that could easily have been written in the United States, the Harris government has embarked on a far-reaching program of welfare retrenchment, benefit cuts, and deregistration, all in the name of workfare. And as if to underline the extent to which the project of workfare has become a multijurisdictional, transnational one, the Harris government will borrow liberally (and explicitly) from Wisconsin, on the one hand, while denying parallels with the more problematic New York experience, on the other. Meanwhile, the British Conservative Party, on the hunt for new ideas, chooses to emulate Harris's "Common Sense Revolution" election platform, including a panoply of harsh-sounding welfare-reform measures, in order to demonstrate its radical credentials. In turn, this is part of a wider strategy to establish "clear blue water" between the Conservatives and Tony Blair's New Labour government back in Britain, where Blair has already gone further than Margaret Thatcher in enforcing work requirements on the unemployed. Completing the circle, the Blair government, for its part, continues to draw inspiration from the U.S. "success story" of work-based welfare reform, while lecturing its European partners that this is the future; get used to it.

These swirling currents of workfare politics are important, not simply because they are creating, lubricating, and animating new channels for transnational "policy transfer," but because in a more profound sense they reveal how the workfare project is internationalizing. Internationalization is occurring in a number of ways. In a relatively weak sense, workfare has found its way on to the policy agenda in all of the prominent international agencies, and in countries as diverse as South Africa and Denmark. It has become one of the coordinates of the debate over the future of welfare and labor-market policy. Moreover, internationalization is also occurring in a much stronger sense, as neoliberal governments in particular have begun to embark on a process of *mutually referential* policy development. The constant churning of the workfare-reform process itself—rather than stable "systems," these are very much policies "in motion"—has the effect of constituting "external" sources of inspiration and legitimacy for "local" reformers. The extraordinarily wide circulation of politically stylized success stories like the "Wisconsin model" has less to do with the effectiveness of Governor Tommy Thompson's PR department than with the fact that a "policy market," of sorts, has been created for such suggestive reform homilies. Such external sources of credibility are especially important in places like Ontario, where the administrative challenges of delivering workfare have been almost overwhelming for the Harris government. Where delivery is difficult, constant reaffirmation that this is the one-best-way in social policy, and that workfare is working in Wisconsin, is needed to keep the reform process in motion.

Of course, none of this would count for much, in Ontario or elsewhere, if the welfare rolls were rising. Broadly favorable labor-market conditions—plenty of "flexible" jobs, falling underlying levels of unemployment, a weakened labor movement—are also key prerequisites for the "effective" delivery of workfare. Contemporary workfare policies rarely involve job creation on any significant scale, along the lines of the old-fashioned public-works programs; they are more concerned with deterring welfare claims and necessitating the acceptance of low-paid, unstable jobs in the context of increasingly "flexible" labor markets. Stripped down to its labor-regulatory essence, workfare is not about creating jobs for people that don't have them; it is about creating workers for jobs that nobody wants. In a Foucauldian sense, it is seeking to make "docile bodies" for the new economy: flexible, self-reliant, and self-disciplining.

This book's overriding objective is to explore this labor-regulatory function both theoretically and empirically. Theoretically, and for that matter politically, workfare is significant because it raises the question of how far the current rough-and-ready correspondence between active welfare/workfare regimes and burgeoning contingent labor markets represents the basis for a new and punitive "regulatory fix" in neoliberalized countries like the United Kingdom, Canada, and the United States. Empirically, there is a need to explore the different ways that this nascent regime of regulation is taking shape under different gender orders, under different labor market and political conditions, and so forth. Although the three countries examined in this book are often grouped together as "liberal welfare states" in much of the literature on welfare-state restructuring, a finer grained level of analysis reveals important differences in the dynamics of the reform process, in gender and race politics, in the scope and potential of progressive countermovements, and so on. The challenge in the analysis that follows has been to pay due regard to these issues without having them overwhelm the central focus of the book: the political–economic dynamics of workfare and its nascent labor-regulatory role.

This focus also has methodological implications, for the concern here has been to explore the different forms and mutations of workfare in a range of settings, not to conduct a formal and symmetrical piece of comparative analysis per se. I did not set out to carry out broadly based and comprehensively structured comparisons of three welfare systems in the midst of restructuring, but sought instead to trace different moments and manifestations of workfare as a regulatory process. This is why different parts of the books are devoted to the "front-end" delivery of workfare as a system of labor control, the political construction of workfare as a policy convention at the national and international scales, the political economy of devolution and program "downloading," the politics of "policy transfer," and the interrelated processes of crisis-induced restructuring, on the one hand, and active institution building, on the other. And rather than privilege one episode or experience of workfarist restructuring, the approach here has been self-consciously more open and exploratory. So, the political economy of workfare is examined, inter alia, in the context of the Harris government's Common Sense Revolution in the province of Ontario, the Blair government's "Third Way" social inclusion program in the United Kingdom, the Dukakis–Weld reforms in Massachusetts, and the Republican *Contract with America*. These are not here as neatly "parallel" experiences of workfarist restructuring, but rather as suggestive episodes in an ongoing process of path-dependent— but mutually referential and unevenly convergent—regulatory reform.

One would expect the politics of workfare to play differently in these different contexts, and indeed they do. But what also emerges across the following chapters is a strong sense of the commonalities and connections, which in turn often highlight more systemic features of workfarism. This concern with the systemic, or protosystemic, character of workfarism has called for an approach that is distinct both from conventional forms of policy analysis, which are so often preoccupied with the specificities of individual programs or policies, and from established methods of welfare-regime analysis, which tend to lean more toward exhaustive taxonomic classification. In contrast, the concern here with the reform process "in motion," and more generally with the always provisional and inescapably contradictory process of constructing workfarism as a regulatory project, has given license to a more roving and theory-driven methodology, which aspires to be analytically strategic but perhaps just as often has had to be pragmatically opportunistic. My hope is that the end product is just as often combative and engaged as it is analytical and distant. It has grown out of an attempt to conceptualize and interrogate workfare as a "living" regulatory phenomenon, stretching the analysis beyond and outside the usual "boxes" of programcentric evaluation or static-system regime studies. In addition to studying workfare programs in situ, I have also tried to capture a sense of what is happening *between* the sites of workfarist experimentation, across the scales of political intervention and program delivery, and behind the backs of policy actors.

Thinking about workfare in this comparative, international way—rather than, as is usually the case, simply as a domestic programming issue—pushes a new set of questions onto the research agenda. It is these questions—concerning, for example, the incipient regulatory logic and contradictions of workfare as a generic policy orientation; the limits and possibilities of transnational policy transfer and learning; the role of political, economic, and institutional contingencies in workfare policymaking; shifting scales, sites, and domains of policy formation, intervention, and reform—that have shaped this book. Necessarily and even deliberately exploratory, the book represents an attempt to "map" the workfare offensive, to locate its leading edges and weak spots, to chart its local variants, and to account for its rise from local experiment to transnational "policy fix." Needless to say, there are many ways to tackle these questions, and the strategy adopted here reflects personal circumstances and choices. My hope in tracking the nascent forms and emerging shapes of the workfare offensive in Canada, the United Kingdom, and the United States is that the outcome conveys an impression of the exceptional depth and reach of this incipient regulatory project. Looking at different sides of workfare in this way means being *more*, not *less*, careful about what constitutes workfarism and what does not. I certainly hope that it does not mean that I will see paranoid visions of workfare wherever I look, although my own transatlantic movements in recent years have tended to be organized around the hot spots of the intensifying political–economic offensive. Coming full circle, the book is being finalized as I arrive back in the United States—to a position at the University of Wisconsin-Madison—ironically one of the global epicenters of workfare policy. It all looks even more vivid and formidable from here.

No doubt the target will continue to move, the fortunes of programs will continue to rise and fall, and the course of welfare/workfare politics will continue to twist and turn, sometimes in unexpected directions. I cannot claim to have definitively captured the full ramifications of this ongoing process, but this book nevertheless represents a sustained attempt to probe the regulatory logics and limits of workfare. If it succeeds in this goal, it will do so by teasing out underlying structures, forces, and contradictions amid a sea of institutional minutiae. There have been plenty of studies of these minutiae and I have no desire to add to them. Instead, *Workfare States* focuses its attention on the "big picture" of the reform process, partly by abstract thinking but also substantially, by demonstrating how these underlying currents are revealed in a wide variety of "small-picture" situations. So, my ultimate objective here is to draw attention to the systemic features of what remains, in many ways, a protosystemic, unstable, and profoundly dynamic policy regime. This means looking for the family resemblances and traits, as well as sketching out the local peculiarities. Perhaps, above all, it involves a search for the *meaning* of workfare, in part by documenting its local translations.

## DEFINING WORKFARE

Twenty years ago the issue of "workfare," which at the time signified a particular type of U.S. work program requiring participants to "work off" their welfare checks, was pretty much a marginal concern for anything other than a specialist audience. Then, workfare seemed to be a rather perverse preoccupation of a small but influential cadre of intellectuals and social visionaries on the U.S. right, who were attracted to the notions of minimalist welfare and work enforcement, but who conspicuously and repeatedly failed in their attempts to translate these predilections and prejudices into a workable program. Yet the struggle over workfare had already begun, as the right recognized that the low-politics workfare message played well with "taxpaying" citizens, while critics on the left made the most of the inflammatory rhetoric of workfare in their attacks on punitive, ill-conceived programming designed to pander to welfare stereotypes rather than respond to real needs or provide real opportunities. Outside the United States, workfare had also become a powerful symbol: reformers studiously avoided the derogatory label while social advocates and anti-poverty campaigners learned to use the term to great effect at the first sign of a "U.S.-style" policy regression.

Today the picture looks very different. While the keyword *workfare* retains many of its pejorative connotations, its various generics such as "welfare-to-work," "labor-force attachment," "active-benefit systems," and "work-first welfare reform" now trip off the tongues of politicians and policymakers across the political spectrum. Work-based welfare reform—along with attacks on fraud, "welfare dependency," and the supposedly stunted work ethics of the poor—have become common currency in what has developed into a bipartisan onslaught against traditional, rights-and-eligibilities-based welfare systems, particularly in neoliberal countries. President Clinton's pledge to "end welfare we know it," and his subsequent complicity in doing just that in the federal welfare reform of 1996, were key moments in this realignment; they were two manifestations of a very broadly based and concerted drift toward work-oriented reform during the 1990s. The subsequent growth in the U.S. economy, and its continued generation of contingent, flexijobs by the million, came at the right time to validate the U.S. workfare message abroad, where prevailing attitudes—at least until recently—were generally skeptical. And at varying speeds and in different ways, a host of neoliberal countries have embarked upon a similar path. Britain and Canada are examined in later chapters of this book, while parallel accounts could be developed for Australia or New Zealand, and even for some of the bastions of state-welfarism in continental Europe which are now beginning to experience growing pressures for work-oriented welfare reform.

The essence of workfarism—as it has emerged in this variegated, transnational form—involves the imposition of a range of compulsory programs and mandatory requirements for welfare recipients with a view to *enforcing work while residualizing welfare*. This does not mean that welfare itself completely disappears, but it does mean that the logic, structure, and dynamics of the system of poor relief are transformed so as to maximize work participation while minimizing "dependency" on welfare. Rather than facilitating eligibility-based claims on welfare entitlements, the logic of the welfare regimes of the postwar period, workfare systems privilege dynamic transitions from welfare *to work*, typically through the combined use of "carrots" in the form of work and job-search programs and "sticks" in the form of benefit cuts for the noncompliant.

Part political ideology, part policy program, part moral crusade, workfare lies at the emblematic center of the contemporary attack on the principles and practices of the welfare state. *Workfare* is a controversial and highly elastic term, referring both to individual welfare-to-work programs and in a more generic sense to work-oriented welfare regimes. It is in the latter sense, as a signifier of a nascent *workfarist* regime, that the term is used here (see also Jessop, 1994; Sayeed, 1995; Shragge, 1997c). So notwithstanding the fact that there are a range of meanings attached to the term *workfare*, those meanings share

> the common thread of the state's transformation of social assistance as an income security program based on financial need, to a program which is conditional on the performance of employment activity in exchange for benefits. (Shragge, 1997a: 13)

More specifically, workfare is defined here as a *political-economic tendency*, one that is associated with a variety of discursive representations, restructuring strategies, and institutional forms. Just as the welfare regimes of the postwar period exhibited a range of forms both internationally and intranationally, so also one would expect the dynamics of the workfare offensive to work themselves out in a series of different ways.

Crude "transition models" of political-economic change are rejected here (see Thrift, 1989; Martin, 1994) in favor of an approach that seeks to hold together a concern with the "structural" and generic features of workfarism combined with a sensitivity to the variability of local outcomes. By way of an examination of welfare/workfare politics in and between the United States, Canada, and the United Kingdom, *Workfare States* sets out to probe the incipient regulatory logic (and emerging contradictions) of workfarism in a range of institutional contexts. While each of these three countries evolved a distinctive welfare settlement, there are striking parallels in the ways the politics of workfare are currently being played out. Discourses of "welfare dependency," that construct the causes of poverty and un(der)employment in terms of individual failings and that legitimate distinctively *anti*welfare restructuring strategies are fast becoming staples of political orthodoxy in these and other "advanced" industrial nations, particularly where neoliberal economic orthodoxies are most heavily entrenched (Jessop and Peck, 2000). Meanwhile, policy "solutions" center increasingly on work and work ethics, as the once broad remit of welfare reform collapses into a narrow preoccupation with welfare *to work*. Crucially, the ideological "decentering" of welfarism often seems to be associated with an institutional analog in the form of decentralization, defederalization, and localization of welfare processing and programming. In a sense, nationally constituted welfare regimes are giving way to locally constituted workfare regimes; uneven spatial development is being established as an intentional, rather than merely incidental, feature of workfare program delivery; and local experimentation is becoming a mainstay of the policymaking process. Under workfarism, geographic variability, "churning" of programs, and a restless search for local "success stories" ripe for replication, are all effectively normalized.

The workfare offensive has rather different inflections in different countries, reflecting political traditions and institutional structures. But more often than not it is present in some form or another. Hence the importance of retaining a grasp on the generic or abstract form of workfare, as well as its more specific institutional variants. Here, workfarism in its generic form is defined in terms of the following three dimensions:

- individually, workfarism is associated with *mandatory* program participation and behavioral modification, in contrast to the welfarist pattern of entitlement-based systems and voluntary program participation;
- organizationally, workfarism involves a *systemic* orientation towards work, labor-force attachment, and the deterrence of welfare claims, displacing welfarism's bureaucratic logic of eligibility-based claims processing and benefit delivery with a more insistent focus on deflecting claimants into the labor market;
- functionally, workfarism implies an ascendancy of *active* labor-market inclusion over passive labor-market exclusion, as workfarism seeks to push the poor into the labor market, or hold them in a persistently unstable state close to it, rather than sanctioning limited nonparticipation in wage labor in the way of welfare systems.

These workfarist principles are becoming embedded in different ways in the welfare restructuring movements currently underway across the United States, in Canada and the United Kingdom, and elsewhere, but as a set of principles it is clear that they diverge significantly from those of welfarism. Highlighting the nascent form of these principles, Table 1.1 summarizes some of the more telling contrasts between established welfare structures and emerging workfare strategies. Where welfare stands for the principles of needs-based entitlement and universality, workfare stands for market-based compulsion and selectivity. Where welfare stands for passive income support, workfare stands for active labor market inclusion. Where welfare constructs is subjects as claimants, workfare reconstitutes them as jobseekers: The status of being *on* welfare is replaced by the transitory experience of being processed (back) into work *through* workfare (see Dean, 1995; Little, 1999). The logic is to "churn" the welfare/workfare population, to hold them close to or push them into the job market, and to systematically remove alternative means of support in order to enforce (low) wage dependency.

Welfare and workfare also imply alternative modes of labor regulation. While welfarism was fundamental to the stabilization of Fordist wage relations, to the regulation of incomes and demand, and to the reproduction of a gendered industrial laborforce (Gough, 1979; Lipietz, 1987, 1992), workfare strategies are being pursued in a very different kind of labor market. There is a brutal but undeniable logic in the way that workfare aggressively mobilizes workers for (minimum) waged work. Under conditions of falling wages, chronic underemployment, and job casualization, workfarism maximizes (and effectively mandates) participation in contingent, low-paid work by churning workers back into

**TABLE 1.1.** Generic Welfare Structures and Workfare Strategies

| | Welfare structures | Workfare strategies |
|---|---|---|
| **Ideological principles** | Entitlement<br>Aid distributed on basis of need | Reciprocity<br>Enforcement of work and work values |
| **Objectives/ rationale** | Reducing poverty through income transfers<br>Responding to manifest social need through entitlements and programming | Tackling welfare dependency through promotion of work/ welfare deterrence<br>Maximizing labor-market participation through labor-market-oriented triage |
| **Dominant discourse** | Needs satisfaction and entitlement<br>Social work/bureaucratic codes and norms<br>Organizationally introspective and systems-focused rather than client-oriented | Work, personal responsibility, and self-/ family sufficiency<br>Business/employment service codes and norms for the job-ready; remedial services for "unemployables"<br>Externally focused |
| **Means** | Passive income support | Active labor-market integration |
| **Labor-regulatory function** | Exclusion from wage labor<br>Socially sanctioned recipient groups defined on basis of ascribed/categorical characteristics | Inclusion into wage labor<br>Market-determined treatment groups defined on basis of job readiness |
| **Subject/state** | Welfare recipient<br>*On* welfare | Job seeker<br>Moving *through* workfare |
| **Social relations** | Determining entitlements of passive subjects | Interventionist case management of active subjects |
| **Hierarchy** | Centralized control<br>Limited local autonomy in program design, entitlement, and eligibility<br>Management by input controls and sanctions | Centrally orchestrated devolution<br>Increasing local discretion over program design, entitlement, and eligibility<br>Management by output targets and incentives |

*(cont.)*

**TABLE 1.1.** *(cont.)*

|  | Welfare structures | Workfare strategies |
|---|---|---|
| Delivery | "Structured bureaucracy," shaped by eligibility rules <br> Line-management ethos <br> Process and input orientated <br> Standardized programs | "Flexible bureaucracy," with increased local discretion and internal competition <br> Local market ethos <br> Output- and outcome-oriented <br> Variegated programs |
| **Work/work program participation** | Limited <br> Voluntary | Extensive <br> Mandatory; ethos of compulsion |
| Contradictions | Welfare dependency <br> Periodic desynchronization of welfare and labor market | Rising social externalities <br> High implementation costs, particularly under conditions of demand deficiency |

the bottom of the labor market, or by holding them deliberately "close" to the labor market in a persistently "job-ready" state (see Swift, 1995). It constitutes its subjects as active agents, denying a stable mode of existence outside the wage-labor market to all but the irredeemably "unemployable." In Offe's (1985) terms, it represents a shift from principles of labor market exclusion to those of labor market inclusion. From the perspective of the OECD, systems of labor-market regulation based on the principle of passive income support are being displaced "by a combination of active reintegration policies, positive incentives to search for work and a safety net in the form of minimum income security" (1990: 88).

This is not to say that the transition from welfare to workfare is a uniform or an inevitable one. Workfare is a contradictory strategy, uneven in implementation, often unpredictable in terms of impacts. The workfare offensive itself is becoming a key site for political struggle and counter-mobilization (see Rose, 1995; Shragge, 1997b). So there is not going to be one, structurally preordained, path from welfare to workfare, but a range of trajectories and blind alleys. If workfarism is to be effectively understood, let alone effectively opposed, careful mapping of a range of contemporary workfare experiments is essential. This means tracing the incipient regulatory logics of established and emerging workfare strategies.

Workfarism may be contradictory, but this does not mean that it will necessarily wither. Contradiction, of course, is a characteristic even of "durable" institutions, like welfare systems. In fact, contradiction often serves as a source of important institutional dynamics itself. So, one of the challenges of this kind of real-time regulatory analysis is both to trace how the logics *and illogics* of emergent institutions are combined, and to explore how they cohere and conflict at the scale at which rule systems are made and enforced. Workfarism is not yet so much a fully coherent regulatory logic as a dominant regulatory strategy, an emerging tendency rather than an achieved structure. It would be wrong to counterpose, in a symmetrical way, the welfare state and the workfare state, because workfarist tendencies remain just that, tendencies. So while some sort of structural transition toward workfarist labor regulation may be underway, it is far from complete. To the extent that a transition is in evidence, it must be understood not as some monolithic transformation, but instead in the more specific terms of the structural and strategic contexts against which workfarist politics are emerging. Hence the need to connect the macro characteristics of workfarism with the specificities of its local manifestations. Local variability itself turns out to be an important part of the story.

Contrary to the aspirations to fair and equal treatment under welfare regimes, where spatial unevenness and local discretion were often constituted as policy problems in their own right or viewed as legacies of pre-welfare practices, workfare makes a virtue of geographic differentiation and subnational devolution. The shift to workfarism is certainly not going to be characterized by homogenization and convergence, as one system is replaced in toto by another. Rather, workfarism implies divergence, differentiation, and the proliferation of workfar*ist* reform paths and strategies. In fact, the very unevenness of the emergent workfare regime is a source of innovation and energy, as translocal fast-policy transfers become one of the principal means of policy development. The landscape of workfare is a restless one, as policies and programs are deliberately churned and persistently rolled over, just like the "clients."

This is one of the many ways in which the logic of workfarism differs fundamentally from that of welfarism. There is a form of coherence in the emergent workfare regime, but it is not reflected in the kind of integrative, coordinating institutions that characterized the welfarist era. In place of the directive, top-down, command-and-control strategies of the welfare state, workfare regimes are associated with fluid, unstable, and multiscalar regulatory configurations. At the national and international level, various kinds of policy intermediaries and advocates—from private consultancies to think tanks and evaluation houses, from reform-minded welfare administrations to transnational regulatory agencies—are assuming a much greater significance as agents of fast-policy transfer. More often than not, they are engaged in spreading messages and learning lessons, rather than delivering policy in the tradition of conventional welfare administrations. At the local level, front-line offices are now themselves engaged—often in a very self-conscious fashion—in the process of policy development. No longer merely the territorial outposts of a centrally managed system, they now have a role in making policy as well as implementing it.

## TRANSNATIONALIZING WORKFARE

Even though the term *workfare* itself remains controversial, even though the performance of work programs is mixed at best, and even though experiences of reform continue to vary from place to place, there is growing evidence that workfare is beginning to take on the form of a transnational regulatory project. Understanding workfare means coming to terms with how, simultaneously, it is internationalizing as a reform generic while at the same time remaining local and paticularized in institutional terms. Amongst other things, this shows how the *politics* of workfare really matter.

Workfare regimes will not be designed on some policymaker's drawing board, then lowered into place as a coherent and fully-functioning "system." Rather they will emerge through the complex and contested processes of political and institutional change and subsequently be mediated through the labor market. Yet while this will mean that the precise form of workfare states is likely to be highly variable, the analytical and political challenge must be to identify typical patterns, common processes, and mutual causalities amidst the noise and idiosyncrasy of the restructuring process. In this respect, a key contention of *Workfare States* is that workfarism occupies a structurally pivotal role in an emerging political-economic orthodoxy. Increasingly, workfarism is taken to signify more than an ideological and institutional attack on welfarism and to imply not simply a critique of the extant system but a rolling forward of new institutions and new norms of regulation. Now more than an institutional component of "welfare reform," workfare is emerging as the regulatory antonym of welfare. Even though the terrain of implementation remains uneven and contradictory in important ways, at the level of regulatory principle, workfarism may be beginning to constitute a codification of a distinctive, alternative regime. The aim of this book is to explore the character of workfare as a regulatory project, both by teasing out the regulatory logic of workfare and by mapping the workfare offensive as it has taken shape over recent decades, and the last decade in particular.

The task here is to trace the uneven emergence and development of workfare strategies in the United States, and reflects also on how workfarism is being "translated" in Canada and the United Kingdom. The American experience is privileged not only because this is the birthplace of workfare but because it is also the place where workfarist strategies are most (regionally) differentiated and have reached their most "advanced" stage of development. Moreover, now that the policy transfer process is itself an international one, the various U.S. models of workfare—such as the Wisconsin and Californian models, and their various derivatives— are increasingly acquiring the status of "reform generics" in policy debates in Europe and elsewhere (see King, 1995; Jones, 1996; Dolowitz, 1998; Ravallion, 1998; Walker, 1998; Haveman and Wolfe, 2000; Jessop and Peck, 2000). In this sense, while the American experience is a distinctive one, its paradigmatic position in the international discourse of workfare means that it is often a harbinger of things to come. This is an assertion which holds both for workfare experiments in particular and regulatory reform in general. Here, the kind of neoliberal strategies pioneered by the United States have been in an ascendancy, not because they are more "efficient" or "functional" than competing approaches, but because in the context of global economic liberalization they have a unique capacity to erode higher-cost and more socially oriented alternatives (see Burawoy, 1985; Esping-Andersen, 1990; Streeck, 1992; Peck and Tickell, 1994). These global conditions place deregulated economies such as the United States at the leading/bleeding edge of regulatory reform now that pressures are building for social and welfare standards to be ratcheted down to the lowest common denominator.

This need not, and in fact will not, mean that an unmediated process of "Americanization" will be set in train in welfare systems around the world. Workfare regimes have never been institutionally uniform. Heterogeneity, unevenness, and complexity are indeed paradoxically systemic features of workfarism. But as a symbol of the Washington consensus on social policy, workfare is exerting a strong influence in international policy discourse (see Ravallion, 1998; Haveman and Wolfe, 2000). One reason for this, aside from the geopolitical power of the United States, is that, like it or not, workfare tells a compelling story. It is a story about the failings of the poor and the virtues of hard work; it is a story which emboldens reformers and wrong-foots opponents; it is a story that chimes with parallel concerns for the desirability of flexible labor markets, governmental austerity, and local discretion; it is a story which many *want* to hear. It would therefore be ill-advised to dismiss workfare as a minor right-wing obsession or a neoliberal policy gimmick. It is more than this, as its paradoxical expansion illustrates. Workfare exhibits a measure of "structural consonance" with prevailing conditions in the globalized/neoliberalized policy community.

Certainly, there is a sense in which workfare strategies are themselves becoming the social policy of choice around the world to complement active labor-market programs and trade liberalization (see OECD, 1990; Teeple, 1995; EC, 1996; Deacon, 1998). Somewhat paradoxically, this is despite the fact that at a practical level workfare programs themselves remain stubbornly difficult to implement, as even their supporters concede (see Nathan, 1988; Mead, 1996b, 1997a). It is for this reason that the twists and turns of U.S. welfare/workfare politics assume a very particular significance. The U.S. experience—in so many ways paradigmatic—of the crisis of welfare and ascendancy of workfare cannot be properly comprehended as a rationalist process of "good" policy driving out "bad." Rather, it is a deeply politicized process, in which the nature of the policy "problem" was comprehensively redefined before being "solved."

Even at home, workfare politics remain somewhat unpredictable, despite the fact that recent experiences in the United States would seem to lend support to the argument that the workfare juggernaut is becoming unstoppable. The recent political push for workfare in the United States was not simply summoned up by reform-minded political elites. In fact, it is the complex outcome of political contingencies, institutional momentum, and structural economic pressures. It has complex roots in more than a decade of state- and federal-level political debate and program experimentation. This turbulent process would eventually culminate in the Personal Responsibility and Work Reconciliation Act (PRWORA). Once enacted, the 1996 legislation triggered a further round of state-level reforms which were facilitated by an expanding job market and consequential reductions in the welfare rolls in virtually every case. If the rolls are falling, of course, almost any reform can be presented as a "success," whether or not the reforms themselves brought about the caseload reduction. Economic conditions have therefore been critical in underpinning the narrative of success that has been woven around the 1996 reforms both nationally and internationally (see, for example, Matthews and Becker, 1998). Correspondingly, continuing economic difficulties in Europe have served further to erode the legitimacy—again, both nationally and internationally—of continental welfare settlements and the "European social model" more generally, even when the ultimate sources of these difficulties lie elsewhere. The long American boom of the 1990s, and continuing economic difficulties in Europe, consequently presents neoliberal politicians with a disarmingly simple tale to tell about the benefits of workfare and economic flexibility.

In this fashion, the politics of workfare can be seen to be economically contingent even if they are not economically determined. They are also strongly conditioned by institutional and (macro)political forces, that saturate and prefigure—but again do not simply determine—acts of political agency such as presidential vetoes. There is, then, a macroregulatory story to be told about workfare, albeit one that is inescapably expressed through the idiosyncrasies and particularities of any such "reform" process. The political-economy of workfare cannot be reduced to a unidirectional process of enacting a grand vision of "post-welfare," but instead finds its expression in the messy histories and uneven geographies of institutional change. For all the simplicity of the workfare narrative, the realities of workfarist policymaking are inevitably more complex, more provisional.

It is for this reason that workfare is conceived here as a regulatory *project*, as a set of political and institutional strategies, rather than as some kind of stabilized, postwelfare *state*. Such may be the longer run outcome of the workfare offensive, of course—hence the need for searching and critical accounts of these ascendant regulatory projects. The current conjuncture might still be most appropriately characterized as one of uncertainty and instability, but these are also precisely the conditions that workfare aspires to make its own, for example by mobilizing labor for low-paid, contingent jobs or, in policy terms, by "churning" programs and systems in an impatient search for effective strategies. This dynamism itself affords workfare a certain degree of stubborn resilience, as in the context of the prevailing economic orthodoxy of neoliberalism it seeks to make a virtue of "flexible labor markets," not to reform them. While the motive forces behind contemporary workfare experiments are primarily political and institutional, there may then be scope for a kind of post hoc economic functionality to emerge as workfare systems tread down into contingent labor markets. First came "McJobs," now there is "McWelfare" too.

There may be a risk here of "naturalizing" workfare, of presenting it as some unstoppable force for work-based welfare reform. There is a still greater risk, however, in failing to see the forest for the trees. For all their idiosyncrasies and institutional specificities, local workfare experiments *are* part of a bigger picture. The argument in *Workfare States* is that while there clearly are important differences in the reform strategies that are being pursued in, say, New York City, Baltimore, Toronto, Wisconsin, or London, there are also a series of basic *workfarist* features that unite these diverse experiments. There are many ways to interpret the workfare narrative, but a narrative there is. The goal of this book is to seek out common threads and underlying features in a way that is sensitive to local and institutional contingencies. It asks whether workfarism can really be shown to have a systemic logic, or whether it represents no more than an opportunistic rollback of welfare entitlements in the context of a (generally) expanding economy.

While this is not the place to answer this question in a comprehensive sense, it should be noted at this stage that these are not mutually exclusive possibilities: it is quite conceivable that a systemic logic may emerge out of a series of opportunistic experiments; indeed, this type of institutional searching is often the way in which new regulatory conventions are formed. And while there are pockets of resistance to workfare (one thinks of New York City and Toronto), it must be acknowledged that, in general, the workfare offensive is still gaining rather than losing ground, at least in neoliberal countries. Moreover, there are precious few extant examples of countervailing trends to the general drift toward mandatory, work-based welfare reform. Basic income strategies, for example, continue to be difficult to operationalize, while local social-economy initiatives have yet to be emulated on a generalized basis. These progressive experiments must be nurtured and sustained, but in this context there is also a need to figure out why it is that workfare—for all its flaws—seems to be winning the argument.

One of the perplexing features of workfare is that, for all its internal inconsistencies and negative externalities, the expansionary momentum continues almost unabated. Hence the need to take workfare seriously as a multilateral regulatory project, rather than simply as a loosely connected assemblage of social-policy gimmicks. This need not mean taking the hype of workfare at face value, but it does underscore the need for a sustained political–economic analysis of the character and potential of the workfare offensive. Waiting in some analytically pure yet politically complacent way for workfare to collapse under the weight of its own contradictions would be a reckless and risky strategy. While the political–economic significance of workfare should not be exaggerated—given that the question of how workfare will *work* on a large scale in countries like the United States, Canada, and the United Kingdom remains a substantially open one—it would be just as ill-advised to underestimate the potency of workfare.

One of the most striking features of the workfare offensive, in fact, has been its capacity to disable and disorganize sources of potential political opposition. Opponents of workfare can easily be portrayed as status quo-minded and even anti-work opponents of change, who often run the risk of implicitly condoning established practices and inequities— such as bureaucratized management, surveillance of clients, and benefit traps—which under normal circumstances they would be the first to criticize. The practice of oppositional politics is also rendered problematic by the localized and variegated form of workfare strategies themselves: the shift toward workfare is very often associated with some form of decentralized delivery, with the result that resistance itself tends to be particularized and locally specific. This fact has surely not been lost on national politicians seeking to "download" responsibility for welfare/workfare to states, provinces, and localities: downloading the programs often means downloading the oppositional politics too. Building concerted opposition to workfare out of a plethora of separate local struggles has proved predictably difficult.

Workfare States seeks to make a contribution to these efforts by presenting a political–economic critique of the recent origins, current form, and future prospects of the workfare offensive. The basic approach, in fact, is to map this offensive. The principal empirical focus is on the United States though some of the wider implications of neoliberal workfare are also explored by way of considerations of more recent workfarist turns in Canada and Britain. These "export models" of workfare share a great deal with their U.S. predecessors but they also show signs of having been "homegrown" as well, emerging as they have done from distinctive institutional and political contexts. This book does not aspire to offer a comprehensive political economy of these welfare states, nor does it attempt an exhaustive documentation of their long histories of welfare politics. At a general level, the classic treatments of these issues, such as Piven and Cloward's (1971, 1993) Regulating the Poor, Gough's (1979) Political Economy of the Welfare State, Offe's (1984) Contradictions of the Welfare State, and Esping-Andersen's (1990) Three Worlds of Welfare Capitalism, deserve to be reread, not simply rehashed.

## WORKFARIST LABOR REGULATION

The more modest goals of this book are organized around the role of workfare as a labor-regulatory institution. As Frances Fox Piven (1999: 87–88) reminds us, "Political talk notwithstanding, welfare is not mainly an institution to regulate individual morality. It is also, and more important, a labor market institution." It follows that work-based welfare reforms bring about changes in the rules and dynamics of the job market, or, as Piven puts it, they "alter the terms of the labor market, especially the lower tiers of the labor market where poor and unskilled women compete for work." The shadow of workfare therefore falls far across the labor market itself, where it helps set the terms and the tone of low-wage employment relationships. In conditioning access to the labor market, workfare also plays a part in determining who gets what, typically with regressive social-distributional consequences. This is one of the reasons why welfare reform is such a deeply politicized process: programs and benefits are often targeted at specific groups (such as lone parents or immigrants), with far-reaching consequences for patterns of labor-market participation. One of the paradoxes of the welfare/labor-market relationship is that those social groups with access to nonwage sources of support are typically treated by employers, unions, and labor-market institutions as semidetached workers, leading to discrimination, exclusion from better jobs, and a pattern of reliance on unstable work that perversely reinforces the need for nonwage benefits while apparently confirming the perception that these are unstable *workers* (see Offe, 1985; Peck, 1996). This underlines the fact that welfare/workfare politics are intricately bound up with the wider political, economic, and institutional forces that produce and reproduce the "contingent workforce," and the relations of the gender, ethnicity, and class that divide and define this workforce.

Workfare regimes, too, are being constructed through these relations. Indeed, one of the reasons for choosing the strategic–comparative method that is put to work here was to raise searching questions about the labor-regulatory logics, effects, and contradictions of workfarism under different (local) configurations of race, gender, and class relations. While not the primary focus my inquiry, these relations clearly animate the wider politics of welfare reform, just as they shape the micro-institutional form of workfare strategies. And in a rather paradoxical way they also help to define what it is that is generic about workfarism and what is peculiar to particular contexts. For example, though the primary targets of recent workfare programming (and rhetoric) have been unemployed young men in the United Kingdom and lone mothers in the United States, many of the institutional and political strategies used in both countries have been remarkably similar. I remember a senior British official saying to me that there was no gender dimension to the Blair government's welfare-to-work program because most of the participants were male! Apart from the obvious error of reasoning, what his comment revealed was a very narrow and programmatic understanding of the welfare-to-work process. A major reason why three-fourths of participants in the United Kingdom's main welfare-to-work program are male is that the benefit system and the low-wage labor market, which between them predetermine participation patterns, are themselves strongly gendered: work-enforcement measures within the benefit system tend to deregister and deter more women than men in situations where there is a plentiful supply of part-time and flexijobs, many of which are in the service sector and are gender-coded as "women's jobs." This tends to reduce the likelihood of sustained benefit claims among young women, rendering long-term unemployment a male-dominated phenomenon. A wider look at the workfarist *regimes* in which programs like the New Deal are embedded—which encompasses the interconnected elements of the benefit system, the low-wage job market, and its associated labor-market institutions—therefore reveals that this is in fact a profoundly gendered structure.

These comments are made here for two reasons. First, they underline the point that uneven social-distribution outcomes are bound up with the process of workfarist labor regulation. Unequal outcomes are not just a secondary by-product of the way that workfare regimes work, but follow from the way that these regimes reorganize the relationship between welfare and (contingent) work. The microsociological outcomes of these processes may be particular to individual places and specific programs, but the general propensity to generate, validate, and reproduce inequality is not. As Nancy Rose (1995) has powerfully demonstrated, historically, work programs have systematically operated to entrench and widen social divides—for example, three-fourths of work-program participants in the 1930s United States were white males, though this was hardly an accurate reflection of the social dimensions of poverty and unemployment at the time. Second, and more broadly, these issues of social sorting and channeling within, prior to, and beyond workfare programs draw attention to the need for a broadly based analysis of workfarism as a regime. While the programs themselves are natural foci for a study of this nature, it is in their complex and dynamic articulations with the labor market that their true effects are revealed. Insofar as workfare programs serve to deter existing and potential welfare claims, for example, they plainly affect the socioeconomic behavior, employment chances, and domestic arrangements of a potentially large and often quite indeterminate "nonprogram" population. Indeed, just like workhouses and prisons, workfare regimes are intended to throw a long shadow, shaping the norms, values, and behaviors of the wider population, and *maintaining a form of order*. Sticking with the penal analogy, what matters in these situations is not just the activities and immediate fate of the inmates, nor the particularities of prison architecture, but the broader social, political, and economic effects of the criminal-justice system. The parallel concern here is with the wider form and effects of workfare regimes, not with the narrow remit of program evaluation.

With this context in mind, *Workfare States* sets out instead to probe the political–economic structures and dynamics of contemporary workfare policymaking, diffusion, and development. Its focus is on the leading (or bleeding) edges of the welfare-/workfare-reform process; its goal is to explore if, and if so how, contemporary workfare experiments express a distinctive workfarist "logic." The voices of policy actors loom large in the account, not because they are the only players in this complex process of institutional, regulatory, and socioeconomic change, but because their words expose critical issues around the rationale, scope, and limitations of workfarism—the central concerns of the book. In the course of five years of research beginning early in 1995, I conducted more than 250 interviews with welfare administrators, work program managers, participants, anti-poverty campaigners, welfare advocates, and researchers for this book and for related projects. I am immensely grateful to all those who found the time to take part, and who have helped— wittingly or not—to shape the arguments in this book. My hope is that their insights infuse a kind of firsthand, practical knowledge into the account that follows, so as to ground the argument in local realities of workfarist programming and restructuring. Too much "academic" writing has lately become impervious to this kind of knowledge, and as a consequence often fails to engage with issues in ways that make sense even to those actively involved in the processes under study. Of course, I can only hope that the approach adopted here—which falls somewhere between critical policy analysis, on the one hand, and institutional political economy, on the other—is more successful in bringing theoretical questions to bear on contemporary, "real-life" concerns. After all, the underlying objective here is not just to critique workfare programs, or even to reform them, but to open up lines of attack that might lead to their transcendence.

## PLAN OF THE BOOK

Beginning with the next chapter, Part I of the book traces the roots of workfare, both historically and theoretically. Chapter 2 establishes the theoretical context by outlining the ways in which different historically and geographically specific patterns, or *regimes*, of regulation assume hegemonic or dominant status. Three such regimes are identified—the workhouse system, the welfare state, the emergent workfare regime— each of which is associated with a particular institutional form and a distinctive mode of labor regulation. The chapter focuses in particular on two themes, which in some senses have been neglected in conventional accounts of the history of poor-relief/welfare regimes: first, the interaction between relief arrangements and the labor market, an institutionally mediated relationship that is viewed in a dialectical, mutually constitutive, and yet nonfunctionalist fashion; and second, the role of uneven spatial development and the scaling (and rescaling) of regulatory institutions under different regimes of regulation and during the periods of crisis and uncertainty that characterize their interstices.

This analytical framework is taken forward to Chapter 3, which considers the U.S. origins and recent ascendancy of workfare in the context of the restructuring of the welfarist settlement. Here, the concern is with the discursive construction of the "reform" process and the range of meanings associated with the regulatory keyword *workfare* under different historical and geographical contexts. Particular emphasis is placed on the highly charged politics of welfare/workfare in the United States, leading up to and during the momentous reforms of 1996. It is suggested that the value-laden yet somewhat elastic language of workfare has played an important role in the constitution of workfarism as a regulatory project.

Part II of the book explores some of the contemporary spaces of workfare in a more empirical context, concentrating on recent experiences of welfare-reform politics and local workfarist experimentation in the United States. Chapter 4 traces the history of welfare/workfare politics in Massachusetts, which has shifted in recent years from the liberal to the radical conservative fringe of the U.S. reform movement. This chapter draws particular attention to the way in which workfare politics are associated with a complex "rescaling" of the processes of policy development and implementation, as in the U.S. case regulatory capacities and discourses are being reorganized across the local-, state-, and federal-level scales.

This theme is also taken up in Chapter 5, which presents a critical analysis of both the methodology and the stylized interpretations of one of the most influential local "models" of workfare: Riverside, California's, Greater Avenues for Independence (GAIN) program. One of the pioneers of the "work-first" or "labor-force attachment" method, which places overriding emphasis on rapid job-market entry for those deemed employable, GAIN has come to epitomize a no-frills, no-nonsense approach to welfare-to-work. It has been praised and emulated not only across the United States, but also in Canada, the United Kingdom, and elsewhere. But in fact the claims that are made on behalf of the Riverside model are exaggerated and distorted, and experience has shown that while it may be possible to replicate some of the program's design features and administrative routines, reproducing its *results* under different labor-market and political conditions is quite another thing. Somewhat ironically, slow progress in achieving comparable results has only increased the thirst for imported policies: perversely, the more mediocre the results, the more frenzied the process of "fast-policy" emulation becomes, a process actively facilitated by consultants, program evaluators, and a range of other governmental and nongovernmental policy intermediaries and brokers.

In Part III, the workfare policy development process is traced offshore, first to Canada and then to the United Kingdom. Chapter 6 traces Canada's path from welfarism to workfarism, which while distinctive has become increasingly referential to, and resonant of, the experience of its southern neighbor. But even if there are strong U.S. echoes in the reform strategies and policy measures that have been adopted in Canada over recent years, the particularities of the Canadian polity have meant that the trajectories of Canadian workfare remain somewhat idiosyncratic. This is illustrated by way of a case study of Ontario, where a radical workfare program implemented by a deeply conservative provincial administration has produced highly contradictory outcomes, so much so, indeed, that the institutional integrity of the program, Ontario Works, has been brought into question, even as economic and political conditions remain broadly favorable to the reformist interests.

In Chapter 7, attention shifts across the Atlantic (and back again), as the resonances and dissonances between the United Kingdom's recent but fulsome embrace of workfare are explored. Chapter 7 focuses on the particularities of the British path to workfare, through the Conservative administrations of the 1980s and early 1990s, which were intrigued by the idea but concerned about the costs of workfare, through to the Blair government of today, which has embraced workfare (in all but name) in its transformative project of "Third Way" modernization. Yet for all the bravado of ministerial pronouncements, Britain's welfare-to-work project remains precariously dependent on facilitative labor-market conditions, which are sufficiently uneven and brittle even at the top of the business cycle to signal danger signs for the future. But just as the United Kingdom's drift toward workfare has been slow, incremental, and somewhat provisional, there remains scope for path-altering adjustments even within the current policy paradigm. These may have to be rapidly enacted if/when the country slides back into recession. Broadly speaking, however, it is clear now that a variant of workfarism has been firmly entrenched in Britain, reinforced by the acceleration in transatlantic policy transfers in recent years. The political, ideological, and stylistic affinities between the Clinton and Blair administrations, in particular, established the basis post-1997 for a far-reaching process of policy learning and emulation in the field of welfare-to-work and labor-market regulation. Even though the institutional differences between the two countries' welfare/ workfare systems remain considerable, reform politics and reform strategies in both have followed a compellingly similar path. But at the same time as this has facilitated accelerated policy transfer—nearly all in an eastward direction—it has also drawn attention to its limits, as economic, institutional, and political contingencies continue to matter in more than trivial ways.

Pulling the main arguments of the book together, Chapter 8 explores the notion of workfare at a more abstract level—defining its tendential regulatory logic and incipient contradictions—before going on to speculate about the future course of workfare politics. The continued ascendancy of workfarist policy strategies appears to be confounding the predictions of those observers who have portrayed workfare as a mere fad of social policy. At an abstract level, workfarism codifies an alternative regulatory logic to welfarism, based on the enforcement of low-waged work and, more generally, on the reproduction of a persistently contingent labor supply. For all the flaws and contradictions of workfarist practice—modest direct-program outcomes, high unit costs, reliance on accommodating job-market conditions—these nascent regulatory functions, coupled with the empirical evidence of the regime's geographic expansion, suggest that it would be unwise to write off workfare as a passing fashion or an unrealizable vision. At the very least, workfare has proved an effective means of disorganizing the defenses of welfarist entitlements and programs—an important factor behind its continued growth. Ultimately, only time will tell whether workfarism itself becomes sufficiently normalized to constitute an alternative and (in the medium term at least) "functional" regime of regulation. There is growing evidence, however, that this process may already be underway. Politically and institutionally, the workfare offensive is still gathering pace; theoretically, there is a brutal logic to the way in which workfare remolds social policy in the interests of short-term job-market flexibility and recasts welfarist entitlements in terms of state-enforced, individualized responsibilities. It may not always work and it certainly is not fair, but it may nevertheless be the shape of things to come.

# Roots of Workfare

# CHAPTER TWO

# Regulation

## *Workhouse/Welfare/Workfare*

[A] great expansion of relief constitutes a "crisis" and pressure
mounts to reorganize the system . . . in the name of "reform."
Similar episodes in the past suggest that such calls for reform
signal a shift in emphasis between the major functions of relief
arrangements—a shift from regulating civil disorder to
regulating labor (Piven and Cloward, 1971: 342).

The publication of Piven and Cloward's (1971) seminal treatment of the
functions of welfare, *Regulating the Poor*, coincided with the apogee of
U.S. welfarism. The immediate historical context of their book was
provided by the "explosion" of the welfare rolls during the 1960s, a
phenomenon attributed at the time to rising benefit levels and—most
notoriously—to alleged dysfunctions in the "Negro family" (Moynihan,
1965). Contrary to the conventional conservative wisdom, Piven and
Cloward demonstrated that the causes of this historic expansion in the
welfare rolls lay elsewhere: in politically mediated responses to the
threats to civil order posed by the modernization of southern agriculture
and by the deepening problem of underemployment in the northern cities. This in turn was seen as a contemporary manifestation of a far
deeper set of historical currents in the political economy of poor relief.
Here, Piven and Cloward detected a cyclical process, as "expansive relief
policies are designed to mute civil disorder, and restrictive ones to reinforce work norms" (1971: xiii). Quite rightly, they sensed at the time that

31

the U.S. system was reaching the top of the cycle. A regressive turn was in the offing.

Reflecting the historic pattern of enforcing work norms as the threat of social disorder receded, localized workfare trials had in fact been underway since the late 1960s—when the term *workfare* was originally coined. More generally, pressure for thoroughgoing "welfare reform" had been building for some time, though the efforts of the Nixon administration in this arena were to be frustrated. While "work incentives" within the welfare system were strengthened in the Talmadge Amendments of 1972, many conservatives would remain dissatisfied with such piecemeal—and manifestly ineffective—responses to the "welfare mess." As Henry J. Aaron was to ask, somewhat plaintively, in 1973, "Why is welfare so hard to reform?" Reform proposals are always hotly debated because they cut to the heart of enduring political tensions around the causes of poverty, the moral status of recipients, the regulation of low-wage labor markets, the condition of urban ghettos, and so forth—not to mention the pronounced race, gender, and class coding of most welfare discourse. As Aaron (1973: 1–2) saw the situation at the start of the 1970s, a consensus had begun to emerge around the critique of welfarism—the main tenets of which were to coalesce into an anti-welfare accord in the 1990s (see Quadagno, 1994; Mink, 1998)—but division remained over the vital question of *alternatives* to welfare (1973: 1–2):

> President Nixon has stated that passage of welfare reform would be the most significant domestic social legislation since enactment of social security in 1935. Many quarrel with his definition of reform, but few question the President's judgement that the existing welfare system requires extensive change. Welfare has been indicted for encouraging family dissolution, promoting illegitimacy, degrading and alienating recipients, papering over the sins of a society that generates poverty, shielding the dissolute and lazy from their just deserts, failing to support life by providing too little assistance, and fostering sloth by providing too much. Conservatives, liberals, and radicals unite in attacking the welfare system but divide over its specific faults. . . . Because the politics of welfare express various attitudes about welfare recipients and about other values, no agreement exists about what constitutes welfare reform even if cost were no object.

One of the reasons welfare was proving so hard to reform in the early 1970s lay in the political legacies of its recent expansion phase: while the liberalization of welfare during the 1960s may have played a role in dissipating social (and particularly urban) unrest (Isaac and Kelly, 1981), it also laid the foundations of new political movements around welfare advocacy and welfare rights (Trattner, 1984). Subsequently, these were profoundly to shape the course of the welfare-reform process, at both the federal and state levels (see Norris and Thompson, 1995). As the workfarist moment in the cycle began to gather pace in the mid-1980s and beyond, the advocacy movements found themselves all but overwhelmed. "Welfare reform," once a site of serial underachievement for policymakers, had become the issue that politicians sought to make their own. By the 1990s, it had become a defining issue of the times.

Yet while the drive for welfare reform became ever more clamorous during the 1980s and 1990s, the issue of welfare reform—in some form or another—had in fact been on the U.S. political agenda almost continuously since the late 1950s (Handler and Hasenfeld, 1991). Welfare consequently earned the reputation as the "Middle East of domestic policymaking" (Corbett, 1995). While most fields of social provision undergo phases of restructuring and reorganization, they also tend to experience periods of stability, consolidation, and incremental change. Not so for welfare, which in the United States at least seems to have been perennially controversial. As social historian Michael Katz (1986: ix) has stated, "Nobody likes welfare." This negativity does not, however, necessarily translate into an effective reform process. There are no permanent fixes to be had here. In the long run, of course, workfare may prove to be just as unpopular. Its current popularity is partly explained by the fact that it appears new and different, and partly because "workfare" has become the discursive vessel for all things *anti*-welfare. But workfare also sends a signal of systemic change. The implication is that this is not just about cleaning up the "welfare mess," but about replacing the welfare *system* with something different. So, political rhetoric increasingly promises to go *beyond reform*, to move toward a new system based on new principles. Clinton's fateful pledge to "end welfare" was, of course, a case in point.

This is not just rhetoric. There are important material as well as discursive shifts underway in the transition from welfare to workfare. Materially, the end of federally policed, needs-based entitlement in the United States in 1996 coincided with the rise of a range of work-oriented systems and the imposition of severe restrictions on both eligibility and benefit levels. Visions of a postwelfare order are also being discursively constructed in ways that begin to constitute their own realities. Discursively, these developments are wrapped in the language of reciprocity, self-sufficiency, and independence through work (in contrast to dependence on welfare), as workfare is presented as a means to liberate the poor from the shackles of the ghetto's "dependency culture."

Only for the most fanatical libertarians, however, does this postwelfare vision imply the removal of welfare altogether (see Tanner, 1995). In the small print of even the most radical "mainstream" proposals provision is made for the "truly needy," those who due to some profound physical or mental incapacity are deemed incapable of work. Once grounds for generalized exemption, childcare responsibilities are for the most part no longer regarded as a legitimate reason for nonparticipation in the labor market, yet even after the 1996 Welfare Act most U.S. states continue to allow mothers of very young children to be exempted from workfare requirements. Exemptions remain, though the broad thrust of policy is unmistakable: mothers of all but the youngest children should be dependent on a man or a wage, not on welfare. As Mink (1998: 23) observes, "Many welfare reformers view work requirements as necessary not because all mothers should be in the labor market, but because *poor single* mothers ought to be."

In the language of social welfare, what is being adjusted here is the age-old distinction between the "deserving" and the "undeserving" poor in the context of changed social and economic conditions. In the language of labor-market regulation, on the other hand, it represents a periodic restructuring of the boundary between the "active" and the "passive" components of the wage-labor force in the context of a shift in the level and composition of labor demand, coupled with changes in the labor supply such as the growth of waged employment among women. For all the political manipulation and institutional idiosyncrasy, welfare and poor-relief systems continue to perform this basic regulatory function in the labor market. Their rules condition who should work and under what circumstances by virtue of the way they ration and regulate access to nonwage incomes. The remainder of this chapter is dedicated to an exploration, in fairly general and abstract terms, of these labor-regulatory roles, and their historical and geographic constitution.

## RELIEF AND REGULATION

Some kind of movement is underway in the complex of social rules and conventions, many but not all of which are enforced though legal sanction, which determine which members of the population should be expected/required to earn a living on the labor market. Most fundamentally, this speaks to the way in which capitalist labor markets, which can never be "managed" in a contradiction-free fashion, are *socially regulated* through ongoing processes of institutional adjustment, political action, and cultural change (see Peck, 1996). Systems of poor relief; the institution of the family; the regime of legal protections for the old, the young, the sick, and the disabled; cultural conventions concerning "appropriate" forms of work for men and women; and deep-seated practices like racial discrimination, combine in complex and indeterminate ways to define what Offe terms

[t]he niches, free spaces and buffer zones . . . in which those who are
. . . propertyless but not wage labourers live. . . . [These] are socially
established through cultural and political norms which more or less
permanently determine which persons living in which conditions are
not required (or allowed) to offer their labour power in labour markets. There is no past or present society where, over a long period of
time, more than half its members have invested their labour power in
money-mediated relations of exchange. (1985: 26)

Perhaps the most impermanent of these "niches, free spaces and
buffer zones" are those systems of poor relief that have acted historically
as a "safety valve" for the labor market. In Piven and Cloward's (1971:
xiii) terms, welfare is a "secondary and supportive institution," expanded
during the hard times of deficient labor demand and retrenched in periods of economic growth when additional reserves of labor must be mobilized. What Piven and Cloward call "cycles of relief" are in fact closely
synchronized with the rhythms of the labor market, albeit in politically
mediated ways. Historically, while the expansion of relief has been
shown to dissipate the threats to social disorder—particularly *urban* social disorder—posed by economic dislocation and underemployment, its
contraction has correspondingly been related to the imperative of restoring "the compulsion to sell labor on whatever terms the market offered"
(Piven and Cloward, 1987b: 11). At a more abstract level, this speaks to
some of the perennial functions of relief/welfare regimes, of which workfare is but the most recent manifestation.

[T]he workhouse as an institution is dead, but as a concept it has been
reincarnated as workfare. These programs act therefore both to regulate labour and to deter other claims for social assistance benefits. . . .
The existence of an unemployed pool of workers creates downward
pressure on wages, and weakens the political and social strength of
workers by increasing the competition for jobs. There is a clear connection, in other words, between those inside and those outside the labour market. . . . The surplus population, though "excluded" from the
labour market, is in other ways attached to it. Workfare policies tie the
surplus population to the discipline of the labour market, and workfare is the means of marshaling them towards it. (Shragge, 1997: 29–
30)

In this sense, welfare reform is also about *reregulating the labor market*.
While debates around welfare reform typically focus on "internal" and
supply-side factors, such as the (excessive) costs of the system or the
(perverse) habits of recipients, in most cases it is clear also that the "external" and demand-side factors, such as the state of the labor market,
are playing an important if often unstated role. While such economic fac-

tors rarely drive the reform process, and certainly do not determine it, they establish one of the *structural contexts* for reform efforts. Welfare-reform cycles and labor-market cycles are not, therefore, functionally or automatically synchronized, but they are undeniably related.

Although cyclical pressures remain in evidence, it is important also to acknowledge the role played by relatively long-term processes of institutionalization, both in relief systems and in the structure of labor markets. Moreover, the prevailing institutional form of relief systems and the dominant mode of labor-market regulation are closely related to one another. This is reflected, for example, in the mutually constitutive relationship between postwar welfare systems—characterized by extensive, entitlement-based provision and the assertion of "welfare rights"—and the distinctive labor-market relations of the Fordist long boom—based on a structure of institutionalized compromises between capital and labor, itself predicated on rising profitability, labor productivity, and real incomes. This was also a period in which regulatory norms relating to welfare entitlements, industrial relations, and labor-market management were entrenched at the national level, as the prevailing dynamic became one of centralization. Generically defined, this Fordist–welfarist pattern of relief-system/labor-market relations can be seen as a historically and geographically distinctive *regime of regulation*. Quadagno had similar, long-term patterns in mind when she observed that "the social organization of production determines the nature and form of relief programs. If poor laws are a product of feudalistic agrarian societies requiring an immobilized labor force, then national welfare systems emerge from the conflicts generated by the commodification of labor under industrial capitalism and the need for a mobile labor force" (1988: 6–7). Likewise, local workfare systems can be seen to reflect responses to the emerging regulatory dilemmas of flexibilized, *after*-Fordist labor markets in which polarizing wages, rising inequality, and contingent employment have become systemic conditions.

The production of such distinctive regimes of regulation—the costabilization of relief systems and labor-market structures—is an iterative, dialectical process, somewhat more complex and indeterminate than Quadagno implies in her statement that "the social organization of production *determines* the nature and form of relief programs" (1988: 6–7, emphasis added). Relief systems shape the way labor markets work, while labor markets shape the way relief systems work. This is a relationship, in other words, that is characterized by complex feedback effects and mutual adjustment, reflecting processes of labor regulation which in their nature are continuous, contradictory, and dogged with unanticipated impacts (Moulaert, 1987; Boyer, 1992; Peck, 1996). The apparent medium-term stability of regimes of regulation, such as that witnessed during the golden age of Fordism and welfarism, is therefore partly illusory, given the constant stresses and strains created by fluctuating labor-market conditions, on the one hand, and politico–institutional pressures, on the other. Ultimately, these stresses and strains may develop the kind of cumulative momentum that can lead to the collapse of the regime itself, as indeed seems to have occurred in the case of the simultaneous crises of the Fordist growth dynamic and the Keynesian–welfarist mode of regulation (Jessop, 1994).

Many have argued that just such a systemic collapse has been underway in the Keynesian–welfarist complexes of North America and northern Europe since the mid-1970s, and that the protracted crisis conditions that have ensued are associated with a search for alternative "institutional fixes," both in the production and wage-labor spheres and in the realm of social policy (see Leborgne and Lipietz, 1992; Jessop, 1994; Peck and Tickell, 1994). The explosion in "welfare-reform" initiatives— just like the rash of experiments with flexible production systems, the rise of labor-market "deregulation" as a policy orthodoxy, and the expansion in contingent employment—should be understood in this *structural* context. They reflect simultaneous moves to deconstruct extant and ostensibly "outmoded" systems and the continuing search for regulatory "solutions." It is this environment that confers special significance on the current phase of the "relief cycle," because what is at stake here is more than a cyclical downswing in welfare benefits and rights, but a structural rollback of an entire regime of social entitlements, supportive institutions, and accepted norms of labor-market behavior.

A decisive question for analysts of this contemporary moment in the long history of social-welfare and labor-market policy—and this is as much a political question as a theoretical one—concerns the long-run significance of the recent turn toward workfare. One of the lessons of historical analysis is that such phases of retrenchment and work enforcement quite commonly follow on the heels of expansions in the relief rolls. So, workfare can be understood *in part* as a cyclical phenomenon, "a secular reaffirmation of the work ethic" (Handler and Hasenfield, 1991: 39) or as a "replay of history" (Piven and Cloward, 1988: 644). From such a perspective, contemporary workfare politics are interpreted as another episode in the long-running dramaturgy of work:

> Historically, in the labor-regulating phase of relief cycles, poor law authorities reorganize relief arrangements to enforce work, both by expelling people from the rolls and by intensifying the degradation of those "impotents" allowed to remain on the rolls in order to reinforce work norms. In the past, the most common method of achieving this objective has been to shut down outdoor relief arrangements and to

> grant relief only in hell-holes called workhouses. . . . The less extreme
> [contemporary approach is] to slash benefits in tandem with falling
> wage levels, to force more of the poor to accept the deteriorating con-
> ditions of market work by driving many of them off relief, and subject
> those remaining on the rolls to "workfare" and other forms of ritual-
> ized degradation. (Piven and Cloward, 1993: 366–367)

The historical parallels are certainly compelling, and no contemporary account of work-based welfare reform can afford to downplay them.
At the same time, however, it is important to recognize that, while history may be filled with echoes, it is never repeated. Although at an abstract level it may be possible to discern certain transhistorical and
pangeographical *tendencies* in the regulation of capitalist labor markets,
concrete expressions of these regulatory imperatives are always and necessarily conditioned by temporal and spatial contexts (Peck, 1996). This
means that each historical chapter of the relief debate, and indeed each
geographical site in which this debate takes place, can be expected to
have distinctive characteristics. Patterns of institutionalization, and the
course of institutional change, will vary over both time and space, as will
political and labor-market conditions. The political economy of workfare, then, will *play* differently in different times and different places, reflecting the path-dependent nature of economic and institutional change.

Analytically, it is necessary to be sensitive both to the historic patterning of relief cycles and to the particular institutional form of anti-
relief/work-enforcing moments in the cycle. Never is this more important (or difficult) than when such moments coincide with wider and
deeper ruptures in the political–economic fabric. The analytical challenge is to discern emerging regulatory structures amid a sea of failing or
redundant institutional experiments. What is more, the straightforward
numerical prevalence of certain strategies—be these inward investment
policies, anti-union measures, or job-search assistance packages—need
not always be a reliable guide to the shape of any emerging "order," for
these may be creatures of the crisis itself rather than constituent elements of some resolution (Tickell and Peck, 1995). While mapping and
enumeration must be part of the process, analysis of emerging regulatory
strategies must concentrate on specifying their "logic" and rationale,
their flaws and internal contradictions, their various material forms and
discursive representations, and their compatibility (or otherwise) with
coevolving strategies and structural constraints. This calls for a close empirical analysis of contemporary experiments, but also underscores the
need for forward-looking and even speculative theoretical work (see
Boyer, 2000). At an abstract level, Jessop (1993, 1994) adopts a similar
approach in his "thought experiments" on the possible forms and func-

tions of the Schumpeterian workfare regime, where a series of potential resolutions to the protracted crisis of Keynesian welfarism are explored with reference to a range of state strategies that are currently in evidence. Hence the need to think across and between localized workfare experiments, reforms in national regulations, and emerging international policy conventions.

With this approach in mind, the remainder of this chapter explores the roles of poor relief in the process of labor regulation, first by examining the form and function of relief-regulation relationships in the operation of labor markets, and second, by bringing in the dimensions of time and space, by drawing attention to the distinctive ways in which relief arrangements have been institutionalized during different historical periods and in different places.

## REGULATING LABOR

Poor relief, or welfare, plays a vital and ongoing—but nonetheless contested and contradictory—role in the regulation of labor markets. Most straightforwardly, it does this by regulating flows of labor around the bottom of the labor market and shaping the conditions under which low-wage labor is bought and sold. In the process, relief arrangements curb and mediate the self-destructive tendencies in labor markets, which would otherwise drive wages below subsistence levels (Offe, 1985). These are forces that extend beyond the relief population, and even beyond the low-wage labor market, because the effects of expansions and contractions in relief ripple through the labor market as a whole. Protections for *low-paid* workers are, in this sense, protections for *all* workers. This is a point that has to be stressed, because it flatly contradicts the conservative (and now the mainstream) critique of welfare as a *creator* of dependency and a *perpetuator* of poverty. What Piven and Cloward term the "Great Relief Hoax" conceals the manifest reality that "people whose labor is of little value in the market are better off when they receive income protections, and that most other workers are also better off when they no longer have to compete with such vulnerable workers" (1987b: 7–8).

In labor-market terms, then, relief systems perform a systemic function by placing a floor under the process of competition, thereby limiting the extent to which workers can be played off against one another to the detriment of their bargaining position. Workfare deliberately and aggressively reverses these conditions. Solow (1998) points to two pertinent shortcomings, for example, in the current U.S. strategy of replacing welfare with work. First, even under highly favorable labor-market conditions, there is little evidence of "slack" in the job market for former welfare recipients, who consequently face tough competition with *existing* workers (most of whom are already in low-paid, unstable jobs) in their attempts to make the transition from welfare to work. Second, as the labor market adjusts to this new influx of workers, the inevitable result is falling wages at the bottom of the employment spectrum. Solow's conservative estimate is that, in principle, wages at the bottom of the U.S. job market would have to fall by 5 percent in order to absorb even two-thirds of the welfare caseload into work. In his view, the minimum wage and other factors may check this wage fall to a certain extent, but only at the cost of increased unemployment and job insecurity:

> Either way, the working poor will pay. . . . [T]he burden of adjusting to any genuine replacement of welfare with work will fall primarily on low-wage workers, especially those virtuous ones who have been employed all along. The burden will take the form of lower earnings and high unemployment, in proportions that are impossible to guess in advance. (Solow, 1998: 32)

## Relief Politics and the Labor Market

Different versions of the Great Relief Hoax have been used at different points in time in the long history of poverty politics, but conservative attacks are invariably most fervent at the peak of the relief cycle, when the welfare rolls are at their most bloated and when the supposed psychoses of dependency threaten to reach epidemic proportions (see Katz, 1986; Heclo, 1994). These conditions are typically associated with a political onslaught against the vacillating work ethics of the poor, a clampdown on relief giving, and the enforcement of both work and work values. At the same time, this is a "moral panic" and a regulatory crisis. The moral panic codifies and rationalizes a political response, be this in the form of "scientific charity" in the late nineteenth century or workfare in the late twentieth century. The regulatory crisis calls for a resynchronization of relief arrangements and labor-market conditions, both quantitatively and qualitatively. In *quantitative* terms, the axiom of "less eligibility" dictates that the conditions of relief must not be allowed to exceed those pertaining in the most menial of jobs. While the manipulation of benefit levels is perhaps the most common contemporary expression of this age-old principle, in its classic workhouse formulation it would also embrace the conditions of employment and the diet of paupers. According to the architect of the principle of less eligibility, Jeremy Bentham, the workhouse should offer no more than "maintenance in the most frugal and least luxurious shape," serving the most basic fare in the most degrading of conditions such that "charity-maintenance, or maintenance at the expense of others, should not be made more desirable than self-maintenance" through wage labor.[1] According to Charles Mott, a disciple of Bentham and a workhouse manager in London in the 1820s and 1830s, where food allowances were regulated down to the half-ounce, any slackening of the doctrine of less eligibility would run the risk of overwhelming the London labor market as a whole, "the pauper population becoming too great for the industrious classes to bear, industry paralyzed, rents diminishing, property absorbed, and all sinking down to a pauper level."[2]

In addition to this quantitative dimension, whereby relief arrangements serve to manage both the flow of labor into the market and the prevailing wage, the regulation of labor is a *qualitative* process too. Poor relief shapes not just the price and amount of labor entering the market, it also conditions the social environment within which these transitions occur. Relief arrangements exert a strong influence over the social distribution of waged work, establishing the conditions under which certain social groups are granted access to the means of subsistence outside the market and in the process shaping the identities and labor-market chances of those "contingent" or "secondary" workers who are expected to have a marginal and/or discontinuous commitment to wage earning (Offe, 1985; Peck, 1996). A persistent theme in relief debates through the centuries is the manipulation of the social and institutional boundaries between those who are expected to work and those who might for some reason be legitimately excused or excluded. Inevitably, these boundaries are somewhat porous, the grounds on which relief systems are so often politically discredited. As Katz (1986: 41–42) demonstrates, the overwhelming majority of those receiving outdoor aid in the nineteenth-century United States were widows, children, the aged, and the infirm, but this did little to prevent periodic attacks on the system as an alleged haven for the able-bodied but workshy:

> [O]pponents feared not the people on relief but those who might be. Outdoor relief was dangerous not because of whom it helped but because of the lesson it taught by example. Its very existence was a threat to productivity, morality, and the tax rate, because the respectable working class just might learn the possibility of a life without labor. As with poorhouses, policy again held the sick and helpless hostage to fears about social order and the need for a dependable, industrious workforce willing to labor for low wages.

The shadow of the poorhouse therefore fell across the low-wage labor market. The establishment of strict discipline in the former is critical to the maintenance of control in the latter. And now, as then, it is clear that the process of making rules for relief is also one of making rules for the bottom of the labor market. Specifically, these rules serve to regulate the social distribution of waged work. For example, ethnic inequality in access to outdoor relief in the nineteenth century, and to welfare in the 1960s, shaped the contours of ethnic segmentation in the labor market in general and the functioning of its low-wage "secondary" sector in particular (Gordon et al., 1982; Cray, 1988; Quadagno, 1994). Likewise, the dualistic structure of the U.S. welfare state—where there is a marked divide between a male-dominated stream of entitlements-based, non-means-tested provision (such as workmen's compensation and social security) and a female-dominated stream of means-tested, discretionary, and stigmatized programs (such as AFDC/TANF and WIC, the food program for women, infants, and children)—clearly reflects gender divisions, but at the same time maps onto the fundamental *labor-market divide* between unstable and exploitative "secondary-sector" work and secure, better paid "primary" employment (see Piore, 1970; Gordon, 1988; Piven and Cloward, 1988). In other words, the structure of labor markets exerts "demand-side" influences on the welfare system. Contrary to the conservative imagination, sporadic work patterns and welfare recidivism are not simply "lifestyle choices" made by some poor people, but reflect the structural realities of life in this unstable segment of the labor market. As Piore (1970: 68) saw it in the 1960s, the welfare system "tends to foster habits of behavior and thought characteristic of secondary jobs and antagonistic to success in primary employment. The personalized, dependent relationship between client and social worker is closely akin to the relationship between worker and supervisor in the secondary sector and totally unlike the institutionalized procedures for job allocation and redress of grievance in primary jobs." And the fact that many workers remained "trapped" in secondary job markets, due to factors like discrimination, means that they invariably need to make periodic recourse to welfare. Here, *employment* is systemically insecure, the underlying causes of repeated welfare use having more to do with structural economic conditions (on the demand side of the labor market) than with individual motivations or social circumstances (on the supply side).

Contributing as they do to the socialization and reproduction of the secondary workforce, relief arrangements exert a profound mediating influence over the social allocation of "good" and "bad" jobs, and over the configuration of power relationships in the labor market (Giddens, 1981; Rueschemeyer, 1986). The labor market must be seen as a domain of power relationships, preeminent among which is the "primary asymmetry" between capital and labor and the various "secondary asymmetries" between different fractions of capital and between different social groups in the workforce (Kreckel, 1980; Peck, 1996). Relief arrangements im-pinge on both these dimensions of power asymmetry in the labor mar-ket. Extensive relief provisions temper the primary asymmetry, to a lim-ited but significant degree, in favor of labor: they provide a temporary shelter from the vagaries of the labor market, allowing workers to exer-cise their strategic option of "exit" from particularly exploitative employ-ment relations, while also permitting labor to "wait" on the margins of the labor market until suitable employment opportunities arise. Relief arrangements therefore allow workers partially to counter one of their fundamental strategic weaknesses in the labor market: their inability to control their own labor supply (Offe, 1985). "The availability of social provision thus strengthens the position of workers by making them more secure, and this is especially important for nonunionized low-wage workers, who are otherwise close to the precipice of sheer want" (Piven and Cloward, 1987b: 6–7). In restricting the labor supply and tightening the labor market, welfare provision consequently attenuates the depend-ency of workers on wage labor.

The fact that access to relief tends to be unevenly distributed among the working class means also that the pattern of secondary power asym-metries is affected too. Those social groups, such as young people, married women, and the disabled, with access (or perceived access) to alternative means of subsistence outside waged employment tend to bear a disproportionate burden of labor-market risks, being discriminated against in hiring, promotion, and firing decisions (ironically *because* they are perceived to have both a weak attachment to the labor force and an alternative means of support). As a result, these groups find themselves systematically excluded from primary-sector jobs and the opportunity of stable employment, because their access (or *potential* access) to non-market means of support—coupled with their other socially ascribed dis-advantages—renders them "unstable" workers in the eyes of employers (Peck, 1996). Such cycles of disadvantage and exclusion are the defining characteristics of what we have come to regard as the "contingent workforce," the economic marginality of which does not stem from bad habits or shortfalls in "human capital" but from the *structural position* of these workers vis-à-vis both the labor market and the relief system.

That the interface of welfare systems and low-waged work is a site of enduring dilemmas of labor regulation should hardly be surprising. The very fluidity of the contingent labor force, the instability and cyclicality of secondary-sector employment, the fluctuating relativities of benefit packages and wages, the changing bureaucratic criteria for relief giving—all these factors pose a constant threat of desynchronization between the labor market and relief arrangements. This is why the process of "welfare reform" is a seemingly continuous one, and why crises of welfare are not so much *resolved* as *displaced*, only to reappear in different forms. It also explains why, historically speaking, labor markets and regulatory systems grew up together, evolving through mutual interdependence and uneasy symbiosis. As Polanyi explained, the idea of a self-regulating "free" labor market—for all its ideological symbolism—implied a stark, and ultimately unattainable, utopia. Historically, the mobilization of wage labor has required concerted, yet invariably problematic, institutional intervention.

> The road to the free market was opened and kept open by an enormous increase in continuous, centrally-organized and controlled interventionism. To make Adam Smith's "simple and natural liberty" compatible with the needs of human society was a most complicated affair. Witness the . . . amount of bureaucratic control involved in the administration of the New Poor Laws which for the first time since Queen Elizabeth's reign were effectively supervised by central authority. . . . Administrators had to be constantly on the watch to ensure the free working of the system. Thus, even those who wished most ardently to free the state from all unnecessary duties, and whose whole philosophy demanded the restriction of state activities, could not but entrust the self-same state with the new powers, organs, and instruments required for the establishment of *laissez-faire*. (Polanyi, 1945: 140–141)

As long as there have been wage-labor markets there has been experimentation in what the Webbs called "statecraft dealing with destitution" (Webb and Webb, 1963: 29). The contemporary interplay between workfare systems and "flexible" labor markets is but the latest chapter in this long history, only serving to underscore Polanyi's point that even the most "deregulated" of labor markets require substantial institutional support in order to operate "freely."

The mutual interdependence of relief systems and labor markets holds important political and analytical implications. Piven and Cloward (1987b:12) remark that "[e]fforts to shape relief arrangements so they would not intrude on market relations virtually define the history of social welfare." Equally, it is important to recognize that these "market relations" do not exist independently of relief systems themselves: political pressure for the "reform" of relief systems, particularly where this is exerted by employers or their representatives, has as much to do with remaking labor-market rules as it does with concerns about social provision per se. "Market relations" are not in this sense outside, separate from, or above state action, just as relief systems are not "external" to the labor market. These two spheres—state and economy, relief systems and the labor market—are fundamentally and irretrievably linked; their logic is a conjunctural one, their structures and dynamics mutually constitutive (see Block, 1994; O'Neill, 1997). "Market forces" are institutionally framed, sustained, and mediated. Therefore, the terrain of poverty politics, poor relief, and welfare reform is not one of "state intervention" in a historically and logically prior "market," but instead must be seen as a site of complex and relentlessly contradictory intersections of labor-market processes and regulatory systems, mediated through the vagaries of politics and the uncertainties of statecraft. The principal victims of this process, of course, are the poor, who repeatedly pay the price for their structural position at this pressure point in the job market.

## Regimes of Regulation

This complex regulatory nexus cannot be reduced to a one-dimensional, quantitative relationship between relief arrangements and the labor market, in which welfare provision is simply rolled back or rolled forward in accordance with labor-market conditions. The qualitative interconnections between the two spheres mean that "labor-market conditions" (and labor-market rules) are *themselves* partly a product of the extent and nature of relief arrangements. In turn, this implies that the character of each upswing or downswing in welfare provision is qualitatively distinctive, institutionally specific, and historically and geographically variable. The seesaw tendencies identified by Piven and Cloward, wherein politically initiated liberalizations of welfare periodically subside into economically oriented downswings of work reinforcement, quite rightly draw attention to the underlying political–economic momentum. But this approach runs the risk of understating the institutional specificities of successive phases in the "cycle":

> The civil disturbances which prompt the liberalizing of poor relief are often short-lived, and the expansion of relief is one reason why. This is the central meaning of our proposition that poor relief moderates disorder. . . . As disorder subsides, elite preoccupation with work discipline comes to the fore. The better off . . . resent the costs of relief [while] employer groups fear that relief undermines labor discipline. Employers have always understood that by shielding working people from some of the hazards of the market, relief reduces the power of employers over workers. Moreover, for just this reason, the very *idea* of social provision is defined as dangerously subversive of market ideology. (1993: 344–345)

These are vital insights, rationalizing as they do the way in which political and economic interests are realigned at different historical moments in the relief cycle. The clear implication, however, is that the regulatory baseline is minimalist, work-reinforcing relief, that there is a kind of regulatory "default setting" that is restored once the immediate threats of social disorder are ameliorated. This itself is a somewhat minimalist reading of labor regulation, for it could be equated with an almost classical rendering of the logical (and historical) priority of the "free" labor market. Of course, poor relief performs a regulatory function even at the peak of its expansionary cycle, though this regulatory function might be regarded as a *qualitatively* different one to that of enforcing low-wage work. During the Fordist–Keynesian era, for example, expansive welfare provisions, varying in form from one country to another, represented an integral element of a macroregulatory conjuncture dedicated to the maintenance of full (male) employment, mass consumption, stabilized social reproduction, and a particular pattern of labor segmentation (see Lipietz, 1987; Harvey, 1989; Esping-Andersen, 1990; Kotz et al., 1994). Even though the U.S. variant of this regime was rather provisional and weakly developed by international standards, its basic regulatory architecture was consistent with the generic features of the prevailing mode of regulation: the U.S. welfare system, for example, was tendentially expansionist, being rooted in principles of needs-based entitlement that were ultimately codified (and struggled over) predominantly, but not exclusively, at the national level.

In a parallel fashion to the workhouse era that preceded it, the welfare era represented a *historically distinctive regime of regulation*. This is most certainly not to deny the strong continuities across these historical periods (see Clement, 1985; Katz, 1989; Handler, 1995; Jacoby, 1997), but to make the rather more subtle point that they each represented a distinctive institutionalization of poor-relief/labor-market relationships. The workhouse regime was definitionally minimalist, structured in accordance with the principle of less eligibility and critically dependent upon the deterrent effect of the poorhouse with its associated ceremonies of degradation. Strictly enforced residency requirements served to immobilize peasant laborers, effectively binding them to the land in a quasi-feudal fashion, as the evolving rules of poor relief were shaped in accordance with the sporadic labor demands of an emerging market (Rimlinger, 1971). The status of the recipients of poor relief was determined by their irretrievably subordinate position in the moral economies of both the old agrarianism and the emerging industrial order (Laslett, 1971), stratified according to elite interpretations of the "deserving" and the "undeserving." Administration was a predominantly local matter, eligibility and benefit levels being determined by local elites and their underlings.

While some of these principles were rescripted in the subsequent welfarist era, the defining institutional characteristics of this pattern of regulation were distinctive in several respects. Social programs were increasingly standardized and bureaucratized, while eligibility gradually became a matter of national entitlement rather than of local discretion. Welfare rights became embedded both in legislation and in the taken-for-granted *doxa* of social progress. In the process, welfare's subject was also remade: the old quasi-feudal dependency was displaced by a new notion of *industrial dependency*. As Fraser and Gordon (1994) explain, the identity of the welfare recipient under industrialism was defined as the wage earner's other, comprising those marginalized or excluded from the "malestream" of the labor market. In the United States, the old distinction between the deserving and undeserving poor was reworked into an institutionalized, "two-track" welfare system, structured in terms of flows into the core and out to the periphery of the waged-labor market rather than on moral grounds (see Gordon, 1988; Piven and Cloward, 1988). The composition and reach of welfare programs and provisions defined the social groups—primarily on the basis of the ascriptive criteria of age, gender, and race—with politically sanctioned alternative roles outside the white, male-dominated core of the labor market, be this the social–reproduction role of the "housewife," or the underemployment and economic peripherality of the African American worker (see Offe, 1985). Simultaneously, this pattern of social exclusion and economic marginalization shaped the distinctive social boundaries of the wage-labor market of the industrial–welfare era. The Fordist labor market, and the welfare regime that supported it, was predicated on virtually full employment for males, the payment of "family wages" for primary-sector workers, and the discontinuous incorporation of various marginalized and socially disadvantaged groups into secondary employment.

It should hardly be necessary to point out that these social presumptions concerning the distribution of paid work, and the institutions that underpin and reproduce them, are deeply structured along race and gender lines. These imprints are also strongly reflected in the structure of welfare regimes and in the course of reform politics (see Quadagno, 1994; Rose, 1995; Orloff, 1996; Lieberman, 1998; Brown, 1999; Mink, 1999b; O'Connor et al., 1999). In countries with liberal welfare regimes (including the United States, the United Kingdom, and Canada), social provision is generally subordinated to the labor market and consists of fairly comparatively minimalist provision for the unfortunate minority without access to waged work. This configuration tends to place women, the disabled, minorities, and poor people in general in an especially precarious position. Sometimes these groups may be specifically targeted for social-policy interventions in ways that compound their marginalization in the labor market; in other instances, the application of formally "race-blind" and/or gender-neutral policies can have profoundly regressive effects. With reference to the introduction of Temporary Assistance for Needy Families in the United States, for example, Orloff (1999a) observes the following social-distributional consequences. First, the 1996 reforms effectively replaced a social right (however limited in scope) with a more restrictive and discretionary regime in which former and would-be welfare recipients are forced to rely on "private" sources of support, such as wage work, charity, and the family. This shift disproportionately disadvantages women and minorities, and those with caregiving responsibilities, because these groups typically have lower incomes, suffer higher incidences of unemployment and job discrimination, and as a result typically have greater recourse to welfare. Second, the replacement of AFDC by TANF means that state support for caregiving and reproduction (again, however limited) has effectively been eliminated. Instead, remaining public support for these functions is restricted to those in employment, negatively impacting those outside the waged sphere, while care services delivered through the market are often beyond the reach of poor households. Third, these reforms marked an important shift in institutional and social conventions concerning the gender division of labor, in that waged work—in addition to unpaid caring work—is now expected of all poor mothers, compounding the stresses associated with low pay, poor-quality childcare, multiple (paid and unpaid) job-holding, and insecure household incomes. The cumulative outcome of these changes is that

> labor market position is increasingly important for life chances as U.S. citizens and residents are less buffered from social inequalities by state policies. Feminist analysis of welfare states in the past has maintained that programs which reward labor market participation advantage men over women, given that men tend to have jobs with higher pay and better conditions than do women. This is still, on average, true. But in the wake of decades of equal opportunity employment and educational policies, in the context of a restructured labor market featuring fewer manufacturing and more service jobs, there is more variation among both men and women. Labor markets don't advantage men and disadvantage women uniformly. Rather, labor market success depends on educational qualifications and cultural capital, as well as the extent to which workers are burdened with or free from caregiving responsibilities. . . . [T]he problem with work requirements for many welfare recipients is the kind of employment they have and the kind of care they can afford for their children. (Orloff, 1999a: 24)

Welfare-retrenchment and/or work-enforcement strategies do not simply shift the boundary between the employed and the nonemployed segments of the labor market in some socially neutral manner. Because this boundary is socially constructed, its movement inevitably entails the re-organization of social relations. And when this boundary movement occurs in the context of liberal welfare/neoliberal workfare regimes, the outcomes are usually measured in terms of deepening social and economic inequalities. Among the neoliberal national states, at least, life chances and residualized social rights are being rendered increasingly contingent on labor-market participation, just as the employment system in these deregulated economies is itself characterized by growing contingency. The outcomes are new and more market-mediated forms of inequality in low-wage labor markets, the swelling of which is being facilitated by state-induced commodification of large parts of the previously unwaged sector and the forced labor supply that this creates.

The outcomes of this process of restructuring are varying spatially, even within the loose grouping of (neo)liberal welfare states. Some of the sources of these variations originate in the labor market itself; others stem from the nature of the reform strategies that are being pursued in different jurisdictions; still others can be traced to the particularities of race, gender, and class politics. A persuasive illustration of the latter "social-shaping" processes can be found in Orloff's (1999b) examination of different "models of motherhood" in the formation of social-policy configurations in Britain, Canada, and the United States. This study placed the United States in something of an outlier position in that state support for (poor) single parents was the norm in Britain and Canada, while the United States was moving decisively toward a model in which paid work was the principal means of support. Even though there may have been a degree of "convergence" on the U.S.-style paid-work model in recent years, it is surely significant that the politics of welfare reform continue to play rather differently in these three countries. Mandatory work programs for lone mothers, for example, remain comparatively controversial in Canada and Britain, where reform-minded politicians tend to tread more carefully around such issues, while in the United States this moment of political sensitivity seems to have been passed some time ago (see Myles and Pierson, 1997; O'Connor et al., 1999; Deacon, 2000).

The boundary between welfare and work is, therefore, socially constructed and perpetually reconstructed. The state is deeply implicated in shaping patterns of labor-market inclusion and exclusion among different social groups. Racial, gender, and generational divides are routinely exploited in this ongoing process of social regulation (see Peck, 1996). Reorganized social relations and uneven social-distributional outcomes are consequently more than side effects in this process of social regulation. Indeed, they are very much bound up in its means and methods. Hence the need to see "welfare reform" as a significant site of social struggle, framed by the shifting imperatives of the labor market, and not just some discrete arena of social-policy intervention. Welfare-to-work is very much concerned with work as well as with welfare. Such is the politicized nature of this process, and the complexity of labor-market responses and feedback effects with which it is associated, that there is an argument for seeing each manifestation of welfare reform as unique, idiosyncratic, and historically and geographically specific. But there is also a "big-picture" story to be told here, one concerning the distinctive, *generic* characteristics of different regimes of regulation.

## Shifting Labor-Market Boundaries

The workhouse, welfare, and workfare regimes represent distinctive institutional/political responses to one of the enduring dilemmas of regulation in capitalist labor markets: that a sustainable social allocation of waged work must be achieved without eroding the imperative to enter the market for the "mainstream" workforce, while recognizing that it is impossible to force the *entire* population into waged employment. This is a delicate balancing act, requiring constant adjustment and fine tuning, and it is one which, historically speaking, has been attempted in a series of different ways. The workhouse model and the welfare model are two of the most clearly delineated generic responses to an enduring regulatory dilemma. They represent historically and institutionally specific attempts to

> overcome this dilemma within the framework of a social order structured by the organizing principle of the labour market [based on] criteria of exclusion or exemption from the labour market that must have two qualities: i) they may not be freely chosen individually and thus potentially unable as a means of strategic withdrawal from the labour market; and ii) they must be selected in such a way that the "exempted" portion of the population . . . is not in a position to place "excessive" demands and politically effective expectations about its need for the means of subsistence on the production and occupation system. (Offe, 1985: 37)

As Offe goes on to point out, both these criteria "correspond to the institutions of the labour market, in which we regularly find special relations of force and control" (37). Welfare regimes perform a critical, *systemic* function in this regard, providing a "safety valve" for the labor market as a whole (not simply an individually exercised strategic option for some of its participants). Those ascriptively-designated social groups granted access to welfare systems, and to other institutional spaces on the outer limits of the labor market, do not, however, find themselves in a privileged position. Quite the contrary. Their access to alternative means of subsistence—itself a typically punitive and degrading experience—labels them contingent, marginal, and secondary workers, against whom discrimination in the labor market is effectively deemed legitimate and even rational (Peck, 1996). Such workers—poor women, ethnic minorities, the disabled—are denied access to stable, primary-sector jobs because they are socially designated in the prevailing regime of regulation as semidetached, peripheral workers, a subordinate position that is both reflected in and validated by the education and training system.

Of course, there are circumstances when this contingent workforce must be mobilized on a large scale, for example, following shifts in the aggregate scale and composition of labor demand. Under these conditions, regulatory institutions such as the welfare system are manipulated so as to encourage job-market inclusion. As Table 2.1 illustrates, a range of regulatory mechanisms might be deployed to facilitate such a switch in emphasis. On the demand side of the labor market, inclusive strategies such as wage subsidies and restrictive working-time legislation can be deployed as a means of mobilizing new sources of labor. On the supply side, relocation and retraining packages can be used to generate positive incentives for inclusion, while the retrenchment of relief systems and the

**TABLE 2.1.** Modes of Labor-Market Regulation

|  | Positive sanctions (incentives) | Negative sanctions (penalties) |
|---|---|---|
| **Labor-market exclusion** | | |
| Demand side | Early retirement schemes | Prohibition of child labor or employment of illegal immigrants |
| Supply side | Paid parental leave; incentives for full-time education and training; self-employment schemes | Extension of compulsory schooling; lowering earning disregards for pensioners |
| **Labor-market inclusion** | | |
| Demand side | Wage-subsidy schemes | Employment quotas; maximum working-hours legislation |
| Supply side | Allowances for continuing education and retraining; relocation assistance | Workfare programs; manipulation of benefit levels/ eligibility and reservation wages |

*Source:* Developed from Offe (1985: 46–51).

implementation of workfare tend to achieve labor-market inclusion by removing alternatives to waged work. Correspondingly, a parallel array of regulatory techniques is associated with the objective of labor-market exclusion, such as early retirement schemes and employment prohibitions on the demand side, or parental-leave arrangements and the extension of compulsory schooling on the supply side.

The process of adjusting and reorganizing the "boundary institutions" of the labor market by way of this repertoire of policy measures is a continuous one, both reflecting and contributing to the unstable disequilibrium of the labor market. Phases of concerted regulatory restructuring tend to be associated either with structural changes in the labor market or with calamitous labor-market "shocks"—such as the mass mobilization of labor during wartime or the proliferation of "makework" schemes during deep recessions (see Labour Studies Group, 1985). Structural change in the labor market typically calls for a fundamental restructuring of boundary institutions and often accompanies a break between regimes of regulation, as *qualitative* reorganization as well as quantitative adjustment is called for. In other words, there is a regulatory imperative not only to numerically *adjust the flows of workers* into and out of wage labor, but also to endeavor to *remake the workers themselves*, their attitudes toward work and wages, their expectations about employment continuity and promotion prospects, their economic identities, and so on. Welfare systems are deeply implicated here, given that their function is not simply to provide a "shelter" from the labor market, but to define and enforce norms of labor-market participation in ways that are inscribed into the very identities of contingent workers. Thus, the practices of "welfare reform" are never just "administrative" processes, but are instead saturated with ideological presuppositions: they are about self-respect and family responsibility, about the moral economy of the poor, about the definition of "independence" and the work ethic itself, about the legitimation of "appropriate" gender roles.

## Crisis and Change in Relief Systems

These regulatory processes are simultaneously structural and personal, mediated as they are through the lived experiences and political struggles of workers. The negative symbolism of relief, for instance, is reproduced through the identities of the poor and their representations in the media. The mirror image of the *dignity* of wage labor is the *stigma* of welfare. So, when the Chicago labor market collapsed in the 1920s, the search for scapegoats focused on the most vulnerable sections of society. For many of the victims of this process, self-organization was the only way to restore dignity. According to a Mexican community leader of the time,

Due to our own negligence . . . we are forced to join the public charities. . . . [O]nly through a strong organization [can we] overthrow the
hostile propaganda voiced in some newspapers who accuse us of being
a burden on the Relief institutions, a menace to public health, and a
hindrance to the stability and advancement of the life of the native
worker. (quoted in Cohen, 1990: 222)

That the shame of the dole should be so acutely felt by the victims of
poverty, even as the Great Depression tore apart the fragile systems of
mutual support and corporate welfare in Chicago, is testimony to the
depth of such convictions. In many ways they belied the condition of
structural crisis that were to lay the foundations for the New Deal. Macroeconomic failure continued to be experienced (and represented) as
personal failure. Between 1929 and 1931, the combined public and private cost of poor relief—partial and patchy though this remained—in
eighty-one U.S. cities rose from $42 million to $170 million (Katz,
1986). Soon, local relief agencies were to be overwhelmed and the stage
set for unprecedented federal intervention in the form of the New Deal.

Such moments of extreme stress in relief systems often reveal a lot
about underlying regulatory dynamics. While the New Deal framework
was modified frequently over the ensuing six decades, its underlying
foundational principles remained intact. The New Deal institutionalized
a pattern of entitlements for different social groups (and with this a particular configuration of labor-market attachments), which essentially
established the parameters for both poverty politics and economic participation until the 1990s. The expansions of the 1960s and the retrench-
ments of the 1980s occurred *within* this framework. They may have challenged it, but they did not rupture it. Cycles of relief did not disappear
altogether, though in an important sense they had become channeled
and institutionalized. Piven and Cloward, for example, characterized the
anti-welfare initiatives of the early Reagan years as an "indisputably . . .
serious effort to *reverse* a pattern of government policy that has developed by fits and starts since the Great Depression" (1985: 2, emphasis
added). They went on to predict that the anti-welfare offensive would
fail, notwithstanding the concerted efforts of powerful business and state
elites, due to the defensive political forces that had become inscribed into
the modern welfare state itself:

Public relief, once the sole form of state intervention to ameliorate
destitution, has . . . come to be embedded in a general structure of in-
come-support programs for a wide range of constituencies, from the
aged to the disabled to the unemployed. The changes in American society that gave rise to this development lead us to the conclusion that
*the cyclical pattern of providing subsistence resources by the state has been
replaced by a variety of permanent income-maintenance entitlements. . . .*

> The political economy of the late twentieth century is not that of either the eighteenth or nineteenth century. The relationship of state to economy has been drastically altered in ways that provide powerful support for the idea that people have a right to subsistence, and particular legislative or executive actions will not distinguish that idea. We believe, in short, that *Regulating the Poor* represents a better characterization of the past than a prediction of the future. (1985: x–xi, emphasis added)

So, the essentially cyclical pattern in relief arrangements had given way to a more stable, institutionally mediated accommodation based around socially legitimate entitlements. The strength of the defensive political interests mobilized around these entitlements was such, Piven and Cloward predicted, that the Reagan offensive would falter and fail. History now shows, however, that the Reagan years marked a radical acceleration in anti-welfare politics, as a wedge was driven between stigmatized welfare recipients (notably those on AFDC) and other entitlement groups. The exploitation of racial and gender divides within and between different entitlement groups played a large part in this, undermining the collective political capacity of welfare recipients (see Quadagno, 1994; Rose, 1995; Gilens, 1996; Mink, 1999a). By the 1990s, and under a Democratic president, this tactical assault on welfare had matured into a new workfarist hegemony and a full-blooded "politics of disentitlementarianism" (Safire, 1994).

While Piven and Cloward may have initially overestimated the defensive capacity of welfare advocates, their observation that the cyclical rhythm in relief arrangements had given way to a more stable, structurally embedded pattern is a telling one. It implies that the emergence of a welfare *state*, as opposed to a contested assemblage of short-term welfare *programs*, represents a qualitative shift in the nature of state–economy relations (see Collier, 1997). Correspondingly, the attack on this system, which has been building continuously now for more than two decades, represents more than another cyclical downturn, but seems instead to presage a profound structural realignment. It is in this context that the contemporary politics of workfare should be understood. Even though the rhetoric of workfare continues to run ahead of its material achievements, both warrant critical scrutiny at the present time for at least two reasons. First, the rise of workfare—its discursive construction as an alternative "system," as a regulatory antonym of welfare, and the embedding of its principles in new legislative frameworks, job-market norms, and administrative practices—is occurring in the structural context of the possibly terminal erosion of welfarist institutions and principles. This need not imply that workfarism is somehow noncontradictory, or that it holds the "solutions" to all the extant regulatory problems (imagined or real) of welfarism, but it does suggest that—as the prevailing political orthodoxy—workfarism is beginning to codify a distinctive regulatory path in the context of a continued search for an after-welfarist fix (see Peck and Tickell, 1994; Jessop and Peck, 2000). It is conceivable, of course, that workfarism will ultimately prove to be a transitory phenomenon, a symptom of the crisis itself, but its continued ascendancy in North America and Europe means that its *potential* role in a new regulatory order at least deserves sustained investigation. Although it has yet to stabilize as a systemic regime, workfare has become associated with a range of strategies that are manifestly, and often *definitionally*, anti-welfare in character (see Table 1.1).

A second reason to take workfare seriously is that its ascendancy has coincided with, and may already be reinforcing, fundamental shifts both in the organization of labor markets and in labor-market policy orthodoxies. The growth of polarized, "flexible" labor markets, particularly in North America and the United Kingdom, has been coupled with a transatlantic policy program dedicated to deregulation, and through this to the reconstitution of "competitive" relations in the labor market (see Tarling, 1987; Harrison and Bluestone, 1988; Boyer, 1988, 2000; Albert, 1993; Hutton, 1995). The story is now a familiar one: wages have polarized and levels of socioeconomic inequality have risen dramatically; permanent underemployment is accepted as a "natural" feature of labor markets; labor unions have fallen under legislative and political attack as the enemies of economic competitiveness; the feminization of the labor force, the growth of dual-income households, and multiple job holding, in the context of falling incomes around the middle and bottom of the income distribution, have overturned the male-dominated, "breadwinner" model of the postwar era; various forms of contingent working, such as part-time, contract, and temporary work, are transforming the meaning of the job itself. In these and other ways, underlying economic tendencies for rising "flexibilization" have been reinforced by changes in policy regimes variously rationalized in terms of accommodating to, or seizing competitive advantage in, this "new order" in the labor market. The politically dominant strand in labor-market policy calls for a rolling program of "deregulation" (especially on the demand side of the labor market), measures to stimulate the adaptability and employability of the workforce, and an overarching emphasis on labor-market inclusion.

Workfare seems to be playing an important role in this wider shift in the "mode of political rationality" (Offe, 1985), in the systematic reregulation of the poor in general and of the contingent workforce in particular. While there are some historical similarities, this strategy is manifestly not the same as the workhouse regime of the nineteenth century, for it is being advanced in contemporary labor markets through contemporary state structures. The workfare offensive is very much a product of these contemporary conditions, not least because its underlying principles have been forged in the context of, *and in opposition to*, those of the Fordist golden age: universal welfare entitlements, real wage growth, and institutionalized worker protection. In this sense, workfarism differs from earlier downswings in the relief cycle for similar reasons that welfarism differed from previous expansionary phases: more than a rollback in benefits and programs, it is a broadly based onslaught against an entire regime of institutionally stabilized and politically embedded regulatory norms and conventions; it is concerned with a root-and-branch restructuring of regulatory structures, not simply an adjustment in priorities or in the scale of provision. The principles and parameters of the welfarist regime of regulation are themselves being challenged. It is no coincidence, then, that the transatlantic policy orthodoxy of flexibly deregulated labor markets now has a social policy analogue in the concerted advocacy of workfare programs (see Deacon, 1997; Dolowitz, 1998; Theodore, 1998; Peck and Theodore, 2000b).

## Workfarism as a Regime of Regulation

The structural significance of workfarism is not merely a function of its self-evident popularity among political elites, but has to be understood in the wider context of its complementarities with ongoing processes of economic and regulatory restructuring. Certainly, workfare cannot be simply bracketed off as an example of social policy innovation; it is deeply implicated in the ways that labor markets are being restructured. While it is important not to overstate the economic functionality of workfarism, it is just as important to recognize that the workfare offensive is occurring alongside far-reaching shifts in the organization of labor markets and in the rationales of labor-market policy. Just as the workhouse and welfare were emblematic of distinctive regimes of regulation, expressing a particular, historically specific pattern of relationships between the labor market and relief arrangements, so also the possibility must be confronted that workfare is beginning to define an alternative, after-welfare regime of regulation.

Hence the need to explore the emerging political–economic "logic" of workfare, alongside a consideration of its evident contradictions and weaknesses. This means taking seriously, if not at face value, some of the epochal claims that are currently being made about the crisis of welfare and the potentialities of workfare. Listen, for example, to two advocates of workfare, of rather different political stripes:

Politics is shifting its focus from class to conduct. The most divisive disputes are no longer about unionism or socialism but rather the problems of new ethnic minorities, usually immigrants, whom many feel threaten the social order. Concerns about social cohesion, as much as economic costs, explain why European welfare states have ceased to grow, just as social reform has halted in the United States. . . . *The old issues were economic and structural; the new ones are social and personal.* . . . In the progressive era, the archetype is the factory worker carrying out a strike or organizing to get out the vote for political parties of the left. The archetypes of dependency politics are much more helpless—the jobless youth of the inner city; the homeless man begging in the better parts of town; above all, the single mother sitting at home on AFDC. . . . Such people have *personal* problems that must be addressed before impersonal reforms of the traditional kind are even conceivable. . . . Motivation is inevitably more at issue than opportunity. (Mead, 1992b: 211–212)

Eventually, replacing welfare with work *can* be expected to transform the entire culture of poverty. It won't happen in one generation, necessarily, or even two. But it will happen. Underclass culture can't survive the end of welfare any more than feudal culture could survive the advent of capitalism. (Kaus, 1992: 129)

So, just as the workhouse and welfare regimes constituted their subjects in socially distinctive ways—first as undeserving poor, then as the wage-workers' other—workfare programs address themselves to the problem of "postindustrial dependency" (Moynihan, 1989). Significantly, while dependency is regarded as an individual, psychological–behavioral condition (see Fraser and Gordon, 1994), it is one with roots in the supposedly systemic dysfunctions of welfarism. Workfarism consequently represents, at least in part, a *corrective* for welfarism. Work obligations under contemporary workfare systems are "cast in rehabilitative terms" (Handler and Hasenfeld, 1991: 202; see also Mead, 1997b), providing opportunities for individuals, enforced by regimes of compulsion and discipline, to lift themselves out of dependency and into the social and economic "mainstream." In Mead's view, they signal more than a switch toward an active and inclusive style of policy, and indeed represent the reconstitution of the *passive* subjects of welfare as *active* subjects of workfare: "The poor . . . are controversial because they do so little to help themselves . . . their actions lack purpose and direction. In dependency politics, the . . . question is how passive you can be and remain a citizen in full standing" (1992b: 213). Under workfare regimes, participation in wage labor is regarded as a prerequisite for citizenship.

Workfarism is centrally concerned with the resocialization of workers for the flexible labor markets of today. It is about establishing new regulatory conventions concerning the nature and value of contingent work and contingent workers; constructing new codes of conduct for those on the edges of the labor market; and rebuilding wage-labor's "boundary institutions." This is why workfare is likely to be more than just a passing phase in social policy. Whether or not the current brace of programs and administrative experiments prove to be durable ones, the emerging norms and conventions of workfarism seem set to play a key role in the restructuring of labor-regulatory systems in coming years.

Arriving as they have in the context of a sustained attack on the philosophy and institutions of welfarism, workfare experiments have a kind of preparadigmatic significance. One indicator of this—and a theme that will be developed throughout the book—is that the attack on welfare and the rise of workfare have been accompanied by a profound *spatial* restructuring of the institutions and political–economic relations of the relief system. The long history of relief arrangements reveals that major shifts in their rationale, scale, and structure are typically accompanied by changes in the spatial hierarchies of regulation (in particular, concerning the relative balance of local and national responsibilities), and in the geographies of relief provisions, on the one hand, and poverty, on the other. Consequently, movements in spatial structures and relations are indicative of the wider pattern of restructuring in relief systems. And here, too, there is evidence that space is being (re)made for workfarism.

## SPACES OF REGULATION

Distinctive spaces of regulation are associated both with the rhythms of relief politics and with each regime of regulation—under the workhouse system, under welfarism, and under the emerging workfare regime. In cyclical terms, expansionary phases tend to be characterized by administrative and financial centralization in relief arrangements, while during periods of contraction it is common to see various forms of decentralization in delivery systems and funding. In Piven and Cloward's (1971) terms, cyclical responses to civil disorder tend to take the form of concerted actions on the part of nation-states and national elites, while labor-disciplining downswings are typically accompanied by the (re)localization in relief arrangements. As Handler and Hasenfeld (1991: 31) put it, "[W]hen issues of labor discipline and social control of deviant behavior are strongest, programs tend to be locally administered." While the threat of *generalized* social breakdown and civil disobedience usually triggers the involvement of national authorities, as occurred for example following the wave of urban riots and political protests in the United

States during the 1960s, once "political stability is restored, relief practices in each locale are re-shaped day by day to meet manpower needs" (Piven and Cloward, 1971: 123). This process, by which relief arrangements are (re)embedded at the local scale, is strongly conditioned by the exigencies of local labor markets, local administrative practices, and local moral codes. This is because

> the moral ambiguity of poverty always threatens the integrity of welfare programs as a system of social regulation. Contending ideologies embedded in welfare policy itself create contradictory regulatory and ceremonial requirements. Moreover, once a class of "deviants" has been created, an enforcement system has to be established requiring the exercize of discretion. Therefore, a major concern in the administration of welfare policy is the allocation of *jurisdictional responsibility*. When there are difficulties in drawing clear lines between different moral/economic subcategories amongst the poor population—say between the deserving and undeserving, or between the employable and unemployable—the jurisdiction of welfare programs is more likely to be local, enabling the local community to sort out the ambiguities. (Handler and Hasenfeld, 1991: 30)

Detailed but nontrivial decisions about the dividing lines between the deserving and the undeserving poor, about the interpretation of eligibility criteria, and about the nature of work-participation requirements, for example, tend for the most part to be devolved to the local level. Unsurprisingly, this leads to an uneven spatial pattern in the de facto form and labor-market impacts of relief arrangements, and to the emergence of distinctive *local* subregimes of labor-market regulation. Within the framework of the nineteenth-century English Poor Laws, for example, the "Manchester Rules" imposed especially harsh local interpretations of work tests and eligibility criteria for outdoor relief, reflecting the city's wider political–economic environment of brutal class discipline and elite governance (Webb and Webb, 1963; Rose, 1971).

Alternatively, the particular ways in which relief arrangements "tread down" into local labor markets can have profound implications not only for program outcomes but also for the functional role of relief itself. The labor-market effects of a welfare-to-work program based on subsidized employer placements, for example, might be expected to vary from place to place: in depressed labor markets the program would serve to contain unemployment in the context of demand deficiency, while in a buoyant labor market its predominant function would be as a filtering and prescreening device for labor-market entrants (Peck, 1990, 1999; see also GAO, 1987; Vartanian, 1999). Not only the effects, but the very viability of welfare-to-work programs are contingent on local labor-market conditions, and this is especially the case where programs emphasize immediate "labor-force attachment" in the face of local job shortages. This is the acid test confronting workfare programs in many British, U.S., and Canadian cities today, where localized "job gaps" and pockets of underemployment remain in evidence even at the top of the business cycle.[3] As Michael Harrington has observed, "[Y]ou cannot dragoon someone into taking a job that does not exist" (1984: 33).

## Geographies of Relief

Complex spatial iterations—around the balance of local jurisdictional authority and administrative discretion, and around the geographical unevenness of policy forms and outcomes—add yet another layer of contradiction and indeterminacy to the ongoing process of labor regulation via poor relief. Hence the continual adjustment both of local relief systems and the wider frameworks in which they are embedded. Geographies of relief, in this sense, are not minor side effects of policy, but are integral to the changing architecture of policies themselves. Spatial variations in policy outcomes repeatedly frustrate the architects of relief policy, as the gap between policy intent and local outcomes is very often a large one. The history of U.S. welfare policy can be told in such terms (see Handler, 1995), as the "formulation of coherent national welfare policy [has proved] extraordinarily difficult, and the amount and kind of assistance offered poor people varies by where they live" (Katz, 1986: x). Just as the structure and dynamics of labor markets vary across space, while processes of economic restructuring inevitably entail geographical unevenness and inequality (Massey, 1995), so also do regimes of labor regulation unfold unevenly across the economic and institutional landscape (Peck, 1996; Herod, 1998). As a result, there is no direct correspondence between the (local) form and function of regulatory strategies, with geographic unevenness in the former confounding the objectives of the latter. Welfare-to-work policies made in London or Washington, DC, for example, rarely look the same in declining cities as they do in the more buoyant suburbs, while at a more finely grained level, outcomes also vary in myriad ways along with the microgeographies of administrative practice, social convention, and labor-market interaction. It is not merely a throwaway statement to observe that "relief in West Virginia is different from that in New York" (Handler and Hasenfeld, 1991: 32). Rather, coming to terms with the admittedly messy geographies of poor relief is essential to understanding both the effects of programs and the politics of "reform."

"New" relief policies, needless to say, are not imposed on a featureless isotropic plain; implementation does not occur on a tabula rasa. On the contrary, the form that "new" policies take on the ground in different local situations will be a result of the way in which they interact with the spatially uneven residues of previous policies, and more generally the inherited geographies of labor markets and their related institutions of social reproduction and regulation (see Peck, 1998). Katz invokes a familiar geological metaphor to draw attention to these historically embedded interactions: "American welfare practice has been constructed in layers deposited during the last two centuries" (1986: ix). Each of these layers, of course, is geographically uneven, and the pattern of uneven development in each conditions the geography of the next. While this layering process is a continuous one, it has been suggested here that it has been punctuated by a number of structural breaks, each reflecting a major regulatory realignment of relief arrangements and labor-market conditions. Each regime of regulation is associated with a characteristic set of spatial structures and relations, albeit in the context of the continual flux of cyclical adjustment. In essence, the workhouse system was locally based and administered, while the prevailing tendency under welfarism was for centralization and increasing national regulation. Correspondingly, the crisis of welfare and the rise of workfare have been associated with the "hollowing out" of national institutions and the emergence of (different forms of) decentralized policy formulation and delivery (see Cope, 1997; Jessop and Peck, 2000). All these, it must be underlined, are no more than tendential patterns—there were repeated attempts to centralize and standardize the workhouse system; welfare provision remained far more uneven in reality than was suggested by its legislative and ideological foundations; and workfare policies remain heavily embedded in different national frameworks and strategies. But it is important not to overlook the general point that distinctive structures of spatial relations have been associated with the underlying logic of these different regimes of regulation.

## The Workhouse Regime

Defining characteristics of the workhouse regime were geographic unevenness and local administration. Typically, it was local elites and their representative overseers who formulated the rules of access to outdoor relief, who applied laws of "settlement" in denying aid to "strangers" from outside the area, who codified the rules and practices of the workhouse, who set the rates, and who translated local moral conventions into local administrative procedures (see Fraser, 1976; Trattner, 1984; Clement, 1985; Katz, 1986; Cray, 1988). Even concerted attempts to centralize the system, such as England's New Poor Law of 1834, did little to alter the stubborn localization of the workhouse regime. As Fraser remarks of the English situation, "At no time in the nineteenth century did the poor relief system achieve even the semblance of uniformity. Variety was the essence of the New Poor Law as of the old" (1976: 17; cf. Williams, 1981). At the same time, local administration was the cause of profound tensions. In England, "the most frequent battle between central and local administration was that between a reforming bureaucracy anxious to raise standards and parsimonious guardians bent on economy" (Fraser, 1976: 20). Emphasizing the commonalties between this and the parallel U.S. system of relief, and in many ways anticipating the circumstances of contemporary workfare regimes, Trattner has pointed out that

> [l]ocal responsibility often led to inadequate and unequal standards, on the one hand, and inefficient and sometimes corrupt administration, on the other. Thousands of untrained and often incompetent overseers of the poor, many of whom were employed on only a part-time basis, did not make for effective administration. More important, because many of the poorer districts had a higher proportion of needy residents and less money to spend on relief than the more prosperous ones, not only was treatment of the poor unequal, but the communities that could least afford it usually had the highest poor rates. (1984: 47–48)

There were also growing contradictions in the way that relief systems intersected with evolving (local) labor markets. Laws of settlement, which restricted relief to local residents, fettered the geographic mobility of labor. Workers who moved to a new area in search of employment were effectively placing themselves outside the relief system and totally at the mercy of the local market (Rose, 1976). This led to deep problems in the regulation of urban labor markets in particular, which relied upon large inflows of workers to feed the factories, but were also prone to violent cyclical swings in business activity and labor demand. Of course, the act of making rules about urban relief was at the same time a process of urban labor-market regulation: the moral and administrative categories of the relief system—concerning marital and family status, length of residency, place/country of origin, and so on—both defined access to extramarket subsistence and determined patterns of participation in wage labor. While over time there was a tendency for these codes of inclusion and exclusion to become embedded in extralocal legislation, economic conventions, and corporate norms (Williams, 1981; Katz, 1986), the degree of local variability in their interpretation and implementation remained high throughout the workhouse era. In the process, urbanization and the expansion of wage-labor markets went hand in hand with the evolution of relief arrangements. Local labor markets and local labor regulation therefore emerged side by side through mutual adjustment. "Relief, in short, served as a support for a disturbed labor market and as a discipline for a disturbed rural society" (Piven and Cloward, 1971: 30–31).

This process of gradually, if unevenly, adjusting relief arrangements was through trial, error, and experimentation beginning to establish the institutional boundaries of the industrial labor market and the socioeconomic identity of the industrial worker. A relatively stable, white, male working class was being constructed, as other groups of workers—children, immigrants, married women, old people, and so on—were variously pushed to the margins of the labor market or excluded from waged work altogether. Relief arrangements and the development of social legislation played a significant part in this process by determining which categories of worker should be granted access to social catchment areas on the edge of the labor market, and by implication, which groups should be excluded from, rendered exclusively dependent on, or discontinuously reliant on, wage-labor. Braverman characterized the process in this way:

> [The] massive growth of institutions stretching all the way from schools and hospitals on the one side to prisons and madhouses on the other . . . represents not just the progress of medicine or education, or crime prevention, but the clearing of the marketplace of all but the "economically active" and "functioning" members of society. (1974: 280)

In this way, the restructuring of "boundary institutions" was beginning to establish the rules of participation of the emerging industrial labor market (Brandes, 1976; Gordon et al., 1982). These, though, were turbulent times: the expansion and modernization of the labor market called for dramatic and often contested organizational changes in the workplace, while the process of urbanization proved to be both a prerequisite for the new regime of labor relations and a source of contradictions. A wave of strikes rippled through major cities in the United States around the turn of the century, for example, and the fledgling corporations responded by suburbanizing production and introducing new systems of workplace control (Gordon, 1977).

In the first decades of the twentieth century, the underregulated labor markets of cities like Chicago were lurching from one crisis to another. Workers struggled to make a living in the face of intermittent unemployment, low pay, sparse and voluntary relief systems, and various forms of mutual support, while the majority of employers continued to hire and fire at will, though some sought to generate a measure of worker loyalty by way of limited "company-welfare" programs (Cohen, 1990; Jacoby, 1997). This fragile matrix of regulatory institutions was scarcely adequate to the task of accommodating even the routine rhythms and disturbances of the urban labor market. It was to collapse altogether in the wake of the stock-market crash of 1929. Within just four years, the national unemployment rate rose from 3 to 25 percent. This unprecedented economic downturn not only brought down banks and corporations, it tore apart the social institutions of the labor market. Relief agencies were quickly overwhelmed as financial support dried up at the same time as the number of displaced workers was spiraling. The costs of relief—the bulk of which was underwritten by overstretched municipalities, townships, and counties—mushroomed, despite the fact that only one-quarter of the unemployed were receiving relief by 1932 (Piven and Cloward, 1971). The relief crisis, which began as a local and even personal phenomenon, had become national and structural in character. The imperative was for some kind of federal response, but this would be to enter uncharted territory.

## The Welfare Regime

When Franklyn D. Roosevelt accepted the presidential nomination of the Democratic Party in 1932, he sensed that "[T]his country needs, and unless I mistake its temper, the country demands bold, persistent experimentation. . . . It is common sense to take a method and try it. If it fails try another. But above all, try something" (quoted in Trattner, 1984: 262). On taking office, Roosevelt acted immediately to initiate large-scale federal aid, soon to be augmented in 1934 with a temporary-work program, the Works Progress Administration (WPA). These steps were bold and conservative at the same time, underwriting what Katz (1986) has aptly termed the United States's "semi-welfare state." While the sheer scale of the New Deal provisions was immense by the standards of its time, so also were the perceived threats to social order. These threats were all the more acutely felt when they started to come from "mainstream" U.S. workers: that prime-age, white, males should find themselves unable to find work and at the mercy of the relief system placed at risk not only a major segment of the core working class but the legitimacy of the U.S.-style free market itself. A national survey of the relief population for the WPA in Washington, DC, had reported the startling finding that "workers on the urban relief rolls in 1934 were not industrial misfits who had never worked nor persons with an irregular work history [but] were a relatively experienced group of workers" (quoted in Katz, 1986: 212). In fact, the typical recipient at the time was a male household head in his late thirties with a prior history of stable manual employment—the paradigmatic industrial worker.

Circumstances dictated that relief provisions, and in particular work programs, had to be expanded enormously. Whenever possible, however, these would reinforce established labor-market and moral codes, and extant patterns of labor segmentation: programs were constructed in such a way that different categories of recipient were channeled into different forms of provision in accordance with their normative labor-market status. Despite the haste in which they were constructed, the new programs carefully streamed participants by gender, race, and occupational status, taking special care to insulate the industrial worker from his "others" (Rose, 1989). Fearful nevertheless of the potentially erosive effects of relief on labor-market discipline, business leaders fiercely opposed the expansion of work programs, particularly where doles outstripped local wage rates, as they did in many parts of the South (Piven and Cloward, 1971; Bremer, 1975; Quadagno, 1984). Considerable tensions emerged between the federal government and state- and local-level interests as the scale of the unemployment crisis drew the Roosevelt administration, rather reluctantly, into further expansion of "temporary" work programs. At their peak in February 1934, the three main programs—the Federal Emergency Relief Administration (FERA), the Civil Works Administration (CWA), and the Civilian Conservation Corps (CCC)—were assisting some eight million households, or 22 percent of the U.S. population (Katz, 1986).

In the midst of this expansion in federally supported work relief, Roosevelt's Committee on Economic Security set to work on the creation of a federal social security framework. The subsequent Social Security Act of 1935 internalized many of the same principles that had shaped the federal government's temporary measures. Indeed, at one level, the content of the act "amounted almost to a catalog of America's social welfare programs" (Berkowitz and McQuaid, 1988). This was clearly the case with respect to the act's welfare provisions, which built upon state and local practice, and remained substantially dependent on local delivery. Nevertheless, a slow and uneven process of federalization had begun. Katz (1986: 246) reports that between 1932 and 1939 the federal share of public-aid expenditures rose from 2.1 to 62.5 percent. More significantly, the Social Security Act began to codify a pattern of welfarist entitlements and a repertoire of welfarist programs at the national level, embedding these in the structures of the federal government and (more slowly) in the labor-market expectations of both workers and employers. These were vigorously resisted by parts of the business community, but found tacit support from others. Some employers realized that a minimalist state-welfare system, topped up where necessary by private arrangements, was preferable to—and might well preempt—more interventionist and socialized alternatives (Jacoby, 1997).

Although by international standards the degree of centralization in the U.S. welfare system was relatively modest—just as, in fact, the U.S. system was underdeveloped on a whole range of measures in comparison with its western and northern European counterparts—centralization became both an underlying tendency and a defining characteristic of postwar welfare regimes (Gough, 1979). In the relatively weak U.S. form of welfarism, centralization was checked at every stage by opposing forces in the business community, in state and local governments, and elsewhere, as were the wider panoply of measures associated with social Keynesianism (Weir, 1992). Throughout the welfare era in the United States, the geographic cleavages in the Democratic Party—specifically, between its southern conservative wing and its more liberal cadre in the northern cities—have played an important part in the politics of welfare reform. Southern conservatives opposed the expansion and federalization of welfare from the New Deal onward, repeatedly insisting on state autonomy and "flexibility," local control over benefit levels, and local discretion in administration as a means of maintaining the region's regressive labor-market norms. The truncated and distorted state of the U.S. welfare system is testimony to the strength of these political forces. It was not until the "welfare explosion" of the late 1960s, fueled by the modernization of southern agriculture and the rise of urban disorder in the northern cities (Piven and Cloward, 1971), that the southern states were drawn—reluctantly and still only partially—into the welfare era.

As Table 2.2 shows, welfare caseloads increased in all areas of the United States during the 1960s, though the highest rates of growth were found outside the South, and particularly in the northern cities. In 1969, 58 percent of the national AFDC caseload was located in urban areas, while the cities had accounted for fully 70 percent of national caseload growth during the 1960s. In contrast, the Deep South contained a smaller share of the national caseload at the end of the 1960s than it had in the beginning, despite its manifest problems of poverty and labor-market adjustment. Piven and Cloward (1971) show, moreover, that 98 percent of the growth in the welfare rolls in the Deep South during the 1960s occurred after the passage of the Civil Rights Act of 1964.

The U.S. experience reveals more clearly than any that the tendential centralization of the welfarist era did not mean uniformity of coverage. While European welfare systems were to come closer to matching aspirations of uniformity with reality (see Esping-Andersen, 1990), in the United States uniformity was scarcely even an aspiration. Here, marked spatial differences in benefit levels, in the balance of federal and state funding, and in administrative practices remained throughout the welfare period (Trattner, 1984; Jones and Kodras, 1990; Cope, 1997). Nevertheless, the prevailing direction of change—most clearly during the 1960s—was toward federalization, as welfare rights and entitlements

**TABLE 2.2.** The Geography of the U.S. "Welfare Explosion"

| | Share of national AFDC caseload 1960 (%) | Share of national AFDC caseload 1969 (%) | Change in AFDC caseload 1960–1969 (%) | Contribution to national AFDC caseload growth (%) |
|---|---|---|---|---|
| Northeast | 23 | 31 | 180 | 39 |
| North central | 23 | 20 | 78 | 17 |
| West | 18 | 22 | 161 | 26 |
| South | 36 | 27 | 54 | 18 |
| Deep South[a] | 12 | 9 | 57 | 6 |
| Other South | 25 | 18 | 52 | 12 |
| Urban areas | 45 | 58 | 165 | 70 |
| Five largest[b] | 17 | 25 | 217 | 34 |
| Remainder | 29 | 33 | 135 | 36 |
| Northern | 37 | 49 | 175 | 60 |
| Southern | 8 | 9 | 121 | 10 |
| Rural and less urban areas | 54 | 42 | 60 | 30 |
| Northern | 27 | 24 | 87 | 22 |
| Southern | 28 | 18 | 34 | 9 |
| U.S. Total | 100 | 100 | 107 | 100 |

*Source:* Calculated from Piven and Cloward (1971: Appendices 1 and 2).
[a]Louisiana, Mississippi, Georgia, Alabama, South Carolina.
[b]Chicago, New York, Detroit, Los Angeles, Philadelphia.

were increasingly codified at the national level, as political and bureaucratic struggles emerged around the national "poverty line," as non-AFDC benefits such as food stamps and Medicaid began to compensate for local shortfalls in cash assistance to the poor, and as new initiatives and directives poured out of Washington, DC, where the War on Poverty was to be declared (though never won). The development of activist groups such as the National Welfare Rights Organization (NWRO) was partially underwritten by the federal government, especially by Democratic administrations anxious to reach out to African American voters in the turbulent cities, where deindustrialization and job dislocation were emerging as major problems (see Bluestone and Harrison, 1982; Wilson, 1987). In the process, welfare "emerged as a national issue [while a] whole array of federally sponsored local initiatives was directed at the inner city. . . . These were intentionally designed to bypass traditional political structures, and a direct relationship was forged between the federal government and the ghettos" (Handler and Hasenfeld, 1991: 116). Subsequently, these Great Society programs, the associated expansion in the welfare rolls, and the later (ill-fated) movement for a guaranteed income would come to define the "entitlement liberalism" of the late 1960s.

## The Crisis of Welfare and the Promise of Workfare

Davis (1996) has argued that the historical significance of entitlement liberalism may lie less with its political accomplishments than with the potency of the countervailing political forces that it inadvertently mobilized. Crucially, the "Conservative reaction . . . included a growing political interest in attaching work requirements to AFDC [which] found substantive expression with Governor Reagan's 'workfare' experiment in California and [Georgia] Senator Herman Talmadge's 1971 bid to improve the effectiveness of the Work Incentive Program" (Davis, 1996: 236). These early forays in the workfare offensive consequently had a particular geography, being spearheaded by traditional opponents of welfare in the West and the South. They also reflect the strong association, in the conservative imagination, between the problem of "welfare dependency" and the moral and economic collapse of the inner city. As Fraser and Gordon (1993) have argued, the transition from one pattern of poor relief to another tends to be associated with a redrawing of the "map of dependency." Thus, the ghetto is rendered the principal site of contemporary "welfare dependency," the rhetorical location for a host of dysfunctional institutions and the home of a disengaged underclass. The promise of workfare, its advocates argue, is that these problems are tackled head on and in situ. Lawrence Mead, for example, makes his case for workfare by observing that

> [i]nstitutions linked to dependency are a presence in and around the ghetto. Here is where homeless shelters and other custodial institutions tend to be clustered, in part because land is cheaper and community resistance less effective. Here, too, most public housing projects are built, and black youth who live in them or on welfare are markedly less likely to be in school or working than others. Here is where welfare is most often long term, which also means it is nonworking. Living in such neighborhoods does seem to add extra pressures towards dysfunction. Youth from heavily poor and black areas are somewhat more likely to drop out of school, become unwed mothers, and earn low wages, even controlling for personal characteristics. Less certainly, they are more likely to get into crime. (1992b: 146)

Here, too, is the familiar slippage between welfare dependency, urban decay, and problems of/in the African American community. Mead's list also represents a catalog of the (ghetto) labor market's "boundary institutions," those social catchment areas on the edge of the waged sphere that regulate processes of work socialization and labor allocation. In their own ways, conservatives also recognize these labor-regulatory functions. Their argument goes that, by enforcing work and reinforcing work values, workfare will bring about the integration of ghetto residents (read: the welfare-dependent African American underclass) into the labor market.

The workfare imperative—to put what Mead calls the "nonworking poor" to work—is sold in terms of the interests of those precariously surviving just one rung up on the urban labor-market hierarchy: the working poor. In a perverse reworking of the axiom of less eligibility, the working poor are represented as the class with the most immediate interest in the radical curtailment of welfare. As Mitchell Ginsberg, former commissioner of welfare in New York City, put it in the wake of Nixon's failed reform effort in November 1972:

> [T]he hatred of welfare is unbelievable. There is a strong mood across the country to crack down, keep people off the rolls. Welfare reform is at a dead end. . . . It is clear that people like me who have been pushing for reform for years obviously haven't made much progress. . . . We underestimated the depth of the opposition. We didn't pay enough attention to the concerns of people who were above the welfare line. The heart of the opposition to welfare comes from people just above it—blue-collar workers, trade unionists, though not labor leaders or high-level businessmen. It is the group below, the lower-middle-income worker. He's the guy who feels welfare is taking it away from him. We will have to pay attention to the ethnic groups who feel more threatened by "them." (quoted in Davis, 1996: 236–237)

Such interpretations did, and still do, play conveniently into the low politics of welfare reform. In reality, of course, those just above the "welfare line" have the most to gain from liberal welfare policies, as these have the effect of placing a floor under wages and conditions in the labor market, prevent the overcrowding of the low-wage sector, and provide a safety net for those falling on hard times. To respond to the deteriorating conditions in low-wage labor markets by retrenching welfare and forcing recipients into waged employment is consequently to do no favors to those immediately above the welfare line. On the contrary, the most likely outcome is that their own jobs become more unstable, competition for whatever work is available intensifies, and wage rates fall along with the welfare line (see Mishel and Schmitt, 1995; Solow, 1998; Peck and Theodore, 2000b). One of the reasons why Ginsberg's argument still works on a (low) political level, however, is that the welfare line is at the same time a color line and a gender line: those below it are still often perceived as the "others" of the "mainstream" worker.

As the United States's poor population has urbanized—73 percent of those in poverty in 1990 were resident in metropolitan areas, compared to 44 percent in 1960 (Danziger and Weinberg, 1994)—a trend which seems to be accelerating in the 1990s (Center on Urban and Metropolitan Policy, 1999), so also the issue of welfare reform has become increasingly bound together with the question of urban labor-market regulation, in a debate galvanized by the specter of the "ghetto underclass." These concerns have also been linked to growing pressure to decentralize programs, a common feature of labor-disciplining downswings in relief cycles, but in this case one that was to develop into a sustained process of defederalization and downloading. While the Nixon administration flirted with decentralization, it was not until the "New Federalism" of Reagan's first term that the issue was placed firmly on the agenda. Advocating the block granting of welfare provisions to the states and a radical expansion in local workfare programs, the Reagan administration sought to rupture the federal infrastructure of the welfare system. An internal administration memo of 1981 echoed an age-old principle of urban poor relief in its assertion that "individual needs for public assistance can be assessed most effectively at the level of government closest to the need" (quoted in Piven and Cloward, 1987b: 24). The concern here, however, was manifestly not with the efficacy of local administration, but with the role of the federal framework itself in the maintenance of welfare rights, entitlements, and standards: "Because individual needs vary, public assistance benefits should not be tied to a federally-determined standard" (24).

While the Reagan administration was only partially successful in its attempts to defederalize welfare, its sustained autocritique of "big government," encouragement of local workfare trials, and cultivation of the "states' rights" movement were to establish the foundations for the antiwelfare orthodoxy of the 1990s. Local experiments with welfare reforms outside the federal legislative framework, which were permitted for research and policy-development purposes under the 1935 act, were encouraged by the second Reagan administration, were expanded under Bush, and proliferated under Clinton (see Wiseman, 1995). Decentralization, block granting, and radical welfare reform were key planks in the Republican's *Contract with America* (see Moore, 1995), prefiguring in so many ways the block-granting PRWORA of 1996. The crisis of welfare, in other words, has involved the "decentering" and "hollowing out" of welfare—institutionally, financially, and ideologically.

The decentering of welfare has occurred on a number of levels. First, decentralization has occurred hand in hand with federal defunding, most notably perhaps under the 1996 act which imposes unfunded work mandates totaling $13 billion, according to the Congressional Budget Office.[4] States and localities are consequently induced to pass on cuts, or to raise revenue locally, if caseloads rise. Either way, a financial climate is created in which subnational jurisdictions must operate under fixed spending limits and in accordance with the (workfarist) dictates of the federal regime (meeting work participation requirements, etc.), or suffer funding penalties. Fortunately, strong economic growth post-1996 provided states with windfall gains in their welfare budgets, as job-market expansion drove down caseloads.[5] Second, decentralization has the effect of dissipating and diluting political opposition, bypassing the Washington-based representation and advocacy system, switching some policymaking and lobbying functions back to the statehouse level, and making the policy-development process itself far more difficult to track, let alone respond to. The machinery of advocacy, campaigning, and representation constructed around the federalizing welfare system is therefore rendered substantially impotent, while the process of wielding external pressure on policymaking becomes contingent on the highly uneven capacities of state- and local-level organizations. Such a fragmentation of political opposition was an explicit objective of right-wing advocates of welfare downloading and the block-grant mechanism.

Third, decentralization intensifies the competition for (dwindling) resources at the state and local levels, systematically biasing policy innovation and program-delivery processes in favor of low-cost options yielding short-term, politically visible results. Comparatively high-cost paths to workfare, such as the Wisconsin or Minnesota models, are therefore rendered vulnerable to competition from lower-cost emulators (see Bush, 1996; Handler and Hasenfeld, 1997). Moreover, while federal policy capacity is in many ways diluted by decentralization, there is continuing scope to deploy arm's-length measures (such as financial incentives, contractual measures, funding pilot initiatives and demonstration projects, etc.), in order to steer the ongoing reform process. The federal government can therefore assume significant new roles as an *orchestrator* of workfarism. Fourth, the methodology of workfare is such that localized program design and enhanced discretion (over such matters as eligibility, service needs, and placement) at the hands of local officials are often regarded as prerequisites for "successful" delivery (see Wiseman, 1989; Handler and Hasenfeld, 1997; Mead, 1997b).

> Workfare has to be delivered at the local level. It is possible to mail checks from state capitals like Sacramento or Madison, but it is not possible to manage job search or training programs from there for recipients who live in Bakersfield or Janesville. Think about it: What

creates glory and press in Sacramento and Madison must be delivered
by people slugging it out in Fresno and Beloit. (Wiseman, 1987: 42)

The administration of workfare is typically a hands-on, local matter. Intensive and active "case management" by field officers is a defining feature of programs such as Greater Avenues for Independence (GAIN) in
Riverside, California, where a supervisor remarked, "Contact! . . . Once a
week, twice a week, there's no such thing as too often . . . it reminds
[participants] that you *care*, and that you're *watching*" (quoted in
Bardach, 1997: 269).

The effects of decentralization are also mediated through the labor
market in at least four important ways. First, the floor under local wages
that was previously maintained—albeit imperfectly and unevenly—by
the federal welfare package is rendered both lower and more uneven by
decentralization. Although states fought successfully to retain control
over AFDC cash-assistance levels right though the welfare era, so as to
maintain the principle of less eligibility with respect to *local* wage rates,
variability in AFDC payments was partly canceled out by topping up via
the food-stamp program and by the nationwide provision of medical
benefits to poor families. Decentralization breaks up this national floor
under the low-wage economy, allowing wages to fall to a lower and yet
more uneven level in line with conditions in local labor markets. Second,
and reinforcing this trend, the generally weaker fiscal capacity of low-
wage states and localities means that scope for defending welfare entitlements and benefit rates is further impeded in precisely those areas where
downward pressures on pay rates and employment conditions are most
concerted. Even where the political will exists to defend welfare provisions—and in many such areas it clearly does not—the financial and administrative capacity needed to achieve this objective may be lacking.

Third, regressive local workfare regimes are likely to become a qualitative indicator of a "good business environment," along with related
proxies of local labor discipline such as low pay rates and right-to-work
legislation. Whether or not conditions in the lower reaches of the labor
market really matter all that much for individual enterprises, the presence of a no-nonsense, work-oriented welfare system will nevertheless
register as emblematic of wider attitudes to labor-market management.
Relatively liberal systems, on the other hand, will tend not only to inflate
local pay rates at the bottom end of the labor market, but may be difficult
to reconcile with claims that states really "mean business" in the relentless processes of corporate attraction and retention. Fourth, state and local administrations are subject not only to financial discipline in the
form of the federal funding framework, but tend in addition to be more
vulnerable to the implicit and often explicit economic discipline of mo-

bile capital. The costs and tax implications of welfare spending enter into the locational calculations of footloose investors, if only in a symbolic sense, while the local fiscal environment (and perceptions thereof) condition the behavior of endogenous firms. The leverage of business lobby groups, moreover, tends to be greater at the state and local levels—where the threat of exit is a more palpable one, creating a downward drag on public spending in general and social spending in particular.

The dynamics of decentralization are consequently played out on a whole range of levels, from the symbolic terrain of the corporate imagination to concrete conditions in low-wage labor markets, from the architecture of funding regimes to the sphere of oppositional politics. Likewise, the prospect of profound regressive change is real at each of these levels, as is the threat of a "race to the bottom" in social standards, regulatory norms, and labor-market practices. The complex of political and economic forces that during the welfare era served gradually to ratchet up benefit and pay levels, and with these the general conditions of existence for both welfare recipients and low-wage workers, seem to have been thrown into reverse in this period of crisis. A dynamic of decentralization had been entrenched. At the same time, this is associated with the breakup and "decentering" of welfarist principles and institutions, on the one hand, and the tendential rise of decentralized workfare regimes, on the other. While disorder and flux continue to reign, it is becoming increasingly clear that these changes—and the distinctive spatial dynamics that underpin them—are more than simply transitory, but are concerned with a systemic reorganization of the regulatory regime. So, for Cope (1997), the rise of workfarism in the United States is part of a wider strategy for the "flexible dispersion of labor."

## Other Paths to Workfare

While the U.S. experience represents the most vivid, and perhaps paradigmatic, case of the crisis of welfare and the ascendancy of workfare, its experience has certainly not been unique. In fact, workfarist tendencies of different kinds can be identified in most of what we have become accustomed to calling the "advanced welfare-state" countries. It has become axiomatic that these systems varied considerably from country to country in terms of their institutional form, their interpenetration with the labor market, their pattern of rights and entitlements, and so on, even though at an abstract, generic level they shared certain common characteristics (Gough, 1979; Offe, 1984; Esping-Andersen, 1990, 1996). Echoing these different historical antecedents, workfare politics and workfare strategies have exhibited different forms in different places, albeit again in the context of certain generic parameters. Later chapters consider the distinctive evolution of workfare in Canada and in Britain. Suffice it to say at this stage that, to the extent that some sort of generalized transition from welfarism to workfarism is underway, this will necessarily take on a geographically specific and path-dependent form. There will not be one but a variety of paths from welfarism to workfarism.

While workfare politics exhibit their most complex form in the United States, parallel developments in countries such as Australia, the Netherlands, and the United Kingdom should not be dismissed as pale imitations of the U.S. "original." Rather, they each have their own roots, inflections, and contradictions. At a broad, generic level, it is already clear that different forms of workfare politics and programming are associated with different kinds of welfare regime:

> Whereas dependency is at the core of the American discussion on workfare, the search for labour market flexibility stands at the forefront in Europe. Distinctions among welfare regimes help us make sense of these differences. Indeed, the dependency argument is not so much North American as it is anchored in the liberal conception of the welfare state. Likewise, labour market arguments are typical of conservative and social democratic welfare states. . . . [While] arguments about workfare abound . . . they vary with the type of welfare states [that] different countries have institutionalized. (Noël, 1995: 54, 57)

Table 2.3 sketches the emerging shape of workfare strategies in the three ideal-typical welfare regimes identified by Esping-Anderson (1990). In the "corporatist" welfare states, such as Germany, France, Italy, and Austria, where the state has historically played a central role in the granting of social rights and the maintenance of status hierarchies, workfare strategies have been state-led and have been concerned to minimize the disruption of established status rights and relativities. Here, workfare has been primarily concerned with *labor-market reintegration*. In the "social democratic" welfare states, such as Sweden, Norway, Denmark, and Finland, where the principles of equality, universalism, and the decommodification of social rights have been taken farthest in the context of maximalist welfare provision, workfare strategies have been oriented to structural adjustment in the context of residualized commitments to universalism and social redistribution. Here, workfare has been about *(re)investment in human capital*. Finally, in the "liberal" welfare states, such as the United States, Canada, Australia, Switzerland, and the United Kingdom, where means testing and limited social transfers reflect a vision of welfare as necessarily subordinate to market allocation, workfare strategies have been at their most developed, reinforcing market "incentives" in the context of an individualized "deficiency-model" analysis of welfare dependency. Here, workfare has been mostly concerned with *labor-force attachment*.

What is striking about these three generic paths from welfarism to workfarism is that they each represent a work-based response to a welfare crisis with roots in the mid-1970s. Although political strategies and institutional reforms vary both between *and within* the three regime

**TABLE 2.3.** Three Worlds of Welfare and Three Paths to Workfare

|  | Corporatist welfare states | Liberal welfare states | Social-democratic welfare states |
|---|---|---|---|
| | | Welfare regime | |
| Rationale | Political stabilization via social protection | Market-oriented system<br>Dominant work ethos | Social citizenship<br>Pursuit of equality |
| Work–welfare regime | Categorical design of social programs<br>Corporatist involvement of labor-market actors | Market/state insurance for majority<br>Means-tested assistance for "marginal" groups<br>Residual and minimalist approach to social programming | Universal programs<br>Generous social provision<br>Commitment to full employment<br>Fusion of welfare and work |
| Labor-market policy | Geared to rise in unemployment<br>Responsive to political power of left | Passive income support<br>Responsive to political and demographic pressures | Extensive, active approach<br>Responsive to countercyclical pressures |
| Ideology | Corporatism, structured skills, and social stability<br>Rights attached to class and status | Social assistance as a temporary, individualist problem<br>Stigmatization of welfare recipients | Universal rights and shared responsibilities; positive welfare orientation |

*(continued on reverse)*

**TABLE 2.3.** *(continued)*

|  | Corporatist welfare states | Liberal welfare states | Social-democratic welfare states |
|---|---|---|---|
|  | **Workfare strategies** | | |
| **Orientation** | Statist Emphasis on labor-market adjustment and skilling Emphasis on work values Tackling structural unemployment | Market Individualist approach: behavior modification and "incentives" Countering "welfare dependency" | Social Labor-market adjustment through social-democratic means Continuing commitment to universalism and social redistribution |
| **Workfare model** | Labor-market reintegration approach Residual commitment to active labor-market policies Differentiated strategy | Labor-force-attachment approach Restriction of welfare entitlements and benefits | Human-capital approach Incorporation of labor-market partners in policy formulation and program delivery |
| **Ideology/ discourse** | Work values with continuing commitment to class/status rights | Moral regulation: family values and work disciplines | Structural reorientation of welfarist approach |
| **Regulatory dilemmas** | Reluctance to commit to large-scale, comprehensive workfare programs Between laissez-faire and adjustment | Contradiction between costs of workfare and objective of reducing social expenditures "Unfunded" workfarism Between social control and laissez-faire | Paternalism Tension between labor-market objectives and individual autonomy Between adjustment and social control |

*Sources:* Developed from Esping-Andersen (1990); Noël (1995); Peck and Jones (1995).

types—as the rather different experiences of the United States, Canada, and the United Kingdom clearly illustrate (see Chapters 6 and 7)—their generic similarities suggest that workfarism is beginning to take shape as an international phenomenon. Of course, the mere presence of such similarities in welfare-reform discourses and strategies need not imply that some universal structural cause is driving the process of institutional change. In part, these similarities reflect the growing international trade in workfare-reform packages themselves, as accelerated policy transfer in this strategically important field becomes increasingly commonplace (Deacon, 1998; Walker, 1998; Jessop and Peck, 2000). The global diffusion of workfare-style discourses, institutions, and policies is a highly uneven one, but is no less significant for this. Indeed, the fact that decentralization and spatial unevenness tend to accompany shifts toward workfare, and may also have a role in *facilitating* these shifts, means that workfare regimes are even "mature" likely to be geographically variable. This is certainly true at the local level, where a number of quite distinctive generic reform strategies have emerged (summarized in Table 2.4), each associated with a multitude of permutations. Analyses of workfarism must therefore be sensitive to the international as well as to the subnational geographies of (anti-)welfare politics and workfare strategies.

## SITUATING WORKFARE

The history of relief arrangements is one of continuities and discontinuities. In addition to the political–economic cycles identified by Piven and Cloward (1971), it is possible also to discern a broad historical–institutional patterning in the relationship between relief arrangements and the labor market—what have been termed here "regimes of regulation." While there are continuities, too, in the ways in which the regulatory relationship between relief and the labor market is expressed, as the residues of past practices can often be seen in contemporary institutional structures and strategies (see Katz, 1986; Bagguley, 1994; Jacoby, 1997), it is important also to recognize that this is not a smooth coevolutionary process, but one punctuated by phases of institutional crisis and wrenching economic change. Such phases typically mark the breakdown of an established poor-relief/labor-market relationship and the search for another. The irreducibly contradictory nature of this relationship, moreover, means that all such periods of institutional searching are uncertain ones, while no resolution to the crisis will be a permanent one. Each period of restructuring in the "boundary institutions" of the labor market—as the perennial nature of welfare reform efforts illustrates all too clearly—tends to call forth unanticipated political and economic effects, leading to a continual process of institutional adjustment.

Such ongoing forms of adjustment are the source of important internal dynamics within regimes of regulation. These, though, are historically distinctive in that they each express a *qualitatively* different relationship between poor relief and the labor market: workhouse regimes

**TABLE 2.4.** Local Forms of Workfare

| | Market model | Local state model | Community sector model | Human capital model |
|---|---|---|---|---|
| Program orientation | Wage labor market | State and quasi-state agencies | Not-for-profit sector | Education and training system |
| Objectives | Assisting rapid transitions into work, by the shortest route | Enforcement of work discipline; lowering cost of basic public services | Work experience, exploiting/developing skills for community benefit | Raising long-term employability and tackling pre-market discrimination |
| Philosophy | Get a job | Earn your check | Repay the community | Go to school |
| Client formation | Jobseeker | Underlaborer | Temporary helper | Trainee |
| Social relations | Business-like, job-placement approach | Bureaucratic and managerialist ethos | Contractualized, community/social-work approach | Developmental ethos; service-delivery approach |
| Program dynamics | Processing-based, highly exposed to labor market | Job slot-based, contingently linked to internal labor market | Placement-based, partially insulated from labor market | Course-based, insulated from labor market |
| Labor-regulatory function | Short-term labor-force attachment | Casualization/restratification of public-sector work | Containment/development of nonprofit economy | Educational and vocational skill formation |
| Labor-market entry | At or near to minimum wage | Undercutting union rates | Subminimum wage | Usually above minimum wage |
| Labor segmentation | Active reproduction of inequalities through privileging of most job-ready | Resegmentation of public-sector workforce through creation of subordinate stratum | Passive reproduction of inequalities through ghettoization/sheltering | Scope to reorder job queue/tackle inequality through positive discrimination |
| Geographic incidence | Strongly ascendant; exurban and small-city origins but often imposed on larger cities | Isolated instances; associated with aggressive/regressive local state management | Relatively widespread, but now less favored; contingent on presence of large not-for-profit sector | Increasingly rare; typically associated with large cities and lagging regions |
| Contradictions | Fuels working poverty by swelling contingent labor supply and depressing wages; high social externalities; residualizes hardest-to-serve clients | High cost, unless predicated on displacement of fully waged workers; vulnerable to labor-union opposition/unionization of workfare workers | Restricted long-term job prospects; sector highly dependent on external funding; vulnerable to disruption by social activists | High unit costs; outcomes may be indirect and long term; internalizes wider social costs, often reflected in high attrition rates |

*Source:* Peck (2000b).

were concerned to secure the brutal incorporation of an immobilized working class into a commodifying labor market, while welfare regimes sought to stabilize certain social norms of inclusion and exclusion in the context of an industrial labor market with close to "full" (male, white) employment, and protosystemic workfare regimes are associated with the restructuring of these regulatory norms in the face of employment polarization, feminization, and flexibilization. Analytically, this approach falls somewhere between those which, on the one hand, see nothing but historical continuity in relief arrangements (and by implication, also, in the institutionalization of labor markets), the character of which simply oscillates in accordance with the cyclical rhythms of the economy and polity, and those, on the other hand, which reduce this complex process of regulatory restructuring into a stage or transition model in which each institutional epoch is replaced in toto by the next. In the reading presented here, processes of cyclical and structural change are seen to be operating simultaneously, and while each regime displays a distinctive regulatory "logic," this necessarily internalizes aspects of past practice while yielding its own institutional patterns, vocabularies of reform, political tensions, economic contradictions, and so forth.

The historical and geographical "edges" of these regimes of regulation are inevitably blurred, they exhibit a certain degree of internal heterogeneity, and the paths between them are many and varied. In the final analysis, it is the way that political struggles intersect with economic imperatives and institutional forms that shapes the emerging regulatory fix. And to reiterate, this is not just a matter of tracing the uneven evolution of social-welfare programs, but of focusing on how these variously mesh with, disrupt, and transform labor-market structures. Continuous change is evident on both sides of this relationship, though there have also been phases of costabilization and mutual interdependence. As Quadagno put it:

> Since the New Deal, the composition of the working class has changed. It is now comprised more of women employed in service jobs than of men in manufacturing jobs. Programs that adequately protected families of fully employed male workers in manufacturing industries from the risks associated with cyclical fluctuations in business and from loss of employment in old age are insufficient to protect part-time employees in low-wage service industries characterized by high labor turnover and the absence of fringe benefits. (1994: 181)

The simultaneous crises of industrial labor markets and welfare systems define the structural context against which workfarist strategies of different kinds are emerging. This structural context, however, does not (pre)determine the nature of political–economic responses, which are likely to be variegated in form, and might range from the relatively progressive to the regressive (see Fraser, 1993; Noël, 1995). Axiomatically, both patterns of labor-market restructuring and paths of regulatory reform are preconditioned by, and mediated by, the inherited institutional form of the welfare state (Esping-Andersen, 1996; Hamnett, 1996). Just as there is no one, universal form of labor-market flexibility, there is no single orthodoxy of labor-market "deregulation," and there is no unidirectional path toward workfare (Peck, 1996)—hence the emphasis in this and subsequent chapters on the *geographies* of workfarism.

While there is widespread acceptance that the turbulent labor-market conditions of the 1930s and the associated frenzy of regulatory reform led to a systemic adjustment in the relationship between poor relief and the labor market (Piven and Cloward, 1985; Berkowitz and McQuaid, 1988), needless to say there is no such agreement on the broader significance of contemporary restructuring processes. Jessop's (1993, 1999) "thought experiment" on the nascent form of a potential successor to the Keynesian welfare paradigm, the Schumpeterian workfare regime, remains perhaps the most ambitious contemporary account. Here, a Schumpeterian strategy for the "promotion of product, process, organizational, and market innovation . . . and the enhancement of the structural competitiveness of open economies mainly through supply-side intervention" is coupled with the workfarist "subordination of social policy to the demands of labour market flexibility and structural competitiveness" (Jessop, 1993: 9). There may be a danger in such an approach of endowing premature political–economic functionality on a set of fragile and contradictory developments, one that Jessop (1995b, 1999) acknowledges (see Peck and Jones, 1995; Carter and Rayner, 1996). And while the present analysis of contemporary shifts in workfare/labor-market relationships is manifestly more restrictive in scope and modest in reach, there is a similar risk, perhaps, of implying that workfarism is somehow an inevitable and predestined "next stage." But workfarism is not the unmediated outcome of the political will of conservative politicians, any more than it is an automatic consequence of economic globalization. Ultimately, workfare is a political choice, not an economic necessity. And as Jessop (1999) emphasizes, there is at the present time not just one but a variety of workfarist strategies and welfare/workfare mixes in evidence, while still more are conceivable. Although the neoliberal form of workfare remains "hegemonic on the international level . . . important counter-currents exist in specific national and regional contexts" (Jessop, 1999: 357).

In this sense, whether one characterizes the present conjuncture as a continuing crisis of the welfare state or as an emerging workfarist regime amounts to more than a semantic distinction. While the former reflects an ongoing regulatory breakdown, the latter at least implies that the outlines of a regulatory *rapprochement* of some kind are beginning to take shape. The account of workfarism presented here is rather more provisional and open than this, reflecting the contradictory nature of the workfarist attempt to restructure the "boundary institutions" of the labor market, the regulatory inconsistencies of flexible labor markets, and the fragile identity of the normative contingent worker. Nevertheless, the regulatory intent of workfare strategies, and the new language of workfarism, are taken seriously. The central questions that *Workfare States* poses concern the extent to which welfarism is in a state of terminal crisis, on the one hand, and the sense in which workfarism might be stabilizing into a new regulatory fix, on the other. This analytical strategy is pursued with a view to opening up, rather than foreclosing, debate around the repertoire of regulatory options that might currently be available.

Regressive workfare models define one path, but they also seem to be indicative of the prevailing direction of change. The dissection of workfare—in all its potentialities, inconsistencies, and contradictions—must therefore be one of the prerequisites for the establishment of a progressive alternative. Workfare ideologues have for several years now been actively engaged in the process of envisioning a future based on radically different regulatory principles in the context of a new kind of (flexibilized and individualized) labor market. Their political ascendancy stands in marked contrast to the apparently stale and retrospective position of progressives, as the left has been backed into the corner of either defending welfarism (itself far from perfect, of course, as progressives would normally be the first to say), standing idly by, or even joining the workfare offensive with all the zeal of converts. Progressives have clearly been losing the battle over ideas, policies, and priorities that is the daily grind of regulatory reform. Clearly, the war over welfare's successor will never be won unless these battles are joined. In addition to engaging with the mundane reality of policy development and critique, this also means getting to grips with what Fraser (1993) calls the "political imaginary of social welfare." The crisis of welfarism has brought forth struggles not only over resources and rights, but also over the *meaning* of welfare and its alternatives (Schram, 1995). So far, advocates of workfare seem to be coming out on top in this process of discursive struggle, seizing the initiative and producing a new vocabulary for that "public sphere [that] is saturated with—indeed, structured by—various taken-for-granted assumptions about people's needs and entitlements . . . assumptions [that] inform the ways in which social problems are named and debated [and that] delimit the range of solutions that are thinkable"

(Fraser, 1993: 9). This process of discursively reframing the object and form of regulation—in which progressive voices have been ruthlessly marginalized—is the focus of the next chapter, which examines where the words of workfare came from and what they have come to mean.

## Notes

1. *The Works of Jeremy Bentham*, ed. John Bowring (Edinburgh, 1843) 8: 401–402, 384; quoted in Cowherd (1977: 93–94).

2. *Extracts from the Information Reviewed by His Majesty's Commissioners as to the Administration and Operation of the Poor Laws* (London, 1833), 332; quoted in Cowherd (1977: 235).

3. See Kleppner and Theodore (1997), Center on Urban and Metropolitan Policy (1999), Turok and Edge (1999), Peck (2000a), and Peck and Theodore (2000b); for a more optimistic view, see MDRC (1999).

4. Children's Defense Fund, *Summary of Final Welfare Conference Bill, Part I* (Washington, DC: Children's Defense Fund, August 8, 1996).

5. This has even led to suggestions that state funding caps should be lowered. Assuming the 1996 spending caps remain in place, then states will have some room for maneuver when caseloads begin to rise again, or when they face growing unit costs in dealing with the "less-job-ready" population. A recession, of course, would place this system under enormous strain very quickly, even allowing for the fact that new participation rules act as a deterrent to new welfare claims.

CHAPTER THREE

# *Workfare*
## *What Does It Mean?*

Workfare. Any public welfare program that requires welfare
recipients to work (work + welfare = workfare) or to enroll in a
formal job-training program. (*Dorsey Dictionary of American
Government and Politics*)

A word is not a crystal, transparent and unchanged; it is the
skin of a living thought and may vary greatly in color and
content according to the circumstances in which it is used.
(Oliver Wendell Holmes, quoted in Rossiter, 1955: 4)

Welfare reform is not only concerned with restructuring institutions and
mobilizing political power; it is also about creating a *language* of reform,
about constructing new vocabularies of regulation. "Workfare" is per-
forming just such a function, as in the space of thirty years it has evolved
from a technocratic term deployed in the process of *intrawelfare* reform,
through to a powerful signifier of a systemic, *after-welfare* "alternative."
Discursive struggles around the meaning and signification of *workfare*
have played a decisive role in reencoding the language of poverty politics, as "old" discourses of needs, decency, compassion, and entitlement
have been discredited, while "new" and reworked discourses of work, responsibility, self-sufficiency, and empowerment have been forcefully advanced. Geography matters here, too, because the ascendancy of *local*
workfare over *federal* welfare (itself now a political attack term) has been
associated not only with a rolling back of the language, routines, and sys-

83

tems of welfarism, but with the rolling forward of radically new institutions and vocabularies of regulation. Although the term continues to be contested, *workfare* is fast becoming the regulatory antonym of *welfare*; in the process, it is playing a part in the way that the program is becoming programmatic.[1]

## WORDS OF WORKFARE

The origins of the term *workfare* lie with a series of work-for-benefits programs developed in the United States in the late 1960s and early 1970s (Shafritz, 1988: 595). But be it as a conflation of "work-for-welfare" or as a synonym of "welfare-to-work," the term *workfare* is "now used in a much broader sense to include, as a condition of income support, the requirement that recipients participate in a wide variety of activities designed to increase their employment prospects" (Evans, 1995: 75). More broadly still, "the embrace of workfare is . . . not just a stance on a particular part of social policy, but also [represents] a rejection of the dominant public ethos on social welfare" (Jacobs, 1995: 14). "Workfare" is used as a discursive counter to established, welfarist norms of public policy, such as passive income support, entitlement, and needs-based provision. Perhaps, then, *workfare* can be seen as the regulatory antonym of *welfare*.

*Workfare* has become a staple of the American political lexicon. Although the term was coined in the late 1960s, its widespread usage began with the early years of the first Reagan administration, before becoming one of the "keywords" of the 1990s. "The language of workfare," as Guy Standing (1990: 678) has observed, "is hazy," but this very haziness tells a story. It reflects how struggles over meaning and social signification are bound together with material processes of institutional and political change. As Raymond Williams has emphasized,

> It is common practice to speak of the "proper" or "strict" meaning of a word by reference to its origins. . . . The original meanings of words are always interesting. But what is often most interesting is the subsequent variation. . . . [It] is necessary to insist that the most active problems of meaning are always primarily embedded in actual relationships, and that both the meanings and the relationships are typically diverse and variable, within structures of particular social orders and the processes of social and historical change. (1983: 20–21, 22)

Rector and Butterfield (1987: 9) observe that "workfare means different things to different people." Its meaning also varies over time and space.

While workfare has acquired the status of a political mantra in the United States, for example, it has remained until recently almost a taboo word in the European social democracies.[2] As the evolution of the term in the United States illustrates, workfare has progressively acquired a more generalized and abstract meaning as time has passed. What began as an experimental modification of a limited number of U.S. welfare programs has matured first into a federal institutional framework and subsequently into an ideological totem, as workfare has come to signify an *inversion* of welfarist principles and practices.

A survey of the incidence of newspaper articles on workfare in the pages of the *New York Times*, the *Washington Post*, and the *Wall Street Journal*, for example, reveals that there were more references to workfare in 1995 alone than there were during the whole period 1971–1980. Figure 3.1 illustrates not only the general ascendancy of workfare rhetoric, culminating in the passage of the PRWORA of 1996, but also the discursive fallout of Reagan's anti-welfare budget of 1981, the discussions around the Family Support Act of 1988, and the far-reaching post-1992 debate over "the end of welfare." In the process, it has become acceptable for Democrats to use the term they once derided, while workfare has come to occupy a key ideological site in the language of the New Right. In 1990, in his capacity as convenor of GOPAC—a Republican Party po-

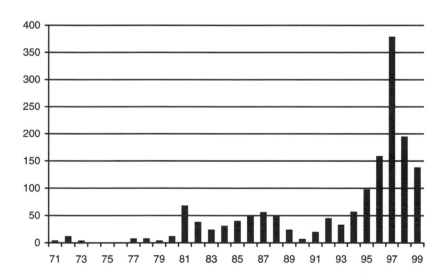

**FIGURE 3.1.** Incidence of references to "workfare" in major U.S. newspapers, 1971–1999. *Sources:* Citations in *New York Times, Washington Post, Wall Street Journal*; LEXIS/NEXIS.

litical training arm and one of the power bases of the right of the party—Newt Gingrich circulated a prescient document entitled *Language: A Key Mechanism of Control* to state candidates. Extracts from his covering letter and from the political glossary itself (Figure 3.2) reveal Gingrich's tactics in what he saw in part as a war of words. On becoming Speaker of the House, Gingrich later explained of the Republican's discursive strategy, "We may have a more limited success in terms of bills, but the whole language of politics will be in the midst of transformation. . . . The real breaking point is when you find yourself having a whole new debate, with new terms. That's more important than legislative achievements" (quoted in Drew, 1996: 14).

Denounced in a *New York Times* editorial as "the worst of American political discourse" (September 20, 1993: A20), the benefits of hindsight reveal that Gingrich was anticipating both the tenor and the terrain of political debate in the 1990s. His bold discursive counterposition of welfare and workfare presaged a root-and-branch ideological and institutional attack on the principles and practices of welfarism. Workfare

---

As you know, one of the key points in the GOPAC tapes is that "language matters." . . . As the tapes have been used in training sessions across the country and mailed to candidates we have heard the plaintive plea: "*I wish I could speak like Newt.*"

That takes years of practice, but we believe that you could have a significant impact on your campaign and the way you communicate if we help a little. That is why we have created this list of words and phrases. . . . Read them. Memorize as many as possible. . . .

**Optimistic Positive Governing Words**
"*these words can help give extra power to your message*"

**Contrasting Words**
"*apply these to the opponent, their record, proposals and their party*"

| | | | |
|---|---|---|---|
| opportunity | *workfare* | decay | *welfare* |
| moral | dream | failure | ideological |
| courage | freedom | collapse | anti-(issue) |
| crusade | pioneer | patronage | stagnation |
| family | building | destroy | greed |
| compete | pro-(issue) | sick | corrupt |
| active | empower | liberal | status quo |
| duty | strength | bureaucracy | taxes |
| care | hard work | unionized | spend |
| tough | incentive | devour | permissive attitude |
| vision | passionate | waste | red tape |

---

**FIGURE 3.2.** Excerpts from Newt Gingrich's *Language: A Key Mechanism of Control. Source:* GOPAC (Bernstein and Bernstein, 1995: Appendix II).

codifies the organizing framework for this attack, not simply as a bureau-cratic–procedural reform, but as an *incipient regulatory critique* founded on the enforcement of work disciplines, the rolling back of entitlement programs, and the ascendancy of behavioral (as opposed to structural) analyses of poverty and unemployment. Speaking in 1992 Gingrich argued that "[r]eplacing welfare with workfare . . . would be a revolution" (quoted in Bernstein and Bernstein, 1995: 26). Just such a revolution was promised to the U.S. electorate in the shape of the *Contract with America*, though according to Gingrich the vexed issue of welfare reform was to prove to be "*the* crisis" of the first hundred days of the 104th Congress (Gingrich, 1995; Drew, 1996). During this important period of the welfare debate, some of its key terms—in every sense of the word—were to be set.

The question of welfare reform lay at the heart of what became a "year-long rhetorical battle over the role of the federal government, a war of words with the Democrats and the Clinton White House that has profound policy consequences" (Maraniss and Weisskopf, 1996: 82). One of the ten bills proposed in the *Contract* was a Personal Responsibility Act (PRA) that would have introduced a two-year time limit on welfare eligibility, denied welfare to teen parents and to additional children born to welfare mothers, and coupled "cut[s in] spending for welfare programs . . . with work requirements to promote individual responsibility" (Gillespie and Schellhas, 1994: 9–10). Of course, Clinton's own reform package had also emphasized work requirements, time limits, and parental responsibility,[3] so in some senses the Republican proposals were not as radical as they sounded. In fact, it was Clinton who was not as radical as he sounded: initially at least, his revolutionary rhetoric concealed an incrementalist reform program. Later, though, Clinton's rhetoric would catch up with him:

> Clinton's slogans were cleverly ambiguous. . . . The President didn't say so, but he was building—quite incrementally and quite responsibly—on the framework of the Family Support Act [while] letting his listeners infer that he intended radical reform with real fall-off-the-cliff time limits. . . . Candidate Clinton, however, had let a powerful genie out of the bottle. . . . When the Republicans gained control of Congress in 1994, the bumper-sticker rhetoric began to matter. (Edelman, 1997: 44)

By the time of the 1996 presidential election, workfare was no longer one of the "wedge issues" that differentiated the candidates in terms of policy substance, although each was keen to appear tougher and/or more radical on the issue of welfare reform. As President Clinton argued in his 1996 State of the Union address, "For too long, our welfare system has undermined the values of family and work, instead of supporting them. The Congress and I are near to agreeing on sweeping welfare reform. We agree on time limits, tough work requirements, and the toughest possible child support enforcement. . . . I challenge Congress to send me a bipartisan welfare reform that will really move people from welfare to work. . . . I will sign it immediately" (*Washington Post*, January 24, 1996: A13). Following his administration's deliberate cultivation of state-reform initiatives, Clinton was subsequently able to boast that "73 percent of welfare recipients nationwide are receiving their benefits under some sort of 'workfare' reform program" (*Asbury Park Press,* March 12, 1996: A1).

The increasingly close alignment of Democrats and Republicans on the issue of welfare reform from the mid-1980s onward came to underpin what has been termed the "workfare consensus."[4] Part of the political dynamic here, most certainly, stems from the fact that few politicians are prepared to defend welfare, either in principle or in practice. Conservatives and liberals have found common cause—and a common *language* of reform—in the issue of "welfare dependency," one where welfare itself displaces poverty as the problem to be tackled (see Fraser and Gordon, 1994; Schram, 1995). The new imperative is to end welfare, not poverty per se; the objective is to correct those individual behavioral dysfunctions—such as moral laxity and inadequate work discipline—that are seen as a *cause* of poverty but more importantly as a *consequence* of the welfare system. For example, in the wake of the Los Angeles riots, Vice President Dan Quayle proposed the "dismantling" of the welfare system: "Our inner cities are filled with children having children . . . with people who are dependent on drugs or the narcotic of welfare" (*San Francisco Chronicle*, May 20, 1992: A1). Senator Daniel Patrick Moynihan, on the other hand, asserts that "just as unemployment was the defining issue of industrialism, dependency is becoming the defining issue of postindustrial society" (quoted in Cloward and Piven, 1993: 693; see Moynihan, 1989). The problem, given that the current system apparently has few (vocal) defenders, is what to do about it. While for many in the Republican and Democratic Parties agree that some form of workfare package is the answer, there are others, certainly on the left and even on the right, who continue to question what Gilder (1987: 20) has called "the unthinking rush to a 'workfare' state."

## The Geopolitics of Workfare Discourse

This chapter traces the roots of the U.S. "workfare consensus" by way of a geopolitical etymology of the keyword *workfare*. The process is an etymological one because the shift toward workfare (and the associated crisis of welfare) must in part be understood as a discursive project. Here, the discursive (re)framing of the policy problem really matters in accounting for the changing *substance* of policy. The process is a *geo*political one because workfare has a geography as well as a history. There is an important sense in which policy knowledges about workfare have been *spatially* as well as socially constructed. There is a renewed ideological faith in "local solutions," reflected in concrete terms, prior to the 1996 act, in the orchestration of state-level experiments under the waiver process, and subsequently in the block granting of welfare provisions to the states. In the process, models and stories of workfare—from California to Wisconsin—have been disembedded from the local contexts on which they are dependent, translated into the kind of universal, technocratic language suitable for "fast policy transfer," and then taken up in a transformative way into national (and international) policy discourses.

Fittingly perhaps, British etymologist Sir Ernest Weekly traced one of the first uses of the word *welfare* (in its contemporary sense) to the industrial Northeast of the United States: "The home of the 'welfare policy' is the city of Dayton, Ohio. . . . *Welfare*, as in 'child welfare,' 'welfare centre,' and so forth, was first used in this special sense in Ohio in 1904" (quoted in Safire, 1993: 866). Appropriately perhaps, there is no comparable "home of workfare policy" today, in part because the turnover of policies and programs is itself accelerating, as state and local policymakers compete to get ahead of the curve in workfare innovation. Such local models of workfare—or more precisely their *representations*—have come to occupy a central place in the current welfare-reform process, undermining federal orthodoxies and discursively levering wider, systemic change.

The spread of workfare discourse has been lubricated by these decontextualized "placeless knowledges"—what Schram (1995: 17) aptly calls "facts from nowhere"—the prevalence of which helps account for the particular form exhibited by the "welfare-reform" debate in the United States. Dehli is describing a similar situation when she explains how it is that through discursive practices, "local and particular experiences are represented and transformed into an extra-local 'documentary reality,' thus facilitating the social organization of management and regulation. . . . [These] processes of policy formulation . . . transform people's experiences of work, economic upheaval and political struggle into administrative categories which can be put to work in state institutions" (1993: 87). In fact, the geographies of workfare and the spatiality of its discourses are distinctive ones, revealing a great deal about the capacities and contradictions of this ascendant regulatory strategy.

## (RE)DEFINING WORKFARE

> In the final analysis, we cannot talk our way out of poverty; we
> cannot legislate our way out of poverty, but this nation can
> work its way out of poverty. What America needs now is not
> more welfare, but more "workfare." (President Richard Nixon,
> televised speech, August 1969; quoted in Nathan, 1986: 107)

Although the earliest recorded use of the term *workfare* has been attributed to civil-rights leader James Charles Evers in 1968, its subsequent
adoption by President Richard Nixon first placed it in the context of federal "welfare reform." As William Safire, Nixon's speechwriter at the
time, later bragged, "I may not have been the first to use the word, but I
had a hand in its nationwide launch and feel a stepfather's pride" (1988:
10). Safire's ambition was that "workfare" would come to define Nixon's
welfare-reform initiative, the rather euphemistically entitled Family Assistance Plan (FAP), subsequently promoted by the president as "the
transformation of welfare to 'workfare,' a new work-rewarding program"
(quoted in Safire, 1993: 885). In fact, the term *workfare* was to fare better
than Nixon's reform package, which was defeated by an unusual coalition of, on the one hand, liberal Democrats and welfare advocates opposed to the bill's work requirements and low benefit levels, and on the
other, southern conservatives concerned that the new provisions would
actually *raise* benefits levels across much of the South (Brodkin, 1995).

Georgia Senator Talmadge proposed a series of amendments to the
FAP that tightened work requirements under the established Work Incentive (WIN) program. This package, which became known as the
Talmadge Amendments, was passed into law in 1971, establishing a
workfare dynamic that has only intensified over the ensuing decades. Requiring work of welfare recipients with schoolage children, the Talmadge
Amendments emphasized immediate job placement over the provision of
education and training services (Rose, 1995). In the contemporary par-
lance of welfare-to-work initiatives, the WIN approach is known as a
"labor-force attachment" or "work-first" approach to workfare, while the
more service-intensive alternative favored by many liberals is termed
the "human-capital-development model" (see Gueron and Pauly, 1991;
Freedman and Friedlander, 1995). Recent struggles over the meaning of
workfare have centered on this binarism, a technocratic reworking of the
old distinction between "hard" and "soft" workfare (see Brown, 1997;
Peck and Theodore, 1998).

Another important legacy of WIN concerns the production and dissemination of policy knowledges. WIN made provision for the development of experimental work programs, notably the Supported Work

Demonstrations (SWD) and the Community Work Experience Program (CWEP).[5] An explicit aim of these local workfare-style programs was to develop and diffuse (work-oriented) policy innovation within the welfare system. Evaluation played a key role here, the Manpower Demonstration Research Corporation (MDRC) being formed in 1974 to monitor and disseminate the results of these early trials. Although the results of the early workfare experiments were, to say the least, mixed,[6] it was already becoming clear that they were building considerable momentum. Under then-Governor Ronald Reagan, the California CWEPs instituted a particularly harsh regime in which eligible participants were rotated through a series of low-grade, low-skill community-service jobs. As Rose (1995: 105) notes, these demonstration projects were to "serve as precursors to the 'workfare explosion' of the 1980s," the fuse for which was to be lit by now-President Reagan.

## Reagan's Workfare Offensive

Once in Washington, Reagan effectively declared war on welfare with the Omnibus Budget Reconciliation Act (OBRA) of 1981. With the objective of encouraging "attachment to the labor force and self-support [while reducing] the public assistance rolls" (President's Statement on the Budget, quoted in Nathan, 1993: 22), OBRA dramatically restricted eligibility for AFDC,[7] cut welfare payments, and offered further inducements for states to develop welfare-to-work programs. These reforms removed close to half a million families from the welfare rolls (Brodkin, 1995), despite being introduced in the midst of a recession. Rector and Butterfield (1987) observe that OBRA had the effect of resuscitating workfare policies, which had been languishing since the mid-1970s.

OBRA stepped up the workfare dynamic both by forcing welfare recipients into low-wage work and by allowing states to extend mandatory workfare programs. According to Mead (1992b: 190), while Reagan began by espousing a traditional conservative agenda on welfare—"cuts, restrictions, devolution to localities"—in retrospect his "main legacy turned out to be the expansion of workfare." By 1985, some twenty-two states had introduced mandatory programs, but these were mostly local demonstrations, with only seven states operating mandatory workfare on a statewide basis (Burghes, 1987; Walker, 1991). The intention, however, was never to move directly toward blanket coverage, but to "cultivate local solutions" to federal work mandates (Oliker, 1994: 201). Again, most of the evaluations of the OBRA experiments were conducted by MDRC (see Greenberg and Wiseman, 1992), the significance of which was soon to become clear.

In his 1986 State of the Union address, Reagan wove together old

and new themes in welfare/workfare discourse, castigating welfare programs for "encourag[ing] dependency and entrench[ing] the very poverty they were intended to alleviate. . . . As Franklin Roosevelt warned 51
years ago: Welfare is ' . . . a narcotic, a subtle destroyer of the human
spirit.' And we must now escape the spider's web of dependency."[8] Reagan called for radical welfare reform, though few anticipated at the time
that the president's "preferences for funding cuts and for decentralized
workfare would spark much reform in a Democrat-controlled legislature" (Oliker, 1994: 197). But the climate had changed, fundamentally
and perhaps permanently: what was to become the Family Support Act
(FSA) of 1988 represented a "remarkable consensus on federally-initi-
ated mandatory workfare" (Oliker, 1994: 197). Crucially, the MDRC's
long-term evaluations of earlier workfare demonstrations were just becoming available. These were to have an inordinate influence on the
course of the policy debate around the FSA, and the subsequent shape of
the legislation, because they appeared to demonstrate that workfare programs did in fact work (Baum, 1991; Haskins, 1991; Mead, 1992b; Nathan, 1993; Oliker, 1994). Couched in the impartial and measured language of quantitative policy "science," the MDRC evaluations took much
of the heat out of a debate traditionally fought out in emotional language
on the partisan terrain of political and moral principle: the FSA debate
became less about words and beliefs, more about numbers and techniques (see Mead, 1992b). This technocratic approach also had the effect
of defusing and dissipating the highly charged race politics of the welfare
debate, which for decades had been articulated around attacks on, and
defenses of, the African American poor (Piven and Cloward, 1993;
Quadagno, 1994).

Reflecting on the lessons of the welfare-to-work evaluations, the
president of MDRC argued for an approach that both

> promotes and also rewards work. Workfare, narrowly defined, does
> the former, but . . . it may not provide enough added income to ade-
> quately combat dependency. . . . "Sticks" may be part of the solution,
> but "carrots" are also merited if work is to be more an alternative to
> than a punishment for being poor. (Gueron, 1987: 38)

The results of the evaluation studies, skillfully marshaled by MDRC,
proved convincing to many Democrats previously skeptical about the
utility (not to mention the morality) of mandatory work requirements.
The authoritative nature of the MDRC studies, in particular their utiliza-
tion of a meticulous experimental design methodology,[9] was such as to
play forcefully and directly into the policymaking process. They pulled
the debate into the field of program implementation and away from is-

sues of political principle: the prevailing (gendered and racialized) interpretation of "welfare dependency," for example, was tacitly accepted, as
strategies became preoccupied with fixing welfare rather than tackling
poverty (see Schram, 1995; Epstein, 1997). But according to Epstein
(1997: 179), in "leading the consensus toward the desirability of the
1988 FSA, [MDRC] were following popular tastes for conservative welfare reform more than the dictates of their experiments." More specifically, the design of the MDRC evaluation program tended implicitly to
favor labor-force attachment over human-capital models of workfare,
given that the selection of research sites was skewed toward the low-cost,
job-search-oriented experiments (Szanton, 1991). Indeed, as Oliker
(1994: 205) saw it, the "goal of providing a clear direction for workfare
reform appears to have been built into MDRC's plan to study the low-
cost OBRA demonstrations."[10] Establishing a pattern for the future, sanitized and technocratic representations of local workfare experiments
were (pre)defining the terrain for national debate and federal reform.

The explanation for this pattern of events lies less with purposeful
and conscious action on the part of those commissioning and conducting program evaluations and more with the particular confluence
of structural conditions around the welfare policymaking process in
the mid-1980s. At the ideological level, anti-welfare rhetoricians—
emboldened by a series of caustic attacks on welfarism and its alleged
perversities from the intellectual right (see Gilder, 1981; Murray, 1984;
Mead, 1986; Olasky, 1992)—became ever more trenchant. In program
terms, the spread of workfare experiments—and the incipient regulatory
critique that they represented—began in effect to concretize an alternative program. This was no longer simply an abstract critique, but also
signified a concrete package of reforms. Workfare experiments appeared
to offer a way out of the "welfare mess," constructing a bridge between
anti-welfare/pro-work rhetoric, on the one hand, and programs that
could be shown to work, on the other. Workfarism, had, in effect, become a simultaneously practical *and* ideological project.

## The Language of Reform

These shifts were also reflected in the politics of evaluation research,
where, according to Schram (1995), an "economistic–therapeutic–mana-
gerial" (ETM) discourse had entered an ascendancy. Focusing on the
generation of "disembodied information" on the economic practices of
poor people and their supposedly Pavlovian responses to policy stimuli,
ETM "imputes to the poor the identity of self-interested, utility maximizing individuals who need to be given the right incentives so that they
will change their behavior and enable the state better to manage the

problems of poverty and welfare dependency" (Schram, 1995: 4). In this way, welfare-policy discourse serves to constitute and reproduce its supposedly dysfunctional subjects/objects of study (see Fraser and Gordon, 1994; Epstein, 1997). ETM can be seen to permeate much of the contemporary research discourse on poverty and welfare, ranging from the hypothetical economic calculi of Charles Murray's (1984) incentives-driven couple, Harold and Phyllis, through the sophisticated empirics of David Ellwood's (1988) work on welfare dynamics, to the sober evaluations of workfare experiments by MDRC. Crucially, the staging of local "demonstrations" in welfare reform, and a particular way of reading their implications, have come to occupy a central place in the ETM paradigm. Local experimentation has become

> an institutionalized part of welfare policy making . . . [reinforcing] the idea that the goal of welfare policy research is to produce decontextualized information about the distinctive behavior of the poor so that the right mix of incentives and penalties can be introduced in order to get the impoverished to change their behavior. Experimentation is entirely consistent with ETM and the way it constructs the poor as deficient subjects of the welfare state. (Schram, 1995: 14–15; see also Brodkin and Kaufman, 1998)

For all its measured neutrality, the methodology of MDRC can be placed within just such a framework. As Nathan (1993: 36) explains, the procedure of the MDRC studies "is that of a classic experiment." There is almost clinical precision in the way that, in the sites selected for study, subjects are randomly assigned to "treatment" (on-program) and "control" (off-program) groups, with the subsequent experiences of the two groups being closely monitored over a period of several years. The objective is to isolate and quantify the "impacts" of work programs on key variables such as earnings, net costs, and employment rates. Program effects—the results of "treatment"—are inferred from disparities in these dependent variables between the control and the treatment groups. The "black box" of local-level causality and contingency remains largely unopened in the MDRC methodology (Oliker, 1994), as causal status is attributed to empirical associations between an isolated group of program variables and labor-market "outcomes." While MDRC is conscious of these limitations, and indeed acknowledges that a range of local-level effects (such as local labor market conditions, the structuring of welfare services, and the nature of the education and training infrastructure) may influence the results of their evaluations (Gueron and Pauly, 1991: 186–189), the reality is that their policy messages are consumed by practitioners and legislators as if all observable effects on client behavior can be attributed to (replicable) program characteristics. Although MDRC staff are themselves always cautious about making such claims, their research has nevertheless fostered the impression among many policymakers that the replication of the features of certain successful programs will lead in turn to the replication of desired program outcomes. Rarely, in fact, is this the case. Local policy systems tend to be heavily "embedded" in local political, economic, and institutional milieux; and although certain aspects of policy procedures and program apparatuses may be "transportable" from place to place, their *outcomes* very rarely are (Peck, 1996). Nevertheless, the rise of ETM practices has facilitated the discursive disembedding of policy practice, a critical prerequisite for the diffusion of workfare.

The danger of constructing policy on the basis of "facts from nowhere" is that serious problems such as the nonreplicability of local models and operational difficulties associated with moving from small-scale local trials to state or even national programs are effectively ignored (see Moffitt, 1992; Oliker, 1994). Sanitized representations of local workfare experiments, couched in the scientific language of the prevailing ETM discourse and bolstered by voluminous quantitative data from MDRC's "experimental sites," profoundly shaped political thinking on workfare at the federal level. But these were not the only "local policy knowledges" to permeate the FSA deliberations in the mid-1980s. Reagan himself insisted that legislation should build on the practical "lessons" of California's workfare experiments, while many of these same experiences became scientifically recodified in MDRC reports (Mead, 1992b; Heclo, 1994; Oliker, 1994). But while representations of "positive" models of reform exerted a strong leverage on the policy debate, so also did the "negative" spatial images of the welfare-dependent ghetto and its supposedly dysfunctional, racially stereotyped residents. As Lawrence Mead, a commentator closely involved in the FSA debate, saw it:

> The disintegrating inner city was in the backs of everyone's mind. Few policymakers imagined they were engaged, as in the progressive era, in redistributing advantages among functioning citizens. Rather, they were mounting what the Ford Foundation experts called a "salvage operation" for poor communities that were falling apart due to drugs, crime, and welfarism. (1992b: 200)

What was clear was that the geography of the "welfare mess" was rather different from the emerging geography of the "workfare solution." Welfare dependency and poverty were conceptualized as largely inner-city problems, reflecting both the reality that poverty has urbanized massively in the United States since the 1960s[11] and the political imagery of President Reagan's vivid attacks on "welfare queens in designer jeans," cruising around the ghetto in their Cadillacs, buying vodka with food stamps.[12] In contrast, the workfarist "solutions" to welfare problems have tended to come from quite different places: largely rural states, small towns and cities, suburban areas, the states of Wisconsin and Minnesota, and the edge city of Riverside, California, being perhaps the paradigmatic locations. This profound spatial disconnect, however, is largely buried under the decontextualized pseudoscience of workfare advocacy.

Geographies of perceived success and failure in welfare reform, moreover, influence the implementation process as well as the wider political climate. As an MDRC evaluator explained:

> "MDRC gets a lot of publicity for their studies. We're funded, in part, to get the results out. I think there has been a change since the . . . results came out of Riverside. . . . [Now] they're very quick to say, the program does work; you all told us that. That also reinforces that there is hope. . . . I know, I read it in the newspapers, we have great impacts. . . . Places like Detroit, there isn't stuff that comes out and says this works in the big cities. . . . What you read is that nothing is working in the big cities and that undermines the few successes you see. . . . In the bigger cities, that's where our evaluations have had most trouble. . . . In a smaller place, they'll try something new, they don't have to wade through so many channels or layers of bureaucracy. But in the big cities, even just implementing an evaluation is incredibly difficult. . . . [There] if you're really trying to foster institutional change, and change the culture of a place—to be more focused on work, as opposed to maintaining income—it's going to be an incredible push to get that message out and cover all the channels."[13]

As the chief negotiators of the FSA, Thomas Downey and Daniel Patrick Moynihan, conceded, the power of MDRC's analyses was such that the debate was soon resolved to issues of "numbers" rather than "principles" (*Congressional Quarterly Weekly Report*, June 25, 1988: 1764). It effectively became a set of negotiations over what *kind* of workfare bill to pass. As Democratic legislator Sander Levin saw it at the time, the FSA "links welfare and work irretrievably. It crosses the Rubicon" (quoted in Mead, 1992b: 199). The passage of the FSA was indeed critical in shifting the discourse of welfare reform away from partisan debates over the desirability or otherwise of workfare *in principle*, and towards a more policy-oriented deliberation of how best to achieve (shared) workfarist goals *in practice*. From the perspective of MDRC, for example, the research-evaluation case for workfare programs had been both made and accepted: "There is a large body of rigorous studies that confirm that welfare-to-work programs produce positive impacts and represent a cost-effective investment of public funds. . . . The key question for such programs in the 1990s is thus not *whether* to implement them, but *how* to design them to be most effective" (Gueron and Pauly, 1991: 249).

## The Short History of JOBS

Bipartisan support for the FSA was constructed around a balance between the raw philosophy of labor-force attachment favored by conservatives and the more service-intensive approach favored by liberals. As Moynihan captured it, "Conservatives have persuaded liberals that there is nothing wrong with obligating able-bodied adults to work. Liberals have persuaded Conservatives that most adults want to work and need some help to do so" (quoted in Mead, 1992b: 201). In the FSA legislation this workfarist compromise was translated into a package of education, training, and childcare services, coupled with stringent work requirements: the Job Opportunities and Basic Skills program (JOBS) was to be administered by states with some degree of latitude over the specifics of program design. JOBS required states to have 20 percent of recipients in workfare programs by 1995, but "[h]ow states do that is largely their own business" (Heclo, 1994: 411).

In fact, the implementation of the JOBS program was even more uneven than this suggested. States and localities pursued a range of strategies within the JOBS framework, some punitive and mandatory, others relatively supportive and voluntary (Handler and Hasenfeld, 1991; Blank, 1994a; Freedman and Friedlander, 1995). Moreover, the fact that JOBS was launched into a recession meant that administrative and financial capacities were overstretched, while the public credibility of most program "successes" was immediately undermined by the fact that welfare rolls tended to be rising rather than falling (Brodkin, 1995). Policy analysts, however, still struggled to see past these unfortunate contingencies. According to Erica Baum, a Moynihan aide and architect of the FSA, for example, there had always been skepticism about the claims made for the Massachusetts workfare program, ET, the effects of which were discounted by virtue of the state's tight labor market (see Chapter 4). The MDRC findings from a range of states, on the other hand, had given Baum "reason to believe that similarly favorable outcomes could be replicated across this diverse country of ours" (1991: 609). Before this question could be answered, however, by the large-scale JOBS evaluation being conducted by MDRC, it was becoming clear that pressure for further reform was again building. The apparent malaise in the JOBS program, and the impending presidential election of 1992, signaled a "resurgence of anti-welfare politics" (Brodkin, 1995: 217).

## READING CLINTON'S LIPS

Bill Clinton entered the 1992 presidential race determined to make welfare reform one of its decisive issues. As governor of Arkansas, Clinton had played an active role in state-level welfare reform, initially through his Arkansas WORK program (see Friedlander et al., 1985; Funiciello, 1993), and later through his chairship of the influential National Governors' Association (NGA) working party on welfare reform (see NGA, 1987; Brodkin, 1995). The NGA's work played into the FSA debate in significant ways, helping establish the political foundations for the workfare consensus and codifying the language (of "mutual obligations" under a welfare "contract") to go with it. Beneath the surface, however, were continuing tensions. Reagan had pushed during the 1980s for a radical devolution of welfare, but having made no progress with Congress, sought to exploit opportunities for state-level reform under an obscure provision of the Social Security Act. Section 1115 of the act permitted the waiver of certain entitlement provisions with a view to allowing local demonstration projects and research trials (Williams, 1994).[14] Many liberals remained profoundly suspicious of Reagan's intentions, a stance subsequently reflected in a considerable degree of skepticism concerning the actual role of such state-level "experiments" (Mead, 1992b; Heclo, 1994). So, while there was near-consensus on a great many issues in the FSA negotiations, there were extreme differences between the conservative and liberal proposals on the issues of devolution and state experimentation: the Republican proposal (HR 3200) had been that unlimited waiver authority be granted to states spanning some twenty-two federal programs, while the more liberal Democratic proposal (HR 1720) had argued for a much more narrowly defined expansion of demonstration projects in prescribed policy areas (Reischauer, 1989). These tensions were to remain unresolved, as the contentious language concerning state experimentation was eventually removed from the FSA. They were to reappear, though, as the welfare debate resumed in the early 1990s.

No doubt mindful of the ensuing election, President Bush had sought to take up the issue of welfare reform in his 1992 State of the Union address, arguing for the need to "replace the assumptions of the welfare state" and seeking to move toward this by making the waiver process "easier and quicker" for states to use.[15] Traveling later in the campaign to Riverside, California, a county that was beginning to demonstrate striking outcomes in its MDRC-evaluated work program, Bush announced further elements of his administration's strategy for welfare reform. Addressing those he called "the most endangered species in California, the taxpayer," Bush espoused a traditional conservative critique of welfare:

> We can't afford the welfare system that we have today. And the taxpayers know it. The recipients know it. *The economists know it.* And welfare is a system that literally wastes millions of tax dollars a year, and we can't afford that. Welfare was designed to be temporary. Temporary.

But today, more than half of all recipients receive a check for at least eight years, and we can't afford that. . . . Welfare punches a hole in the heart of the American Dream. . . . We need to say, "Get a job or get off the dole" (Applause).[16]

Putting his faith in the "real action" taking place at the state level, legitimized by the discourse of economics and the practices of experimental evaluation, Bush pledged his administration's support for the governors' welfare reform efforts. "I put my trust in the states more than Washington. That's the philosophical underpinnings of our approach to welfare. And so, a big part of our effort is to give states the freedom to make the changes they want. New ideas, new opportunities, new flexibility" (Federal News Service, July 31, 1992).

In contrast with Bush's relatively cautious validation of existing state reforms, candidate Clinton seized the political advantage with his portentous proposal to "end welfare as we know it."[17] This tapped in a calculated way into frustrations over the apparent failure not only of welfare in general but more particularly of the last iteration in the reform process, the FSA. Clinton's presidential victory in 1992 meant that Bush was never able to claim the credit for his strategy for welfare reform, summed up by Heclo (1994: 415) as "federalism by waiver." Nevertheless, the cumulative effect of the Bush waivers was significant, for it had ascribed new legitimacy to state-authored reforms while granting waiver requests at such a rate as to generate real political momentum. According to Wiseman (1993: 18), this added up to a "major change in the landscape of welfare reform."

## Clinton Waivers

Clinton's approach to welfare and welfare reform was complex, reflecting recent policy legacies and his own role within them. On the one hand, he professed support for the FSA, ruing the fact that it was never fully implemented, but continuing to adhere to its underlying (workfarist) principles.[18] On the other hand, he appealed to anti-welfare sentiments in his attempt to justify more far-reaching reform.[19] The organizing principles of Clinton's approach—despite these contradictions—remained essentially workfarist. As the president said in a speech to the NGA in February 1993, "We must begin now to plan for a time when people will ultimately be able to work for the check they get, whether the check comes from a private employer or from the United States taxpayers (Applause)."[20]

Under the Clinton administration, however, the issue of federal welfare reform was soon to take second place to healthcare reform. Welfare reform would instead have to be encouraged by "remote control": from an early stage, Clinton was keen to maintain the momentum of state-level reform, clearly seeing this activity—as Reagan and Bush had before him—as broadly consistent with his administration's objectives. In a speech before the nation's governors, within weeks of taking office, Clinton sought to encourage further experimentation under the waiver system. Just like Bush, he too placed explicit faith in the method of the "experiment":

> On welfare reform as on health care reform, there are no top-down, made-in-Washington solutions that will work for everyone. The problems and the progress are to be found in the communities of this country. . . . My view is that we ought to give you more elbow room to experiment. . . . I [will] approve waivers of experiments that I [do] not necessarily agree with. . . . And the only thing I want to say, to ask you in return, is let us measure these experiments and let us measure them honestly so that if they work, we can make them the rule.[21]

The experience of the waiver system, under Bush and subsequently under Clinton, was however substantially different to the ostensibly systematic process of experimental evaluation. Under both administrations, waivers were granted almost indiscriminately (Greenberg, 1995; Wiseman, 1995), resulting in a "checkerboard of mini-welfare reforms all over the nation" (Towns, 1995: 6), generating a raft of would-be policy orthodoxies around issues like time limits and family caps, but providing surprisingly little reliable data on what works and what does not (see Brodkin and Kaufman, 1998). The entire process, in fact, was politically mediated and structured, for all the studied deference to the evaluation data. The primary criteria for approving waiver requests were cost-neutrality (a principle introduced by the Reagan administration in 1987), coupled with a requirement that a suitable evaluation framework was in place (Bane, 1995). These ostensibly "passive" criteria, however, led to a number of distortions in the welfare-reform process. Four stand out.

First, the cost-neutrality principle meant that states were induced to seek rapid-return, cost-cutting, and relatively low-risk strategies, rather than approaches that might yield longer term benefits but that required larger upfront investments. In terms of workfare models, this favored labor-force attachment over human-capital models and punitive over supportive approaches. Notwithstanding the inevitable variety in the specifics of state experiments, the overall direction of the welfare-reform process was thus effectively predetermined: toward punitive measures aimed at reducing the welfare rolls (by whatever means, though preferably in the short term), and away from service- or support-intensive approaches. Second, and relatedly, the kind of policy knowledges that this process produced were equally distorted. The preferred evaluation method, that of random-assignment experimentation pioneered by MDRC, focused on the tracking of outcomes. Seldom, if ever, was the black box of process opened to discover *how* these outcomes were achieved. Typically, waivers permitted states to introduce not one but several policy innovations at the same time, with the result that—even at the end of the evaluation period—it was difficult or even impossible to assign an achieved outcome to an ultimate single cause. Was the observed fall in the welfare rolls, for example, caused by the deterrent effect of mandatory workfare, or by the imposition of a two-year time limit on welfare, or, for that matter, by a tightening of sanction rules or by growth in the local economy?

Third, political cycles are shorter than evaluation cycles. State governors tend to reap the political benefits of welfare reform at the very beginning of the process, usually at the time of its announcement (Wiseman, 1995), particularly where this can be presented as a radical plan that has had to be vigorously negotiated with Washington bureaucrats. In contrast, the equivocal and often modest outcomes of a four- or five-year evaluation of the same plan are likely scarcely to even register with the electorate (or the governor's successor). By this time, the earlier reforms will have become part of the environment. Political capital can only be reaped by those who are one step ahead of the policy orthodoxy, inducing state politicians to pursue ever more radical measures in order to place themselves at the "leading edge" of the reform process. The issue of time-limited welfare, for example, was championed by Clinton and by other governors in the early 1990s; was the subject of nineteen waiver applications; and had already become part of the wider rubric of welfare reform, becoming a key element of the PRWORA, *before* any systematic evaluation evidence was available (Greenberg, 1996). There was consequently an internal dynamic in the waiver process that bred both serial reproduction of certain "innovations," while impelling the adoption of yet more radical or punitive measures. By definition, these had to exceed the regulatory envelopes established both by federal legislation and by state/local practice. Consequently, as David Ellwood observed in 1992, state experimentation tends to be inherently radicalizing:

> The politics of Congress and the uncertainty about the impact and appropriateness of various changes will force a national program to be pale and cautious. But some states will be willing to be quite bold. From them, we can learn about a true transformation of the welfare system. (quoted in Williams, 1994: 36, n 150)

Fourth and finally, the increasing unevenness of the welfare system itself became a source of new political dynamics. The opening up of the waiver process has led to a "reassertion of the older, pre-1960s tradition of state variation in welfare assistance" (Heclo, 1994: 411), a crucial difference being, of course, that the welfare gains achieved during the civil-rights era—which were reflected in increasing federalization—were now being actively *reversed* (Piven and Cloward, 1993). The political dynamics that once worked to ratchet welfare standards upward appeared to be operating in the opposite direction (Peck, 1996). Whereas unevenness in state welfare systems was previously portrayed as a policy problem, the remedy for which was the inscription of basic standards into federal law,[22] the same phenomena were later being used to justify defederalization. This was clearly illustrated in the debate around "welfare magnets," or what President Bush flippantly called "welfare shopping,"[23] as researchers in the mid-1980s were called upon to address the question of whether geographic variations in welfare-benefit levels were causing the poor to migrate to (relatively) high-benefit states.

> Traditionally, the purpose behind such research was to make the case for more national standards in AFDC payments. By the 1990s, however, use of such research findings had switched to a more immediately appealing issue in statehouse politics: how to restrict benefits for immigrants from lower benefit states. This magnet fear, plus the exit threat from businesses and others objecting to higher taxes, means that the states are not so much running independent experiments as jockeying for comparative advantage in holding down both welfare benefits and the taxes needed to pay for such services. (Heclo, 1994: 411)

Despite the finding that the level of such (welfare-induced) migration is comparatively modest (see Peterson and Rom, 1990), both California and Wisconsin were subsequently granted waivers to cut benefits to migrants from states with lower benefit levels, even though there was "clear reason to believe that a court would find them unconstitutional" (Greenberg, 1995: 11).

It was against such a backdrop that Clinton's reform efforts were defined. Their centerpiece was time-limited eligibility, along with expanded workfare programming, some additional training, and tougher sanctions against noncompliance (Cloward and Piven, 1993). As Dionne (1996: 133) has observed, the proposed two-year cutoff was the one issue that could not be compromised in the administration's negotiations over welfare reform in 1993–1994, as "[o]nly this would send the signal that Clinton had kept his promise to 'end welfare as we know it' and establish a new moral basis for public assistance." While this strategic emphasis on time limits is understandable, given that it was always the most innovative element in Clinton's plan, its prominence reflected the fact that the administration was already becoming a prisoner the president's own rhetoric. Having promised to end welfare, and having urged the states to explore radical reforms, nothing less than a draconian transformation would do. Yet, as the contradictions of Clinton's position began to accumulate, it was to become clear that there would be no welfare reform package in the 103d Session of Congress. Ironically, welfare reform was to become a victim of the panic over deficit reduction, to which *in the long term* it was of course intended to contribute. Large-scale cuts in the February 1993 budget undermined the welfare-reform effort, almost before it had begun (Woodward, 1994).

> [O]nce Clinton's welfare task force went to work, it could not simply devote its energies to fashioning the new welfare system. It spent months looking for budget cuts to finance the training and job creation that Clinton had promised as part of his effort to move welfare recipients to work. Many of the cuts the task force examined were in existing programs for the poor [arousing] intense opposition within the heart of the Democratic Party. Liberals charged that Clinton was putting new burdens on the backs of the poor in order to finance a program that was putatively designed to help them. (Dionne, 1996: 130–131)

While the failure of Clinton's initial welfare-reform effort was in this sense predetermined, its search for a means to couple deficit reduction and workfare was to set the stage for a yet more regressive turn in welfare politics. Radical welfare reform was a centerpiece of the House Republicans' *Contract with America* on which the Republicans successfully campaigned to take control of both Houses of Congress in 1994.

## COSTLY RHETORIC

> It is our goal to replace the welfare state. Not to reform it, not to improve it, not to modify it, to replace it. To go straight at the core structure and the core values of the welfare state, and replace them with a much more powerful, much more effective system. (Newt Gingrich, speech to Young Republicans Leadership Conference, 1992, quoted in Bernstein and Bernstein, 1995: 28)

Taking advantage of the disarray in the Clinton administration over the issue of welfare reform and exploiting the ground that Clinton had conceded to the right in his anti-welfare/pro-workfare rhetoric, the *Contract with America* sought to end welfare even as Clinton knew it. Codified in terms established by the Republican right's then-guru, Newt Gingrich (1984, 1995), the *Contract* proposed a Personal Responsibility Act that would end the entitlement status of AFDC by block granting residual welfare provisions to states. Railing against the perceived perversities of the welfare system, the House Republicans alleged that

> [g]overnment programs designed to give a helping hand to the neediest of Americans have instead bred illegitimacy, crime, illiteracy, and more poverty. Our *Contract with America* will change this destructive social behavior by requiring welfare recipients to take personal responsibility for the decisions they make.... [It will] reduce illegitimacy, require work, and save taxpayers money. (Gillespie and Schellhas, 1994: 65)

The PRA would cap spending, time-limit welfare (to a *maximum* of five years, including up to two years on work programs), prohibit welfare for mothers aged under eighteen and noncitizens, and promote the extension of welfare-to-work programs (costed at $10 billion) so as to move welfare recipients into work "as soon as possible" (Gillespie and Schellhas, 1994: 71), setting a federal work-participation requirement but otherwise assuring states that the "federal government will not meddle in other parts of the program" (72).

The PRA represented a strategic coup on the part of the House Republicans, turning Clinton's rhetoric against the Democrats and leaving liberal reformers in the "awkward position of criticizing Republican welfare reforms as 'mean-spirited,' while defending their own initiatives— that first launched and legitimated time limits, family caps, and state discretion to reduce or eliminate benefits to entire categories of the poor" (Brodkin, 1995: 218). The Republicans were able, in effect, to reposition and consolidate their anti-welfare/pro-workfare position as a "mainstream" one, capitalizing on the momentous series of rightward shifts in policy orthodoxy since the passage of the FSA. Ironically, the provisions of the 1988 legislation on work participation were not scheduled to come fully into operation until 1995, by which time the center of gravity in welfare-reform efforts had moved markedly in the wake of waiver liberalization, the Clinton campaign of 1992, and the *Contract*. In the absence both of new federal legislation and of conclusive program evaluations, the terrain of debate had been transformed. Language played a key part in this transformation.

## The Rhetoric of the Right

The first Clinton administration witnessed a sea change in welfare politics. Even in the Senate, Republicans had begun to use workfare rhetoric much more aggressively. Launching the Republicans' welfare proposals in January 1994, Senator Alfonse D'Amato, for example, insisted:

> [L]et me say workfare not welfare. I think if you were to speak to welfare recipients and canvas them, they want the opportunity to pull their own weight, and that is what this bill is designed to do. . . . [It] goes a long way towards creating a state where it is no longer the welfare state but it is the workfare state. . . . I'm looking at some of the differences in the states in welfare. When just last year, the federal government finally gave a waiver to Wisconsin to implement the workfare programs, they have now cut off two entire counties from welfare because the workfare program is working. Preliminary reports from Iowa show that a majority of people that are in the workfare program are actually in real jobs. An Ohio workfare program demonstration achieved extraordinarily high participation rates. This is working. Workfare is working. So, the federal government can take a lead from the states and make something that not only will lower the cost to taxpayers, but again—getting back to that goal of giving each person the ability to be self-sufficient and proud that they are working to support their families.[24]

In the House debate following the Republicans' congressional victory, early in 1995, emotions reached fever pitch. As Drew recalled it, the welfare debate

> was uglier than any in memory—Democrats . . . invoked the specter of Hitler, while Republicans likened welfare recipients to animals—and House members knew they had ventured into new territory. The last shreds of civility were gone. . . . Ways and Means Committee chairman Archer, normally a most civil man, said the emotional level of the debate was driven by "the dying throes of the federal welfare state." Archer had a point. This wasn't any old bill: it represented a fundamental shift in policy, and in authority. (1996: 145)

The Republican welfare-reform plan proposed a radical devolution to the states, a cornerstone of the *Contract*'s overall philosophy (Maraniss and Weisskopf, 1996). But the strategy was not without its contradictions, for all the (premature and often unfounded) talk of reforms alleged to be "working" at the state level. The issue of costs touched a nerve. As Heritage Foundation researchers had argued some time before, "conservatives are talking through their hats when they claim that workfare makes people independent and cuts costs immediately" (Butler and Kondratas, 1987: 145). But still there was an attempt to play the issue both ways. Speaking on NBC's *Meet the Press*, Gingrich had earlier responded to the assertion that workfare strategies are costly and problematic—due to the commitments that they entail in terms of childcare, transportation, education and training provision, and even job creation—by arguing:

> That's not true. Governor Tommy Thompson has implemented work-fare and learnfare in Wisconsin; he has both saved money and changed behavior. Governor John Engler is implementing a variation of it in Michigan—he is both saving money and changing behavior. Governor Bill Weld is implementing it in Massachusetts—he is both saving money and changing behavior. . . . You could adopt workfare this spring, you'd be saving money by June.[25]

Nevertheless, the Republicans were clearly treading a fine line in seeking to move toward workfare without, first, incurring additional costs, or second, facilitating the expansion of (work-oriented) welfarism in a different form, replacing the entitlement to a welfare check with a new entitlement to a government-financed job. Given their overriding priority of deficit reduction, there were clearly political risks inherent in invoking the notion of workfare. As Republican senator Trent Lott revealingly said of liberal proposals, for example, "If we did everything the Democrats are talking about, we'd end up with welfare reform that costs money" (*Tennessean*, September 13, 1995: 8A). Perhaps the most taxing problem in this mode of welfare reform—particularly for conservatives—is how to enact work programs without incurring heavy spending commitments (Butler and Kondratas, 1987; Rector and Butterfield, 1987; Dionne, 1996; Drew, 1996). More fundamentally, some intellectuals on the right had been warning of slippage that can occur between the super-ficially attractive rhetoric of workfare and the potentially costly realities of workfarist commitments (Gilder, 1987; Rector and Butterfield, 1987; Tanner, 1995). According to George Gilder, "all this tough talk of 're-sponsibility,' 'obligation,' and 'duty' is just so much conservative patina on the hard metal of government jobs and day-care entitlements. [Work-fare] . . . would set the stage for a drastic expansion of the American wel-fare state. . . . [It] flunks the minimal test of a pro-family policy. . . . Workfare usurps the two human roles that most inexorably depend on moral commitments and difficult sacrifices by fathers and mothers: rais-ing children and providing for them" (1987: 20–21).[26]

It is in this context that the language of reform assumed an in-creased significance, as Republicans seized opportunities, on the one hand, to hem in Clinton with his own rhetoric, and on the other, to roll forward an anti-welfare movement as a discursive project. In the process, "welfare state" became an attack term (Safire, 1993),[27] one that few Dem-ocrats dared to utter except in distancing themselves from its principles and practices (Drew, 1996). These were precisely the grounds on which

Senator Bob Dole sought to challenge Clinton's 1996 State of the Union address, chiding the president for his apparent reluctance to live with the consequences of his own rhetoric: "The president has chosen to defend with his veto, a welfare system no one can defend—for it is a daily assault on the values of self-reliance and family" (*Washington Post*, January 24, 1996: A15). While these words have been less than entirely convincing when uttered by Senator Dole, himself once dubbed by Gingrich "[t]he tax collector for the welfare state" (quoted in Rodkey, 1995: 21), they had begun to acquire a deeper resonance on the right of the party where they were increasingly ascribed programmatic status.

## Tongue of Newt

At the center of this discursive project of welfare reform in the period leading up to the 1996 reforms was Newt Gingrich, a politician who undeniably understood the importance of words and the power of carefully constructed discursive strategies (Maraniss and Weisskopf, 1996). "The thing that shocks people," he once said, "is that I mean what I say. I don't use hyperbole" (quoted in Rodkey, 1995: 43). As Dionne explained at the time, Gingrich

> speaks incessantly about replacing the "welfare state" with an "opportunity society," knowing that the word "welfare" is now associated in the public mind with dependency, sloth and illegitimacy. His rhetoric is built around a careful study of the impact of words and their reception by the public. . . . When he compare[s] the "liberal welfare state" with the "conservative opportunity society," each word in each phrase amounted to a pair. "Liberal" was contrasted with "conservative" (there are more self-identified conservatives than liberals), "welfare" with "opportunity" (no contest between those two), and "state" with "society" (because . . . he wants to move attention away from the government's role and toward the social forces outside government). He identifies all government with the word "bureaucrats" and seeks to cast all choices about spending and taxes as a decision between giving money to those "bureaucrats" or letting citizens use the money themselves. (1996: 208)

This discursive strategy was taken a step further in the House Republicans' sequel to the *Contract*, *Restoring the Dream*, edited by Stephen Moore of the right-wing libertarian think-tank the CATO Institute.[28]

*Restoring the Dream* deploys the issue of "welfare reform" as an entry point for a root-and-branch critique of the principles of the liberal welfare state and, ultimately, to envision an alternative social structure: "It is not our goal to create a cheaper welfare state. It is not money we are trying to save—it's minds and lives" (Moore, 1995: 164). This is not simply about reform, but about a "wholesale transformation" from the old principles of the welfare state to the new principles of the "opportunity society." For Gingrich, welfare reform was a key plank of the wider strategy "to repeal the New Deal, smash the welfare state, and break the national power of the protectors of federal programs" (Drew, 1996: 143). As the unashamedly radical *Restoring the Dream* put it,

> [T]he government structures erected in Washington over the past quarter century must be entirely uprooted. . . . [They are] financially and morally bankrupt. The welfare state is not fixable because the model is wrong at its very foundation. It needs to be replaced with a new structure emphasizing dignity, hope, and individual responsibility. (Moore, 1995: 164–165)

*Restoring the Dream* goes on to codify, by way of a series of linguistic dualisms, the basic differences between the (supposedly) failing liberal-Democratic model of the welfare state and the new Republican opportunity model. Emphasizing work, family, and individual responsibility, along with localized and market-based solutions, this version of the opportunity society is constructed from a set of principles not only different from, but deliberately antagonistic to, a particular construction of welfarism as hopelessly centralized, bureaucratic, and disempowering (see Table 3.1).

Continuing an established trend in anti-welfare rhetoric (Heclo, 1994; Dionne, 1996), *Restoring the Dream* implicitly addressed itself to white suburban voters—the "taxpayers"—while presenting cities and "low income neighborhoods" as the locus of the problems to be fixed. Cities were constructed as the principal sites of welfare statism and dependency, as places where "Liberalism's fixes—welfare, urban handouts, public housing, the Department of Education—are now visible and widely acknowledged failures" (Moore, 1995: 38). Significantly, the chapter entitled "Building an Opportunity Society took aim at three issues—anti-poverty programs, the public school system, and the inner cities—overlaying the arguments around each in subtle yet revealing ways. Thus, the strategy to "bring capital and capitalism back into our struggling inner cities" (Moore, 1995: 164) was predicated upon an attack on welfarism: "The culture of poverty perpetuated by the current welfare state—perhaps more than any single factor—is devastating the physical, economic, and moral infrastructure of cities. A genuine culture of opportunity will take root in our inner cities, if we end welfare as we know it" (Moore, 1995: 185).

For the Republican right, then, the "culture of opportunity" is per-

**TABLE 3.1.** The Opportunity Society as a Discursive Project

|  | Liberal-democratic welfare statist model | Republican opportunity society model |
|---|---|---|
| **Power structure** | Empowers bureaucrats to make decisions for the poor | Empowers the poor to make decisions themselves |
| **Ethic** | Perpetuates an ethic of victimization; crowds out civic responsibility | Cultivates an ethic of personal responsibility; creates space for civic responsibility |
| **Governance** | Relies on centralized command-and-control structures | Relies on localized and market-based solutions |
| **Programming** | Expensive, uncoordinated, and value-void programs | Supports work, family, and personal responsibility |
| **Behavioral norms** | Rewards socially irresponsible behavior; welfarism as corrupting and entrapping | Encourages socially productive behavior; liberation |
| **Ideology** | Culture of dependency, poverty, and violence; counterculture value system; needs-based entitlement | Replaces dependency with work; reasserts American civilization; reciprocity |

*Sources:* Derived from the House Republicans' *Contract with America* (Gillespie and Schellhas, 1994) and *Restoring the Dream* (Moore, 1995).

ceived as the "natural" order to which urban societies will tend once ridded of the perverse interventions of the welfare state. This "natural" order is conceived as a domain of presocial, extrastate relations rooted in the organizing principles of *work*—hence the rhetorical attractiveness of *work*fare in contradistinction to welfare. Work, moreover, defines the *active* persona of the responsible and "independent" citizen, again in deliberate contrast to the *passive* role ascribed to "dependents" of the welfare state. These discursive dualisms are also gender encoded in the sense that the masculinism of work—what Gingrich (1994: 191) refers to as its inherent "muscularity"—is sharply contrasted to the implicitly feminine ministrations of the overbearing "nanny state."[29] For Gingrich, work and work*ing* are the cornerstones of "American civilization"; working is about "the sense of energy, the pursuit of happiness . . . it's an active verb—not happiness stamps, not a department of happiness, not therapy for happiness" (1994: 191).

Embedded within this wider ideological framework—and resituating social-policy concerns firmly within the context of work and responsibility—the House Republicans' proposals for welfare reform were rooted in the following six principles:

1. Require work for benefits.
2. Turn back most of welfare to the states to encourage experimenta- tion and cost-effectiveness.
3. Stop subsidizing illegitimacy.
4. Make welfare a temporary safety net, not a lifetime support system.
5. End the open-ended entitlement feature of welfare by block grant- ing programs to the states and establishing enforceable spending caps.
6. Renew the vital role of private institutions such as charities, Boys and Girls Clubs, and neighborhood groups to serve as support net- works. (Moore, 1995: 170)

Despite his professed sympathies with large parts of the Republican proposals, President Clinton twice vetoed welfare-reform bills that had passed House and Senate during 1995.[30] Commenting on his second veto decision, and exploiting the Republicans' tactical weakness over the cost of enforcing work mandates, Clinton argued that the welfare-reform bill "does too little to move people from welfare to work. . . . Americans know we have to reform the broken welfare system, but they also know that welfare reform is about moving people from welfare to work, not playing budget politics" (*Congressional Quarterly Weekly Report*, January 13, 1996: 103).

## Policies that Work

The stage was therefore set for welfare reform to play a key role in an- other presidential election, the Clinton–Dole contest of 1996. Here, there were tactical weaknesses on both sides. It was clear that there were ten- sions between the Republican Party's moderate pragmatists and radical ideologues with respect to the issue of workfare. Fearful, perhaps, of an electoral backlash against the *Contract*, some emphasized the place of workfare within a program of reform, while others continued to push for the full realization of the *Contract*. These differences were displayed in the May 1996 dispute between D'Amato and Gingrich over the Republi- cans' electoral strategy:

> [Gingrich] ought to concentrate on basic 101 communication. We want workfare, not welfare. . . . Less than 10 percent of the people knew anything about the Contract With America. And by the way, there's some good things in the Contract With America. But what we have to do is get back to reality. People don't want a revolution. They

want an evolution. They do want change. They want smaller government, less government. They want workfare, not welfare. (Senator Alfonse D'Amato)[31]

I don't think we went too far [in the 1994 congressional elections]. I think voters want a balanced budget. They want tax cuts. They want less litigation. They want less red tape. They want power shifted back to the states and out of Washington. And they want workfare instead of welfare. . . . I think people are going to get it and they're going to understand there's a party that wants less power in Washington and a party that wants more power in Washington, and I think that's going to be the choice, and I think, on balance, most people in this country would like to see us have lower taxes, less red tape in Washington, less bureaucracy, and return more power back home. (Representative Newt Gingrich)[32]

More cautiously, Bob Dole reassured voters that "we're looking at meaningful policies like workfare. . . . We understand what works."[33] The question of what works, however, continued to be a contentious one, particularly with respect to work requirements. For example, workfare advocate Lawrence Mead observed of the Republican proposals that their main effects would be on the "leading states in welfare reform, rather than the large urban states with the largest caseloads."[34] He went on to explain that the work mandate was seriously underfunded. Mead's concerns reflect a recognition that the federal welfare-reform process is increasingly modeled on the experience of a small number of nonurban reforms—based particularly on labor-force-attachment approaches to workfare that are likely to be sensitive to local labor-market conditions. Hence the interest in the ubiquitous "Riverside model." But as MDRC's Judith Gueron concedes, "[I]t is unclear whether Riverside's success can be replicated in diverse communities around the country, particularly in inner-city areas."[35] Achieving successes in urban areas, in fact, has become one of the main challenges of the post-1996 period, as "welfare reform's most consequential test is taking place in the nation's big cities" (MDRC, 1999: 1). Again, subnational experiences of welfare reform leave a strong imprint on national debates.

## THE QUIET REVOLUTION

[The *Contract*] signaled an important change in the political landscape of America—a fundamental shift in power away from Washington, D.C., back to state and local governments and communities. This comes after sixty years of the courts and Congress eroding the power of states and concentrating public

policy decisions in the nation's capital. . . . Governors will need
to craft efficient state and local programs based on ideas and
models that work. . . . [W]e must significantly redesign income
maintenance programs to encourage work, to support stable
families, and to promote parental responsibility. (Governor
Tommy Thompson, nd: 1, 17)

As the 1996 presidential campaign gathered pace, there was an important
sense in which, despite all the talk of Washington's legislative logjam, de
facto welfare reform was already substantively underway at the state
level. As a result, much of the politics of welfare reform had also "re-
verted to the subnational level" (Heclo, 1994: 411). States at the leading/
bleeding edge of anti-welfare politics—such as California, Wisconsin,
and Massachusetts—had been pushing through real reforms, though
quite often these had been restricted to localized trial sites. Just as importantly, these states were active agents in rescripting the language of the
debate, as the disaggregation of "welfare dependency" and "workfare"
rhetoric in Figures 3.3 and 3.4 illustrate. The very unevenness of rhetoric

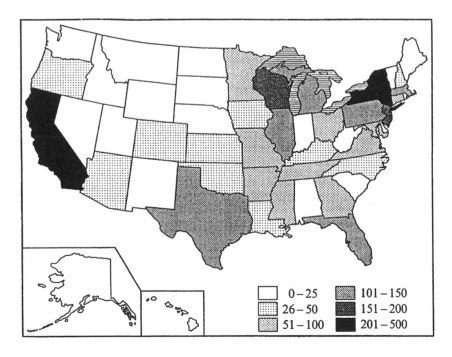

**FIGURE 3.3.** A discursive map of "welfare dependency." *Sources*: Citations to
"welfare dependency" in major U.S. newspapers, 1971–1996; LEXIS/NEXIS.

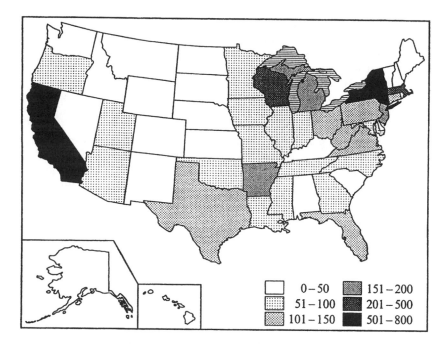

**FIGURE 3.4.** A discursive map of "workfare." *Sources*: Citations to "workfare" in major U.S. newspapers, 1971–1996; LEXIS/NEXIS.

and practice generated its own anti-welfare dynamics, as the race to the bottom was joined by more and more states.

The space for this subnational resurgence in anti-welfare politics was opened up by the Section 1115 waiver process. In the wake of the failure of his own early reform efforts, Clinton sought to add further impetus to the state-level reform process when he again met the NGA, in July 1995, to announce a streamlining of his administration's welfare policy. Deferring to the pragmatic lessons of state experiments, the president emphasized that "we shouldn't just wait around for the congressional process to work its way through. We can do more based on what States already know will work." Effective immediately, waiver requests would be approved on a fast track if they incorporated one or more of the following five administration strategies:

> First, requiring people on welfare to work and providing adequate child care to permit them to do it. Delaware recently got an approval to do this, so have several other States. Why not all 50?
>
> Second, limiting welfare to a set number of years and cutting peo-

ple off if they turn down jobs. Florida got approval to limit welfare . . .
so did 14 other States. Why not all 50?

Third, requiring fathers to pay child support or go to work to pay
off what they owe. Michigan got approval to do this, so did 13 other
States. . . . Why not all 50 States?

Fourth, requiring underage mothers to live at home and stay in
school. . . . Vermont got approval to [do] this, so did five other States.
Why not all 50?

And finally, permitting States to pay the cash value of welfare and
food stamps to private employers as wage subsidies when they hire
people to leave welfare and go to work. Oregon just got approval to do
this, so did Ohio and Mississippi. Arizona and Virginia can do it as
well. Why not all 50 States? This so-called privatizing of welfare reform helps businesses to create jobs, saves taxpayers money, moves
people from welfare to work, and recognizes that in the real world of
this deficit we're not going to be able to give a lot of public service jobs
to people who can't go to work when their time limits run out. I think
this has real promise. (President Bill Clinton, 1995)[36]

By way of this more *dirigiste* approach to the waiver process, Clinton
sought actively to structure state-level reform efforts in line with his administration's priorities, while keeping the federal safety net—threatened
by the Republicans' block-grant proposals—at least formally intact. He
continued: "[I]f you pass laws like these or come up with plans like these
. . . you send them to me, and we will approve them within 30 days.
Then we will have real welfare reform even as Congress considers it."

## Workfare by Waiver

While not all of the waivers approved by the federal government prior to
1996 involved workfare (in the narrow definition), they clearly reinforced the workfarist dynamic in several important ways: first, they compromised the integrity of the (admittedly weak) federal structure upon
which welfarism in the United States was constructed; second, they further opened up the policy space at the state level to experiment with new
ideas, framed within the important constraint of cost-neutrality; third,
they raised the stakes in welfare-reform efforts by linking visible/audible/
legible reform efforts with state-level political advantage. According to
Wiseman (1995: 13), "Governors are now compelled to be welfare
reformers . . . voters want welfare reform, and it is not happening in
Washington. Waiver based demonstrations make governors look good."
Fourth, they all started from a base of the workfarist structure laid down
in the FSA, variously undermining welfarist principles and practices
from this point of departure. As Greenberg (1995: 15) explains, once

"the media began identifying 'welfare reform' states as those that had filed waiver applications or had begun operating demonstration programs [this shifted attention from] the extent or quality of the state's implementation of the Family Support Act. Indeed, a state that can only point to its accomplishments in implementing the Family Support Act tends to be quite vulnerable to the charge that it is not 'doing' welfare reform."

But while the federal government played a vital role in creating the space (and some of the shape) of the welfare-reform movement, through its use of the waiver system, the words and deeds of governors had a significant effect on this process. A genuine dialectic of reform came into operation, as state- and federal-level developments began to condition and configure one another. In a glimpse of the block-granted future, the subnational politics of welfare reform began to generate their own dynamics, on this occasion assisted by a radicalized NGA (see Thompson, nd). In February 1996, the NGA unveiled their own welfare-reform proposals, modeled on the previously vetoed HR 4 bill, but designed to respond to some of the Clinton administration's reservations and thereby break the stalemate in Washington. The governors called for additional funding, particularly in support of welfare-to-work objectives, but retained the controversial block-grant provisions (Katz, 1996a). It was on these latter grounds that the administration initially rejected the proposal with Department of Health and Human Services secretary Shalala insisting that it allowed states too much discretion over programs (Katz, 1996b). Later speaking of this decision, Shalala explained:

> By block granting . . . welfare, the governors put at risk the most vulnerable children in our society. . . . I won't pretend to you that we aren't looking for some kind of transitional program [but] there must be some fundamental law of the land that protects children and protects their families as they are going through this transition [from welfare to work]. It ought not to make a difference if you're poor in one part of the country versus another part of the country in terms of the ability of your family to get some help to move back into the workforce.[37]

As the Clinton administration began to define its defensive posture in terms of the case for a minimalist safety net (avoiding, where possible, the politically inflammatory words "federal" and "entitlement") and the needs of children (around which the Democrats had had some success in portraying the House Republicans as excessive), it seemed to many that the battle had already been lost over the emerging form of workfarism. When, in May 1996, Clinton sought to steal the Republicans' thunder by endorsing a waiver application from the state of Wisconsin, he again heaped praise on the "quiet revolution" of state-level welfare reforms, pledging to "reform welfare state by state, if that's what it takes."[38] In response, Dole attacked the "killing compassion of the welfare state" as liberalism's "greatest shame," pushing for strict two-year time limits and a drastically reduced federal role: "[W]e cannot reform welfare on one waiver at a time. . . . In a Dole administration, no state will have to play the waiver game. Washington does not have all the answers. The federal role should be limited . . . problems are best solved . . . at the local level (Applause)."[39]

## Federalizing Reform

In July 1996, the House and Senate both passed modified welfare reform bills, thrusting the issue again into center stage of presidential politics. Both bills did away with the federal entitlement to welfare, block granting the remaining provisions to the states. Newt Gingrich described the House bill as a "strong welfare reform bill that emphasizes real work requirements; that returns power to the states; that cleans out the federal bureaucracy and federal red tape and federal micro-management," while Trent Lott observed that the Senate bill would "end welfare as a . . . way of life. It is historic. If you really want welfare reform, this is it" (*Washington Post*, July 24, 1996: A1). Critics insisted that the bills were chronically underfunded and punitive, and that they spoke more to election-year politics than to "real" reform. Democratic senator Carol Moseley-Braun attacked the legislation as "rhetoric raised to the level of policy" (*New York Times*, July 24, 1996: A1), while Senator Edward Kennedy fumed: "[O]ur Republican friends have absolutely no interest in real reform if it costs money. The proposal before us is not welfare reform. It is nothing more than legislative snake oil. . . . [T]his may well be the most cruel and extreme measure of the entire Republican Revolution."[41] Revealingly, there was less explicit talk of workfare—still a word with which conservatives are more comfortable than liberals—during this round of the debate, as the House Republicans and the president focused on their common political interest in finally passing a welfare-reform bill.

As the president considered whether he could risk another veto, he no doubt reflected on how his earlier rhetoric of "ending welfare as we know it" has come back to haunt him. Urging a presidential veto, a *Washington Post* editorial described the bill as "a terrible piece of legislation [that] provides too hard a shove and too little help." Riding high in opinion polls but with several months to go before the election, Clinton faced what the paper called "a defining moment in his presidency."[42] In

August 1996, on the eve of the Democratic convention, Clinton defined his presidency by signing the bill. In effect, the PRWORA enforces workfare on the cheap, implicitly providing incentives for the retrenchment of state's residual welfare commitments while favoring low-cost, labor-force-attachment approaches over more service-intensive alternatives (see Children's Defense Fund, 1996; Handler and Hasenfeld, 1997; Mink, 1998). The act presages an era of yet more radical (and punitive) welfare reform at the state level, initiating a defederalization dynamic that will be immensely difficult to reverse under current and foreseeable political conditions.

## THE POLITICS OF "DISENTITLEMENTARIANISM"

In the wake of the passage of the PRWORA, it is clear that there is now a genuine engagement with what Safire (1994: F4) has called the "hard part" of the reform process: the politics of "disentitlementarianism." In popular prejudice, entitlement has become synonymous with a "something-for-nothing" philosophy, part of the discredited culture of welfarism. So while Clinton was said to have supported the principle of entitlement, this was not something he was "willing to say publicly—or fight for" (Drew, 1996: 149). Instead, his lame and ultimately futile defense of residual welfarist principles was framed in the coded language of the "safety net" and the moral imperative to "protect children." But recall that even Ronald Reagan, long-time advocate of decentralized workfare, was loathe to take issue with the principle of entitlement: his welfare-cutting Budget Reform Plan of 1980 said of safety-net provisions that "these commitments transcend differences of ideology, partisanship, and fiscal priorities" (quoted in Carleson and Hopkins, 1981: 10). Sixteen years later it had become politically infeasible for Clinton to defer to such sacred principles. Instead, he found himself confined to advocacy of *his* version of workfare by way of the coded language of defending children and enforcing work, in the hope that the former might legitimate the retention of some kind of state-level "entitlement," while the latter invoked a more robust commitment to support services than Republicans dare endorse. Yet the punitive act of 1996 stands as testimony to the fact that the momentum of reform seriously outran the Clinton administration's rearguard defenses of *relatively* "soft" workfare. With their attack on the principles of federalism, the Republicans truly have—in Gingrich's words—gone "straight at the core structure and the core values of the welfare state" (quoted in Bernstein and Bernstein, 1995: 28).

   The fundamental strategy of the Republican right—effectively realized in the 1996 act—was to rupture the federal superstructure of welfarism, around which the fragile gains of the 1960s in benefits and entitlements were consolidated, and on which much of the contemporary politics of welfare advocacy are predicated. As Gingrich pledged on the first day of the 104th Congress, the House Republicans would "decentralize welfare back to the states . . . break up the Washington logjam, shift power back to the 50 states, break up all the liberal national organizations—and make them scramble back to the state capitols in Texas, Georgia and in Missouri" (*Washington Times*, January 4, 1995: A11). But while the Gingrich revolution stalled as a political project during the presidential campaign of 1996—as its author was first pushed to the sidelines, later banished permanently—this may paradoxically have been as much a measure of the success of the Republican right as of its failure. As Clinton stole the Republicans' clothes on welfare and on many other issues, so key elements of the *Contract* were effectively mainstreamed: the critique of "big government," the preoccupation with deficit control, the advocacy of states" rights, the language of work, responsibility, and opportunity—all have apparently become entrenched as consensual principles.

The Republican strategy also seems to have been successful in dissipating the power of the liberal opposition and the welfare-advocacy movement, opening the space for yet more radical reform at the local level. Its method of rolling back federal welfarism while rolling forward local workfarism has an important discursive as well as material component. In part, the debate over welfare reform has been about rescripting poverty politics, replacing "old" discourses of federalism, needs, and entitlement with "new" discourses of localism, work, and empowerment. To an extent, this can be seen as a reworking of age-old motifs in poverty politics, where work enforcement and the principle of "less eligibility" have been perennial themes (see Piven and Cloward, 1993; Handler, 1995).

Yet the contemporary workfare offensive represents a qualitatively distinctive strategy because it is eroding historically embedded welfarist principles (albeit in their relatively limited U.S. form) that many considered to be effectively irreversible, and because it is being advanced in the context of disturbingly complementary developments in flexibilizing, modern-day labor markets. The dominant signifiers in this contemporary debate have been welfare and workfare, the relative fortunes of which speak to a far-reaching political transformation. Hence the degradation of welfare into a political attack term and the ascent of workfare from a program of reform *within* the welfare system to a codification of an *alternative to* this system. The broadening and deepening of the meaning of workfare consequently reflects a slow transformation in its role as a discursive signifier and political trope, from intrawelfare reform through anti-welfare strategy to putative postwelfare structure.

Of course, there is still ambiguity, as there is with all such keywords. Recall that Clinton first sought to sell his welfare-reform proposals as neither a conservative nor a liberal idea, *but as both.* Beneath the discursive consensus on workfare are serious disagreements over how "hard"/ "soft" or punitive/supportive the new regime should be (see Rector and Butterfield, 1987). For Brodkin (1995: 217), this "ambiguity is not without its political advantages, enabling an apparent consensus to form around 'workfare,' while sidestepping fundamental differences between workfare as punishment and workfare as a social service." The very elasticity of workfarist language has created the space for consensus building around work-oriented welfare, which in turn has contributed to the political momentum behind welfare reform since "everyone agrees" that the system is broken. Moreover, as the welfare debate has progressed, so its accompanying ETM discourse has evolved to underpin the new "consensus." Thus, contrary readings of workfare-as-punishment and workfare-as-social-service have been rescripted in the technocratic language of policy evaluation as a distinction between "labor-force-attachment" and "human-capital-development" approaches to welfare-to-work programming, just as the erosion of federal standards was initially concealed by the language of program flexibility and local experimentation. Materially and discursively, the federal government has become an active agent in its *own* "hollowing out" (see Jessop, 1995a; Dicken et al., 1997), as local stories of "successful" workfare experiments, coupled with a federally orchestrated and incentivized reform process, have served to erode welfarist structures "from beneath." This is not a smooth and contradiction-free process—witness, for example, the continuing spatial disconnect between the (real and imagined) geographies of the "welfare mess" in places like inner-city Baltimore or New York City and those of the putative "workfare solution" in places like suburban California or rural Wisconsin—but it is nevertheless a process that has real political and institutional momentum.

For all workfare's haziness, however, it continues to perform important discursive work in remaking the subjects of policy and the nature of the policy problem. The words "workfare" and "welfare dependency" function to reconstitute the problem of poverty as a problem of welfare, thereby achieving the simultaneous objectives of directing reform efforts in a regressive direction (against welfare), rendering tractable the immediate policy objective (dismantling welfare), and creating the space for an alternative model (building workfare). This is, of course, a common strategy in state restructuring, as policy problems and political interests are systematically reconstituted by the state, in part, to make them (appear) satisfiable (Offe, 1984; Jessop, 1990). For example, Reagan's attack on poverty in the early 1980s was coupled with an administration critique of the notion of a national "poverty line" and the imposition of (lower and more uneven) "state need standards" (Carleson and Hopkins, 1981), just as the British Labour Party's embrace of workfare has coincided with debates over the definition of poverty and the meaning of welfare (Stephens, 1995; Brindle, 1996; 6, 1997). According to Tony Blair, by the early 1990s in Britain too

> welfare [had become] a term of abuse. It [was] associated with fraud, abuse, laziness, a dependency culture, social irresponsibility encouraged by welfare dependency. Welfare was blamed as the problem not the solution. . . . We are creating a welfare system which is "active" not "passive," genuinely providing people with a "hand up" not a "hand-out." Previous governments were satisfied simply to dole out money. . . . That is not our approach. We believe that the role of the welfare state is to help people help themselves, to give people the means to be independent. We are creating an active welfare state focused on giving people the opportunities they need to support themselves, principally through work.[43]

Yet while political rhetoric continues to drive the workfare debate, systematically channeling and constraining policy options, it is important to recall that the material achievements of the program are no more than modest and often highly questionable. Active policies like workfare are costly to deliver, such that their implementation is likely to be accompanied by increases in public spending, notwithstanding the politicians' claims to the contrary. Their effectiveness is also highly contingent on local labor-market conditions, a stubborn fact that program's politico-technocratic translation into ostensibly "transferable" policy models can only partly obscure. There is no evidence, moreover, that workfare reduces poverty. Rather, it is a regulatory regime designed to remove the alternatives to *working* poverty, by eroding welfare and enforcing work. As Katz has observed, "Workfare is a nonresponse to the structural sources of poverty in America. It addresses the politics of poverty, not its roots" (1989: 232).

But workfare has also become more than this. It is beginning to evolve beyond its earlier logic as an intrasystem reform program, designed to bring about a reorientation of an extant policy regime. Words of workfare are now being deployed to envision an alternative mode of regulating the poor. Needless to say, the poor are not regulated by political discourse alone. One of the distinctive features of workfare regimes, though, is the way that the apparently free-floating rhetorics of welfare denigration and work exhortation are connected powerfully to the daily material practices of workfare programming. Indeed, qualitative studies of "front-end" program delivery often draw attention to the way in which heavily loaded welfare/work dualisms are used to manipulate the behavior and self-image of clients (see Bardach, 1997; Edin and Lein, 1997; Little, 1999; Weaver, 2000). The codification of "welfare blues/advantages of work" drawn from Little's ethnographic study of a vocational counseling class, which is reproduced in Table 3.2, reveals remarkable echoes of "elite" political rhetoric. This is a measure neither of the perceptiveness of politicians nor of the gullibility of welfare recipients, but speaks instead to the deep currents of socialization and (neo)liberal ideology into which such discourses tap.

For their part, politicians are wont to oversell new policies and legislation and overpromise on results, as each reform is rendered a moment of great historical import. The history of welfare reform—perhaps more than any other field of social policy—is littered with such misplaced hyperbole. But the cumulative effect of more than a quarter century of slowly intensifying workfare rhetoric—coupled with the accelerating dissemination of local workfare practices and the radical implications of the PRWORA—is such that epochal claims about the end of welfare no longer seem quite so far-fetched. Despite the continuing modesty of its material accomplishments, workfare *as a discursive strategy* has played a key part in this process. Reflecting on the ascendancy of this portentous keyword, William Safire (1988: 8) observed that *workfare* "filled a void," be-

**TABLE 3.2.** Constructing Choices, Constructing Dependents

| Welfare blues | Advantages of work |
|---|---|
| Not enough money | Independence |
| Feel shameful/embarrassed | Money—regular paycheck |
| Often you get a "hard time" | Personal growth |
| Long waiting periods to be served | Insurance: life and medical |
| Caseworkers are sometimes mean; | Respect |
|   they don't always do their jobs | You know who and what you are |
| Discrimination |   dealing with |
| A lot of appointments | Income tax refunds |
| You have to justify your life to | Child support full payments |
|   someone | Savings/investments |
| Always request same documents | Travel |
| | Self-esteem rises |
| | Meet different types of people |
| | Vacation and sick days |

*Source:* Little (1999: 170).

coming as much "a part of today's language as the ancient word it was bottomed on." Initially, workfare filled a void in the sense that it provided a discursive framework for the systematic organization of anti-welfare sentiments and reform proposals, but it has subsequently outgrown this role. Workfare is no longer simply about rolling back the language and practices of welfarism; increasingly it prefigures the rolling forward of new institutions and vocabularies of regulation. One of the functions of the fuzzy language of workfare has been to hold together a range of contradictory and contending forces that are inevitably released by such a process of regulatory restructuring. Struggles over the meaning of workfare will continue, not least at the subnational level, where a range of differing strategies are being pursued. In the wake of the 1996 act, the next round of the welfare-reform debate is shaping up as a competition between a range of *local* variants of workfare. As poverty politics have been rescaled, so the meaning of workfare is being contested anew at the state and local levels.

## Notes

1. An earlier version of this chapter was published as "*Workfare*: A Geopolitical Etymology," *Environment and Planning D: Society and Space* (1998) 16: 133–161. I am grateful to Pion Limited, London, for permission to reproduce it here.

2. See Safire (1988: 8) on the rise of workfare, "this ugly duckling of a neologism, derided at launch, neglected by word mavens," in the United States. See Stephens (1995) and Wood (1995) on the United Kingdom.

3. On the Clinton package, see Greenberg (1993, 1994).

4. See Block et al. (1987), Butler and Kondratas (1987), Gilder (1987), Block and Noakes (1988), Nathan (1993), and Deacon (1994).

5. SWD provided twelve to eighteen months of employment in supervised work situations, focusing on long-term welfare recipients, young school dropouts, unemployed ex-offenders, and former addicts; while the more punitive CWEP required welfare recipients to "work off" their benefits, usually in public-sector or nonprofit agencies (Rose, 1995).

6. According to a Department of Labor review in 1978, CWEPs were "costly, inefficient, and resented by work supervisors as well as participants" (quoted in Rose, 1995: 106). An earlier review of the California workfare experiment, in 1972, had concluded that the program "did not prove to be administratively feasible and practical" (*U.S. News and World Report*, September 7, 1981: 63; see also Goodwin, 1983).

7. AFDC was restricted to families with gross incomes no greater than 150 percent of the "state need standard," a state-set poverty measure mostly lower than the official federal poverty threshold.

8. Public Papers of the Presidents, February 6, 1986, Pub. Papers 163: "America's Agenda for the Future."

9. According to a key Democratic staff member, the strength of the MDRC approach was "[e]xperimental design, experimental design, experimental design! That's what mattered to me," while a Republican staffer agreed: "You just couldn't question the [MDRC] results" (quoted in Szanton, 1991: 598).

10. According to Block and Noakes (1988), there were two further methodological flaws in the MDRC approach: their experiments were based on new claimants and excluded mothers with children under six years of age. The focus on new claimants tends to underrepresent long-term welfare users (the welfare dependent of policy concern and political rhetoric), while the exclusion of mothers with children under six effectively discounts around two-thirds of the AFDC caseload. Both groups would require greater service intensity (i.e., with childcare and other support services) to make the transition from welfare to work, which would inevitably raise the cost of a more comprehensive program, while also probably depressing the positive outcomes achieved in such partial welfare-to-work trials. There is every reason to expect, then, that as workfare trials are generalized to larger scale initiatives, cost-per-participant would rise as positive outcomes fell. Raw "labor-force-attachment models" would consequently appear more viable than actually they are.

11. Danziger and Weinberg (1994: Table 2.4) report that in 1960, 26.9 percent of the poor population were resident in central cities but by 1990 this figure had risen to 44.4 percent. The share of the poor population resident in nonmetropolitan areas, on the other hand, fell from 56.1 percent to 27.0 percent over the same period. Whereas in 1960 one-third of the nonmetropolitan population was categorized as poor, by 1990 this figure had almost halved, to 16.3 percent. These trends seem to be accelerating post-PRWORA, as the residual welfare population is increasingly trapped in the inner cities (Center on Urban and Metropolitan Policy, 1999).

12. *Washington Post*, November 13, 1979: A18. Reagan, of course, was famous for his use of (often unsubstantiated) "anecdotage" in reply to serious policy questions. Perhaps most notoriously, he once responded to questions about budget cuts with an anecdote about a welfare recipient using food stamps to buy vodka (see Safire, 1982; Pear, 1983). According to Reese (1982: 20), "In the public mind the welfare queen and the welfare mother are now one and the same, a view reinforced by a President who draws sweeping conclusions about budget deficits from a possibly apocryphal tale about a young man who buys vodka with change from his food stamps. Indeed, a new generation of American taxpayers has begun to vent its frustrations against the welfare state—a generation, says [Senator Paul] Tsongas, that has grown up reading not about hungry poor people but 'about abuses in the food-stamp program.' Ronald Reagan shares the concerns of that generation, and has made the 'waste, fraud and abuse' in social programs a primary target of his budget cuts." As Edsall (1991: 214) has argued, "The continuing vitality of this coded language—a language of 'groups,' 'taxes,' 'big government,' 'quotas,' 'reverse discrimination,' 'welfare,' and 'special interests'—became critical to the maintenance of the conservative presidential major-

ity in the latter half of the 1980s, as the utility of other weapons in the Republican populist arsenal diminished."

13. Senior MDRC evaluator #7, interviewed by Jamie Peck, November 1995; see also Berlin (1997).

14. Early waivers under Section 1115 were granted to California, New Jersey, New York, Ohio, Washington, and Wisconsin, subsequently some of the most proactive states on the issue of welfare reform.

15. While Bush espoused anti-welfare rhetoric, his approach to reform was for the most part a reactive one: "Ask American parents what they dislike about how things are going in our country, and chances are good that pretty soon they'll get to welfare. Americans are the most generous people on Earth. But we have to go back to the insight of Franklin Roosevelt who, when he spoke of what became the welfare program, warned that it must not become 'a narcotic,' and a 'subtle destroyer' of the spirit. Welfare was never meant to be a lifestyle. It was never meant to be a habit. It was never supposed to be passed from generation to generation like a legacy. It's time to replace the assumptions of the welfare state and help reform the welfare system." His approach was to create more space for the states to innovate: "States throughout the country are beginning to operate with new assumptions that when able-bodied people receive Government assistance, they have responsibilities to the taxpayer: A responsibility to seek work, education, or job training; a responsibility to get their lives in order; a responsibility to hold their families together and refrain from having children out of wedlock; and a responsibility to obey the law. We are going to help this movement. Often, State reform requires waiving certain Federal regulations. I will act to make that process easier and quicker for every State that asks for our help" (Public Papers of the Presidents, January 28, 1992, cite 28 Weekly Comp. Pres. Doc. 170: "Address Before a Joint Session of the Congress on the State of the Union").

16. Federal News Service, July 31, 1992: Remarks by President Bush to community service organizations at Riverside Convention Center, Riverside, California, emphasis added. For early coverage of Riverside's "success," see *Los Angeles Times*, 26 April 1992, and Izumi (1992).

17. U.S. NewsWire, September 11, 1992: "Remarks by Gov. Clinton at the Clayton County Office of Family and Children's Services." While Clinton continually stressed the importance of moving welfare recipients back into the workforce, it should be acknowledged that this workfarist refrain appeals to some of the longest standing convictions in welfare policy. Clinton continued: "Spending a couple of thousands dollars a year on a welfare recipient today; helping that person to become independent, to lead their children in a different direction; to open up new avenues of possibility; will mean more incomes and more taxes, and less dependence in the future." To be sure, this is a long-established philosophy: "To cure paupers and make them self-supporting, however costly the process, must always be economical as compared with a smaller but constantly increasing and continual outlay for their maintenance" (Abbott, 1937: 161).

18. "The Family Support Act embodies a principle which I believe is the basis of an emerging consensus among people without regard to party or without regard to their traditional political philosophies: we must provide people on wel-

fare with more opportunities for job training with the assurance that they will receive the health care and child care they need when they go to work and with all the opportunities they need to become self-sufficient. But then we have to ask them to make the most of these opportunities and to take a job" (Federal News Service, February 2, 1993: Remarks by President Bill Clinton to the National Governors' Association meeting, J. W. Marriott Hotel, Washington, DC).

19. "No one likes the welfare system as it currently exists, least of all the people who are on it. The taxpayers, the social service employees themselves don't think much of it, either. Most people on welfare are yearning for another alternative, aching for the chance to move from dependence to dignity" (Federal News Service, February 2, 1993: Remarks by President Bill Clinton to the National Governors' Association meeting, J. W. Marriott Hotel, Washington, DC).

20. Federal News Service, February 2, 1993: Remarks by President Bill Clinton to the National Governors' Association meeting, J. W. Marriott Hotel, Washington, DC.

21. Federal News Service, February 2, 1993: Remarks by President Bill Clinton to the National Governors' Association meeting, J. W. Marriott Hotel, Washington, DC.

22. As Williams (1994) points out, such concerns with "temporary and local pressures" were central to the decision to federalize welfare in 1935.

23. Federal News Service, July 31, 1992: Remarks by President Bush to community service organizations at Riverside Convention Center, Riverside, California.

24. Federal News Service, January 27, 1994: Press conference on welfare reform.

25. Reuter Transcript Report, February 21, 1993.

26. Gilder is as trenchantly anti-workfare as he is anti-welfare: "55 percent of all women with children hold jobs. Why not welfare mothers? The reason is simple. They are on welfare in the first place because they would or could not get jobs that remotely compete with welfare benefits. On the whole, white or black, these women are slovenly, incompetent, and sexually promiscuous. To bring them into the workforce would require heroic efforts: enriching welfare with day-care, education, and training, and then cutting off benefits and granting government-subsidized jobs run by disciplinarians who can require more work effort. . . . [I]f welfare meant a greased pole to employment training, free day-care, and a government job, most of the population would join. . . . The welfare state has already deprived . . . children of their fathers. The workfare state proposes to take away the mothers as well" (1995: 25).

27. According to Safire (1993: 866), "welfare" has become synonymous with "creeping socialism," while when used in this context, the word "state" is seen to have a "totalitarian connotation."

28. CATO, which has close links to the Republican freshmen, is skeptical of workfare programs, instead advocating the termination of federal funding for welfare: "Individuals unable to support themselves through the job market should look to the resources of family, church, community, or private charity" (CATO Institute, 1995: 178).

29. According to Republican governor Tommy Thompson of Wisconsin,

one of the leading innovators in welfare reform, "In order for us really to effectuate meaningful change . . . you have to come to Washington on bended knee and say, 'Mother may I try something new?' And then Washington will give you a reduced waiver" (CNN, *Inside Politics*, May 7, 1996, transcript #1167). On masculinism in welfare-reform practice and discourse, see Fraser and Gordon (1994), Tickell and Peck (1996), and Weinroth (1997).

30. Welfare-reform bills were passed by the House (March 24, 1995) and by the Senate (September 19, 1995). These measures were first vetoed when presented as a component of a budget reconciliation bill (HR 2491) in December 1995 and subsequently as a freestanding welfare reform bill (HR 4) in January 1996.

31. CNN, *Inside Politics*, May 3, 1996, transcript #1163.

32. Federal Document Clearing House political transcripts, March 21, 1996: "Delivers remarks at a conference of the National Newspaper Association."

33. Federal Document Clearing House political transcripts, October 23, 1995: "Wilson endorses Robert Dole's candidacy to be President of the United States," Washington, DC.

34. Federal Document Clearing House Congressional Testimony, December 6, 1995, Lawrence M. Mead, House Ways and Means Human Resources Review of Welfare Changes (HR 4).

35. Federal Document Clearing House Congressional Testimony, February 28, 1995, Judith M. Gueron, Senate Labor Impact of Welfare Revisions.

36. Public Papers of the Presidents, July 31, 1995: Weekly Comp. Pres. Doc. 1342; "Remarks to the National Governors' Association in Burlington, Vermont."

37. Speaking at Coalition on Human Needs "Welfare to Work" conference, Washington, DC, March 29, 1996.

38. Federal News Service, May 18, 1996: "President Clinton's Weekly Radio Address."

39. Federal News Service, May 21, 1996: "Speech by Senate Majority Leader Robert Dole: Welfare and Welfare Reform."

40. CNN, *Capital Gang*, July 21, 1996, Transcript #50–2.

41. Congressional Press Release, July 22, 1996: "Statement by Senator Edward M. Kennedy on the welfare bill."

42. Quoted in *Washington Post*, July 31, 96: A26.

43. Beveridge Lecture, Toynbee Hall, London, March 18, 1999.

# PART II

# Spaces of Workfare

# CHAPTER FOUR

# Postwelfare States?

## *Geopolitics of "Reform"*

Public relief which seeks only to relieve distress ends by
creating the pauperism which it was designed to remove.
Outlays so great betray a fatal weakness in our social
structure—a weakness to be coped with only by striking at its
causes. Pauperism is due in greatest measure to a lack of
mental capacity in the individual to support himself and his
dependents. His trouble is largely hereditary. He is brindle
stock. To relieve him, that he may propagate more of his strain,
is to perpetuate the problem of pauperism. . . . When
Massachusetts followed the practice of taking a drab to the
almshouse for her lying-in, thereafter relieving her of her child
and sending her out again to the roadside to get another, it was
thereby placing a premium upon the birth of the handicapped
and in great measure fostering the fool. (Kelso, 1922: 194)

There is nothing new in individualistic and behavioral accounts of the
causes of poverty. The design of welfare systems has always reflected received views concerning the appropriateness of work requirements/
expectations for different social groups, related assumptions about which
segments of the poor population are more or less "deserving" of public
aid, and more particularly, profoundly gendered attitudes toward assumed work roles inside and outside the home. With the oldest welfare
system in the United States, Massachusetts has experienced just about
every iteration in these age-old debates. While at times state and local
authorities have adopted a hard-line approach, Massachusetts has for

most of the time since the New Deal stood for liberal social values and a comparatively generous welfare settlement. In fact, for much of this time, the state has been a symbol of the most progressive strand in U.S. social-welfare provision. But in the early 1990s, when the election of a Republican governor, William Weld, coincided with growing anti-welfarism at the federal level, things began to change, dramatically. Weld instigated a root-and-branch autocritique of the state's welfare policies, driving through a series of measures that were soon to place Massachusetts at the bleeding edge of the national "welfare-reform" movement. As a local welfare-rights advocate described the situation, "Massachusetts had one of the most liberal, generous [welfare] programs. Now we have one of the most punitive, harsh ones."[1] In this most recent iteration in the long history of Massachusetts welfare politics, the hard-liners are again in the ascendancy. Echoing nineteenth-century accounts of the intergenerational transfer of dependency and pauperism, the Weld administration drove through a radical welfare-reform package in 1995 that dramatically curtailed access to welfare and sharpened work requirements, ostensibly in the interests of the children of the poor.[2]

> The current welfare system not only fosters parents' dependence on welfare as a way of life, it can also affect children. . . . Children that grow up in families and communities where their parents and neighbors do not work fail to realize that other opportunities are available to them, and often adopt welfare dependence as an acceptable lifestyle. . . . The availability of welfare benefits and other welfare supports for teen parents has also helped to fuel births to unwed teens. . . . Massachusetts' [plan] seeks to reorder the priorities of the welfare system. By reintegrating [public aid] recipients into the work force, we can begin to break the cycle of dependence and eliminate the inequities wrought by our current system. (Commonwealth of Massachusetts, 1995: I-3-4)

The Massachusetts reform plan was trumpeted as "among the boldest and far-reaching in the nation," replacing "traditional cash assistance with work or community service requirements" for all able-bodied welfare recipients with schoolage children (Commonwealth of Massachusetts, 1995: I-1). But while the Massachusetts welfare reforms are in many senses radical, they also reflect how far the center of political gravity had shifted—even prior to the PRWORA—to the right across the country. Here, mutually reinforcing developments at the federal and state levels have served to entrench a regressive reform dynamic throughout the welfare system. It is no longer adequate for policies to be "sound," "appropriate," or even "well founded"; now they must be "bold" and "far-reaching."

In fact, the Massachusetts reform package—which was to earn the epithet *Weldfare*—represented a cocktail of some of the most ambitious measures that were being proposed at this strategically important time, that is, immediately prior to the passage of the PRWORA: benefits were reduced and "incentivizes" were built into earnings allowances; work was vigorously enforced, while those failing to find work after a specified time were required to undertake mandatory community service; anti-fraud measures were toughened; children born to mothers on public aid were denied benefits (the "family cap"); recipients failing to immunize their children against a range of diseases specified by the Department of Public Health had their benefits reduced, as did those whose children had unexcused absences from school ("learnfare"); subsidies and tax breaks were offered to employers to recruit welfare recipients; paternity requirements were extended; and welfare was denied to teen parents living independently and to those not in receipt of, or registered for, a high school diploma.

## LOCATING MASSACHUSETTS

In the context of the national reform movement, Massachusetts is perhaps more of a radical emulator than a genuine innovator, but the state's political significance and the cumulative stringency of its recent reform program have certainly played a part in establishing a new standard of punitive programming against which other reforms have been judged.[3] Significantly, it also prefigured the PRWORA of 1996, in terms both of timing and content. Massachusetts was one of the states that shaped the agenda for welfare reform during Clinton's first term, contributing to the clamor for federal reform, which in turn was facilitated by the Clinton administration's liberalization of the waiver process. Prior to 1996, the politics of reform were very much played out *between* Washington and the states. Nevertheless, it was politically convenient for all concerned, including President Clinton himself, to represent reform as a "bottom-up" process:

> The state-based reform we have encouraged has brought work and responsibility back to the lives of 75 percent of the Americans on welfare. . . . [State-level] reforms . . . are very encouraging for two reasons. First, they give us hope that we can break the vicious cycle of welfare dependency. And, second, because they make it clear that there is now a widespread national consensus shared by people without regard to their political parties on what welfare reform should look like. It should be pro work, pro family, pro independence, responsible. Welfare should be a second chance, not a way of life.[4]

The respective dynamics of state- and federal-level politics tellingly illustrate the way in which the contemporary onslaught against welfare is associated—perhaps contingently, perhaps necessarily—with different forms of decentralization, defederalization, denationalization, localization, regionalization, and "hollowing out" (see Jessop, 1994; Jessop and Peck, 2000). The Massachusetts case highlights the way in which regulatory reforms commonly entail changes in, and challenges of, the *spatial constitution* of the objects and subjects of regulation, the extant pattern of federal–state/central–local regulatory relations, and the related geographies of policy, institutions, and governance. This is not just to say that policy reforms yield uneven spatial effects (though they certainly do), but to make the broader claim that the process of reform itself is necessarily bound up in shifting spatial relations, that it involves changes in the prevailing "spatial-institutional fix" (see Jones and Kodras, 1990; Peck and Tickell, 1994). The erosion of federally or nationally constituted welfare regimes alongside, and partly *through*, the rise of locally constituted "workfare" systems exemplifies the way in which the "reform" of policy and the remaking of regulatory relations tends to be associated with changes in the geography of the policy apparatus, narrowly conceived, and more broadly in the structural orientation and strategic emphases of the state itself.

Focusing on the case of Massachusetts, these themes are addressed in this chapter by way of a consideration of the intrinsic spatiality of welfare/workfare politics. It will be suggested that the process of welfare reform has been driven in a sense *neither* by Washington *nor* by the state governors, but instead has emerged out of a complex series of political interactions between the federal, state, and local levels. Particularly important to the way that the United States has lurched toward its after-welfare settlement is the way in which a series of distinctive "models" of reform—established in state- and local-level "experiments"—have been taken up, in a highly politicized and ultimately transformative way, into wider policy discourse and practice. Such has been the intensity of competition between different state and local models of welfare reform that the process has in fact begun to generate its own momentum, as the extant system and its underlying principles have been rapidly destabilized through a *federally orchestrated* process of erosion "from below."

The Massachusetts experience is revealing in this sense, because the state's profile in wider welfare-reform debates has always been a distinctive one, and more specifically because its switch from a liberal to a punitive regime over the last decade both conditioned, and was conditioned by, the changing policy climate at the federal level. This period has also witnessed Massachusetts's switch from its 1980s role as a policy innovator and "exporter," when the state pioneered voluntary and service-intensive approaches to welfare reform, to a 1990s role as a policy imitator and "importer," with a reform program representing a bold amalgam of the most far-reaching state experiments from around the country. The account here is divided into two phases: first, the period from the late 1970s to the early 1990s, during which Washington sought to stimulate experimentation in welfare reform through demonstration projects and waivers from federal law, associated with the rise and fall of "new-style" workfare in Massachusetts; and second, the period since 1992, in which state-level reform and experimentation became effectively endemic, culminating in the current "block-grant" regime, which Massachusetts had partly anticipated in its earlier shift toward *Weldfare*.

## MAKING NEW-STYLE WORKFARE

State-level welfare politics come in fifty flavors, reflecting as they do a wide range of local economic, political, and institutional conditions. Yet they are also strongly influenced by the rhythms of federal reform politics. Intense periods of activity at the state level often occur when the federal reform process has stalled. So it was that an important legacy of Nixon's failed reform effort was the revitalization of WIN in the early 1970s. For the most part, these work-welfare projects were small-scale local trials that—especially in their California variants—favored minimalist "hard-workfare" approaches (Hayes, 1984; Rose, 1995). Most quickly became mired in administrative problems (Wiseman, 1989). At the time, states like Utah, Texas, and North Carolina were at the forefront of the reform process, though it was not long before some of the northern—and traditionally pro-welfare—states like New York, New Jersey, Connecticut, and Massachusetts began to follow suit. Massachusetts barred all "employable" persons from its General Assistance (GA) rolls in 1975, and subsequently showed great interest in emulating Utah's tough and mandatory approach to workfare.[5] Unlike Utah, however, Massachusetts had large welfare rolls—in 1978, it was the highest ranked state in both welfare spending and in the size of the caseload relative to the overall population. It also had a formidable tradition of welfare-rights advocacy. Nevertheless, the state's political leadership continued to press for the implementation of some kind of workfare program. The *Economist* observed that

> Massachusetts . . . has become a surprisingly conservative state. . . .
> [It] is not the liberal bastion in its domestic affairs outsiders imagine it

to be. . . . [Governor] Dukakis has had fairly broad support for his "workfare" proposal, which, if approved by federal officials, would force some men with families now receiving welfare to work three days a week for 13 to 26 weeks to earn their welfare cheques. Unlike President Carter's proposed welfare reform plan, the workers would not even be paid the minimum wage. (1978: 32)

But the impetus for change here was not solely a state-level one; the federal regulatory framework was also being revised, and with it the scalar constitution of the reform process. Reagan's OBRA legislation of 1981 encouraged states to develop a new set of local *demonstration* projects (the broader intent being clear) as a means of driving forward the process of welfare reform.

## OBRA Demonstrations

OBRA "gave states the workfare toolkit" (Wiseman, 1989: 19), initiating a range of strategies for reforming welfare at the local level through the introduction of work, training, or community-service requirements, most of which were mandatory for welfare recipients. Despite the fact that few such programs had achieved anything but the most modest of results in the past, under OBRA (and with 90 percent federal funding) they were to lay the foundations for the dramatic increase in local-level workfare experiments during the 1980s (Burtless, 1995; Rose, 1995). These demonstrations represented a stubborn institutional critique of the AFDC program (see Table 4.1).

The landscape of the welfare-reform process began to change. OBRA had triggered an unprecedented phase of experimentation with alternative policies and programs, and even though many of the individual experiments failed, their cumulative effect was to create the impression of growing pressure for reform on the part of the states (see Epstein, 1997). In Brodkin and Kaufman's (1998: 1) view, the orchestration of demonstration projects, their promotion through the ostensibly apolitical evaluation literature, and the subsequent emergence of state "success stories" had a major effect on U.S. poverty politics because they "narrowed the boundaries of policymaking, reinforcing conservative tendencies that have [subsequently] limited the range of policy possibilities."

Bearing in mind the subsequent course of welfare politics, the 1981 act proved to be decisive in a number of ways: First, it switched the political momentum of the reform process from the federal to the state level, sidestepping the intractable problems of steering reform through the complex of entrenched interests and oppositional forces in Washington, and opening up the space for state governors to initiate local solutions to the "welfare mess." Second, for all the rhetoric of states' rights, this was no straightforward process of defederalization. Clear parameters were set by Washington, which meant that the overall direction of the reform process was in an important sense predetermined: the demonstrations would seek generally low-cost ways of enforcing work, drawing on different combinations of job-search and community-service requirements. Third, within these parameters, states would have the freedom to explore alternative program designs and different mixes of sanctions and supportive services, with the effect of generating a repertoire of (costed and evaluated) restructuring strategies. In time, the very presence of these "local solutions" would make the process of systemic federal reform all the more inevitable, both as symbols of the states" hunger for reform and as prima facie evidence that these are "ideas that work."

The Massachusetts experience through the 1980s would show, however, that opening up the space for state-level reform can have unpredictable consequences. Initially, the path of least resistance was followed. Dukakis had lost the 1978 election to a conservative Democrat, Edward J. King, who then moved to realize his predecessor's posturing on workfare. In the immediate aftermath of OBRA, King launched his Work and Training Program (WTP), a paradigmatically tough program that aggressively sought to place welfare recipients in work, immediately sanctioning the grants of recalcitrant participants. Significantly, the senior administrators hired to run WTP had been recruited from California, a state with a long tradition of no-frills workfare experiments. But for all this, WTP was doomed to failure. It was quickly besieged by welfare advocates, who would eventually have WTP's sanctions policy reversed in the courts, while at the policy level the program was soon to buckle under the pressure of a coordinated attack from a coalition of labor, human-services, church, and welfare-rights groups (Savner et al., 1986). This was a portentous moment, since King failed to win reelection in 1982 partly as a result of his administration's disarray over workfare (Nathan, 1993). Equally important was the subsequent campaign to lift welfare recipients "Up and out of poverty," which drew the anti-WTP coalition into an increasingly close working relationship with the incoming Dukakis administration, one of the first acts of which was to appoint a task force to restructure WTP. The outcome was a new approach based on supportive services rather than financial sanctions: the new "soft workfare" program, Employment and Training Choices (ET), was launched in 1983 (Mandell and Withorn, 1993). A new welfare commissioner was appointed, whose slogan was "Send the Californians back to California" (Nathan, 1993).

**TABLE 4.1.** OBRA Work-Welfare Demonstrations

| State | Program | Start date | Features | Evaluation |
|---|---|---|---|---|
| Arizona | Work Incentive Demonstration Program | 1982 | Job-search, training, and placement assistance | Manpower Demonstration Research Corporation (MDRC) |
| Arkansas | WORK Program | 1982 | Job-search assistance and work experience | MDRC |
| California | San Diego Employment Preparation/Experimental Work Experience Program (EP/EWE) | 1982 | Two-track system: job search only and job search plus community service | MDRC |
| California | San Diego Saturation Work Initiative Model (SWIM) | 1985 | Successor to EP/EWE program, augmented with more comprehensive services | MDRC |
| California | Greater Avenues for Independence (GAIN) | 1985 | Variable, from job search-focused to service-rich programs | MDRC |
| Florida | TRADE Welfare for Work Program | 1984 | Range of wage-subsidy schemes | Florida Department of Health and Rehabilitative Services |
| Illinois | WIN Demonstration Program (WDP) | 1984 | Minimum-service two-track program: job search and job search plus work experience | MDRC |
| Maine | Training Opportunities in the Private Sector (TOPS) | 1983 | Work experience and on-the-job training for volunteers | MDRC |
| Maryland | Baltimore Options | 1982 | Two track: service-rich and minimalist | MDRC |

| State | Program | Year | Description | Research Organization |
|---|---|---|---|---|
| Maryland | Basic Employment and Training (BET) | 1982 | As Baltimore Options, though requiring up-front job search | MDRC |
| Massachusetts | Employment and Training Choices (ET Choices) | 1983 | Range of training, placement, and general-education services for volunteers | Pioneer Institute for Public Policy Research |
| Minnesota | Community Work Experience Program | 1983 | Job search and community service | Minnesota Department of Human Services |
| New Jersey | Grant Diversion | 1984 | On-the-job training for volunteers | MDRC |
| North Carolina | Community Work Experience Program | 1982 | Two track system, job search only and job search plus community service | North Carolina Department of Human Resources |
| Ohio | Community Work Experience Program | 1984 | Combining job search. community service, and on-the-job training | Potomac Institute for Economic Research |
| Oregon | JOBS | 1982 | Mandatory job search | Oregon Department of Human Resources |
| Pennsylvania | Community Work Experience Program | 1982 | Community service | Pennsylvania Department of Public Welfare |
| South Carolina | Community Work Experience Program | 1982 | Community service | Clarkson Co. |
| Utah | Emergency Work Experience Program (EWEP) | 1983 | Replaced welfare grants with work requirements plus some services | Social Research Institute, University of Utah |
| Virginia | Employment Services Program (ESP) | 1983 | Job search, community service, and miscellaneous training | MDRC |
| Washington | Applicant Employment Services | 1982 | Mandatory job search | Washington Department of Human Services |
| Washington | Community Work Experience Program | 1982 | Two track: job search and community service | Washington Department of Human Services |
| West Virginia | Community Work Experience Program | 1982 | Mandatory community service | MDRC |

*Source:* Derived from Greenberg and Wiseman (1992).

## ET Choices

ET was to be a voluntary program. Its philosophy was different from those California-style workfare experiments predicated on the principle of mandatory participation. It is important to emphasize, however, that the form of ET was not simply a product of Dukakis's own liberal instincts—after all, in the 1970s he had made much of the need to get tough on welfare—but instead was shaped by the legacy of Massachusetts welfare politics. As Nathan has explained, "[T]he liberal political values on social issues that we associate with Massachusetts, and the way Governor King's WTP program bumped up against these values, were underlying factors in the decision to highlight voluntarism under Dukakis's successor program" (1993: 43). As a result, the defining feature of the new program was that it would sell work rather than sanction welfare:

> [ET] did not attempt to serve as a deterrent or to control the behavior of the recipients by imposing a work requirement, and it did not penalize the able-bodied poor for not working. Instead, it attempted to induce the able-bodied poor to enter the labor market by offering an array of services, including extensive education and training. . . . ET represented a symbolic departure from WIN by viewing welfare recipients as potential customers to be attracted to the program. (Handler and Hasenfeld, 1991: 188–189)

At least initially, the performance of ET Choices was promising. In its first eighteen months of operation, fifteen thousand welfare recipients were moved into paid employment and the welfare rolls shrank by eight thousand, though crucially this was in the context of a booming labor market (at the time, Massachusetts's unemployment rate was the lowest of all the industrial states). And the program was costly—initially $3,000 per job placement, later rising to $5,000—reflecting its service-intensive approach and relatively significant commitment to training. This was not so much of a problem when the welfare rolls were falling and for all intents and purposes the program could be represented as a "success." According to a favorable evaluation in the *Economist*, the only real obstacle that might have prevented ET from meeting its ambitious employment targets was the capacity of the program itself: "The main constraint is not the local job market but the 15,000-place capacity of the state's employment programmes" (1985: 36). Yet while the expanding Massachusetts labor market was able to absorb large numbers of former welfare recipients, it was only doing so at relatively low wages. In the mid-1980s, a Massachusetts mother of two children leaving welfare would double her cash income by entering a job at $5 per hour, but would almost certainly lose health and other benefits in the process. Taking these lost benefits into account, this woman would be worse off in work unless she could find childcare for less than $25 per week. Nevertheless, the *Economist* concluded positively by pointing out that the "Massachusetts experience suggests that the quality of support services may be more important than either money or compulsion in luring welfare recipients, particularly single parents, out to work" (38). Widely touted, in fact "surely the most publicized welfare program in the country," ET seemed also to be well received locally, "Massachusetts [being] one of the few states where a welfare program seems to be a political asset for state politicians" (Wiseman, 1989: 29). "Soft workfare," it seemed, was working.[6]

## The Politics of ET

In the wider context of the OBRA demonstrations, ET was located on the liberal wing of the movement toward new-style workfare. New-style workfare differed from its predecessors in that, rather than simply requiring recipients to "work off" their grant, a range of sanctions and supports were utilized in the effort to move participants from welfare to work. This approach has two advantages for advocates of workfare: first, costs are generally lower than on the "old-style" community-service-based programs, particularly where emphasis is placed on up-front job search; and second, programs need not simply be punitive, but can be represented as offering new opportunities for participants to escape poverty through their own efforts (Block and Noakes, 1988). Not surprisingly, this was a seductive package for many New Democrats, who saw the political possibilities of combining rights-and-responsibility rhetoric with activist but no-nonsense programs, and perhaps—in the most favorable circumstances—bringing about falling welfare rolls and cash savings. But if liberals were going to cross the Rubicon, joining conservatives in advocating workfare, their approach still had to be a distinctive one. In the mid-1980s, the issue for liberals was no longer whether or not to support the principles of workfare *vis-à-vis those of welfare*, but one of deciding which *form* of workfare to support. Hence the Dukakis administration's repeated attempts to link the performance of ET to its distinctive features *vis-à-vis the other OBRA demonstrations*: voluntary participation and service intensity. "[T]he success of the ET program is based on the philosophy that welfare recipients should have the same employment opportunities available to other people and that they will make use of those opportunities if necessary support services are available" (Commonwealth of Massachusetts, 1986: 4; see also Ammott, 1986).

Others were not so easily convinced. Critics from the right-wing Heritage Foundation argued, perhaps with some justification, that

Dukakis had misappropriated the term *workfare* in order to disguise "recycled old approaches, which drape themselves in the workfare mantle ... to justify traditional and ineffective social policies" (Rector and Butterfield, 1987: 7). Workfare, they maintained, should be cost-*saving*; so by definition ET's heavy investments in education and training marked it out as something different. More tellingly, Rector and Butterfield also observed that the actual impacts of ET could not be assessed with any certainty because "the state has refused to permit controlled experiments" (1987: 10; see also Baum, 1991; Oliker, 1994). In contrast, far more influential at the time were the program evaluations provided by MDRC (see Gueron, 1987). Both in their methods of analysis and in the selection of research sites (which was skewed toward low-cost, job-search-oriented programs), the MDRC evaluations implicitly favored "harder" and less service-intensive versions of workfare (Block and Noakes, 1988; Szanton, 1991; Epstein, 1997). In addition, there was some concern—even among those predisposed toward the "softer" approach of ET—that the apparently positive results of the Massachusetts program were critically contingent upon the state's buoyant labor market and so as a result would not be easily "transferable" (O'Neill, 1990; Baum, 1991). Moreover, for all the program's emphasis on supportive services, there was a strong sense in which its functioning mirrored that of the labor market: ET's performance-based funding system led to "creaming," as most job-ready clients were the first to be hired (O'Neill, 1990); racialized and gendered patterns of recruitment and retention tended to be reproduced, rather than countered; while employment probabilities were also systematically related to job histories, durations of unemployment, and education and training (Urban Institute, 1990).

As searching questions were being raised about the actual achievements of ET, the process of welfare reform was about to enter another decisive phase. In 1985, the National Governors' Association (NGA) took up the issue of welfare reform, appointing a task force to construct the foundations of a bipartisan approach to workfare. It was headed by Governor Bill Clinton of Arkansas. The NGA's work would form a central plank of the "workfare consensus" that would become the FSA of 1988, which for the first time devoted mainstream federal funding to workfare programming under the JOBS program. While Piven and Cloward (1993: 387) have claimed that ET was one of a handful of programs that "became the model for the work provisions" in the FSA, in fact the linkages were rather nebulous. Certainly, ET bolstered the conviction among New Democrats that "soft workfare" could work, contributing at an ideological level to the workfare consensus by shoring up its more liberal wing. But legislators remained rather skeptical about the achievements of the program itself, largely due to the absence of the kind of "scientific" evaluation provided by MDRC for so many of the other OBRA demonstrations (see Table 4.1). According to an aide to Senator Daniel Patrick Moynihan, recruited to draft the FSA legislation, "[W]e took particular note of MDRC's findings and did not rely much on the claims of success being made on behalf of Governor Dukakis's much discussed [ET] program. . . . Without the same sort of rigorous research design employed by MDRC, it was impossible to say how many Massachusetts welfare recipients would have left the AFDC rolls for jobs anyway, even if ET had not existed" (Baum, 1991: 609). Indeed, O'Neill's evaluation of ET would later conclude that the program "had no discernible independent effect on reducing the AFDC caseload; rather, it was [due to] local economic conditions" (Handler and Hasenfeld, 1997: 62).

Somewhat perversely, the service-intensive approach of ET was portrayed in the FSA negotiations as somehow "more embedded" in local conditions (and hence less portable) than were the other OBRA demonstrations, most of which tended to emphasize the kind of low-cost, job-search-based strategies that are manifestly contingent on local-labor market conditions (see Table 4.1). A more telling explanation for ET's failure to play in the FSA debate was its supporters' insistence on the decisive role of voluntary participation. In this sense, the Massachusetts model stood for the principle of *supporting* welfare recipients' transitions into waged work, in contrast to the ascendant approach of *mandating* participation in work programs. Again, the politicization of the evaluation process was such that the critique of ET was distorted to suit the emerging consensus around mandation, despite the fact that quite different conclusions could be drawn from the same evaluation studies:

> The failure of ET . . . encouraged O'Neill [the program's evaluator] to support other conservatives . . . in calling for more restrictive welfare-to-work programs that provide low-paying jobs and low-cost services. . . . Yet the same findings might argue for a more generous approach, such as a national jobs program. . . . If anything, the failure of the manpower training experience argues forcefully for a more direct strategy of job creation. [The impacts of this] are hard to know, except for the near certainty of its great expense and political unpopularity. (Epstein, 1997: 178)

While the eventual design of the JOBS program would be sufficiently elastic to permit the deployment of ET-style support services, the FSA framework formally eschewed ET-style voluntarism. The reasons for this went to the heart of the FSA debate and the newfound workfare consensus. The political bargain struck by Democrats and Republicans had been that liberals would concede the principle of compulsion if conservatives dropped their opposition to the provision of supportive services (Mead, 1992b). The post-1988 federal framework consequently appeared to split the Massachusetts model straight down the middle. And critically, the relative strengths of mandatory versus voluntary programs—the challenge of ET—was never fully tested (see Wiseman, 1989; Handler and Hasenfeld, 1997; Brodkin and Kaufman, 1998). The moment had passed.

While in practice JOBS proved to be less mandatory than the FSA legislation suggested, with many states' administrative procedures effectively softening the edges of the federal law (Handler, 1995), the movement away from ET-style voluntarism and service intensity was soon gathering pace. Welfare rolls were rising due to deteriorating labor-market conditions, which was translated politically into growing irritation with the apparent failure of more costly (i.e., service-intensive) JOBS programs. This represented a particular problem in Massachusetts, because the earlier success of ET had been claimed on the basis of falling caseloads; so once these began to rise the program's legitimacy was duly undermined (Wiseman, 1989). Meanwhile, MDRC's evaluations began to tend strongly in favor of tougher, low-cost, minimalist approaches, epitomized by the Riverside GAIN program. And the wider political climate was also changing. Having conceded the principle of mandatory workfare, the Democratic Party began to drift away from structural/social analyses of poverty toward an individual-deficit model, just as its center of political gravity began to shift from the traditional liberalism of the northeastern states to the conservatism of the New Democrats in the South (see Kodras, 1997). This was to find its most vivid expression in the ascendancy of Bill Clinton and his anti-welfare presidential campaign of 1992. In program terms, the "tough-love" approach of the New Democrats would further discredit service-intensive methods, now portrayed as overweening, costly, and inefficient.

By the time Clinton entered the White House, the ET philosophy was dead in Massachusetts. The program's legitimacy had been undermined by rising welfare rolls, related to the slowdown in the state economy, while the gubernatorial elections of 1991 saw a swing to the right. The new governor, William Weld, got straight to work on the welfare system. His approach, as one of his senior managers in the welfare administration explained, was to be radically different:

> "Look, for sixty years we've done welfare the way it's always been done, with a federal approach to this thing, and it's got nothing but worse. I don't know how we cannot try some new approach to this thing . . . *at least* have this experiment. . . . It's the end of the way it's

been done for sixty years . . . the pendulum is swinging to the point where we're saying to individuals, you've got to be responsible for your actions. That had never happened before; somebody would come in and say, 'I want welfare, I meet the requirements, give it to me.' This whole shift to individual responsibility was something that was missing from the old programs."[7]

Reflecting the new priorities, the Department of Public Welfare was renamed the Department of Transitional Assistance (DTA). A major legislative overhaul was initiated. *Weldfare* was taking shape.

## MASSACHUSETTS'S AFTER-WELFARE SETTLEMENT

One of Bill Clinton's first acts as president was to address the NGA on the subject of welfare reform, where he encouraged governors to step up their reform efforts under Section 1115 waiver provisions. These efforts would generate a repertoire of reform strategies, which were serially reproduced and developed right up until the passage of the PRWORA in 1996. As Clinton would boast during the 1996 presidential election campaign, "[I]n the last three years, my administration has granted 38 states welfare reform waivers, clearing away federal rules and regulations to permit states to build effective welfare reforms of their own. . . . So the states can keep on sending me these strong welfare reform proposals, and I'll keep on signing them."[8] The shape of the 1996 legislation was in many ways evident in this accumulated pattern of waiver applications, the basic outlines of which had been established even before Clinton took office. Lawrence Mead's survey of "changes in local welfare policy" in the final months of the Bush administration, for example, led him to identify the following common strands:

- **Cuts in benefits**. The California proposals include a 10 percent across-the-board reduction in AFDC benefits, and Michigan and Massachusetts have curtailed general assistance.
- **Time limits on benefits**. Some states, including Vermont, have discussed limiting how long a mother could draw AFDC benefits unconditionally.
- **Workfare**. Several states propose to reward recipients who participate in welfare employment programs with higher benefits and/or to penalize those who do not participate.
- **Learnfare**. Several states propose to require that welfare adults, particularly teen mothers, stay in school on pain of a reduction in their benefits. Wisconsin, in addition, requires that welfare parents keep their children in school.

- **Child limitation**. The California and New Jersey plans seek to limit the size of welfare families by denying welfare mothers additional benefits if they have further children while on the rolls.

- **Marriage promotion**. Economic incentives are proposed to encourage welfare mothers to marry. For example, the mothers could keep more of their current welfare benefits than is now permitted.

- **Other restraints**. Various stipulations tied to benefits include requirements that mothers secure health care for their children and that teen mothers continue to live with their parents. (1992a: 14; see also Wiseman, 1993; NGA, 1994)

Mead went on to identify three factors behind the states' advocacy of welfare reforms of this kind: first, they were for the most part inspired by previous workfare experiments (which in his opinion were "widely viewed as effective") in that they sought variously to build on work mandates by extending benefit conditions into other spheres such as the regulation of children's schooling and the domestic lives of welfare recipients; second, states were seeking to extend control of recipients' behavior from the public domain of waged work to the private sphere, so as to intervene in the "troubled" family lives of poor people; and third, they implied a widespread "repudiation of voluntary methods," as states have reacted to the "failure of voluntary social programs to halt the violence, child abuse, and school and employment problems in low-income areas" (14–15). As the NGA has observed, there was soon "striking consensus among states on the changes needed to encourage work and reduce reliance on welfare" (1994: 1).

Echoing familiar themes in the right-wing critique of the Great Society (see Murray, 1984), the turn against voluntarist welfare programming was justified by workfare advocates on the grounds that the very *persistence* of social problems like drug abuse and crime (or, for that matter, economic problems such as poverty and fluctuations in the business cycle, insofar as these would swell the welfare rolls) was somehow conclusive evidence both of the failure of "liberal" policies like AFDC and ET and of the dysfunctional behavior of their clients. Moreover, in the realpolitik of welfare reform, those policies that happen to be in place when the rolls are rising tend automatically to be branded as failures (the fate of many JOBS programs launched into slackening labor markets in the early 1990s). The backlash against JOBS set the critical context for many states' impatient search for something new. In Mead's view, this is why "local leaders want to get tough," as the new consensus had it that "merely to dole out benefits is simply not enough to deal with [the] problems [of the poor], which today are due as much to disorder as to material need" (1992a: 15).

## Getting Tough in Massachusetts

These arguments found a receptive audience in many statehouses across the country, not least in Massachusetts, where Weld's welfare administration became absorbed in a mission of self-transformation. Established practices, and the entire check-printing rationale of the old bureaucracy, became discredited by their association with the failed regime of welfarism. Few inside or even outside the administration would take the risk of defending welfarist principles in general or past practices in particular. By definition, this meant defending the indefensible, the status quo. As the momentum built, the process of welfare reform in Massachusetts would go through a series of iterations, beginning with the "most employable" of the welfare population: single adults on the GA program. As a senior official recalled,

> "Prior to the governor [Weld] coming into office, [GA] had been growing at a phenomenal rate. We were approaching almost forty thousand cases and an expenditure of close to $200 million a year. . . . So when the governor came in he immediately asked the department to come up with a plan to address that, and we did. . . . [GA] was changed and we cut both the population and the expenditures in half. During that period, however, as in any time you try to change anything, the advocates—or the people who don't want to see change—complained and demonstrated and protested and basically made the complaint that people would be dying in the streets if we took the drastic steps to reduce that program. Of course, none of that ever materialized. . . . And that kind of set the tone."[9]

The reform of GA—justified, apparently, on the grounds that the program was being heavily used—"set the tone" for subsequent welfare reforms in Massachusetts in two important ways. First, it demonstrated that the Weld administration would not balk at draconian measures oriented explicitly to deregistering recipients, with little regard for their subsequent fate. After all, work—of any kind—*had* to be better than welfare. Reflecting the strong libertarian strand in Weld's thinking (see Tanner, 1995), the Massachusetts approach was to effect exits from welfare (read: liberation from dependency and exposure to the opportunities of work) with the minimum of service support. A senior DTA official would even dismiss, as excessively interventionist and "coddling," the paradigmatic exemplar of hard workfare, the Riverside GAIN program. The following observation underlines the extent to which state-level officials were engaged in monitoring and learning from "competing" programs, while also benchmarking the stringency of their regime against those in other jurisdictions:

"I read a number of the Riverside articles. . . . You have got to help people, but helping isn't always coddling, you know, it can be abrupt. . . . Here we seem to be taking a more distant approach, so that, hey, that's *your* job, you have got to do that. It's not *my* job to find you a job, it's *your* job to find you a job."[10]

Second, the GA reform exposed critical weaknesses in the welfare-advocacy movement—which as one DTA official observed had always been "very strong and very united in their opposition to what they call workfare"[11]—because the advocates proved ineffectual in their initial opposition, while tactically miscalculating in their prediction of dire *and visible* social consequences. According to one strategically placed official, while welfare advocates had "always had a major political voice in this state," their invocation of "death on the streets" had proved unfounded: "They have been yelling so often about the sky falling in that it's falling on deaf ears. . . . They don't have any influence on us, and they don't have any influence on the governor, and I believe that their influence on the legislature is minimal, very small."[12]

The Weld administration's apparent "success" in overwhelming the advocate community and neutralizing opposition to program changes may have had less to do with superior tactics or strong policies than with the wider political climate around the reform process. When, in the next critical moment in the state's step-by-step, cumulative approach to welfare reform, mandatory community service for AFDC recipients was introduced in January 1994, the administration drew strength and legitimacy from the federal legislation—the FSA—while taking pride in implementing the policy in the teeth of opposition from advocates, on the grounds that this showed that the reforms were biting. One of those centrally involved explained that

"we were pioneers in a way, and set a trend [in] the community-service requirement. . . . Community service is known around here as workfare. I'm sure it's known around the country as workfare. But here our advocates are very vocal about workfare and 'slavefare,' they call it everything. . . . I don't think we would have been able to do it alone, without the federal legislation, because the advocate community in this state is very strong. But we started it, we started it with opposition from the social-services community out there. . . . We proved the advocates wrong."[13]

No doubt recalling the sorry fate of Governor King's workfare initiative of the early 1980s, the DTA has been especially careful to minimize the scope for lawsuits, to which all such programs are vulnerable, given the

relatively broad discretion that they place in the hands of frontline officials.[14]

For advocates, the very scale and momentum of the reform process
presented major problems of strategy and organization. As the Weld administration worked through seemingly endless permutations of their
welfare-reform proposals, each with its different emphases, likely impacts, and design features, advocates found that their resources and energies were soon overstretched, faced as they were with the need constantly to change tactics, to remobilize around different issues, and later
in the campaign to fight on several fronts simultaneously. As two advocates recalled,

> "What happened is that so many things came out, and you'd win one
> small victory, sort of focus your energies there and you might get
> somewhere, but then at the time you're putting your energy there,
> there are ten other things that have come along. It was too big, too
> fast, and there were just so many things going on. It was very cynical.
> For years we've been fighting this same thing, and it's just sort of crept
> up each year so it's bigger and bigger, and it got to the point that it was
> *so* big."[15]

> "Our agency, we were just trying to hold the line, you know? There
> was a lot of denial. There were already a lot of primary providers
> swamped and overwhelmed with what they had to do. . . . You just
> couldn't possibly keep up. . . . It was hard at the time, but you really
> needed to be standing up. . . . Nobody wanted to take it on. And there
> was already a lot of rhetoric and propaganda out there about the wel-
> fare system doesn't work, it has to be reformed, there are abuses, blah,
> blah, blah. So nobody was really able to muster a great challenge. [We]
> didn't have a chance. . . . It was too much for people."[16]

Social-services activists were confronted by a particularly acute form of
one of the perennial contradictions of welfare advocacy: the challenge of
balancing the defense of those reliant on the existing system while remaining above charges of vested interest, or worse still, portrayal as an
apologist for past practice. In fending off repeated waves of regressive reform on grounds of principle and practice, advocates ran the obvious
risk of appearing to be defending the status quo. The administration
could therefore denigrate advocates not only as "welfare pimps," but also
as unconstructive opponents of change itself.

Thus the juggernaut of reform soon outran and outflanked the
opposition. In stark contrast to the Dukakis reforms of the early 1980s,
the imprint of the advocacy movement is scarcely, if at all, distinguish-

able in the Weld reforms. Instead, these took their inspiration and their cues from other sources: first, from the constantly evolving repertoire of state strategies, given that by 1994 all forty-eight states responding to an NGA survey of welfare reforms had undertaken initiatives "beyond those required under federal law" (NGA, 1994: 3); second, from the sustained critiques and counterproposals of the Republican right, as codified in the *Contract with America* and the work of numerous right-wing think-tanks such as the American Enterprise Institute, the Heritage Foundation, the Hudson Institute, and the Cato Institute, which have fostered prolifer-ated state-level support and dissemination networks in recent years; and third, from a revisionist reading of Dukakis's policy failures, on the basis of which the Weld administration would claim that both voluntarism and service-intensive methods had been shown to fail.

## Reform, Off-the Peg

Clearly though, much of the inspiration, if not the impetus, for the Weld reforms came from outside Massachusetts, reflecting the rapid diffusion of reform strategies, mechanisms, and policies both "vertically," between the federal and the state levels, and "horizontally," between the states themselves. Through this kind of "fast policy," states have been able to acquire reform policies "off-the-peg," tailoring them to local circum-stances and packaging them together in different ways. This partly ex-plains the conundrum, noted by Norris and Thompson (1995: 229), that the "politics of welfare reform in the states [is both] remarkably similar and remarkably different." Policies are diffusing rapidly, yet for different reasons their local implementation and representation remain highly un-even. Implementation varies spatially owing to the complex institutional and labor-market interactions that condition the execution and ultimate impacts of work-oriented welfare programs, reinforced by the path-de-pendent nature of local policy systems. Representation remains uneven, first, due to the natural inclination of state politicians to claim the credit for new initiatives, and second, as a result of the current ideological pre-disposition—fostered both in Washington and in the states—for "local solutions." Thus, the Weld program—despite the obvious borrowing from elsewhere of certain policy strands, such as learnfare (Wisconsin) and the family cap (New Jersey)—was represented as both homegrown and innovative. One of its authors explained it like this:

> "Call it arrogance . . . but we didn't look at other states at all. . . . The senior managers in this agency have been in this system for a good long time, and we pretty much *knew*. We'd read the literature, we'd read what was coming out of Washington, those kinds of things, and

we had an idea what was going on in other states, but we never wanted to model ourselves after any particular state. . . . One of the things about Massachusetts, when Dukakis was Governor in the '80s, he set about in his own way with welfare reform. We were one of the leading states in terms of providing retraining services and education services to welfare recipients. The rest of the country, as I see it, was just getting . . . to that point, where we were back in the '80s. What we did was we sat down and looked at the success, or lack of success, of those programs that we had in the '80s. That's why we decided that wasn't the way. We shouldn't be emphasizing this education and training business, but what we should be pushing on is work. In the '80s, there was a lot of the services . . . and yet you still saw that core of welfare cases that would continue to be there. My judgment was that what we should try to do was get to them. And one of the ways of getting to them was to have a strong work requirements."[17]

As Handler and Hasenfeld (1997: 76) observe in their review of welfare-reform initiatives around the time of the PRWORA, "Massachusetts has taken the lead in tough welfare reforms." Ironically, Massachusetts could represent itself as the vanguard of the conservative reform movement in the 1990s precisely *because* it had played such a prominent role in the liberal movement of the 1980s. The comprehensive reform package passed by the state legislature in February 1995, summarized in Table 4.2, earned the state national prominence, more by virtue of its sweeping nature than by its specific innovations in policy. Although the package was vigorously negotiated with state legislators, one of its architects claimed that "as a whole, it came out weighted more to what we wanted than what the legislature wanted."[18] Having agreed to a handful of concessions proposed by the legislature, such as the Full Employment Program and additional exemptions under the time-limit rules, Weld eventually forced its passage by threatening to withhold half the state's welfare budget for the coming year.[19]

There followed several months of waiver negotiations with the Department of Health and Human Services (HHS) in Washington. This slowed down the reform process but played favorably into the wider political strategy of presenting the governor as a radical reformer at loggerheads with Washington bureaucrats wary of "real" reform. The main sticking point in the Massachusetts waiver application was the uncompromising nature of its time-limit provisions (see Table 4.2). Having themselves advocated time limits, senior figures in the Clinton administration found themselves in the awkward position, in the run-up to the passage of the PRWORA, of encouraging state-level reforms while also seeking to soften their more punitive elements. In particular, HHS sought to widen the scope for exemptions around the states' time-limits propos-

**TABLE 4.2.** Summary of Massachusetts's Welfare Reform, 1995

| Measure | Features |
| --- | --- |
| Work requirements | Able-bodied AFDC parents who are nonexempt and whose child of record is of school age must work 20 hours per week. This will include approximately 20,000 recipients. |
| Time limits | Assistance is limited to 24 months in a 60-month period. |
| Exemptions | Those recipients exempt from the time limit and work requirement include: <br>• disabled parents <br>• parents caring for disabled children or a disabled spouse <br>• parents with a child of record under the age of two <br>• women in their third trimester of pregnancy <br>• parents with any child under three months <br>• parents under 20 attending high school <br>• caretaker relatives |
| Benefit reduction | In order to encourage employment, all nonexempt recipients will be subject to a 2.75 percent reduction in cash assistance benefits (approximately $15 per month for a family of three). |
| Work incentives | All families subject to the 2.75 percent benefit reduction will be permitted to retain more of their earned income. The current four-month £30 and one-third disregard is increased to $30 plus one-half of earned income. In both cases, the deduction will remain in place for as long as a family is eligible for assistance. |
| Community service | Able-bodied recipients with schoolage children who seek paid employment but cannot find it must work a minimum of 20 hours in a community-service position in exchange for assistance. |
| Employer subsidies | The Full Employment Program is established to help finance employment opportunities for welfare recipients. Recipients who volunteer for the Full Employment Program will receive wages from their employer, plus a supplement from the Department, if necessary, to bring their income up to the level of AFDC and Food Stamp benefits. The state will pay participating employers $3.50 per hour for each recipient for a period of nine |

| | |
|---|---|
| Teen parents | months, and $2.50 per hour for three additional months. An employer who hires a former recipient into nonsubsidized employment receives a state tax credit of $100 per month for a maximum of 12 months. As a condition of eligibility, parents under the age of 20 must have a high school diploma or GED, or be in a program to obtain one. In addition, they will be required to live in the home of a parent or responsible adult relative or, if there is abuse or neglect at home, in a supervised, structured setting. |
| Paternity establishment/ child support | The plan strengthens requirements for establishing paternity, and requires the Department of Revenue to certify the cooperation of program participants. To encourage responsibility on the part of absent parents, courts are authorized to order community service when a noncustodial parent is in contempt of a child-support order. |
| Learnfare | Children under the age of 14 will be required to attend school. When a child misses eight days of school within three months without an acceptable excuse, the child will be placed on probation. The child's portion of the grant will be reduced after three unexcused absences in a month during a probationary period. |
| Family cap | The Commonwealth will no longer provide benefits for additional children born to welfare recipients (with exceptions in extraordinary circumstances). |
| Immunization requirement | Failure to provide proof to the Department that children have received necessary immunizations will result in the parental portion of the grant being reduced. |
| Direct payment of rent | If a recipient falls behind six weeks or more in rental payments, the Department is required, at the request of the landlord and after a hearing, to deduct the recipient's rent from her grant money and pay it directly to the landlord. Exceptions are made in the case of landlord/tenant disputes. |
| Assets | The allowable asset level for recipients is increased from $1,000 to $2,500. |
| Treatment of motor vehicles | The permitted value of a motor vehicle is changed from an equity value of $1,500 to a fair market value of $5,000. |
| Anti-fraud | The program establishes wage assignment in cases of fraud or other payments, increased penalties for individuals who commit fraud, and denial of benefits for individuals with outstanding warrants. |
| Direct deposit of benefits | Recipients with bank accounts will be required to receive benefits through direct deposit. |

*Source:* Derived from Commonwealth of Massachusetts (1995: 1-5-I-7).

als, which were becoming fashionably draconian. There were political costs in this, however, as Republicans would use every opportunity to present the Clinton administration as prevaricating in the face of "real" reform proposals, many of which, after all, seemed to be guilty of nothing but taking the president at his word.

For some time, the Republican strategy at the federal level had been predicated on the reforms of a number of leading governors, including those of the Weld administration. Although their agenda was clearly ideologically driven, this provided an opportunity to portray Republican reform proposals as concrete and grounded. The agenda of the right was to build on the reform repertoire at the state level, albeit within the critical parameters of enforcing work *while cutting costs*. This would serve the twin objectives of eroding the federal welfare settlement while demonstrating to skeptics that the rhetoric of workfare could be turned into a reality, if only Washington would get out of the way. So, Newt Gingrich would argue that "all the President has got to do is call in Thompson, Weld and Engler and ask them how to do it. They're already doing it in their states and we could be doing it in Washington."[20]

In fact, what Thompson, Weld, and Engler were doing in their states was precisely what Washington allowed them to do, either under closely specified waivers or under the latitude of the FSA. But as Gingrich's remarks make only too clear, there was a strong political dynamic built into this process. Advocates of radical reform were able to tap into widespread frustration over the "failure" of welfare, turning this powerfully against the present custodians of the system in Washington. Meanwhile, Republicans in Washington took to measuring the processing time of the waiver applications of key states, such as Wisconsin, citing delays as evidence of the Clinton administration's lack of resolve. Governor Weld would also extract political advantage from the waiver negotiations by publicly removing the controversial time-limit provisions in anticipation of carte blanche under a future block-grant regime.[21] Thus Weld was able to simultaneously demonstrate a tough posture on welfare reform and an ability to get things done, while appearing one step ahead of the bureaucrats in Washington. His actions also contributed to the mounting pressure for a block-grant regime, which the NGA was later to take up nationally in its (ultimately successful) bid, early in 1996, to resurrect the legislative process in Washington (see CBPP, 1996).

In an echo of the FSA negotiations, the NGA would again perform a decisive function by taking the lead in drafting a bipartisan bill (albeit one, in this case, substantially skewed toward earlier Republican proposals) that would eventually pave the way for federal legislation. As the election campaign had intensified, it had become clear that Clinton and the House Republicans had a shared interest in passing some kind of bill, as this would keep Clinton's 1992 campaign pledge to enact far-reaching reform while also converting a key element of the *Contract with America* into legislation. In fact, the passage of welfare-reform legislation in the midst of the 1996 campaign allowed both Clinton and the House Republicans to demonstrate that they could "walk the walk" as well as they "talked the talk" on welfare reform. No matter that the bill was seen to be a flawed and underfunded one, even by many of those who voted for it, the overriding imperative was for decisive action: the time had finally come to realize the rhetoric of workfare. According to one of the bill's Democratic supporters in the House, "This is a bad bill but a good strategy. In order to continue social and economic progress, we must keep President Clinton in office. . . . We had to show Americans that Democrats are willing to break with the past, to move from welfare to workfare."[22]

Undoubtedly, the significance of the PRWORA extends far beyond the short-term calculations of electoral politics, for it represents the culmination of more than two decades of sustained, if uneven, pressure for radical welfare reform. Waivers had been eroding the federal system for some time, but prior to the 1996 act had at least occurred within the context of national standards, safeguards, and requirements. By rupturing this federal framework, the block-grant provisions in the act presage a profound turn in both the symbolism and the reality of "welfare" in the United States. Certainly, the process of "reform" in the U.S. welfare system has been a highly uneven but almost continuous process since the early 1990s. But this unevenness—and indeed the *meaning* of unevenness itself—was set radically to change once the states were formally handed the mandate for reform. According to Kilborn (1996: A10), we are witnessing the beginning of "a new chapter in the welfare reform debate, one that will be waged outside of Washington."

The PRWORA clearly reflects key aspects of the states' reform agenda—given that its specific measures have been mostly tried (if not fully *tested*) in a range of state-level reforms (see Table 4.3)—but more importantly places a new regulatory framework around the process of state experimentation. A new "standard" for welfare and welfare reform has been established, against which states are rapidly realigning themselves. States have already moved to reposition themselves variously on the punitive and ameliorative edges of the new welfare system: a few are acting to temper and restructure federal provisions, while the majority— including Massachusetts—are taking steps to ensure that their provisions will be tougher and more stringent than the (constantly shifting) federal norm (see Table 4.4). The race to the bottom seems already to have been joined, as the "*floor*" of needs-based entitlement, which characterized the old AFDC system, has been replaced in the block-grant regime with a

**TABLE 4.3.** Summary of Federal Welfare Reform, 1996

| Measure | Features |
|---|---|
| Eligibility | Terminates federal Aid to Families with Dependent Children (AFDC) program and needs-based eligibility. The new program, Temporary Assistance for Needy Families (TANF), will be operated by states under a new regime of block grants. States gain control of eligibility rules, benefit systems, administration, and program design. |
| Spending cap | Establishes a permanent federal spending cap on welfare. There is a small contingency or "rainy-day" fund for states requiring temporary increases in federal assistance. |
| Time limits | Sets a federal maximum lifetime timelimit of five years, but allows states to impose shorter limits. Permits states to exempt no more than 20 percent of the caseload from the time limit. |
| Work requirements | Requires recipients to begin working two years after receiving aid. Failure to work to lead to benefit reduction or termination. In order to avoid funding penalties, states must meet stringent federal targets for work (or work program) participation. For example, 50 percent of single-parent families must be working at least 30 hours per week by 2002. Offers only limited funding for work programming, leaving a funding shortfall of $13 billion, according to the Congressional Budget Office. |
| Community service | Recipients must participate in community service after receiving two months of TANF assistance. |
| Single parents | Permits states to deny aid to unwed mothers under the age of 18. Provides incentives for reducing illegitimacy rates. Benefits may be cut where single mothers fail to provide adequate information on the identity/location of the child's father. |
| Immigrants | Denies most welfare benefits, including Medicaid, cash assistance, and Supplementary Social Security, to future legal immigrants for five years. Permits states to extend these exclusions. |
| Spending cuts | Anticipates spending reduction of $55 billion over six years, primarily due to cuts of $23 billion from the food stamp program, savings from the denial of aid to immigrants, and reductions in child-nutrition programs. |
| Drug users and dealers | Convicted drug users and dealers are denied cash benefits and food stamps. States are allowed to override this ban. |
| Teen parents | Requires recipients under 18 to live at home or in a structured setting. They must also attend school or an alternative education/training program once their child reaches 12 weeks of age. State requirements may be more stringent. |
| Program design | States are afforded broad discretion in program design and delivery, including privatization and various forms of outsourcing/contracting to local agencies and organizations. |

*Source:* Derived from Personal Responsibility and Work Opportunity Reconciliation Act of 1996.

**TABLE 4.4.** Selected Features of State Welfare Reforms (for 30 States in November 1996)

| Reform | States |
|---|---|
| Family cap: denial of benefits for children born to parents on aid | California, Florida, Indiana, Massachusetts, Mississippi, Nebraska (five counties only), New Jersey, South Carolina, Tennessee |
| Restriction of benefits for new state residents | California, Florida, Maryland, New York, Wisconsin |
| Requiring work earlier than the 24-month federal mandate | Alabama, Arizona, California, Kentucky, Mississippi, New Jersey, New York, Ohio, South Carolina, Tennessee, Wisconsin |
| Community service: affirming federal requirement of community service after two months of TANF | Alabama, Florida, Massachusetts (similar provisions covered by existing waiver), Mississippi, New York |
| Community service: opting out of federal requirement of community service after two months of TANF | Connecticut, Kentucky, Maryland, Missouri, Oklahoma, Oregon, Tennessee, Texas |
| Prematurely cutting benefits to immigrants, relative to the TANF schedule | Alabama, Kentucky, Louisiana, South Carolina, Wyoming |
| May provide additional benefits to immigrants, in addition to those required by TANF | Connecticut, Florida, Indiana, Maine, Massachusetts, Michigan, Missouri, Nebraska, New Jersey, New Hampshire, New York, Ohio, Oregon, Tennessee, Texas, Utah, Vermont |
| Work requirement: will eliminate all cash assistance as sanction for failure to participate in work | Connecticut, Florida, Louisiana, Maryland, Massachusetts, Mississippi, New York, Oklahoma, Oregon, South Carolina |
| Child-support enforcement: will eliminate all cash assistance as sanction for failure to cooperate with child-support enforcement | Alabama, Louisiana, Maryland, Mississippi, South Carolina |
| Learnfare: elimination or reduction of benefits if child does not attend school | Florida, Maryland, Massachusetts, South Carolina |
| Immunization requirement: elimination or reduction of benefits if children do not receive preventative healthcare | Florida, Louisiana, Maryland, Massachusetts |
| Elimination or reduction of benefits if recipients fail to provide Social Security numbers and/or fingerprints | New Jersey, New York, Oregon |
| Time limits: 60-month lifetime limit/accordance with TANF guidelines | Alabama, Kentucky, Maine, Maryland, Michigan, Mississippi, Missouri, Nebraska, New Jersey, Oklahoma, Wyoming |
| Time limits: additional restrictions and/or shorter time limit than TANF guidelines | Arizona, Connecticut, Florida, Indiana, Louisiana, Massachusetts, Oregon, South Carolina, South Dakota, Tennessee, Utah |

*Source:* Derived from Children's Defense Fund (1996).

155

*"ceiling"* of spending caps and work participation requirements. Under the old system—in which the dynamic was for federalization—incentive structures and federal matched-funding provisions had the effect of ratcheting up welfare standards (with the intent of lifting welfare standards in general, and those in the South in particular). Under the block-grant regime, this incentive structure has been all but reversed, as the imposition of spending caps alongside exacting work-participation requirements has created a climate of defunding and regressive policy experimentation.

> Block grants and the recision of entitlement strengthen the discretion of states. States are no longer obliged to provide assistance to *all* needy families, even if all of them meet state eligibility criteria. . . . [Yet while the PRWORA] offers many options to states—thereby creating many dangers for individuals—it is far from a restoration of states' rights. A state *must* do certain things in exchange for its block grant. It must also *not* do certain things even if local majorities want to. A state cannot offer assistance on more generous or equitable terms than are stipulated in the [act]. . . . If a state wants to suspend the work requirement, whether because remunerative employment is unavailable or because single mothers already have one job in the home, it would have to support recipients wholly on its own. (Mink, 1998: 63, 65–66)

A new dynamic of defederalization and uneven development is therefore being released, one that history shows tends to lead to socially regressive outcomes (see Piven and Cloward, 1985). By implication, the scope and definition of "radical" welfare reform has changed. Importantly, the federal government has a major hand in this, as the author and enforcer of the rule system within which the states now operate. In the block-grant era, federal orchestration of the state-level reform process continues, albeit in a less explicit and direct fashion than in the era of demonstration projects and waivers under AFDC.

The politics of welfare reform is also undergoing a qualitative change, as states confront the vexing issues of implementation. Under the block-grant regime, state welfare policies will need not only to be fine sounding, they will also need to show results. So while Governor Weld declared himself "delighted" with the federal reform package, now that he finally could implement Massachusetts' two-year time-limit proposals (quoted in the *New York Times*, August 1, 1996: A9), he also no doubt realized that with the newfound flexibilities came new responsibilities and new risks. As a local advocate observed prior to the passage of federal legislation, while the Weld administration was able to reap the short-term political advantages of falling rolls, the real challenge lies in the medium- to long-term *effects* of the Massachusetts reforms:

"Right now, Governor Weld keeps telling us how everything is work-ing because they have [fewer] people on the rolls than they did two years ago, which has more to do with economics and teen parents be-ing scared off and stuff. A lot of this will show up over time, as people start having problems. . . . The time-limit problem won't show up until the end of the time limit. . . . The problems people are having right now are going to show up with people dropping out, people living on less money because they're sanctioned for one reason or another, grid-lock in shelters. It won't be like a major crisis with everyone showing up in the street all at once. It'll be people living even more substan-dardly."[23]

Under present conditions, the most likely impact of the Massachu-setts reforms is this: There will be an attenuated squeeze on aid recipi-ents, some of whom will drop out of programs and go to work, while others—perhaps most—will fashion some means of getting by at the in-terstices of the (residualized) welfare system and the (contingent) labor market. Of course, long-term welfare usage was never as serious a prob-lem under AFDC as the political rhetoric suggested (Blank, 1997), with most recipients moving in and out of work on a regular basis and in a fashion that said more about the deficiencies of systemically unstable, low-wage labor markets than it did about their "dependent" lifestyles. If there is "chronic dependency" here, it is chronic dependency on contin-gent work, a condition certain to intensify following the implementation of welfare reforms based on minimally serviced "labor-force attachment." In the process, much of the cost of falling welfare rolls will be effectively externalized and/or individualized, as recipients are induced to renegoti-ate domestic coping arrangements and income-packaging strategies—under conditions even less favorable than before—across the porous boundaries of welfare and work.

## Workfare on a Rainy Day

Strongly favorable economic conditions have postponed, but certainly have not resolved, the underlying tensions and contradictions of PRW-ORA's federally imposed ceiling on TANF expenditures. Unless the busi-ness cycle has been banished along with welfare, the realities of down-loading in the context of capped spending will one day have to be confronted. Under PRWORA, little additional funding could be sought from the federal government if a recession were to drive up the welfare rolls. The "rainy-day" provisions in the federal legislation earmark only $2 billion over five years to compensate for fluctuations in the business cycle.[24] In the three years of the early 1990s recession, however, federal welfare spending rose by $6 billion, suggesting that there is a major shortfall in the new contingency fund. This was the basis of Ohio Republican Governor Voinivich's earlier opposition to block grants, which when coupled with federal spending caps would, he claimed, "constitute the single most burdensome unfunded mandate on already strained [state] budgets" (quoted in *Washington Post*, March 26, 1995: C5). In contrast to the AFDC system, in which spending would automatically rise and fall in line with need, the block-grant regime leaves it to the states to "decide who to serve. Unless Congress votes to increase the grant during recessions, states will end up trying to cope with more people in need while their budgets are being squeezed by falling tax revenues" (Marshall, 1996: B1, B3).

The synchronization of business cycles and welfare caseloads highlights a central flaw in the supply-side reasoning on which the current reform movement is predicated. State welfare rolls may fluctuate by as much as 15 percent over the business cycle (Marshall, 1996), suggesting that the size of caseloads is a function of the availability of jobs rather than a by-product of the personal dysfunctions of aid recipients (unless the sum of human fecklessness also happens somehow to be economically pro-cyclical). Welfare reforms such as those of the Weld administration, however, rest on just such a behavioral explanation of welfare use, constructing "solutions" accordingly, in terms of changed attitudes, redoubled job search, restrictions on aid, and so forth. Indeed, the very methodology of "mandatory 'community service' (a.k.a. workfare) . . . implies that recipients are shirkers who stay on the rolls longer than necessary in order to avoid work" (Fraser, 1993: 16–17). Issues around the availability, pay, accessibility, and quality of jobs, where they are acknowledged at all, are assumed into insignificance under this individual-deficit approach to welfare reform. In considering its reform proposals, the Weld administration consequently saw no need for an analysis of the capacity of the state's labor market to absorb an influx of displaced aid recipients. Instead, the rather complacent assumption, typified by the following exchange between senior officers of the DTA's employment team, was that "everybody knows the jobs are there":

OFFICER #4: I think the governor is very, very clear that the jobs are there [for welfare recipients]. Very clear.

OFFICER #2: If you take the philosophy that any job's a good job, then the jobs are there. I mean, there's no doubt about it, there are a lot of jobs out there, but what it will mean is that we will probably have to supplement them with welfare grant for a while. I think there are certainly are jobs there. The main thing is trying to get people to accept some of those jobs. That's the task.

OFFICER #3: Some of these questions nobody knows the answer to. That's the problem. There's usually more jobs out there than we think there are, especially if the question is, do people get the job they want, the job they prefer, or the job they have to take? There's a mountain of difference there. But on the other hand, when you already have an unemployment rate—What is it, 5.5 percent, something like that?—the unemployment rate is supposed to mean that people are looking for jobs and can't find them, that's what that rate is supposed to reflect. But [the unemployed] don't *have* to take jobs either, they're free to have reservations about which job they want and which they don't. So how do you crunch all those factors and say, are there *really* enough jobs out there? I don't think anybody knows.

OFFICER #2: So it gets back to an economics question. What's unemployment? I don't know.

OFFICER #3: I don't think we have to know the answer to the question. It's full steam ahead; you have to go to work. Who cares? Why waste time with an unanswerable question? Let's get on with it.[25]

The critical issue of the availability of jobs for welfare recipients is consequently reduced to an article of faith by advocates of such reforms, a position that ignores the reality of severe shortfalls in low-wage entry-level jobs, even under current conditions (Blank, 1994b; Mishel and Schmitt, 1995; Bernstein, 1997). This act of denial may not have been exposed for what it is during the theatrical posturing of the welfare-reform debate, but it is certain to become a—if not *the*—key issue in the new politics of implementation. The Economic Policy Institute estimated that wages in Massachusetts's low-wage labor market will fall by 11.6 percent as a result of the forced influx of former welfare recipients, at a cost to the state in terms of lost wages of just under $1 billion (Mishel and Schmitt, 1995).

Massachusetts is currently in the throes of a reckless social experiment. With the public and political acts of debate, reform, and legislation concluded for the time being, the DTA now has to set to work on the personal and procedural task of *delivering reform* in what Nathan (1993) calls the "shadow land" of implementation. At present, the DTA has the advantage of relatively favorable aggregate labor-market conditions, though the low-wage segment is certain to become much tighter. Whereas, in the 1980s, the limits to reform were apparently set by the size of the state's workfare program, in the 1990s they are to be determined by the (largely unknown) absorptive capacity of its local labor markets. At present, such concerns are effectively defined out of existence by the DTA, which is setting about the reform process with vigor. Now that winnowing down the welfare rolls is a policy end in itself, welfare recipients are finding themselves propelled into the labor market in the position of indentured laborers, with no realistic alternative but to accept whatever the (local) market offers. The Massachusetts reforms are instilling a brutal form of labor-market discipline, reinforced by what many advocates describe as a climate of fear:

"They'll be told you have to get a volunteer slot or go to work. People give up. They just drop out, you know, and they're in sweatshops or living with relatives, or stuff like that. . . . People get very discouraged."[26]

"Welfare reform has gotten so it has become a licence for social workers to say whatever nasty things they want. . . . I got a call from a person who said, 'I'm going to have to do a work requirement if I don't get a job.' I said, 'Well, there may be some ways to go around that.' They just said, 'I'm just getting such an attitude from my social worker that I'm going to go out and get a job. I can't put up with this any more.' The stories are just horrible. . . . The climate out there is really ugly."[27]

And yet for some frontline workers, what others see as signs of arbitrariness they interpret as long-overdue discretion:

"The change of name of our agency from Public Welfare to Transitional Assistance was really one of the kickoffs. . . . It's interesting how quickly that took hold, especially for our field folks—who deal one on one with recipients every single day—who were really very happy about the welfare-reform changes that were coming. In many instances they were disappointed that they weren't tougher."[28]

Perhaps the main outcome of this early stage of implementation has been to deregister current and to deter potential welfare users, to deploy bureaucratic procedures as a means of driving women back into the wage labor market. There are already clear indications that high sanction rates are contributing strongly to caseload declines, both nationally and more specifically in Massachusetts, where the sanctions policy is relatively strict (see Rector and Youssef, 1999; Schott et al., 1999; Walters, 1999).

The Massachusetts reforms outlined in Table 4.2 can be seen as a bureaucratic–procedural strategy for redrawing the social boundaries of the waged sphere with a view to expanding the supply of (low-)wage-dependent workers. The approach is a reckless one in the sense that, at least in the DTA, there is no clear appreciation of what the social limits—or even the social consequences—of this process of induced low-wage dependency might be. As Blank (1994b: 65) has observed of such methods, "Attempts to simply cut women off welfare without making other services available will merely cast them and their children into an increasingly hostile labor market where many less-skilled persons in single-adult families cannot earn enough to survive on their own." Massachusetts is destined to be one the first states to discover the costs of this approach.

## MAKING SPACE FOR THE WORKFARE STATE?

Welfare reform is neither a "top-down" nor a "bottom-up" process. In a complex and perplexing sense it is both. The United States's after-welfare settlement was neither made in Washington and imposed in some unmediated fashion across the country, nor is it the aggregate outcome of statehouse reforms in Boston and elsewhere. Rather, it is better understood as an uneven, inchoate, and unstable process of regulatory reform, within which the decisive causative influences have stemmed from political interactions and policy relays between the federal and the state levels. The policymaking process, in this sense, has been a *dialectical* one. Four key moments in this dialectical process have been identified in the course of the analysis given here.

First, in the 1970s, came a series of state and local demonstration projects, initiated at the federal level as part of an attempt to break the stalemate around welfare reform. Massachusetts figured in these debates to the extent that, with its comparatively generous benefits and high caseloads, the state was regarded as one of the primary sites of the "welfare mess." Toward the end of the period, however, the implementation of GA reforms in Massachusetts sent out the signal that there was a thirst for reform even in this bastion of liberal programming. Second, in the 1980s, the Reagan administration sought to broaden the scope and reach of reform demonstrations under OBRA, presiding over the proliferation of state- and local-level experimentation with a view to translating conservative critiques of welfare into "working models" of reform. During this period, Massachusetts's ET Choices initiative became the epitome of service-intensive, voluntarist programming, exerting some influence on the shape of federal legislation but waning in significance as the emphasis began to shift toward lower cost and more punitive workfare programs.

Third, in the 1990s, the liberalization of the waiver system—first under Bush and more proactively under Clinton—led to widespread opt-ing-out from federal provisions, as the process of state-by-state welfare reform became effectively systemic. Now under Republican control, Massachusetts was quick to join the frontrunners is this reform move-ment, taking advantage of the anti-welfare climate by negotiating one of the most broad-ranging reform packages. Because this drew on an estab-lished repertoire of reform measures, Massachusetts's distinctiveness dur-ing this period lay less with policy innovation than with the very breadth and boldness of its reforms. Fourth, after 1996, Massachusetts is poised to be one of the first states to feel the full effects of thoroughgoing reform under the block-grant regime, although the sustainability of its post-welfare settlement remains substantially in question. The future viability of the regime of temporary assistance in Massachusetts will depend criti-cally on the way the new regime treads down into different local labor markets, and on the wider social consequences of this forced expansion of the contingent labor supply.

The Massachusetts reforms' liability to failure is a real one for the simple reason that past experiences of work-based welfare reform—as even its promoters concede—show that the costs of new programs tend to be higher, and the results more modest, than the initial fanfare sug-gests (see Butler and Kondratas, 1987; Gueron, 1987; Kaus, 1996). Ac-cording to commentators such as Wiseman (1989: 14), "[W]ork pro-grams offer a useful opportunity for incremental welfare reform, but unanswered questions about the organization and consequences of such programs necessitate a cautious approach to program development and merchandising." As frontline welfare advocates will also point out, while anti-welfare rhetoric may suffice during the reform process itself, it is no substitute for workable policy:

> "[The Massachusetts reform program] is not just mean-spirited, it's also ill-conceived, and not well implemented. . . . It's not as though the low-income population hasn't been scrutinized to death for ten to fif-teen years. Study after study after study. . . . There isn't really any ratio-nale. This is mostly a value-based, emotional argument that has won over that says that people that are poor, it's their fault, that's about it. It's really contrary to just about every study, if the goal is to lift people out of poverty. But they've used all the rhetoric, skillfully, to say, this will be the jump-start, to lift people out of poverty. And it couldn't be more contrary in practice. I don't think the general public, however, in any way shape or form, has a full understanding of that."[29]

Drawing its legitimacy from the frustrations of past welfare-policy failures, and to some degree from anti-welfare sentiments in the wider population, the U.S. welfare-reform process became by the early 1990s a self-referential and ultimately self-actualizing one. State reform begat state reform, to the point where the federal system had all but ruptured. Washington lawmakers, it seemed, needed only set the final seal on this tumultuous process of de facto reform. But the PRWORA took the process a step further, entrenching a decentralization dynamic that may not be easy to reverse. The new federal regime initiated a proliferation of competing local-workfare regimes, based on different institutional mixes of mandatory work and minimalist aid. The states are taking the lead in a kind of decentralized socioregulatory experiment, with the perhaps forlorn hope that there will be more (local) successes than failures in this search for a sustainable postwelfare settlement. In place of the grand federal designs of the Great Society is a patchwork of local programs based on "policymaking-by-doing."

## Dialectics of Workfare

Although this decentralization trend does not mean the end of Washington's influence in the U.S. welfare system (far from it), it does signify an important shift in the prevailing pattern of policy dialectics. While the recent history of welfare/workfare politics has been dominated by relays between Washington and the states, in the unfolding phase of implementation, state–local relations are set to assume increased importance. Certainly at a discursive level, the state and local scales are being constructed as the primary domains of regulation, but there is also an important sense in which the methodology of workfare *requires* localization, particularly with respect to the implementation of intensive forms of individualized "case management" (see Wiseman, 1987; Weaver, 2000). And as the regulatory apparatus localizes, so also does the nature of the regulatory *processes*. There are powerful resonances here with recent theoretical work on the emergent form of "hollowed-out" workfare states (Jessop, 1994), where "hollowing out" is taken to refer not simply to unidirectional and unambiguous shifts in the balance of power between spatial levels of the state apparatus, but signifies changes in the spatial form of institutional and political–economic relationships themselves. Thus, spatial reconfigurations are profoundly caught up in the complex *qualitative* restructuring of state strategies and capacities (Jessop, 1995a). The block granting of welfare does not represent the end of "big government" per se, though it does imply complex changes in the spatial composition of state functions. A deeply politicized process, this rescaling of regulatory capacities and propensities must be understood in the context of contending political–economic forces in the conception and implementation of "welfare reform":

[A] favorite device for managing political conflict in the United States is delegation to lower units of government. The structure of the U.S. welfare state demonstrates this pattern: when there is agreement on the "deserving poor," programs are relatively transparent and administered at upper levels of government. The most prominent example is the Social Security pension system. Conversely, when programs are conflictual and morally ambiguous—for the "undeserving poor, they are usually at lower levels of government, such as AFDC, unemployment, and general assistance. This arrangement suits upper-level politicians who want to avoid conflict; they prefer a symbolic "solution" but, in effect, delegate administration; a successful delegation is one that stays delegated. The welfare-to-work programs are prime examples. Upper-level politicians promise to get welfare recipients to work. It is the field-level officials who have to resolve the conflicts between the demands of local labor markets, the employability of recipients, and need. TANF continues [this] delegation process. (Handler and Hasenfeld, 1997: 208)

In this sense, America's postwelfare settlement remains a distinctly unsettled one. The process of downloading responsibility may meet certain (federal- and state-level) political objectives in a situation in which economic growth is robust, but the political, economic, and social costs of this process will not be easy to manage at the local level. This is all the more true in those states—such as California, Colorado, Indiana, New York, and Ohio—that are anticipating these pressures through *further* devolution, to the local level (see Havemann and Vobejda, 1997). This, of course, is only likely further to entrench the decentralization dynamic within the welfare system, while doing nothing to ameliorate the effects of regressive localization: as Handler and Hasenfeld (1997: 208) conclude, "Counties may compete with each other to provide the lowest benefits in order to discourage 'welfare magnets,' thus setting off a race to the bottom."

Both the *spatial form* (the complex of federal–state–local regulatory relationships) and the *local functions* (the architecture and orientation of frontline systems) of the U.S. public-aid regime are in the process of being transformed by welfare reform and the rise of workfare. As proponents like Lawrence Mead see it, for example, workfare implies the emergence of new forms of governmental action:

[State proposals for welfare reform] represent a sharp departure from the economic discourse that normally surrounds social policy in Washington. When federal politicians discuss helping poor people, the debate is about "doing more" for them versus "doing less." . . . The argument is about the scale of the antipoverty effort. It taps into the great partisan dispute over the proper role of government in society, which goes back to the New Deal or before. The new proposals, however, change the character of government much more than its scale. The aim is to get recipients to do something more to help themselves. If they do . . . a new social contract is realized, in that the recipients satisfy more of the common expectations of citizenship in return for rights. Changing the economic cost of welfare is secondary. (1992a: 15–16)

Moreover, just as the crisis of welfare has in part been scripted by nation-states themselves, so also are these processes of hollowing out, defederalization, and localization in part self-imposed. The recent history of U.S. welfare reform illustrates only too clearly how nation-states have become active agents in their *own* hollowing out. In the process, new spaces of workfare politics are being opened up, and it will be in states like Massachusetts that they first begin to take shape. Under the fragile postwelfare settlement, the states must take the responsibility as well as the credit for their far-reaching reforms, as President Clinton made clear in choosing directly to address the country's governors on the occasion of the effective repeal of the New Deal: "The governors asked for this responsibility. Now they've got to live up to it. . . . [T]here is no longer a system in the way" (quoted in *New York Times*, August 23, 1996: A10).

## Notes

1. Massachusetts welfare advocate, interviewed by Jamie Peck, February 1996.

2. An abridged, early version of this chapter was published as "Postwelfare Massachusetts," *Economic Geography* (1998) 74 (Special issue for the annual meeting of the AAG): 62–82. I am grateful to the editors of *Economic Geography* for permission to reproduce parts of this article.

3. "Governor Weld has not only joined the pack [of radical welfare reformers], but for a couple of years has been trying to lead the pack, with efforts to cut benefits in Massachusetts, introduce time-limits, and other schemes for modifying the behavior of welfare recipients" (Antipoverty campaigner, New York City, interviewed by Jamie Peck, February 1996). See also *Washington Post*, February 25, 1995: A1; March 26, 1995: C5.

4. *Federal News Service*, May 18, 1996: President Clinton's Weekly Radio Address.

5. *U.S. News & World Report*, July 18, 1977: 81: "When States Tell People They Must Work for Welfare."

6. As Dukakis stated in 1985, "of all the things we've done in the past three years, I don't know of anything more important than ET. . . . This issue of work and welfare has been called the Middle East of domestic policy. Everybody talks

about it; nobody does anything about it" (quoted in *Boston Globe*, October 30, 1985: 17).

7. Senior official #4, Massachusetts DTA, interviewed by Jamie Peck, February 1996.

8. *Federal News Service*, May 18, 1996: President Clinton's Weekly Radio Address.

9. Senior official #2, Massachusetts DTA, interviewed by Jamie Peck, February 1996.

10. Senior official #1, Massachusetts DTA, interviewed by Jamie Peck, February 1996.

11. Senior official #3, Massachusetts DTA, interviewed by Jamie Peck, February 1996.

12. Senior official #5, Massachusetts DTA, interviewed by Jamie Peck, February 1996.

13. Senior official #5, Massachusetts DTA, interviewed by Jamie Peck, February 1996.

14. "What we worry more about now is being sued. You know, what's going to be the next lawsuit? [Advocates] can't get us on anything that we've got in policy; they're just waiting for us to do something wrong. So far—knocking all kinds of wood—that hasn't happened. That's why we have a legal department, to make sure that those things don't happen" (Senior official #3, Massachusetts DTA, interviewed by Jamie Peck, February 1996).

15. Massachusetts welfare rights advocate, interviewed by Jamie Peck, February 1996.

16. Manager, nonprofit human service agency, Boston, MA, interviewed by Jamie Peck, February 1996.

17. Senior official #5, Massachusetts DTA, interviewed by Jamie Peck, February 1996.

18. Senior official #6, Massachusetts DTA, interviewed by Jamie Peck, February 1996.

19. "Basically, the governor stood his ground. . . . [He] took it on himself to say, 'I am only gonna fund the welfare program for half a year . . . and when that half a year is up, if there's not a new law, then welfare is no longer in existence in this state.' . . . He had the constitutional authority to do this, at least he felt he did, it was never challenged. So, eventually, he forced the hand of the legislature" (Senior official #5, Massachusetts DTA, interviewed by Jamie Peck, February 1996).

20. Newt Gingrich, NBC, *Meet the Press*, February 21, 1993, Reuter Transcript Report.

21. "We felt very, very strongly, and continue to feel very strongly, that the two-year limit was just that. . . . The feds wanted what we considered major loopholes in that limit. . . . The governor basically gambled. His estimation was that Congress was going to pass a welfare-reform bill . . . and there would be block grants [and he] would have his own say on what this two-year limit would look like. So he said, 'Instead of haggling and fighting over this two-year limit, let's just go ahead and implement everything *but* the two-year-limit. I will get

that once the federal legislation is passed' " (Senior official #5, Massachusetts DTA, interviewed by Jamie Peck, February 1996).

22. Representative Gary L. Ackerman (D-NY), quoted in *New York Times*, August 4, 1996: A12.

23. Massachusetts welfare rights advocate, interviewed by Jamie Peck, February 1996.

24. Initially only $1 billion was allocated to this fund. It was raised following pressure from the states and the NGA (see CBPP, 1996).

25. Interviewed by Jamie Peck, February 1996.

26. Manager, nonprofit human service agency, Worcester, MA, interviewed by Jamie Peck, February 1996.

27. Welfare rights lawyer, Massachusetts, interviewed by Jamie Peck, February 1996.

28. Senior official #1, Massachusetts DTA, interviewed by Jamie Peck, February 1996.

29. Manager, nonprofit human service agency, Worcester, MA, interviewed by Jamie Peck, February 1996.

CHAPTER FIVE

# Local Discipline
## *Workfare at Work*

> Our experience in working with welfare recipients indicates
> that members of multi-generational welfare families and long
> term welfare recipients do not possess work ethics or a strong
> desire to support themselves or their dependants. Others may
> have an incomplete set of work ethics. The Department's Work
> Ethics Education Program is intended to instill or maintain a
> full measure of work ethics in the welfare population by means
> of a complete multi-media educational program. (Work ethic
> educational materials brochure, Riverside Department of Public
> Social Services 1996)

The marketing section of the Department of Public Social Services for
Riverside County, California, sells a full range of "work ethics educational materials," including bumper stickers, campaign buttons, and motivational posters, some of which "depict the value of work in a humor-
ous manner, others are more serious," while a work-ethics CD—written,
arranged, and performed by the staff of the welfare office—contains mu-
sic "intended to assist in the strengthening of work ethics and to encourage those individuals who are employable to be positive, have hope and
to believe they can have a wonderful new future by seeking to improve
and develop themselves" (Riverside County DPSS, 1996: 2). These make
nice souvenirs for the hundreds of policy tourists who visit the Riverside
program each year. The main reason for these visits, however, is to learn
abut how they *do it* in Riverside County . . . how they designed and de-

livered what has become the paradigmatic "work-first" workfare program.[1]

The Riverside approach is an institutional manifestation of the no-frills "true" workfare model envisioned but never actually realized by Ronald Reagan: it sets out deliberately to destabilize the experience of welfare receipt, propelling its "clients" into low-wage work in the open labor market with the minimum of delay, the minimum of cost, and the minimum of support. Riverside's active enforcement of daily job search, its remorseless inculcation of pro-work messages, and its relatively high "success rate" in moving individuals from welfare to work have placed the program at the leading edge of workfare experimentation in the United States. Riverside County's welfare department was catapulted to a national prominence in the early 1990s when initial evaluations of its version of California's GAIN program revealed that exceptionally high levels of welfare-cost savings and postprogram employment were being achieved in this "edge-city" location east of Los Angeles. This led California governor Pete Wilson to characterize Riverside as a "dream county" for welfare reform (*San Francisco Chronicle*, April 20, 1995: A25). One of six counties to be studied in MDRC's three-year evaluation of the GAIN program, Riverside was distinctive in its exhaustive emphasis on placing welfare recipients in a private-sector job—*any job*—as quickly as possible. This "work-first" approach downplayed the role of basic education and training services in the transition from welfare to work, and in contrast with the more services-oriented approach to GAIN favored by the remainder of California's fifty-eight counties, concentrated on the inculcation of a strong "employment message."

While the Riverside approach is certainly distinctive in the sharpness of its employment focus, its initial rise to prominence was almost entirely due to an extremely favorably evaluation by MDRC. Tracking the experiences of an experimental (on-program) group and a control (off-program) group over a period of three years, MDRC revealed that the Riverside program generated average earnings gains of $3,113—or 49 percent—for experimentals relative to the control group, while reducing welfare payments by an average of $1,983—or 15 percent—for experimentals compared to the control group (Riccio et al., 1994b). Perhaps most striking from a policymakers' point of view was that, for every public dollar invested in the Riverside program, $2.84 was returned in the form of reduced welfare costs and increased tax receipts. Given that this is a "standard of success by which few social programs are assessed," the Riverside results appeared truly remarkable, in fact "the most impressive . . . yet observed for a large-scale welfare-to-work program" (Riccio et al., 1994a: 3).

These results secured Riverside's reputation as the "most touted welfare-to-work program in the nation" (*U.S. News and World Report*, January 16, 1995: 30). Although MDRC was quick to emphasize the dangers of "overpromising" on the basis of the Riverside results (*San Francisco Chronicle*, January 24, 1995: A2), the genie was already out of the bottle. Politicians at the state and federal level seized on the Riverside model as evidence—finally—that workfare worked; delegations of visitors from around the United States, and from overseas, poured into the Riverside GAIN offices. All came in search of the "secret" of the Riverside model. And according to the program's managers, this boiled down to nothing more complicated than a direct and unequivocal *enforcement* of the U.S. work ethic. As Lawrence E. Townsend Jr., director of Riverside County DPSS and chief architect of the Riverside model, argued in testimony before the U.S. Senate:

> There is a foundation of belief upon which the employment-focused program in Riverside County is based. . . . Work is inherently good for individuals and each day in employment is a good day. . . . In America's past there was a belief that if you worked hard, did good work, and were reliable, you would eventually prosper. This belief is still valid. Proof of this is evident in the success of our GAIN clients. . . . Employment, however modest, teaches and reinforces very basic, yet essential, skills necessary for acquiring and retaining employment that many people take for granted but not all of us have, such as: setting the alarm clock; getting to work on time; accepting supervision; learning to complete tasks reliably; getting along with co-workers; and dressing appropriately for work.[2]

Riverside has become more than a program; in many way it has come to symbolize a *philosophy*. From the outset, Riverside's strategy was to position itself as the paradigmatic example of an employment-oriented, work-first approach. The clear intent here was to trial an extreme form of the work-fist method, as a senior manager involved in the initial design of the program emphasized: "We really wanted to test whether a rapid-employment model would work. . . . We didn't want just to do a lukewarm, average attempt to run a program . . . because I thought at that time that it really could have some impact, and so therefore . . . we had to give maximum effort to find out if this method worked or not."[3]

What California's Republican governor, Pete Wilson, liked about the Riverside approach is that it cut costs while aggressively enforcing a vision of the work ethic commensurate with the realities of the (low-wage) labor market:

> If you simply say we are going to educate you and train you but never require that you go to work, a lot of people are never going to go to

work. [The Riverside model] is, I think, creatively impatient . . . it's
the right thing. It's sort of like having a mother or father in the household who's saying, get out and get a job, go ahead and better your lot
by getting some additional education but in the meantime start paying
some rent.[4]

The Riverside approach seeks to overcome what for the right is the central
paradox of workfare, that for all its rhetorical attractiveness, implementation tends to be considerably more costly than passive income support (see
Rector and Butterfield, 1987; Tanner, 1995). It differs from more traditional approaches to workfare (based on the mandatory participation of
welfare recipients in community- or public-service jobs) by effectively
mandating rapid entry into the wage-labor market, at whatever wage and
under whatever conditions: go to work, or face sanctions. The Riverside
approach is to minimize the welfare caseload while imposing work, *and
work values*, through forceful applications of the economic whip of the local labor market, backed up by the unambiguous use of local administrative authority. The apparent success of the Riverside program in efficiently
cycling large numbers of welfare recipients into the labor market has ex-
cited considerable interest, for it offers the promise of enforcing work while
cutting costs. Such is the degree of fit between the contemporary political
economy of welfare restructuring and the character of this "local solution,"
it increasingly seems that "Riverside is the future":

> Both the Massachusetts and the Wisconsin reforms are very tough, but
> they are also very expensive. . . . [Moreover] patience and money
> quickly become scarce commodities among politicians, especially
> when local economies begin to decline. . . . It seems safe to predict
> that expensive parts of state programs will not last and the Riverside
> model will prevail. . . . It is cheaper to require welfare recipients to en-
> gage in job search and accept entry-level, low-wage jobs. Economically
> and politically, this strategy is preferable to an investment in education
> and training. The state saves money and upholds the politically popu-
> lar norm of the work ethic. . . . Riverside is the future. (Handler and
> Hasenfeld, 1997: 76–77)

This chapter presents a critical analysis of Riverside's "work-first"
approach to workfare, outlining its methodology, considering its role in
the process of labor control, and drawing out some of the wider political
and policy implications. These extend beyond the welfare population,
and for that matter the immediate considerations of "welfare reform," because they appear to presage the installation of a new regime of labor
control, locally applied (see Jonas, 1996; Peck, 1996). Riverside's "work-
first" method has the effect of imposing a new set of regulatory norms on

local labor markets: go to work, or else. In many ways this may seem brutally "functional" in highly flexibilized local labor markets, where jobs are relatively plentiful but low paid and dead end, but it is just plain brutal when imposed on job-starved, inner-city areas. Essentially, the Riverside strategy is about enforcing both work and the ideology of work in the context of an emerging moral panic around the work ethics of the poor and the continued deterioration of low-income labor markets. As one of the program's senior managers explained,

> "Employment, that's education itself. . . . It's also socialization, you learn self-discipline and those sort of traits. You learn how to temper your personality. . . . I think we sort of got off the track, probably in the sixties, about the value of work. . . . We forgot that employers do education and training on the job, training people in their way of do-ing things . . . and how really important that is. Instead we had gov-ernment doing it, or sending them off to school."[5]

Despite its rapid ascendancy to an effective "policy of choice," the Riverside approach is riven with contradictions and tensions, especially when viewed from the perspective of big-city welfare systems. But here there may be a mesolevel analogue to the regulatory role of the Riverside strategy within local labor markets"subordinating the poor to unequivo-cal dependency on low-wage work—its effect within the wider political economy of U.S. welfare reform being to subordinate the cities to an un-yielding regime of marketized workfare. As an MDRC evaluator saw the situation, "You're going to have ideas and policies imposed on cities be-cause they've worked in places like Grand Rapids, Michigan, and River-side, California, when the population of folks that you need to serve [in big cities] is quite a lot different, and the whole organization of labor markets is different."[6]

## THE METHOD AND THE MESSAGE

Riverside's unequivocal "employment message" permeates every aspect of the program, from its internal staffing practices to the management of its basic education services, from induction seminars to case closures. This is a high-expectations regime, in which the expectation is that all participants are on their way off welfare and into a job. The forcefully ar-ticulated ideology of the program is clearly reflected in the material prac-tices of caseworkers and in the design of the program's organizational technologies (see Weaver, 2000). The difference this has made is a palpa-ble one. According to MDRC president Judith Gueron,

More than any other place I know of, this program communicates a message of high expectations. When you walk into a GAIN office in Riverside, you are there for one purpose: to get a job. At orientation, job developers announce job openings; throughout, program staff convey an upbeat message about the value of work and people's potential to succeed. If you are in an education program ... you are not marking time, as you can in some locations. You know that if you do not complete the program, or at least make progress in it, staff who are closely monitoring your progress will insist that you look for a job. Finally, if offered a job by a job developer, you have to take it or have your grant reduced. . . . Under this regime, welfare *feels* temporary.[7]

In terms of the methodology of program delivery, Riverside achieves this strong employment focus by heavily privileging the job-search component of its program. Its approach has been, in effect, to minimize reliance on basic education and training components while maximizing the flow through job-search functions into work. Education and training are not seen as ends in themselves but as atge means to rapidly secure work: "Clients who are in basic education or training understand that they are there to improve their skill level so they can effectively enter the labor market" (Riverside County DPSS, 1994: 4).[8] Riverside's instrumental and minimalist approach to education and training is reflected in its comparatively low unit costs: across the six sites studied by MDRC, the net cost per experimental in the GAIN program was $3,422, ranging from a low of $1,597 in Riverside to a high of $5,597 and $5,789 in Alameda (Oakland) and Los Angeles, respectively—the latter two sites serve more disadvantaged populations and rely more on education and training than Riverside (Riccio et al., 1994b).

## Wal-Mart Workfare

In process terms, the Riverside approach is to exert a constant downward pressure on costs by paring support services to the minimum required to place clients in jobs. The stated principle, according to one senior official, is

"the greater good for the greater number. So I've got to keep my investment in service restricted to the most minimal level it could possibly take in order to get a person a job. So how *few* services can I render and still get somebody employment, so that we can reach out and touch many more welfare recipients' lives? . . . We had to become a kind of Wal-Mart organization. We had to keep our costs down, our overhead down, and deal in volume. And we had to have satisfied customers, which is the business sector, if we're going to get repeat business."[9]

The analogy with no-frills, high-volume retailing is apt in the sense that the objective is to move as much "merchandise" as possible at the lowest feasible cost. Consequently, the bottom line is what the (labor) market will bear, not what investments in participants might otherwise be desirable. The Riverside approach is to fix what needs fixing in order to get a client employed, not to provide an education and training service. As one of the program's managers explained:[10]

> "If you have an automobile that does not start, do you pull the engine out and put a new engine in, pound the dents out, paint it and put new tires on it? Or do you just look at the spark plugs and the points and do the most minimum thing to make the car run? So using a practical approach here, if [the recipient] can't get a job, is it because they can't sit up in a chair right, that they don't know how to market themselves? If so, that's *all* we're going to do. Why should we do more if that's all it takes to get somebody a job?."[10]

The centerpiece of the Riverside program is the job-club/job-search function, into which all GAIN participants without compensatory education needs are immediately inducted. This intensive element of the program contains many familiar elements, such as guidance on the completion of applications and search techniques, but also seeks to strike at the heart of the "pathologies" ascribed to the welfare population by drawing attention to the "differences between a working lifestyle and a welfare lifestyle. . . . The participant is encouraged to look at what he/she can do *now* as a start toward a working lifestyle" (Riverside County DPSS, 1994: 7). The objective here is no less than a thoroughgoing overhaul of the clients' attitudes, behavior, and self-image, as themes from dress code to posture, telephone manner to interpersonal style are all addressed. One of the Riverside staff explained: "Some of them just need some motivation, they need an opportunity to see the world differently, they need an opportunity to understand that you have to shine your shoes when you go for a job interview, that you have to say yes sir, no ma'am, that you have to deal with the world in a certain way if you want someone to see you as an employable candidate. That's kind of what job club and job search is all about."[11]

For the most part, the tone is very upbeat and positive, consistent with the goal of building self-esteem and motivation. But the issue of motivation is a double-edged sword, given that the majority of participants are mandated to attend the program, with the threat of benefit sanctions being a real (and often used) one. As the department's director has put it,

It is not optional. You don't have the luxury, if you're a welfare recipient, to stay home. In fact, we insist that you come here, and we use motivational techniques in sales, in marketing, about the wonderful things that employment can do you for you, but if they don't even come and show up, we will cheerfully reduce their welfare grant.[12]

In the more restrained language of GAIN's official documentation, "If necessary, immediate and timely action, sometimes resulting in financial sanction, is taken to obtain a satisfactory level of participation by the client" (Riverside County DPSS, 1994: 4). Of the eight largest counties in California, Riverside has the highest rate of sanctions for noncompliance, while it is also known to make considerable use of presanction "conciliation" procedures (Bardach, 1993).[13] As a senior DPSS executive put it, "We're not hesitant here to use the stick. . . . It's done to ensure that people understand that they have an obligation to their children, to themselves, to move forward, and to find a way to get off aid." Likewise, a colleague emphasized that he made it clear to his clients that "[y]ou're going to have to work your butt off. . . . You're going to have to do it *yourself.*"[14]

The mix of subtle and not-so-subtle forms of compulsion is also evident in the style of the program and the approaches adopted by case managers. When participants enter the job club, for example, they are issued a terse set of "Job Club Rules":

1. Be on time—8.30 to 12.30
2. Dress for success
3. Full class participation
4. No criticisms
5. No food
6. No drink
7. No gum
8. Daily job search

While the Riverside program represents itself—to both clients and to the outside world—in the language of "empowerment," "independence," and "self-sufficiency," there is also an important sense in which its methodology is about coercion, discipline, and conformity. The foundation of the Riverside approach is a "basic work ethic," employment being viewed as a "gradual socialization process" to which GAIN's ostensibly dysfunctional and "welfare-dependent" clients must be subjected if they are to achieve "self-reliance": "Employment, however modest, teaches GAIN clients employment discipline, such as setting the alarm clock, getting to work in time, learning to complete tasks, accepting supervision and a chance to learn that they can be useful and successful" (Riverside County DPSS, 1994: 1). This transition will not be accomplished, GAIN staff insist, unless clients are willing to change not only their behavior but also their physical appearance. Figure 5.1 displays the strict dress code that is enforced by program staff.

Three distinctive features of Riverside methodology reinforce this climate of compulsion and contribute to the distinctive "feel" of the program. First, the case-management style is intensive and strongly client-focused. Second, the processes of job development are aggressively pursued. And third, the program is represented to clients as a transitional one, as though they are not so much *on* welfare as *moving from* welfare to work.

---

## MANDATORY DRESS CODE

*PROPER DRESS* for men and women (respectively) for interviews or participation in a Job Club/Job Search activity is as follows.

| MEN | WOMEN |
|-----|-------|
| Shirt and Slacks | Skirt and Blouse |
| Appropriate Shoes | Dress |
| Socks | Nylons (Hose) |
| Neat and Clean | Neat and Clean |
| Clean Fingernails | Appropriate Shoes |

### IMPROPER DRESS

ABSOLUTELY:  NO Spandex pants (short or long)
NO Short skirts (must be at least knee length)
NO Shorts
NO Tank tops
NO Theme tee shirts
NO See-through tops
NO Hats
NO Sun dresses
NO Mid-rift tops
NO Extreme hairstyles
NO Tennis shoes
NO Jeans/Levis

Appropriate dress is necessary to participate and be successful in your job

---

**FIGURE 5.1.** Riverside GAIN dress code. *Source:* Riverside County DPSS.

## Managing Cases

The client-focused case-management approach utilized in Riverside has the effect of transforming claimants' experiences of welfare receipt and program participation. Each participant is assigned a case worker who will take a close personal interest in his/her *daily* activities. As an employment counselor explained, "I am always visible to my clients, checking on them in Job Club/Search on a daily basis. . . . I call participants regularly and follow up on their job search" (quoted in Riverside County DPSS, 1994: 34). This intensive monitoring and supervision of clients represents a marked change from the traditional social relations of welfare, in which involved clients are almost anonymously processed through "the system." Under the active and participatory Riverside approach, the philosophy is quite different:

> It's really simple; you've got to be all over every client like flypaper! Every day. "Okay, you said yesterday you were going to do this and this, what have you done today?" (Director, Riverside DPSS, quoted in Bardach, 1993: 19)

> "We're contacting them by phone, reminding them they're scheduled for the appointment. 'I can't get there.' Well we can send you a bus ticket. We'll get you here."[15]

This system of intensive case management is in turn driven by a performance-contracts regime in which GAIN staff are themselves assessed and rewarded on the basis of their record in achieving job placements.[16] Each employment specialist, for example, must achieve a minimum of fourteen (previously twelve and before that ten) monthly job placements, while those who place thirty or more recipients are rewarded by a commendation from the director in the form of a gold eagle lapel badge (Riverside County DPSS, GAIN Handbook, Section 42–18). These performance standards are considered to be the "primary measure of success."[17] Riverside's job-placement targets—which are calculated for district offices and the county program as a whole too—have been steadily increasing over time, subjecting GAIN staff to a form of "speed-up" as their work rate gradually intensifies (Bardach, 1993).

## Developing Jobs

Active job development is one of the hallmarks of the Riverside program. GAIN staff are all hired with a view to developing jobs for clients, including scanning newspapers and looking out for "help wanted" signs. Program staff are also very carefully selected.[18] Private-sector marketing techniques are used to promote both the general concept of GAIN and the specific merchandise of the "job-ready" applicant, who can if necessary be with an employer that very afternoon. Employers' needs and preferences are paramount, with program staff "thoroughly screening participants prior to referral for a hiring interview" and being "sensitive to the needs of the employer" (Riverside County DPSS, 1994: 8). "Job-readiness" is the overriding goal. This may imply some adjustment of expectations on the part of employers, but its main effect is to require transformed attitudes and behaviors on the part of clients. As two Riverside managers explained,

> "Initially, it's real hard to overcome the stereotypical concept of what an AFDC recipient is. As [job developers] are able to break that, they can be more and more successful in [obtaining placements]. They have to be careful about who they send. They have to make sure these people are job-ready. But the employers [say] you don't have to train the person technically how to do a job, you need to send me someone who's ready to work, will show up on time, won't give the supervisor any grief."[19]

> "Job-ready doesn't mean that they are trained to do something, it means they are ready to work. . . . A large portion of our clients are not in general terms job-ready, and that's why they get a job, they lose a job, because they're not going to take any stuff off anybody, and if they want to go home, they go home, and if they don't want to come in, they just don't show up. This is the basic problem that we're talking about with low-income, welfare-type people . . . it's the attitude that has to be overcome. And the way we've gone about doing that is by constant pressure, relentlessly applied. Until they get a job, and they hold a job. Or they leave the area!"[20]

The program consequently operates largely on employers' terms, a fact that is drilled into clients. From a client's perspective, this approach is reflected in the ethos of the program, that conformity, deference, and rapid job entry are everything. Working with the grain of employers' preferences means, of course, that discriminatory practices are likely to go unchallenged. And this method fosters the impression that the "right attitude" is *all* a person needs to get a job. By implication, those clients who are unsuccessful in finding work must have the "wrong attitude." This approach absolutely subordinates the goals and aspirations of welfare recipients to employers' demands in particular and to the imperatives of contingent work in general. Moreover, the distribution of employment is ultimately determined by market criteria, which are variously anticipated, mimicked, enforced, and ultimately reproduced by the program itself. The program's advocates are often quite candid about this. As Brown (1997: 8) explains, "a work first model generally begins with the expectation that everyone is capable of finding work and lets the job market itself—through job search activities—determine who is employable."

Each client also knows that, once hired, failure to conform with employers' requirements is likely to lead to their dismissal and replacement, given that there is always a ready supply of GAIN participants to take their place. Anyone who has been through this program knows that substitution is a palpable and constant threat. As an employment specialist explained:

> I listen to what employers need in terms of an employee, and then I try to meet their needs. . . . I can't guarantee that a person is going to work out at the job. No one can guarantee that, but I can guarantee if someone doesn't work out I can replace them with another worker. (quoted in Riverside County DPSS, 1994: 47)

GAIN participants are also put under considerable pressure to develop their *own* jobs. The job-search component of the program is a strict regimen of supervised daily vacancy searching and cold calling. Participants are required to cold call employers from the GAIN office, each being stationed (for several hours per day) in a booth containing a telephone and a telephone directory that is backed by a mirror so as to permit the self-monitoring of poise and telephone manner. Again there are targets: participants are expected to make at least twenty-five calls per day to new employer contacts, at least three days a week, while making at least fifteen personal visits to employers' premises each week. Each participant is expected to generate at least five positive job leads per day.

Induced to regard "any job as a good job," Riverside GAIN participants usually find themselves rapidly reintegrated into the labor market, albeit typically in a low-wage, "entry-level" job. The philosophy here, based on a package designed by private welfare-to-work consultants Curtis & Associates, is that each job is a "learning experience" and that participants are more likely to be able to move into a better paying job if they are already in work. This stepping-stone approach is explained here first by Dean Curtis, cofounder of Curtis & Associates, and second by a Riverside job developer:

> What people on welfare need are jobs, and they need them right away. We believe that anyone can be successful with just what they bring in the door. Expect a lot, and you'll get back a lot. It always works. . . . Self-sufficiency is what people really want. . . . The thing that welfare

agencies have to do is change their own attitudes about people and to stop treating them like they are weak and wounded. Experience, age, education, appearance—none of that matters. It's attitude.[21]

My philosophy is any job that will get you back out into the job market, it's going to have some potential. You might be really nice to a customer that you're giving a Big Mac to, and they might be the president of some company that wants to hire you. You just never know.[22]

The willingness to subordinate job placement to the short-run opportunity set presented by the flow of vacancies, coupled with the aggressive way in which participants are propelled into the job-search process, explains much of the extraordinary success achieved in Riverside in moving welfare recipients into work. The Riverside program, for example, serves only 4 percent of the state's GAIN caseload, but accounts for some 19 per cent of all job placements achieved.[23] Thus, the strategy is predicated on the twin assumptions that the local labor market has the capacity to absorb a continuous flow of welfare recipients and that such transitions can be achieved with fairly minimal support (see Hogan, 1996; Brown, 1997; cf. Peck and Theodore, 1999, 2000b). According to Mead, the strength of "[e]fficient programs like Riverside" is that they "stress placement in *available* jobs with the minimum of extras."[24]

Once a client is placed in employment, the labor market—or so the theory goes—should do the rest. Those with the ability will move on to a better job; those without will learn to cling on to what they have got; neither will regard welfare as a viable option any longer. The corpus of research on labor segmentation, of course, shows that labor markets do not function in this way: many of those entering the secondary labor market will remain trapped there, often irrespective of their skills and attitudes (see Harrison, 1972; Gordon et al., 1982). Yet as an MDRC evaluator conceded, in an "atmosphere in which people really *will* be constrained to accept entry-level employment," this situation has not been confronted: "One of the assumptions of the labor force-attachment-model is that people will move up from their entry-level jobs into jobs that offer more fringe benefits, higher salaries, etc. I don't think we know an awful lot about mobility in that way."[25]

Yet, at an ideological level, these arguments continue to carry great weight. It was, after all, Charles Murray who in the context of the U.S. welfare debate sought to resuscitate this "stepping-stone" approach to advancement via low-wage work:

[F]or a person with limited education and talent, the most reliable way out of poverty is to acquire . . . a low-income job; keep working as steadily as possible through a succession of such jobs as to acquire some skills and a good work record; and thereby eventually move into a relatively secure job with a decent wage. . . . The reforms of the 1960s . . . [discouraged] this slow, incremental approach . . . [by making] welfare a more attractive *temporary* alternative to a job . . . [undermining] acculturation to the demands of the workplace—arriving every day at the same time, staying there, accepting the role of subordinate . . . [and diminishing] the stigma associated with welfare [while] simultaneously devalu[ing] the status associated with working at a menial, low paying job. (Murray, 1985: 443–444)

The problem of poverty, for Murray, becomes an issue of incentives: welfare had distorted the traditional incentive structure faced by the poor— because "we—meaning the not-poor and the un-disadvantaged—had changed the rules of their world" (428), so the solution had to be to invert this incentive structure so as to encourage work, not welfare. "True" workfare does this, according to Mead (1992b: 172), by creating a strict "structure of compliance" so that work, in effect, becomes the only option.

## Feeling Temporary

The GAIN methodology ensures that participants experience a "push" from welfare as well as a "pull" from the labor market. According to Judith Gueron, one of the main impacts of the "tough and conservative" Riverside model is that "welfare *feels* temporary."[26] A strategy commonly deployed by Riverside caseworkers is to "motivate" participants by portraying an image of an uncertain future on welfare. Long before time-limited welfare became part of federal law, the *threat* of termination was frequently invoked in Riverside as a means of destabilizing clients. Two caseworkers explained their strategies:

> For each individual you learn strategies that tend to influence/impact your participant effectively. For example: . . . AFDC is changing drastically and it might not be around nor as dependable as it has been. I advise them of the proposed welfare changes by President Clinton, for a 2-year limit of AFDC. I urge them to start *now* and get a job! (quoted in Riverside County DPSS, 1994: 34)

> I draw a line on a chart, for "welfare" going down: The governor proposes a cut in the grant; your child turns 18; another child goes to live with her father . . . then I draw another line starting just under the welfare line but going up: You get a raise; you quit and get a better paying job; you get a promotion . . . Well, maybe the best the line will

do is stay flat, but unlike welfare it won't go down. (quoted in Bardach, 1993: 7)

The manifest intention here is to destabilize the welfare experience and to package a scenario of threats and opportunities that point only in one direction: off welfare and into work. As a senior DPSS executive put it, "I don't believe in stable welfare. . . . It causes people to drop out of school, enter crime, become involved in drugs, the whole thing. It's a terrible punishment to inflict on somebody."[27] The objective is to tip the balance in the trade-off between welfare and low-paying work unequivocally in favor of work. To do so, of course, is to recall perhaps the oldest principle in the provision of relief to the poor: the system of public assistance should in no way interfere with the imperative to work. Piven and Cloward (1993: 34) define this workhouse principle as one designed to "spur people to contrive ways of supporting themselves by their own industry, *to offer themselves to any employer on any terms.*"

## WORK-FIRST LABOR REGULATION

The Riverside model deploys a package of (often very) short-term services, backed up by tough sanctions, to effect the rapid reintegration of welfare recipients into the labor market. It seeks to create a secure and regular labor supply for what are for the most part insecure and irregular jobs. As Jamie Swift (1995: 176) has explained of similar programs, their effect is to "handcuff" the poor to the bottom of an unstable labor market, "holding them close in the labor market's gray area between bad jobs and welfare." The penal analogy is entirely appropriate here, given both the direct and the indirect roles played by sanctions in the Riverside model. Yet as a senior manager insisted, "The purpose of sanctions is not to punish but to shape behavior" (quoted in Bardach, 1993: 18). By implication, however, such behavioral changes would not be forthcoming unless a real threat of sanctions was present. As Lawrence Townsend explains,

Some clients need more encouragement than others to participate. Some . . . resist participation in GAIN. For some of these AFDC clients, once they understand their participation is mandated, they dive into the process wholeheartedly. Some of our most interesting success stories are individuals who were initially hesitant about participating. A small proportion of able-bodied AFDC clients believe society should support them. For this small number, sanctions may be necessary. If, after extensive counseling, pleading, offers of assistance in person, by letter, and by phone, we continue to be met with noncooperation, we sanction the recalcitrant clients. While sanctions are applied to only a small proportion of the caseload, *the existence of sanctions is important to the success of our approach.*[28]

Similarly, program participants are left in no doubt at all concerning the significance of the sanctions policy. Forceful reminders are ubiquitous. Use of sanctions procedures is routine. When clients enter the job club, for example, they are handed a photocopied sheet that states: "You are required to attend class EVERYDAY. If you have one or more excused absences, we will be having your GAIN counselor meet with you to discuss your attendance problem and to explain conciliation/sanction procedures."

## Shaping Behavior

At one and the same time, the Riverside model of workfare is concerned with the realpolitik of institutional change and with a set of deeper issues relating to the philosophical bases on which public assistance is provided and received. According to Wiseman (1987: 41), "Workfare changes the nature of the welfare bargain. It does this not simply by conditioning welfare receipt on work, as in the simplest of work requirements, but by conditioning welfare receipt on participation in a detailed, supervised program of preparation for self-support." Building on this notion of reciprocity, the Riverside philosophy forcefully advances an essentially behaviorist analysis of, and putative solution to, poverty and unemployment. If, as in the Riverside approach, deference, compliance, and the imposition of conventional codes of dress and manners are held up as the means to effect transitions from welfare to work, so by implication are assumed personal deficits in these areas constructed as the *causes* of labor-market disadvantage. Consideration of the quality and quantity of jobs, and indeed the entire realm of labor-market policy, are effectively rendered irrelevant by this mode of reasoning. Instead, imputed behavioral dysfunctions of the poor and unemployed themselves are presented as the source of the problem in need of treatment. This is one of the articles of faith in the Riverside program, such that when the local unemployment rate rose following a wave of defense-related closures, the job-placements targets for GAIN staff were actually *increased* by management.[29]

Another article of faith is that participants must be *compelled* to receive the necessary treatment. Rules are strictly enforced within the GAIN program, but an equally important effect of mandation is that the very *threat* of compulsory participation induces some welfare recipients to deregister. In fact, there tends to be a significant dropout rate at all stages in the administration of workfare programs, an effect that Mead (1992b: 172) terms the "workfare funnel." Riverside staff drew attention to this deterrent effect in different ways:

> "There is some subset that we don't really understand yet. They're working already and it's not reported. What the [GAIN process] does is flush that to the surface. They say, oh yeah, I'm going to work to-morrow, and they've been working for three months. But they haven't told us, and they aren't going to tell us because they'll go to jail! . . . So people go to work literally before they have any real contact [with the GAIN program itself] but much more of that happens after they have been involved with [the program]."[30]

> "Sometimes they go to work when they get a letter from GAIN saying that they're coming in [to begin the program]. *They know.* And like all communities, there's a lot of communication. I'm sure in the AFDC community, they know. So here's a letter from GAIN. They're going to put me through this process. And they begin to look for work. . . . Some people go to work so that GAIN will not bother them any-more."[31]

"Motivation" in the Riverside program is consequently secured not simply through esteem building but also through the deliberate exploita-tion of uncertainty and fear, coupled with the systematic erosion/with-drawal of alternative means of subsistence. These work-enforcing mea-sures, particularly when combined with time-limited welfare, lie at the heart of an emerging "active" mode of labor regulation. In contrast to the welfarist paradigm of passive-income support, such active systems im-pact not only the "financial plight of the unemployed, and . . . their job prospects, but also . . . those attitudes, affects, conducts and disposition that present a barrier to the unemployed returning to the labour market, and alienate them from social networks and obligations" (Dean, 1995: 572; see also Offe, 1985).

## Reproducing Contingent Workers, Reproducing Contingent Work

As the centerpiece of an "active" regime of labor regulation, workfare aims to secure no less than the basic social reproduction of the contin-gent workforce. Workfare seeks to compensate for the weakened "wage pull" of contingent labor markets, the capillary action of which is dimin-ished by chronic job instability, poor benefits, and low pay. Willfully mis-interpreting this as a motivational problem, and conveniently sidestepping the structural economic explanation, workfare seeks to counteract the weak pull of contingent work by inducing a strong push from welfare. Absent an adequate supply of decent-paying jobs, this has far-reaching and adverse effects both on the "self formation" of welfare recipients, who are forcibly engaged in the governance of their own subordination to contingent work (Dean, 1995), and on the structure of labor markets, reinforcing the downward drag of pay and conditions (Peck, 1996).

Yet, clearly, this does not solve the problems of poverty and under-employment; it merely displaces them. Using what they describe as "conventional economic assumptions," the Economic Policy Institute calculated that the PRWORA will result in severe labor-market problems. Although widespread unemployment and job displacement are perhaps the most likely outcomes of the attempt to drive welfare recipients into the labor market, the Economic Policy Institute study "takes congressional welfare reform at face value," assuming that an influx of just over one million former welfare recipients will compete directly for jobs with existing low-wage workers: the result is that wages in the low-wage labor market fall by an average of 11.9 percent, and by more in states—like California—where there is a large welfare population (Mishel and Schmitt, 1995).[32] Widespread job dislocation can also be expected to occur. The Illinois Job Gap Study revealed, for example, a serious shortage of entry-level jobs in many parts of the state, and following the entry of welfare recipients into this crowded labor market the situation can only be expected to have deteriorated further. The Illinois study estimated that under these conditions there would be four workers chasing every entry-level job in the state and six for every such vacancy in Chicago (Carlson and Theodore, 1995).[33] Under such conditions, downward pressure on wages and conditions is certain to follow.[34]

Even in the relatively favorable local economic environment of Riverside, the research evidence revealed that the main effect of the "work-first" approach was to *accelerate* reentry into the labor market at poverty wages.[35] Here, the GAIN program can be seen to be not only exploiting but in fact underwriting, *and even subsidizing*, labor-market insecurity and employment contingency. As a senior DPSS executive conceded, while the program manifestly cannot create jobs, it could nevertheless exploit turnover through aggressive job placement:

> "What we've found is that there is always job turnover. So even if there weren't enough jobs, are we going to doom a certain number of people to a life on welfare, or would it not be better to have a population that has familiarization and capability for employment? I think there's also an unfilled job market, it's what I call the delay factor. . . . By aggressive job placement, if jobs that normally have two months of vacancies

before they're refilled, if I can shorten that to two weeks on the average, there's more employment in total. So we got fairly good at finding
job openings fairly fast, and getting clients into them fast. So while we
didn't create additional jobs, we were able to harness more employment because with the unfilled factor we shortened that time frame."[36]

As Mark Greenberg has explained, "[T]he Riverside approach generally did not result in raising wages for those who entered employment;
in contrast another county (Alameda) was successful in helping its participants enter into higher-paying jobs, though with a program that was
far more costly than Riverside."[37] Likewise in Michigan, where Riverside-
style "labor force attachment" (LFA) measures were trialed alongside education and training-oriented "human capital development" (HCD) programs—each serving a similar client groups—an evaluation has revealed
that while the two groups achieved the same employment rate, the LFA
group achieved fewer hours of work and consistently lower earnings: 30
percent lower at both initial placement and ninety days after placement,
the average wages of the LFA group were only 85 percent of the poverty
rate for a family of two and just 56 percent of the poverty rate for a family
of four (Eberts, 1995). The critical weakness of HCD approaches, however, is that in terms of short-term accounting frameworks they are more
expensive to operate than LFA models (see Peck and Theodore, 1998).

## Cutting Costs

Under pressure to reduce costs and improve (short-run) outcomes, Los
Angeles, Alameda, and numerous other counties have abandoned their
HCD strategies in favor of a Riverside-style approach, it having been
deemed that the latter method delivers the kinds of results—low-cost job
reentry—that matter. The apparent conclusiveness of the MDRC study
gave many counties no real alternative, as program managers both inside
and outside Riverside came to understand:

> "[After] the second-year study came out we thought, wait a minute,
> we're looking bad here. Not bad, bad, but not like Riverside. . . . So we
> went down there. . . . [Afterward] we thought maybe we need to re-
> tool a little bit, but our advisory council wasn't quite convinced. After
> another year we really got the writing on the wall and now have been
> really trying to retool to make it much more of a proactive, you know,
> get-a-job-now kind of program. But we will be forever remembered
> from the MDRC study because we went for what was called the hu-
> man-capital-development [approach]. . . . But we had to turn around
> because of the cost of the program. . . . There is value in training, but
> we simply cannot spend that much money on those few people, espe-

cially in view of welfare reform. . . . [Now] you have got to make people self-sufficient as quickly as possible."[38]

"A lot of counties—Santa Barbara and San Mateo are two real good examples—have just turned around 180 degrees from the approach they were using before. Some counties are sticking to the tried-and-true, they feel tried-and-true, approach of human-capital development . . . which is fine, it's got some real strengths, but if you look at the costs involved and the kind of money that's coming at us in the federal welfare reform, you can discuss it all you want but there's no money to do human capital development; it's not there. But at $1,166 per employment placement, that's a number you can do a lot with. You can move a lot of people through the program."[39]

More formally, legislation passed in the State of California in 1995 (based on the recommendations of a GAIN working party chaired by the then-director of Riverside DPSS Lawrence Townsend) embeds numerous features of the Riverside model in the state framework, notably mandatory up-front job search, extended stays in job club/search, and a deprioritization of provision for the most needy (State of California AB 1371; GAIN Advisory Council, 1994). As two interviewees in the state administration pointed out, both the philosophy and the method of Riverside are therefore being generalized:

"The counties . . . will have more flexibility in terms of the individuals they can serve. Right now, we have a requirement that—if they only have so much money to serve individuals—we have them focus on what we call the long-term recipients, the person that's been on aid for a long period of time. That's prevented a lot of counties from being able to intervene early on with someone who's just come on aid. There's been a tension for many years between that requirement and counties' ability to intervene early on. . . . [Now] they may be able to get them back into a job more quickly."[40]

"We're trying to break free from this one-size-fits-all approach to welfare delivery. . . . There could be significant proportions of the population that really don't need a lot of intensive services. . . . A job, a better job, a career. . . . What we're really saying is that we have to get people into jobs quickly because the most important thing they have to learn is how to work."[41]

As the Riverside methodology becomes more and more generalized, so its labor-regulatory effects will become correspondingly widespread. As the state official quoted above argued, the GAIN program should not be concerned with providing what recipients might want—improved education and training and the chance of a better job—but instead should focus on what employers want: "What they need is someone who . . . will show up on time and has a good attitude."

## Reregulating Labor Markets

Under the increasingly LFA-oriented GAIN program, welfare recipients are being pushed into the cracks and crevices of the local labor market. In the short run, the Riverside strategy is self-evidently contingent on the capacity of the local labor market to generate suitable (low-wage) work. An MDRC evaluator observed that

> "sometimes in these job clubs they list on a blackboard the most re-
> cent jobs people got. . . . I would say that almost half of them are in
> the service industry, either maids at hotels or busboys, things like this,
> or in fast-food restaurants. These are not great jobs. These are jobs that
> have high turnover and are also very sensitive to how the economy is
> going. . . . So you're very sensitive to the fine-tuning of the local labor
> market, and the bottom line is that they are just not good jobs."[42]

In the longer run, of course, one might expect the labor market itself to adjust to the availability of this new labor supply, as employers begin to tailor their employment policies in accordance with changing local conditions. The likely effects of this are that conditions deteriorate markedly in the lower tiers of the labor market, and *stay* deteriorated. Perversely, the (workfarist) labor supply then begins to generate its own (contingent) labor demand, creating the conditions for a medium-term regulatory realignment in the labor market.

Expanding the supply of contingent labor in such a way is likely to lead to falling wages, greater job instability, and a deterioration in workplace conditions. "Work-first" workfare not only facilitates but *drives* labor-market trends in this direction by creating a new category of forced labor, compelled to accept low-wage work. And this affects more than just program participants, because the *threat* of workfare also alters the job-market behavior of the poor. The impacts of workfare consequently extend beyond the welfare population to encompass low-wage workers in general, as the regulatory rules for the bottom tiers of the labor market are effectively rewritten in employers' favor. Workfare consequently plays a role in changing the rules concerning welfare *and* work, to enforcing the latter by transforming the former. In effect, a new regime of labor discipline is being enforced, as the poor are given no alternative but to cycle between jobs, either "voluntarily" or with the "assistance" of a program like GAIN. As Cloward and Piven (1993: 696) explain, such policies represent a "symbolic crusade directed at the working poor rather than at those on relief, and the moral conveyed is the shame of the dole and the virtue of labor, no matter the job and no matter the pay."

Interpreted at this broader level, the "Riversidization" of the U.S. welfare system not only represents a turn in policymaking fashion, it also can be seen in the context of the installation of a harsh regime of labor regulation. This highlights the potential role of workfare as a regulatory support for the split-level labor market in the U.S., a political response to localized shortages of decent-paying jobs for entry-level workers and the rupturing of upward mobility. In the process, the old welfarist settlement-with its "culture," its associated institutions, and its regulatory norms-is actively eroded/partially replaced in what is a deliberate and explicit regulatory project. Two GAIN managers explained it like this:

> "We know we're changing society, one client at a time, in a desirable direction. . . . We think our society's been going in the wrong direction, and we think if we can get people instead of turning to welfare turning back to work, the way things used to be . . . we're enabling people to find out how good they are and how they can fit into society."[43]

> "A lot of people say there aren't any jobs. Well, people still get jobs . . . they're not all great jobs, but as [California's director of welfare] Eloise Anderson said—and it was a real eye-opener—she was talking to a group of GAIN participants from San Diego and she said, 'You're on welfare, why shouldn't you take a minimum-wage job? What's wrong with this picture?' It's just a matter of rethinking the whole way of doing business and our attitude to our clients. . . . And really assist them on all levels, not just say well here's your check, but just really change the whole culture."[44]

The Riverside model, in this sense, represents a form of economic conscription, a means of enforcing work and its associated disciplines in the context of flexibilizing labor markets. Here it is "work" itself, rather than just the work ethic, that is failing, as the problems of falling wages and insecure employment further erode the capillary processes that have traditionally operated to draw the poor into the bottom of the labor market *above the welfare line*. The brutal "solution" represented by the Riverside approach is to intensify the "push" from welfare into work, the imperative being to accept the jobs, working conditions, and wages that happen to be on offer—in other words, to accommodate the labor supply to the prevailing local conditions of labor demand. Under the Riverside model, welfare recipients are aggressively "jobclubbed" into private-sector jobs. This has the effect, within local labor markets, of driving down both the reservation wage of the unemployed and the prevailing market wage for low-paid workers, while also further destabilizing contingent employment. While welfare-to-work programs may not have been designed with this purpose in mind, they nevertheless can be seen to be dispensing such regulatory functions.

## SELLING RIVERSIDE:
## DISCOURSE AND DELIVERY

The Riverside model has become much more than a "successful" approach to welfare-to-work programming. It has become a powerful symbol in the politics of workfare and welfare reform. Riverside exerts an inordinate influence in these debates, and also in the day-to-day practice of policy implementation, because it is an institutional realization of a series of passionately held beliefs on the right of American poverty politics. Previously, when politicians such as Ronald Reagan espoused the discourse of punitive workfare, of replacing welfare checks with paychecks and setting the poor to work, they were oftentimes to be accused not only of dogmatism but also of a lack of pragmatism. The tough rhetoric of workfare was one thing, implementation was quite another (Nathan, 1993). The arrival of the Riverside model, however, and in particular its glowing evaluation by MDRC, dramatically realigned the rhetoric and the reality of workfare. Riverside appeared to demonstrate that not only could tough love sound good, it could also be translated into a workable—and cheap—program.

The significance of the Riverside model lies with the set of fundamental ideological currents into which its "jobs, jobs, jobs" philosophy taps. It has conferred legitimacy on the "old-style" model of workfare always favored by conservatives and in so doing has made a decisive contribution to the long-running struggle over the *meaning* of workfare in America. The ascendancy of Riverside marks a watershed in this struggle, for it appears to lay to rest the "softer" and more service-intensive versions of workfare, such as Massachusetts's ET Choices. The evaluation literature's telling distinction between rapid-employment LFA programs and more traditional, education, and training-based HCD approaches to welfare-to-work programming echoes what Brodkin (1995) characterizes as the old political fault line between "hard" and "soft" workfare. In this context, "labor-force attachment" may have become a politically correct pseudonym for workfare-as-punishment, market-style.

This same fault line was also evident in the debates around the establishment and early development of California's GAIN program. According to former Governor Deukmejian,

"[W]e originally intended GAIN to place a heavy emphasis on job-seeking up front. . . . California cannot afford this kind of welfare system. We must go back to basics. We need to give a hand to those who cannot help themselves for a short period of time, until they can make it on their own. In turn, those we help must help themselves. We need to rededicate ourselves to the original intent of the GAIN approach. GAIN should be transformed into a true "workfare" program, where the immediate priority is to remove people from welfare rolls and put them on payrolls as quickly as possible. . . . [All] participants should be required to look for jobs before being diverted into any education or training program. Let the job marketplace, not case workers, determine who is employable. . . . I am [also] proposing that measures be strengthened to require mandatory participation in GAIN; under the current system, they are too lax. (1990: B7)[45]

In the 1990s version of the hard-versus-soft workfare debate, Riverside signifies a sanitized version of the punitive approach. And despite the relative modesty of its material achievements, it has emerged as the working definition of "welfare reform with results."[46]

## Riverside Goes Generic

One of the architects of the Riverside model, consultant Dean Curtis, contends that "[t]he results are coming in across the country that this employment-first approach is the way to go."[47] The Riverside approach (or one of its euphemisms) has been cited in scores of congressional hearings and policymakers' conferences since the early 1990s. The efficacy of the model was further underlined when MDRC presented some of the initial findings of its nationwide evaluation of the JOBS program. Conducted in seven sites, including Riverside, the evaluation comes down strongly in favor of the LFA approach: Freedman and Friedlander (1995: ES-3, ES-9), while conceding that the preliminary nature of their results "may stack the deck against the HCD approach," nevertheless tellingly conclude that "well-implemented, highly mandatory JOBS programs that use job search followed by a range of short-term education, training, and other services to promote rapid job entry—the Labor Force Attachment model—can produce dramatic reductions in welfare receipt and substantial increases in employment and earnings."

Nowhere had the case for LFA approaches been made more strongly than in the GAIN evaluation, which starkly contrasted the HCD approaches of Los Angeles and Alameda (Oakland)—both underresourced, big-city programs that concentrated their efforts on the most hard-to-serve client group of long-term recipients—so unfavorably with the low-cost, high-output Riverside program. This presented an opportunity to reestablish workfare as a punitive, "no extras" strategy. For example, California's director of welfare, Eloise Anderson, has insisted that workfare strategies based on the Riverside model be deployed so as to create "strong incentives for recipients to enter the *real workforce*," seeing this as a route to her ultimate goal of "reject[ing] the philosophy of entitlement."[48] Her deputy director of welfare programs, Michael Genest, argued that this entails a wider and deeper cultural reorientation of the welfare system:

> It is extremely important to change the culture of applying for or receiving welfare by setting the expectation that applicants or recipients make every effort to join or rejoin the workforce as soon as possible. Exemption and deferral criteria must be narrowly defined and limited just to those individuals who are truly unable to work or benefit from the program.[49]

Cultural and administrative accounts of the success of the Riverside model have established this strategy as a reform generic in welfare-to-work programming. It has come to define the standard for a "high-performance" welfare-to-work program, as the lessons from Riverside have been translated into programmatic prescriptions for welfare reform. Testifying before the Senate Committee on Labor and Human Resources, MDRC's Judith Gueron cautioned, however, that "Riverside's GAIN program has not eliminated welfare or transformed the earnings potential of welfare recipients. More people got jobs than would have gotten them without the program, and got them sooner, but they were usually not 'better' jobs and families were rarely boosted out of poverty."[50] She went on to describe the positive features of the Riverside approach in terms of a series of (at least potentially transferable) generic practices:

- Priority on the JOBS program by the most senior officials in the agency.
- A strong commitment and adequate resources to serve the full mandatory population (not just those who volunteer or appear to be more job-ready).
- A pervasive emphasis on getting a job quickly, even a job that is relatively low paying and even for people placed in education and training activities.
- A mixed strategy, emphasizing structured job search ("job clubs"), but also making substantial use of basic education.
- The active use of job developers to establish a close link to private-sector employers and to help recipients locate work.
- A willingness to use sanctions (i.e., grant cuts) to enforce the participation mandate.

- A cost-conscious management style, reflecting a recognition that time is money and that moving people quickly toward the goal of employment will increase the program's cost-effectiveness.
- An outcome-focused management style, including job-placement standards for case managers.[51]

Less that two weeks later, Lawrence Mead advised the Senate Finance Committee against the Clinton administration's welfare proposals, which would spend "unnecessary sums on public jobs, training, [and] childcare" and would permit the "big cities [to] go on allowing vast numbers to pursue higher credentials, usually to little good, in place of working."[52] Mead effectively rejected the HCD approach—which MDRC had earlier found tended to be more commonplace among those big-city welfare systems confronted with "highly-disadvantaged welfare populations, poor local labor markets, [but] readily available education and training resources" (Hamilton et al., 1994)—in favor of a "high-performance" approach emphasizing the following (Riverside-style) characteristics:

- High participation: clients must participate actively in the program, not simply sign up.
- Actual work or looking for work, as against education or training.
- Tight administration, with clients closely supervised and sanctioned if uncooperative.
- Minim[al] delay between client going on welfare and being referred to JOBS.
- Enrol[ing] high proportions of recipients referred to JOBS, not allowing them to drop out.
- Plac[ing] high proportions of participants in motivational training and job search.
- Downplay[ing] education and training in advance of work.
- Enforc[ing] these rules with case managers who followed up on clients closely.
- Minimiz[ing] the use of government jobs.[53]

Subsequently, Mead (1997b: 56) argued that "[w]illingness to enforce participation and work is the major feature that explains the superiority of . . . Riverside." Echoing the experience of ET Choices in Massachusetts and the skewed debate around the FSA, interpretations of program effectiveness tend to be strongly conditioned by the prevailing political climate: apparently, programs work because they are mandatory; they fail because they are not mandatory enough. However, others have maintained—more convincingly—that such is the level of complex contingency and unattributable causality in the GAIN evaluation data that there is in fact "no consistent relationship between the enforcement of mandatoriness through the use of sanctions and program outcomes" (Handler and Hasenfeld, 1997: 86). Nevertheless, mandation remains a strong element of the Riverside "message." This message is all the more potent because it seems to be one that many people—from federal politicians to commissioners of welfare to frontline workers—have been waiting to hear. As Mead has conceded, "[S]omehow the political process takes a certain direction, and operators at all levels get the message. . . . The idea of enforcing work has taken hold as if by an invisible hand" (quoted in Bardach, 1997: 278).

More concretely, policy brokers like MDRC are now actively engaged in promoting "work-first," both as a coherent philosophy and as a transferable package. MDRC's "How-To Guide" defines a stylized version of the Riverside method in the following terms:

> What defines [work-first] programs is their overall philosophy: that any job is a good job and that the best way to succeed in the labor market is to join it, developing work habits and skills on the job rather than in a classroom. Work first programs share a strong message that, for participants, employment is both the goal and the expectation. Work first programs seek to move people from welfare into unsubsidized jobs as quickly as possible, and job search itself is a central activity in these programs. However, work first is more than just job search. Work first programs generally begin with job search for most participants, using the labor market itself as a test of employability. Then, for those who are not able to finds jobs right away, work first provides additional activities geared toward addressing those factors which have impeded employment. These activities might include education, training, work experience, or other options. In the context of work first, they are generally short term, closely monitored, and either combined with or immediately followed by additional job search. (Brown, 1997: 4)

While stressing that "there is no exact recipe for implementing work first," Brown nevertheless goes on to describe a series of essentialized program features, administrative routines, and reform philosophies that are ripe for wider exploitation. The MDRC guide acknowledges that advocating "a single model would be of little use, because no single model would work everywhere"; but by defining "work-first" in a sufficiently elastic fashion and by breaking the model down into its necessary components, it becomes possible to isolate the "key ingredients [along with] some ideas on how to mix them together" (Brown, 1997: 6). So, the product cannot quite be bought "off-the-peg," but with a modicum of tweaking and customization, a policymaker can usually find the right mix: "Given your own situation, you may want to add more or less of some ingredients, or alter the recipe in other ways. . . . [The] guidelines here will point you in the right direction" (Brown, 1997: 6–7).

## Riversidization

The Riverside story has indeed taken hold in welfare administrations across the United States, and even beyond. Michigan, New Jersey, Georgia, Indiana, Texas, North Carolina, Mississippi, Oregon, and Maryland are among the states that have embraced a work-first, labor-force-attachment approach. The PRWORA's capped spending regime and high work targets, coupled with generally buoyant labor-market conditions, represent conditions highly favorable to the proliferation of Riverside-style systems. Indeed, even before the passage of the PRWORA, it was clear that, "thinking in Washington and among many states is moving in the direction of short-term job search assistance as the preferred way off welfare" (Eberts, 1995: 1). The Riverside approach and its various generics—defined both as an implementation strategy and as a general philosophy—are consequently disseminating rapidly. MDRC continue to argue for the LFA method, which strikes a positive chord with many policy advocates and commentators (see Hogan, 1996; Raspberry, 1996). This approach is also being actively touted in Canada, the United Kingdom, and elsewhere (see Labour Party, 1996a; Mitchell, 1996; Vosko, 1998; Peck and Theodore, 2000a). It is hardly an exaggeration to say that "work-first" is now being held up as the "one best way" in orthodox welfare-reform circles (see Holcomb et al., 1998; HM Treasury, 2000). At an administrative level, work-first practices are diffusing rapidly across welfare administrations, it slogans and programming routines—"every job is a good job," finding the shortest path to employment—cropping up all over the place (see Borland, 1998; Grubb et al., 1999; Little, 1999; Rodgers, 2000). Since "work-first" has been firmly established in the welfare-to-work lexicon, explicit deference to the Riverside model is no longer particularly necessary. In the words of the MDRC manual (Brown, 1997), the key questions now seem to be about "how to" rather than "why to" implement "work-first."

The MDRC's evaluation results fed directly into the competitive process that had become the welfare-reform movement by the mid-1990s. As a senior welfare administrator in Maryland commented, "We were really able to use the results from MDRC, the results from Riverside, that, together with what other states are doing. . . . They'd say, that's what they're doing in Virginia, so we're right at the forefront of social policy. . . . It's a political process, but informed by facts, at least if they're used to prove a point."[54] Meanwhile, other jurisdictions were buying heavily into the philosophy as well as the method of the Riverside model, as HCD approaches became rapidly discredited. A New Jersey official explained:

> "Generating checks is an important function, but there has not been sufficient focus in our view on the actual solutions—placing people in jobs, making direct connections with the labor market, economic self-sufficiency. . . . Our human-capital investment approach [is changing] to a direct-labor-market-attachment [approach]. In the past, we somewhat denigrated, or didn't aspire to place people, in the jobs that were available. We wanted good jobs. And we spent a lot of time on training and education. . . . The thought now is that . . . labor-market attachment is most important, the philosophical view that there is dignity in all work and sometimes we find that the best preparation for a job is a job. . . . The effort here is to send a strong message of high expectations, that this is a temporary program and for most people there is an expectation that people will move off it. . . . Based on the experience nationally of places like Riverside, California . . . we've put a lot of effort on immediate job placement."[55]

For some, however, a lingering concern was that states would read selectively from the Riverside script, using this to justify the installation of punitive regimes based on the cursory treatment of participants and oriented principally toward deregistration. According to a well-placed HHS administrator in Washington,

> "That's going on right now, a Riversidization. It's happening everywhere. . . . It's a happening through a confluence of different things. One is the research results. . . . The second thing is the economy is good and people see that there are jobs out there and they're not afraid of sending people out there looking for jobs. . . . What worries me a lot more is that some states don't go to Riverside . . . that they just go to cheap programs. . . . Telling people to go out and make five employer contacts isn't going to have any effect [alone]. You need more than that. You may not need [Wisconsin's] W2, but you need something that serious[ly] shows people how to look for work, connects them, monitors them whether they're doing it or not, sanctions them if they're don't. . . . It takes investment. My personal biggest fear in all of this is that the investment side will go away. It'll be the conservative rerun of the '70s: it'll be we'll just manipulate the benefit structure, we'll cut people's benefits, rather than we'll do the things that research shows *will* make a difference."[56]

Even very-well-implemented clones of the Riverside model, however, will not winnow the welfare rolls down to nothing. A rump of claimants will remain that the market continues to reject, for whatever reason. There is clearly a danger that the Riverside method imparts a gung-ho attitude in welfare administrations: "This may be hurting now, but we *know* it will be good for you in the long run." As the HHS official continued,

> "The program at Riverside works because you motivate people. . . . Serious labor-force-attachment approaches really work for a number of reasons. One is that they get people jobs faster than they would have [otherwise]. They ferret out people who are already working. . . . If you put it all together in a well-implemented package, it does seem to me that you can realistically think about reducing 20–30 percent [of the rolls]. Beyond that, I think that's another issue. There's a segment of the caseload that's going to have a hard time. The value of their labor is not the minimum wage, or only in exceptional circumstances. . . . That segment of the population, we either provide a dignified existence for them and their children . . . or we say that's too expensive . . . they get cut off and who knows what happens to their kids. . . . There's a low-skill segment of the population which we're going to have to face up to."[57]

There may be many reasons, of course, why a Riverside approach might fail to achieve significant results in other locations. True, there is certainly likely to be a "low-skill segment" within every caseload, but a host of other factors also shape employment chances. The shortcomings of the Riverside approach are perhaps most apparent in large cities, which not only tend to have weaker local labor markets—cutting the ground immediately from under the "any job is a good job" method— but which also experience intractable social and political problems around issues like poverty, racism, and bureaucratic reform. According to an evaluator at MDRC, an organization invited to carry out very few studies by big-city welfare administrations,

> "My work on [welfare programs] in New York City led me to understand the vast political complexities involved in programs in large cities. . . . One of the things that we have not talked about a great deal in broadcasting the Riverside results is that a relatively minor proportion of the Riverside population is African American. And the discrimination that blacks face in the labor market . . . is not something that we have looked at."[58]

## WORKFARE VERSUS THE CITIES

While there is clear evidence here of Riverside "going generic," also notable is the fact that this edge-city location occupies a particular location in the *geography* of workfare politics. The United States's central cities may be the epicenters of the "welfare mess," both in terms of the spatial distribution of recipients and the loaded political imagery of "welfare-dependency," but they are also places where reform efforts repeatedly flounder. As an MDRC evaluator explained of the situation in Detroit, another of the sites in the national JOBS evaluation:

> "Detroit is a kind of mess. There's a lot of reasons for that. They have a kind of New York City–New York State relationship. Detroit is the biggest thing going in Michigan, but at the same time I'm not sure the politicians are trying to influence Detroit residents. They're trying to influence everyone else in the state, so I think Detroit often doesn't get their share of state revenues. The administrators get a sense of that too. You know, keep this city under control; beyond that we don't care. [It's] a typical big-city program. . . . I'm not sure there's much there to emulate."[59]

To invert the euphemistic language used by Bardach (1993) in describing the Riverside model, Detroit represents an example of a *"low* expectations" welfare program in which the daily features of the system feed back into poor staff morale and the branding of recipients themselves as failures. The MDRC evaluator continued:

> "There has been a change since the . . . results came out of Riverside. . . . [Now] they're very quick to say, the program does work; you all told us that. That also reinforces that there is hope. . . . I know, I read it in the newspapers, we have great impacts. . . . Places like Detroit, there isn't stuff that comes out and says this works in the big cities. . . . What you read is that nothing is working in the big cities and that undermines the few successes you see. . . . In the bigger cities, that's where our evaluations have had most trouble. . . . In a smaller place, they'll try something new, they don't have to wade through so many channels or layers of bureaucracy. But in the big cities, even just implementing an evaluation is incredibly difficult. . . . [There] if you're really trying to foster institutional change, and change the culture of a place—to be more focused on work, as opposed to maintaining income—it's going to be an incredible push to get that message out and cover all the channels."[60]

A colleague agreed that "the big cities [will not] be the places where you're going to see the first round of innovation" because in this situation systemic change is extremely difficult, for administrators as well as participants:

> "It's like any other very big organization, they don't move very quickly and they can't change very quickly. In New York especially, it's such a

struggle just to manage the size of the programs, that to mount any kind of change that would be a citywide change, when you're sitting on the inside, looks like it's just impossible. So within cities you may see little pockets of let's try this and let's try that, but you never get a real sense of whether it's anything you could ever really take to scale and do for the entire caseload. . . . It will just take a lot longer to get things started and get changes in places in New York City than it will in smaller counties and smaller cities, but at the same time there are time limits and of course the clock is going to be ticking."[61]

The problems faced by big-city welfare systems such as those of Detroit and New York City, of course, extend far beyond "getting the message out." Manifest conditions here mean that short-term, low-cost "solutions" are not easily found. Delivery systems are overloaded, labor markets are often in structural decline, client groups are both large and multiply deprived, political capacity and will is often absent in welfare administrations accustomed to a "low-expectations" regime of systemic failure and crisis management. Riverside's promotional videos tend not to play well here because there is an understanding that the answers are not *anything like* so simple. But while there is recognition (at least in some quarters) that the "urban welfare mess" is deeply entrenched— either economically and socially, as liberals would have it, or culturally, as conservatives would have it—there is comparatively little awareness of the parallel embeddedness of the "exurban workfare solution." It is no coincidence that workfare's "reform generics" virtually all originate from exurban or small-city locations, where the welfare population is relatively small, where labor markets tend to be rather more dynamic, and where welfare administrations are rather more fleet of foot.

    Much of the "success"—and maybe even the viability—of the Riverside model is predicated on a very particular set of local conditions. Around the time of the MDRC evaluation, conditions may not have been perfect for welfare-to-work programming, but in many ways they were conducive. The local labor market expanded by 4.4 percent (31,300 jobs) between 1990 and 1994, following the influx of a large number of small manufacturing and service firms, making for an unusually turbulent employment situation in which the rate of turnover of vacancies (and therefore the labor market's absorptive capacity) is especially high. The area experienced strong population growth in the early 1990s (16 percent in 1990–1994), but also relatively high unemployment (rising from 2.6 percent to 10.5 percent over the same period) and falling per-capita income. According to the County Economic Development Agency, the local labor force is "low skilled" and has a "poor work ethic" but remains highly "trainable" (Economic Strategies Group, 1995).[62] The local labor regime therefore combines a climate of tough discipline with a buoyant supply of contingent work—pretty favorable conditions under which to develop a workfare system based on the rapid placement of participants in low-skill, low-paid jobs.

Indeed, the fact that the Riverside evaluation suggested such positive results in the face of a downturn in the local labor market may speak more to the weaknesses of the "work-first" method than to its strengths. As Epstein (1997: 174) points out, it is quite conceivable that "many GAIN registrants had been displaced from steady employment by the local recessionary labor market," with the result that "Riverside County's GAIN program simply might have exploited temporal employment fluctuations" in order to achieve its results. Under this scenario, the Riverside model would have done no more than hasten the reemployment of the most employable in the context of an earlier downturn, pushing recently displaced—and relatively skilled and motivated—jobseekers to the front of the local jobs queue. Viewed in the context of the wider political economy of the local labor market, the Riverside results look rather different. Epstein continues:

> The real Riverside story might be much less virtuous than MDRC's tale of scientific benevolence in which a wise county adopted humane and useful job search strategy to prevent the unemployed from becoming long-term welfare recipients. Rather, because the GAIN program favored AFDC registrants over other low-income job seekers, the latter nonwelfare population spent down their already meager resources to become eligible for welfare. Thus, GAIN came to serve the conservative desires of the local community: an expanded pool of low-wage workers, downward pressure on wages, low welfare dependency, and a diminishing tax burden. (Epstein, 1997: 174)

Local political and institutional conditions were also conducive. California has a relatively decentralized welfare system in which county administrations have historically played an important role not only in delivery but also in program design, development, and innovation. This was an essential prerequisite for the establishment of a distinctive Riverside approach in the early years of GAIN. The pro-work, anti-welfare approach of the Riverside program is also consonant with the prevailing social and political ethos in this tract of conservative suburbia (see Jonas, 1997), where there is no real tradition of welfare-rights advocacy or anti-poverty politics and where the degree of empathy, among the general population, with the "nonworking poor" is strictly limited. This is the kind of place, in other words, where "hard workfare" belongs. It is the kind of place where people are inclined to accept the political construction of the poor as an economically dysfunctional *and culturally separate* class and to take at face value the right-wing rhetoric that "welfare recipients respond very favorably to authoritative social messages" (Rector and Butterfield 1987: 8).

But while this message may be favorably received in California's edge cities, it translates less well in the big cities of the North and East, where LFA approaches—along with their underlying philosophies and socioeconomic prerequisites—remain somewhat incongruous. The major cities have tended to rely on HCD approaches for good reason: the paucity of inner-city jobs and the manifest needs of their large welfare populations. To implement LFA approaches in such contexts would be to take a quite unprecedented leap in the dark with respect to welfare policy (see Weir, 1998). Yet this is precisely the challenge that MDRC has set itself. The early results are as yet inconclusive, although MDRC is characteristically optimistic about the possibilities (see MDRC, 1999).

"Work-first" in the big cities might effect a brutal reengagement with the labor market for the most "job-ready" of recipients, but the threat of large-scale social dislocation would be real. For the most part, city jurisdictions have been wary of taking this risk, though some—such as Baltimore and Los Angeles—are moving in this direction. The regulatory environment created by the PRWORA, however, is such that more and more urban welfare administrations will be forced down this path, perhaps not against their will but often against their better judgment. There is certainly a sense in which Riverside-style incentives are written into the rules of the PRWORA, both for welfare recipients and for welfare administrations (see Brown, 1997). As Bardach (1997: 270), puts it, "The 1996 welfare reform bill essentially tells welfare recipients 'Work or else!' In effect, it gives state welfare agencies an analogous message: 'Get those people to work, or else.' "

## GO TO WORK, OR ELSE: TOWARD "TRUE" WORKFARE

Although real doubts remain over how far it is possible to reproduce the Riverside model—or its effects—in other locations, the terrain of the U.S. welfare system is already being remade in its image. For all its faults, it would appear that Riverside really is the future. In the context of the PRWORA, its attractions are easy to see: it is cheap and it appears to "work" (at least where success is measured in terms of speedy reentry into paid employment). The rise of Riverside also taps into a deep current of frustration about the intractability of the U.S. "welfare mess," venting this in the form of a reactionary turn toward punitive workfare, albeit subtly repackaged in the euphemistic language of labor-force-attachment strategies, high-expectations welfare systems, and work-first programming. Riverside has become a metaphor for this contradiction-riven transition, offering the spurious promise that not only will everything work out, it will also be cheap.

To be sure, the history of U.S. welfare reform is littered with such unfounded panaceas, but few before could claim the kind of legitimacy that comes with MDRC's stamp of approval. This has engendered a degree of political potency in the Riverside model that in some senses is unprecedented. According to one well-placed commentator, close to Washington decision making,

> "In truth, I think some of the MDRC research has been a disservice to the system because it has shifted the entire thing into a jobs-first, work-first mode. . . . [Their recent research] has reinforced the idea that human capital doesn't pay off . . . and by now they have built up such credibility on Capitol Hill that when MDRC says it, my god, we're going to do it. I think that gave enormous impetus to this whole-work first thing."[63]

A perverse side effect of the MDRC research on tough, work-first programs has been to confer the respectability of an experiment on almost any punitive turn in welfare-to-work programming. Never before has anti-welfare dogma been so easily translatable into a program of reform: "true" workfare has thus been transformed from a perverse preoccupation of the right-wing fringe to an ostensibly operational orthodoxy of the policy mainstream. The fault here should not be laid exclusively at the door of evaluation researchers, but rather must be traced more deeply to the political–economic context of the welfare-to-work movement. As Epstein (1997: 175) observes, "It is notable that GAIN achieved so little and ominous that this over-rated activity would so profoundly influence national policy. Yet GAIN's utility may lie less in its production function as a manpower program and more in its ceremonial role of justifying a socially efficient national policy toward underemployment, unemployment, and poverty." Of course, it matters what the MDRC evaluations did and did not say, but more important in many ways were the ways in which the Riverside results were consumed, and acted upon, by the policymaking community. An MDRC evaluator explained:

> "This was something MDRC was very unprepared for, kind of an inversion, if you will, of how our results were interpreted by policymakers. Whereas in the 1980s, modest but positive results were cheered and applauded by everyone who was used to a history of no results at all from [welfare-to-work] programs, suddenly the debate turned around 180 degrees and even with the Riverside program the

argument became, well, if your results are *only* going to be what Riverside got, if you *only* reduce the rolls by that much, or if you only increase employment by that much, that's insufficient. We need much more radical kinds of reforms."[64]

The radicalizing momentum of the U.S. welfare-reform movement, now being translated to the international scale, makes light of issues such as demand-deficient unemployment and local economic and institutional embeddedness. Instead, each "successful" program is deconstructed down into ostensibly transferable components—leadership, performance contracts, job-club design features, income disregards—ready for shipping. Mobilizing the message becomes more important than weighing the evidence, as a proselytizer for the Riverside philosophy observed:

"We've been coaching Los Angeles County, and their results are up 200 per cent. San Bernardino has adopted some of our methods, and now they're pushing us in terms of job numbers. . . . Part of it is political and management will. It's transferable if they really wish to move people off of welfare soon. If they're required to do it, and can still afford to remain with the old methods, they may give lip service to it, but the results won't be as good. So the leaders involved have to really *want* to get people into employment as soon as possible. If they truly desire that . . . yes it is transferable. . . . It has mostly to do with desire, unless you *have* to do it. . . . [With] block grants, change is even more inevitable, because if you're locked at [previous year] expenditures and the population is growing and you have inflation, you really *have* to do something."[65]

For all the windy rhetoric about leadership in welfare reform, the plain fact is that the structural context established by the PRWORA makes the slide to Riverside-style programming all the more inevitable.

The Riverside model embodies both a cultural critique of and an institutional alternative to the welfare system, mounted by way of a celebration of low-wage work. It mandates working poverty rather than providing any kind of solution to the problem of poverty itself. While Riverside's GAIN program was propelling people into work, it was not lifting them out of poverty. In this respect, the MDRC results were in fact far more inconclusive than at first they seemed: the Riverside experimentals were only $52 per month better off than their counterparts in the control group; two-thirds of the experimentals were not working at the time of the year-three interview; and almost half never worked during the entire three-year period (Handler, 1995; see also Epstein, 1997). As MDRC's Judith Gueron has conceded, if ending poverty rather than tackling "welfare dependency" is the goal, then Riverside does not provide the answer: "[T]he downside to Riverside is that families weren't moved out of poverty. People didn't get better jobs. If that's your goal, you have to make a larger investment to get there."[66] The Riverside model is typical of a form of welfare-to-work policymaking that speaks to the *politics* of poverty, not to its underlying causes; just as its methodology is addressed more to the *stereotype* of the dependent, work-fearing welfare recipient than to the realities of poor people's lives and contingent employment. In the largely symbolic terrain on which the U.S. welfare-reform debate has been played out, such "success stories" have nevertheless acquired an enormous potency, particularly where they are cloaked in the language of scientific evaluation.

Riverside's administratively unyielding method of microregulating the poor puts people to work, not in simulated but in "real" jobs. The fact that these are not good jobs, its proponents insist, is beside the point. The PRWORA's implicit validation of Riverside-style programming, and the deepening hegemony of LFA methods, means that we may now be witnessing the installation of the kind of "true" workfare regime envisaged by Ronald Reagan, but on a much broader scale, both geographically and in terms of rates of mandatory participation. Reagan's vision of decentralized workfare as the norm rather than the exception is consequently being realized, as more and more states subscribe to the Riverside philosophy and its associated mode of labor discipline. According to a GAIN regional manager, this is as simple as it is brutal: "It's something any ten-year-old kid could tell you, but a doctorate in sociology can't: If you want people to get off welfare, you stay on their backs until they get a job."[67] While a host of evaluation studies has calculated to the nearest cent the costs of such methods of "getting on the backs" of welfare recipients, virtually none have explored the wider social and labor-market implications of this quick-fix approach to labor-force attachment. The United States continues to drift in this direction, apparently oblivious to the likely costs of adopting the Riverside method on a comprehensive basis. This is a risky strategy because the effects of *large-scale* LFA programming are simply unknown, especially in the nation's big cities. But the move is advocated nevertheless: according to another proponent of the work-first approach, Will Marshall of the Progressive Policy Institute, "The only way to find out how well labor markets absorb people moving off the welfare rolls is to try."[68]

The fact that strong labor-market growth in the second half of the 1990s served to accommodate this strategy should not divert attention away from the risky nature of its underlying premises. The work-first method appears to have been validated in this large-scale "field trial," but the real challenge for policymakers is whether such systems can be made to work in foul weather as well as in fair. In fact, both supply- and demand-side constraints operate to limit the scope and effectiveness of these approaches. On the demand side, a strong vacancy flow is a prerequisite, implying that a growing and/or turbulent labor market is necessary in order to make work-first programs work. In a circular fashion, however, these programs may be operating to lubricate the transition to just the kind of contingent job-market conditions they need. If labor-market contingency rates continue to rise, and if Riverside-style programs of one kind or another continue to socialize and acclimatize participants for a life of irregular work, then a perverse kind of equilibrium may be created in some local labor markets. Nevertheless, the fact remains that a generalized economic downturn would surely throw this fledgling system into some disarray. Short of a quantum shift toward contingent employment, these demand-side constraints would suffocate the program, as job availability declined at the same time as worker displacement and program demand rose.

On the supply side, work-first programs enforce an uncompromising form of market-mediated selection: they let the job market decide who is the most "employable." The distributional consequences of this are to be found in the reproduction, and sometimes the magnification, of preexisting labor-market inequalities, as traditionally disadvantaged groups are pushed to the back of the employability queue. Ultimately, this creates capacity constraints for work-first programs because the flipside of catering to the most job-ready is that, over time, the residual welfare-client group is increasingly disadvantaged and "hard to serve." The individuals that work-first leaves behind tend to have multiple employment barriers and social needs, such as to render ineffective work-first's quick fixes. And the longer work-first programs operate, of course, the more likely it is that they will have to reach down into this hard-to-serve/hard-to-employ client group. As many U.S. program managers now characterize the situation, this residualized one-third of clients are much more difficult to shift than the rest: conventional accounts have it that, after PRWORA, one-third of welfare recipients were easy to place as they were effectively ready for work already; the middle one-third needed "activating" with incentives, deterrents, and services; and as for the remaining one-third, perhaps they will need something different? In many U.S. states, where the welfare rolls have fallen by between one-half and two-thirds, the limits of allowing the market to cherry-pick the caseload are becoming apparent. So, another structural constraint of work-first is being exposed.

But if program managers and participants know this, that knowledge has yet to permeate the political sphere. Here, particularly in the United States, welfare reform is talked about as if it was a "done deal."

So, in the 2000 presidential elections, welfare reform was relegated to a side issue, and was mainly discussed in the past tense: candidate Gore spoke of the "next step in welfare reform: help[ing[ responsible parents, crack[ing] down on deadbeats,"[69] while candidate Bush, when dealing with poverty and welfare issues at all, addressed himself to those "above welfare's assistance, but beneath prosperity's promise."[70] In retrospect, the second Clinton term may be remembered as a long interregnum between the legislative moment of reform and the need to deal with the consequences. Just as in Canada and the United Kingdom, reforming politicians in the United States have been able to ride the business cycle while deferring the costs. And work-first in so many ways represents the administrative essence of these peculiar conditions. But the experiment has yet to run its course, as Clinton's successor will no doubt find out.

## Notes

1. An early version of this chapter was published as "Workfare in the Sun: Politics, Representation, and Method in U.S. Welfare-to-Work Strategies," *Political Geography* (1998) 17: 535–566 (Copyright 1998). I am grateful to Elsevier Science for permission to reproduce it, in revised and updated form, here.

2. Federal Document Clearing House Congressional Testimony, February 28, 1995, Lawrence E. Townsend Jr., U.S. Senate Labor and Human Resources Committee.

3. Senior executive #1, Riverside DPSS, interviewed by Jamie Peck, October 1995.

4. Quoted from *MacNeil/Lehrer NewsHour*, August 1, 1995, transcript #5283.

5. Senior executive #1, Riverside DPSS, interviewed by Jamie Peck, October 1995.

6. Senior program evaluator #4, MDRC, interviewed by Jamie Peck, November 1995.

7. Federal Document Clearing House Congressional Testimony, March 15, 1994, Judith M. Gueron, House Ways and Means/Human Resources Welfare Revision (emphasis added).

8. Uniquely, Riverside has negotiated performance-based contracts with its educational providers, thereby translating its outcomes-driven methodology to basic-education provision too: "The school providers get paid for the student progress, in other words, as the student achieves different grade levels they get paid. They don't get paid for hours in the seat. . . . So they have a very, very strong incentive to move these people, and see that they progress. If they're not progressing, then they're back to us saying, hey, you need to deal with this person, they're not doing it" (Program specialist, Riverside GAIN program, interviewed by Jamie Peck, October 1995).

9. Senior executive #1, Riverside DPSS, interviewed by Jamie Peck, October 1995.

10. Senior executive #1, Riverside DPSS, interviewed by Jamie Peck, October 1995.

11. This respondent continued: "For people that still don't have a job at the end of [job club] and part of that is an attitude problem . . . they put them back through a much more intensive, attitude-focused five-day process to help them overcome their problem with the world" (Senior executive #2, Riverside DPSS, interviewed by Jamie Peck, October 1995).

12. Quoted from *MacNeil/Lehrer NewsHour,* August 1, 1995, transcript #5283.

13. Bardach explains that the conciliation process involves "official notification of failure to participate and a demand for improvement which, if not met, would eventually lead to a sanction. . . . As one caseworker in Riverside County remarked, 'They have to have some kind of disruption in their lives to face up to some responsibility' " (1993: 18).

14. Senior executive #2, Riverside GAIN program, interviewed by Jamie Peck, October 1995; senior manager #1, Riverside GAIN program, interviewed by Jamie Peck, October 1995.

15. Manager #2, Riverside GAIN program, interviewed by Jamie Peck, October 1995.

16. While MDRC was somewhat equivocal about the specific role of Riverside's "personalized" case-management system in generating the program's strong impacts, opting instead to attribute these to a particular *constellation* of factors, including case-management style (Riccio et al., 1994: 294), others insist that this is the critical ingredient. According to Richard Nathan, for example, it is imperative "that there are case managers for all employable welfare families. That person should not be allowed to have more than 100 cases. This is the Riverside, California 'GAIN' model. These front-line case managers are essential to reducing welfare. They need to have the time and resources to do their job. . . . [It] is a big proposition to assure effective case management. But without some attention to the 'Who' and 'How' of welfare reform, we are putting too much reliance on preachments and prohibitions from on high. Such implementation activities are the short suit of American government. More hard thinking needs to be given in the current welfare-reform debate to this implementation dimension of reform, particularly as it applies to the state role of moving welfare family heads into the labor force" (Federal Document Clearing House Congressional Testimony, April 27, 1995, Testimony on an Alternative to the House-Passed Welfare Reform Bill, U.S. Senate Committee on Finance).

17. Federal Document Clearing House Congressional Testimony, February 28, 1995, Lawrence E. Townsend Jr., Labor Impact of Welfare Revisions, U.S. Senate Labor and Human Resources Committee.

18. According to Townsend, GAIN staff "must be top performers from other programs; they should not have had failures in their own employment history; they should be well groomed; they should have a positive and enthusiastic disposition. Extensive training is provided for GAIN staff to increase the likeli-

hood they can meet the performance expectations" (Federal Document Clearing House Congressional Testimony, February 28, 1995, Lawrence E. Townsend Jr., Labor Impact of Welfare Revisions, U.S. Senate Labor and Human Resources Committee).

19. Senior executive #2, Riverside DPSS, interviewed by Jamie Peck, October 1995.

20. Manager #1, Riverside GAIN program, interviewed by Jamie Peck, October 1995.

21. Quoted in *San Francisco Chronicle,* June 6, 1995: A1.

22. Quoted from *MacNeil/Lehrer NewsHour,* August 1, 1995, transcript #5283.

23. Federal Document Clearing House Congressional Testimony, March 20, 1995, Will Marshall, Senate Finance Welfare Revision—Work Programs.

24. Federal Document Clearing House Congressional Testimony, March 9, 1995, Lawrence M. Mead, Senate Finance Welfare Revision (emphasis added).

25. Evaluation researcher #3, MDRC, interviewed by Jamie Peck, November 1995.

26. Federal Document Clearing House Congressional Testimony, February 28, 1995, Judith M. Gueron, Labor Impact of Welfare revisions, U.S. Senate Committee on Labor and Human Resources; Federal Document Clearing House Congressional Testimony, March 15, 1994, Judith M. Gueron, House Ways and Means/Human Resources Welfare Revision (emphasis added).

27. Senior executive #1, Riverside DPSS, interviewed by Jamie Peck, October 1995.

28. Federal Document Clearing House Congressional Testimony, February 28, 1995, Lawrence E. Townsend Jr., Labor Impact of Welfare Revisions, U.S. Senate Labor and Human Resources Committee (emphasis added).

29. "The real reason we increased the [job-placement] goal when the unemployment rate went up is that we didn't want our staff to engage in a process of excuse making. Because once they start saying that outside forces could be used as an excuse not to do the right thing for our clients, that sets up a whole wave of excuse making for nonperformance" (Senior executive #1, Riverside DPSS, interviewed by Jamie Peck, October 1995).

30. Senior executive #2, Riverside DPSS, interviewed by Jamie Peck, October 1995.

31. Senior manager #2, Riverside GAIN program, interviewed by Jamie Peck, October 1995.

32. Wages in California were projected to fall by 17.8 percent and in New York by 17.1 percent.

33. The ratio of workers to entry-level jobs paying wages as high as the poverty level in Illinois was yet higher (7:1), while there were estimated to be between thirty-three and two hundred abd twenty-two job seekers for every entry-level job paying a "livable wage."

34. There is now a broad consensus on this issue, extending of course to those advocates of reform who emphasize the role of welfare-to-work programs in dissipating inflationary tendencies (read: suppressing wages). For

commentary, see Shankman (1995) Theodore (1995), Tilly (1996), Bernstein (1997), Kleppner and Theodore (1997), Solow (1998), and Peck and Theodore (2000).

35. Federal Document Clearing House Congressional Testimony, March 15, 1994, Judith M. Gueron, House Ways and Means/Human Resources Welfare Revision; Federal Document Clearing House Congressional Testimony, January 18, 1995, Mark Greenberg, House Economic and Education Opportunities Committee, Welfare Revision.

36. Senior executive #1, Riverside DPSS, interviewed by Jamie Peck, October 1995.

37. Federal Document Clearing House Congressional Testimony, January 18, 1995, Mark Greenberg, House Economic and Education Opportunities Committee, Welfare Revision.

38. Senior manager, Alameda GAIN program, interviewed by Jamie Peck, December 1995.

39. Senior executive #2, Riverside DPSS, interviewed by Jamie Peck, October 1995.

40. Senior manager #2, GAIN program, State of California, interviewed by Jamie Peck, December 1995.

41. Senior manager #1, GAIN program, State of California, interviewed by Jamie Peck, December 1995.

42. Senior program evaluator #1, MDRC, interviewed by Jamie Peck, November 1995.

43. Senior executive #1, Riverside DPSS, interviewed by Jamie Peck, October 1995.

44. Senior manager, Alameda GAIN program, interviewed by Jamie Peck, December 1995.

45. He continued: "In a key compromise we accepted in order to enact the legislation, a provision was added that basic education ... would be provided to people who needed this training before they had to seek work. It was estimated that 20 percent of GAIN registrants would need such education. Instead, since the program began in 1986, more than 60 percent of GAIN registrants, including some who would prefer to work, are being identified as needing basic education, rather than being placed in the job market. This is the primary reason that the program is costing much more than expected."

46. See, among many, Porter (1990), Handler (1995), Department of Labor (1995), Brown (1997), and Handler and Hasenfeld (1997).

47. Quoted in *Omaha World Herald*, September 22, 1995.

48. Federal Document Clearing House Congressional Testimony, August 9, 1994, Eloise Anderson, House Ways and Means/Human Resources Welfare Revision (emphasis added).

49. Federal Document Clearing House Congressional Testimony, January 19, 1995, Michael Genest, House Economic and Educational Opportunity Committee, Subcommittee on Post Secondary Education, Training and Lifelong Learning.

50. Federal Document Clearing House Congressional Testimony, February

28, 1995, Judith M. Gueron, Labor Impact of Welfare Revisions, U.S. Senate Committee on Labor and Human Resources.

51. Federal Document Clearing House Congressional Testimony, February 28, 1995, Judith M. Gueron, Labor Impact of Welfare Revisions, U.S. Senate Committee on Labor and Human Resources.

52. Federal Document Clearing House Congressional Testimony, March 9, 1995, Lawrence M. Mead, Senate Finance Welfare Revision (emphasis added).

53. Federal Document Clearing House Congressional Testimony, March 9, 1995, Lawrence M. Mead, Senate Finance Welfare Revision.

54. Senior official, Maryland welfare administration, interviewed by Jamie Peck, July 1996.

55. Senior welfare administrator, New Jersey, interviewed by Jamie Peck, April 1996.

56. Senior research manager, HHS, Washington, DC, interviewed by Jamie Peck, December 1995.

57. Senior research manager, HHS, Washington, DC, interviewed by Jamie Peck, December 1995.

58. Evaluation researcher #3, MDRC, interviewed by Jamie Peck, November 1995.

59. Senior program evaluator #2, interviewed by Jamie Peck, November 1995.

60. Senior program evaluator #2, interviewed by Jamie Peck, November 1995.

61. Senior program evaluator #4, MDRC, interviewed by Jamie Peck, November 1995.

62. Some 13 per cent of Riverside's workforce is classified as "low skilled," compared to 9 percent for Los Angeles County and 7 percent for Orange County, while average hourly wage rates are $0.70 lower than in LA County.

63. Senior program evaluator and political adviser, Washington, DC, interviewed by Jamie Peck, June 1996.

64. Senior program evaluator #3, MDRC, interviewed by Jamie Peck, November 1995.

65. Senior executive #1, Riverside DPSS, interviewed by Jamie Peck, October 1995.

66. *San Francisco Chronicle*, January 24, 1995: A2; *MacNeil/Lehrer NewsHour*, August 1, 1995, transcript #5283.

67. Quoted in *Los Angeles Times*, April 26, 1993: A1.

68. Federal Document Clearing House Congressional Testimony, August 16 1994, Will Marshall, House Ways and Means/Human Resources Committees, Welfare Reform Revision: Limiting Cash Payments.

69. www.algore.com/briefingroom/releases/pr_102099_welfare-reform.

70. www.georgebush.com/speeches/newprosperity.

# PART III

# Echoes of Workfare

# CHAPTER SIX

# Canada's Path

## Permeable Welfare/
## Fragile Workfare

[The] world has changed faster than our programs. In the last decade especially, the sheer relentless force of technological, economic and social change has reshaped our lives and our livelihoods. Government policies and approaches have been too slow in responding. . . . The next generation of social programs must not just share wealth, and protect those who are disadvantaged among us, they must actively create opportunity for Canadians and, in so doing, help drive economic growth. . . . [The] key to dealing with social insecurity can be summed up in a single phrase: helping people get and keep jobs. . . . Increasingly our competitors are not the enterprises and workers down the street or in the next province, or even across the border, but those across the ocean. . . . To make the most of our future, we need more jobs. And that means pulling in more investment from inside Canada and abroad to create jobs. We need to be an investment magnet. Key to this is to overcome Canada's "skills deficit"—to offer the best-educated, best-trained workforce in the world, and that must be our common goal in the coming years. (HRD Canada, 1994a: 7–10)

"The status quo is not an option," a Canadian government discussion paper on the future of the country's social security system has insisted. "Changes in our economy, in our families, in our workplaces, in our communities, and in the financial standing of our country are too dramatic to allow us to tinker at the edges of social policy and programming" (HRD Canada, 1994a: 8–9). The report went on to assert that social policy and welfare reform, themselves rapidly melding into the ubiquitous discourse of an active labor-market policy, are increasingly subject to the imperatives of international competition. In terms of the social and labor-market policy agenda in Canada, workfarist refrains are becoming more and more commonplace, as Canadians are increasingly told that the welfare system is too generous, particularly in the context of international economic competition, while those who can work ought to be at work. Echoing the increasingly ubiquitous international discourse of welfare reform, there is talk of benefit dependency, the unsustainable cost of fraud, and the pressing need for systemic change. Yet these easy soundbites are considerably more difficult to translate into policy in the context of structural unemployment, weak growth, and continuing interjurisdictional tensions over appropriate roles within a reformed welfare/workfare system. While the political pressure for reform has become palpable in Canada, this has yet to be translated into a coherent program of welfare restructuring. The dominant direction of change is certainly workfarist, but a combination of ill-conceived reform strategies, federal–provincial disputes, and political opposition continues to check and constrain the reform process.[1]

This chapter examines Canada's distinctive path toward workfarism in the context of the protracted restructuring of the country's "work–welfare regime" (see King, 1995). Due to its particular institutional arrangements and political traditions, Canada has not followed the U.S. route toward workfare, one based on the parallel evolution of work-based social-policy programs and a fundamentalist political attack on welfarist principles, but instead has taken a rather different (not to say more complex) path. Canada's meandering path toward workfarism has been characterized by a series of multilateral policy shifts and drifts, in labor-market and training programming, in the employment-insurance regime, in the financial framework of the welfare system, and in experimentation with welfare-to-work schemes. In the process, provincial experimentation and federal reform have *jointly* served to advance a workfarist agenda, albeit in a lurching and intermittent fashion.

The shadow of U.S.-style workfare looms large here, though. Sherri Torjman (1998: 5) notes that "[a]ny social program that has its roots in the US tends to be viewed by many Canadians with suspicion, if not hostility," yet for all the institutional and cultural resistance to U.S.-style workfare in Canada, the message and the method seem to be spreading. Certainly, the form of workfare debates in Canada reflects the nature of Canadian politics, but these are increasingly penetrated by U.S. influences. U.S. programming terminology, and indeed even the inflammatory term "workfare" itself, now peppers Canadian policy discourse. The Canadian welfare system, it seems, is on the cusp of structural change.

## TOWARD CONTINENTAL WORKFARE?

For all the talk of globalization in Canada, much of the competition that the country faces is originating from just south of the border. And just as the North American Free Trade Agreement (NAFTA) has accelerated and deepened the process of economic continentalization, so also it seems that pressures are mounting for a "downward convergence" in social policy.[2] Indeed, Kreklewich (1993: 263) has argued that NAFTA "formally institutionalizes neoconservatism within the macroeconomy of North America." Despite the concerted cultural, institutional, and political resistance to "Americanization" in Canada, it is becoming clear that the United States is now the principal referent in terms of welfare reform (see Ralph et al., 1997). This does not mean that the two systems are converging in some uncomplicated fashion, though is does signal a shift in the prevailing ideological and practical bases of social-policy reform. Certainly, there is in Canada plenty of direct advocacy of U.S.-style programming, including workfare, but there are also robust debates around the risks inherent in workfarist strategies.[3] In one sense, the Canadian debate around workfare is more explicitly ideological and partisan than its contemporary U.S. counterpart, though as Evans (1995: 97) ominously notes, "the flavour of the workfare debate is similar to that which surrounded the US Family Support Act in 1988." Although Canadian debate has yet to take the kind of technocratic, almost postideological turn that occurred in the wake of the FSA, there are first signs that this is beginning to occur as the drift to workfarism intensifies. Also reminiscent of the United States, the Canadian welfare-reform debate reflects and expresses growing fears of urban social dislocation—often with a racial inflection:

> What can Canada learn from the United States about welfare and its reform? Some Canadians' instinctive response is likely to be "not much." For them, our more generous social programs fundamentally differentiate the two countries and make Canada's public policy unambiguously superior to that of the United States. . . . Probably our more generous social policies explain, in part, the absence in Canadian cities of large districts with the level of violent crime and social distress that exist in US urban ghettos. But—and it is a major but—comparisons such as these are dangerous. Their effect is to lull Canadians into parochial smugness. How many Canadians are aware that unemployment among aboriginals in western Canadian cities is as widespread as among US urban blacks and that the proportion of Canadian aboriginals living in cities has tripled over the past three decades? If Canadians want better policy to address aboriginal poverty, they are foolish to ignore the history—both the successes and the failures—of US

policies that have addressed similar problems of urban unemployment. (Richards and Vining, 1995: 1–2)

For all the mixed messages and serial underachievement of U.S. policy in this area, however, a familiar set of "lessons" must apparently still be taken on board. Here, the language and political practices of "scientific" evaluation threaten also to dislodge and defuse some of the acrimonious ideological debates around welfare reform in Canada. And even if the programs themselves do not appear to work, that apparently only underscores the need for more extensive and concerted experimentation. As Richards and Vining conclude:

> We think the workfare-training experiments appear promising. To some extent, they offer win–win outcomes: they raise the net earnings of participants and generate net savings for taxpayers. . . . We believe the US experience with welfare reform and its analysis are clearly relevant to the current Canadian social policy debate. Yet, as the Americans are the first to admit, much uncertainty remains over optimum program design . . . [as indicated by the] MDRC experimental evaluations. . . . In Canada, as in the United States, the need is for more experiments and rigorous evaluation and for fewer ideological battles. (26–27)

Workfare experiments continue to proliferate in Canada—not least in Ontario, where the ideological and political battles have, if anything, intensified. Concerted opposition to workfare has emerged in Toronto, though the resolve of reformers seems also to be hardening. Echoing some of the earlier U.S. incursions into workfare programming, local and provincial experiments remain highly politicized and often controversial, yet at the same time they have been shaping the terms of the debate. Advocates of progressive, expansionist, or developmental welfare meanwhile have been pushed onto the back foot. Moreover, the structural contexts of these debates has changed markedly over recent years, not least by virtue of the NAFTA-induced restructuring of the Canadian political economy and, in the field of social policy itself, the emerging "workfare consensus" at the international scale, especially among the G7 countries. But even if the structural context seems set for a transition toward workfare, this does not make the programs themselves easy to deliver, as the government of Ontario has conspicuously discovered.

## Provincial Workfarism

The Ontario Conservatives, elected in 1996, passed legislation based on a "plan to convert welfare to work" by way of mandatory workfare programming. The government's intention is to "restor[e] welfare to its original purpose: a transitional program of last resort to those truly in need, with a stepping stone back to work and independence" (Ministry of Community and Social Services, 1998: 1). Since its launch, however, the province's workfare program, Ontario Works (OW), has been mired in implementation problems. Its initial design relied on placements in community organizations, ironically the source of considerable opposition to the principles of workfare. Having been handed this opportunity to disrupt and delay the OW's implementation, social activists have mounted an effective campaign against what has been characterized as a "punitive and degrading vision of workfare" (Workfare Watch, 1996b: 1).

Yet it would seem that, in Ontario, at least, conservative elements in the media and the electorate have been convinced of the vision of workfare even as the practicalities remain unresolved. As the workfarist momentum builds, each successive implementation failure is greeted by a hardening of resolve rather than a rethinking of underlying principles. Drawing on parallels with the United States, and reminding its readers that "[w]orkfare is inspired by a different philosophy than Canada's traditional welfare system," the *Globe and Mail* editorialized along the lines that problems in the OW program were merely "fixable" design flaws, the solution to which lay with privatization:

> Welfare reform needs more flexibility and experimentation, not more bureaucracy. . . . [P]rivate-sector firms have not been given enough of a chance to act as placement agencies for program participants in the paid job market. Such companies, paid on the results they produce, have been a key element in the success of several schemes in the U.S. It will take years before we can say with confidence whether or not Ontario Works lives up to its name. That does not mean, however, that the program's obvious design flaws cannot be fixed, thereby increasing the chances that the ultimate verdict will be a favourable one. (*Globe and Mail*, July 31, 1998: A14)

And fixing "design flaws" in workfare programs invariably means looking south of the border. So as Williamson (1999: 13) rhetorically asks,

> The question is, should Ontario still look to Wisconsin as a model for its workfare program? It's hard to see why not. Sadly, in Ontario we're still stuck in the old philosophical fight over whether it's cruel to have people work for benefits. Maybe the U.S. experience is just a uniquely American quirk—something that would never happen here. . . . [But] we ignore the lessons of the most powerful economy on Earth— including the quirky ones—at our peril.

Prior to the Ontario experiment with workfare, Alberta and Quebec had been operating a number of pseudoworkfare schemes for several years (Reynolds, 1995; Murphy, 1997). Until 1996, extensive and explicit deployment of mandatory work programs was prohibited by federal law, a fact that restrained—though did not entirely prevent—workfare-style experimentation (NCW, 1997; Pulkingham and Ternowetsky, 1998). But the pressure for radical welfare reform had been building for some time at the provincial level, especially in Alberta, where the radical Conservative government of Ralph Klein (dubbed "Canada's Reagan") made the editorial pages of the *Wall Street Journal* on the strength of a gung-ho strategy of deregulated economic expansion and minimalist welfare (Fund, 1995). Alberta has sought to create "incentives to work" by cutting welfare payments (by 20 percent for a single person), and placing those that are unable to find paid employment in a range of workfare-style programs. The ostensible objective here has been to restore the principle of less eligibility: according to social services minister Mike Cardinal "Albertans can no longer afford social service programs which provide welfare recipients with a higher standard of living than that of working Albertans." His stated purpose, however, is "not to make welfare unbearable. . . . But it has to be uncomfortable enough that people will try to find an alternative way of living."[4] Correspondingly, the role of work programs was rationalized by ministers in the now-familiar, derogatory fashion: welfare recipients would have to learn how to get out of bed each day and how to maintain basic standards of personal hygiene. Again, these initiatives had more to do with the mythology of welfare dependency than real conditions in low-income communities, less still the real causes of poverty and unemployment. Even before the welfare cuts, for example, the provincial minimum wage (itself the second lowest in Canada) was 60 percent higher than the benefit level; after the cuts, it was 90 percent higher (Murphy, 1997). This hardly seems a case of high benefits impeding the operation of the labor market.

The Alberta reforms "worked" in the sense that the province's welfare rolls fell dramatically, partly aided by labor-market expansion but also assisted by outmigration to neighboring provinces. Such was the hostile reaction to the latter policy—which saw seven hundred Alberta families per month heading west in 1995—that the British Columbia government introduced a welfare-residency requirement in December 1995.[5] Alberta's welfare-reform policy, later to earn the ironic epithet *busfare*, was characterized by British Columbia premier Mike Harcourt as "give people tickets and point on the road map to British Columbia" (*Edmonton Journal*, November 25, 1995: A9). British Columbia's response to its newfound status as a "welfare magnet" was to attempt by way of a three-month residency requirement to build a "welfare wall" along the

Albertan border, but this contravention of the Canada Assistance Plan was later ruled illegal by the federal government, fueling further federal–provincial tensions in the field of welfare policy (*Economist*, May, 1995). Prior to the Conservative victory in Ontario in 1996, the Alberta regime clearly lay at the extreme fringe of social-policy reform in Canada. More recently, this kind of radical project has begun to define the dominant direction of change. After Thompson (1968), Denis interprets this as an authoritarian project dedicated to a root-and-branch restructuring of the "moral economy" of contemporary Canada, a state-authored offensive concerned to reimbue the fundamental values of self-sufficiency and work discipline. In Alberta, the strategy has been

> not only [to] eliminate the social programmes associated with the welfare state, but also [to] replace utterly the moral and material culture of the welfare state with an authoritarian culture of business competition. . . . It is not just public budgets that are being slashed—it is also a way of thinking, a cultural framework, that is being drilled into the heads of Albertans. . . . Seen from within the culture of hyperliberalism, cutbacks . . . are a positive good: welfare recipients—no less than offenders—had to be reformed, had to take responsibility for their own lives. By forcibly putting them on the road to recovery, the government shows all Albertans the way home . . . so that Alberta may become itself again. (Denis, 1995: 376, 380)

As Mike Cardinal has argued, "It's tough love, but we have no choice. Alberta's way is what has to happen all across the country" (*Financial Post*, June 24, 1995).

## Federal Workfarism?

Coupled with a shift to a more permissive federal regime after 1996, provincial reforms in Alberta, Ontario, and elsewhere have fueled an ascendant politics of workfare in Canada. By the mid-1990s, according to Monique Jérôme-Forget, president of the Institute for Research on Public Policy, " 'Workfare' "—the scare quotes are still in regular usage in Canada—"has emerged as a pivotal issue in the debate over income security reform" (1995: 3). When Prime Minster Crétien controversially announced in an interview at the end of 1993 that the unemployed should be enrolled in training programs or community projects if they want to continue to receive unemployment insurance or welfare payments (York, 1994), he was merely underlining his administration's support for what was fast becoming a mainstream, but muted, workfarist position. In fact, the origins of this newfound policy orthodoxy in Canada can be traced to the mid-1980s (Mitchell, 1990; Muszynski, 1985; McBride, 1992). Philp has observed that there is a "growing consensus that social programs must be reformed. . . . Foremost [here] is a change in thinking on unemployment insurance and welfare—a philosophical shift toward saying that for those who are able to work, financial assistance is not a right but a privilege to be earned" (1994: A1). This emerging hegemony was reaffirmed in the federal government's enthusiastic endorsement both of "active labor market policies that will help the unemployed to search more effectively for jobs and [of reforms designed to ensure that] social support systems create incentives to work" (G7 Jobs Summit communiqué, March 1994, quoted in HRD Canada, 1994a: 29).

Yet if there is an emergent workfare consensus in Canada, it is taking on a different form from its counterpart south of the border. Certainly, there has been a concerted "hardening" in federal and provincial attitudes toward welfare policy, as budget cuts coupled with the downloading of programs and responsibilities have been the prevailing pattern during the 1990s. These changes have seen successive federal governments "backing away from a leading role in social policy [as] Ottawa cut its spending for social programs to the bone and left provincial and territorial governments to cope with the problems dumped in their laps" (NCW, 1997: 1, 3). Certainly there are echoes of the U.S. debate, and of U.S. reform strategies, in the aggressive advocacy of "flexibility," "decentralization," and "local discretion" in welfare policymaking, moves that so often seem to accompany the erosion of welfare and the rise of workfare (see Torjman, 1997).

At the federal level, the abolition in 1996 of the Canada Assistance Plan (CAP), described by one well-traveled public servant as "the TransCanada highway of social welfare,"[6] and its replacement with a "block-funding" regime called the Canada Health and Social Transfer (CHST), terminated the principle of needs-based welfare provision while paving the way for further funding cuts. This critical reform also allowed provinces "to impose work-for-welfare programs and to disqualify certain groups from applying for welfare" (NCW, 1997: 4). More pointedly, "CHST now permits the institutionalization of 'workfare' " in Canada (Pulkingham and Ternowetsky, 1998: B6). It also erodes the fundamental federalist–welfarist principle of interregional income transfer (see Théret, 1999). Some hemmed in by their own financial problems, some politically predisposed against welfare anyway, provinces have responded by toughening their welfare regimes, rather than by seeking in any serious way to compensate for federal cutbacks. And in provinces like Ontario, this downloading dynamic has been accelerating, as the provincial government has sought to offload the costs of welfare/workfare to municipalities (see Torjman, 1997). The objective here is clear:

The programs which will be downloaded are ones where costs are likely to increase. . . . Workfare and downloading have a common starting point in federal policy. . . . [They] are essentially two parts of a program to push municipalities to undertake further cuts in welfare. Downloading saddles municipalities with unmanageable costs, creating pressures for setting standards and eligibility criteria for social assistance [at the local level]. Workfare provides an administrative mechanism which permits municipalities to cut people off assistance. (Workfare Watch, 1997: 2)

Following a familiar theme in workfare politics, many of these provincial and local-level restructuring initiatives have taken advantage of expanding labor markets in driving down welfare caseloads. In the longer term, however, the nature of the Canadian welfare caseload appears to present some severe structural challenges to workfare strategies because it tends to be dominated by the unemployed, usually accounting for more than half the caseload, and people with disabilities, who account for around one-fourth (NCW, 1998). Moreover, welfare has been playing an increasingly important role in the labor-market coping strategies of displaced workers, as eligibility for Employment Insurance (EI, formerly Unemployment Insurance, or UI) has declined, ironically, as a result of shortening job tenures, increased economic insecurity, and the growth of contingent employment. The residualization and localization of welfare is consequently occurring within an economic environment that may be favorable in the short term, but which in the longer term is riven with tensions and contradictions.

A similar point might be made about the political environment in Canada, where there is a long history of federal–provincial and interprovincial struggle over legislative, regulatory, and financial responsibilities in social and labor-market policy. In terms of welfare provisions, just as the generally expansionist momentum from the 1960s onward was associated with tendential federalization, so the emergence of workfarist politics has coincided with strong and growing pressures for defederalization and downloading. Yet in this and other ways, while it is clear that the Canadian experience exhibits certain similarities with U.S. welfare/workfare politics, the trajectory has been distinctive. If fully fledged workfarism is the future in Canada, it is a future that has yet to arrive. At present, it is more appropriate to view workfarism as a prevailing political dynamic rather than as a functioning alternative regulatory system, because in Canada workfarist politics remain as concerned with the deconstruction of the extant welfare regime as with its reconstruction (see Sayeed, 1995; Richards et al., 1995). One might expect that workfarist dynamics will intensify under these conditions, as they have done in the United States, but it would be wrong to regard Canada as simply "lagging" behind the United States in this (or other) respects. Rather, welfare/workfare politics are taking their own course in Canada, being shaped perhaps above all by the institutional and political character of the country's federal settlement and, more generally, by the nature of its political and economic relations with the United States.

As Noël (1995) emphasizes, the particular shape that workfare takes in Canada, as it does elsewhere, tends to reflect the political traditions and institutional legacies inherited from the welfare-state era. In the Canadian case, this means that the politics of workfare are complex, emerging as they have done from a "hybrid" welfare-state model that combines United States-style market liberalism with elements of European-style conservatism and social democracy:

> Essentially liberal, the Canadian welfare state gives priority to market mechanisms, especially for the provision of income security. At the same time, Canadian institutions embody elements of the universalism typical of social democratic welfare states, as well as a few conservative features. Social protections less related to the labour market, in particular, can be met with social democratic, universal programs— health care and education, for example. In income security, there are also conservative elements: the family, for instance, is often privileged. Overall, however, labour-market failures are compensated by insurance or means-tested programs. This reliance on liberal solutions for labour market issues means that Canadian debates on workfare are likely to be liberal debates. (Noël, 1995: 58)

More generally, the particular manifestation of workfarism in Canada can be seen to reflect the political–economic regime of "permeable Fordism" that underpinned the country's development path during the postwar period (Jenson, 1989). As Théret (1999: 493) observes, in contrast to the United States, Canada "gradually equipped itself with a developed welfare state that has had major redistributive effects at both the inter-individual and the interregional level." And just as Canada's permeable Fordism was structured around the institutions and relations of federalism, so its experience of workfarism is being structured by this legacy. It is now becoming clear that a potentially far-reaching spatial reconstitution of Canada's work–welfare regime is underway, as welfarism is being decentered both politically and institutionally.

## PERMEABLE FORDISM AND PERMEABLE WELFARE

Canada's postwar growth regime, characterized by Jenson (1989) as "permeable Fordism" was distinctive in both political and economic terms.

The country's unique experience of Fordism—defined generically as an institutionally mediated coupling of mass consumption and mass production on the one hand, and Keynesian welfare regulation on the other—was a reflection both of its particular political–economic legacy and its unique mode of insertion into the global economy. More specifically, the dominating economic and political presence of the United States had fundamental effects both on the orientation of Canada's economy and the structure of its state. As Jenson (1989: 78) puts it, Canada's Fordism "was designed domestically but always with an eye to the continental economy." This variant of Fordism was "permeable" in the sense that international—and more particularly, continental—relations profoundly structured the country's development path and the structure of its accumulation system. This was also reflected in Canada's distinctive pattern of social regulation.[7] In contrast to the majority of Atlantic Fordist countries, Canada's permeable Fordism was not inscribed in social democratic, corporatist, or partisan institutions. Instead, the wage relation remained substantially privatized, while the class compromise came to be mediated through the institutions of federalism and the ideological project of nation building:

> The social compromise . . . which institutionalized fordism depended less on partisan politics than on federal–provincial negotiations. No class compromise was organized in the party system between left and right parties; its crucial ideological underpinning lay elsewhere. Nor was it a fordism in which the state gained a determinant role. Canada's permeable fordism was based on a discourse of nation-building, and social justice through nation-building was the primary theme. (Jenson, 1990: 662)

While the Canadian state deployed Keynesian strategies of macroeconomic management, these were not immediately coupled with the extensive development of welfare functions. Again, relations with the United States were to play an important role in shaping state structures and strategies. In particular, the pattern of labor regulation in Canada was strongly influenced by U.S. industrial relations and labor-market practices (Wolfe, 1989; Mahon, 1991), though the late-developing system of welfare-entitlement programs was more generous than its U.S. counterpart (O'Connor, 1989). It was only in the 1960s, in fact, that spending on social programs began to rise significantly, as public-sector employment was expanded, and as welfare entitlements were standardized on a national basis. The landmark legislation of this period was the Canada Assistance Plan (CAP), which extended welfare entitlements to all those deemed "in need," while technically outlawing mandatory workfare programs (Hum, 1983; Lightman, 1991).

Within certainly federally defined parameters, the costs of the almost open-ended commitment to welfare that were enshrined in the CAP were to be shouldered jointly by the federal government and the provinces. This further contributed to what was already becoming a complex pattern of "jurisdictional entanglement" (McBride, 1994) around work–welfare responsibilities and functions in Canada.[8] At the same time, the institutions of federalism acted as the displaced nexus of the Canadian class compromise and the repository of the contradictions of labor regulation under permeable Fordism (Jenson, 1990). While unemployment insurance had been a federal responsibility since the Second World War, labor-market programs, workforce preparation, and job training have emerged not so much as shared as contested policy domains. According to McBride's assessment, "federal–provincial conflict in these areas has been quite intractable" (1994: 268).

## From Crisis to Federalization

Behind these conflictual federal–provincial relations lay a deeper set of contradictions relating to the uneven spatial development of the Canadian social formation. "The lottery of resource distribution and the effects of industrialization via branch plants," Jenson (1990: 670–671) has argued, "mapped a regional cleavage into the heart of the Canadian working class and recreated, through time, a framework which interpreted class through the lens of region." This, in turn, is reflected in a spatialized politics of representation, which Jenson refers to as a "space-sensitive societal paradigm." Real and perceived differences in political–economic interests have subsequently placed continuous strain on federal–provincial and provincial–municipal relations, while contributing to the fragility of the nation-building process. The crisis politics of the 1930s depression forged the political contours of the permeable Fordist era in general and structured the spatial constitution of the work–welfare regime in particular. In the context of burgeoning demand for poor relief, the 1930s witnessed a failed attempt to federalize the system of unemployment insurance, foundering on a declaration of *ultra vires* by the Judicial Committee of the Privy Council anxious to defend provincial jurisdictions in the face of what was seen as creeping federalism. Given that provincial governments had previously devolved much of the responsibility for relief to municipalities, the costs of widespread unemployment and poverty quickly accumulated in the form of municipal debt (Rea, 1985; Banting, 1987). This was subsequently to trigger a "Relief from Relief" movement on the part of overburdened municipal governments (Taylor, 1987).

The uneven development of the work–welfare regime in Canada

during the depression years consequently contributed to the mounting political and fiscal pressures for federalization. The devolution of welfare commitments to the municipal level, coupled with large-scale and regionally concentrated unemployment, "completely unbalanced fiscal capacity within the Canadian federal system . . . and this general imbalance was exacerbated by the regional incidence of welfare needs" (Banting, 1987: 62). It became imperative that the resolution to the crisis took account of the weak fiscal capacity of the poorer provinces and municipalities. The strategy adopted was a "massive centralization of responsibility for income security" (Banting, 1987: 63), one that reinforced the emerging ideologies of nation building and Keynesianism during and after the Second World War. The institutional and fiscal foundations for this process had been laid by the 1937 Royal Commission on Dominion–Provincial Relations (the Rowell–Sirois Commission) which advocated a thoroughgoing reform of federal and interprovincial relationships through the introduction of a system of "equalization" transfers between the provinces. The commission "attempted in its fiscal proposal to provide both for a more equitable distribution of governmental burdens and social service benefits throughout Canada and to make possible a revenue system and fiscal policy designed to stimulate rather than depress the national income" (Rowell–Sirois Report, quoted in Yalnizyan, 1994: 68).

The growing influence of Keynesianism and the associated centralization of regulatory responsibilities brought about a transformation in the work–welfare regime: from the principles of means-tested "relief" to those of social insurance and universal entitlement (Rice, 1985). The commission's intention was clear: to regulate federal–provincial relations in such a way as to secure the basis for wages and welfare standards to be ratcheted upward from a newly constituted national "floor." An imperative for the commission was the leveling out of taxation rates (and social-service standards) between the provinces in order to ameliorate the tendency for mobile capital to flow to low-cost, low-tax locations. This, of course, would have had the effect of destabilizing provincial finances, while engendering a downward drag on wages and welfare.[9] The federalization of the Canadian work–welfare regime in the 1940s placed a brake on this process, underwriting a leveling out of social and welfare standards between the provinces and accounting for a growing proportion of the social wage (see Bakker, 1991; Cohen, 1991). The significant and growing role of federal dollars in this can be illustrated by the case of Ontario. Here, overall spending on welfare (including UI, family allowances, and old-age security) increased in real terms from Cdn$54 per capita in 1948 to $205 per capita in 1971, while the effective federal share of this expenditure rose from 84 percent to 92 percent over the same period (Rea, 1985).

## From Crisis to Defederalization

Just as the institutions of federalism—and the associated complex of federal–provincial–municipal relations—were central to the construction of Canada's work–welfare regime, so also they have been deeply implicated in its deconstruction. Reforms of the UI system in the mid-1970s authorized the switching of UI funds into active labor-market programs, such as job training (Pal, 1983). In general, however, most attempts to reorganize the welfare system during the 1970s became mired in federal–provincial wrangles. The momentum of reform gathered in the 1980s, as monetarist-inspired critiques of the UI regime, first from a UI Task Force (in 1981), then from the Macdonald Commission (in 1985), and finally from the Forget Commission (in 1986), attacked the system for inhibiting labor-market flexibility and geographical mobility (see McBride, 1992). A focus of attention for all three reviews was the functioning of the UI system in regions afflicted by structural unemployment and underemployment, where UI was seen to be impeding labor-market efficiency and adjustment. Regional variations in the form and functions of UI, of course, followed from the federal commitment to fund the system according to demand, but were subsequently bolstered by a series of enhancements to the program designed to aid lagging regions. In addition to the "stabilizer" effect of welfare spending, which flowed automatically to those individuals, and therefore those regions, which met federal standards of need, certain forms of semipermanent supplementary provision—such as fishermen's benefits—were also put in place for lagging regions. Thus, to question the role of UI in regions of chronic unemployment was to question a fundamental welfarist and indeed federalist principle: as Kerans (1990: 55) saw it, "To attack regional variations in the Canadian UI program [in the manner of the Macdonald and Forget Commissions] is to attack the Canadian welfare state at its heart."

Ultimately, Forget and Macdonald were unsuccessful in their attempts to reform the UI system, as the federal government bowed to "tremendous counter-pressures from affected provinces, regions, unions, employers, and social advocacy groups" (Pal, 1988a: 11). Despite the significance of this tactical victory, it was perhaps premature to conclude, as Pal did, that the system of UI "is now so deeply embedded and widely embedded in the Canadian political economy that fundamental change would seem virtually impossible" (11). In fact, Forget and Macdonald were to play a pivotal role in shifting the ideological climate around Canada's work–welfare regime, establishing as they did the main tenets of a tenacious neoliberal critique of the program (Kerans, 1990; McBride, 1992). As Banting observed, despite the fact that "the political sensitivity of the [Forget] program may well doom such ideas in perpetuity . . . they had come to constitute the established agenda among policy planners by the mid-1980s" (1987: 191).

The center of political gravity around work–welfare issues had consequently shifted as neoliberal doctrines became more prevalent. In Canada, as elsewhere, this has been associated with an essentially behaviorist explanation of unemployment and its supposed solutions. As Lightman (1995: 177) sees it, "Policymakers' focus on the supply of, rather than the demand for, labor seems to place responsibility for unemployment on lazy individuals, rather than on a sick economy." Thus, the emerging workfare consensus in Canada emphasizes the need to create "incentives to work" as a means of combating "welfare dependency," along with its supposedly debilitating moral and economic side effects.[10] The workfare offensive has also taken on a regionalized form. In 1990, the federal share of funding for UI was withdrawn, transferring the costs of regional extend benefits and fishermen's benefits to premium payers—to employers and employees—thus abdicating responsibility for regional and structural imbalances in unemployment and economic well-being (see CLMPC, 1994a; Rutherford, 1996b). The 1990 reform also expanded the role of "developmental uses" of UI in active labor-market programs, job training, and worker mobility, while withdrawing direct federal funding for these activities (see CLFDB, 1993; HRD Canada 1994b). Workfarist reforms have been strongly encouraged in lagging regions, following the federal government's desire to bring about

> change in the UI system so it is tilted towards more active job training and away from simply passive income support. . . . The government wants to engage the provinces on this issue of income support and is willing to try a number of experiments, particularly in regions of the country—such as Atlantic Canada—where dependency on government is so pervasive and economic development is lagging. (Toulin, 1994: 17)

Just as federalization proceeded hand in hand with the expansion of welfare during the era of permeable Fordism, so the critique and restructuring of the work–welfare regime since the mid-1980s has been associated with "rising tensions between federal and provincial programs" (Banting, 1987: 82; see also Muszynski, 1985; Rice, 1985). And as the momentum of the workfarist movement has gathered, so too has the federal settlement been brought increasingly into question. The implications of this situation go far beyond the concerns of welfare reform, and strike at the heart of the postwar growth paradigm and its associated mode of regulation: "The crisis of fordism in Canada, given the particularities of the fordist paradigm, is, then, a crisis of the political arrangements of federalism" (Jenson, 1989: 69). Or as Rutherford puts it, if Canada's permeable Fordism was an "institutional renegotiation of federalism . . . its crisis in the labour market is expressed in a decentralization of labour market responsibilities" (1996b: 34).

## Toward Local Workfare

The process of "decentralization" in the Canadian work–welfare regime has been an uneven and institutionally variegated one, involving a range of developments from the localization of delivery systems to the handing down of un- or underfunded federal mandates, from the renegotiation of shared federal–provincial fiscal responsibilities to the orchestration of provincial and local experimentation in policy systems and governance structures.[11] For example, the 1994 social security review posed the problem in the following way:

> Social security reform requires going beyond the content of policies and programs to find ways to modernize how they are managed and delivered. . . . If there is one feature of Canadian politics that most people are tired of, it is the constant tug of war between federal and provincial governments over questions of jurisdiction. . . . This situation can and must change. . . . The provinces and territories, local communities and private groups have undertaken many innovations over recent years in searching for better ways to deal with long-standing social problems. Such experimentation must continue to flourish. (HRD Canada, 1994a: 26–27)

Workfarist experiments—involving mandatory participation in training or employment programs—have been underway for some time in New Brunswick, Newfoundland, British Columbia, Saskatchewan, Alberta, and Quebec (NAPO, 1989, 1995; NCW, 1997). Lightman's view at the beginning of the 1990s was that the CAP had "prevented widespread experimentation with mandatory work-for-welfare . . . [while] those programs which have occurred are hard to document, poorly evaluated, and generally of minimal impact" (1991: 133). Yet while the latter observation may still be true, it did not prevent the proliferation of workfare experiments in Canada, even prior to the abolition of CAP. Although workfare programs continue to yield no more than modest results in terms of successfully (and sustainably) moving people from welfare to work, their symbolic and ideological significance can hardly be overstated. Of course, this is the terrain on which the case for workfare is typically advanced, as this case "has more to do with values, norms, and ideology than with any rational or empirical assessment of cost, investment in human capital, work, productivity, or employability" (Lightman, 1995: 153).

As a potent political mantra, workfare has come to define one of the central terrains of struggle around the crisis-ridden work–welfare regime in Canada. Advocating the benefits of training and the value of hard work, as if deficiencies in these areas were somehow the cause of Canada's structural economic problems, have become the means by which the ideological attack on the welfare state and its underlying principles are waged. There has been a great deal of advocacy of active labor-market programs, but for the most part this signifies no more than a shallow and underfunded form of supply-sidism in training policy, coupled with work-oriented welfare reform. In this context, provincial governments have been deploying workfarist rhetoric as a kind of neoliberal figleaf for an (underresourced) active labor-market policy. One reason these policies have achieved little in practice is that structural weaknesses in Canadian labor markets have remained largely unresolved (see Betcherman, 1996; Rutherford, 1996b). Blaming the victims of unemployment may be feasible as a short-term political strategy, but it is manifestly flawed as a functional labor-market policy.

> Rather than spending the bulk of their efforts on labour market policies which would lead to more jobs and better jobs for more people in the population at large, most governments confine themselves to trying to get able-bodied people on welfare into jobs that do not exist. When all else fails, they come up with euphemisms for welfare programs built around words like "opportunity" and "independence" or call out the fraud squads to exaggerate the surprisingly small amount of cheating in the system. . . . *The stark reality is that welfare reform without job creation simply does not work.* That reality applies to all governments in Canada, regardless of their political or ideological views and regardless of the types of programs they are promoting. It applies as much to extreme measures such as workfare as it does to moderate measures such as training and career counselling. (NCW, 1997: 110–111, emphasis added)

Yet the supply-side drift in Canadian policy continues unabated, more often than not now accompanied by harder edged workfare programming. As New Brunswick premier Frank McKenna explained: "I have this absolutely dominating belief that in this chicken-and-egg conundrum of whether you should have jobs or training first, the answer is that you need the training first. If you have the training, the jobs will take care of themselves" (*Globe and Mail*, January 16, 1993). Subsequently, however, the New Brunswick government was attacked for running the "stingiest social assistance program in Canada [while] vowing to show the country how to get people off the welfare rolls" (*Globe and Mail*, February 12, 1994). The introduction of a new workfare program, NB Works, coupled with a tightening of benefit rules, left "[m]any assistance recipients . . . balking at participating in programs because they fear the jobs do not exist and they do not want to do menial tasks so that they can continue to receive benefits" (*Globe and Mail*, February 12, 1994). The reality of programs like NB Works is that they deflect attention away from structural weaknesses located on the demand side of the economy by individualizing the problem of unemployment both in discursive and administrative terms (see Mullaly, 1997). Yet clearly, deflecting attention from problems is not the same *as solving* them.

While as recently as 1991 federal Conservatives rejected the notion of mandatory workfare as an electoral liability (Taylor, 1995), such has been the change in Canada's political climate that similar proposals now strike a positive chord with the current Liberal administration. So Professor Judith Maxwell, then chair of the Economic Council of Canada, hardly caused a stir when she asserted that "no Canadian under the age of 25 should be eligible for unemployment assistance," proposing the formation of a "job corps" for unemployed young people on the grounds that "[w]e shouldn't be paying them to be idle when they are in their formative stages" (quoted in Philp, 1994: A4). Perhaps a little militaristic for federal government tastes, this proposal did not make much headway. Instead, the federal HRD minister, Lloyd Axworthy's preference was for an incentives-based program: "Here's your choice: If you don't want to continue in school or work as an apprentice or an intern or in an on-the-job training program, or do full-time community-service work, if you want to go skiing, that's your business. But there will be no income security for you" (quoted in Philp, 1994: A4).

In this fashion, the dynamics of workfare politics are being worked out through the institutions of federalism, as federal and provincial governments each chide one another into taking yet more radical steps. In a parallel to the U.S. situation, the dialectics of reform are working themselves out *across* the federal/provincial divide. The federal government's UI reform package significantly reduced funding for the program, committing half of the "savings" to premium cuts while channeling some of the remainder into welfare-to-work initiatives. The general pattern has been for the negotiated devolution of responsibilities in labor-market policy, and in training and welfare-to-work programming, but the federal government has also at times advocated the radical decentralization of delivery systems to the local level. One proposal involved the establishment of "employment kiosks" in order to bring employment and training services to locations such as shopping malls. Apparently oblivious to such instances of administrative gimmickry masquerading as substantive reform, some were to draw historical parallels with the nation-building (and welfare-building) efforts of the Pearson administration: "Scaling down the welfare state to function at the civic level might seem a less inspiring task than Pearson's creation of grand national systems. There may never be statues on Parliament Hill to those who oversee such a transition. A modest bust in some town square, just across from the employment kiosk, might be more appropriate" (Geddes, 1995: 19).

More substantially, the transformation of UI to *Employment* Insurance has been accompanied by a significant individualization of labor-market risks, as EI eligibility has dwindled, as benefit levels have been cut, and as reliance on welfare—as the program of last resort—has increased. While 88 percent of unemployed workers received insurance-based benefits through UI in 1990, this had fallen to 43 percent in 1997 (NCW, 1997). This is increasing the strain on provincial welfare programs: UI reforms pushed 30,000 workers from the insurance system to the welfare system in Quebec between 1990 and 1994, while in Ontario less than 30 percent of unemployed people received EI in 1997, compared to 65 percent at the start of the previous recession in the province (Government of Quebec, 1996; Workfare Watch, 1997).

It is consequently important to recognize that while provincial governments vie to seize the political initiative on work–welfare reform—most notably under the Progressive Conservative regimes in Alberta and Ontario—the parameters of the restructuring process and the direction of change itself continue to be defined, at least in part, at the federal level. This is no straightforward process of the devolution of power—or, for that matter, a simple transition from federal welfare to provincial workfare—but in fact involves the reconstitution of federal–provincial relations and the adoption of discourses of flexibility and decentering. To take one example, the 1994 federal budget announced a new program for the support of innovative approaches to work–welfare reform, to be developed in "partnership" with the provinces and territories, and focusing on:

- exploring ways to help people move from welfare to work;
- testing new options for reform in training and learning, income security and social services;
- finding more cost-effective approaches to labour market programming. (HRD Canada, 1994a: 26)

The federal government also "invited" provinces and territories to enter into three-year Labour Force Development Agreements with a view to "harmonizing services at the local level" (HRD Canada, 1994a: 40). This triggered ongoing negotiations around the devolution and territorial restructuring of a range of work–welfare policy functions such as:

- strategic planning for employment development services, including institutional, project-based, and workplace training;
- managing the purchase of institutional training;
- planning and implementing a network of "single window" offices, bringing together unemployment insurance, training, welfare, and other labour market programmes;
- managing a range of other federal programmes, such as Canada Employment Centres and co-operative education. (HRD Canada, 1994a: 40; see also CLMPC, 1994b; Sharpe and Haddow, 1997)

Clearly the intent has been that a federally orchestrated process of local work–welfare experimentation will play a part in levering wider regulatory and policy reform. As Dehli (1993) has explained, such local "stories" of labor regulation often acquire a discursive resonance as they are taken up into wider debates around (alternatives in) labor-market policy. It would be quite wrong, then, to dismiss local work–welfare experiments as *merely* local experiments. Self-evidently, they have material effects on "local people," but more broadly, they open up the political and institutional space for extralocal change. Still sensitive about U.S. imports, especially in highly charged fields like social policy, Canadian governments have set about the task of growing their own welfare-to-work programs.

## Local Policy Knowledges and Regulatory Reform

An important feature of workfarist experimentation, and one that is quite clearly evident in Canada as it has been for some time in the United States, is the manner in which local programming and local-level reforms are self-consciously deployed with a view to influencing the wider reform agenda. Irrespective of whether these have been cultivated and funded by extralocal agencies (as many in fact have), "local" policy knowledges tend to acquire a powerful discursive resonance in reform debates. Almost irrespective of their substantive nature, they tend to carry with them the *feel* of "grounded," practical experience and of "bottom-up" policy development; they present a means of challenging philosophical, ethical, and theoretical opposition by way of the assertion of "real-world" empirical understanding. This is certainly one of the reasons why local "models" and policy ideas have been so effective in framing, channeling, and levering wider regulatory reform, even if in a conveniently circular fashion they are merely confirming and concretizing the predispositions of national policymakers (see Theodore and Peck, 1999). Local policy knowledges, as Dehli explains in the Canadian context, consequently perform "a particular kind of epistemological and political work, creating rationales for changes in labour market policy formation, and in modes of regulating education and training for future and incumbent workers" (1993: 106). This is how contemporary shifts toward "local flexibility," "experimentation," and "performance incentives" in the Canadian work–welfare regime should be understood. They are being deployed deliberately as a means of leveraging regulatory reform, to widen the repertoire of concrete reform strategies, and simultaneously to "feed" and animate the reform movement. The federal orchestration of local regime competition, and the permissive attitude toward growing spatial differentiation in welfare rights and workfare requirements that has accompanied this, is consequently playing a role in the "presystemic" drift toward workfarism in Canada. In this context, political and cultural resistance to Americanization in Canada may in a paradoxical fashion be facilitating the shift to workfarism at the same time as it acts as a brake on continental policy transfer, as the difficulties associated with importing "off-the-shelf" imported models mean that added impetus is given to the cultivation of "homegrown" *local* models of workfare.

Moreover, this increasingly insistent search for "local solutions" is reinforcing the drift toward defederalization. Just as an upward regulatory ratchet operated through the underwriting of provincial fiscal capabilities during the welfarist era, so the downward ratchet of the ensuing crisis period is associated with the centrally orchestrated erosion of the work–welfare regime from beneath. If the Canadian accumulation system has been characterized by its permeability "from above," given its subordination to continental imperatives, then the unfolding crisis of the Canadian welfare state can perhaps be viewed in terms of permeability "from below," as institutional structures and systems of entitlement are systematically eroded and restructured at the local and provincial scales. In more specific institutional terms, Lightman has explained how the CAP imposed a "heavy restraining influence" on provincial work–welfare reform not so much by federal diktat and prohibition, but through the establishment of regulatory and fiscal incentives and disincentives: "to designate certain benefits shareable [in financial terms] not only encourages the province to head in those directions but also necessarily impedes (and almost precludes) non-shareable activities" (1991: 134). Previously ineligible for federal shared-cost support, mandatory workfare schemes were consequently effectively barred under the CAP. With the abolition of CAP and the institution of block funding under CHST, this incentive structure is all but inverted, especially where work programming serves to meet the shared federal–provincial imperative to reduce deficits by reducing welfare rolls.

The simultaneous rise of "deficitist" politics and workfarist strategies was more than coincidental: scaremongering around the former has legitimated decisive action in the latter, as the "Common Sense Revolution" of the Harris regime in Ontario illustrates all too clearly:

> Under the pretext that crisis is fraught with urgency, Harris implicitly argued that there was no time for delay, for protracted discussion, analysis and all those "nasty" habits of a professional and intellectual elite, which he deemed both plaintive and ineffectual. With the ideology of deficitism at hand, he could readily dismiss the voices of discontent (those "special interest groups"), and judge their claims as self-indulgent. . . . Harris's denunciation of the welfare recipient as a social "other" served as a receptacle in which to eliminate all doubts, interrogations, and contestations of his policies. Fanning the resentments of the middle class against that most hated of government practices—heavy taxation—Harris solidified a prejudice against the welfare state and its recipients using this antipathy as yet another commonsensical argument against his critics. (Weinroth, 1997: 65–66)

Continuing concerns about cost control, however, raise one of the fundamental contradictions of workfarism: while radical workfare programming certainly speaks to the (self-imposed) demand for urgent, decisive action, the policy itself is invariably very costly to implement. This has certainly permeated the policy debate in Canada, where the U.S. experience has been cited as evidence that the annual per capita cost of workfare programs is between US$1,000 and $7,000 higher than that of "passive" income support (Valpy, 1995; see also Simpson, 1995; Pulkingham and Ternowetsky, 1998). While in some circumstances this kind of argument might undermine the case for workfare, it has also been playing a role in shaping the course of "intraworkfare" politics in the sense that it is one of the justifications used for moving toward LFA strategies and away from more service-intensive HCD approaches. While the latter previously found favor in Canada, reflecting the tradition of modest but not insignificant governmental involvement in the provision and funding of training programs (see Rutherford, 1996a; Sharpe and Haddow, 1997), they have been criticized by business lobby groups for their high costs and because program outcomes tend neither to be predictable nor immediate (Cook, 1995).

While a labor-force-attachment model may gain support due to its lower cost structure, the narrow basis on which such costs are calculated suggests that this path, too, is likely to be problematic. "Savings" on welfare costs, calculated on the basis of simply moving people off welfare, do not take account of externalities associated with working poverty or—yet worse—with complete loss of income (where claimants are simply sanctioned off welfare due to some administrative misdemeanor without a job to enter). Welfare "savings" may consequently become simply displaced as "new" costs in the form of increased homelessness, ill health, criminality, or foster care. HCD models of welfare-to-work are politically vulnerable as these costs tend to be "internalized" within programs themselves, not least because participants tend to spend longer periods of time on HCD as opposed to LFA programs, but also because some of the more service-rich HCD strategies seek explicitly to tackle a range of barriers to employment (Peck and Theodore, 1998). In putting participants straight to work as rapidly as possible, LFA methods effectively externalize these costs as far as workfare administrations are concerned, though they are costs that are likely to manifest themselves in other ways, often in other arms of the state apparatus. Although there are those who continue to advocate HCD-style approaches in Canada (see Torjman, 1996, 1998), the general drift of policy is toward low-cost, market-oriented provision, which for all its flaws is perhaps better suited to the prevailing (neoliberalized) political–economic context. Crucially, this shift has been compounded and legitimated by improving labor-market conditions—as employment growth has occurred, so short-term strategies like LFA programs yield rapid results (in terms of welfare deregistration), while keeping costs down.

So, workfare strategies do not simply present "internal" problems for the state; they are critically dependent on "external" economic conditions. Those programs that appear to "work"—in the sense that their introduction happens to coincide with falling welfare rolls—tend to do so in the context of relatively buoyant regional labor markets. Welfare-to-work strategies do not work where there is a shortage of work. Just as Riverside's effectiveness was predicated on churning in its low-wage labor market, so Alberta's program was judged a "success" because the province enjoyed a burst of job growth at precisely the time its government sought to "incentivize work," while Quebec's workfare strategy foundered on a sluggish labor market.[12] For critics such as NAPO president Jean Swanson, this reveals the reality that "workfare is a cheap-labour strategy, a strategy that won't create jobs . . . [but] will reduce wages and working conditions of people who already have jobs" (*Globe and Mail*, June 10, 1995: D7). As Alberta's social services minister has conceded, workfare programs are no panacea, but have a role to play in driving welfare recipients into jobs under certain labor-market conditions:

> Welfare is not the best way of dealing with poverty and unemployment. Workfare is not the best alternative either, but it's a better one than paying people to do nothing at home. We may always need a jobs corps [workfare] program because there will be pockets in the province that just won't have the jobs that are needed. Workfare is a cush-

ion. We don't have money to pay young, healthy people to do nothing when we have deficits and need to help those who truly need it. We must get everyone working who can work. (Mike Cardinal, quoted in *Financial Post*, June 24, 1995: 19)

Here, workfare programs are located within a wider workfarist strategy aimed simultaneously at minimizing welfare rolls while imposing a new "moral regime" in the Canadian labor market. Yet despite all the political rhetoric around deficit reduction, "tough love" welfare reform, and "world-class" training, fundamental questions of program costs, delivery systems, and displaced externalities often remain unanswered (see Turk, 1992; Simpson, 1995; Rutherford, 1996a; Workfare Watch, 1999a). Even advocates of the workfare philosophy have begun to realize that its implementation as a workable program can be an "administrative nightmare" (see Corcoran, 1995; Walker, 1995). The scene is therefore set for a contradictory and contested transition from welfare to workfare in Canada. Nowhere are these tensions more clearly evident than in Ontario, which rather like Massachusetts has experienced a rapid transition from traditional welfarism through soft workfare to hard workfare, precipitated by what David Brown (1995: 59) provocatively called a "U.S.-style welfare explosion" in the province.

## IN AND AGAINST ONTARIO'S WORKFARE STATE

According to the *Toronto Star*, workfare was the "visceral issue" of the 1995 Ontario election campaign (May 25, 1995: A1). The Progressive Conservatives, who would subsequently assume power in the province, campaigned on a manifesto of radical reform styled the *Common Sense Revolution*. With unmistakable echoes of the *Contract with America*, the Conservatives' manifesto proposed a radical program of reform, with workfare as its centerpiece. On welfare, they asserted that "the best social assistance program ever created is a real job. . . . [W]e must move to control costs and help people return to the workforce . . . [while investment] will go into 'workfare' and 'learnfare' programs that link welfare with work and education" (Ontario Progressive Conservative Party, 1995: 9). On the defensive, the incumbent New Democrats (NDP) attacked these proposals as authoritarian, impractical, and doctrinaire, but quickly appeared to be losing the argument. The Conservatives played directly to anti-welfare sentiments, focusing on issues such as fraud while repeatedly emphasizing the scale of the "welfare problem" in Ontario. At the time, the province contained more than one-third of the nation's welfare population, and the cumulative effect of a series of rate increases since the mid-1980s had meant that its benefit levels had become relatively high (Simpson, 1995; Sabatini, 1996). Indeed, as the Conservatives were keen to point out, with a gesture toward economic continentalization, benefits were then among the highest not only in Canada but in North America (*Toronto Star*, July 22, 1995: A10). That rising benefit levels and growing concerns about fraud should coincide, in the 1990s, with an expansion in the rolls, played into the hands of conservative critics, even though the underlying reasons for the caseload expansion had more to do with economic dislocation than with "welfare dependency." As a senior official in Ontario's welfare administration explained,

> "We had about 5 percent of people on assistance throughout just about the whole postwar period. . . . In 1985 there was still only 5.5 percent of the population on social assistance. By 1991 it was one in seven. That's quick! . . . Frustratingly, the reasons [for this] were heterogeneous . . . and many of them are not related, but they all end up in the same bottom-line figure. And people say, well *something's* wrong. . . . People believe that the reason it's gone up is because of abuse and fraud."[13]

In the context of electoral politics, the "bottom-line" figures tended to set the parameters for the debate. None of the major parties were prepared to defend the principles of welfare, or the integrity of welfare recipients themselves, in the face of a high caseload. So while workfare was the issue that publicly divided the Ontario parties, their positions were not nearly so polarized as the political rhetoric suggested. While each of the three main parties had a distinctive position on workfare as a narrowly defined program, in fact they all subscribed to workfarist principles of one sort or another. All three parties promised welfare cuts and a further crackdown on fraud, in each case underpinned by a workfarist policy orientation: while the Progressive Conservatives opted for a tough anti-welfare line and straightforward work compulsion via workfare, the Liberals offered the veiled threat of "mandatory opportunities," while the NDP continued to emphasize the role of training initiatives such as jobsOntario within an environment of creeping compulsion (Rusk, 1995; Sheldrick, 1998). In effect, this narrow suite of policy options boiled down to a choice between traditional and "new-style" workfare.

## Not-Workfare and the NDP

From the center-left, the NDP had in fact backed itself into a quasi-workfarist position by the early 1990s. During its period in office (1990–1995), the NDP had sought progressively to integrate welfare and labor-market policy, framing its responses to poverty, unemployment, and workforce preparation in discourses of competitiveness and flexibility (see Albo, 1994; McBride, 1996), but also seeking ways to drive down the welfare rolls. As a senior welfare administrator observed, "in 1993, when the NDP started to look at welfare reform, even though there wasn't the language of workfare, the desire was [to] shrink the welfare system."[14]

As the NDP would discover, welfare reform is often a slow and contested process, but while their concrete achievements in this field were destined to be no more than modest, they did succeed in changing the terms and the tone of the welfare debate in Ontario. As the appropriately titled *Turning Point* policy statement of 1993 had explained:

> One out of every nine dollars Ontario spends goes towards a welfare system that entrenches poverty and keeps recipients on the margins of society. The extraordinary cost would be money well spent if it represented an investment in helping people enter or re-enter the labour market. Right now, the system locks recipients into a lifestyle of dependency. (quoted in Sabatini, 1996: 218)

In advancing such arguments about welfare dependency and the need for active labor-market integration, the NDP signaled their intention to commodify welfare through the promotion of labor-force attachment. This approach was criticized by social-advocacy groups and elements in the labor movement, who were to play no small part in stalling and averting the subsequent reform process, for eroding the fundamental principle of needs-based entitlement and enforcing work in the absence of the necessary, comprehensive program of service supports. As Sheldrick has explained,

> *Turning Point* represented a fundamental shift in the purpose and function of social assistance in Ontario. Responding to a period of economic crisis and restructuring brought about by free trade, globalization, and a decrease in federal transfer payments, the Ontario state sought to transform social assistance into a labour market device that would assist in the flexible deployment of labour as a mechanism of competitiveness. . . . In order to achieve this restructuring, however, concepts of income security would have to be abandoned in favour of benefit rates substantially below minimum rates of pay in the labour market and compulsory job placement schemes to subsidize employers would have to be adopted. (1998: 53–54)

Despite having established the philosophical case for workfare, the NDP would never move to implement a fully fledged workfare program.

The negative political symbolism of workfare was such, in fact, that a concerted move in this direction would have ruptured the fragile social compact on which the NDP's power rested. Workfare represented one of the lines in the sand in the NDP's social-democratic flirtation with neoliberalism, the transgression of which would not be tolerated, even by a labor movement largely resigned to the constraints of market-oriented pragmatism. As a senior NDP policy adviser explained, workfare was not seen as politically feasible in Ontario at the time, for while it would have powerful advocates, there would also be fierce opposition: "The workfare stuff is going on in New Brunswick and elsewhere. It was not a possibility here under this [NDP] government. . . . That was never part of [our] approach. You know the labor movement would have gone bananas if we'd talked about that."[15] Under the NDP, then, the move toward workfare seems to have been checked largely by *external* political constraints, the administration having clearly indicated its desire to shift away from "passive" welfare programming, where feasible. As well-placed observers in the policy community saw the situation at the time:

> "[Workfare] is less conceivable in Ontario. Ontario is more politicized because of the Free Trade Agreement and the recession . . . and the labor movement has a broader base."[16]

> "Partly because the NDP was in power, there was a sense that it wasn't a serious worry in Ontario, the move to workfare. Now there were some serious rumblings in the Ministry of Community and Social Services about doing that, but I don't think that was seen to be a major danger."[17]

Workfare politics were confined to mere "rumblings" in part because the NDP had begun to concentrate on the "positive" and facilitative side of the workfare agenda: the development of an active labor-market strategy. In the wake of the influential report *People and Skills in the New Global Economy* (Premier's Council, 1990), political energies had been focused on the creation of an Ontario Training and Adjustment Board (OTAB), an arm's-length body that would develop a "partnership" approach to job training and labor-force adjustment involving business, labor, and equity-group interests (see Dehli, 1993; Rutherford, 1996a; Wolfe, 1996).

Informed by what Albo (1994) has termed a "progressive competitiveness" model of economic adjustment (see also Mahon, 1991), OTAB came to epitomize the NDP's parallel commitments to social partnership and economic modernization, in which a dynamic training regime would provide the basis for high-technology, high-wage expansion. The funding of OTAB, its governance structure, and the suite of work–welfare programs that it inherited from the provincial government, were arguably never commensurate with the scale of such a task.[18] Its experience was one of seeking to develop a progressive, social-partnership approach to labor-market policy in a harsh political and economic environment. Pre-occupied with administrative, representational, and procedural issues under the NDP, then abruptly abolished by the Progressive Conserva-tives, OTAB was to become a victim of the very climate of short-termism, cuts, and undercutting that the Premier's Council had set out to transfor-m. But this brief experiment in labor-market institution building was not without its longer term consequences. According to Dehli (1993: 87), OTAB lay at the center of a wider strategy concerned to promote alterna-tive "frameworks for thinking about and explaining the effects of eco-nomic change [representing these] as matters of the deficiencies in knowledge and skills of individual workers in an increasingly competi-tive and aggressive world." Similarly, Mahon (1991: 327) observed that the philosophy of the Premier's Council report, subsequently institution-alized within OTAB, could be expected to "do little to halt the slide into a two-tiered economy" under NAFTA and its associated "regime of regula-tion by market forces."

This may be to exaggerate the irretrievably regressive nature of the OTAB experiment, and active labor-market programming in general, which certainly has progressive *potential* even if this is not always real-ized in reality (see Wolfe, 1996). More significant, certainly, in the subse-quent slide to workfare in Ontario, was the NDP's adoption of anti-wel-fare rhetoric, its resort to "dependency" analyses of welfare usage, and its preoccupation with welfare fraud. According to Sheldrick (1998: 60), this laid the "political and social groundwork for a backlash against so-cial assistance recipients," upon which the Conservatives would later capitalize, and hence it played a role in "facilitat[ing] the implementa-tion of regressive workfare policies."

## The Common Sense Revolution

With the 1995 election won, the Conservatives set about the task of wel-fare reform with vigor, announcing a 21.6 percent cut in benefits which, despite its adverse affects on one million claimants, was the subject of celebration by the financial community (*Toronto Star,* July 22, 1995: A10, E1). The plan was to phase in workfare during 1996 through a network of fourteen to twenty regional centers across Ontario and relying heavily on the suite of local jobs programs that were already in place (see Rutherford, 1996a). But opposition to the new initiative remained strong, while it became clear that many of the municipal authorities charged with its delivery at the local level harbored considerable reservations about both the principle and the practice of workfare. Partly as a result of this, but also due to the complexities of building a new management and tracking system for the program, implementation proved to be much slower than anticipated (*Globe and Mail*, July 29, 1998: A3).

Devolution alone was clearly not enough to animate and sustain the new system. Instead, many local authorities felt that they were simply being exploited in a clumsy process of downloading:

> "What's been downloaded is responsibility. Financial responsibility. . . . But the policy manual for the Ontario Works program, it's eight hundred pages long! In my conversations with delivery agents, they're very clear that the discretion under this program . . . is much narrower than ever it was under the old programs. . . . The rhetoric is interesting—we're going to put this into the hands of the people, they're local, they know their caseload, they know what they need to do; we have to untie their hands—when in reality this thing is very tightly prescribed. . . . On the ground, it is a completely different system from what it is on paper. You know, it's a personalized, idiosyncratic system where your relationship with your [case]worker is everything. And what the law says hardly matters. . . . So the idea of centralizing control and making the program very narrow and prescriptive is a double-edged thing." (Social advocate #3)[19]

> "We are used to being creative and in an employment program you have to be. You have to be able to respond fairly quickly and be innovative. With this program [OW], we found there was a lot of . . . micromanaging by the province." (OW program manager #1)[20]

Ontario Works also met explicit political resistance, particularly from the social-advocacy community. Given Ontario's relatively progressive tradition on welfare issues (Rea, 1985), its strong labor movement, and its active network of community and grassroots organizations, it was always likely that the Conservatives' workfare plans would be contested. The new government's first social services minister, David Tsubouchi, seemed to acknowledge as much when he underlined his resolve to deliver a "real" workfare program in Ontario: "I may have [to get] community support, but that isn't my primary goal. When I refer to the dignity of a job, that's what I mean, the dignity of a real job" (*Toronto Star*, September 17, 1995: A1). Despite this single-minded determination, the Conservatives' plans for delivering workfare were to be checked by community and social-advocacy organizations in a number of ways. A highly effective Workfare Watch campaign lobbied against the government's workfare proposals, drawing extensively on research evidence from the United States and elsewhere to discredit the program, and galvanized opposition at the local and provincial levels.[21] More directly, pressure was brought to bear on those community organizations prepared to offer placements under the OW program in an attempt to choke off the supply of workfare slots. Many of those agencies that did agree to participate in OW as placement providers would find their board members and senior staff being lobbied immediately to reverse the decision, while some labor unions threatened to withdraw funding from participating agencies. The Ontario Coalition Against Poverty (OCAP) also wrote to all such agencies in uncompromising terms, threatening various forms of direct action should these pleas go unheeded:

> We have learned that your agency has decided to accept workfare placements. . . . As you must be aware, workfare is not a voluntary system. Agencies that sign up for it will monitor and file reports on people that may lead to suspension or cancellation of their benefits. In agreeing to become involved you are, moreover, opening the door for the massive extension of this incontrovertible abuse of welfare recipients. If workfare is allowed to grow, it will spill into the broader public sector and even be made available to private businesses. The kind of exploitation that has become rampant in places like New York City could become part of life here if people like you are allowed to carry out [Premier] Harris's dirty work for him. However, we have no intention of letting you get away with this. . . . This deserves nothing less than public condemnation.[22]

This direct-action strategy has been effective in constraining the expansion of workfare, especially in Toronto, where the initiative has become profoundly politicized. As the Harris administration has struggled to roll out the infrastructure for the new program, fears have again been raised that private-sector placements would be deployed on a large scale, reversing an earlier commitment that the program would not be allowed to displace waged jobs (see Workfare Watch, 1998b). Although the administration has made very little progress on this front—there were only two hundred such placements in September 1999—the symbolism of the move may be just as important, in that it again suggests a hardening, and an expansion, of the workfare strategy (*Toronto Sun*, September 3, 1999: 7). This raises the prospect of direct confrontation with labor unions as well as social-advocacy groups, though it may be the only way that the Harris government can deal with the intractable administrative and political problems that have been associated with its workfare strategy. As the social services minister Janet Ecker complained, "Anyone who thought this process was going to be short, sweet and simple doesn't know much about the welfare system in Ontario" (*Globe and Mail*, July 30, 1998: 7).

While the Ontario government has secured the support of the municipalities in delivering OW (see *Globe and Mail*, August 20, 1999: A9), the City of Toronto—which has the lion's share of provincial welfare cases—continues to voice concerns. This partly reflects the politically controversial nature of workfare in the city, but it also says something about the challenges of delivering a program like OW in an urban context. As one senior administrator explained,

> "We have fourteen welfare offices across the city and a caseload of currently about 82,000 [or 180,000 individuals]. . . . In the smaller places, with a smaller caseload, you can spend time with your client in order to make sure there is proper placement . . . whereas in big systems, you don't have the resources to do [that], resulting in less time with the client. . . . [Moreover] in Toronto, [OW] has been an uphill battle, just because of the controversy of it."[23]

The initial piloting of OW in municipalities outside Toronto was, in this sense, partly deliberate. As one local observer explained, "They were looking for municipalities with kind of compliant local politicians, who would be happy to go along with this. . . . All the organized resistance of the big unions and the advocacy groups and so forth is going to be strongest in the urban centers."[24] While the economic climate has initially favored such downloading strategies, as caseloads fell sharply post-1995, some local governments have begun to consider establishing their own "rainy-day" funds in anticipation of harder job-market times ahead.[25]

The future course of workfare politics in Ontario is far from set, despite the fact that much of the current debate concerns the practice and delivery of workfare rather than its underlying principles. In an unusual twist of neoliberal logic, the Ontario Conservatives originally opted for community-based workfare because to permit private-sector placements would be to distort the "free" functioning of the labor market. More pragmatically, private-sector provision might also smack of the kind of jobs-based interventions previously favored by the NDP and OTAB, but attacked by the Conservatives in opposition. The Conservative government's later decision to explore the possibility of private-sector placements must be seen in the light of the opposition mobilized by social-advocacy groups, though it also reflects the political lessons learned from places like Wisconsin, the destination of a ministerial visit in April 1998 (see Workfare Watch, 1998a).

This highlights one of the ways in which workfarist policy messages are increasingly being transferred "interlocally," by way of direct policy contacts between subnational administrations (see Jessop and Peck, 2000). In this case, there are also growing signs that OW is moving toward the kind of "work-first"/LFA approach that has become so en-

trenched in the United States. OW formally emphasizes driving participants down the "shortest route to employment," providing minimalist
services that amount to "no more than is required to support moving toward the achievement and maintenance of employment" (OW program
guidelines).[26] The lingering issue of private-sector placements, while certainly raising questions for free-market purists about "interference" in
the labor market, can nevertheless be rationalized in these terms. As a
Conservative minister conscious of these very tensions chose to put it,
"This is to be a program that provides people on welfare with [a] stepping stone into a permanent job. It's not to subsidize employers" (quoted
in Workfare Watch, 1998b: 1).

Programs like W-2 and OW are persistently vulnerable to the accu-
sation that they represent a relatively costly means of securing employment for those, in accordance with the principles of work-first, who were
in any case the most employable, and therefore most likely to leave the
welfare rolls unaided. This is certainly an important strand of the Ontario debate, though there is also a sense in which explicit concerns
about costs are receding. Certainly as long as favorable labor-market conditions continue to assist in driving down the welfare rolls, there is a feeling in some quarters that workfare is quite simply a price worth paying
in order to enforce work norms and "activate" welfare recipients. An official from Ontario's welfare department drew a telling comparison with
the cost of prisons:

> "You find that people aren't worried about the cost. If you say, should
> we have more civil servants they say no. If you say, should we have
> more people checking up on welfare they say yes. . . . What if it isn't
> cost-effective? It doesn't matter. It's just like putting people in pris-
> ons. . . . If they don't behave properly, then they've got to be *gotten* to
> behave. . . . So I don't think costs even enter the equation. It's more
> [concerned with] having people behave properly. . . . The problem is
> located with them [recipients] as opposed to any systemic problem.
> These are people who won't be part of the system. So we'll get all over
> them and we'll spend twice as much as we'll ever make, but it just
> doesn't matter."[27]

Cost-per-place or cost-per-job calculations of the "effectiveness" of
workfare clearly do not capture these wider deterrent/enforcement effects
of workfare strategies. For every individual on a workfare placement, there
might be two or three former welfare recipients induced to enter low-wage
employment in order to avoid workfare. The economics of the program,
therefore, look quite different if it is viewed as a labor-regulatory strategy
with wide-ranging effects across the lower reaches of the labor market,

rather than simply as a narrowly conceived form of social-policy intervention. However, both orthodox evaluation techniques and mainstream political discourse tend to focus on the latter, narrow measures of program costs, perhaps because any wider method of accounting might also expose the deleterious *social* costs of work enforcement.

There are also significant consequences for the structure of the welfare caseload. Here, workfare plays an important role in inverting the incentive structure of traditional welfare systems, aggressively reordering eligibility structures in terms of the market-orientated criteria of "employability" (see Peck and Theodore, 2000a). This shift was explained by an Ontario welfare official in terms of a fundamental restructuring of institutional incentives for welfare recipients:

> "A lot of it has to do with reconceiving the nature of the caseload and using different organizing principles for it. [The traditional welfare] system looks upon groups in terms of a hierarchy of deservedness, of categorical eligibility, which puts disabled at the top, mothers somewhere in the middle, and young single employables on the bottom. . . . The whole idea now is to reorganize the caseload according to those people—whether they are disabled, single parents, or employables— who are most job-ready, those who are job-ready with a little help, those who are job-ready with a lot of help, and then a small tier at the bottom who will never be able to make it. So, it's to completely reorganize that tiering away from target groups, because what happens is you have a built-in set of institutional incentives to move yourself up through the welfare hierarchy. Single parents whose children are becoming older always start to discover aches and pains that will get them on to the disability."[28]

Under a workfare regime, the old incentive structure that was believed to cause recipients to gravitate toward the most "secure," stable, and "hassle-free" reaches of the welfare system is purposefully destabilized, to be replaced by an alternative set of calibrations based on relative degrees of employability and "distance" from the labor market (which can, of course, be measured in social terms or by way of unit program costs). According to its advocates, workfare consequently strikes directly at the perverse institutional incentives that create "welfare dependency," even though the program itself acts on only a small proportion of the total caseload. As the Ontario welfare official continued,

> "So [recipients are] always trying to go from the most stigmatized to the least stigmatized, and from more intervention to less intervention—in other words, they [welfare caseworkers] get out of your

life—and finally, you get more money, and the money is more stable, and is less prone to discretion. We have the most discretion over the sixteen- and seventeen-year-olds: they've got to be living right, they've got to be with adults, they've got to go to school, blah, blah, blah. If you're in the disabled category, there's the least discretion, you just get your money. . . . To change the system, you have to get institutional rewards to raise [claimants] from the less employable to the more employable, therefore participation allowances and things like that. [Under the old welfare system] we paid people to become less and less active. . . . [Now] we're trying to put in a system that will pay people to be more active, so the institutional rewards are more for activity planning, getting back to work."[29]

Workfare programming must therefore be understood in the context of the wider transformation of Ontario's welfare system. The fundamental principles of traditional welfare delivery are challenged by the systemic orientation toward work, as social assistance becomes, in effect, subordinated to labor-market policy. As Workfare Watch (1999a: 3) points out, "Workfare . . . transforms the basis of social assistance, from a system based on need, to one based on deservedness—proven through employment activities. . . . Ontario Works completes the transformation, making social assistance an instrument of labour market adjustment, almost to the exclusion of any other purpose."

The long-run effects of this systemic shift are difficult to predict, grounds on which the provincial government is often accused of recklessness. As a senior official involved in delivering OW at the local level asked, "What happens to people once they get off? Do they really stay off, or do they come back on? Do they get better paying jobs? Or do we have more crime in the future? . . . Those things take a long time to determine. I mean, what will our society look like in ten or fifteen years?"[30] Yet for all the inequities and flaws in the current system, others detect an emergent, brutal logic in forcibly driving the poor into the margins of the labor market. As a Toronto-based social activist put it,

"They know they are shuffling the deck of who is occupying the low-wage labor market. But what they are doing is making sure that a lot more people maybe share in that, so they don't get this permanent underclass [of] long-term excluded [people]. Everybody gets a shot now and then to be in the labor market for a little while, interspersed with periods on social assistance, but you minimize the number of hard-core marginalized people. . . . You are well beyond simply controlling the low-wage labor market. You have got to keep a whole population under social control here."[31]

Superficially at least, it seems difficult to square such arguments concerning the supposed "logic" of workfare with the prosaic realities of political incompetence and delivery problems. Paradoxically, however, the practical achievements of programs like OW are often less important than the political and ideological messages that they convey. It is on this symbolic terrain that the politics of workfare in Ontario are currently being worked out. And it is becoming clear that there are internal dynamics in the political process that are serving to sustain the policy of workfare, even as the program itself falters and misfires.

## Political Dynamics of Workfare

Even though the Ontario Conservatives have repeatedly stumbled and fumbled in their implementation of workfare, this does not mean that the wider regulatory project will be easily derailed, either by administrative incompetence or by political opposition—both of which are present in this case. The deterrent/enforcement effects of workfare, coupled with swinging benefit cuts, and assisted by growth in contingent employment, are all working to secure the broader objectives of this regulatory project, even as implementation problems continue to dog the program itself. And while the network of community activists and trade unionists in the province has achieved some notable victories in terms of the OW program, the wide-ranging regulatory shift that OW epitomizes will be less easy to contest. This task will be made more difficult still if the welfare rolls continue to fall in Ontario, allowing the Conservatives to continue to present the program as a "success" even in the face of its manifest shortcomings. With the welfare rolls having fallen for nineteen consecutive months—amounting to a 425,000 reduction in the number of claimants since June 1995—Community and Social Services Minister John Baird claimed in September 1999, "Our government is making steady progress in the area of welfare reform. We are offering people a hand up, to break the cycle of welfare dependency and help get them back to work" (Ministry of Community and Social Services, 1999). This was a message that had played well in the 1999 provincial election, which saw the Progressive Conservatives returned to power. An election-year brochure produced by the Conservatives sought to encapsulate the message that workfare was working: with no mention of implementation problems, shortages of workfare slots, or other distracting details, the line was a simple one: "jobs up, welfare down," these are the benefits of "turning welfare into workfare" (Ministry of Community and Social Services, nd).

The coincidence of falling welfare rolls and a forcefully articulated workfare policy is providing the Conservatives with a very effective message, even as the capability to deliver the program eludes them. This message has helped the Conservatives win two successive elections in the province. The greater the controversy around the program, the more powerful the message becomes. And opposition has been sustained and serious: OW has been boycotted by the United Church of Canada on the grounds that it is immoral to "force the poor to work" (Asling, 1997);[32] the Harris government has been censured by the United Nations for violations of human rights in denying OW participants the right to strike or join a union (*Toronto Star*, December 8, 1998: 1); an attempt unilaterally to impose work requirements on native bands was declared unconstitutional under the Indian Act (*Toronto Star*, August 26, 1999: 1); and the Conservatives have been ridiculed for insisting that OW participants be bussed out to work on farms-so-called farmfare—as a substitute for migrant workers (Woodcock, 1999).[33] Nevertheless, in its role as a political strategy, workfare continues to be perversely successful:

> When his critics ridicule workfare and compare it to slavery, it reinforces Harris' standing with those inclined to vote Tory. It also deflects attention away from what would otherwise be a big problem for the Tories with their supporters. That is, they've never delivered on workfare. Not even close. Harris is in a no-lose situation. By talking up workfare, he solves two political problems at once. He pays lip service to a program that is hugely popular with that part of the public which supports him, while the left's overreaction diverts his constituency from the fact the program itself has failed. (Goldstein, 1999: 15)

While the headlines proclaim that workfare has driven more than 400,000 people off welfare—and supposedly into work—numbers on the workfare component of OW remain tiny in comparison, at just six thousand in July 1999. In fact, during 1998–1999, only 2–5 percent of welfare recipients were actually on workfare assignments (depending on the method of counting), yet the program retains its totemic status. As an otherwise characteristically sober evaluation by the OECD (1999: 109) concluded, "The design and delivery of Ontario Works is far removed from the political rhetoric." In fact, the Ontario government's approach to welfare-to-work continues to be almost breathtakingly brazen. For all the great claims that are being made for OW, there are no plans to commission an independent evaluation. Meanwhile, official pronouncements contain a bewildering mix of anti-welfare sentiment, recycled PR, and self-servingly selective statistics (see Ministry of Community and Social Services, 2000). Much is made of the new "zero tolerance" attitude to welfare fraud, the "serious and enforced" approach to mandation, and the defining role of OW as "the new way of delivering welfare and employment services in Ontario" (Ministry of Community and Social Services, 2000: 10, 21, 12), but the relatively modest scale/outcomes of these initiatives *relative to* the overwhelming size of the deregistration effect underlines the fact that much of this is symbolic politics. The Ontario Conservatives are engaged in an ideological reregulation of the low-wage labor market, banging the drum of workfare as loudly as possible in order to maintain downward pressure on the welfare rolls.

Repeatedly embarrassed by the modest actual size of the workfare-community service caseload, the Harris government has variously concealed and embellished participation statistics, stretched the definition of the program, and noisily telegraphed its raising of municipal placement targets. According to Amdur (2000: D4), "Participation in workfare has been so poor, the [Harris] government has chosen to expand the meaning of the phrase." Municipalities charged with the delivery of the scheme have found that they have been allowed to use increasingly flexible definitions of "community-service" participation by a provincial administration determined to see targets being met and the "work for welfare" message sound credible. Behind the smoke and mirrors, as the OECD (1999: 111) saw the situation, "mandatory work placements are currently limited in Ontario . . . [yet their] existence acts as a deterrent."

The Conservatives' unambiguous message is that workfare itself—and, by implication, their own political resolve in the face of defensive interests—has transformed the experience of welfare: Premier Mike Harris insists that "I am determined not to let anyone fall through the cracks. We cannot, and will not, give up on anyone who remains on welfare" (*Canada NewsWire*, May 15, 1999). In contrast to the situation in 1995, when the Conservatives came into office and one in eight of Ontario's population was on welfare, the situation has been turned around, the politicians claim, with one person "escaping dependency" *every five minutes* following the introduction of workfare.[34] Despite the absurdity of the claims made for OW, formal political opposition has been muted. So, while Liberal leader Dalton McGuinty criticized the program during the 1999 election campaign on the grounds that "Workfare is a slogan, it's not a job placement program in Ontario," his lame alternative was simply to "fix workfare" by injecting more funding and stepping up private-sector participation.[35]

So, despite the small scale and almost untraceable direct achievements of OW, "[r]hetorically at least, workfare remains the centrepiece of welfare reform" in Ontario (Workfare Watch, 1999a: 3). This creates tactical difficulties for social activists, because attacks on the program are typically used by the Harris administration to affirm and bolster its political support. In much of the media, the complaints of social advocates simply lend credence to the Conservatives' argument that the program is hurting/working. The conundrum is, as one social activist explained, that to attack the program in a high-profile way is to at least imply that it is working, that it is having significant effects:

> "The dilemma for us has been sitting here knowing the thing is a catastrophe on the ground, but the government continues to try and claim credit. Do we shut up? . . . I mean if they continue to be embarrassed with this program, what comes after it could well be worse. Who knows? And we've got welfare legislation that makes anything possible at this point."[36]

While there may also be risks for the Conservatives in exaggerating the effectiveness of OW,[37] at a more strategic level the workfare message has credibility because the wider panoply of workfarist reforms are yielding results.

The OW program itself is in many ways an emblem for a wider and deeper restructuring strategy concerned to deter welfare claims and pursue deregistration as ends in themselves. So, the savage 21.6 percent cut in welfare benefits implemented in October 1995 brought about the largest monthly reduction in the caseload in twenty-five years, when 35,000 individuals left the rolls immediately following the rate reduction (AOHC, 1995). Behind the daily travails of the OW program, then, lies a much broader strategy of welfare dismantling.

> "They changed the definition of spouse in the house, . . . they made it much more difficult for sixteen- and seventeen-year-olds to get on state assistance, they made it easier to kick people off assistance, they lowered asset levels, and things like that. . . . They cut benefits. . . . As soon as you lower the maximum benefit levels [some claimants] would become entirely ineligible. . . . Then, you know, the change in climate, which is hard to quantify. The negative climate is much worse at the level of the local office, where people actually have contact with the welfare system. So how many people leave because they can't take the hassle any more? Or never apply, because they have been discouraged by that climate?" (Social advocate #3)[38]

> "[Benefits] are now well below New York, Pennsylvania, our so-called competitors. Now really we're in line with Alabama and Georgia. . . . A climate gets created that means that a lot of people are no longer eligible, or are very reluctant to even think about welfare. . . . A lot of it is chill. There's a chill been established." (Social advocate #2)[39]

> "The government has been really successful at shaming the social-assistance recipient. . . . They've reduced rates to where it's subsistence at very best. It's made it very difficult for some client groups to even

access the system. . . . They have marginalized a lot of people. . . . They feel that they need to get off the system even if they can't work." (OW Program manager #1)[40]

Indeed, the very breadth of this reform package is one of the factors behind the implementation problems of OW—local welfare administrations having been literally overloaded with a series of reforms in law, policy, and practice.[41] So while the threats of anti-poverty advocates have certainly checked the expansion of workfare in Toronto, slow initial progress was also partly attributable to (short-term) implementation problems, many of which have subsequently been resolved. As basic organizational problems are slowly ironed out, however, other issues of a more intractable nature have been emerging on the horizon. Reflecting a classic neoliberal dilemma over workfare (Noël, 1995), the Conservatives' failure adequately to fund childcare provision threatens to undermine the very transitions into work they seek to encourage. According to an independent evaluation commissioned by the Ministry of Community and Social Services, which described the wider system of supports and incentives around the OW program as "perverse," childcare shortages would cause many recent leavers to be forced back on to the welfare rolls (*Globe and Mail*, September 27, 1999: 1).

## Workfare Discourse

There is little sign of the heat being taken out of the workfare issue in Toronto. Indeed, it has become a staple of contemporary political debate. By way of illustration, one measure of this is the frequency of references to the word *workfare* in the *Toronto Star*: hardly mentioned at all during the 1980s, during which time it was mostly discussed as a "foreign" phenomenon, the word *workfare* appeared in print once every 91.2 days over the period 1985–1992; by the mid-1990s, however, *workfare* had become very much a "local"—and highly controversial—phenomenon, its frequency of citations rising to once per 1.7 days over the period 1993–1999.[42] And the very proliferation of workfare discourse performs political work of its own. As one local observer put it, "The word [*workfare*] is politically potent. And what you do after that is probably not important."[43]

With no sign of the workfare issue beginning to hurt the Harris administration, opposition forces have begun to advance a dual strategy. The threat of direct action against placement providers continues, as social advocates focus on blocking workfare in the nonprofit sector, while labor unions maintain a watchful eye on private-sector placements. This strategy is being complemented by a sustained attack on workfare as a policy measure, based on close monitoring of the U.S. evaluation evidence. So when ministers invoke the Wisconsin experience (of supposedly successful programming), advocates counter with stories of failure from elsewhere: as one social activist explained, "They don't talk about New York. *We* talk about New York!"[44] This represents an attempt to match the fast-policy characteristics of workfarism with an equally potent form of "fast opposition."

Learning how to make the most of the technocratic evaluation literature—as an obstacle to, rather than as a facilitator of, reform—is proving important here, as is networking with other locally and nationally based opposition groups outside Canada. Otherwise uninspiring evaluation studies and implementation lessons can in the "wrong hands" be turned against the program itself. While in some senses this reflects the growing sophistication of the social-advocacy movement, it also follows from a frank assessment of the limitations of media-oriented, "cry-wolf" strategies, which in an anti-welfare political climate may actually be counterproductive. Instead, as one protagonist explained, the strategy has involved working at the weak spots of Ontario's favored approach of work-for-welfare in the nonprofit sector:

> "We didn't go out and just rail at people and say workfare is slavery, or anything like that. It was just here is what we know about programs like that. Here is what they do and here is what they don't do. Here is what the law says, and here are the real administrative and legal implications of an organization that is contemplating participating. . . . We use all the MDRC stuff to show that nowhere, with the exception maybe of Los Angeles and New York City, is pure work-for-welfare anything other than a marginal part of welfare-to-work programs. Nowhere are there significant numbers of workfare placements in the not-for-profit sector. . . . Most organizations in the not-for-profit sector are very small. They just don't have the capacity."[45]

As the Harris administration, either through incompetence or deliberate provocation, repeatedly inflames the workfare debate, it seems that the political theater of workfare is rendering the program almost invisible itself. Yet as a broadly based strategy, rather than a narrowly defined policy, workfarism really is transforming the nature of social assistance in Ontario. In the name of workfare, eligibility is being restricted and a philosophy of deterrence is being normalized; large-scale deregistration and the commodification of poverty are the outcomes. And still, on the symbolic terrain of workfare politics, the Conservatives continue to take the fight to the opposition. Perhaps the most vivid portrayal of this was the passage of Bill 22 in November 1998, which in direct contravention of

Article 8 of the U.N. Covenant on Economic, Social, and Cultural Rights denies workfare participants the right to

1. Join a union.
2. Have the terms and conditions under which he or she participates [in OW] determined through collective bargaining.
3. Strike. (Legislative Assembly of Ontario, 1998: paragraph 1[2])

Even though the practical impact of this legislation may not be particularly significant—given the modest size of the OW program—it nevertheless stands as a potent symbol of a radically reformed set of job-market and welfare norms. Bill 22 underlines the role of workfare in codifying/enforcing new rules and expectations for those on the margins of the labor market: political–economic rights must be *earned*; those lacking economic "self-sufficiency" are effectively excluding *themselves* from such rights . . . until they get a job.

## BEYOND THE SAFETY NET

Commenting on some of the early signs of work–welfare restructuring in Canada several years ago, Drache (1991: 266) observed that "renewed calls for limiting benefits and tightening work search requirements [reveal] the extent to which government as well as business consciously link the need to restructure social programs to a strategy to facilitate a qualitatively different kind of trade-centred flexibility." For some, there are signs that this project may be stabilizing into an "institutional fix" at the continental level, as since the 1980s both the state and business in Canada have been actively exploring

> the parameters of an alternative model of development that builds on the continentalism of permeable Fordism but abandons the latter's more progressive features. The moves toward privatization, deregulation, "targeted" (as opposed to universal) social programs, and contracting out—hallmarks of neoconservatism throughout the West— thus form part of a broader package including the consolidation of a continental mode of regulation that would incorporate the Canadian economy into the regime of polarized growth that has already taken root in the United States. (Jenson and Mahon, 1993: 81)

Like its neighbor to the south, Canada has allowed the social safety net to be unpicked incrementally, province by province. Ontario may be at the forefront of this process at the present time, if for no other reason than the confrontational and media-oriented nature of the Harris strategy, but it is not alone. Other provinces are jostling for the mantle, too. For its part, the federal government has repeatedly sent signals that it expects to see continuing reform, validating ongoing experiments while remaining at least one step removed from the dirty business of implementation. While in many senses the action remains at the local level, the importance of federal-level initiatives and discursive shifts should not be underestimated.

A key moment, certainly, was the abolition of CAP, which dramatically rewrote the rules of Canadian federalism, the rules on which the country's welfare settlement had been based. Indeed, the federal government's intent to animate debate around welfare reform had been clearly evident for some time. The green paper of 1994, *Improving Social Security in Canada,* portrayed the situation in the now-familiar language of "difficult choices," but again the response from social advocates and labor unions was characteristically principled and robust. Prior to the Harris government's effective "mainstreaming" of workfarist rhetoric (if not practice), the punitive signifiers of *workfare* were still tactically useful in checking social-policy regression:

> The traditional approach to social security has centered on providing income support and basic services to those in need. This "safety net" approach is incomplete. Too often it short-changes people by dealing with the symptom of their income insecurity, not the causes. . . . [For] those who have the potential to help themselves, improved government support must be targeted at those who demonstrate a willingness and commitment to self-help. . . . Any reformed social security system must meet the test of affordability . . . entailing making difficult choices about the best use of available funds. (HRD Canada, 1994a: 25–26)

> The green paper considers forcing people to work for welfare and unemployment insurance benefits. This is called workfare. . . . Workfare is punitive, it keeps poor people in poverty and it allows government to blame the poor for an unemployment problem they have not created. . . . The federal government must be much clearer about what it means by training and employment services. If it means genuine support that responds to the need of poor people and includes a job at the end, NAPO will completely support these measures. If it really means allowing the provinces to implement workfare programs, NAPO must and will strongly oppose any such action. (NAPO, 1995: 19, 22–23)

In another critical submission on the green paper, the Canadian Auto Workers (CAW) attacked workfare programs as an "economically perverse social experiment," concluding: "We cannot overemphasize the depth of our anger and opposition to this policy direction" (CAW, 1994: 11). The CAW, perhaps more than most, are sensitive to the disempowering effects of decentralization, given the powers of leverage that this confers on actors operating at the provincial and federal scales. As a CAW official explained, "Within our own union we have a clear history around what happens when you allow whip-sawing. . . . We broke away from the United Auto Workers in the [United] States precisely because of this notion of competition at the local level, concession bargaining and whip-sawing."[46]

Workfarist tendencies in Canada must consequently be understood both in the concrete reform strategies of individual provinces and more widely in terms of the general political climate of neoliberal downloading. Increasingly, downward pressure on welfare is being exerted on a continental scale. The regressive dynamic feared by the Rowell–Sirois Commission in the 1930s has been released, albeit in a different form, as standards are being ratcheted down at the provincial level by governments seeking to reduce welfare rolls/costs and flexibilize labor markets. The "national standard" of welfare entitlements and benefits, once seen as a "floor" upon which provinces should build, is being reconstructed as a "ceiling" that no province dares to exceed (see National Council of Welfare, 1995). In the Canadian case, work–welfare reforms, the current conjuncture of deficit politics, workfare experimentation, weakened political opposition, and administrative decentralization may presage a period of rapid and regressive change. Unevenness in welfare provision, and in the meaning of welfare itself, seems set to increase, as provinces and localities engage in competition for dwindling resources. As an Ontario labor union official explained,

> "The model that is being driven by federal government [is based on] a downloading of responsibility. . . . This [is not] about developing coherent labor-market policy, this was about downloading, about shifting responsibility and about privatizing. . . . If you have a series of autonomous structures, then governments can pilot various initiatives, disconnected from others, and just constantly drive their agenda very effectively."[47]

In what may prove to be a sign of things to come, for example, the Conservative premiers of Alberta and Ontario argued strongly at the 1996 provincial summit for a radical decentralization of social programming (*Globe and Mail*, August 22, 1996: A1). While this particular proposal was defeated by a coalition of poorer (and more "welfare-dependent") provinces, it is indicative of just the kind of centrifugal pressures that led to the block granting of welfare in the United States: first, the federal framework is liberalized; second, subnational and local experimentation is encouraged; third, demands for greater flexibility and autonomy build from below; and fourth, the federal framework is breached. Apparently ignoring the lessons from the past, conservative provinces like Ontario seem prepared to trade federal resources for provincial flexibility. Here, and in a familiar fashion, political careers are being made through the language of tough-love welfare reform. Although, as the Ontario experience shows only too clearly, workfarist rhetoric continues to be difficult to realize as a workable program, the clear danger is that underfunded decentralization leads to a primitive form of workfare (or minimalist welfare), effectively by default. There are certainly many who fear that Canada may be on the brink of some kind of "race to the bottom" in regulatory standards, or even, with a downturn in the economy, a 1930s-style relief crisis.

Centrally orchestrated local workfare experiments seem set to erode the foundations of the Canadian welfare state "from below," as regulatory restructuring is accomplished not simply by federal government fiat, but through a more complex process of centrally initiated and guided reform, combined with provincial initiative and response, and local delivery. Through these developments, the established pattern of socioinstitutional relations that came to define the work–welfare regime during the permeable Fordist era is being transformed. So also the system is being reconstituted *spatially*. To characterize this as a transition from federal/national welfarism to local workfarism is to capture the broad direction of change, but the process is certainly more complex and perhaps more provisional than this implies. There are several intersecting strands to this process of spatial reconstitution, as federal and provincial governments have played an active role in first, reorganizing the territorial hierarchies of regulatory functions; second, fostering local regulatory and institutional experimentation; third, constituting competitive relations between (local) arms of the state and delivery agencies; and fourth, exposing welfare recipients and other unemployed workers—sometimes aggressively—to *local* market disciplines and regimes of control.

Just as in the United States, it is clear that much of the debate around workfare in Canada has been strongly conditioned by the low politics of opportunism and scapegoating. Even though Canada's experimental forays into workfare at the provincial level may be on the verge of yielding nontrivial regulatory effects in the labor market, there is little evidence that workfare is being conceived politically as a regulatory project. Instead, the interventions have often been symbolic or plain clumsy, but they have nevertheless being pursued with considerable zeal. Moreover, the predominant orientation of reform has been almost universally neoliberal and workfarist, albeit with a range of inflections and intensities. So the prospect of a new regulatory alignment is not just so much fanciful theorizing. There is growing acknowledgment of the significance of these developments in Canada, even though the prospect of severe social dislocation may also be a real one. Ontario's perversely robust experiment with workfarism certainly raises this prospect. To take another example, Murphy's analysis of the "workfare myth" in Alberta leads him to conclude that

> government elites seem determined to continue propagating the hoary myth of self-reliance as justification for destroying the last vestiges of a national social safety net. They obviously haven't been reading their history books. Welfare was developed not as part of some communist plot, but rather as a system which could assure the social stability necessary for production. As the ties are cut which bind the poor to the rest of the population in a common society, any incentive they have to follow society's rules is also eliminated. The prospect of a vicious circle of inchoate resistance and state repression, which inevitably springs from such circumstances, gives little cause for comfort. (1997: 127)

No doubt workfarism in Canada will continue to meet concerted political opposition; and there are some who believe that it may even buckle under the weight of its own contradictions. Experience elsewhere suggests that it would be unwise for the opponents of workfare to rely on such structural illogics to bring down this emergent project, yet it may also be true that Canada's underlying economic problems mean that this is one place where the contradictions of workfare are likely to be especially vividly exposed.

## Notes

1. This chapter draws in part on "From Federal Welfare to Local Workfare? Remaking Canada's Work–Welfare Regime" in *An Unruly World? Geography, Globalization and Governance*, ed. A. Herod, S. Roberts, and G. Ó. Tuathail (London: Routledge, 1998), 95–115. I am grateful to International Thompson Publishing Services Ltd for permission to reproduce parts of this chapter here.

2. See Betcherman (1996), Merrett (1996), Mishra (1996), Drache (1996), T. Clarke (1997), Régimbald (1997), and Théret (1999).

3. See Richards et al. (1995), Sayeed (1995), SPCMT (1996a, 1996b), and Shragge (1997c).

4. Quoted in Murphy (1997: 119); see also Denis (1995: 378).

5. Under the ruling, newly arrived immigrants were not allowed to claim welfare benefits in British Columbia until they had been resident for three months. The provincial government claimed it would save Cdn\$25 million per

year as a result of the policy (NCW, 1997), though welfare advocates immediately attacked the measure as unlawful (*Maclean's*, December 18, 1995: 16).

6. Senior officer, Ontario Ministry of Social Services, interviewed by Jamie Peck, January 1996.

7. See Cameron (1986), O'Connor (1989), Wolfe (1989), and Jenson and Mahon (1993).

8. See Pal (1988b), Muszynski (1985), Rice (1985), Simeon and Robinson (1990), and McBride (1992).

9. The commission was concerned about the "readiness of industry in one province to complain if it is taxed for social services which are provided out of general taxation in other provinces or are not provided at all in other provinces. Even if there are offsetting advantages by way of the better health of employees, or their freedom from anxiety, and even if in the long run the employer's contribution may in the course of wage bargaining come to fall on the employees, the employer is . . . placed in a position of competitive disadvantage in comparison with employers in provinces where there are not contributory social services" (Rowell–Sirois Report, quoted in Banting, 1987: 65).

10. See Courchene (1987), Yalnizyan (1994), Morrison (1997), and Régimbald (1997).

11. "Pilot projects for reforming social-assistance programs will be popping up all over Canada in the coming months while Ottawa and the provinces plan a major overhaul of the system. . . . [At a recent meeting] the provinces were given the green light for their various experiments in reforming government assistance schemes. . . . Ottawa has assured the provinces that they will get help for projects that experiment with the delivery of social services—adding work-incentives systems and co-ordinating unemployment and training, for instance" (*Globe and Mail*, February 15, 1994; see also York, 1994: A4).

12. See Taylor (1995), Walker (1995), Murphy (1997), and Shragge and Deniger (1997).

13. Senior officer, Ontario Ministry of Community and Social Services, interviewed by Jamie Peck, January 1996.

14. Senior welfare administrator, Toronto, interviewed by Tod Rutherford and Jamie Peck, July 1998.

15. NDP adviser, Ontario, interviewed by Jamie Peck, April 1995.

16. Equity group representative, Canadian Labour Force Development Board, interviewed by Jamie Peck, April 1995.

17. Ontario trade union official, interviewed by Jamie Peck, March 1995.

18. Initially, some twenty-seven programs were transferred to OTAB from several provincial government ministries, the shortcomings of which—in terms of their inadequacy in meeting labor-market needs—had of course been a key factor in the initial decision to create OTAB (see Premier's Council, 1990; Wolfe, 1996).

19. Community organizer, Toronto, interviewed by Tod Rutherford and Jamie Peck, July 1998.

20. Program manager #1, municipal authority, Ontario, interviewed by Tod Rutherford and Jamie Peck, July 1998.

21. See SPCMT (1996c) and Workfare Watch (1996b, 1998a, 1999a).

22. Extract from OCAP's letter to workfare-placement providers, 16 December 1997; see also OCAP (1997).

23. Senior welfare administrator, Toronto, interviewed by Tod Rutherford and Jamie Peck, July 1998.

24. Social activist #3, interviewed by Tod Rutherford and Jamie Peck, July 1998.

25. See "Rainy Day Welfare Fund Suggested for Region," *Record* (Kitchener, Ontario), January 30, 1999: 3.

26. Quoted in Workfare Watch (1999a: 3). As one well-placed respondent explained of the Ontario Conservatives, "They are very anti-training, so all the training agreements that we sign up with agencies, they have to demonstrate that it's the shortest route to a job. . . . It's much tighter [than the previous regime]" (Senior welfare administrator, Toronto, interviewed by Tod Rutherford and Jamie Peck, July 1998).

27. Senior officer, Ontario Ministry of Social Services, interviewed by Jamie Peck, January 1996.

28. Senior officer, Ontario Ministry of Social Services, interviewed by Jamie Peck, January 1996.

29. Senior officer, Ontario Ministry of Social Services, interviewed by Jamie Peck, January 1996.

30. Program manager #1, municipal authority, Ontario, interviewed by Tod Rutherford and Jamie Peck, July 1998.

31. Social activist #3, interviewed by Tod Rutherford and Jamie Peck, July 1998.

32. Premier Mike Harris responded to the church boycott by accusing church leaders of "wanting to keep members of society dependent on government" (*London Free Press*, August 18, 1999: A11).

33. Premier Harris asked, "Isn't it a tragedy that we have one million people sitting at home and drawing benefits and we are importing labour on a temporary basis like this?" (*Ottawa Sun*, September 4, 1999: 13).

34. "From Welfare to the Workforce: The Plan Is Working," *Canada NewsWire*, May 15, 1999.

35. "McGuinty Vows to Fix, Not Scrap Workfare," *London Free Press*, May 29, 1999: A4.

36. Social activist #3, interviewed by Tod Rutherford and Jamie Peck, July 1998.

37. "Their polling, their focus groups tell them that workfare is popular. They told them before the election and they're still telling them, and therefore they've got a problem. Because they have to keep pushing it, they have got to keep saying that we have achieved success, but the reality is that the emperor has no clothes" (Social activist #2, interviewed by Tod Rutherford and Jamie Peck, July 1998).

38. Interviewed by Tod Rutherford and Jamie Peck, July 1998.

39. Interviewed by Tod Rutherford and Jamie Peck, July 1998.

40. Interviewed by Tod Rutherford and Jamie Peck, July 1998.

41. "They are trying to change a [welfare] program into an active labor-market, work-orientated program. They've changed all the regulations [and] at

the same time, they're trying to tighten up eligibility everywhere. . . . So, the biggest problem is the workload problem. . . . We are trying to make the OW program work, while we're also looking at all the basic regulations. . . . The minister now finally herself has recognized that they have been moving much too quickly and there are glitches, there are problems. . . . They are attempting to reform the whole system. So it's just gotten so big" (Senior welfare administrator, Toronto, interviewed by Tod Rutherford and Jamie Peck, July 1998).

42. Source: calculated from LEXIS/NEXIS.

43. Social activist #3, interviewed by Tod Rutherford and Jamie Peck, July 1998.

44. Social activist #2, interviewed by Tod Rutherford and Jamie Peck, July 1998.

45. Social activist #3, interviewed by Tod Rutherford and Jamie Peck, July 1998.

46. On whip-sawing, see also Holmes and Rusonik (1991).

47. Ontario trade union official, interviewed by Jamie Peck, March 1995.

# CHAPTER SEVEN

# Another New Deal

*Workfare, United Kingdom Style*

> Now at the close of the 20th century, the decline of old
> industries and the shift to an economy based on knowledge
> and skills has given rise to a new class: a workless class. In
> many countries—not just Britain—a large minority is playing
> no role in the formal economy, dependent on benefits and the
> black economy . . . detached not just from work, but also from
> citizenship in its wider sense. . . . Earlier this century leaders
> faced the challenge of creating a welfare state that could
> provide security for the new working class. Today the greatest
> challenge for any democratic government is to refashion our
> institutions to bring this new workless class back into society
> and into useful work, and to bring back the will to win. (Tony
> Blair, speech at the Aylesbury Estate, June 1997)

Following the British Labour Party's landslide victory at the polls in May
1997, Prime Minister Blair chose the occasion of his first major speech
outside Parliament to address the question of welfare reform. Speaking at
a run-down London housing estate—a carefully chosen site the symbolism of which was clearly not lost either on local residents or on the wider
national audience—Blair insisted that there would be "no no-go areas for
New Labour."[1] On the contrary, his would be an activist, reforming, modernizing administration, one prepared not only to "think the unthinkable" in its review of policy options, but also to do it. At the heart of this
radical program sat welfare reform, "the single most important policy

that separates Blair from Old Labour" (Teles, 1997: 23). Blair's tough talk on welfare showed that his administration would not balk at offending the "Old Labour" sensibilities of traditionalists and those on the left of the party; his speech at Southwark was calculated to draw a line under the rights-and-entitlements approach to welfare reform while marking out the territory for the new "radical center" in British politics.

According to John Kay (1998: 35), "Welfare-to-work . . . represents the largest ideological shift by New Labour and most clearly epitomises the Third Way." Significantly, welfare reform is defined by New Labour both as a political and as an economic project; it is concerned with re-connecting the poor with waged work in the context of a changing labor market; and it is about transforming the behaviors and perceptions of a distinct social group—a *class*, no less—alledgedly rendered dependent and dysfunctional by economic change. The task for government is seen as one of radical and work-reinforcing institutional reform; the (recipro-cal) task for welfare recipients is to respond enthusiastically to these new opportunities. While the prime minister conceded that "[t]he task of re-shaping welfare to reward work is daunting," he nevertheless maintained that this was the issue on which his administration should be judged: "This will be the Welfare to Work government."[2]

Perhaps Blair's government has been reassured by the fact that it is not alone in its search for a postwelfare settlement. But it is choosing its allies carefully. When Tony Blair addressed the Party of European Socialists' Congress in June 1997, he chose not to build bridges with left-of-center parties across Europe but instead to lecture delegates about the disabling costs of welfare and the virtues of deregulated labor markets.[3] In marked contrast, the visit to London one week earlier of President Clinton had been seized upon as an opportunity to cement a political alliance between the United Kingdom and the United States: the two leaders pledged to make common cause of welfare reform and active labor-market policy-making, exploiting their successive presidencies of G8 in 1997 and 1998 to drive forward what Blair described as "a common agenda, and a shared de-termination to tackle the problems we all face, to identify what reforms have worked where, what reforms have failed and how we can learn the les-sons of both success and failure. . . . We have a shared language. We have a shared outlook."[4] According to Robert Walker,

> The acceptance of the flexible labor market and, by implication, low wages, combined with proactive measures to encourage workers to ac-cept them, positions New Labour closer to Clinton Democrats than to social democrats on continental Europe. . . . Blair's speeches, and the writings of his close colleagues, resonate with a pot-pourri of US influ-ences. . . . Blair seems to accept that welfare has become a problem

rather than a solution, destroying the work ethic and other family values . . . [proposing] an agenda forged from a heady mix of US social
liberalism and communitarianism, combined with British Christian
Socialism. (1998: 35)

Close political affinities (of a rather different kind), coupled with a
lubricated policy-transfer system, had of course been a feature of the
Reagan–Thatcher era of the 1980s (see Jones, 1996; Dolowitz, 1998), but
in some ways the less explicitly ideological alliance between Clinton and
Blair may have proven to be more radical, at least for the United Kingdom. While, during the 1980s, the degree of receptivity to U.S. policy innovations in the United Kingdom was marked in areas such as urban
policy and local economic development (see Barnekov et al., 1989; Jonas
and Wilson, 1999), the process of policy transfer in the welfare and labor-market spheres was always more cautious and provisional. At the
center of this hesitancy was resistance to what was almost universally—
and typically also pejoratively—referred to as "U.S.-style workfare," opposed by both the right and the left for rather different reasons: "[T]he
right dislikes the expense involved setting up training schemes, while
the left sees any element of compulsion as anathema" (Digby, 1989:
114). Always nervous of the public-expenditure implications of seeming
to endorse a role for the state as "employer of the last resort," the
Conservative governments of 1979–1997 never fully bought into the
workfare philosophy. Incremental shifts toward workfare certainly did
occur—specifically in the progressive tightening of the benefits regime
and the effective mandate of labor-market programs—but every movement in this direction met vociferous opposition from welfare campaigners inside and outside the Labour Party. In fact, to castigate Conservative
reforms—such as the tightening of work-availability rules under Restart
in 1986, or the introduction of the benefits-plus Employment Training
program in 1988—as "a step closer to U.S.-style workfare" was almost
guaranteed to secure maximum political (and media) impact. So, while
the institutional characterizations of the welfare system and the political
context of the welfare settlement are both quite different in the United
Kingdom and the United States (see King, 1995), the politics of the reform process have been such that successive policy shifts in Britain are
invariably calibrated against the U.S. situation.[5]

Interpreting workfare politics in the United Kingdom can be perplexing because it appears to combine strong echoes of the U.S.-style
workfare with equally strong resistances to the same phenomenon.
Indeed, there are many echoes of the Canadian situation in this simultaneous vulnerability/resistance to "Americanization." Any potential
movement towards fully fledged workfare systems was held in check

during the 1980s and early 1990s by two quite distinct political forces: the expenditure-conscious right of the Conservative Party and the anti-compulsion left of the Labour Party. Meanwhile, advocacy of workfare was a fringe concern of the Conservative left and the Labour right (see Heseltine, 1990; Field, 1995). By the time of the 1997 General Election, however, cross-party support for workfare-style reforms had emerged (see Convery, 1997). Britain, it seemed had fashioned its own version of the "workfare consensus," as the manifestos of the three main parties made clear:

> The best way to tackle poverty is to help people into jobs—real jobs. The unemployed have a responsibility to take up the opportunity of training places or work, but these must be real opportunities. The [Conservative] government's workfare proposals . . . fail this test. Labour's welfare-to-work programme will attack unemployment and break the spiral of escalating spending on social security. (Labour Party, 1997: 19)

> Although governments cannot create jobs, they can help people train and find work. . . . We will always help those in genuine need: in return, the unemployed have a responsibility to look for work and accept a reasonable job offer. That belief underpins our new Jobseeker's Allowance which ensures that no-one can refuse reasonable work opportunities and remain on benefit. (Conservative Party, 1997: 11)

> We will enable long-term unemployed people to turn their unemployment benefits into "working benefits" paid to an employer to recruit and train them. We will break open the poverty traps that stop unemployed people from working. (Liberal Democratic Party, 1997: 17)

This chapter traces the roots of Britain's newfound "workfare consensus," focusing on the transition between the Conservative government's incrementalism during the 1980s and early 1990s and the new Labour government's radicalism in the late 1990s. It will explain why the political embrace of workfare in Britain was initially such a tentative one, and why the late conversion of New Labour to workfarism has been such a fervent one.

## CREEPING COMPULSION: CONSERVATIVE INCREMENTALISM

Until the late 1970s, the political convention in the United Kingdom had been that if the level of unemployment should pass one million, the government of the day would fall. And certainly this was one of the factors behind the collapse of the Labour government in 1979. But the incoming Thatcher government overturned these political conventions by presiding over an explosion in unemployment during the 1980s. The Conservatives' monetarist strategy for controlling inflation had sent the country into deep recession in the early 1980s, leading to a shake-out of manufacturing jobs and a rapid acceleration in the level of unemployment to over three million. Pragmatically, the Conservatives initially responded to the unemployment crisis by reworking and expanding the suite of labor-market programs for young people and the unemployed inherited from the previous Labour administration. A range of schemes had been established under the Manpower Services Commission (MSC) during the 1970s to deal with what was regarded at the time as a *temporary* downturn in labor demand: a package of relatively small-scale employment subsidy, work-experience, and job-creation schemes had been launched as "counter cyclical measures" (MSC, 1976).

The very stubbornness of the unemployment problem, however, led to a reconsideration of both the design and the rationale of the program. Measures for young people, for example, were coordinated and consolidated under the 1978 Youth Opportunities Programme (YOP), which by focusing on remedial workforce preparation began to displace a demand-side rationale (temporary employment opportunities in response to a cyclical shortage of jobs) with a supply-side one (instruction in work and social skills in response to a deficient work ethic among the young). This new philosophy was to be pursued with evangelical zeal by the Conservatives, who constructed an active program of labor-market flexibilization around large-scale training and "employability" schemes for young people and unemployed adults (see Robertson, 1986; Finn, 1987; Peck, 1994), replacing YOP with the Youth Training Scheme (YTS) in 1983.

The scale of the programming effort increased in lockstep with the mushrooming unemployment problem, as the Conservatives—for all their rhetoric of free-market deregulation—found themselves steering a highly interventionist labor-market regime. While cash benefits on youth schemes were held well below market rates, adults on schemes such as the Community Programme (CP) were paid the going "rate for the job" (on the insistence of labor union representatives within the MSC), and participation remained voluntary. While the unemployed were certainly induced to enter programs, or where possible waged work, rather than to remain on benefits, the early 1980s regime was a *relatively* passive one. Urban riots at the start of the 1980s and the widespread collapse of manufacturing economies dictated that the benefit regime be operated in a comparatively liberal manner, at least for the time being. This hardly sat easily with the Conservatives' political instincts, but pragmatism and expediency suggested a more cautious approach. If there had to be labor-market programs, however, at least they would de (re)designed in such a

way as to complement and strengthen market forces, rather than to replace them. Schemes were "designed to work with the grain of the market, so as to encourage more realistic wage levels and more flexible
working patterns" (Treasury, 1984: 3). Thus far, the coercive integration
of the unemployed into the labor market was largely an aspiration of
government policy rather than a reality. The overriding imperative remained one of containment.

## Stricter Benefits

Significantly, it was not until the mid-1980s, when unemployment finally
began to fall as the economy entered a cycle of growth, that more punitive and restrictive measures were introduced. A series of legislative reforms and incremental shifts in policy and practice were to fashion what
became known as the "Stricter Benefit Regime." Under the Restart program initiated in 1986, those unemployed for more than six months
were called in to JobCentres where they were required to demonstrate
the *active* steps they were taking to find work. Refusal to cooperate, or to
join designated programs, would result in benefit sanctions. What became known as the "restart effect" would induce claimants to leave the
rolls: an evaluation revealed that Restart participants were 5 percent less
likely to continue claiming benefits than an "off-policy" control group
(White and Lakey, 1992). Subsequently eligibility rules and "availability-
for-work" tests were repeatedly tightened. The effect was to discipline
those in the lower reaches of the labor market as well as the unemployed
themselves (both of which, of course, are traditionally highly dynamic
and closely interlinked groups). For example, benefit penalties and exclusion periods were extended for those leaving paid employment "voluntarily"—a common method of exit from secondary employment,
where workers have little in the way of formal protection (see Daniel,
1981)—a system which in 1981 was dubbed "the English version of
Workfare" by Peter Barclay, then chair of the Social Security Advisory
Committee (quoted in Digby, 1989: 113).

While generally intensifying the pressure to move off welfare—
and into work, onto other benefits, into "inactivity" or the informal
economy—the restructuring of the benefit system also imposed a regime
of compulsion around government-training, job-search, and work-
experience programs. Young people were the first to fall under attack
here, as the 1988 Social Security Act removed sixteen and seventeen
year-olds from eligibility for cash benefits. This meant that YTS, which in
1986 had been extended from a one- to a two-year program and which at
the times was providing more than 350,000 places nationally, was effectively compulsory for young people. While technically at least participa-

tion in YTS was voluntary, the removal of benefits made what was tortuously termed the "guaranteed option" of a place on the scheme a last resort that few were in a position to refuse. So, even at this stage, with unemployment falling and the Conservatives at the peak of their political strength, explicit compulsion was never stated policy. Michael Portillo, then under secretary of state for health and social security, offered the following convoluted account during the committee stage of what was to become the 1988 Social Security Act:

> I entirely rebut the . . . repeated allegation about compulsion. It is true that we are withdrawing income support from 16 and 17-year-olds who have left school, are not in work and have not taken up a YTS place, but the choices for young people are still there. They can stay at school. They can go to college. They can, if they are lucky, take a job. Or they can take a YTS place that is on offer to them. I persist in saying, therefore, that there is no compulsion. We are talking about the guaranteed option of a place on a YTS and the response of the Government and the taxpayer to that new situation. (quoted in King, 1995: 171)

Finding a later echo in Canadian Liberals' talk of "mandatory opportunities" for welfare recipients to participate in training and employment schemes, the notion of a "guaranteed option" of a YTS place reflected a reluctance fully to commit to a workfarist strategy at this time in the United Kingdom. Establishing a pattern that was to run through to the New Labour period, it was already clear that de facto compulsion was more acceptable for some groups (notably, young people) than for others (like lone parents and the disabled). Portillo himself, in fact, would remain somewhat ambivalent about workfare, preferring to manipulate the benefit system so as to enforce work, compel participation in labor-market programs, and deregister recipients; he would later sanction experimental trials, but remained unwilling to incur the public-spending commitments, or to countenance the extensive state role in the labor market, implied by full-blown workfare.[6]

## Dismantling Labor-Market Corporatism

While in the run-up to the 1987 General Election, ministers stressed that there were "no plans to introduce a workfare type programme in this country" (David Young, quoted in Digby, 1989: 114); the clear thrust of policy continued to be workfarist. The launch by the returning Conservative government of the Employment Training Program (ET) in 1988, in which participants were paid only £10 on top of benefits, seemed calculated to provoke a major confrontation with those labor unions and local authorities that for some time had been leading the campaign against workfare, with the active support of the Labour Party through the "Charter Against Workfare."[7] Alongside the introduction of ET, the government proposed also to restructure the MSC so as to dilute labor-union representation, renaming it the Training Commission (see Ainley and Corney, 1990). Infuriated at the proposals, commission member Ron Todd of the Transport and General Workers Union (TGWU) declared that a more appropriate name for the new body would be the "Workfare Commission." Subsequently tendering his resignation from the Training Commission, Todd attacked ET as "the British version of Workfare" (quoted in Jones, 1997: 105). The TGWU would then coordinate the campaign against ET with the Trades Union Congress, which voted to oppose the scheme at its 1988 annual conference. The then-leader of the Labour Party, Neil Kinnock, had urged the TUC to "resist the slide to workfare,"[8] but many delegates recognized that the unions' role within the commission had for some time been largely symbolic and defensive, given the government's increased propensity to impose its will on this supposedly arm's-length organization.[9]

The government's response to the TUC boycott of ET was breathtakingly radical: it eliminated the fledgling Training Commission, reabsorbing its national coordination role into the Department of Employment while decentralizing its remaining functions to a newly created network of locally based, employer-led Training and Enterprise Councils (TECs). Inspired by the United States Private Industry Councils (PICs), TECs were constituted as private companies operating on contract to the Department of Employment to deliver a range of training, employment, and enterprise programmes at the local level, including ET and the repackaged youth scheme, YT (see Jones, 1996, 1999). The contractual framework in which TECs were embedded was designed to mimic the market, rewarding rapid, low-cost (re)integration of program participants into employment (Peck and Jones, 1995). As such, it served to further entrench a workfare dynamic in U.K. labor-market policy, drawing TECs into the role of low-cost servicers of the welfare-to-work transition. What was being enforced here was often not work per se, but participation in low-grade training schemes and various forms of simulated work or "make-work." This was appropriately characterized by Jones (1999) as "trainingfare."

## Toward Workfarism

Unemployment rose sharply again in the recession of 1990—1993, but on this occasion the government's response was rather more flexible and variegated. The network of TECs proved adept in the expeditious delivery of new programs, contributing also to policy innovation through their role in local-level piloting and experimentation. The newly created Employment Service that had been formed to integrate the management of job-placement services (through JobCentres) and the unemployment-benefit system, was itself delivering a range of job-search and motivational programs under the Stricter Benefit Regime. Summarized in Table 7.1, the package of measures on offer at this time nearly all had their origins or inspirations in earlier U.S. initiatives (see King, 1995; Dolowitz, 1998), representing the selective appropriation of key elements of the U.S. workfare repertoire (see Walker, 1991). Rarely, if ever, were these initiatives—such as job clubs, benefits plus "training" schemes, and motivational programs—"imported" in a direct, lock-stock-and-barrel fashion; instead, they were selectively integrated within the evolving British institutional system. Over the decade since the mid-1980s, the orientation of this complex, multiagency system had become increasingly workfarist, as the uneven fall in unemployment had presented opportunities to shift away from the previous schemes-based orthodoxy of national, stand-alone "special employment measures" toward an increasingly integrated, locally flexible, benefits-and-programs regime. As Fletcher observes,

> since the mid-1980s "Workfare" ideas have steadily become more influential. Such ideas emphasise individual rather than social causes of unemployment. In this context, re-motivational measures are ideal because they are comparatively cheap, easy to administer and help to place the onus of finding work squarely on the unemployed. (1997: 178–179)

Paralleling the gradual shift toward labor-force attachment models of workfare in the United States, there has been a tendency in the United Kingdom to make increased use of job-search counseling and motivational programs, which may cost as little as 5–10 percent of the cost of training-based programs (see ERGO, 1992; Meager, 1997). This reflected the Conservatives' goal of inducing the unemployed to deregister and/or to enter work, but only where this could be achieved on a low unit-cost basis. Elaborate labor-market-adjustment programs or high-quality training/education provision were, realistically, never part of the picture.

The barrage of labor-market measures deployed in the United Kingdom by the early 1990s were clearly workfarist in the general sense in which the term is used here. Benefit eligibility had been reduced and for those "inside" the system had been rendered increasingly conditional on a range of actively-seeking-work tests and behavioral requirements.

**TABLE 7.1.** Programs for the Unemployed, 1994–1995

| Program | Function | Delivery | Number of places (000) | Cost per place (£) |
|---|---|---|---|---|
| **Remotivation programs** | | | | |
| Job clubs | Improves basic job-search skills of the unemployed | Employment Service | 257 | 196 |
| Jobplan | Helps the unemployed assess their skills and strengths and examine new options in either work or training | Employment Service | 250 | 127 |
| Job-review workshop | Provides the unemployed with an opportunity to reassess the type of work they are looking for and explore alternative options | Employment Service | 40 | 80 |
| Job-search seminar | Assists the unemployed to improve their job-search skills | Employment Service | 65 | 75 |
| Job Interview Guarantee | The JIG preparation course addresses interview techniques | Employment Service | 300 | 6 |
| Restart courses | Job-search training | Employment Service | 144 | 98 |
| **Training programs** | | | | |
| Training for Work | Vocational training and work experience for those unemployed for 6 months or more; participants receive an allowance equal to benefit plus £10 | TECs | 280 | 2,475 |
| Youth Training | Two-year training program for 16- to 17-year-olds | TECs | 232 | 2,831 |
| **Employment subsidies** | | | | |
| Workstart | Employer subsidy paid on recruitment of long-term unemployed (2 years plus) | Employment Service | 1.2 | 2,340 |

*Source:* Adapted from Fletcher (1997).

Summarizing the aims of Conservative employment and welfare-policy reform during the 1980s and early 1990s, Dean and Taylor-Gooby point to three central themes:

> to strengthen work incentives, which means widening the gap between benefit levels and earnings; to direct spending accurately to defined groups of needy people, which means greater use of means-testing and of restrictions on entitlement; and to simplify the administration of the system, while intensifying the measures to stop fraud and regulate claimants' lives which are required by the other two objectives. Policies to create more jobs take a second place to policies designed to compel people to take whatever jobs are available, and training schemes are incorporated more tightly into the system of labour discipline. Social security for unemployed people changes its character. From being an apparatus designed to maintain the incomes of those out of work, it becomes a system designed to force people into work. (1992: 55)

Labor-market programs, even where their internal rules determined participation to be "voluntary," were operated within a climate of compulsion enforced by the benefits system. Over time, programs were increasingly subordinated to the demands not only of labor markets in general but of *local* labor markets in particular, becoming systemically oriented to low-cost, labor-market integration. The British work–welfare regime consequently exhibited the fundamental features of workfarism by the mid-1990s: it combined coerciveness, conditionality, and compulsion. Of course, this was not "U.S.-style workfare" as such. Because workfare regimes are heavily embedded and path-dependent, "U.S.-style workfare" can only exist in the United States. As Walker (1991: 2) has observed, "The long history of workfare in the USA and the current consensus of support, [based] on a symbiotic compromise between different political traditions, makes the concept as American as blueberry pie." Rather more formally, the *concept* of workfare is an abstraction from the specificities of workfarist practice, in the United States or elsewhere; its different national (or local) variants represent specific and institutionally embedded conjunctures of workfarist practices and structures. As a *concept*, workfare is of course highly transferable. The British version of blueberry pie may not taste exactly like the U.S. original, but it certainly shares many of the same ingredients—mixed rather differently.[10]

The British variant of workfare, at least in its early form, very much reflects its distinct political–economic origins. First, it emerged in the context of an inherited pattern of large-scale labor-market programming for young people and the adult unemployed, initially taking the form of reorienting existing schemes rather than constructing new ones (see

Robertson, 1986; Peck, 1994). Second, the gradual emergence of work-farism was shaped both by economic conditions and by the Conservative government's political–economic response to mass unemployment, vividly revealed in Chancellor Lamont's infamous remark in the midst of the early 1990s recession that unemployment was a "price well worth paying" for the effective control of inflation (Glynn, 1994; Grieve Smith, 1997). The policy orientation had since the early 1980s generally been one of containment, though downswings in the level of unemployment in the late 1980s and again in the mid-1990s were, significantly, both associated with a heightened emphasis on labor-market (re)integration. Third, there was a reluctance to fully embrace workfare rhetoric in the Conservative Party, in part due to anxieties about public-expenditure implications, and in part because one of the primary political motivations for more activist approaches to unemployment is to play to the populist concern that this will root out "scroungers" and those "fiddling the system" (Mead, 1996a; Novak, 1997). The preoccupation with the work ethic in U.S. workfare discourse simply was not present in anything like the same way in the British debate under the Conservatives—a fact reflected in the typically pejorative connotations of "U.S.-style workfare." Fourth, the ascendancy of workfarism U.K.-style occurred in the context of a distinctive pattern of institutional restructuring, framed by the rise, neoliberalization, and fall of the MSC, the launch of TECs, and the construction of an activist Employment Service (King, 1993, 1995; Jones, 1996). Workfarism in the United Kingdom has emerged as a complex *interinstitutional* phenomenon, rather than as a clearly identifiable "project," "scheme," or "initiative." This is arguably the reverse of the U.S. situation, where the term originally denoted a specific program and only later would acquire the wider, systemic meaning.

These antecedents partly explain why the initial emergence of work-farism in the United Kingdom, in the decade following the mid-1980s, was so nebulous. In the realm of political representation the phenomenon was never actually *named* as workfare; indeed, there was little or no explicit recognition that diverse reforms in the training system, in social security law and practice, and in labor-market programming were even connected, let alone part of some grand (workfarist) design. Retrospectively, Dolowitz (1998: 173) makes such a claim, asserting that Britain had a "fully functioning workfare regime by 1990," though his account is largely based on an assessment of the *cumulative* significance of what were (for the most part) piecemeal, workfare-style reforms. There is something to be said for this argument, though it must be acknowledged that workfarism lacked any serious systemic coherence at this time. In fact, it would take another decade, and the election of a Labour Government, to set in train this systemic transformation.

The partial, fragmentary, and tendentious nature of workfare in the

United Kingdom prior to the mid-1990s is reflected in the fact that, throughout this period, critics were able to mobilize potent political capital simply by virtue of labeling an initiative or reform as "workfare." In addition, the legacy of large-scale, scheme-based interventions seems to have led both critics and advocates to associate workfare with a single, monolithic program. So it is notable that *Workfare* is often rendered as a proper noun in British political discourse, in contrast to its more genericized usage in the United States. Writing in 1991, Robert Walker appropriately characterized the British variant of workfarism in the following way:

> Workfare has not been implemented in the United Kingdom and, while the idea has attracted much comment, there are as yet no plans to introduce such as system. [W]orkfare, in its ideologically "pure" form, is in fact rare in the United States. Instead, a range of work–welfare measures have been implemented which are in varying degrees mandatory. . . . [T]he reality of American workfare is a set of services and obligations which are very similar to those already available in the United Kingdom. . . . In some respects, the current combination of employment and social security policies places Britain further along the road *towards* workfare than many states in America. . . . While the British system is clearly not workfare, many of the elements of American work–welfare schemes are already in place. (1991: 49–50)

This is more than an arcane exercise in policy semantics, for what Walker is describing here are the elements of a *protosystemic* workfare regime. Of course, this is not yet a "system" in any absolute sense, but it clearly exhibits presystemic qualities in its incorporation of aspects of workfarist practice, embedded within a regime of creeping compulsion.

By the time Britain was coming out of the early 1990s recession it had become clear that many of the most important parts of the workfare jigsaw had been put in place. The social security system had acquired a more activist and individually interventionist methodology, labor-market programs had been realigned to respond to the short-term needs of local economies, nonbusiness interests had been substantially purged from governance structures at the local and national levels, and the labor market itself had been substantially deregulated and flexibilized. The Conservatives had inherited, and developed, a welfare system that was arguably more concerned with minimizing fraud than maximizing work, subsequently bolting on a series of job-search and "training" programs in an incremental and often economically contingent way. In the early 1990s, this remained some way from a coherent and integrated workfare regime, though many of its constituent elements were in place. The stage was now set for workfare politics to take on a far more explicit form in the United Kingdom.

## RADICAL CONSENSUS: ENDING BEVERIDGE

The first phase of workfarism in the United Kingdom was characterized by a series of incremental attempts to construct a framework of compulsion around a suite of (inherited, but modified) labor-market programs. The second and still ongoing phase, which cannot be dated precisely but began in the early to mid-1990s, witnessed a much more direct and explicit engagement with the politics of workfare. In different ways, both major political parties began to move in this direction, challenging the hitherto sacrosanct principles of the Beveridgean welfare state (see Fraser, 1984). The debate began with less of a bang than a whimper, when Prime Minister John Major finally broached the taboo subject of workfare—albeit cautiously and almost hesitantly—in a speech to the Carlton Club in February 1993:

> I increasingly wonder whether paying unemployment benefit, without offering or requiring any activity in return, serves unemployed people or society well. Of course, we have to make sure that any conditions imposed improve the job prospects of the unemployed people and give good value to the country. But we have already introduced this principle, for example through Restart, in a limited sense for the long-term unemployed. I believe we should explore ways of extending it further. (*Guardian*, February 4, 1993: 20)

This short passage from Major's speech caused something of a political storm, for while the word itself had not been used, critics seized immediately upon its workfarist connotations. Labour's social security spokesperson, Donald Dewar, insisted, "What the unemployed want is work and new skills. What is unacceptable is workfare by any name" (*Independent*, February 4, 1993: 1). Seeking to extract maximum political advantage from the situation, Dewar called on Peter Lilley, secretary of state for social security, to explain to the House of Commons "what this deliberately obscure passage actually means" (*Independent*, February 4, 1993: 4). But with the cabinet apparently divided over workfare, government sources moved quickly to dampen speculation around far-reaching welfare reform.[11] The prime minister's speech, it was insisted, was supposed to have been about crime and the inner cities (themselves familiar themes in many a workfare litany).[12]

Amid the confusion, claim, and counterclaim in this opening moment of the new phase of the workfare debate, U.K.-style, it had become clear to some that a symbolically important point had been passed. As a leader in the *Independent* (February 5, 1993: 18) put it, "The provocative Americanism 'workfare' has not passed the Prime Minister's lips, but something akin to it has been forced on to the political agenda." Certainly workfare continued to aggravate the anti-interventionist sensibilities of the Conservative right, who remained opposed to the program on the grounds of public cost and market distortion,[13] but the discursive foundations of the debate were beginning subtly to change. As rightwing policy advocate Graham Mather explained:

> In 24 hours, Workfare has lurched from a faintly remembered 1980s nostrum to a top-of-the-news shock horror, and, after hasty corrective briefing, back into the realm of medium term policy possibilities. . . . It is a symptom of the inadequacy of the way in which we discuss and make policy in Britain that the Workfare idea, and the limited steps towards it primarily during the late 1980s, have been confined to the files of a few specialist writers and technical journals. The concept is less dramatic, more conventional, less economic and more moral and social than this week's headlines suggest. (1993: 21)

More telling in retrospect was the fact that the ascendant, "modernizing" wing of the Labour Party was also beginning to choose its words more carefully. Peter Mandelson, architect of the subsequent "Blair revolution," wrote in a letter to the *Independent*, "On the subject of 'workfare,' the Labour Party needs to abandon its knee-jerk responses and wake up to the fact that there is a world beyond Westminster crying out for action for the unemployed. . . . Everyone must abandon slogans and start some real thinking instead."[14]

## Modernizing Welfare Policy

As Peter Mandelson was all too aware, the Labour Party had only three months before established the Commission on Social Justice to undertake a far-reaching review of the changing relationship between work and welfare. Precisely fifty years after the Beveridge Report, *Social Insurance and Allied Services*, had enshrined the principles of Britain's postwar welfare settlement (Beveridge, 1942), the new commission was charged with the responsibility for presenting policy options for the redesign of the welfare state in line with contemporary economic and social "realities." Guided by the enduring principles of social justice, its terms of reference nevertheless urged a radical review of existing policies, institutions, and priorities:

- To consider the principles of social justice and their application to the economic well-being of individuals and the community;
- To examine the relationship between social justice and other goals, including economic competitiveness and prosperity;

- To probe the changes in social and economic life over the last fifty years, and the failure of public policy to address them adequately; and to survey the changes that are likely in the foreseeable future, and the demands they will place on government;
- To analyse public priorities, particularly in the fields of employment, taxation and social welfare, which could enable every individual to live free from want and to enjoy the fullest possible social and economic opportunities;
- And to examine the contribution which such policies could make to the creation of a fairer and more just society. (Commission on Social Justice, 1994: 412)

The commission would subsequently walk a fine line between fairly traditional Labour Party positions and radical "modernization." So, emphasis would be placed on demand-side causes of unemployment—in particular the collapse of male-held, manufacturing jobs—while at the same time issues like "welfare dependency" were also placed on the agenda; there would be skepticism concerning deregulationist and (some) supply-side strategies for combating unemployment, but it would be matched with an insistence on the need for greater flexibility in benefits systems (see Balls and Gregg, 1993). At a more discursive level, the commission's report deployed the language of intervention alongside the distinctively U.S. vernacular of welfare reform. For example, there are unmistakable echoes of Clinton rhetoric in the commission's call for a transformation of the welfare state "from a safety net in times of trouble to a springboard for economic opportunity. . . . The welfare state must enable people to achieve self-improvement and self-support. It must offer a hand-up, not a hand-out" (Commission on Social Justice, 1994: 1, 8).[15]

The commission examined the option of workfare—narrowly defined, as the requirement that welfare recipients "work off their grants in unpaid jobs" (Commission on Social Justice, 1994: 182)—concluding that it should be rejected on the grounds that the principle of compulsion would inevitably undermine both the credibility and the work-reinforcing goals of the program:

> There is a real danger . . . that if young people are offered the choice between workfare or inadequate training and the loss of their benefits, they will reject both workfare and benefits and choose a third way—the cash-and-crime economy. . . . Workfare . . . tries to make unemployment disappear by converting it into public works programmes paid at benefit plus a weekly top-up. But the long-term unemployed, like everyone else, want to work for wages, not for benefit or benefit-plus. As Alan Sinclair, founder of the Wise Group stressed to us "We have got to get people out of 'Giroland' " (Commission on Social Justice, 1994: 182–183).

Work rather than workfare was the commission's preferred option; policies would need to wean the unemployed off their "Giro" (welfare) checks, and off the benefit culture. Their recommended welfare-to-work strategy combined wage subsidies for the long-term unemployed with significant investments in childcare and training, backed up by an active "reemployment" service. Self-employment would be encouraged, while steps would have to be taken to create "intermediate labor markets"—inspired by the Wise Group model in Glasgow, where unemployed people are trained to work in the local "social economy"—in areas of particularly high unemployment. Although the commission clearly acknowledged the role of Britain's "jobs deficit" in causing unemployment, its welfare-to-work proposals were nevertheless strongly oriented toward the objective of "improving employability" because "in the end employment goes to the employable" (Commission on Social Justice, 1994: 175).

More accurately, of course, employment tends to go to the *most* employable; it is a supply-side fallacy to suggest that improving employability will increase the aggregate level of labor demand, that is, the number of jobs in an economy. In isolation, supply-side measures are more likely to impact the social *distribution* of work at a given level of labor demand. In this sense, they may alter the relationship between welfare and work by reducing the duration of both employment and unemployment spells for those at the bottom of the labor market; the effect is to reduce "duration dependency" through a subsidized process of labor-market "churning" (see Balls and Gregg, 1993; Hutton, 1996). The clear danger in this kind of zero-sum redistribution is that policies achieve tentative reattachments to the labor force at the expense of employment insecurity; labor-market instability, poverty, and indeed welfare dependency are not "solved" by such measures, they are for the most part simply redistributed among the same "at risk" groups (see Peck and Theodore, 1999).

The work–welfare proposals of the Commission on Social Justice consequently represented a break both with the Keynesian welfarism of Britain's postwar settlement and with the neoliberalism of the Conservatives. According to William Walters, they epitomize a new strand of thinking on welfare reform: *human capitalism*. Alongside complementary positions, such as those of former U.S. labor secretary Robert Reich and the European Commission's social policy directorate,[16] the Commission on Social Justice argued for labor-market integration via enskilling as the solution not only to unemployment but to a range of social problems afflicting the "nonemployed":

> Like neo-liberalism, human capitalism holds that wealth and prosperity depend ultimately on the capacity of individuals, regions, and nations to respond to the demands and opportunities that an increas-

ingly global and competitive economic environment present. Both reject the premise they associate with the "Keynesian welfare state"—that welfare can be engineered by extra-economic means, by "social" technologies. However, human capitalism differs when it insists that competitiveness requires a dense mesh of extra-economic institutions. As a political framework it requires a state that is variously described as "enabling," "entrepreneurial," "catalysing." But it also requires various economic agents. The essentially negative tactic of deregulation will not suffice. (Walters, 1996: 212)

Although the translation of the commission's specific proposals into Labour Party policies was disrupted by the death in 1994 of John Smith, and his replacement as Labour leader by Tony Blair, both continuities and discontinuities would be evident in Labour's subsequent approach. The overall emphasis on what Walters terms "human capitalism" was retained, and at least at a rhetorical level the role of skills and training would be stepped up. But there would be no new training tax, no new obligations on employers to invest in skills, no increases even in the basic rate of income tax. Instead, working within the same tight public-spending parameters as the Conservatives, a future Labour administration would eschew the party's tax-and-spend image in favor of a new approach combining fiscal prudence and low-inflation growth. In effect, the shadow chancellor, Gordon Brown, pledged to operate a broadly similar macroeconomic management regime as the Conservatives, albeit one complemented by a more activist range of policies for tackling unemployment, his belief being that the maintenance of economic growth would alone be insufficient to solve the problems of the long-term unemployed (*Independent*, November 24, 1994: 12).

But the new Labour's leadership's embrace of an active labor-market philosophy would take it much closer to workfarism—and to a U.S.-style welfare-to-work approach—than the Commission had recommended. As political journalist Stephen Castle predicted at the time, "anxious to break the dependency culture [Blair] may want to go further towards US-style workfare than the commission" (*Independent*, October 23, 1994: 2). Indeed, a member of the commission observed that the rapidly shifting position of the leadership on welfare in general and compulsion in particular was an early signal of the shape of things to come from New Labour: "The Commission were criticized by many of the left [for] being modernizers. Within a year, really, of Blair becoming leader it was like we were classed as Old Labour! Quite extraordinary. So I see it as a touchstone of the speed with which Blair pulled the Party to a different position."[17]

One month after the publication of the commission's report, in November 1994, Gordon Brown produced a shadow budget intended to highlight the differences between Labour and the Conservatives in the sphere of labor-market policy. Brown's ambitious jobs package was based around a series of "roads into work," including tax breaks for employers recruiting from among the long-term unemployed and a series of benefit reforms designed—in another imported phrase—to "make work pay." Most controversially, the new programs would be compulsory for benefit recipients, though Brown was at pains to insist—inevitably—that they were not workfarist. In contrast to the Conservatives' approach, Brown argued that mandatory participation should be understood not so much as brutal "compulsion" but more in the context of a new (moral) framework of reciprocal rights and responsibilities: "The Tories [sic] option is simply to penalise the unemployed while shifting nearer to workfare. Labour says the obligation on the unemployed to seek work must be matched by government action actively to promote new opportunities" (*Guardian*, November 25, 1994: 7).

Critically, the Labour Party leadership had now accepted the defining workfarist principle of compulsion, albeit with a veneer of communitarian rhetoric (see Driver and Martell, 1997). Under Blair's self-styled *New* Labour, there would be a commitment to "think the unthinkable" across a range of policy areas, welfare being perhaps the most sensitive. With some echoes of the way in which a workfarist consensus was fashioned in the U.S. Democratic Party, Labour's embrace of workfarism was built around a complex—and in some cases fragile—coalition of political interests. The advocacy of "tough love" was a measure—for the party's leadership at least—of the ideological distance between "New" and "Old" Labour (see Dickson, 1997; Teles, 1997; Kay, 1998), while skeptics on the left of the party were generally prepared to remain pragmatically silent as long as they saw scope for new programs and resources. The left had long argued for a large-scale response to unemployment. It appeared that under the Blair–Brown proposals they would get this, but it would be enveloped in the new language of rights and responsibilities. Labour's workfare compromise would bring together a commitment to an ambitious welfare-to-work program with an obligation on the unemployed to take up these new opportunities. According to New Labour's most fervent advocate, Peter Mandelson,

> It is a crucial New Labour commitment that society must accept a serious obligation to find work for the young unemployed. This will end the long years of Conservative complacency and neglect. In these circumstances the young unemployed themselves have to accept obligations too. . . . It is not right that some people should collect the dole, live on the black economy, and then refuse to cooperate with society's efforts to reintegrate them into the labour market. It is dishonest and corrosive of our attempt to build a sense of mutual obligations in the

community. In circumstances where new opportunity is being offered and refused, there should be no absolute entitlement to continued receipt of social security benefits. . . . Such a tough discipline is necessary to demonstrate the seriousness of the government's efforts and break the culture of hopelessness, idleness and cynicism which a concentration of hard-core unemployment has bred in the many estates throughout Britain where a generation has been brought up on the dole. Young unemployed people, when asked, support these principles. To them it is not "workfare." It *is* fair, and it offers work. (Mandelson and Liddle, 1996: 102)

Despite what had become almost ritual protestations to the contrary, it was clear that Labour's new position on unemployment and welfare was workfarist in all but name. The responsibility for action is portrayed as a societal rather than simply as a governmental one (with the attendant moral connotations); the goal is not to create jobs but to assist the unemployed to *find* work; the unemployed themselves are no longer portrayed, in the Old Labour convention, as the unfortunate victims of deindustrialization and job loss, but as active agents in a dysfunctional economy of benefit dependency, fraud, and illegal work; it is seen as axiomatic that the unemployed should be "obliged" to "cooperate" with those making a genuine attempt to wean them off the dole. This amounts to an active, supply-side strategy for labor-market reintegration based on the principle of compulsion. It is manifestly workfarist.

Labour's strategy for funding its welfare-to-work initiative was also ingeniously consistent both with the ideological principles of New Labour and with the imperatives of electoral pragmatism. The new program would be funded by a "windfall tax" on the privatized utilities, widely regarded by the public as profiteering and unaccountable, rather than from general taxation revenues. This strategy, initially formulated under John Smith's leadership (see *Guardian*, January 20, 1993: 20), would enable Labour to represent welfare-to-work as the classic free lunch: there need be no increases in middle-class taxation; the injection of "new money" from the privatized utilities would front-load the program, which in due course would become self-financing as welfare rolls and costs fell. Details of the proposed welfare-to-work program were announced in November 1995. The grandly titled "New Deal" for the unemployed would offer four options for those aged eighteen to twenty-five who had been out of work for six months or more: a subsidized employer placement, voluntary-sector work, education and training, or a position on a new "environmental task force." In what was to become something of a political mantra for New Labour, there would be no "fifth option" of a life on benefit: those refusing places would be docked 40 percent of their benefit. This element of coercion caused a serious rift in the Labour Party, as it was claimed that the principle of compulsion had been imposed by the leadership in the absence of consultation with the membership (Wintour, 1995). Left-leaning labor unions, such as the Transport and General Worker's Union, joined advocates for the unemployed in opposition to Labour's explicitly coercive approach,[18] but others noted Labour leadership's growing confidence in advocating this new form of "social moralism" in the face of such resistance (Rentoul, 1995). Out of the malaise of the post-Thatcher era, a new form of conviction politics was taking shape. As Gordon Brown insisted at the launch of the New Deal,

> In return for offering an opportunity provided by society as a whole, we should expect people to exercise responsibility, so this is not some electoral gimmick. This is my genuine belief that rights in a modern society should be matched by responsibility. . . . This is not a lurch to the right by the Labour Party. This is the Labour Party setting out the philosophy of a party supported by a decent hard working majority. (*Guardian*, November 10, 1995: 1)

Increasingly, critics within the Labour Party would be branded as "Old Labour," as opponents of change itself, by an emboldened leadership. Their accusations of workfarism, however, continued to aggravate a nerve. According to Gordon Brown, "This is not workfare in the sense that it is understood—as the penalising of the unemployed for being unemployed, and asking people to work in return for their benefit" (*Guardian*, November 10, 1995: 6).

While the Conservatives attacked Labour's proposals as bureaucratic and interventionist, they must have sensed also that the opposition's radicalism was overshadowing the government's more tentative approach. Treasury minister Angela Knight complained that "Gordon Brown's 'make work' schemes won't create real jobs. . . . It's businesses which create jobs, not governments" (*Financial Times*, November 10, 1995: 8). In truth, the Conservatives had been feeling their own way toward workfare, though in the kind of muddled and contradictory fashion that had become a characteristic of the Major administration. On the more interventionist left of the Conservative Party, the growing influence of the deputy prime minister, Michael Heseltine, was reflected in the deployment of a series of local workfare experiments. Heseltine had been arguing for workfare since the 1980s—floating the idea in 1988 that "[w]e should now link social security entitlement to the recipient's willingness to participate in the schemes which are available. Somewhere between the Swedish Right to Work and the American Workfare [program] we should find a British model" (*Independent*, November 15, 1990: 27)—but this was a concept somewhat out of step with the Conservatives' free-market majority.

On the deregulationist right of the party, employment secretary Michael Portillo and social security secretary Peter Lilley steered through a fundamental overhaul of the benefits system in the context of falling unemployment after 1993. The new benefits regime, passed into legislation in 1995, would "help the jobseeker and motivate the job-shy" (Peter Lilley, quoted in *Independent*, October 25, 1994: 1). The Jobseeker's Allowance reduced benefit eligibility while compelling active job search, with its proponents "emphasis[ing] the responsibilities of unemployed people—to take every advantage of the opportunities open to them to get back to work. Our proposals . . . aim to ensure that the link between looking for work and receiving benefit is clear" (Lilley and Portillo, 1994: 2).

## From Claimant to Jobseeker

The Conservatives were to reserve their most far-reaching reorganization of the benefit system until what proved to be their last year in office. Implemented nationally in October 1996, the Jobseeker's Allowance (JSA) presaged a radical restructuring of the benefits regime. As social security secretary Peter Lilley explained, the intention of JSA was to transform the benefits system from one that perpetuated dependency to one that rewarded work: "The Jobseeker's Allowance . . . gives extra help to those who want to get jobs and makes it a bit tougher for those who are workshy . . . who don't try."[19]

Under JSA, eligibility for benefits was narrowed and means testing expanded, but more important was the way in which the new benefit system enforced the requirement that unemployed people—as a condition of benefit—engaged in an *active* process of job search. Individually tailored "jobseeker's agreements" specify the steps that each claimant will take—on pain of sanction or termination—to secure work. Employment secretary Michael Portillo was reportedly unable to resist a "wry smile [about] how little attention his bill to introduce [JSA] was attracting. . . . JSA will mean a sharp cut in dole payments for tens of thousands and a dramatic acceleration of the drift towards a compulsory workfare system" (Milne, 1996: 17). In no less sweeping terms, the chief executive of the Employment Service, Mike Fogden, would describe JSA as "the most significant event in the history of the public employment service since the Beveridge reforms were introduced in 1948."[20]

Just as the benefits regime had been tightened during the slow recovery from the early 1980s, falling unemployment after 1992 again opened up the political space for narrowing eligibility and "promoting work." Thus, the JSA reforms "mark a further important step in the Government's wide-ranging labour market reforms [which] lie behind the substantial fall in unemployment that has occurred since December 1992" (Employment Department Group/Department of Social Security, 1994: 4). This argument is as fallacious as it is circular. One of the reasons why unemployment appears to have fallen so much in the United Kingdom—particularly in comparison with other European countries, as the Conservatives were keen to point out (Conservative Party, 1997)—is the deregistration effect of the stricter benefits regime itself, not to mention the thirty-two changes in the method of counting the unemployed that were brought in during the 1980s and 1990s.

When in April 1996 the "official" unemployment count stood at less than two million, economists at the HSBC banking group calculated the "real" unemployment level in the United Kingdom at four million (*Guardian*, April 16, 1997: 13). At the time, the independent Unemployment Unit calculated that half of the 360,000 fall in registered unemployment over the previous six months was due to deregistration effects under JSA, while Simon Briscoe, UK economist at Nikko bank stated, "We cannot emphasise strongly enough how distorted these numbers could be. . . . [T]he introduction of the JSA and the benefits hotline have made interpretation of the monthly unemployment figures impossible."[21] For many of the poorest households in the United Kingdom, there had in fact been no "recovery" from the early 1990s recession at all: the Employment Policy Institute calculated that the share of all households with no wage earner actually rose from 17.5 percent at the beginning of the "recovery" to 19.3 percent in 1996 (*Guardian*, April 15, 1997: 21).

The cumulative effect of serial restrictions on benefit eligibility, the tightening of "availability for work" tests, and straightforward downward pressure on the level of dole payments was to force hundreds of thousands of people off welfare. Many went into low-waged work, others into various forms of "economic inactivity" (including registration on long-term sickness and disability benefits), yet others into the "informal" economy. For all the Conservatives' preoccupation with "disincentives to work," the residualized benefits system of the mid-1990s did relatively little to protect the unemployed from the vagaries of the labor market. Conservative chancellor Kenneth Clarke justified benefit restrictions in terms of the age-old principle of less eligibility—endorsing measures to "ensure that those on benefits do not have a more comfortable lifestyle than those who are supporting themselves of modest incomes."[22] The evidence, however, revealed precious little scope for "comfortable lifestyles" on welfare. The "reservation wages" of the unemployed had fallen dramatically under the Conservatives, tracking the decline in benefit levels, such that a person leaving the dole queue for work in 1995 would on average be paid £100 per week, a fall of 12 percent in real terms since 1980 and less than half the mean pay rate across the labor market as a whole (Gregg, 1997). Similarly, OECD data showed that the replacement ratio in the United Kingdom—the ratio of unemployment benefits to wages—fell from 43 percent in 1972 to 28 percent in 1980, then to just 16 percent in 1990 (Berry et al., 1995).

Research commissioned by the Department of Social Security also revealed that the reality of unemployed people's lives bore little resemblance to the stereotype of the work-shy "scrounger" that had become not only the focus of political rhetoric but a primary object of government policy. Shaw et al. (1996: 152) found that "[m]ost claimants do look for work and approach the labour market flexibly with modest reservation wages. Some may be demoralised by long spells on Income Support, but few give up looking for work." While the burden of government policy toward unemployment—exemplified most clearly by JSA—constructed worklessness as an individual, behavioral problem, the fragility of the welfare-to-work transition apparently had more to do with a weak job market, coupled with unsupportive social arrangements (such as the shortage of low-cost childcare provision). Echoing research in the United States (see Blank, 1997), the report showed that the population of benefit claimants was in fact a highly dynamic one: over a two-year period, one-third of Income Support recipients exited the system, with most entering jobs, though one-fifth would be back on benefit within six months. While behaviorists would interpret such a problem of repeat usage in terms of recidivism, causality lies with the unstable and very low-paid nature of the jobs obtained by former welfare recipients. For all the government's talk of a booming economy, the report found that "[s]hortage of work opportunities is a major barrier to moving off Income Support and, in general, [recipients'] perspectives of the labour market are bleak" (Shaw et al., 1996: 153). Subsequent research would show that those who did successfully transition from welfare to work typically did so by way of contingent jobs: part-time jobs, temporary positions, and self-employment accounted for fully three-fourths of the jobs entered by unemployed people, according to White and Forth's (1998) longitudinal study.

## The JSA Method

With strong echoes of the California GAIN methodology,[23] the JSA regulations render eligibility to benefit strictly conditional on the completion of a "Jobseeker's Agreement," which commits each claimant to a pattern of active jobseeking behavior. Claimants must sign a declaration to the effect that they understand their benefit eligibility will be affected if they (1) do not do enough to find work (2) are not deemed available for work (3) act in any way to reduce their chances of getting work, or (4) become incapable of work. They are then required to make detailed statements concerning their availability for work and job-seeking activities (see Figure 7.1). Employment Service regulations require most claimants to make themselves available for work immediately (i.e., in less than twenty-four hours) and for a minimum of forty hours per week (some exceptions are made for those with caring responsibilities, or mental or physical disabilities). Unpublished guidelines on interviewing policy for frontline-eligibility workers also call for specifically *measurable* and *timebound* activities to be identified in the Jobseeker's Agreement:

> Make sure the jobseeker knows that they will be asked regularly to show what they have done to find work, and that this will take into account what they agreed in their Agreement. Advise them to keep a record of what they do to look for work. . . . Making Agreements measurable will help when it comes to discussing what they jobseeker has done to find work, for example:
>
> a "phone at least 2 employers a week";
> b "look in the Echo every Tuesday and Thursday";
> c "register for sales work with People Power Agency by 13 May";
> d "construct a CV based on advice given today. This will be reviewed on 17 December";
> e "attend interview at Local Training on Friday 30 November at 12 noon to join bricklaying course" . . .
>
> Making activities timebound will make for easier follow-up at fortnightly reviews and subsequent advisory interviews, for example:
>
> a "visit at least 2 employers every week";
> b "look in The Anytown Star every week";
> c "attend classes for reading and writing at Adult Education Centre every Thursday 7PM–9PM starting on 12 April. Teacher's name is Jean Haslam."[24]

Jobseeker's Agreements are reinforced where necessary by the Jobseeker's Direction, a new power that enables benefit advisers to require specific actions on the part of claimants to "improve their employability through, for example, attending a course to improve jobseeking skills or motivation, or taking steps to present themselves acceptably to employers" (Employment Department Group, 1994: 21). As Murray (1995) points out, this could include requiring jobseekers to alter their dress and physical appearance. Failure to comply with a Jobseeker's Direction is linked directly to benefit sanctions under JSA. The JSA sanctions policy is intended not only to minimize abuse and tighten eligibility, but also has the "important role [of] reinforcing incentives for unemployed people to take the right steps to get back into work" (Employment Department Group/Department of Social Security, 1994: 25).

The further tightening of conditionality rules under JSA had the effect of mandating employment and training programs—even those that in terms of their own rules were technically voluntary (Finn, 1995a, 1995b). The overriding imperative was clearly to initiate transitions into work. The introduction of JSA reduced benefits for many claimants (in comparison with the previous system of unemployment and supplementary benefits), while extending the scope of means testing. It served to pressurize claimants to accept whatever work might be available locally: the JSA White Paper stated unequivocally that JSA claimants "will be required to be available for *any work which they can reasonably be expected to do*" (Employment Department Group, Department of Social Security, 1994: 17, emphasis in original). As the Employment Service's unpublished guidance on interviewing policy has it, the range of jobs a claimant is looking for

> may vary as unemployment lengthens, for example, at the end of a permitted period jobseekers are expected to broaden their job search and be prepared to accept a wider range of jobs and rates of pay. . . . [M]ake sure the jobseeker understands that if they do not find work they will be expected to widen the types of job they are willing to accept. (1996: 16)

A new computer system, the Labour Market System, was introduced to facilitate the referral of JSA claimants to job vacancies and places on government schemes. As Murray (1996) notes, this system can be used to test claimants' availability for work as well as to facilitate actual referrals. The scope for deregistration by way of this computerized "work test" may be one of the reasons behind the increasing disjuncture in employment and unemployment flows since the introduction of JSA, as the rate of off-flow from the register has outstripped the sluggish expansion in aggregate employment in many areas (see Peck and Tickell, 1997). A growing number of people are being forced into the netherworld *between* welfare and work, in effect creating a forced-labor supply for the lower reaches of the labor market. According to Murray (1996: 27), the benefit regime is "now dedicated to the aim of forcing the unemployed into low-paid work or onto Government schemes, which in turn are increasingly devoted to this sole objective." Or as Novak (1997: 102) sees it, JSA "effectively signals the mass means-testing of the unemployed and the imposition of new forms of regulation and control on their behaviour."

*Jobseeker's*
**Allowance**

*Jobseeker's* **Agreement**

**Jobseeker's Agreement**

This Jobseeker's Agreement sets out
- when I can work
- the types of job I am willing to do
- what I am going to do to find work and increase my chances of finding work.

I, or an Employment Service adviser, can ask for it to be changed at any time. If we cannot agree about changing the Agreement, an independent adjudication officer will be asked to look at it.

If I am not satisfied with their decision, I can have it looked at by another adjudication officer. If I am still not satisfied, I can appeal to an independent tribunal.

**Availability for work**

I understand I must
- be available for work
- (unless the limitation is for health reasons) have a reasonable chance of getting work if I limit
  - the kind of work I am willing to do
  - the rate of pay I will accept
  - where I am willing to work
  - the hours I am willing to work
- be capable of work.

**Permitted period**

* I know I can limit myself to accepting work in my usual job and at my usual wages from     /     /
           to            /     /
After this I will be interviewed about broadening my availability and job search.

**Actively seeking work**

I understand that I must actively seek work. I will be asked regularly to show what I have done to find work. I have been advised to keep a record of what I do to find work.

**Jobseeker's Allowance**

I understand my allowance may be affected if I
- do not do enough to find work,
- am not available for work
- reduce my chances of getting work, or
- become incapable of work.

If this happens, I will be told and my case may be sent to an independent adjudication officer for a decision.

If I am not satisfied with the decision, I can appeal to an independent tribunal.

I understand that this is general information and not a full statement of the law.

* The adviser has read this Agreement to me.

| Jobseeker's signature | | Adviser's signature | |
|---|---|---|---|
| Date | / / | Date | / / |
| | | Adviser's name | |
| | | Phone number | |
| * Delete as appropriate. | | TAM date | / / |

**ES 3**

*(continued)*

**FIGURE 7.1.** Jobseeker's Agreement. *Source:* Employment Service.

**Name** [                                                    ]

The types of job I am looking for
[                                        ]  SOC [        ]

I am willing and able to start work
☐ immediately      ☐ within 48 hours
☐ within 24 hours  ☐ after giving a weeks notice

I want to limit the days and hours I am available for work
No ☐
Yes ☐

I am available for work these days and these hours

| | Earliest start time | Latest finish time | Most hours I can work |
|---|---|---|---|
| Monday | [        ] | [        ] | [        ] |
| Tuesday | [        ] | [        ] | [        ] |
| Wednesday | [        ] | [        ] | [        ] |
| Thursday | [        ] | [        ] | [        ] |
| Friday | [        ] | [        ] | [        ] |
| Saturday | [        ] | [        ] | [        ] |
| Sunday | [        ] | [        ] | [        ] |

Most hours I can work each week [        ]

Other agreed restrictions on my availability
[                                        ]

**FIGURE 7.1.**  (*cont.*)

**NI number** [                          ]    **Claim file/cycle** [        ]

**What I will do to identify and apply for jobs**

○ Write to at least ___ employers a week

○ Phone at least ___ employers a week

○ Visit at least ___ employers a week

○ Contact the Jobcentre at least ___ times a week

○ Ask family, friends and people I have worked with before

○ Look in these newspapers and trade papers

**How often I will look**

[                          ] [            ]

○ Register with these employment agencies and contact them ___ times a week

[                                      ]

**Other activities including any steps to improve my chances of finding a job**

[                                      ]

**FIGURE 7.1.** *(cont.)*

The tightening of benefit conditionality under JSA, and the associated intensification of pressure on the unemployed to enter the low-wage labor market (if necessary via government schemes), defined the Conservatives' path toward workfare in the mid-1990s. While a prominent Conservative right-winger, Francis Maude, had earlier caused something of a furor when he declared that "the principle of Workfare is an excellent one and is a Christian approach to providing help to people" (*Guardian*, August 12, 1992: 2), the government's approach was in general more cautious and qualified. Employment secretary Michael Portillo stated that to describe the JSA provisions as "workfare" was just so much "loose talk." Portillo's definition, in contrast, was anything but loose:

> To me, "workfare" means that the state will be the employer of the last resort, committing itself to provide work for any who are without it. That implies a bigger role for the state than I am willing to contemplate. (Michael Portillo, 1995)[25]

> But I do not shy away from saying that financial provision is there for those who need it—that is to say because they cannot support themselves—and they must be able to demonstrate that by their willingness to work. That can include being required to take work that is offered to them on penalty of losing their benefit. If that to some spells workfare, so be it. (Michael Portillo, 1995).[26]

Critics saw no need to observe these definitional conventions. The Trades Union Congress denounced JSA as "another step to workfare in the UK" (TUC, 1994a: 1), while Ruth Lister, a member of Labour's Social Justice Commission, portrayed the new benefit regime, in the context of increasing conditionality since Restart in 1986, as "a quantum leap down the road which leads to Workfare-style schemes" (*Financial Times*, October 5–6, 1996: 4).

## The JSA Consensus

Meanwhile, Labour's official line on JSA was at first ambiguous and muted. According to Novak (1997: 108), the party "effectively stifled criticism [of JSA] from within its own ranks," observing that shadow employment secretary Michael Meacher's pledge to abolish JSA was quickly retracted (see *Red Pepper*, June 1996: 27). Tony Blair was reported to have personally overruled moves within the shadow cabinet to propose the abolition of JSA, "keen," according to the *Financial Times*, "to avoid any charge from the Conservatives that his party would be soft on welfare recipients." But by the time JSA was introduced, the official Labour position was that the system would be "reviewed."[27] In a key decision, the party leadership would in the face of shadow-cabinet opposition pledge to retain the JSA framework (McSmith, 1997). This was a reflection of Tony Blair and Gordon Brown's increasingly hard line on welfare-to-work issues, but it may have also been influenced by electoral calculations. A Mori opinion poll had revealed that two-thirds of the British electorate were in favor of workfare, and while support for compulsion was lower among Labour voters (55 percent), Labour's electoral strategy dictated that the party had to make major inroads into the conservative "Middle England" vote to be assured of victory.[28]

Still some seven months away from the General Election, it had become clear that the positions of the two main parties on benefits reform had converged to the point that they were almost indistinguishable. The battle within Labour's shadow cabinet to restore some of the benefit cuts brought about by the JSA reforms had been lost (*Daily Telegraph*, June 25, 1996: 2), while the party's premanifesto discussion document, *Getting Welfare to Work: A New Vision for Social Security* (Labour Party, 1996a), underlined the extent to which so many issues in the welfare-reform debate now commanded bipartisan support. Labour announced, and then regularly reiterated, that it would instigate a (further) crackdown on benefit fraud, maintaining that £1 billion in social security savings could be secured in this fashion (*Financial Times*, June 11, 1996: 20). Drawing inspiration from GAIN in California and from recent Australian reforms, Labour also argued that the benefit system should become more proactive and *personalized*, in the interests of promoting transitions from welfare to work (Labour Party, 1996a). Pledging now to work with new powers introduced under JSA, and echoing earlier proposals from rightwing Conservatives like Peter Lilley (1995), Labour would also propose to deploy local pilots and trials in the search for workable strategies:

> The Tory government had produced a small number of reforms, ostensibly to tackle benefit barriers to work, some of which have been welcomed by Labour. But many government policies have reduced work incentives. . . . The government had itself used pilot schemes to test the viability of new employment schemes. Our proposals follow this precedent. . . . [There must be] a move away from rigid, national programmes processing large numbers of job seekers with little regard for individual needs or local circumstances. A new approach is needed which brings resources for jobs and benefits close to the communities they exist to serve. (Labour Party, 1996a: 1, 4)

Social security secretary Peter Lilley had himself called for piloting powers in the Jobseekers' Act to be used in a similar way, emphasizing the need for a "cautious, pragmatic approach . . . piloting changes locally be-fore applying them nationally. . . . Local pilots can pave the way for changes in nationwide rules and conditions" (1995: 48).[29] In the U.K. context, this means more than a subtle shift in the methodology of policymaking, for it goes to the heart of the principles of universalism and uniformity that have defined the Beveridgean welfare state (see Fra-ser, 1984). Peter Lilley certainly saw a role for localization in challenging some of these principles, given that "Britain has had one of the most cen-tralised and uniform benefit systems in the world" (1995: 48), while leftwing Labour MP Jeremy Corbyn attacked his own party's proposals on precisely the grounds that to compromise the principles of uniformity and universality would signal the effective undoing of the system (*Daily Telegraph*, June 25, 1996: 2).

The debate—or rather lack of it—around the Jobseeker's Allowance laid the foundations for Britain's workfare consensus. The Labour leader-ship clearly saw an activized benefit system of this kind as an important component of its welfare-to-work proposals, and may even have been re-lieved that the legislative initiative in this sensitive area had been taken by the Conservatives. This would allow Labour to focus on its more "positive" programs, around which it might build support for welfare re-form across the wider party. As for the Conservatives, JSA represented an important milestone in a gradually intensifying, yet still very much incrementalist, approach to welfare reform. The intention was that JSA would form the cornerstone of "a more unified system of in-work and out-of-work benefits" (Employment Department Group/Department of Social Security, 1994: 11). During the last two years of the Major admin-istration, the Conservatives would move to extend the range and breadth of in-work benefits, such as Family Credit and Earnings Top-Up (see Murray, 1995),[30] but they would also begin to take important steps to-ward explicit workfare programming. While the Conservatives' approach would continue to be, in Peter Lilley's words, "cautious and pragmatic," a key factor behind the new piloting powers in the JSA legislation was to facilitate experimentation with workfare at the local level (see Kirkbride, 1995; TUC, 1995).

## EXPLORING LOCAL WORKFARE

Sir Ralph Howell, Member of Parliament for the constituency of North Norfolk, had long been an advocate of workfare within the Conservative Party. For the most part something of a fringe figure, Howell found him-self increasingly a focus of attention in the mid-1990s as work-for-benefit schemes came under serious scrutiny by the government. Although the

Conservatives had maintained a watching brief on U.S. workfare experiments throughout the 1980s (see Casey, 1986; Walker, 1991), they had been reluctant to commit. As unemployment peaked in the early 1990s recession, the government had launched Community Action and, in Sir Ralph's own constituency, North Norfolk Action, both voluntary programs providing work experience and (limited) on-the-job training on community projects.[31] Workstart, a job-subsidy scheme for the very long-term unemployed, was also introduced—again on a relatively small scale—at this time.[32] Of wider significance than these modest programs, though, was the fact that the all-party House of Commons Employment Committee had finally agreed to conduct an investigation into workfare. Prompted by the proposal of a Right to Work Bill by Sir Ralph and independent-thinking Labour MP Frank Field, which would impose a duty on the secretary of state "to offer work instead of income support or unemployment benefit to persons who would otherwise be without work" (House of Commons, 1995: 1), the committee undertook an analysis of workfare experiments overseas, including a study visit to the United States, while reviewing recent experiences and future prospects for work–welfare initiatives in the United Kingdom (see Employment Committee, 1996).

While clearly aware of the range of meanings attached to the term *workfare,* the committee opted for a relatively restrictive definition:

> Proposals aimed at [turning welfare into work] are often loosely called "workfare." The term may be used quite restrictively to mean requiring recipients to work in order to "earn" their benefit, with the state, in effect, acting as the employer of people who cannot find other jobs—as the employer of last resort. Often associated with this are proposals to guarantee the unemployed work or work experience, either subsidised or fully funded, with the private sector, voluntary sector or the public sector. . . . The term "Workfare" may also be more loosely applied to cover any situation where payment of benefit is made conditional upon a claimant agreeing to undertake some form of "activity" which may simply involve intensive job search. In our inquiry we have considered both the more precise and the looser concepts of Workfare . . . but we have used the term "Workfare" to mean a system in which recipients of unemployment benefits are required to work in order to "earn" their benefit. (Employment Committee, 1995: vii–viii)

On the broader, or "looser," definition of workfare, the committee found clear evidence that the benefit system had been subject to increasing conditionality since the early 1980s (see Table 7.2). This increasingly coercive regime was most vigorously enforced against young people, the

**TABLE 7.2.** Conditions Attached to Receipt of Unemployment Benefits, 1982—1996

| Condition attached to receipt of benefit | Date introduced | Method of introduction |
|---|---|---|
| Abolition of compulsory registration at JobCentres/ Introduction of availability testing | October 1982 | Response to the Rayner Report: Payment of Benefits to Unemployed People |
| Introduction of compulsory Restart interviews | July 1986 (for people unemployed 12 months or more) March 1987 (for people unemployed 6 months or more) April 1988 (interviews held every six months of unemployment) | Training for Employment (White Paper 1988) |
| Introduction of Claimant Advisers to follow up Restart interviews | October 1986 | Department of Employment unemployment review |
| Extension of period for which benefit can be disallowed (from 6 to 13 weeks) | October 1986 | Social Security Act 1986 |
| Restart interviewees required to complete questionnaire | April 1988 | Training for Employment (White Paper 1988) |
| Extension of period for which benefit can be disallowed (from 13 to 26 weeks) | April 1988 | Training for Employment (White Paper 1988) |
| Introduction of New Client Advisers to interview those making fresh claims | April 1988 | Training for Employment (White Paper 1988) |
| All new claimants interviews. Availability test every 6 months | 1988 | Employment in the 1990s (White Paper 1988) |
| To receive benefit claimants must show they are "actively seeking work" | October 1989 | Social Security Act 1989 |
| Tightening conditions for requalifying for unemployment benefit | October 1989 | Social Security Act 1989 |

*(continued)*

**TABLE 7.2.** *(cont.)*

| Condition attached to receipt of benefit | Date introduced | Method of introduction |
|---|---|---|
| Requirement on new claimants to complete a Back to Work Plan and attend a review after 13 weeks | October 1989 | Social Security Act 1989 |
| Compulsory attendance at Jobplan Workshop for all those unemployed for 12 months (refusing all other offers of assistance) | April 1993 | |
| Claimants to enter into a formal contract, the Jobseeker's Agreement, in order to receive the new Jobseekers Allowance | October 1996 | Jobseekers Act 1995 |

*Source*: Employment Committee (1996).

Employment Department conceding to the committee that the removal of benefit entitlements to sixteen- and seventeen-year-olds eligible for Youth Training had "something in common with proposals for replacing benefit for certain groups with a right to a place on a temporary work scheme" (quoted in Employment Committee, 1996: xxiii).

On the tighter definition of workfare programming, the committee described the government's approach as "half-hearted," concluding that only in its newly unveiled Project Work (PW) program had the Conservatives "introduced (albeit only as a small scale pilot scheme) something which comes close to classic 'workfare' " (Employment Committee, 1995: xxvii, xviii).[33] Launched in April 1996, PW was piloted in Hull and parts of Kent, with plans to extend the scheme nationally after June 1997. PW required unemployed people aged eighteen to fifty who had been out of work for two years to take part in a thirteen-week program of assisted job search followed, if necessary, by a further thirteen weeks of work experience. Participants were paid £10 per week on top of benefits, with failure to comply resulting in automatic benefit sanctions. Denounced by the Unemployment Unit's Paul Convery as a "fake work" scheme, PW nevertheless marked a "pretty decisive step towards workfare" (*Guardian*, December 2, 1995: 9). Establishing yet another definitional nuance, employment minister Ann Widdecombe said in evidence to the Employment Committee that "by workfare"

> I understand large scale, national probably compulsory schemes. I do
> not want that and nobody I know in Government wants that. That is
> what I understand by workfare. People are using workfare to describe
> some of our programmes, but they are not workfare at all. (quoted in
> Employment Committee, 1996: xxxiii)

The Employment Committee remained somewhat skeptical about the design of PW, instead recommending that "the Government experiment with combinations of the Workstart job subsidy programme and the WISE Group's Intermediate Labour Market to achieve the delivery of a nationwide programme of Government-subsidized or Government-funded employment for unemployed individuals" (1996: li). Significantly, the committee also accepted the (diluted) workfarist principle that "people in receipt of unemployment benefit have an obligation to taxpayers to look for what work is available" (Employment Committee, 1995: l).

In its formal response to the Employment Committee, the government reiterated its opposition to "workfare in its purest sense, and other proposals which involve universal or very large-scale programmes of state-provided work, because such programmes tend to distort private sector activity and damage the job-creating capacity of the economy" (Education and Employment Committee, 1996: iii). Far from providing a solution to welfare dependency, the government argued, such schemes might generate new forms of dependency on state-provided work. Instead, the approach should be to combine measures to increase labor-market flexibility with a macroeconomic regime oriented to economic growth. In terms of welfare-to-work programming, the government stated that experimental pilots would continue, and be generalized if successful, but always within the context of an ongoing commitment to "tailoring programmes to individual circumstances and local conditions" (Education and Employment Committee, 1996: iv). The government's basic position, then, was that incremental development of the current suite of locally delivered programs operated by TECs and the Employment Service would continue (see Jones, 1997).

Pressure for a shift in policy was building, however. Cross-party support for the Howell/Field Right to Work proposals, coupled with the Employment Committee's recent endorsement, signaled an important shift in workfare politics. In July 1996, a group of one hundred and thirty-four backbenchers, drawn from all three major parties, demanded that the government undertake an independent evaluation of the costs of a large-scale workfare program. The government's agreement to commission an evaluation study was greeted by Labour's Frank Field as "a real breakthrough," though he acknowledged that the scale of the task—with

2.2 million registered as unemployed—would mean that the program would have to begin as a voluntary one until enough workfare slots had been created so as to make compulsion meaningful (*Independent*, July 26, 1996: 1). While the government's stance remained officially noncommittal, the *Independent* detected a significant shift in policy, its front page declaring "Workfare revolution to be costed by Major."

## Lean Welfare?

The Conservatives' shift toward workfare would, however, be conditioned more by the political timetable than by evaluation schedules. The deployment of pilot initiatives under the Conservatives—particularly in potentially controversial areas like workfare—often had more to do with a reluctance to commit politically than with any genuine commitment to policy learning through local experimentation. Correspondingly, the expansion of "successful" programs need not imply that evaluations had proved favorable (often, in fact, full evaluations would never be completed), but instead meant that the political decision had been deferred. This was to be the experience with Project Work. At the time of PW's launch the government stated that "potentially these pilot programmes offer a change of a very major significance" (quoted in Murray, 1995: 37).

Local workfare trials had been underway in Hull and Kent for just six months when the prime minister announced at the Conservative Party conference that the scheme would be significantly expanded. Coincidentally, the Jobseeker's Allowance also came into force during conference week, presenting Major with an opportunity to talk tough on the issue of welfare reform. In order to create what he called a "lean welfare machine," there would be another crackdown on benefit fraud, while PW would be extended to cover between 50,000 and 75,000 long-term unemployed people in five cities (*Financial Times*, October 8, 1996: 10). Addressing his comments to the "hard-working classes," the prime minister promised a new "Contract for Work" in which workfare programs would be used to help the unemployed move from "dole to dignity" (*Daily Express*, October 8, 1996: 6). Up to £100 million would be made immediately available for the expansion of PW, rising to £500 million, should the Conservatives be returned to power at the General Election, when the scheme became a national one. The costs of the new work program, it was anticipated, would be compensated for by reductions in the total welfare bill.

Lagging some way behind Labour in opinion polls, the Conservatives were revealing more than a hint of recklessness in their eleventh-hour embrace of workfare. Clearly anxious, though, not to appear bereft of radical ideas after seventeen years in office, and perhaps more pertinently not wanting to be portrayed as softer on welfare than Labour, the government was finally prepared to make a financial commitment to workfare. And while the political spin was that the program would eventually be self-financing, the actual achievements of the pilots suggested otherwise. At the time for the announcement of PW's expansion, only two hundred and eighty-two scheme participants had left benefit for employment in the pilot areas, a figure that the secretary of state for education and employment Gillian Sheppard rather implausibly described as "encouraging" (*Daily Telegraph*, October 8, 1996: 10).

What was "encouraging" in PW for the secretary of state was not the scheme's limited success in steering participants into work but its effectiveness in deregistration. Subsequent figures would show that while the employment rate of participants had barely passed one in ten (by February 1997, just seven hundred of sixty-eight hundred PW participants had entered jobs), a rather larger number were effectively deregistering themselves from the benefit system by refusing to participate in the program (*Guardian*, February 24, 1997: 1). This was proof positive, in the government's eyes, that the scheme was flushing out "scroungers," although in truth deregistration may have been occurring for a variety of reasons. The government's (very) preliminary evaluation of PW concluded that while "many [participants] have found jobs . . . a noticeably higher number have simply ended their claim on referral to mandatory work experience [suggesting] that the approach is particularly effective in deterring those whose claims *are not genuine*."[34] Workfare's deterrent function—the so-called workfare funnel (Mead, 1992b)—was clearly coming into play in the PW pilots, on the basis of which the government was anticipating dramatic reductions in the welfare rolls as the scheme was extended. As the government declared in the PW launch documentation, "for those who have lost heart or motivation, [this scheme] may be just the impetus they need" (quoted in Murray, 1995: 38).

Although the evaluation evidence on mandatory programming remained, at best, inconclusive (Murray, 1996; Finn, 1995b), the Conservatives concluded that it no longer brought with it the political risks they once feared, particularly since Labour too had now accepted the principle of compulsion. Reflecting the changed climate, even Prince Charles was to join the workfare consensus, calling for mandatory community service for young people in the midst of the election campaign, and in contravention of the constitutional custom that precludes the royal family from making "political" statements.[35] Suitably emboldened, the Conservatives would in their election manifesto finally commit themselves to the "nationalization" of workfare in the form of a radical expansion of PW, coupled with a "Britain Works" scheme—modeled on the America works program in the United States (see Nye, 1996)—which would bring private- and voluntary-sector innovation into the welfare-to-work process at the local level.[36] The Conservative "workfare revolution" was, however, not to be. Following the party's crushing defeat in the May 1997 General Election, the initiative was to pass to a new government with yet more radical plans.

## MAKING A NEW DEAL: THE NEW LABOUR PROGRAM

The promise to "get 250,000 under-25 year-olds off benefit and into work by using money from a windfall levy on the privatised utilities" (Labour Party, 1996b: 39; 1997: 40) had been one of Labour's five main election pledges. It had been clear from some time now that Labour meant business on the issue of welfare reform. As Tony Blair had said at a private dinner with Lord Rothermere, proprietor of the Conservative-supporting *Daily Mail*, in 1995, "We all agree that the welfare state has got to be radically reformed. Who is going to do it? You may find I am the only one with the will to do it."[37] Reflecting the extent to which New Labour had bought into conservative arguments about the causes and cures of "welfare dependency," the new strategy would be premised on reintegrating what Tony Blair called the "workless class" into the labor market. As the manifesto baldly stated it, the solution to poverty lay with "help[ing] people into jobs" (Labour Party, 1997: 19). While a jobs orientation of some kind has existed for a long time, both in the rhetoric and in the practice of the British welfare state, the arrival of New Labour brought a sharp shift toward binary narratives of welfare dependency on the one hand and work/independence on the other. As Deacon (2000) notes, a feature of post-1997 welfare politics in the United Kingdom has been the focus on dependency and work at the expense of more traditional concerns such as affordability and entitlement:

> Labour's benefit-to-work strategy is at the heart of our approach to welfare reform. . . . We want to create an active society, not a dependency state. . . . Labour believes that the benefit system should offer people a hand-up, not just a hand-out. (Labour Party, 1996a: 16–17)

An early decision of the new prime minister underlined just how radical the overhaul of the welfare state would be: the new number two at the Department of Social Security, with special responsibility for welfare reform, would be Frank Field, a man described by Tory MP David Willetts as "many Conservatives' favourite politician" (Willetts, 1996: 31). Just a few weeks earlier, Field had praised the Conservatives' Project Work scheme for exposing fraudulent claims (*Observer*, May 4, 1997: 3), a characteristic comment from a politician typically described as "maverick." In an early iteration of the "underclass" debate in the United Kingdom, Charles Murray (1990: 80) said that "[w]hen it comes to policy, Frank Field is the iconoclast and the optimist, moving far afield from Labour doctrine in order to engineer schemes for dealing with single-parent families and integrating young men back into the labour force."

Field's well-established argument had for some time been that "the centre can no longer hold" on welfare, that what was required was no less than a full-frontal attack on the dependency culture and the perverse incentives of means-tested benefits by way of a "remoralisation of welfare" (see Field, 1995; Alcock, 1997). Calling for an end to piecemeal, incremental reforms of the benefits system, Field insisted that the "idea that income support should be paid while people await a return to the labour market is no longer appropriate—nor is it a desirable objective in an age of widescale fraud" (1996: 33). While Field proclaimed himself to be aware of "the danger[s] of trying to transpose an American vision [of welfare dependency] on Britain" (1990: 37), his analysis of the crisis of welfarism in the United Kingdom is nevertheless distinctly resonant of the conservative critique:

> [T]he current welfare status quo cannot hold. . . . [W]elfare does not operate in a social vacuum. It influences character for good or ill. Because of the growing dominance of means tests, welfare increasingly acts destructively, penalising effort, attacking savings and taxing honesty. The traditional cry that means tests stigmatise is now a minor issue. They do for some, but this is simply no longer the main issue. Means tests are steadily recruiting a nation of cheats and liars. Hence the urgency for reform. (Field, 1996: 11)

Field's recruitment into the key strategic post for welfare reform in the new Labour government underlined just how far the party line had shifted during the three years of Blair's leadership.[38] The 1994 Commission on Social Justice, which had of course been charged with "thinking the unthinkable" on welfare reform, in retrospect seemed positively cautious. As former commissioner Ruth Lister pointed out on the eve of the General Election, "Things have shifted so far that already it feels as though it reported in another political time."[39]

## New Labour Goes to Work

As the new government set about its business, it soon became clear that the epochal claims of political commentators were far from exaggerated.

Leading figures from the business world were recruited to head task-forces on welfare-to-work and the reform of the tax and benefits sys-tems.[40] Taking up familiar themes in workfare rhetoric, Blair's administration portrayed the welfare system as irretrievably flawed, costly, and even unnatural and ungodly; the values of work (and by implication, low-waged work) were forcefully propounded; and, contrary to the principles of social insurance and mutualism, divisions between those paying for ("taxpayers") and benefiting from ("dependents") the system were exposed and exaggerated:

> We have reached the limits of the public's willingness simply to fund an unreconstructed welfare system through ever higher taxes and spending. (Tony Blair, 1997)[41]

> What we should be about is turning life-long dependency tickets into real opportunities. From the beginning of creation, people have always wanted to work, and it is inconceivable that fundamental human nature has been rotted by a 50-year-old welfare state. (Frank Field, 1997)[42]

The new government scheduled an early budget, described by the prime minister as "the Welfare to Work Budget,"[43] to set in train its program of welfare reform. In its efforts to shed the old tax-and-spend image, Labour pledged to work within the Conservatives' very restrictive public-spending targets during its first two years in office. There would, however, be one notable exception: the welfare-to-work program would be funded by way of a £5.2 billion hypothecated tax on the privatized utilities. As this was widely regarded as a once-only "special tax," levied for a very particular purpose, it would attract relatively little criticism. In funding its New Deal program for the unemployed in this way, however, the government was sending two important political signals: first, that the costs of welfare reform could be substantially front-loaded, to the extent that they would not represent an *ongoing* commitment from the taxpayer; and second, that welfare reform would not be a burden on "mainstream" taxation, because middle-class income tax rates would remain unchanged.

Couching his remarks in terms of the imperatives of globalization,[44] the chancellor introduced the New Deal program in the context of a radical modernization of the welfare state:

> For millions out of work or suffering poverty in work, the welfare state today denies rather than provides an opportunity. It is time for the welfare state to put opportunity again in people's hands. . . . Taken together [the New Deal's] comprehensive and ambitious initiatives

mean that, from now on, no section of society should suffer permanent exclusion. For too long, the United Kingdom has been united only in name. From today, ours is a country where everyone has a contribution to make.[45]

The main elements of the New Deal would be: a £3.15 billion program of subsidized private-sector employment, voluntary and environmental work, and education and training, for unemployed eighteen- to twenty-five-year-olds; a £350 job subsidy scheme for long-term unemployed adults; and a £200 initiative to help lone parents back into work (see Table 7.3). While the chancellor stressed the element of choice in the New Deal's provisions for young people—where the four components of the program are tellingly characterized as "options"—he also reiterated the point that "[t]here will be no fifth option—to stay at home on full benefit" (*Financial Times*, July 3, 1997: 16). Pointedly, when benefit eligibility was removed for sixteen- and seventeen-year-olds—making the Youth Training Scheme effectively mandatory—Conservative minister Michael Portillo had also talked in terms of a "guaranteed option" of a YTS place (quoted in King, 1995: 171).

Complementary changes in the structure of the tax and benefits system would have to await the outcome of previously launched policy reviews, but the clear intention on the part of the government was not simply to "bolt on" the new programs to the old structure, but to transform the structure itself. As the chancellor had earlier declared, "I am not interested in measures that just alleviate the problem of youth and long-term unemployment for a few months. I'm interested in developing a welfare state built around the work ethic" (*Observer*, May 11, 1997: 1).

## The Work-Ethic State

While the New Deal provisions in the July 1997 Budget only marked a first step in this direction, an indication of the government's resolve came in the announcement that the provisions for young people and the long-term unemployed would be strictly mandatory. In what was described by John Rentoul as a further "shift in the direction of US-style 'workfare' " (*Independent*, July 3, 1997: 11), the New Deal would mean, in Gordon Brown's words, that when the unemployed "sign on for benefit they will be signing up for work."[46] Under New Labour, however, this was not to be portrayed as straightforward workfare, but in the more ambiguous language of compulsion-as-reciprocity. As Tony Blair put it in his Aylesbury Estate speech,

> The basis of . . . modern civic society is an ethic of mutual responsibility or duty. It is something for something. A society where we play by the rules. You only take out what you put in. That's the bargain. . . . Where opportunities are given, for example to young people, for real jobs and skills, there should be a reciprocal duty on them to take them up.[47]

Reflecting both political sensitivities and a reluctance to commit to a major expansion in childcare provision, arrangements for lone parents under the New Deal would be (initially at least) voluntary. Nevertheless, social security secretary Harriet Harman insisted that regarding the exchequer costs of children brought up "dependent on benefit . . . We believe that work is the best form of welfare for people of working age-and that includes lone parents."[48]

While some quarters of the conservative press were skeptical about the viability of Labour's new "make-work scheme," they were heartened by the tough line on mandatory participation.[49] Welfare advocates voiced concerns about the regime of coercion constructed around the New Deal, which was even more stringent than the JSA framework.[50] As an editorial in the *Financial Times* warned, "[T]he government needs to be cautious about the heightened level of compulsion [associated with the New Deal]. Among the unemployed are alcoholics, drug addicts and social incompetents, whom private sector employers will do everything they can to avoid [and who may] cause trouble when dragooned into work."[51] The right-wing Institute of Directors also voiced concerns: 71 percent of its members in a 1997 survey feared that New Dealers would be "unwilling conscripts."[5] A clear danger in Labour's proposals was that the most disadvantaged participants, and those regarded as "problem cases" by employers, would be filtered off into the least desirable of the New Deal options, the environmental task forces and voluntary-sector placements. In the implicit hierarchy of New Deal options, these could, in effect, become "sink schemes," leading the sanctions policy to backfire when "[p]resented with a choice between weeding verges and making a living from crime, some might plump for the latter" (Thomas, 1997: 8).

It is difficult to escape the conclusion that the rigid insistence on compulsion under the New Deal derives largely from the ideological predilections of the Labour leadership rather than from the kind of practical knowledge of on-the-ground programming that otherwise is lauded by New Labour. On the left, resistance to compulsion had been an almost reflex response for many years. As the *Charter Against Workfare*, which was endorsed by the National Executive of the Labour Party in 1988, explained the position, "People should join [programs] because they want

**TABLE 7.3.** Labour's New Deal Program

| Eligibility | Programming | Delivery | Timetable | Cost |
|---|---|---|---|---|
| **New Deal for young unemployed** | | | | |
| Unemployed for more than 6 months and aged 18–25 (180,000–250,000 client group) | Four options:<br>• Subsidized job with an employer (£60 per week subsidy for 6 months; also £750 per person training allowance)<br>• full-time education and training<br>• Voluntary-sector job<br>• Environmental Task Force<br><br>"There is no fifth option": those refusing all four options will suffer benefit sanctions<br><br>Employer placement seen as first choice and Task Force as last resort | Delivered by Employment Service with national, regional, and local partners Business Task Force, headed by Sir Peter Davis, chief executive of the Prudential Group, will advise on development of program and monitor effectiveness (from January 1998) | From January 1998, 10–15 Pathfinder areas will pilot the scheme (accounting for 10% of client group)<br>National rollout, April 1998 | £3.15 billion (to 2002) |
| **New Deal for long-term unemployed** | | | | |
| Unemployed for 2 years or more (350,000 client group) | Employers paid £75 per week subsidy for 6 months | June 1998 | | £350 million (to 2002) |

| Programme | Target group | Provisions | Coordination | Location / rollout | Funding |
|---|---|---|---|---|---|
| **New Deal for lone parents** | Lone parents whose youngest child is in 2nd term of full-time schooling (500,000 client group) | Help with job search, training, and childcare<br><br>Lone parents on Income Support will be "invited" to JobCentre to develop an individual "action plan"<br><br>New Deal participants will be fast-tracked for Family Credit and child maintenance<br><br>Voluntary participation | Coordinated by DSS<br><br>50,000 young people under New Deal will be encouraged to train as childcare workers | From July 1997, 8 pilot areas covering 40,000 lone parents (Cambridgeshire, Warwickshire, Cardiff, Sheffield East, North Cheshire, North Worcestershire, Clyde Valley, North Surrey)<br><br>National rollout, October 1998 | £200 million (to 2002)<br><br>With additional funding for childcare through family credit, housing benefit, council tax, and National Lottery |
| **New Deal for disabled** | Those in receipt of disability and incapacity benefits | | | | £200 million (to 2002) |
| **New Deal for schools** | School infrastructure, IT and equipment | | | | £1.3 billion (to 2002) |
| **University for Industry** Public–private partnership | | | | | £5 million to assist with start-up costs |

*Source:* Budget *Red Book* (July 1997).

to, not because they fear they will lose all or part of their benefits if they don't. Compulsion is a recipe for lower standards, resentment and discrimination" (quoted in King and Wickham-Jones, 1999: 62). Recall also that the Commission on Social Justice came out against the principle of compulsion, citing Frank Field's (then) concern that "trying to force people into a scheme by threatening to reduce their benefits is counter-productive, since [it] simply becomes a very expensive system of monitoring" (quoted in Commission on Social Justice, 1994: 182).

Rather than slide toward mandation, the Commission on Social Justice was one of many groups, including several major labor unions, most of the leading left-of-center think tanks, and the Labour Party's own Regional Policy Commission, to recommend experimentation with intermediate labor market (ILM) models, as pioneered by the Wise Group in Glasgow.[53] The Wise Group model was subsequently cited in Labour's *Road to Manifesto* document as an example of "world's best practice" in welfare-to-work programming (Labour Party, 1996a: 9). ILM proposals would subsequently receive positive support from David Blunkett, then shadow secretary of state for education and employment, who emphasized his opposition to "cheap and compulsory workfare schemes" (*Observer*, October 6, 1996: B6). Indeed, the philosophy of the ILM approach, as the Wise Group's Alistair Grimes (1996: 4) characterizes it, has always been very much an antiworkfarist one: "[I]f workfare is compulsory work for benefits, the Intermediate Labour Market is voluntary training and work experience for an income."

Although important questions concerning the scope for transferring (or even "nationalizing") the Wise Group model have yet to be addressed,[54] it is clear that its practical achievements are real ones, with real lessons. Learning such lessons, as the prime minister maintained in his Aylesbury Estate speech, would be a hallmark of New Labour's approach to government:

> Unless Government is pragmatic and rigorous about what does and does not work, it will not spend money wisely or gain the trust of the public. The last government did little serious evaluation of its policies for poverty, and didn't even know how many people have been on welfare for 10 or 20 years. Its policies were driven by dogma, not common sense. . . . Our approach will be different. We will find out what works, and we will support the successes and stop the failures. We will back anyone—from a multinational company to a community association—if they can deliver the goods. We will evaluate our policies and . . . where appropriate we will run pilots, testing out ideas. . . . We will, in short, govern in a different way.[55]

Under no illusions about the scale of the task ahead, the Wise Group's chief executive Alan Sinclair was nevertheless initially optimistic after the chancellor's launch of the New Deal program, insisting that "[w]e've never tried anything on this scale in Britain and we have to suspend cynicism and accept this is a remarkable change from a previous government which never bothered its shirt tails about the problem" (*Guardian*, July 3, 1997: 17). But once it became clear just how tough the compulsion regime would be under the new program, many—including Sinclair—began to express doubts. Speaking after the sanctions policy had been announced, Sinclair described the New Deal's stringent participation rules as "either unnecessary or just a bit daft. . . . In my experience, and I meet lots of long-term unemployed people . . . the overwhelming majority of them are absolutely desperate for work. There's no need to use compulsion."[56]

But the sanctions policy was clearly going to be a nonnegotiable element of the welfare-to-work package. To concede to pressure from the left and the social-advocacy community to water down or reverse the policy would have meant appearing "soft" on workfare in the eyes of the electorate and the media. So as a symbolic policy it had to be defended. At a practical level, however, the earlier decision to retain JSA was probably more important in enforcing work compulsion on a generalized basis, as JSA effectively defines the framework of participation rules *around* the New Deal. The fanfare around "no fifth option," in fact, reflected Labour's determination to make the compulsion issue its own and to drive home its tough-love credentials. JSA rules would have made the New Deal a de facto mandatory program anyway, so "no fifth option" was as much to do with political theater as with practical programming.

This also reveals how ideological arguments for compulsion can often overwhelm the (often compelling) evidence of practical experience. See Murray (1995, 1996) and Unemployment Unit (1996).[57] While before the General Election Labour deployed "phrase[s] of sophisticated ambiguity," emphasizing the mutual obligation on the part of the unemployed and the absence of a "fifth" option of nonparticipation on benefit (Convery, 1997: 8), as the party in power it has had to confront not only the reality of compulsion but the challenges this presents for program implementation. These challenges are not inconsiderable, given that so many welfare-to-work programs founder at the implementation stage. The National Institute for Economic and Social Research (NIESR) predicted, prior to its launch, that the New Deal would generate 250,000 net new jobs per year along with annual savings (after three years) of £2 billion (*Observer*, June 29, 1997: B1), but these forecasts were made without the benefit of information on how the programs will be operated in practice. NIESR's assumption must have been that program outcomes are "automatically" secured in a linear and predictable way from policy inputs. Implementation is therefore deemed unproblematic, while geographic variations in program design, management, and outcomes cannot be taken into account. These are serious omissions, given the unequivocal evidence from previous welfare-to-work initiatives—in the United Kingdom and elsewhere—of large "implementation gaps" and significant spatial unevenness in labor-market outcomes. Postscheme job-placement rates for participants on YT (the national training program for sixteen- to eighteen-year-olds, operated at the time by TECs), for instance, ranged from over 70 percent in Hertfordshire and Surrey to less than 33 percent in Merseyside and Glasgow (*Working Brief*, March 1996). So, the "same" program can be associated with different outcomes in different places, depending on how it is managed locally and on how it interacts with local labor-market conditions (see Peck and Haughton, 1991; Peck, 1999; Martin et al., 2000). Contrary to the essentialized image of welfare-to-work programs fostered in the evaluation literature (and peddled by consultants), these are not administrative "packages" that are easily portable from place to place with replicable results. They are, in fact, deeply embedded in local political and economic conditions, such that *yielding outcomes* tends to be very much a local matter, even if program routines and strategies are imported from elsewhere (Theodore and Peck, 1999).

## Delivering the Deal

Far from being a second-order concern, the issue of implementation strikes at the heart of program viability and legitimacy.[58] And given that the Labour government has staked its credibility on the New Deal, this represents a significant political risk. As Dennis Snower, previously a high-profile supporter of the Howell/Field Right to Work Bill, said of the New Deal:

> These policies play for high stakes. In a few years' time these measures may have paid for themselves or turned out to be disastrously expensive; they may have reduced unemployment or spawned endless schemes that keep people out of the unemployment statistics without giving them jobs. . . . The Government has shown creativity in its opening moves to promote employment and equality. The challenge now is to be aware of the dangers ahead and to sort out the details of policy and design in the light of good economic sense. In employment policy, as in brain surgery, details can be crucial. (1997: 17)

Snower identified three "economic diseases" that might undermine the New Deal: First, if the government allowed too many participants to enter local-government programs or education and training schemes, "public-sector bulge" would lead to financial crisis; second, the proliferation of small-scale initiatives, local pilots, and program options runs the risk of "labyrinthitis" and fostering bewilderment among both program participants and employers; and third, the danger in mandatory initiatives is that people are forced into "jobs for which they are unsuitable, unproductive or unmotivated" (Snower, 1997: 17). The way to minimize these risks, Snower argued, is to ensure that welfare-to-work initiatives are embedded within a coherent employment and training policy, that they are market-based, and that schemes are voluntary. By definition, the New Deal violates Snower's final principle; only experience will tell if the program operates in accordance with his other criteria.

One key advantage that the government had at the time of the New Deal's launch was an expanding labor market. When the provisions for young people were first announced, in November 1995, the client group of eighteen- to twenty-four-year-olds unemployed for over six months was 241,000; by the time the program was launched, latest figures showed the size of the client group had shrunk to 172,000 and was continuing rapidly to fall (TEN, 1997). The supposedly stubborn and culturally entrenched problem of "welfare dependency" seemed to be disappearing in front of ministers' eyes, and largely of its own accord, even as the government planned to roll out the new program. Conservatives argued that falling unemployment removed the very rationale of the New Deal,[59] though Labour's continuing commitment to what Walter (1996) calls "human capitalism" led the government to defend the role of such interventions, even in the context of a growing labor market. These were needed, according to minister for employment and welfare to work Andrew Smith, to enhance the "employability" of young people by "equipping them with the skills they need to succeed."[60]

> "It's the right time to introduce a welfare-to-work policy when the country is doing well because, first of all, it gives you breathing space to establish structures and practices and culture changes if you need to. For instance, in persuading employers to take unemployed people on, they're more likely to do it now when they need staff, they need a workforce, they are desperate to fill vacancies. We have a record level of vacancies at the moment. So they are much more likely to give it a go."[61]

At the very least, and more cynically, implementing the New Deal in the context of falling unemployment would almost certainly ensure that the program came in under budget, while maximizing the political scope for representing it as a "success." An expanding labor market would also impinge on the economic calculations of those involved in the program: employers would be creating more new jobs, thereby increasing the supply of subsidized private-sector placements as well as serving as a source of demand for New Deal leavers; young unemployed people may be more likely to join the program under such circumstances, though they might also respond to the deterrent effect of compulsory schemes by moving directly into less-desirable jobs on the open labor market. Either way, the program has a greater chance of being judged a success under conditions of economic growth. The Trades Union Congress (TUC) conceded as much when in their early opposition to Conservative workfare proposals they argued that "a period of high unemployment is the worst possible time to introduce workfare and other forms of benefit coercion" (TUC, 1994b: 7). The TUC went on to recite the following extract from the Beveridge Report, which envisaged benefit conditionality but saw this in the context of historically low levels of unemployment:

> The proposal of this report accordingly is to make unemployment benefit after a certain period conditional upon attendance at a work or training centre. But this proposal is impractical if it has to be applied to men by the million or the hundred thousand. (Beveridge, 1942: paragraph 440, quoted in TUC, 1994b: 7)

If, as has become conventional wisdom, Labour remains in office for at least ten years, they would do well to heed Beveridge's warning. No matter how successful are Chancellor Brown's macroeconomic policies, they are unlikely to do away with the business cycle altogether. And while Labour entered office with registered unemployment at a six-year "low" of under two million, a wider count encompassing unregistered jobseekers and those on government schemes took the total amount of "slack" in the U.K. labor market to over five million (*Working Brief*, August–September 1997). The United Kingdom's "Americanizing" economy therefore exhibits *simultaneous* expansion and decay: while "overheating" is evident in the macroeconomic indicators, as even with well over million (officially) on the dole, the chancellor is besieged with calls to dampen down the growth rate, persistent problems of underemployment, low wages, and low skills continue to point to weak labor-market performance. In labor-market policy terms, then, there are clearly no signs for complacency. Far from it, the fact that growth alone is insufficient to solve employment problems calls for redoubled efforts in the labor-market policy sphere, while also raising searching questions about the scope for tackling poverty by driving the unemployed into the (bottom of the) job market.

But New Labour is unlikely to usher in a major shift in established principles of labor-market policy in the United Kingdom. There will be no reversal of the Conservatives' "deregulation" program. On the contrary, the new government promised to *build upon* the underlying principles of labor-market "flexibility," not to overturn them. As the prime minister stated in his Malmo speech of June 1997:

> People criticise some of the right-wing governments of Europe for being too tough. I would criticise them for being old-fashioned and for not having the vision to understand change. For us and Europe, jobs must be the priority; to create jobs we must be competitive; to be competitive in the modern world, knowledge, skills, technology and enterprise are the keys, not rigid regulation and old-style interventionism. . . . Employability—knowledge, technology and skills, not legislation alone—is what counts.[62]

So while Labour's welfare-to-work initiative clearly echoes some of the more interventionist policies favored by "Old Labour" supporters, the program is framed within a market-complementing approach that privileges supply-side over demand-side strategies and that accepts the imperatives of "flexibility" as not simply inevitable but positively desirable. An early priority of the Blair government was to embed these principles in the employment policy guidelines of the European Union (EU), which were under negotiation during 1997. Britain argued strongly, and successfully, for an unequivocal "employability" focus in EU social policy.[63]

Perhaps the most unequivocal statement of this position came—characteristically—from Peter Mandelson. Announcing a plan to establish a social-exclusion unit at the heart of the government's policymaking system, Mandelson contended in a Fabian society lecture that "a permanently excluded underclass actually hinders [economic] flexibility." Combating social exclusion, he maintained, would be the overriding strategic objective of the Blair government, but all new initiatives would be premised on the foundation of a flexible labor market:

> [F]lexibility in its own right is not enough to promote economic competitiveness. It is the job of government to play its part in guaranteeing "flexibility plus"—plus higher skills and higher standards in our schools and colleges; plus partnership with business to raise investment in infrastructure, science and research and to back small firms; plus an imaginative welfare-to-work programme to put the long-term unemployed back to work; plus minimum standards of fair treatment at the workplace; plus new leadership in Europe in place of drift and disengagement from our largest markets. This is the heart of where New Labour differs from both the limitations of new right economics

and the Old Labour agenda of crude state intervention in industry and indiscriminate "tax and spend." (Mandelson, 1997: 17)

The strategy would not be about changing the way the labor market operated, but instead would be concerned with ensuring that the excluded should be rendered "employable" in the context of shifting economic exigencies. Rejecting the canons of redistribution and intervention, New Labour would tackle social exclusion by way of labor-market inclusion (backed up with a little coercion). The answers, moreover, would lie not *within* but *beyond* the welfare state: as Mandelson emphasized, "The people we are concerned about will not have their long-term problems addressed by an extra pound a week on their benefits" (1997: 17).

Mandelson's launch of the social-exclusion unit was held to represent "an exposition of a revolution: in the philosophy and practice of provision, in the conception of the welfare state, in the methods and ethos of addressing poverty, even in the structure of government itself" (Lloyd, 1997: 14). Notwithstanding the fact that changes of government are very often occasions for misplaced hyperbole, all the indications are that New Labour will match its words with actions. Minister for welfare reform Frank Field would even float ideas like devolving welfare budgets to the local level: local benefits offices should be encouraged, he argued "to develop a personalised service with their customers which supported and encouraged those anxious to return to work, while at the same time constructively countering the antics of those who, for whatever reason, decided that work was not an option for them" (Field, 1997: 13). Field argued that decentralization—and the radical institutional restructuring that implied—was in fact a *precondition* for putting the government's welfare-reform program into practice:[64]

> If we don't think seriously about how [welfare] reforms are delivered, then the mechanisms of delivering those reforms might well destroy the point of the reform itself. . . . So institutional reform isn't a secondary matter, it's as important as, it is part of the reform process itself. There will need to be a total commitment and drive, which there is from the very top, from the Prime Minister, for seeing both the programme through and the means for delivering that programme.[65]

As key prime-ministerial advisers like Geoff Mulgan—who, along with Field, has called for an engagement with Charles Murray's critique of welfarism—will repeatedly argue, a program of radical reform requires an equally radical shakeup of the Beveridgean fiefdoms that are the Whitehall "spending departments," followed by the empowerment of proactive, cross-departmental agencies at the local level (see 6, 1997;

Lloyd, 1997; Regional Policy Commission, 1996; Demos, 1996).[66] The intention is to capacitate, animate, and galvanize local agency in the interests of tackling welfare dependency and encouraging work. As Lloyd (1997: 15) summarizes Mulgan's thinking, in order make Labour's (workfarist) bargain with the socially excluded "deliverable, a welfare state that had been constructed as a centralised and standardised bureaucracy must be devolved down to local authority areas, which are in turn given a large degree of latitude [so as to] allow intervention at an early stage to *prevent* the fall into the [welfare] net." Thus, New Labour's road to workfarism via orchestrated decentralization begins to take shape.

## Conviction and Contingency

While New Labour's plans were clearly carefully laid, they have not always followed a predictable course. The leadership has continued to struggle in its attempts to articulate an overall philosophy for welfare reform that does not immediately trigger confusion, anxiety, and opposition. The two senior ministers nominally in charge of the welfare-reform project, Harriet Harman and Frank Field, were both sacked in the first of Blair's cabinet reshuffles, to be replaced by the more cautious Alistair Darling. There have been backbench revolts over proposed cuts in lone-parent benefits and widespread public concern about plans for pension reform. Yet the New Deal retains its flagship status, for all of this.

Continued growth in the labor market has certainly helped, but any student of British economic history knows that such conditions cannot be assumed to be permanent. According to John Gray, the Blairite fusion of economic and social liberalism—epitomized so clearly by the New Deal—could easily break up if there were to be a change in the economic fundamentals:

> The New Deal aims to find work for all who are capable of it. It proposes to do this by reskilling the unemployed and matching their new skills with opportunities in the labour market. Like previous policies, but more vigorously, it makes acceptance of work a condition of receipt of benefit. . . . Forcing the unemployed to take work, however, presupposes that there is work to be had. Fairness and common sense demand that, if the unemployed are obliged to work, society is obliged to provide them with it. And that obligation can be discharged only if the state is ready to step in as employer of last resort. But that it precisely the solution that is ruled out by market liberalism. (1998: 29)

The Blair government, however, seems to have predicated much of its economic and social policymaking on the assumption that steady labor-market growth will continue indefinitely, having come to power at a moment in which "a long economic boom and the economic prestige of the right combined to give neoliberal orthodoxies an ephemeral authority they did not deserve" (Gray, 1998: 29). The decisive strategic vulnerability of the New Deal stems from its contingent relationship with the labor market: designed as a fair-weather policy, it could follow the market down into recession:

> There are many signs that economic life is returning to its normal bumpiness. And when it does the British liberal consensus will be thrown into disarray. We do not need a crisis in the world economy for this to happen. A run-of-the-mill recession, with unemployment rising steadily for some time, will be quite sufficient. Policies such as the New Deal will be heavily compromised if the next downturn is significantly sharper, deeper or longer than presently expected. Public spending plans will need to be revised radically, and promises about not increasing taxation will be considerably harder to keep. (Gray, 1998: 29)

While concerns about the onset of recession in the United Kingdom have ebbed and flowed, there remains an underlying anxiety that the end of the New Deal's honeymoon period is overdue.

There are real concerns about how the New Deal will fare under less conducive labor-market conditions. Even under "boom" conditions significant "job gaps" confront jobseekers in Britain's big-city labor markets, where the New Deal faces an uphill challenge (Holtham et al., 1998; Peck, 1999; Turok and Edge, 1999). While Employment Secretary David Blunkett has poured scorn on those "gloom merchants" in the City of London who were predicting that unemployment would rise sharply in 1999–2000 (*Guardian*, August 12, 1999: 21), it should not have escaped his attention that City economists were not the only people saying this. Indeed, both the Organisation for Economic Co-operation and Development (OECD) and Blunkett's own department have for some time being making very similar unemployment forecasts. This underlines the political risks in claiming credit for the New Deal, as ministers have been doing, on the basis of falls in the monthly unemployment count. When unemployment rises again should the New Deal be automatically branded a "failure"? Rising joblessness would certainly change the economic (and perhaps political) context in which the New Deal operates. Resting heavily as it does on assisted job search and subsidized employer placements, the New Deal is far from recession-proof. On the contrary, as a supply-side initiative, it is deeply reliant on prevailing demand-side conditions in local job markets (see Turok and Webster, 1998). The New Deal cannot create jobs, but instead works actively to take advantage of *existing* job-market opportunities by raising the "employability" of participants. Where these opportunities are lacking, there is some scope to compensate through the provision of voluntary-sector and environmental-taskforce places, but as ministers and program participants seem to agree, these are not sustainable, long-term alternatives to "real jobs."

The phenomena of spatially concentrated poverty and underemployment have been a central concern of the Social Exclusion Unit and is a key factor behind the proliferation of geographically targeted, "zone"-based policy initiatives under New Labour (see SEU, 1998). It also informed the thinking of New Deal planners, for whom the flexible framework of the program would allow the balance of options to vary from place to place in accordance with local economic conditions:

> "[There is] in-built flexibility. You have four options and you cover an entire cohort [which] is what's different about the New Deal. It offers a guarantee to everybody in a particular group, but the nature of that guarantee changes, the mix of options will be different, in different areas. That's the way the New Deal will be different in Middlesbrough than it is in Glasgow or Tunbridge Wells. . . . It doesn't mean you need a different policy in Glasgow than in Tunbridge Wells, it just means that you set a framework which provides a different sort of pattern of activity."[67]

Of course, the New Deal will not simply be "different" in high- as opposed to low-unemployment areas. Its job subsidy-based and vacancy-following methodology means that the program will assume a quite different character under depressed as opposed to buoyant labor-market conditions (Peck, 1999). In prosperous areas, the New Deal will operate in the favorable context of dynamic labor markets coupled with a small client group. Achieving positive outcomes in this context will not be especially difficult. But in areas of structural economic decline, the New Deal will be confronted by the doubly challenging conditions of sluggish, low-demand labor markets and a large client group, many of whom will have spent long periods of time out of work. The operation of labor markets, both historically, on the cumulative size and composition of client groups, and contemporarily, on the availability of subsidized employment, will therefore exert a profound influence on the character of the New Deal.

## From Central Control to Local Learning?

Great store has been set by the New Deal's potential to evolve and learn, particularly in response to *local* experiences. Yet it remains to be seen how far the reins of central control will be slackened, if indeed they are at all, as the New Deal evolves. Traditions of highly centralized policy-making linger on with the New Deal, while the Blair government's preoccupations with firm political control and command-and-control delivery systems also echo long-established conventions in British politics:

> New Labour has no patience for whingers or shirkers. But the political vision is far from Thatcherite. Underpinning the individualistic, mobile, competitive society is a *dirigiste* workfare state which would have warmed the cockles of Beatrice Webb's heart. . . . [New Labour's] workfare state comes straight out of the old Fabian stable of top-down social engineering. It rests on the premise that government at the center not only can, but should remake society to fit an *a priori* grand design. To succeed, the policies that emanate from it will have to be pushed through with as much centralist zeal as the Thatcherites displayed 15 years ago. (Marquand, 1998: 20–21)

Certainly, at the present time, there is an extremely high level of central-government micromanagement in the field of welfare-to-work—through bureaucratic, financial, and policy channels. Reform advocates argue, however, that national policymakers, accustomed to traditions of top-down policy development, are learning how to trust local partnerships and delivery agencies. As one such policymaker put it, "There is a tension between the national picture and the local picture running through the New Deal but I don't think it's damaging. . . . We're all learning about the way it works, particularly within the Department [for Education and Employment] where we've been used to, certainly on the employment side, tighter [central] control."[68] National policy is set to evolve to take greater account of local-level inputs, as it has become clear that this is one of the ways that the roll-out system will be able to "learn."

> "It's one of the ways we are jealous of the United States, for its capacity to innovate and experiment. . . . The original New Deal as it was in the [1997 General Election] manifesto was in some ways a classic traditionalist policy, top-down, nationally defined. . . . It still is substantially that, but with scope for local variation. We have taken that a stage further by bringing in the private sector in to lead in ten of the New Deal areas solely so as to see if they come up with any better ways of doing things which can then be woven back into the system or replicated. . . . In a sense we're trying to reshape the welfare and jobs framework so it can innovate and learn quickly, rather than all policymaking to happen at the center."[69]

Blair has repeatedly stressed that his government is oriented toward practical solutions, having spent much of its time in opposition searching for "ideas that work." While some elements of "best practice" have been culled from British experimentation in welfare-to-work, Labour ministers have at different times actively promoted various U.S. state and local programs such as Riverside GAIN, which an early policy document listed as an example of "world's best practice" (see Labour Party, 1996a) and Wisconsin's W-2 program, which has been the subject of intense study (and debate) by ministers and MPs (see Rogers, 1997; House of Commons, 1998; Theodore, 1998). Even if concrete instances of policy transfer in these cases may have been limited, their assessment by British policymakers and advisers certainly contributed to the boldness and rapidity of the New Deal implementation process. The shortening of policy cycles through the elimination of program pilots, the elimination or short-circuiting of evaluation timetables, and the immediate rolling out of national policy through untested local-delivery partnerships, suggests that the Blair government is satisfied that it has identified appropriate welfare-to-work strategies (the "ideas that work"). All that now needs to be worked out is their *implementation*:

> "The breakneck speed of implementation has been such that the ideas of, let's say, technology transfer, of cross-fertilization, of better techniques for spreading best practice, have been second order to having *any* practice. . . . I think of it more as a road test. Is the wheel gonna fall off? It's not 'Are we gonna have this car?' We've got the car, but we need to run it quickly, before the rest of them come on the highway, to make sure that the gears shift."[70]

However, as is becoming increasingly clear, the more mundane and politically unattractive task of actually sharing best practice among local delivery agents and informing local-level implementation will not automatically take care of itself. Just as innovation may need to be fostered through institutional change, so too must the capacity to share and receive information. Simply devolving *responsibility* for program design and delivery from more centralized to more localized institutions does not guarantee that innovative practices will emerge at the local level, or that they will be disseminated effectively through the system.

Welfare-to-work under New Labour has become associated with a shortening of policy cycles, as established aspects of program implementation such as piloting, evaluation, and program feedback have been dispensed with in the interests of political expediency. In part, this has been justified on the grounds that formal program evaluation is too slow a process, though more experienced observers note wryly that this brand of conviction policymaking rarely culminates in successful programming. There are consequently political risks inherent in the fast-policy process, for all the touching faith that ministers seem to have that some spontaneously evolving process of local-program innovation will drive subsequent policy in the direction of best practice.

There is certainly a possibility that the preferred strategy of devolving responsibility for future innovation to local partnerships will lead to uneven, rather than necessarily best, practice. Firstly, previous experience in the United Kingdom reveals that local partnership-style negotiation often leads to anemic, lowest-common-denominator policies, rather than highly innovatory developments. According to one strategically placed actor with extensive experience of partnership working in Glasgow, "Partnerships often prosper around things that people can agree about, not necessarily what is absolutely the best project to do."[71] Second, the partial privatization of the New Deal delivery system may impede, rather than accelerate, the flow of innovatory practice, given that privatization also tends to be associated with reduced transparency and proprietorial defenses of knowledge. Third, the matrix of manifestly "successful" local programs in the United Kingdom is an extremely sparse one (Finn, 1996; Gardiner, 1997), in part due to the tradition of unimaginative, centrally-designed initiatives and in part due to the limited local policy capacity and underdeveloped infrastructure of many areas. With its highly centralized systems, the United Kingdom has less experience than most countries of reflexive, local-level policy development. As a result, many policy innovations in the area of welfare-to-work may continue to be imported, and then filtered down through centralized policy systems, rather than home-grown (see Peck and Theodore, 2001).

## Learning from America?

There is now widespread agreement that the degree of U.S. influence on U.K. welfare-reform debates and discourses, welfare restructuring strategies, and welfare-to-work programming is both significant and growing.[72] It must be emphasized, however, that this is a highly politicized arena, such that the nature of the comparative lessons that are drawn tends to reflect ideological orientations and political predispositions. So, critics of U.K. policies—both under the Conservatives and under Labour—have tended to draw particular attention to U.S. echoes and parallels, often deploying the politically loaded and—in this context—pejorative term "US-style workfare" to considerable effect as a symbol of punitive programming.[73] Meanwhile, advocates of reform tend to be much more circumspect about the origins of policy innovations, often purposefully highlighting non-U.S. influences wherever possible, and emphasizing the extent to which systemic and institutional differences between the United Kingdom and the United States militate against direct policy transfers (see Dolowitz, 1997, 1998).

So commonplace have become observations that the Blair government is engaged in an "Americanization" of the British polity, that policymakers have tended increasingly to adopt a strategy of denial and studied skepticism toward those who would "accuse" them of importing U.S. models. For example, one strategically placed civil servant, while conceding that lessons were being drawn from the United States at a political and strategic level, insisted, "But [it's] not *just* America. We took a strong interest in the Australian experience . . . and countries like Sweden have been trying active labor-market policies for decades. . . . The model that we looked at closely is Sweden, Denmark a little bit, Holland a little, but mainly Sweden, that's were the job subsidy was first tried. Australia also, with the Job Compact."[74] Yet as John Philpott (1997: 65) has observed, while "Mr Blair would no doubt distance himself from the US term 'workfare' as used by Professor Lawrence Mead with its connotation of unemployed people forced to work for their Giro [dole] cheque . . . there is a certain resonance between Mead's arguments and the Labour government's employment policy agenda, not least in relation to the so-called New Deal for young unemployed people."

Notwithstanding these manifestly strong connections, one of New Labour's most prominent supporters, Anthony Giddens (1998), goes out of his way to stress the *Swedish* origins of current British welfare-to-work policy, in a way that says more about the political sensitivities around Americanization than it does about the realities of the policy-transfer process. But as a former member of the Commission on Social Justice explained,

> "Clearly, the workfare approach . . . has been influenced by the States more than the Swedish model. . . . We're facing that direction in terms of pulling away from a whole continental European, more universalistic approach. . . . They're not going full-scale in that direction, but . . . they're looking more to the States than continental Europe. Although they say very clearly in the Green Paper that's not the model they want, of a residual welfare state—and I'm sure it isn't. But I think there is a danger that a two-tier welfare state is going to emerge which is more American than it is European. . . . I'm sure all that's right but at the same time, if we talk about moving in a direction, that's the *direction* we're moving in. That doesn't mean we're moving lock, stock, and barrel. You know, we'll wake up tomorrow and we've got an American system, but it does seem to me that's where the balance of the shift lies."[75]

Part of the problem here is the implicit literalism in the term "policy transfer," which tends to suggest the importation of fully formed, off-the-shelf policies, when in fact the nature of this process is much more complex, selective, and multilateral. While there are occasional attempts to clone policies on a comprehensive basis—one thinks, for example, of the very close initial modeling of the TECs on the U.S. Private Industry Councils (see King, 1995; Jones, 1999)—more commonplace in many ways are *selective* transfers of particular administrative practices or techniques, of branding ideas or discursive formulations, and of political lessons concerning the management of the reform process itself. There is quite compelling evidence of U.S. influence on U.K. policy debates on all of these levels in the field of recent welfare-to-work policies. But an essentialist, policycentric account of this phenomenon is not at all convincing. What has changed most dramatically here is not the quality of the U.S. export "product" but prevailing political–economic conditions within the United Kingdom itself, many of the roots of which can be traced to the "modernization" of the Labour Party under Blair's leadership. As one seasoned observer remarked,

> "It's funny. If you were to say, three years ago, where do left-of-center people look, do they look to North America or to Europe, you'd say it was the latter, without a shadow of a doubt. Where were the Conservatives looking? They were plainly looking at North America for the opposite reason left-of-center people were looking at Europe. Because Europe appeared to be a more consensual, social-democratic kind of economy. . . . [They] were talking about social exclusion even then. . . . The Conservatives didn't like that, they didn't feel at all comfortable with that. . . . It was only about three years ago that British Labour people started to look at North America . . . it's quite recent but it happened very, very quickly. . . . They saw things that went with the grain of what they were thinking."[76]

The United Kingdom has become so much more receptive to U.S. policy influences in large measure due to the closer political alignment of New Labour and the New Democrats (see Marquand, 1998). And it is *within this context* that the more mechanistic and concrete forms of policy transfer, as well as the more nebulous flows of policy languages and styles, tend to take on an ideological and structural significance that for the most part they lack in cases of one-off transfers between politically unaligned countries. In the case of welfare reform, what have been imported from the United States are not so much individual "policies that work" but more general *political strategies* of reform management-focusing, for example, on issues of "welfare dependency," the virtues of work, and so forth—coupled with a selective reading of key policy lessons. As a senior Treasury official explained, "There is [a U.S.] influence, not so much on the detailed design of individual programs, but I think the general approach. The way that the welfare debate in America has been changed by Clinton has been quite influential on a high-level political plane with people over here. . . . We keep an eye on the debate in America. We've relied quite a lot on the evaluation evidence from people like MDRC."[77]

Perhaps the most significant individual "lesson" to be learned from the United States has concerned the role of compulsion, though arguably this has been more of a political lesson than a programming lesson, given that the U.S. evaluation evidence concerning compulsion is nowhere near as conclusive as many reform advocates have claimed.[78] Nevertheless, such is the controversial nature of the compulsion issue in the United Kingdom, support for mandation having effectively become a litmus test of New Labour credentials (see Teles, 1997),[79] it has been politically advantageous to present this as a *practical* policy lesson from the United States (or more specifically, from Wisconsin) rather than as a matter of ideological principle. But again, the broad political alignment between Britain and the United States under Blair and Clinton has facilitated this kind of transatlantic pragmatism, whereas previously issues such as compulsion would have been regarded as no-go areas of partisan and *principled* opposition. As two senior policy actors saw it:

> "Wisconsin, far and away, has been most talked about over here basically because of the compulsion element. . . . Quite a few ministers have been over to Wisconsin and [senior officers from Madison] came over here. Its interesting to see how it has worked over there, but I don't think you can import wholesale like that over here because our social structure is very different, our economic fundamentals and our traditions and conventions are very different, and the culture generally is very different. So I think we can learn lessons, but I don't think you can import wholesale."[80]

> "Nobody went over to the States and looked at one type of welfare reform . . . and said, this is the model. There are lots of different models that are relevant. For example . . . you've got a whole bunch of people going up to Wisconsin and looking at it and saying, shit, this is kind of hard line but there are a few things that work."[81]

There is an understandable reluctance among many of those involved in British welfare-to-work policymaking to concede that the U.S. experience is being learnt from in any way but selectively. At one level, of course, it is a truism that *systemic* policy transfer is politically and practically infeasible. Labour ministers seem to be almost as anxious about the potentially negative connotations of the U.S. "model" of welfare reform as were their Conservative predecessors, but, like the Conservatives, they have nevertheless continued to pursue a strategy of piecemeal *but incremental* policy transfer.

Surely it is no coincidence, either, that Labour should have pressed so hard for work-based welfare reform in the favorable labor-market conditions that accompanied its rise to power. And here, lessons were certainly being learned from the United States and elsewhere concerning the structural sequencing of welfare-to-work interventions. Echoing the methodology of work-first strategies in the United States, and learning from the troubled implementation of earlier Australian reforms (see Finn, 1997), Labour focused its initial programming efforts on the most employable client group, young people, whose labor market reentry could be facilitated at generally lower cost than groups such as lone parents, unemployed adults, and the disabled. As Conservative critics have (somewhat impishly) asked, why should a government determined to tackle social exclusion focus its efforts and resources on those *most* likely to secure employment in the absence of public support?[82] Labour had clearly learned lessons about how to maximize the (short-term) employment impacts of welfare-to-work programming. Specific lessons were also learned, again from the United States, in terms of the promotion of welfare-to-work as a concept within the business community, where high-level corporate support has been secured through promotional campaigns and business breakfasts with senior cabinet ministers.

More fundamentally, there are also first indications that concerted efforts are being made to open up the space for *local* policy development under the New Deal, drawing on the more heterogeneous and dynamic tradition of "bottom-up" development within the U.S. federal system. While the U.K. system remains very heavily centralized, there is certainly a growing acknowledgment that the route to sustained policy innovation and development should be through some form of decentralization, albeit with a firm central steer. And along with this comes a corresponding emphasis on the cultivation of *local* policy capacity and leadership. As a senior member of the New Deal Task Force put it, "I suspect the reason for wanting that [decentralized] model is based on U.S. experience. I'm not sure to what extent in any detail we've been looking at building on what they've done . . . but the drive for it being a local program I think has come from the States because that's what works."[83]

It must be acknowledged, however, that the historically centralized structure of the British state, coupled with the limited capacity for significant political agency at the local level, means that localized policy experimentation in the United Kingdom is likely to remain substantially different from, and generally less developed than, its U.S. counterpart. The local partnership arrangements that have been brought into being under the New Deal are highly dependent on centrally-dispensed funding streams and, as single-policy, ostensibly "temporary" creations, may in their current form lack the institutional robustness necessary for long-term innovation. As a result, the central government is likely to remain the principal animateur and orchestrator of the welfare-to-work effort in the United Kingdom. Even if this role is modified to take account of policy initiatives percolating up from the local level, central government agencies will retain their dominant function as the "clearing houses" of the policy-development process, conferring the status of favored (and therefore funded) policies on some innovations, while disregarding others. At the present time, it is difficult to conceive of a situation in the U.K. welfare-to-work system, for example, in which concerted political pressure could be mobilized at the local level in order to bring about a radical shift in the national regulatory or funding framework, commensurate with the palpable pressure exerted by some U.S. states for block-grant powers prior to the 1996 legislation.

These deep-seated institutional discontinuities between British and U.S. state structures may go some of the way toward explaining why the policy-transfer process appears such a shallow one in so many respects. There is certainly a feeling in some quarters that the U.S. policy repertoire can be picked over and selectively incorporated in a kind of cafeteria fashion, often absent the deeper lessons concerning the historical antecedents of contemporary U.S. policy.[84] Just as importantly, it is clear that there are some nontrivial European inflections in the U.K. welfare-reform debate, not least the overriding concern with social exclusion, which while partly symbolic may also be exposing alternative development trajectories and progressive opportunities that seem now to be largely absent from the U.S. debate (see Amin et al., 1999; Peck, 1999). As two senior figures in the policy community saw it:

> "There are important aspects of the European model that are getting injected into the [debate]. Some of them are more symbolic than real. . . . Putting in a minimum wage and signing the Social Chapter are strongly symbolic moves that say that we think that a flexible and adaptable labor market is a good idea, but only so far."[85]

> "In terms of welfare-to-work, I think some of the transfers have been exaggerated partly because the U.S. *labels* have been used. . . . Actually in content they have every bit as much a relationship to Scandinavian models, the Netherlands, and so on. . . . So, if you're asking how does it transfer across the Atlantic, well it changes dramatically because there's an entirely different welfare system, I mean men get the dole here, things like that, and because there's been so many years of policy influence, as well, from other European models. . . . That often gets misinterpreted by observers who are looking for [evidence of] a straight transfer."[86]

While the United Kingdom may currently occupy an intermediate position between the continental European tradition and the U.S. tradition with respect to welfare and employment policy, this very hybridity, coupled with the profound economic and political pressures for ongoing reform that are present on both continents, means that this situation is neither a stable nor an entirely predictable one. In this sense, the reform strategies pursued in the United Kingdom are likely themselves to have a bearing on parallel developments in other countries, certainly in continental Europe,[87] and maybe also—in a perversely circuitous fashion—on subsequent reforms in the United States.[88] The precise course of Labour's welfare-modernization project, as the partial retreats over lone-parent and disability-benefit cuts and the sackings of Frank Field and Harriet Harman illustrate, is certainly not set in stone. Perhaps rather than the grand designs of Frank Field, the preferred course will now be more incremental. Indeed, borrowing terminology again from Clinton's welfare speeches, the prime minister has characterized the approach of the current social security secretary, Alistair Darling, as that of "a quiet revolutionary."[89] The future pattern of events in the United States will have a bearing here, in that the coming years may well be decisive in determining whether the "American model" continues its ascendancy as an international reform exemplar, or whether it falters, fails, and becomes discredited. For the time being, the two countries seem to have embarked on a process of joint workfarist policy development. So, when in September 1999 the Blair government introduced its "Working Families Tax Credit," a policy measure directly lifted from EITC in the United States, the *Wall Street Journal* at least was under no illusions about what was happening. It's headline baldly proclaimed, "Britain launches workfare subsidy."[90]

## A Third Way to Workfarism?

The parallel welfare-to-work strategies that have been set in train by the Blair and Clinton governments give concrete expression, of a kind, to recent claims that a Third Way policy orthodoxy is under construction. Yet, at the same time, this critical field of reform exposes many of the limitations and contradictions of such active forms of social interventionism, when operated in the context of a neoliberal economic policy framework. Welfare-to-work strategies do not create jobs, and they struggle to achieve results in situations where local economies are sluggish. If, as some commentators are predicting, recession cannot be far away for both Britain and the United States, the apparent new orthodoxy of work-based welfare reform may prove to be a short-lived one. As the United Kingdom is only in the very first stages of implementing welfare reform, such short-term economic contingencies may exert a significant influence on the future course of policy. In this context, the snake oil of quick-fix welfare reform will have been exposed for what it is: an opportunist policy predicated on the continued buoyancy of labor markets. Passing familiarity with the long history of structural economic problems in the United Kingdom should caution against placing much faith in supply-side "solutions," even if they can be shown to "work" elsewhere.

Because the welfare-to-work client group is largest in those parts of the country where the labor market is weakest, the New Deal will have least purchase as a policy tool in those places where it is needed most. In the northern cities, Conservative "training" schemes in the 1980s were vilified for offering "training without jobs"; the New Deal may simply raise "employability without jobs" in the same areas. Large-scale unemployment is a problem of the very recent past in the United Kingdom, and it *remains* a problem in many cities and lagging regions, even in the midst of the current "boom." In this context, it is complacent and unrealistic to argue that there are no demand-side causes of unemployment in such areas, that the root causes of urban unemployment lie with "welfare dependency" alone.

But just as a narrow reading of the causes of unemployment and poverty has been given new credence by the Blair government, so also there are risks in exaggerating the impact of flagship policies like the New Deal when the determinants of change are both more complex and more economically contingent. Piachaud (1999a) observes that the Blair government is actually making some early progress toward reducing poverty—an explicit prime-ministerial target—but much of this progress can be attributed to tax-and-benefit changes that have resulted in "redistribution by stealth," coupled with continuing job-market growth. The role of welfare-to-work measures here is far from self-evident, though Piachaud believes that they may have helped at the margin. The greater difficulty stems from the straightforward paucity of jobs in many areas, given that benefit levels continue to be held well below the poverty rate.

> Overblown New Deal rhetoric will not magic most pensioners and disabled people from welfare to work. For most of those in poverty, what is most crucial is the level of income support. The minimum income provided for most of those who do not have employment is far below the poverty level. (Piachaud, 1999b: 3)

Welfare-to-work has become a repository for so many of Labour's aspirations, it is difficult to escape the conclusion that its fate and that of the Blair government will be closely entwined. As Barnett and Wintour (1998: 17) have said of the New Deal, "If it succeeds, the Labour government will work. If it falters, Mr Blair correspondingly fails. The stakes could not be higher."

While most would accept the argument that some form of modernization is necessary for the continued effectiveness, and perhaps even viability, of any welfare system, there are clear dangers in engineering an approach that is too closely reliant on short-run economic conditions. In some senses, however, it seems that the long-run objective in the United Kingdom is to fashion a U.S.-style welfare system as a counterpart to the increasingly flexibilized and individualized—some might say "Americanized"—labor market that has been emerging in Britain for some time. What is increasingly clear is that the policy "problem" is seen to lie on the supply side—with the preparedness of unemployed people to accept "flexible" jobs—rather than on the demand side of the labor market, with the economic, political, and regulatory factors behind this process of contingent job creation itself.

Reflecting on the U.S. experience, the House of Commons Social Security Select Committee also framed its discussion of policy options and imperatives in light of changing labor-market circumstances. Low unemployment, at least in some parts of the country, was seen to open up a window of opportunity for experimentation in welfare-to-work:

> We recognise that the British economy does not have the demand for labour that the American economy provides. The British labour market has, however, undergone profound changes: there is overall employment growth and an increase in part-time, temporary and more flexible work patterns. These labour market changes provide the right opportunities to reform the social security system. We believe that the British social security system should be more closely tailored to work requirements for claimants. (House of Commons, 1998: x)

## BRITAIN'S WINDING PATH TO WORKFARE

Lawrence Mead has observed that, in the United Kingdom, "the main upset over welfare appears to be the feeling that many people are 'fiddling' the benefits, that is getting aid illegally," and correspondingly the principal impetus for workfare is to "police the benefit system, to 'smoke out' people who work 'off the books' . . . rather than, as in the US, to enforce work as an end in itself" (1996: 30). This observation exposes the distinctive roots of Britain's newfound workfare consensus, which are to be found with concerns strictly to regulate the use of welfare in the context of mass unemployment. The origins of workfarism, U.K.-style, lie in this essentially negative conception of the "welfare scrounger," one that drove the Conservatives, in the final months of the Major administration to the ludicrous lengths of instigating a crackdown on "workshy" disabled people and conducting random roadside checks for benefit fraud in areas of high unemployment.[91] In his role as chair of the House of Commons Social Security Committee under the Conservatives, Frank Field had played a major role in "mainstreaming" the issue of benefit fraud; his committee's antifraud investigations had "done more than anything else to create a near consensus between the parties over an issue which until recently was generally regarded as the province of the far right and the tabloid press" (Deacon, 1996: 2).

The Conservatives' welfare-to-work strategy was never a fully coherent and integrated one, divided as it remained between a progressive tightening of the benefit regime on the one hand and the marketization of labor-market programs on the other. For all the bravado of Thatcherite rhetoric, the Conservatives adopted an incrementalist approach that at times bordered on the cautious and defensive. At least until the mid-1990s, critics' charges of compulsion and the calibration of every policy change in terms of a shift towards "U.S.-style workfare" were clearly seen—by both the government and its opponents—as hurting the Conservatives politically. But perhaps more pertinent here was the Conservatives' perception of the administrative, as opposed to political, costs of workfare: while comfortable enough with the principle of compulsion, the Conservatives remained anxious about the cost implications of conceding a role for the state as "employer of last resort." Only toward the very end of their eighteen-year rule did they begin to experiment with workfare programming in an explicit way, though in retrospect this looks more like a case of affected radicalism in the face of Labour's sweeping seizure of political initiative.

As Mead (1996) suggests, the Conservatives' stance on workfare was always a qualified one; uncomfortable with the (work)-ethical case for workfar*ism*, they would continue to operate with a literal, narrow, and program-oriented conception of workfare. In opposition, Labour's position was essentially similar. So, while the Conservatives declared themselves to be against "very large-scale programmes," instead favoring small-scale schemes and pilot projects tailored to "individual circumstances and local conditions" (Education and Employment Committee, 1996: iii–iv), Labour would also advocate initiatives sensitive to "individual needs [and] local circumstances" over "rigid, national programmes" (Labour Party, 1996a: 4). But although Labour's language was initially cautious, this belied the radicalism of the "Blair revolution," which would soon be challenging the welfarist principles that the Commission on Social Justice had ventured only to "modernize." Once in power, the scale of New Labour's ambitions quickly became apparent:

> The days have gone when Labour regarded unemployment as a flaw of the market economy, a flaw that could be rectified or reduced through public sector projects financed through progressive taxation. Now unemployment is seen as a product of flaws within the welfare state, which create perverse incentives and in turn produce dependency in welfare recipients. . . . [T]he New Deal involves a different way of looking at the jobless. At one time they were seen as victims of a wicked system . . . but with welfare-to-work in place they will be transformed into recipients of opportunities which carry obligations and responsibilities. And that has already justified imposing sanctions on the young that go beyond what the Conservatives were willing to contemplate. (Dickson, 1997: 19)

The Labour Party had laid the foundations of Britain's welfare state in the wake of its landslide election victory of 1945. Half a century later an even greater landslide would present New Labour with a mandate for radical reform. Tony Blair's self-styled "Welfare to Work Government" would immediately set about the task, demonstrating in its New Deal for the unemployed how the soft words of communitarianism would be married with the hard actions of mandatory programming. The full scale of Labour's ambitions in the area of welfare reform has yet to be revealed, though all the indications are that supporting—or if necessary compelling—transitions into work will be at the heart of the strategy.

There have been both continuities and discontinuities in Labour's approach to workfare. Labour built on the Conservatives' approach by tightening the regime of compulsion established under JSA and by adopting a pragmatic methodology in terms of the specifics of program design (see, e.g., ES/DfEE, 1997). As welfare to work minister Andrew Smith has argued, the government can only justify its "tough position on sanctions" if the objective of quality programming for all participants is fully met:

> To deliver this high quality programme, the framework must be flexible. I am not interested in parachuting in rigid Whitehall blueprints, but would much rather see innovative local solutions, guided by our broad outline [and] effectively meeting local needs. . . . We want the New Deal to build upon what works.[92]

By launching the New Deal, Labour entered a qualitatively new phase in workfare politics. The Blair government has fully embraced both the policy commitment to large-scale, active programming and the ideological commitment to a work-ethic rationale. The divergences between U.S.-style and U.K.-style workfarism, so succinctly identified by Mead (1996), have therefore been dramatically eroded. While the British approach remains a distinctive one—shaped as it is by legacies of extensive labor-market programming and benefit system-based coercion—the Labour leadership's active promotion of a workfarist, rights-and-responsibilities philosophy represents a significant break with the Conservatives' cautious and piecemeal approach.

The ideological repackaging of workfare by New Labour, even though the word itself is still only used pejoratively, is significant because it allows new initiatives to be promoted in a positive light. In contrast to the Conservatives' essentially defensive approach, New Labour has clearly joined the workfare offensive: the old policy rhetoric of fighting fraud is being displaced by a new discourse of promoting independence. This shift is more than a semantic one, but this remains a field in which terminology matters. One well-placed observer—noting that the word *workfare,* while hardly ever uttered in public by ministers, was occasionally used as a symbol of political machismo in closed-door meetings—felt that the substantive changes had already run far ahead of the discursive niceties:

> "It's difficult to see the New Deal for young people as anything other than a clear and fairly explicit variant of workfare, given that workfare is rarely implemented in its harshest, strictest form of, you know, work and you get cash. It's normally a portfolio of options. So it seems to me that the New Deal is workfare. It's quite interesting that the label is not used, or it's casually used . . . but broadly it's a nonword. . . . It's a lovely word at one level because it's overidentified. It has different meanings for different people. But I think in the British debate it's been, broadly speaking, used as a term of abuse."[93]

While the limits of the Conservatives' political ambition and appetite were captured by John Major's eleventh-hour vision of "lean"—and, one might reasonably add, mean—welfare, it would be left to New Labour to establish welfare reform as a (potentially) *transformative* project. New Labour has accepted many of the basic principles, and even some of the moral tone, of a Murrayesque critique of welfare. Welfare dependency, rather than poverty per se, has become the explicit focus of policy: the poor behave "inappropriately" because they inhabit a world of perverse incentives, an incentive structure that must be transformed if they are to achieve "independence"; the solutions must be about work and work ethics, definitionally absent in the disenfranchised and dysfunctional "class" of the workless poor; strategies must be flexible, active, and local, almost the mirror image of the rigid-bureaucracy, passive-dependency stereotypes of welfarism.[94] The notion that the welfare state *must* be modernized if it is to survive (in any form) has now also become a political staple:

The welfare state now faces a choice of futures. A privatised future, with the welfare state becoming a residual safety net for the poorest and most marginalised; the *status quo*, but with more generous benefits; or the Government's third way—promoting opportunity instead of dependence, with a welfare state providing for the mass of the people, but in new ways to fit the modern world. . . . We propose a . . . modern form of welfare that believes in empowerment not dependency. We believe that work is the best route out of poverty for those who can work. We believe in ensuring dignity and security for those who are unable to work because of disability or because of caring responsibilities, as well as those who have retired. This system is about combining public and private provision in a new partnership for the age. (DSS, 1998: 19)

Although the political and institutional dynamics behind workfare are clearly different in Britain and the United States (Nathan, 1988; Walker, 1991; Dolowitz, 1998; Deacon, 2000), a telling lesson from the United States is that once left-of-center parties join the workfare consensus the entire basis of political debate—and the range of policy options—shifts dramatically. The debate becomes less concerned with the relative merits and problems of welfarism vis-à-vis workfarism, focusing instead on the narrower terrain of exploring alternative paths *away from* welfarism and toward some form of work-oriented regime. As New Labour's conviction and confidence have hardened, the Conservatives have (predictably perhaps) lurched further to the right on the issue of welfare, pledging in October 1997 to introduce a "can work must work guarantee." Explicitly borrowing ideas from the Ontario Conservatives, William Hague's *Common Sense Revolution* policy platform included proposals for daily signing at benefit offices, a "one strike and you're out" policy for those refusing to accept a job, and privatization of the JobCentre network (Conservative Party, 1999).[95]

While this kind of workfare consensus has held away in the United States for more than a decade now, it has only recently begun to take shape in Britain. True, benefit coercion has been a strong—and strengthening—feature of the British work–welfare regime since the mid-1980s (Dean and Taylor-Gooby, 1992; King, 1995), but it is only really in the rise to power of Tony Blair, since 1994, that Britain's truncated workfare debate began to exhibit the features of a comprehensive and internally coherent program of transformative action. Thus the focus of debate has begun to move away from the (Conservative) preoccupation with the sheer size and cost of the welfare state and toward a (New Labour) concern with its underlying incentive structure. Quite aptly, as Mead (1986: 3) once put it, "The main problem with the welfare state is not its size but its permissiveness."

It would be wrong to jump to the conclusion that the formation of some kind of realigned political consensus makes the transition from welfare to workfare an inevitable one. Agreeing on the principles of reform is one thing; getting the new system to work is another. As Deacon (2000: 8) notes, having declared "its determination to 'think the unthinkable,' the Blair administration has subsequently been in earnest pursuit of the workable." There are still significant obstacles to, and contradictions within, the nascent workfarist project in the United Kingdom. The path-dependent nature of workfarism means that these take different forms in different places. In the United Kingdom, workfare is perhaps especially fragile due to a series of political, institutional, and economic conditions. While the Blair revolution is firmly entrenched in both the Labour Party and in government itself, oppositional forces are likely to grow in strength over time. Opposition to the principle of compulsion remains strong in the trade-union movement, among advocacy groups, in local authorities, among voluntary-sector providers, and not least among the unemployed themselves.[96]

While, for the time being, an uneasy truce continues to prevail, this is by no means guaranteed to hold, particularly as shortcomings in program implementation or outcomes become apparent. And at least a far as potential participants are concerned, government claims that the New Deal will bear no resemblance to what Frank Field (1995: 15) once called the "Mickey Mouse training courses" of old are unlikely to ring true. They have heard this too many times before (see Finn, 1987; Mizen, 1995). The sheer scale of the New Deal will inevitably make quality control difficult, just as it raises the political risks associated with failure. As Dickson (1997: 18) points out, "with more than £3 billion in windfall revenue, a lot should be achieved [but] failure would be all the more ignominious." A windfall can only be spent once; replacement funding from mainstream taxation, should the program falter, would not be easy to justify with the electorate.

There are also risks at the institutional level. Writing some time ago, Richard Nathan (1988: 17) pointed out that "transform[ing] institutions . . . is the key to workfare, however defined," yet in Britain his impression was that "the bureaucracy, if anything, will be even harder to change than the American." The JSA framework will certainly help facilitate the transition to workfarism in Britain, but there is a great deal to do before the locally networked, activist institutions envisioned by some New Labour gurus become a reality. The fact that the New Deal is being deployed in the context of an uneven and underdeveloped institutional base means that the scope for implementation failures is clearly a wide one. The government repeatedly claims that it is willing to listen to those with on-the-ground experience (ES/DfEE, 1997), and there are some promising experiments that might be built upon (Simmonds and Emmerich, 1996; Fleming, 1997; Haughton et al., 2000), but there are no off-the-peg solutions ready and waiting in Glasgow or elsewhere (Finn, 1996). For all the optimism of ministerial announcements and the manifest political will to effect change, much will rest on ultimately unpredictable developments in the "shadow land" of implementation.

And finally, the state of the economy will also be critical. Long-term unemployment is a stubborn and deep-seated problem in many parts of Britain, not least in its northern and western fringes, where even workfare advocates like Mead (1996) concede there is a shortage of jobs. Delivering work-based welfare reform in such areas represents an enormous political challenge. Soaking up excess labor onto environmental task forces and voluntary schemes may be the way that the New Deal meets its short-term objectives—of enrolling claimants into the program—but this strategy cannot work in the long term if private-sector labor demand in these areas remains weak. Worse still, the integrity of the program as a whole could clearly be compromised if the *national* economy were to slow down. The Blair government currently has the key advantage of labor-market expansion (albeit highly uneven), but a change in the macroeconomic climate could see postprogram unemployment rates soar. In these circumstances, the New Deal might itself be consigned to the dustbin of failed "schemes."

It should not be forgotten, moreover, that there is a long-established relationship between economic cycles and shifts in welfare policy (Piven and Cloward, 1971). While there is strong evidence in the United Kingdom of a cumulative, and perhaps structural, transition toward benefit conditionality and work programming, as creeping compulsion has been accompanied by creeping workfarism (Jones, 1996), there are also indications of Piven–Cloward cycles. So, the more radical reform measures have tended to occur in the context of falling unemployment, first in the post-1986 downswing (e.g., Restart in 1986, the Social Security Act of 1988, and TECs in 1988) and subsequently in the post-1933 downswing (e.g., the JSA proposals of 1994, Project Work in 1995, and the New Deal in 1997). While politicians of all stripes have displayed a touching faith that the last recession *really will* be the last, the emboldening effects of a growing economy should blind no one to the possibility that recession may return. And programs conceived in the good times may not always survive the bad.

The British path toward workfare has been uneven and economically procyclical but it also has been incremental and cumulative. Perhaps the key moment in this was the recent transition from piecemeal experimentation with workfare under the Conservatives to a full-fledged adoption of workfarist principles by the New Labour government. What was once located at the radical fringes of the Conservative program of benefit coercion has come to represent an ideological cornerstone of the New Labour credo. While the word itself is still primarily associated with *critiques* of policy, its various euphemisms signify an important shift in the center of gravity of British welfare politics. The United Kingdom is in the process of scripting its own translation of "workfare." What only ten years ago was defined narrowly as an administrative program, and a questionable "foreign" one at that, has emerged as one of the organizing frameworks for a putatively transformative "reconstruction" of the welfare state.

## Notes

1. Tony Blair, speech at the Aylesbury Estate, Southwark, June 2, 1997.
2. Tony Blair, speech at the Aylesbury Estate, Southwark, June 2, 1997.
3. "We understand that economic stability is the prerequisite for radicalism in social policy rather than an alternative to it. We must be the parties of fiscal and economic prudence. Combined with it must be reform of the welfare state. The public simply won't pay more taxes and spend more to fund an unreconstructed welfare system . . . . We are spending. We are taxing. But we have more poverty and inequality. . . . Welfare has become passive; a way of leaving people doing nothing, rather than helping them become active" (Tony Blair, speech to the Party of European Socialists' Congress, Malmo, June 6, 1997).
4. Tony Blair, Downing Street Press Conference with President Bill Clinton, May 29, 1997.
5. See Burghes (1987), Burton (1987), Digby (1989), Walker (1991, 1998), Deacon (1994), Wood (1995), Employment Committee (1996), Dolowitz (1998), House of Commons (1998), Matthews and Becker (1998), and Jones (1999).
6. See Grove (1995: 251) and *Independent*, May 20, 1996: 11.
7. See Charter Against Workfare (1987) and Jones (1997).
8. Quoted in TUC (1988: 480).
9. See Benn and Fairley (1986), Finn (1987), and Ainley and Corney (1990).
10. Recall Brown's (1997) similar evocation of culinary metaphors in her discussion of work-first policy transfer within the United States (see Chapter 5).
11. David Willetts, MP, a former member of the No 10 policy unit, said workfare would be tantamount to "nationalising unemployment," while Patrick McLoughlin, the employment minister, had insisted in November 1992 that there were "no plans to introduce a compulsory workfare scheme," warning that it would "increase levels of benefit dependency": a scheme "which forces people to work in jobs that they do not want and does little to improve skills or motivation does not enhance either the efficiency or the adaptability of the labour market" (quoted in *Independent*, February 5, 1993: 3).
12. As the *Independent's* Anthony Bevins saw it, "The theme to which the

Prime Minister returned repeatedly during his speech to the Tory club was crime and its roots. Contrasting the impact of the free market and socialism on communities, Mr. Major said 'the big problem' was in the inner cities, rather than the suburbs, small towns and villages. 'It is from the inner cities, where the state is dominant, that businesses have fled. It is in the inner cities that vandalism is rife and property uncared for. It is here that fear of violent crime makes a misery of old people's lives.' . . . Labour, he added, sought to explain the difference between the inner cities and the more peaceful and prosperous suburbs, towns and villages in terms of wealth and poverty. But the Prime Minister condemned that as an insult 'to those families who may face all the problems of unemployment and yet do not resort to crime' " ("PM Blames Socialism for Crime," *Independent*, February 4, 1993: 1).

13. As a *Guardian* leader described it, Major's brief fling with workfare was a symptom of the drift that had characterized his administration: "The subject captured headlines, not surprisingly as it is an important, difficult question deserving serious debate. But now you see it, now you don't. By mid-morning there was an official denial that it meant anything remotely like Workfare. By question time Mr. Major was scouring the thesaurus for ways of saying it was only an option. What benefit has there been to Britain from such a cock-eyed approach?" (*Guardian*, February 5, 1993: 20).

14. *Independent*, February 6, 1993: 13; see also Mandelson and Liddle (1996: 99–102).

15. "I want to give people on welfare the education and training and the opportunities they need to become self-sufficient. . . . I think all of us want what most people on welfare want, a country that gives you a hand up, not a hand out" (Federal News Service, February 2, 1993, Remarks by President Bill Clinton to the National Governors' Association meeting, J. W. Marriott Hotel, Washington, DC).

16. See Reich (1992, 1999), Baily et al. (1993), EC (1994, 1999a, 1999b); cf. Dehli (1993), Gordon (1996), and Crouch et al. (1999).

17. Member of Commission on Social Justice, interviewed by Jamie Peck, May 1999.

18. Bill Morris, general secretary of the Transport & General Workers' Union, reiterated his union's opposition to "the unemployed being pushed into workfare for their benefits" (November 11, 1995: 26), while Dan Finn of the Unemployment Unit wrote in the *Independent* that "it has been profoundly dispiriting to see senior Labour shadow ministers scoring cheap points by peddling gross stereotypes about the young unemployed. This has given a green light to those advocating a workfare regime and has done serious damage to the hard-won credibility of many in the Labour Party who have worked to protect high-quality programmes for the unemployed" (November 14, 1995: 16).

19. Quoted on Radio 4's *Today* program, October 9, 1996.

20. Quoted in *Inside ES*, October 1996: 1.

21. Quoted in *Guardian*, February 13, 1997: 19; see also Employment Policy Institute (1996) and Peck and Tickell (1997). Piloted in twenty-one areas of the United Kingdom from April 1996, the benefits hot-line was launched nationally in August 1996 with a major "Beat the cheat" advertising campaign encouraging the public to report suspected benefit cheats. Billboard and newspaper advertisements listing the hot-line telephone number asked, "Know a benefit

rip-off? Give us a telephone tip-off." A Department of Social Security official drily observed that "[w]e've been surprised at people's enthusiasm to shop their neighbours. Many people who are legitimately claiming benefit, or who are working hard, feel angry at others who abuse the system" (quoted in *Sunday Telegraph*, August 4, 1996: 1).

22. Quoted in *Working Brief*, December 1996–January 1997: 3.

23. On the Conservative's interest in the work-first method of the Riverside GAIN program, see Mitchell (1996). Social security minister Andrew Mitchell was also attracted to the notion of placing JobCentre staff on performance-related contracts, linked to their success rates in placing claimants in work (*Sunday Times*, June 30, 1996: 24). There has been a long-standing interest in GAIN: Secretary of State for Employment Normal Fowler visited the program prior to the introduction of Training and Enterprise Councils in Britain in 1988 (see Dolowitz, 1997).

24. ES unpublished guidance on interviewing policy (1996: 20–21).

25. Quoted in *Hansard*, Debates 252, 10 January 1995: column 52.

26. Quoted in *Guardian*, January 11, 1995: 6.

27. *Financial Times*, July 10, 1996: 6; Chris Smith, shadow social security secretary, quoted in *Guardian*, October 7, 1996: 4.

28. *Observer*, October 6, 1996: 36. A decade earlier support for workfare in Britain was at 50 percent in opinion polls (see Burton, 1988).

29. In the JSA White Paper, the need for piloting powers was explained in terms of the complex interactions between benefit-incentive structures and claimants' behavioral modifications: "Benefits for the unemployed can easily have unintended behavioural consequences. . . . However, it is difficult to predict what the effects of any particular set of rules will be. . . . The Government therefore proposes to introduce a power to pilot rule changes locally before national implementation" (Employment Department Group/Department of Social Security, 1994: 16). The roots of this kind of thinking clearly lie in part with the likes of Charles Murray (1990: 80–81), who stated in an earlier intervention in the U.K. welfare debate that "complex social programmes intended to change human behaviour tend not to work out the way they were planned."

30. Reflecting the "stepping-stone" approach advanced by Charles Murray (1985: 443–444), Peter Lilley explained that "Earnings Top-Up . . . is a scheme to try to boost the earnings of those who take modestly paid jobs, so they get on the ladder of employment, they get starter jobs and they move up. Rather than destroy those jobs with a minimum wage, so there are no bottom rungs on the ladder and people can't get on the ladder of employment" (quoted on Radio 4's *Today* program, October 9, 1996).

31. See D. Finn, "North Norfolk Action and Supportive Caseloading: The Lessons Learned," *Working Brief*, October 1995: 20–21.

32. See D. Finn, " 'Workstart' Employment Subsidies," *Working Brief*, October 1995: 15–17.

33. Employment minister Eric Forth would later concede in a Commons debate that even PW represented a "half-hearted" response on the part of government (quoted in *Guardian*, April 10, 1996: 6).

34. Department for Education and Employment press release, quoted in *Working Brief*, November 1996: 4, emphasis added.

35. *Guardian*, February 20, 1997: 9; cf. Prince's Trust, 1996, and Prince's Trust Volunteers, 1996.

36. Conservative Party, 1997: 11; see also *Financial Times*, December 13, 1996: 8.

37. See D. English, "Tony at Our Table," *Guardian*, October 6, 1995: 19; J. Peck, "Loose Talk and Tight Firsts," *Guardian*, August 7, 1996: S2.

38. David Willetts, one of the most astute Conservative observers of the welfare debate, observed in March 1996 that while Field had been "reduced to a voice in the wilderness of leftwing social policy . . . [t]his may be changing. He has more access to Tony Blair than previous leaders" (*Guardian*, March 26, 1996: 16).

39. Quoted in *Financial Times*, 29 April 1997: 23; see also Deacon (1996). Other former commissioners, in contrast, were more willing to move with the tide: newly elected Labour MP Patricia Hewitt praised Chancellor Gordon Brown's initiation of the "joined-up policy thinking needed to transform the welfare state into a 'Welfare to Work State' " (quoted in *Guardian*, May 13, 1997: 15).

40. The tax-and-benefits task force is headed by Martin Taylor, chief executive of Barclays Bank (see *Guardian*, May 20, 1997: 19), while the welfare-to-work task force is chaired by Peter Davis, chief executive of Prudential insurers and previously a leading member of the Welfare Reform Group, a group of insurance companies involved in the discussion of radical privatization plans under the Conservatives (see *Financial Times*, July 1, 1996: 18). Ian Robinson, chief executive of Scottish Power, was appointed to head the welfare-to-work task force in Scotland (*Financial Times* July 4, 1997: 6). On the new Labour task forces and advisory groups in general, see Daniel (1997).

41. House of Commons debate on the Queen's Speech, quoted in *Financial Times*, May 15, 1997: 1.

42. Quoted in *Observer*, May 18, 1997: 26.

43. Speech at the Aylesbury Estate, Southwark, June 2, 1997.

44. "The central purpose of this Budget is to ensure that Britain is equipped to rise to the challenge of the new and fast changing global economy. . . . The impact of the global market in goods and services, and of rapidly advancing technology, is now being felt in every home and ever community in our country. New products, new services, new opportunities challenge us to change; old skills, old jobs, old industries have gone and will never return. . . . Our creativity, our adaptability, our belief in hard work and self-improvement, the very qualities that made Britain lead the world in the 18th and 19th centuries, are precisely the qualities we need to make Britain a strong economic power in the 21st century" (Gordon Brown, budget speech, quoted in *Financial Times*, July 3, 1997: 15).

45. Gordon Brown, budget speech, quoted in *Financial Times*, July 3, 1997: 16.

46. Gordon Brown, budget speech, quoted in *Financial Times*, July 3, 1997: 16.

47. Speech at the Aylesbury Estate, Southwark, June 2, 1997.

48. Quoted in *Financial Times*, July 3, 1997: 24. As Harman later ex-

plained, "[W]e are not going to tackle social exclusion and poverty by tax and spend. We will tackle them by welfare to work, encouraging savings and reforming the welfare state" (quoted in *New Statesman,* November 28, 1997: 8).

49. As an editorial in the *Daily Mail* grudgingly acknowledged of the New Deal, "At a time when Britain's job-creating economy is the envy of Europe, there is something distinctly dated about this long-rehearsed, if well-intentioned, plan to contrive work experience for the young unemployed. What is reassuring is that, if they spurn this heavily subsidised, bureaucratically clumsy chance to acquire the work habit, it seems they will lose up to 60 percent of their benefits. Who knows? Maybe only a New Labour Government can get that tough with these youngsters that are work-shy!" (July 3, 1997: 12).

50. See TEN, 1997; *Working Brief,* August–September 1997.

51. *Financial Times,* July 4, 1997: 23.

52. Seventy-three percent were concerned that candidates would be "unsuitable," 60 percent that they would "lack skills," and 24 percent that they would be a "disruption to the workplace" (Institute of Directors survey, quoted in *Observer,* January 4, 1998: 17).

53. See also Grimes (1996), Finn (1996), Region of Policy Commission (1996), and Simmonds and Emmerich (1996).

54. As Finn (1996: 34–35) concludes after having reviewed the experience of Wise and other local initiatives, "there is no single local project in the UK which could simply be multiplied into a national scheme to relieve unemployment. Moreover, even if the best programmes currently operating in the UK were made national, they would provide only a partial solution to the problems facing the country in terms of unemployment." Prior to the General Election, Conservative employment minister Eric Forth stated that "I understand that the costs per opportunity, or per job, in the Wise scheme, which is often quoted to me, could be as high as £10,000 or even £14,000 per job. Now, that may well be able to be afforded on a very small scale in one part of the country. I don't think anybody could replicate that right across the country. So I'm not sure it has lessons for us at all" (quoted on Channel 4's *A Week in Politics,* March 8, 1997). Labour's training and employment spokesperson, Steven Byers, conceded that "[t]he Wise Group costs are high and we would want to reduce those. We feel that by having a national programme, then we'll get the benefits of the economies of scale." He went on the emphasize the Labour Party's position on compulsion: "Provided it is a job, a real job, with real wages, we feel that if the person refuses to take up a genuine offer, then there should be a benefit sanction following from that refusal."

55. Speech at the Aylesbury Estate, Southwark, June 2, 1997.

56. Quoted on Radio 4's *Sunday* program, July 6, 1997.

57. See Murray (1995, 1996) and Unemployment Unit (1996).

58. As Lawrence Mead has observed, implementation matters; those programs he considers to be most effective combine "help and hassle," but do so in a way that facilitate exits from welfare as early as possible in the claim period: "The sanction is removal of benefits, but if you administer it well you do not actually get there" (quoted in Fleming, 1997: 19). Labour indicated that it planned to tackle the implementation issue under the New Deal by pursuing a multifac-

eted approach, drawing on private, public, and voluntary agencies at the local level, and subsequently inducing competitive relations between them (see Fleming, 1997; Peck, 1999a).

59. Shadow employment and training minister David Willetts said: "The unemployment figures are further evidence of the healthy state in which we left the economy. Our policies have been getting people off welfare and into work without having to spend billions of pounds on ill-targetted programmes" (quoted in *Guardian*, August 14, 1997: 2).

60. Speech to the First New Deal national design workshop, Birmingham, July 28, 1997.

61. Ministerial adviser #2, Department for Education and Training, interviewed by Nikolas Theodore, May 1998.

62. Speech to the Party of European Socialists' Congress, Malmo, June 6, 1997.

63. "Employability" was established as one of the "four pillars" of EU social policy in December 1997, along with entrepreneurship, adaptability, and equal opportunities. In this context, employability means "how to cover the skills gaps in Europe and create attachments to the world of work for the young and long-term unemployed and other groups who are less competitive in the labour market so they do not drift into exclusion" (EC, 1999b: 14).

64. Having discussed his ideas with local benefit staff in Exeter, Field said, "We've got a large number of people managing huge budgets. So in Exeter the budget is £170 million, but we don't in any way allow [local offices] to manage or control that budget. So I couldn't say to people here, your budget is £170 million, is it feasible if you managed it in your own way, rather than us telling you how to manage it from the centre [you could spend around £15 million on local priorities] whatever was thought to be the right way to move from welfare dependency to creating opportunities? There's no way under the present set-up that that can happen. . . . If it doesn't happen I don't see how we're going to be able to deliver the sorts of reforms we want to deliver. So it's clearly got to be on the agenda. Quite how we do it is the next stage" (Radio 4's *World at One* program, August 6, 1997).

65. Frank Field, Radio 4's *World at One* program, August 6, 1997.

66. Mulgan has distanced himself from the moralizing aspects of Murray's work on the underclass, insisting that his work is of "little use in advancing social policy and the acceptance on both sides of the Atlantic of the need to balance rights and responsibilities" (Letter to *New Statesman*, September 12, 1997: 36).

67. Senior official, Treasury, interviewed by Jamie Peck and Nikolas Theodore, June 1998.

68. Senior official, New Deal Task Force, interviewed by Jamie Peck, November 1997.

69. Senior adviser, No 10 Policy Unit, interviewed by Jamie Peck and Nikolas Theodore, April 1998.

70. Senior adviser, New Deal Task Force, interviewed by Jamie Peck, November 1997.

71. Director, community enterprise agency, Glasgow, interviewed by Jamie Peck and Nikolas Theodore, December 1997.

72. See King (1995), Deacon (1997, 2000), Dolowitz (1998), Hirsch (1998), Theodore (1998), Walker (1991, 1998), King and Wickham-Jones (1999), and Peck and Theodore (2001).

73. See Charter Against Workfare (1987), Digby (1989), Finn (1995), Jones (1996), and Peck (1999a).

74. Senior official, Treasury, interviewed by Jamie Peck and Nikolas Theodore, June 1998.

75. Member of Commission on Social Justice, interviewed by Jamie Peck, May 1999.

76. Director, national advocacy organization, interviewed by Nikolas Theodore and Tod Rutherford, April 1998.

77. Senior official, Treasury, interviewed by Jamie Peck and Nikolas Theodore, June 1998.

78. See Oliker (1994), Epstein (1997), Handler and Hasenfeld (1997), and Brodkin and Kaufman (1998); cf. Rogers (1997) and Mead (1997a).

79. Social security secretary Alistair Darling was clearly addressing the left of his own party when he stated at the Labour Party conference: "When we set up the New Deal, we said there could be no fifth option to stay at home when you could work. People said that was harsh. It isn't. We've cut youth unemployment by 60 percent. . . . Now we're going further. . . . A new culture. New rights. New responsibilities. Some people say it's a tough approach. I don't. It's the right thing to do. It's easy to send out a Giro [benefit check]. But a Giro won't get you a job. Or improve your skills. So we need to do more. We are doing more. We are helping people to help themselves. Help that was never there before. That's what people want. Their government working for them. . . . We live in a changing world. And the welfare state must change with it. There are difficult decisions. And we've got to face up to them" (September 27, 1999).

80. Ministerial adviser #2, Department for Education and Training, interviewed by Nikolas Theodore, May 1998.

81. Director, national advocacy organization, interviewed by Nikolas Theodore and Tod Rutherford, April 1998.

82. David Willetts, speaking on Radio 4's *File on 4* program, November 5, 1997.

83. Interviewed by Jamie Peck, November 1997.

84. "A mistake has been made that what is happening under Clinton is welfare reform and that nothing happened prior to that. Whereas there are probably seven or eight years now of lessons of ET Choices, of GAIN, of Riverside, and so forth, that are much more relevant in terms of having a greater opportunity to step back and say what worked and what didn't. . . . I think [the situation under PRWORA] is horrifying personally. It's all gravitated to the lowest common denominator and all the incentives for excellence, all the incentives for investment, seem to me have been removed" (Senior adviser, New Deal Task Force, interviewed by Jamie Peck, November 1997).

85. Director, national advocacy organization, interviewed by Nikolas Theodore and Tod Rutherford, April 1998.

86. Senior adviser, No 10 Policy Unit, interviewed by Jamie Peck and Nikolas Theodore, April 1998.

87. "We were struck by the [1998] State of the Union address how much the flow was now actually going the other way, in terms of some of the ways in which the issues were framed, the packaging of the policy, and so on. . . . I think it's a period of pretty fruitful interchange and I suspect the next phase of welfare-to-work there may well be some parts of the U.K. experience being looked at by U.S. states . . . but it's probably premature to make that judgment" (Senior adviser, No 10 Policy Unit, interviewed by Jamie Peck and Nikolas Theodore, April 1998).

88. "Because the UK is a large country [within Europe], when it starts talking about some of the welfare-to-work principles . . . that has an influence on Germany and France in a way that the smaller countries don't. Rightly or wrongly, I think we do see the UK as a modernizer within Europe in relation to those large countries" (Senior adviser, No 10 Policy Unit, interviewed by Jamie Peck and Nikolas Theodore, April 1998).

89. Tony Blair, Beveridge Lecture, Toynbee Hall London, March 18, 1999.

90. *Wall Street Journal*, September 8, 1999: A19. On the origins of WFTC, see T. Bewick, N. Theodore, and M. Nimmo, "Can the Tax System Make Work Pay?," *Working Brief*, December–January 1997–1998: 19–24, and A. van Doorn, "Making Work Pay Through Tax Credits," *Working Brief*, April 1999: 11–13.

91. Stricter medical tests were introduced with a view to deregistering supposedly "workshy" claimants of incapacity benefits after April 1995, though an internal evaluation early in 1997 found that the new procedures were excessively costly to implement relative to the fall in registration (*Guardian*, February 13, 1997: 11). Meanwhile roadside checks of the benefit status of car drivers and passengers under "Operation Tinstar" were defended by the Benefits Agency as a cash-saving strategy (*Observer*, February 2, 1997: 1).

92. Speech to the First New Deal national design workshop, Birmingham, July 28, 1997.

93. Adviser to DfEE and DSS, interviewed by Jamie Peck, February 1999.

94. "The fact that the current system rewards lying, cheating and deceit is indicative of the revolutionary change which . . . a welfare reconstruction would bring about in this country. Welfare reconstruction would have a major impact on the ghettos. It would begin to set people free to build their own lives modelled on life outside the ghetto. . . . For far too long welfare has been seen exclusively in terms of combating poverty. The failure of this strategy has been abject. A totally new perspective is required. There are simply not enough votes in an old-fashioned anti-poverty strategy" (Field 1995: 20).

95. The Tories also promised to reduce the tax take under a future Conservative government, apparently oblivious to the cyclical pressures on public expenditure generated by (even minimal) welfare provision. Citing public expenditure trends under the first Thatcher government, the *Guardian* branded this a measure of such impracticality that "[n]ot even the reintroduction of the Poor Law would achieve such reductions" (October 5, 1999: 21).

96. See TUC (1995), Unemployment Unit (1996), Eling and Hewitt (1997), and TEN (1997).

CHAPTER EIGHT

# Conclusion
## *Workfare States?*

> Today's welfare reform is an exercise, not in economic transfers,
> but in statebuilding. . . . Welfare is changing from a subsidy
> into a regime. . . . [The] real agenda is statebuilding. State and
> local administrators are striving to get control of their
> caseloads. They are building a welfare state that is able to
> govern as well as support people. (Mead, 1996b: 588, 598)

There are many states of workfare. This book has mapped some of them.
It has not proved possible to establish a once-and-for-all cartographic
"fix" on workfare because—by definition, or at least in terms of the definition proposed here—the landscape of workfare is a fluid one. The regulatory project that is workfare is not simply about replacing welfarist institutions and conventions with a parallel set of fully coherent and
functioning workfarist ones. Workfare is not some deus ex machina,
lowered into place spontaneously to solve the contradictions of welfarism, flexible labor markets, and urban social dislocation. Rather,
workfare ideologies and strategies have emerged unevenly and iteratively,
as the outcome of years of institutional experimentation, policy reform,
and political struggle. And still, what we have come to understand as
workfarism remains unstable and contradictory. If this can be characterized as a process of "statebuilding," in Mead's (1996b) words, then it is
an ongoing one. It reflects a continuing process of institutional searching
and political–economic response, under which sustainable "solutions"
remain elusive. One only has to go to New York or Toronto to see this.

341

Yet, at the same time, workfare-style strategies have become the common sense of the age. Some variant of workfare is the policy of choice for most neoliberal states at the present time, while for other countries it represents—depending on one's point of view—either a palpable external threat or a seductive alternative. While it may not yet be truly hegemonic, workfare certainly represents a dominating strand in international policy discourse, one of the key coordinates around which reform strategies are plotted.[1] In more concrete terms, workfare has become the institutional codification of work-oriented welfare reform—and as such must be understood as *both* a reactive reform strategy *and* as a would-be successor to the welfare state. Part critique, part alternative, workfare's international allure is to some degree rooted in the fact that it is a policy that appears to "fit" the current political, social, and economic climate. Structurally, workfare seems in some respects to be the logical social-policy complement to flexible labor-market policies. In the here and now, its appeal is also related to the fact that the latest iteration of reform has coincided with an unprecedented economic boom in the United States. This configuration, however, is not entirely coincidental. As Piven and Cloward (1993) have so forcefully shown, the politics of workfare are themselves cyclical; the historical record reveals that work is most aggressively enforced when its availability increases. The significance of the current "upswing," however, is that the nature of work is changing too, as "flexible" jobs, fractions of jobs, and "McJobs" have become an almost permanent and near-ubiquitous feature of the labor market. Hence the sociological interest in the "new insecurity" as one of the defining features of the age (see Sennett, 1998; Bourdieu, 1998).

In this context, workfare strategies are becoming normalized as a means of enforcing labor-market participation in a climate dominated by underemployment, low pay, work insecurity, and low-grade service employment. This raises the prospect of a medium-term regulatory accommodation between activizing forms of social policy and flexibilizing labor markets. These two developments—which do not have a unifying, overarching, "functional" logic in any simple sense, but exhibit distinctive origins and dynamics—may be on the way to becoming mutually reinforcing. More than just a theoretical possibility, this logic of mutual reinforcement is evident at the level of policy development and advocacy. Workfare strategies appear to make sense when the labor market is generating large numbers of contingent jobs; the presence of such jobs facilitates the deregistration of welfare recipients; which in turn means that the policy is perceived as successful. Never mind that the argument is circular, that the jobs are unstable and poorly paid, that the programs are clumsy and often ineffective, the overall picture continues to appeal to politicians as an alternative to "welfare dependency."

Chancellor Gordon Brown, for example, places his government's welfare-to-work strategy at the heart of his vision of "full employability" Britain:

> A high and stable level of employment is our goal. Not jobs for life which no government can promise to deliver, but job opportunities for all throughout all their working life. And this is our challenge: if those who can work take the responsibility to work, if employers take the responsibility to train and to invest, and if all of us show the same responsibility in pay, then Britain can deliver, in our generation, employment opportunity for all. . . . Not just for one brief shining moment when the figures look good . . . but high and stable levels of growth with high and stable levels of employment.
>
> That is why we . . . are extending the New Deal, its rights and its responsibilities, to help more young people, and the long-term unemployed—helping lone parents and the disabled who want to work. That investment in work is now saving money on benefits. . . . I believe our duty is to make the New Deal a Permanent Deal—rights backed by responsibilities—[n]ot just for the young today, but for all who should be in jobs today and in the future.[2]

While the Blair government has been making the most of the following wind of labor-market growth in rolling out its welfare-to-work strategy, it has done so in a way acutely conscious of parallel developments across the Atlantic. While the structural weaknesses in the U.K. labor market, even at the peak of the economic cycle, mean that the goal of marrying active welfare with flexible work will be more of a challenge than in the United States, policy advocates continue to drive the debate in this direction. Neoliberal debates about social and employment policy are becoming distinctly internationalized. So, in his account of the U.S. "economic miracle," McWilliams pointedly draws attention to the way in which "aggressive management and the ever-present fear of losing one's job have been combined with tough welfare regulations" to minimize wage pressures and to facilitate growth. He insists, moreover, that in the United States,

> The improvement in employment prospects is most marked for those in the least good positions, whose equivalents in the UK have been unaffected so far by New Labour's New Deal. Indeed, the combination of a strong growing economy and minimum welfare is so far the only policy that has proved successful anywhere in the world in providing a practical escape route from the underclass. (McWilliams, 1999: B7)

On the face of it, the U.S. evidence is compelling. The national welfare caseload shrank by half in the latter part of the 1990s. Not surprisingly, reformers have been quick to take the credit for this. In a report published by the London-based Adam Smith Institute, it is argued, for example, that PRWORA

> forced even the most reluctant states to submit plans for welfare reform. The sweeping change has had an impact nation-wide, and even states that are not aggressively pushing welfare-to-work are experiencing significant caseload declines. . . . No other American public policy initiative has ever had comparable results. (Matthews and Becker, 1998: 2)

According to this view, the most important changes have followed from legislative reform, tough work-enforcing policies, and concerted political will to "end welfare as we know it." Matthews and Becker (1998: 2, 14) go on to insist that, "[t]he primary difference between successful and unsuccessful states is the policies adopted and the diligence with which they are implemented. . . . When states adopt incentives that encourage people to take a job and help them make the transition so they can keep it, the welfare caseload drops dramatically." Yet evaluation studies continue to reveal that even the most radical state reforms are only accounting for a small component of welfare caseload reductions, whereas strong employment growth is by far the most important factor. Ziliak et al. (1998) demonstrate that no less than 78 percent of the caseload reduction between 1993 and 1996 was due to business-cycle conditions, while only 6 percent could be attributed to the effects of (waiver-based) welfare reforms. Even according to the more conservative calculations of the Council of Economic Advisers (1997), which has been criticized for exaggerating the effects of early reform efforts, 44 percent of the caseload reduction was accounted for by economic growth (cf. Martini and Wiseman, 1997).

While calculations of the relative contributions of "economic" and "policy" effects in welfare-caseload reductions will always be a matter of judgment, most estimates in the United States are assigning between one- and two-thirds of 1990s roll reductions to labor-market conditions (Blank, 2000). And one of the most telling facts is that some of the sharpest caseload reductions actually *preceded* the passage of PRWORA in 1996 (Ellwood, 2000). But the deeper issue that lies behind these debates is that welfare policy itself is at least partly procyclical (see Piven and Cloward, 1971), so posthoc econometric hairsplitting may be missing the point: one reason why this entire sequence of work enforcing/ supporting policies has been pursued—from welfare waivers to tax credits to PRWORA and beyond—is that underlying economic conditions permitted and facilitated their implementation. This does not mean that policies are just reflexively responding to the economic cycle, but it does underline the crucial interdependence between the labor market and welfare/workfare policymaking. After all, essentially similar labor-market conditions have accompanied the British and Canadian reforms too. In Britain, for example, sustained falls in youth unemployment predated the rollout of the New Deal, for which political credit was nevertheless claimed (see Peck, 2000a).

Although it may be unrealistic to expect modesty and circumspection from politicians in such contexts, no amount of triumphalism will disguise the fact that these programs will function differently when (or where) the economic fundamentals change. Talk of some future recession is now often swatted aside as another example of carping from the usual suspects, confounded by too many good-news headlines, but there is more at stake here than this. As Blank (2000: 16) has observed of the United States, "State TANF programs are designed to work in an environment where jobs are readily available." When, or again where, this condition does not hold, some searching questions will be asked of TANF programs. And as Ellwood (2000: 193) has remarked, "[T]he next recession will likely put low-income families at far greater risk than ever before."

It is still too early to calculate the full effects of the 1996 federal reforms in the United States, both due to the recent timing of many state- and local-level policy changes and because unusually strong economic growth has manifestly been such as dominant factor in caseload reductions. Surely, the effects of welfare reform will not really be known until the new regime has been tested at the bottom of the business cycle as well as at the top. However, even at this early stage, some clear trends are beginning to emerge. Welfare reform is having a strong deregistration effect, but in many areas only a minority are entering jobs, while substantially fewer are entering *sustainable* employment, or being lifted out of poverty. Primus et al. (1999) observe that in aggregate terms people are leaving the welfare rolls in larger numbers than they are leaving poverty, highlighting the persistence of working poverty even amid an unprecedented economic boom (see also Loprest, 1999; Acs et al., 2000). These contextual circumstances are leading more cautious policy commentators to call for restraint from those who would proclaim the success of the 1996 reforms. The picture is certainly more complex than the political shorthand of "replacing welfare with work" suggests, as economic growth coupled with the cumulative effects of a series of policy shifts have functioned *together* to drive down the welfare rolls. According to Blank, this outcome

> is the result of a conflux of events that came together at the same time: a strongly expanding economy, substantial revisions in public assistance that emphasized work and reduced benefit eligibility, and major

policy changes that increased the returns to work and the subsidies to support work, particularly among single mothers. . . . In the absence of a robust economy, the legislated changes in 1996 would likely have had much weaker effects. But in the absence of the 1996 reforms, the magnitude of caseload decline and labor force increases is also likely to have been much smaller. (2000: 16, 18)

As Walters (1999) explains in relation to the policy side of this account, it is the combination of strictly enforced sanctions and unyielding work requirements that have been playing the most important role in driving down the welfare rolls. In this context, the actual enforcement of time limits are rarely proving necessary; it is the *message* that they convey that is important. According to welfare policy advocate Toby Herr,

> Time limits take a very complicated message about new programs and new expectations and make it simple for both the client and the caseworker. . . . The clock is ticking, and you have x amount of time until you lose your grant.[3]

Workfarist policies, generically defined, are therefore contributing to a climate in which deterrence and diversion from welfare prevails. In practice, welfare recipients are being forced into the bottom of a crowded job market and left to fend for themselves. Moreover, welfare-to-work outcomes in the United States are proving to be geographically uneven, and again, in ways that often say more about local *economic* conditions than about the effectiveness of local programs.

Brookings Institution studies of welfare caseload trends across twenty-three states are finding that urban areas—which exhibit the highest concentrations of poverty and welfare cases—are already lagging badly in terms of caseload reductions (Katz and Carnevale, 1998; Center on Urban and Metropolitan Policy, 1999). As the national caseload has fallen across the United States, the residual welfare population is becoming increasingly concentrated in the cities, particularly those with weak economies and continuing unemployment problems. Welfare-to-work efforts have been effective in moving the most "job-ready" welfare recipients off the welfare rolls, but a substantial residual group remain, often "trapped" on welfare due to an absence of local job opportunities. Elements of this "trapped" population may be confronting an alarming future without welfare *or* work:

> The most work-ready people are being placed in the available jobs, while the least work-ready remain on the rolls or in workfare jobs with little promise as the welfare clock continues to tick. Unless they improve their skills and overcome their other barriers to work during the

limited time they have on welfare, these individuals will leave welfare
with little chance of self-sufficiency. (Katz and Carnevale, 1998: 14)

Perhaps it is the case that, even in the United States, the workfare strategy is beginning to bump up against some of its structural limits in localities where job markets are comparatively weak. The fact that a similar
story can be told in Canada and in the United Kingdom only serves to
underline the point: employability-based programs will yield only limited effects when operated in slack labor markets (see Lerman et al.,
1999; Vartinian, 1999; Martin et al., 2000; Peck and Theodore, 2000a,
2000b). The case of the cities is an important one because it draws attention to potential flaws in both the economic and the political logics of
workfare. The cities are the places where workfare is meeting its most explicit political resistance; it is here also that implementation problems
tend to be most acute; and urban labor markets often have limited absorptive capacity.

A paradox of employability-based strategies is that they tend to be
most effective for those already nearest the front of the employment
queue, sharpening up the job skills and work attitudes of the most job-
ready, while offering much less to those facing significant barriers to employment (such as discrimination, disability, or lack of childcare). U.S.
programs have made predictably rapid inroads into the job-ready element of the welfare population, but they have been of little assistance to
the hardest-to-employ (from a job-market perspective) or the hardest-to-
serve (from a social-policy perspective). Expressed spatially, this sorting
process is liable to generate a residualized rump of welfare recipients,
stranded in those urban areas where the job market is weakest.

But while the cities may be the sites of some of the more telling contradictions and tensions in the workfare offensive, only in an absolutist
reading of workfare would these be considered terminal problems for the
emergent regime itself. After all, only in the most exaggerated proposals
are residual welfare functions abandoned altogether (see Tanner, 1996).
The practical effect of workfare strategies, more typically, is to minimize
and residualize welfare provision, and to restructure the incentive structure in terms of the principles of employability. Now, cities may be the
most difficult locations in which to advance these principles, but they are
*imposed* on cities nonetheless. This is clearly the case in Ontario, where
each implementation failure or act of political resistance in Toronto
seems only to result in a hardening of resolve on the part of the provincial government. This is a situation that, broadly speaking, also holds for
the New Deal in the United Kingdom, which works actively to take advantage of *existing* job-market opportunities by raising the employability
of participants. If the private economy is weak at the local level, public-

or voluntary-sector placements may be used as substitutes, but practically speaking these are often some distance (in every sense of the word) from "real" job opportunities.

But excavating the underlying logics and tendencies of workfare means getting *behind* the effects of individual programs in particular places to explore threads of continuity and connection. The regulatory project of workfarism is not reducible to the aggregate effects of workfare programs. As it has been described here, the logic of workfarism is a putatively systemic one. It is concerned, inter alia, with shifts in local and extralocal rule systems, in the goals of policy, in the constitution of the policy "problem," in discourses of reform, in models and scales of intervention, in the pattern of incentives, and in normative expectations of work and welfare. Individual workfare programs lie at the emblematic center of this regime, but they represent a part, not the whole. The regime does have concrete expression in policies and programs, but it is also reflected in (changed) attitudes and norms.

Take the case of the deterrent effect of workfare. Experience shows that what Mead (1992b: 172) calls the "workfare funnel" operates in such a way that a certain proportion of potentially eligible participants drop out at each stage in the induction process: when individuals are first informed about program requirements, when they are called in for interview, when they are due to commence a program, at actual placement, and so forth. Others will avoid making welfare claims in the first place in order to evade mandatory work or to "bank" eligibility for a rainier day. So perhaps a little paradoxically, critics' claims that workfare is not working because comparatively small proportions of the client group are actually placed in workfare slots at any one time—recall the criticisms of the small size of the Ontario Works program and of high dropout rates in the New Deal in the United Kingdom—may be missing the (wider) point. Parenthetically, conventional program-evaluation methodologies, which assume that workfare is applied as a quasi-clinical "treatment" to a fixed set of participants, completely fail to capture the wider effects of workfare. So the effects of PRWORA will clearly be radically underestimated—and misrepresented—if assessments focus on those allocated to work programs. The big picture is one of deterrence: "What nobody anticipated," according to Walters (1999: 24), "was the huge number of people who would simply walk away from welfare upon learning about the new quid pro quo of work for benefits."

Workfare is not just about changing the individuals who are on programs, it is concerned to change the rules of the economic and social worlds in which these individuals—and others like them—live. Mickey Kaus expresses this more pithily than most:

> Workfare should not be a short-term program to existing welfare clients, but a long-term program to destroy the culture of poverty. . . . [W]hat's most important is not whether sweeping streets or cleaning buildings helps Betsy Smith, single teenage parent and high school dropout, learn skills that will help her find a private sector job. It is whether the prospect of sweeping streets and cleaning buildings for a welfare grant will deter Betsy Smith from having the illegitimate child that drops out of her school and onto welfare in the first place—or, failing that, whether the *sight* of Betsy Smith sweeping streets after having her illegitimate child will discourage her younger sisters and neighbors from doing as she did. (1986: 27)

The "effects" of workfare programs are not confined to participants, or even to past participants, but extend deep into the "deterred" population (and those, in turn, with whom they live and/or compete in the labor market). Moreover, just as the workhouse cast a long shadow across the working poor in the nineteenth century, the very presence of workfare programs contributes to the climate of strict market discipline in contemporary labor markets. The result is that employers—whether they are hiring current or former workfare workers or not—find that they are able to access a "flexible" pool of employees who have no alternative but to accept what is on offer. Workfare maintains order in the labor market in an analogous fashion to the way in which prisons contribute to the maintenance of social order: as well as disciplining the individuals directly concerned, they symbolize the price that has to be paid for breaking the rules. Prisons can have this effect, even if a (relatively) small proportion of the population is incarcerated. So can workfare systems. Workfarism is a strategy for policing the boundaries of the labor market:

> The main task of social policy is no longer to reform society but to restore the authority of parents and other mentors who shape citizens. Government has no easy way to do that, but the best single thing it can do is to restore order in the inner city. Above all, it can require that poor parents work. . . . The source of bondage for today's seriously poor is no longer social injustice but the disorders of their private lives. For these Americans, the way forward is no longer liberation but obligation. (Mead, 1997a: 15)

> Workfare can be understood as a disciplinary program in the Foucauldian sense. . . . Public assistance in the U.S. is stigmatized and its recipients branded. Dependency discourse constructs a limited field of possibilities for participants, and workfare aims to mold its clients into "docile bodies"—self-disciplining wage workers. (Little, 1999: 164)

Workfare is playing a part in shaping norms of labor-market socialization and participation. Where practicable, welfare is effectively removed from the option set of "employable" individuals, rendering them effectively dependent on (low-) waged employment. At the very least, the experience of welfare claiming is sufficiently destabilized so as to induce persistent insecurity and a generalized liability to deregister. In turn, the very existence of this induced labor supply is likely to further erode pay levels and working conditions at the bottom of the labor market, the mechanism that Mead (1992b: 87) refers to when describing how a pool of "willing but underemployed workers" can in effect "create its own demand." Workfare strategies therefore contribute to the social reproduction, over a relatively short time period, of the kind of contingent labor supply that is ripe for exploitation by bottom-feeding employers. In this respect, workfare may be playing a part—by purposefully generating a persistently contingent labor supply lacking effective recourse to nonwage forms of subsistence—in the proliferation of contingent work.

This could in fact represent a form of *workfarist equilibrium*, with a brutal logic but a logic nonetheless. In contrast to the welfarist dynamic, in which the establishment of a "floor" of welfare standards effectively set (and pushed) the standard at the bottom of the labor market (inter alia, in terms of pay, the ratio of workers to jobs, and determinations of "acceptable" workplace conditions), the workfarist dynamic pulls in the opposite direction, drawing down conditions in the lowest reaches of the labor market, as uncommodified shelters from wage labor are closed off and as former welfare recipients are compelled to accept whatever the market makes available to them locally. The question, then, of what it is that workfare actually *does* must be extended to include these wider labor-regulatory effects.

## FUNCTIONS OF WORKFARE

Writing about the origins of welfare in Massachusetts, when the dominant direction of transatlantic policy transfer was quite different from that of today, Kelso (1922: 1) remarked that conventions of poor relief and governmental action often had origins that were diffuse and oblique:

> Though their emergence be sometimes quick, the abiding tenets by which man governs himself do not spring full-armed from the mind of any one person, king or spiritual leader though he be: they are the sum total of the feelings and desires of generations in the mass. They are custom become law.

Certainly, the task of tracing the origins of governing regimes is usually assisted by historical analysis, which can reveal patterns, trends, and rhythms in the policy process that are difficult to discern for contemporary observers, even for key actors in the process itself. The real-time study of regulatory projects like workfare, however, is inevitably more hazardous: in contemporary analyses of policy regimes "in movement," there is always a danger that a contingent side effect or experimental cul-de-sac will be mistaken for a meaningful structural moment or a transformative episode. There is a basic analytical asymmetry, then, between the retrospective study of welfare-state systems and the necessarily tendentious and exploratory examination of emergent workfare regimes (see Jessop, 1992). As Altvater (1992: 22) tellingly observes, whereas the "process of [institutional] destruction is more or less obvious and identifiable, it is much more difficult to deduce the generation of new social forms of regulation [which] can only emerge as the outcome of conflicting tendencies of progressive acts and regressive setbacks."

The approach adopted here—involving a series of theoretically informed explorations of suggestive empirical trends, nascent institutional forms, shifts in discursive representation, and political–economic developments in a range of settings—may have some utility in highlighting the emergent characteristics of workfarism, but it necessarily remains subject to the analytical constraints highlighted by Altvater. All that can be said is that the analytical risks are known; they cannot be suspended. In this context, perhaps the most hazardous task is to explore, and to speculate about, the embryonic regulatory *functions* of workfarism, and to do so in a way that is not functional*ist*.

It would be to misread the origins of workfarism, in fact, to exaggerate the economic logic of workfare—as a regulatory strategy for managing the contradictions of contingent labor markets—when its associated processes of reform and experimentation, at least in the early years, were so explicitly animated by political and institutional pressures. Workfare, then, should not be seen as a spontaneous response on the part of the state to the social-reproduction needs of a flexibilizing labor market. Nevertheless, flexible labor markets and work-oriented welfare-reform strategies did, historically speaking, evolve together, with each influencing the other in a symbiotic fashion. It was perhaps only in the 1990s that it first became apparent that these might have begun to evolve a shared, conjunctural logic—as developments in one sphere began to rationalize, legitimize, regularize, and naturalize developments in the other. The persistence of, and structural expansion of, contingent labor demand in a sense facilitates and validates workfarist strategies, especially those focused on rapid employment entry for those deemed job-ready. This does not mean that workfare strategies are economically determined or economically driven, but it does mean that they are economically contingent. More than this, in fact, they certainly impact the labor market—by shaping screening, recruitment, and employment systems; influencing job design and workforce-management strategies; normalizing conventions of flexibility and market discipline; and so forth. So, labor-regulatory effects *are* associated with workfarism, even if these effects are often tendentious, sometimes contradictory, and always variable in outcome.

Rather than conduct the discussion here solely in terms of labor-regulatory effects such as deterrence and discipline, which while powerful are also somewhat nebulous from an analytical point of view, the focus will be placed on some of the concrete, program-related impacts of workfare. One way of illustrating these impacts—which it should be reemphasized will always exhibit rather different forms in different places—is to consider the specific job-market consequences of work-first programming. Epitomized by the Riverside GAIN program, this approach represents the leading edge of workfarist regulatory reform, while quite clearly being the ascendant policy of choice at the international level. In terms of the interface between the labor market and workfare programs, work-first approaches self-evidently operate very "close" to the job market. They variously assist, pressurize, and accelerate employment (re)entry, exploiting the short-term turnover of vacancies to bring about exits from welfare. Both philosophically and organizationally, these programs are, as Mead (1997b: 72–73) puts it, "suffused with the work mission." The dominant social relations, allocation systems, and dynamics of work-first programs are therefore closely intertwined with the labor markets in which they operate. This represents a highly dynamic form of "embeddedness," in which programs aspire—quite literally—to read, internalize, and move with the market.

The work-first mechanism is one of the principal means by which localized workfare systems are being trodden down into local labor markets, resulting in a melding of institutional and market dynamics. Through this labor-regulatory process, workfare regimes are beginning to reach deep into contingent job markets, triggering processes of mutual adjustment. So, the screening, selection, allocation, and discrimination systems associated with the lower end of the labor market are reflected in the organization of work-first programs—with their systemic emphasis on "employability," "job-readiness," and anticipating employers' needs— while the operation of the programs themselves subsequently serves to restructure and reinstitutionalize channels into employment. While in some senses it is accepted as a self-evident fact that job-market rules and disciplines should shape workfare programs—after all, this is central to their rationale and philosophy—it has been less clear, until recently, how workfare programs are beginning reciprocally to condition labor markets.

A number of distinct labor-market effects of work-first programs can be identified (see Peck and Theodore, 2000b). First, a defining characteristic of such programs is that they direct participants into low-grade, high-turnover jobs. The methodology of work-first emphasizes the achievement of job-readiness in the context of currently available vacancies. This close tracking of vacancy flows means that these programs interface with the labor market in very particular ways. On the demand side, because contingent job vacancies turn over more frequently than those in the more stable, "primary sector" of the labor market, coupled with the fact that primary-sector jobs tend to be comparatively scarce in areas of concentrated poverty and underemployment, the profile of employment opportunities available to most program participants is heavily skewed toward contingent employment. Given that constant pressure is exerted on participants to enter jobs at the first opportunity, the typical pattern is for most to enter the "secondary" labor market. On the supply side, the prevailing social and labor-market characteristics of the client group tend to reinforce and even rationalize this subordinate mode of labor-market entry: most former welfare recipients have personal attributes that render them "at risk" in the labor market. Many are vulnerable to racial and gender discrimination, or have caring/domestic responsibilities that define them as "marginal" workers in the eyes of employers. Most will have low levels of educational attainment and formally recognized vocational skills. And most will have discontinuous work histories, often including previous periods in low-paid, unstable work (see Burtless, 1994; Eden and Lein, 1997).

Second, work-first methods, and the majority of workfare programs more generally, tend to privilege the *initial* transition into the job market. Overriding priority is placed on securing the first job after welfare, on the presumption that this will provide a "stepping-stone" to better paid, more secure employment. For the most part, the experience of former welfare recipients does not square with this notion of progression (Herr et al., 1996). Most former welfare recipients remain trapped in low-paid secondary employment, while many others return to the welfare rolls following job loss (see Handler, 1995). Yet because work-first defines the initial transition into work as the decisive moment of intervention, these problems tend to lie outside the frames of reference of workfare discourse and evaluation. The vision of policymakers and the practical orientation of programs is instead on the first destination after welfare, the systemic logic of work-first workfare being to *activate* such transitions (rather than necessarily to sustain them).

Third, work-first programs tend to exacerbate, rather than to counteract, "churning" in the lower reaches of the labor market. By inducing a constant, mostly one-way flow from welfare into entry-level jobs, work-first programs intensify competition for work on the supply side of the labor market, while (in the short term at least) the number of job openings is likely to remain largely fixed. This leads to endemic problems of displacement and substitution, where program participants obtain jobs at the expense of other (secondary-sector) workers (Solow, 1998). Employment rates may be increased marginally through this form of intervention, as work-first effectively reduces access to "stable" welfare, while concomitantly increasing the level of dependency on contingent employment. More generally, however, the aggregate effect of work-first may well be to further destabilize contingent employment by increasing the substitutability of labor at the very lowest wage levels. Perversely, then, work-first may achieve its short-term employment goals of raising employment rates for designated groups at the expense of long-run job security, or indeed by detaching other groups of workers from waged employment. It represents an effective subsidy to marginal employers—who are relatively more dependent on "market supplies" of labor and who recruit from the external market more frequently—while also acting as an accelerator of churning.

Fourth, by pressurizing rapid transitions into employment, work-first programs constitute a forced-labor supply for jobs in the lowest reaches of the labor market, which in turn generates a "drag" on pay and conditions. In the medium term, some employers may expand their use of contingent workers in order to take advantage of this new labor supply. Moreover, the limited bargaining power of those currently in contingent jobs stands to be further eroded by the constant flow of former welfare recipients into the labor market, especially as these "new" workers are compelled to accept jobs as rapidly as possible, irrespective of pay and conditions. As the work-first mantra has it, "*any job* is a good job" as far as this client group is concerned. The policy-induced crowding of low-wage labor markets consequently engenders a downward pull on wages and regulatory standards.

Fifth, an important aspect of the "market-following" methodology of work-first is that programs tend to work with the grain of prevailing market criteria concerning the social distribution of work. Eschewing positive actions to tackle inequality and discrimination, these programs accept as given established conventions concerning recruitment and selection, while seeking to accommodate employers' definitions of job-readiness. Typically, this entails a strong emphasis on the correction of "inappropriate" attitudes among program participants. This may be tackled quite aggressively, as in the Riverside GAIN program, for example, or there may be a looser and more passive submission to private-sector recruitment criteria, as is the case with the British New Deal. Employers' definitions of "employability" consequently permeate the internal structures of work-first programs, such that most will tend to reflect and reproduce existing patterns of labor-market inequality.

Sixth, labor-market inequalities are variously anticipated, mirrored, and sometimes amplified by programs' internal streaming and selection procedures. Work-first programs are invariably hierarchicalized in accordance with the degree and forms of intervention deemed to be required by different participants. The programmatic focus is on guiding the most employable down the shortest—and least-cost—route to a job. And although policymakers always resist such characterizations, residual provision is usually made for "sink schemes," the function of which is to absorb those participants who have been unable to access employment (on terms determined largely by employers). While the work-first philosophy tends to equate this fate with individual failure—reflecting deficient attitudes, poor job skills, or inadequate "employability"—the tendency for the aggregate scale of such nonmarket provision to vary quite systematically with local unemployment rates underlines the fact that demand-side factors are also at work here. Where there is a shortage of local jobs, basic education programs and various kinds of "fake-work" schemes perform a "warehousing" function.

Seventh, internal program hierarchies are closely related to different patterns of intervention and service delivery. Work-first systems tailor interventions in accordance with the (often coincident) demands of cost minimization on the one hand and the requirements of contingent labor markets on the other: substantial intervention is dedicated to "resocializing" welfare recipients for work through counseling, job clubs, structured job search, and bureaucratic surveillance; minimal resources are dedicated to human-capital development; and no consideration is given to stimulating labor demand, save the marginal effect of minimizing the time that unfilled vacancies remain on the local job market. In this way, work-first programs acclimatize participants to contingent work, while at the same time systematically removing the means of "sheltering" from the contingent labor market. In this context, the aspirations of participants are reckoned to be "realistic" as long as they are suitably low. If not, they are to be adjusted through judicious combinations of what Mead (1997b) calls "help and hassle."

Eighth, work-first policies are basically concerned with making the most of low-skill, low-wage job markets, not with changing them. Consequently, their deployment actually increases the risk of long-run skills erosion, both for individual welfare recipients and in the labor market overall. In their efforts to achieve immediate labor-force attachment, work-first programs dispense with the goal of appropriate skills matching, as participants are pushed to accept the first job on offer. For the individual, this can lead to disjointed occupational progression; poor returns on education, training, and work experience; and the atrophying of skills sets, thus reducing the likelihood of subsequent job-market progression. As education and training programs are eliminated, or access to them is greatly restricted, there become even fewer avenues for jobseekers to overcome deficiencies in their education, to receive vocational training, or to retrain following job loss. Because the work-first method attends only to current labor-supply concerns in the context of prevailing demand conditions, it is blind to the long-run consequences of this orientation.

And finally, ninth, work-first systems are predicated on specifically *local* labor-market conditions, such that their outcomes are quite different in buoyant as opposed to depressed job markets. Indeed, real questions remain about whether work-first systems, most of which were developed in suburban or exurban locations, will even work in troubled, inner-city labor markets or in economically lagging regions. In some senses, the purchase of the work-first policy package is weakest in precisely those areas where effective welfare-to-work programs are needed most: high-unemployment areas. Definitionally, these are not job-creation programs; they offer only residualized, inferior, and compensatory provision to those that fail the employability test, even though, in high-unemployment areas, demand conditions dictate that the number of such "failures" will inevitably be high.

In summary, the dominant function of work-first workfare is to compel program participants into accepting—and learning to live with—contingent jobs in the context of prevailing conditions in local labor markets. Work-first systems forcibly attach welfare recipients to the lower end of the labor market both by eroding welfare entitlements and by actively managing the transition into an initial job. In contrast to the welfarist logic of providing temporary "shelters" *outside* the labor market for designated social groups, this workfarist logic dictates that targeted social groups are driven *into* the labor market, where they are expected to remain, notwithstanding systemic problems of underemployment, low pay, and exploitative work relations. Work-first programming itself plays a role in naturalizing these conditions.

Work-first workfare makes a virtue of the job market as it finds it, molding potential workers accordingly. Demand-side conditions may remain pretty much as they are. That is, unless there is any truth in the macroeconomic argument for welfare-to-work. U.K. treasury adviser Richard Layard is one of those who advances this case:

> Most opposition to active labour market measures is based on fears of displacement and substitution. In their extreme form these derive

from the "lump-of-labour fallacy": there is only a certain number of jobs so if we enable $X$ to get one of them, some other person goes without work. It is easy to see how the confusion arises. In the most immediate sense the proposition is true. If an employer has a vacancy and, due to a job subsidy, $X$ gets it rather than $Y$, then $Y$ remains temporarily unemployed. But by definition $Y$ is inherently employable. If he [sic] does not get this job, he will offer himself for others. Employers will find there are more employable people in the market and that they can more easily fill their vacancies. This increases downward pressure on wage rises, making possible a higher level of employment at the same level of inflationary pressure. Active labour market policy increases the number of employable workers and thus reduces the unemployment needed to control inflation. (1997: 196–197; see also Layard, 1998; cf. Peck and Theodore, 2000a)

The basic argument here is that downward wage pressure—exerted at the very bottom of the labor market, and at the expense (literally) of the lowest paid—will relieve inflationary tendencies, thereby stimulating employment growth. While wage suppression and work inducement are undeniably features of workfare-style regimes (and in some ways Layard is being quite candid in conceding this), the wider macroeconomic case is more dubious. Indeed, Robert Solow (1998: 32) dismisses it as a "forlorn hope." Realistically, workfare measures do not create employment in the short run. The aggregate number of jobs in the low-wage labor market is fairly static in the short term: the main effect of work-first measures is to intensify competition for *existing* vacancies. This only deepens the problems of underemployment, exacerbating churning effects and further destabilizing existing jobs. The medium- to long-run effects on the contingent job market are—if anything—even more disconcerting. Employers are likely to take advantage of the presence of a forced contingent-labor supply by depressing wages and perhaps, at the margin, creating some additional flexijobs (often at the expense of the erosion of primary-sector employment). Consequently, the principal labor-market impacts of workfare are likely to be felt in terms of the further erosion of pay, working conditions, and job security in the contingent economy. In this sense, both the direct and the indirect costs of workfare are disproportionately shouldered by the working poor, both the "old" working poor of existing contingent workers and the "new" working poor of former welfare recipients.

Work-first workfare is consequently associated with a perverse form of the orthodox adage that supply creates its own demand. Under workfare, an expanded and persistently insecure contingent labor supply, actively driven into employment, serves to undercut existing conditions, while creating a situation favorable to further expansion in the (relative or absolute) size of the contingent sector. If there is "job creation" here, it takes the form of employers adjusting job designs to take advantage of a "new" labor supply. Layard's view that workfare raises the aggregate level of employability, the benefits of which ripple through the labor market in a benign fashion, reveals a failure to grasp both the dynamics of labor-market segmentation and the prosaic realities of labor-market programming. Past experience of programs designed to drive the unemployed into the lowest reaches of the labor market, and then to hold them there, suggests that relatively little is achieved in terms of the alleviation of poverty, skill shortages, or structural unemployment.[4] Rather, the low-wage labor supply is forcibly swelled at the expense of both low-paid workers and (former) welfare recipients. So, workfarist measures do not so much raise the level of employability across the labor market as a whole as increase the rate of exploitation in its lower reaches.

Crucially, even flawed or poorly implemented programs will yield many of these labor-market effects. This is the paradox of programs like Ontario Works, which for all their clumsiness and ineffectiveness *qua programs* nevertheless help to bring about reductions in the welfare rolls by bouncing individuals off the caseload and deterring future claims. Supposedly "effective" programs, like Riverside, may achieve more, of course, albeit in terms of their own (implicit) objectives of enforcing contingent work. But as these programs inspire their imitators, and as new permutations of their work-first approach are developed in different local contexts, so the labor-regulatory effects of workfare are increasingly generalized. In this sense, the workfare offensive remains a highly differentiated one in terms of its institutional form and local effects, but in more generic terms a nascent regulatory logic is nevertheless discernable. It rarely looks nice, but at a basic level there is a sense in which it *works*.

Yet to reiterate, just because workfare strategies may be associated with certain economically functional tendencies, this does not mean the account here is clumsily functionalist. The regulatory project that is workfare was not straightforwardly willed into being through brute political force or automatically secured through economic necessity. Instead, it has emerged through three decades of regulatory struggle and iterative development. To the extent that this regulatory project has begun to gel in a quasi-functional fashion with parallel shifts in the organization of labor markets, this is a post hoc functionality.

## GEOPOLITICS OF WORKFARE

There is in workfare policy an institutional analogue to the phenomenon of churning in the labor market: the more that individual programs founder or underperform, the more aggressive and impatient the reform process tends to become. Workfarism is associated with an institutional dynamic of perpetual reform, revision, and redesign. Geographic differentiation is both a reflection of this situation, and a spur to future restructuring strategies: there is always another "local success story," it seems, just around the corner. Brodkin and Kaufman (1998) persuasively argue that a narrative of success has been woven into a series of politically orchestrated workfare experiments, the actual achievements of which have been almost universally questionable and/or have been predicated on propitious labor-market conditions. In general, U.S. reforms have since the 1980s been running way ahead of the evaluation evidence: in the clamor for "ideas that work," conventional wisdoms have been established prematurely, including in key policy areas such as the supposed superiority of mandatory programs, the aggregate employment and earnings effects of welfare-to-work across local labor markets, impacts on poverty alleviation, and so forth. There are few, if any, definitive answers to these questions. As the United States awaits conclusive signs of the long-run effects of the 1996 reforms, it is sobering to reflect that many of the defining features of the new orthodoxy—such as time limits on benefits, compulsory participation, and work-first programming—remain substantially untested on a generalized scale. In a sense, block-granted welfare in the United States *is* the experiment.

Yet while the policy analysts look on, the "experiment" is having real effects in the here and now. Not only are the lives of millions of past, present, and future recipients being transformed, the workfarist policy message is itself provoking further rounds of reform, both between localities and in the international arena. And here, the United States is again a leader of sorts. Whereas once the defining workfarist principle of mandation set the standard for a certain kind of radical welfare reform, national states that have now passed this point—such as Canada and the United Kingdom—will often be found flirting with the "next stage" of reform: the imposition of time limits. It is a measure both of the continuing differences between the three national regimes examined here and of the compelling power of the Washington consensus that Britain and Canada have yet seriously to address the issue of time limits. The telling point, however, is that in both countries time limits are being discussed, albeit only in those elite circles in which policy wonks ply their trade. The hushed tones that informants use in discussing such radical policy scenarios reflect real—not imagined—political sensitivities in the two countries. And those who would dismiss this simply as empty talk should recall that it was not so long ago—in fact, only in the early to mid-1990s in Britain and Canada—that proposals for widespread mandation were barely even mainstream, and would often be rejected as politically impractical.

The mainstreaming of workfarist discourse and practice, of course, hardly ever occurs by way of quantum shifts in policy. Instead, change is typically more incremental and more complex. The course of workfare politics has run differently in Canada, the United States, and the United Kingdom, as powerful legacies of path-dependency remain alongside revealing convergences in rhetoric and practice. So this is not, nor is it ever likely to be, a story of simple convergence toward a unitary workfarist model, but an uneven process of mutually referential adjustment. In this context, PRWORA retains a talismanic significance, as a truly radical moment of reform. As Rodgers (2000: 5) puts it, "PRWORA completely changes the philosophy of welfare policy." While this may understate some important continuities with past U.S. practice, it quite correctly draws attention to the potentially phase-shifting consequences of work enforcement by way of devolution to the states. The variegated and competitive local reform dynamic that this entails threatens to leave the postwelfare United States in a perpetual state of destabilization and experimentation. This, in turn, facilitates a continuation of the cafeteria-style reform process established under the waiver regime, broadening and deepening the workfarist repertoire and creating the basis for further rounds of fast-policy transfers. Facilitated by an increasingly technocratic and essentialist evaluation literature, plus the earnest endeavors of consultants, this fast-policy regime has taken on an international—and in an important sense interlocal—character (see Jessop and Peck, 2000; Peck and Theodore, 2001).

The defining significance of devolution in the post-PRWORA era underlines the profound sense in which the political economy of workfare is an intrinsically spatialized and scale-sensitive one. It is surely not simply coincidental that workfarist reform efforts are invariably accompanied by, and often indeed are achieved through, some form of decentralization, defederalization, denationalization, or devolution in policy-development and delivery systems. Although this may mean different things and may take different forms in each national context, devolution is invariably present. In many ways, this (re)turn to localized delivery should not be surprising, for the long history of poverty politics reveals that periods of welfare retrenchment and work enforcement typically entail a shift to local administration (Piven and Cloward, 1993). The contested and uneven shift from welfarism to workfarism has been associated with a host of changes in the spatial hierarchy of delivery systems, in patterns of uneven development at the international and subnational scales, and in modes of regulating the poor at the local level. In a rather stylized way, it is possible to visualize the welfare/workfare transition in terms of, on the one hand, the critique, rollback, and deconstruction of *national welfarism* (both as a system of institutions and entitlements, and as an ideology) and, on the other hand, its tendential re-/displacement by a highly differentiated regime of *local workfarism* (again, as a system of institutions and entitlements, and as an ideology). Workfarism as a regulatory strategy is both predicated upon, and achieved through, the localization/uneven development of labor-market and social-policy governance structures. Hence this book's insistent focus on spatial constitution of the welfare-reform process and the emerging geographies of workfarist politics. Local idiosyncrasy and geographic inequality are not simply exceptions to the general rule; under workfare, they *are* the rules.

Among the wide range of such spatial and scalar transformations the following seven developments are perhaps most significant. First, the workfare offensive—as an ideological movement and as a regime of concrete reform measures, policy generics, and restructuring strategies—is increasingly assuming the character of a transnational regulatory project, particularly among neoliberal countries, where not only conservatives but most labor and social-democratic parties now embrace workfarism in some form or another. Workfare has become a cornerstone of the neoliberal regulatory "fix" advocated in international forums, such as G7 and the World Bank, where the United States is also—not entirely coincidentally—a dominating presence. Understandably, these are usually "diluted" representations of workfare, reflecting their negotiated nature. A feature of workfarism is that its *local* manifestations are usually more punitive and hard-edged; this is the scale at which workfare "works" as an operational program. Regulatory frameworks and conventions at the national and international levels act to set the tone and establish the broad tendencies within workfarism, but they are at least one step removed from the local scale at which workfare is delivered, and where it yields its effects. Hence the increased importance of cross-locality policy transfers, many of which today are also international.

Second, "fast-policy" transfers of high-impact local workfare experiments in places like Wisconsin are assuming increased significance at both national and international scales. Disembedded readings of these "local success stories" are being taken up in a transformative fashion into workfare discourse. The comparative evaluation of different local "models," program methodologies, and delivery strategies is itself playing an important role in widening the workfarist reform repertoires available to national and local policymakers, strengthening their capacity to lever (local and extralocal) institutional change. A distinctive feature of the policy-development regime under workfare is that while program delivery is increasingly decentralized to the local level, this occurs in the context of a self-consciously *comparative* approach vis-à-vis other local experiments. In this sense, the process of policy development is neither "top-down" nor "bottom-up" in the conventional sense, but is being structured around *interlocal* policy transfers, variously orchestrated by, and articulated through, the nation-state, international agencies, and (public and private) policy-advocacy organizations. The process is also "fast" in the sense that normal policy formation–evaluation–reform cycles are shortened, as the long grind of policy development is progressively displaced by a new preoccupation with imported, off-the-peg strategies, accelerated learning, and rapid delivery.

Third, there has been a marked decentralization of delivery systems and an associated reorganization of federal and national regulatory frameworks. This phenomena is sometimes referred to provocatively, but perhaps a little misleadingly in this case, as "hollowing out." It is rather misleading because national states retain key functions as regulators and rule setters in workfare regimes, even if program delivery, aspects of policy development, and many of the political struggles around the new system have been aggressively downloaded to the local level. In fact, workfarist politics are a prime example of the discursive "self-abasement" of the national state (see Denis, 1995), in which extranational market forces are portrayed as inexorable, while decentralization strategies are used to open up the space for (often weak and defensive) local responses based on marketization, liberalization, and regulatory undercutting.

Fourth, the methodology of workfare—based as it is on increased levels of "discretion" for local administrators and the "intensive case management" of clients—typically entails the localized microregulation of the job-search, family, and even procreative behavior of welfare recipients. As the Riverside philosophy demonstrates so forcefully, workfare strategies imply the replacement of arm's-length modes of regulating the poor via bureaucratic means with a more aggressive form of hands-on, "paternalist" micromanagement. As Mead (1997b: 63) blithely explains of such methods, "[C]ase management is rule enforcement. Staff members do have to relate to their clients as individuals, not as numbers, but mainly to check up on them. Just doing this appears to be strongly motivating." Workfare systems achieve their results as much by getting on the backs of their "clients" as through the provision of services or programs. They are concerned, in this sense, with the micromanagement of expectations.

Fifth, spatial unevenness and local distinctiveness in welfare/workfare systems, service delivery, and entitlements are increasing. Indeed, notions such as national eligibilities and rights, national need and service standards, and national poverty lines are fast becoming anachronistic, as rights and responsibilities are increasingly being determined (or manipulated) at the local level. While spatial unevenness in servicing and outcomes was for the most part an unintended, residual, and/or unwanted feature of welfare systems, workfare regimes make it a goal and a virtue.

But, under workfare, the benign language of "local needs" and "flexible delivery" often clouds the geographic inequities that are entailed. Access to programs and services, the quality of provision and support arrangements, residual entitlements, and even eligibility itself increasingly vary from place to place.

Sixth, this growing unevenness and localization has implications for the form, scale, and content of oppositional politics. Because programs and systems vary from place to place, so often do the political and policy issues with which they are associated. There is a certain logic to responding to workfare at the local scale—the scale privileged in the workfare policy process—but this can also undermine the potential foundations of cross-locality, generalized opposition to workfare. Established oppositional and defensive forces, developed during the welfare era, tend to be anchored at the national or federal level. These are usually by-passed by localizing workfare regimes, often intentionally. The emergence of particularistic, local struggles against workfare (in its specific local forms) may be creating new opportunities for political mobilization at the local scale (e.g., alliances of labor unions and grassroots community groups), but alone they are unlikely to shift the course of workfarism as a "multiscalar" strategy. There may be some "local victories," where oppositional resources and networks are strong, but for these to really count ways have to be found to "scale them up." Like the forces they confront, oppositional politics will need to become multiscalar and multilayered.

And finally, seventh, local workfare regimes render residual welfare entitlements more directly contingent on local job availability (in that if there *are* jobs available to individuals, welfare will not be), coupled with prescribed forms of job-search behavior. Local workfare systems are being forcefully embedded into local labor markets, with the result that distinctly economic dynamics and impulses now play a more explicit role in determining eligibility (e.g., through the enforcement of "employability" criteria) and programming (e.g., through the deployment of work-first methods). This tendential "marketization" of welfare represents an important development. Economic and social policy became increasingly separated during the Keynesian–welfarist era, resulting in "the relative decoupling of welfare policies from the circuit of capital" (Jessop, 1994: 256). Indeed, as Tony Blair has observed, "By the 1970s, economic policy and social policy were becoming divorced. Welfare policy— redistribution, social security—were seen almost as antithetical to sound economic policy."[5] Under workfarism, economic and social policy are being recoupled, particularly *at the local scale*. The strategies, institutions, and goals of these two, once-distinct, policy fields are being melded in local workfare regimes. As well as rendering welfare eligibility and service mixes increasingly contingent on local economic conditions, this is also contributing to growing spatial unevenness in modes of local labor-market governance (see Peck, 1996; Martin, 2000).

These developments underline the character of workfare as a complex, multilateral, uneven, and multiscalar regulatory project (Jessop and Peck, 2000). The prevailing dynamics here are for the *downscaling* of regulatory functions, institutions, administrative procedures, and programming, though national states retain important roles in steering and orchestrating policy development, and in the "metagovernance" of local workfare regimes. This is the case even in the United States, where the federal government's role has not been removed but remade: PRWORA replaces the welfarist *"floor"* of needs-based entitlement with a workfare-style *"ceiling"* of spending caps, regulatory maxima, and work-participation requirements. So, national states remain key actors in the reform process, though increasingly their role takes the form of orchestrator or animateur of a tendentially decentralizing system, in contrast to the more directive and bureaucratic approach typical of welfare regimes. National states are in many ways the principal authors of the workfare script, although this tends—quite intentionally, in fact—to be read in different ways in different places. They have led the (auto)critique of welfarism and have deliberately opened up the space for local experimentation with workfare programs. In the process, national states have become agents in their own "hollowing out."

The political implications of this are nontrivial. While the politics of workfare advocacy have assumed an increasingly aggressive, generic, and transnational form, for the most part anti-workfare politics remain defensive, particularized, and localized. Indeed, explicit objectives around the weakening, division, and localization of sources of political opposition are often reflected in welfare-restructuring strategies. It seems that once the national defenses of welfarism have been breached, the path is opened decisively to downscale residual welfare and emergent workfare functions. This involves reregulation not only at the state and local scales but also at that of the individual *bodies* of welfare recipients—given the preoccupation in U.S. reforms, for example, with regulating the reproductive as well as the productive lives of welfare recipients, through such measures as the denial of aid to teen parents, "man in the house" rules, learnfare, family caps, and so forth. This downloading of risks and regulatory responsibilities to the level of the individual is also evident in workfare's labor-regulatory functions, because as the epitome of supply-side policymaking it seeks to make a virtue of individualized, "flexible" labor relations. The ideology that frames these programs, indeed, is rooted in the notion of *independence* through wage labor.

Yet because workfare is prosecuted as a variegated strategy, the downscaling process is heterogeneous in form and uneven in effects.

Crucially, this tends to render anti-workfare politics contingent on preexisting and locally variable capacities for resistance, primarily at the urban scale. Here, resistance typically comes through some form of coalition between labor unions, anti-poverty campaigners, social-service advocates, and community organizations, which tend to operate in different combinations—and in pursuit of different strategic lines—in different places. For example, in New York City, where workfare is delivered through public-sector placements, resistance has emerged in the form of unionization of workfare workers, drawing on the joint organizational capacities of public-sector unions and community groups, and political mobilization has also occurred through the associated Workfairness campaign. Meanwhile, in Toronto, where workfare was introduced in the form of placements in the nonprofit sector, a network of social-advocacy and welfare-rights groups, with the support of some of Ontario's industrial unions, have established Workfare Watch, a lobbying and campaigning initiative, while taking steps to prevent community agencies from participating in the program.

There is an important sense, then, in which local political struggles usually reflect—though are not *determined by*—the local form of workfare strategies. Where workfare slots are located in the public sector, the strategy is exposed to the threat of unionization; where workfare relies on nonprofit-sector placements, then the obvious line of resistance is to choke off the supply of places through social-sector campaigning and lobbying; where workfare is oriented to wage employment in the external labor market—in many ways its tendential form—resistance is rendered difficult due to the diffuse and individualized nature of this strategy, but may take the form of boycotts, unionization drives, or research-based campaigns. At the very least, different workfare strategies call for different forms of local political response; they are also differentially vulnerable to disruption, reform, and implementation failure at the local level, depending on their (inherently unpredictable) interactions with local political, economic, and institutional structures. And, of course, the geography of oppositional politics also reflects the uneven terrain of *preexising* political forces and resources at the local level. In Baltimore, for example, responses to workfare have been shaped by previous patterns of activism around the city's "Living Wage" campaign.

So, the urban politics of workfare tend to be just as variegated as workfare strategies themselves. Downloading welfare/workfare functions often seems to mean downloading oppositional politics as well. Constructing effective opposition to workfare out of a series of particularized local struggles has proved predictably difficult, though there are some early signs of cross-locality networking and some attempts to develop cross-scalar campaigns, linking local to wider struggles. While at the present time resistance to workfare tends to be somewhat sporadic and localized, it is possible that recent developments in places like New York City and Toronto will prefigure more generalized oppositional movements. After all, for all its political support and institutional weight as an ascendant regulatory project, workfare remains contradictory, unstable, and in some senses vulnerable: to adverse economic conditions, to implementation failures, and to political resistance.

While it is critically important, in this context, to appreciate the scale and scope of the workfare offensive, this should not be allowed to breed political fatalism. Local resistance is important symbolically and materially, but pressure also has to be brought to bear on the extralocal rule systems that sustain workfarism. Certainly, simply to wait for the workfare regime to collapse under the weight of its own contradictions would be as politically complacent as it is intellectually arrogant. There has to be *engagement* with the politics and policies of workfare, both at the level of the minutiae of individual, local reform programs and at the level of ideological principle. In many ways one of the most pressing challenges facing opponents of workfare lies in the (re)connection of these levels: how to defend welfare rights without looking like apologists for a flawed status quo; how to engage in the process of policy formation without being dragged into some quasi-workfarist compromise; how to build bridges between local oppositional movements and to "jump scale" to the national and international arenas in which workfare policy conventions are being made; how to take on transcendent neoliberal rule systems as well as concrete programs; how to turn strategies of defense and resistance into progressive and purposeful alternatives.

In offering a sustained critique of workfare as an emergent regulatory project, this book has gone some of the way to exposing the metalogics of workfarism, while documenting a few of its chameleon-like local manifestations. It has not been explicitly concerned with developing alternatives to workfarism, but in mapping some of the leading edges of regulatory change it represents a modest contribution to this wider project. In this era of slippage and compromise, there is a pressing need to defend the principles of equity, sustainability, and social justice, to stand the ground in the face of manifest regression. This does not mean opposing reform for its own sake, but it does mean retaining a clear oppositional stance against work compulsion and the enforcement of working poverty. Welfare systems do need to be reformed, but not in ways that simply bend to the imperatives of flexible labor markets; they should instead play an active role in reforming and remaking these labor markets, underpinning decent wages, a fair distribution of work, and employment security. It is time to reform work as well as welfare. It is time that the old principles of less eligibility were replaced by a new emphasis on more equity.

Writing more than a decade ago, during an earlier phase of intense social-policy regression, Block et al. (1987a: xiv) observed how many liberals had failed to mount a "strong and principled defense of the welfare state," having apparently "fallen into theoretical and moral disarray." In the ensuing years, the confidence and determination of pro-workfare "reformers" has only hardened, while opposition has continued to fracture and in some instances capitulate. In the process, the workfare offensive has been gathering pace just as it has gathered converts. The fast-policy regime of workfarism has taken on the form of a formidable regulatory project. Responding to this means coming to terms with the strength, scale, and multifaceted nature of the workfare offensive, as well as searching for the weak spots and progressive openings. This has been the goal of *Workfare States*, but in many ways it is a task that is only just beginning. The process of regulatory struggle remains just that: a struggle. And there may yet be surprises in store for the architects of workfare. True, the policies are fast, but so are the politics.

## Notes

1. On different aspects of the influence of workfare and active employability measures in international policy discourse, see Besley and Kanbur (1993), Deacon (1998, 2000), Ravallion (1998), Walker (1998), EC (1999a, 1999b), ILO (1999), and Haveman and Wolfe (2000).

2. Speech to the Labour Party conference, September 27, 1999.

3. Quoted in Walters (1999: 21–22).

4. See Finn (1987), Handler (1995), Tilly (1996), and Blank (1997).

5. Beveridge Lecture, Toynbee Hall, London, March 18, 1999.

# References

6, P. 1997. *Escaping Poverty: From Safety Nets to Networks of Opportunity*. London: Demos.

Aaron, H. J. 1973. *Why Is Welfare So Hard to Reform?* Washington, DC: Brookings Institution Press.

Abbott, E. 1937. *Some American Pioneers in Social Welfare*. Chicago: University of Chicago Press.

Acs, G., Phillips, K. R., and McKenzie, D. 2000. *Playing by the Rules But Losing the Game: America's Working Poor*. Washington, DC: Urban Institute.

Agnos, A. 1995. A welfare model for all of the U.S. *San Francisco Chronicle* April 20: A25.

Ainley, P., and Corney, M. 1990. *Training for the Future: The Rise and Fall of the Manpower Services Commission*. London: Cassell.

Albert, M. 1993. *Capitalism vs. Capitalism*. New York: Four Walls Eight Windows.

Albo, G. 1994. "Competitive austerity" and the impasse of capitalist employment policy. In *Socialist Register 1994: Between Globalism and Nationalism*, eds. R. Miliband and L. Panitch, pp. 144–170. London: Merlin Press.

Alcock, P. 1997. Making welfare work—Frank Field and New Labour's social policy agenda. *Benefits* 20: 34–38.

Altvater, E. 1992. Fordist and post-Fordist international division of labor and monetary regimes. In *Pathways to Industrialization and Regional Development*, eds. M. Storper and A. J. Scott, pp. 21–45. London: Routledge.

Amdur, R. S. 2000. Why the workfare program is failing. *Ottawa Citizen* January 6: D4.

Amin, A., Cameron, A., and Hudson, R. 1999. Welfare as work? The potential of the UK social economy. *Environment and Planning A* 31: 2033–2051.

Ammott, T. 1986. *ET: A Model for the Nation? An Evaluation of the Massachusetts Employment and Training Choices Program*. Cambridge, MA: New England Regional Office, American Friends' Service Committee.

369

AOHC [Association of Ontario Health Centres]. 1995. *Workfare in Context*. Etobicoke, Ontario: AOHC.

Asling, J. 1997. *United Church Takes Stand against Workfare*. Camrose, Alberta: United Church of Canada.

Bagguley, P. 1994. Prisoners of the Beveridge dream? The political mobilisation of the poor against contemporary welfare regimes. In *Towards a Post-Fordist Welfare State?*, eds. R. Burrows and B. Loader, pp. 74–94. London: Routledge.

Bakker, I. 1991 Canada's social wage in an open economy, 1970–1983. In *The New Era of Global Competition: State Policy and Market Power*, eds. D. Drache and M. S. Gertler, pp. 270–287. Kingston and Montreal: McGill-Queen's University Press.

Baily, M. N., Burtless, G., and Litan, R. E. 1993. *Growth with Equity: Economic Policymaking for the Next Century*. Washington, DC: Brookings Institution Press.

Balls, E., and Gregg, P. 1993. *Work and Welfare: Tackling the Jobs Deficit*. Commission on Social Justice Discussion Paper 3. London: Institute for Public Policy Research.

Bane, M. J. 1995. Reviewing the waiver review process. *Public Welfare* 53: 7–9.

Banting, K. G. 1987. *The Welfare State and Canadian Federalism*. Second edition. Kingston and Montreal: McGill-Queen's University Press.

Bardach, E. 1993. *Improving the Productivity of JOBS Programs*. New York: Manpower Demonstration Research Corporation.

———. 1997. Implementing a paternalist welfare-to-work program. In *The New Paternalism*, ed. L. M. Mead, pp. 248–278. Washington, DC: Brookings Institution Press.

Barnekov, T., Boyle, R., and Rich, D. 1989. *Privatism and Urban Policy in Britain and the United States*. Oxford, UK: Oxford University Press.

Barnett, A., and Wintour, P. 1998. Blair's big gamble. *Observer* January 4: 17.

Baum, E. 1991. When the witch doctors agree: The Family Support Act and social research. *Journal of Policy Analysis and Management* 10: 603–615.

Benn, C., and Fairley, J. (Eds.). 1986. *Challenging the MSC*. London: Pluto Press.

Berkowitz, E., and McQuaid, K. 1988. *Creating the Welfare State: The Political Economy of Twentieth-Century Reform*. Second edition. New York: Praeger.

Berlin, G. 1997. MDRC welfare evaluation project focuses on cities. *Poverty Research News* 1(3): 9–10.

Bernstein A. D., and Bernstein, P. W. (Eds.). 1995. *Quotations from Speaker Newt: The Little Red, White and Blue Book of the Republican Revolution*. New York: Workman.

Bernstein, J. 1997. *The Challenge of Moving from Welfare to Work*. EPI Issue Brief #116. Washington, DC: Economic Policy Institute.

Berry, R., Kitson, M., and Michie, J. 1995. *Towards Full Employment: The First Million Jobs*. London: Full Employment Forum.

Besley, T., and Coate, R. 1992. Workfare vs. welfare: Incentive arguments for work requirements in poverty alleviation programs. *American Economic Review* 82: 249–261.

Betcherman, G. 1996. Globalization, labour markets and public policy. In *States against Markets: The Limits of Globalization*, eds. R. Boyer and D. Drache, pp. 250–269. London: Routledge.

Beveridge, W. 1942. *Social Insurance and Allied Services*. command 6404. London: HMSO.

Blair, T. 1997. It's our duty to reform Britain's welfare state. . . . Nothing's going to stop me. *Sun* December 23: 8.

Blank, R. M. 1994a. The employment strategy: Public policies to increase work and earnings. In *Confronting Poverty: Prescriptions for Change*, eds. S. H. Danziger, G. D. Sandefur, and D. H. Weinberg, pp. 168–204. Cambridge, MA, and New York: Harvard University Press and Russell Sage Foundation.

———. 1994b. Outlook for the U.S. labor market and prospects for low-wage entry jobs. In *The Work Alternative: Welfare Reform and the Realities of the Labor Market*, eds. D. S. Nightingale and R. H. Haveman, pp. 33–69. Washington, DC: Urban Institute Press.

———. 1997. *It Takes a Nation: A New Agenda for Fighting Poverty*. New York and Princeton, NJ: Russell Sage Foundation and Princeton University Press.

———. 2000. Fighting poverty: Lessons from recent U.S. history. *Journal of Economic Perspectives* 14: 3–19.

Block, F. 1994. The roles of the state in the economy. In *The Handbook of Economic Sociology*, eds. N. J. Smelser and R. Swedberg, pp. 691–710. Princeton, NJ: Princeton University Press.

Block, F., Cloward, R. A., Ehrenreich, B., and Piven, F. F. 1987a. Introduction. In *The Mean Season: The Attack on the Welfare State*, F. Block, R. A. Cloward, B. Ehrenreich, and F. F. Piven, pp. ix–xvi. New York: Random House.

———. 1987b. *The Mean Season: The Attack on the Welfare State*. New York: Random House.

Block, F., and Noakes, J. 1988. The politics of new-style workfare. *Socialist Review* 88(3): 31–58.

Bluestone, B., and Harrison, B. 1982. *The Deindustrialization of America: Plant Closings, Community Abandonment and the Dismantling of Basic Industry*. New York: Basic Books.

Borland, J. 1998. *Welfare Reform in California*. Sacramento: State Net.

Bourdieu, P. 1998. *Acts of Resistance: Against the New Myths of Our Time*. Cambridge, UK: Polity Press.

Boyer, R. (Ed.). 1988. *The Search for Labour Market Flexibility: The European Economies in Transition*. Oxford, UK: Clarendon Press.

———. 1992. *Labour Institutions and Economic Growth: A Survey and a "Regulationist" Approach*. No. 9218. Paris: CEPREMAP.

———. 2000. The diversity and future of capitalisms: A "Régulationist" analysis. In *Capitalism in Evolution*, eds. G. Hodgson and N. Yokokawa, London: Elgar.

Brandes, S. D. 1976. *American Welfare Capitalism, 1880–1940*. Chicago: University of Chicago Press.

Braverman, H. 1974. *Labor and Monopoly Capital: The Degradation of Work in the Twentieth Century*. London: Monthly Review Press.

Bremer, W. 1975. Along the "American Way": The New Deal's work relief programs for the unemployed. *Journal of American History* 62: 636–652.

Brindle, D. 1996. The end of the welfare state. *Guardian* May 8: 1, 4.

Brodkin, E. Z. 1995. The war against welfare. *Dissent* Spring: 211–220.

Brodkin, E. Z., and Kaufman, A. 1998. *Experimenting with Welfare Reform: The Political Boundaries of Policy Analysis.* JCPR Working Paper #1. Chicago: Joint Center for Poverty Research, University of Chicago.

Brown, A. 1997. *Work First: How to Implement an Employment-Focused Approach to Welfare Reform.* New York: Manpower Demonstration Research Corporation.

Brown, D. M. 1995. Welfare caseload trends in Canada. In *Helping the Poor: A Qualified Case for "Workfare,"* J. Richards, A. Vining, D. M. Brown, M. Krashinsky, W. J. Milne, E. S. Lightman, and S. Hoy, pp. 37–90. Toronto: C. D. Howe Institute.

Brown, M. K. 1999. *Race, Money, and the American Welfare State.* Ithaca, NY: Cornell University Press.

Burawoy, M. 1985. *The Politics of Production: Factory Regimes under Capitalism and Socialism.* London: Verso.

Burghes, L. 1987. *Made in the USA: A Review of Workfare: The Compulsory Work-for-Benefits Regime.* London: Unemployment Unit.

Burton, J. 1987. *Would Workfare Work?* Employment Research Centre Occasional Papers in Employment Studies 9. Buckingham, UK: University of Buckingham.

———. 1988. Workfare: Ethics and Efficiency. *Economic Affairs* April–May: 17–21.

Burtless, G. 1995. Employment prospects of welfare recipients. In *The Work Alternative: Welfare Reform and the Realities of the Labor Market,* eds. D. S. Nightingale and R. H. Haveman, pp. 71–106. Washington, DC: Urban Institute Press.

Bush, A. 1996. Replacing welfare in Wisconsin. *Public Welfare* 54: 16–23.

Butler, S. M., and Kondratas, A. 1987. *Out of the Poverty Trap: A Conservative Strategy for Welfare Reform.* New York: Free Press.

Cameron, D. R. 1986. The growth of government spending: The Canadian experience in comparative perspective. In *State and Society: Canada in Comparative Perspective,* ed. K. Banting, pp. 21–51. Toronto: University of Toronto Press.

Carleson, R. B., and Hopkins, K. R. 1981. Whose responsibility is social responsibility? The Reagan rationale. *Public Welfare* 39: 8–17.

Carlson, V. L., and Theodore, N. C. 1995. *Are There Enough Jobs? Welfare Reform and Labor Market Reality.* Chicago: Center for Urban Economic Development, University of Illinois at Chicago; Chicago Urban League; Office for Social Policy Research, Northern Illinois University.

Carter, J., and Rayner, M. 1996. The curious case of post-Fordism and welfare. *Journal of Social Policy* 25: 347–367.

Casey, B. 1986. Back to the Poor Law? The emergence of "workfare" in Britain, Germany and the USA. *Policy Studies* 7: 52–64.

CATO Institute. 1995. *The CATO Handbook for Congress: 104th Congress.* Washington, DC: CATO Institute.

CAW [Canadian Auto Workers]. 1994. *Submission to the Standing Committee on Human Resources Development.* North York, Ontario: CAW.

CBPP [Center on Budget and Policy Priorities]. 1996. *The Governors' Welfare Proposal*. Washington, DC: Center on Budget and Policy Priorities.

Center on Urban and Metropolitan Policy. 1999. *The State of Welfare Caseloads in America's Cities: 1999*. Washington, DC: Brookings Institution Press.

Charter Against Workfare. 1987. *Charter Against Workfare: A Statement of Principles*. Manchester, UK: Manchester City Council: Unemployment Unit, Centre for Local Economic Strategies; Transport & General Workers Union.

Chaze, W. L. 1981. From state officials, few cheers for "workfare." *U.S. News & World Report* September 7: 63.

Children's Defense Fund. 1996. *Selected Features of State Welfare Plans*. CDF Legislative Update, November 19. Washington, DC: Children's Defense Fund.

Clarke, J. 1997. Fighting to win. In *Open for Business, Closed to People: Mike Harris's Ontario*, eds. D. Ralph, A. Régimbald, and N. St-Amand, pp. 157–164. Halifax, Nova Scotia: Fernwood.

Clarke, T. 1997. The transnational corporate agenda behind the Harris regime. In *Open for Business, Closed to People: Mike Harris's Ontario*, eds. D. Ralph, A. Régimbald, and N. St-Amand, pp. 28–36. Halifax, Nova Scotia: Fernwood.

Clement, P. F. 1985. *Welfare and the Poor in the Nineteenth-Century City: Philadelphia, 1800–1854*. Rutherford, NJ: Associated University Presses.

CLFDB [Canadian Labour Force Development Board]. 1993. *Report of the Canadian Labour Force Development Board on the Unemployment Insurance (UI) Developmental Uses Plan for 1994*. Ottawa: CLFDB.

CLMPC [Canadian Labour Market and Productivity Centre]. 1994a. *Joint Statement on Unemployment Insurance Issues*. Ottawa: CLMPC.

———. 1994b. *The Roles of Government: Supporting Business–Labour Approaches to Economic Restructuring*. Ottawa: CLMPC.

Cloward, R. A., and Piven, F. F. 1993. Punishing the poor, again: The fraud of workfare. *Nation* May 24: 693–696.

Cochrane, A., and Clarke, J. (Eds.). 1993. *Comparing Welfare States: Britain in International Context*. London: Sage.

Cohen, L. 1990. *Making a New Deal: Industrial Workers in Chicago, 1919–1939*. Cambridge, UK: Cambridge University Press.

Cohen, M. 1991. Exports, unemployment, and regional inequality: Economic policy and trade theory. In *The New Era of Global Competition: State Policy and Market Power*, eds. D. Drache and M. S. Gertler, pp. 83–102. Kingston and Montreal: McGill-Queen's University Press.

Collier, K. 1997. *After the Welfare State*. Vancouver: New Star Books.

Commission on Social Justice. 1994. *Social Justice: Strategies for National Renewal*. London: Vintage.

Commonwealth of Massachusetts. 1986. *The Massachusetts Employment and Training Choices Program: Program Plan and Budget Request, Fiscal Year 1987*. Boston: Executive Office of Human Services, Department of Public Welfare.

———. 1995. *Welfare Reform '95*. Boston: Executive Office of Health and Human Services, Department of Transitional Assistance.

Conservative Party. 1997. *You Can Only Be Sure with the Conservatives: The Conservative Manifesto 1997*. London: Conservative Central Office.

———. 1999. *The Common Sense Revolution*. London: Conservative Central Office.

Convery, P. 1997. Election debate: The parties' policies in focus. *Working Brief* April: 6–8.

Cook, P. 1995. Spend UI savings anywhere but Ottawa. *Globe and Mail* August 18: B2.

Cope, M. 1997. Responsibility, regulation, and retrenchment: The end of welfare?. In *Changing American Governance*, eds. L. Staeheli, J. E. Kodras, and C. Flint, pp. 181–205. Thousand Oaks, CA: Sage/Urban Affairs Annual Review.

Corbett, T. J. 1995 Welfare reform in Wisconsin: The rhetoric and the reality. In *The Politics of Welfare Reform*, eds. D. F. Norris and L. Thompson, pp. 19–54. Thousand Oaks, CA: Sage.

Corcoran, T. 1995. Why workfare won't work. *Globe and Mail* June 7: B2.

Council of Economic Advisers. 1997. *Explaining the Decline in Welfare Receipt, 1993–1996*. Washington, DC: Council of Economic Advisers.

Courchene, T. J. 1987. *Social Policy in the 1990s: Agenda for Reform*. Toronto: C. D. Howe Institute.

Cowherd, R. G. 1977. *Political Economists and the English Poor Laws: A Historical Study of the Influence of Classical Economics on the Foundations of Social Welfare Policy*. Athens: Ohio University Press.

Cray, R. E., Jr. 1988. *Paupers and Poor Relief in New York City and Its Rural Environs, 1700–1830*. Philadelphia: Temple University Press.

Crouch, C., Finegold, D., and Sako, M. 1999. *Are Skills the Answer?* Oxford, UK: Oxford University Press.

Daniel, C. 1997. May the taskforce be with you. *New Statesman* August 1: 27–31.

Daniel, W. W. 1981. *The Unemployed Flow*. London: Policy Studies Institute.

Danziger, S. H., and Weinberg, D. H. 1994. The historical record: Trends in family income, inequality, and poverty. In *Confronting Poverty: Prescriptions for Change*, eds. S. H. Danziger, G. D. Sandefur, and D. H. Weinberg, pp. 18–50. Cambridge, MA, and New York: Harvard University Press and Russell Sage Foundation.

Davis, G. 1996. *From Opportunity to Entitlement: The Transformation and Decline of Great Society Liberalism*. Lawrence: University Press of Kansas.

Davis, M. 1993. Who killed LA? A political autopsy. *New Left Review* 197: 3–28.

Deacon, A. 1994. Justifying "workfare": The historical context of the debate. In *Unemployment and Public Policy in a Changing Labour Market*, ed. M. White, pp. 53–63. London: Policy Studies Institute.

———. 1996. Editorial introduction. In *Stakeholder Welfare*, IEA Health and Welfare Unit, pp. 1–5. London: Institute of Economic Affairs.

———. (Ed.). 1997. *From Welfare to Work: Lessons from America*, Choice in Welfare #39. London: Institute of Economic Affairs.

———. 1998. *Welfare reform in the 51st state? The influence of US thinking and experience upon the welfare debate in Britain*. Paper presented to the annual conference of the Association for Public Policy Analysis and Management, New York, October 29–31.

———. 2000. Learning from the US? The influence of American ideas upon "New Labour" thinking on welfare reform. *Policy and Politics* 28: 5–18.

Deacon, B. 1998. *Global Social Policy*. London: Sage.

Dean, H., and Taylor-Gooby, P. 1992. *Dependency Culture: The Explosion of a Myth*. Hemel Hempstead, UK: Harvester Wheatsheaf.

Dean, M. 1995. Governing the unemployed self in an active society. *Economy and Society* 24: 559–583.

Dehli, K. 1993. Subject to the new global economy: Power and positioning in Ontario labour market policy formation. *Studies in Political Economy* 41: 83–110.

Demos. 1996. The return of the local. *Demos Quarterly* 9. London: Demos.

Denis, C. 1995. "Government can do whatever it wants": Moral regulation in Ralph Klein's Alberta. *Canadian Review of Sociology and Anthropology* 32: 363–383.

Department of Labor. 1995. *What's Working (and What's Not): A Summary of Research on the Economic Impacts of Employment and Training Programs*. Washington, DC: U.S. Department of Labor.

Derber, C. 1996. *The Wilding of America*. New York: St. Martin's Press.

Deukmejian, G. 1990. Clear away obstacles to workfare. *Los Angeles Times* July 27: B7.

Dicken, P., Peck, J., and Tickell, A. 1997. Unpacking the global. In *Geographies of Economies*, eds. R. Lee and J. Wills, pp. 158–166. London: Arnold.

Dickson, N. 1997. Welfare to where? *New Statesman* August 1: 18–20.

Digby, A. 1989. *British Welfare Policy: Workhouse to Workfare*. London: Faber & Faber.

Dionne, E. J. Jr. 1996. *They Only Look Dead: Why Progressives Will Dominate the Next Political Era*. New York: Simon & Schuster.

Dolowitz, D. P. 1997. British employment policy in the 1980s: Learning from the American experience. *Governance* 10: 23–42.

———. 1998. *Learning from America: Policy Transfer and the Development of the British Workfare State*. Brighton, UK: Sussex Academic Press.

Drache, D. 1991. The systematic search for flexibility: National competitiveness and new work relations. In *The New Era of Global Competition: State Policy and Market Power*, eds. D. Drache and M. S. Gertler, pp. 249–269. Kingston and Montreal: McGill-Queen's University Press.

———. 1996. From Keynes to K-Mart: Competitiveness in a corporate age. In *States against Markets: The Limits of Globalization*, eds. R. Boyer and D. Drache, pp. 31–61. London: Routledge.

Drew, E. 1996. *Showdown: The Struggle between the Gingrich Congress and the Clinton White House*. New York: Simon & Schuster.

Driver, S., and Martell, L. 1997. New Labour's communitarianisms. *Critical Social Policy* 52: 27–46.

DSS [Department of Social Security]. 1998. *New Ambitions for Our Country: A New Contract for Welfare*. Command 3805. London: HMSO.

Eberts, R. W. 1995. *Welfare to Work: Local Observations on a National Issue*. W. E. Upjohn Institute Employment Research #2. Kalamazoo, MI: W. E. Upjohn Institute.

EC [European Commission]. 1994. *European Social Policy: A Way Forward for the Union*. Luxembourg: Office for Official Publications of the European Communities.

————. 1996. *Employment in Europe 1996*. Luxembourg: Office for Official Publications of the European Communities.

————. 1999a. *Employment in Europe 1998*. Luxembourg: Office for Official Publications of the European Communities.

————. 1999b. *Five Years of Social Policy*. Luxembourg: Office for Official Publications of the European Communities.

Economic Strategies Group. 1995. *Riverside County: Economic Development Strategy, Phase I Report*. Riverside, CA: Riverside County Economic Development Agency.

*Economist*. 1978. Massachusetts: The streetcar conservative. *Economist* January 7: 32.

————. 1985. The workhouse makes a comeback. *Economist* May 11: 35–38.

————. 1995. Unimpressed in the Canadian west. *Economist* December 23: 49.

Edelman, P. 1997. The worst thing Bill Clinton has done. *Atlantic Monthly* March: 43–58.

Edin, K., and Lein, L. 1997. *Making Ends Meet: How Single Mothers Survive Welfare and Low-Wage Work*. New York: Russell Sage Foundation.

Edsall, T. B. with Edsall, M. D. 1991. *Chain Reaction: The Impact of Race, Rights, and Taxes on American Politics*. New York: Norton.

Education and Employment Committee [House of Commons]. 1996. *Government Response to the Second Report from the Employment Committee Session 1995–96: The Right to Work/Workfare*. Second Special Report. London: HMSO.

Eling, S., and Hewitt, T. 1997. Local authorities join forces against Project Work. *Working Brief* June: 7.

Ellwood, D. T. 1988. *Poor Support: Poverty in the American Family*. New York: Basic Books.

————. 2000. Anti-poverty policy for families in the next century: From welfare to work—and worries. *Journal of Economic Perspectives* 14: 187–198.

Employment Committee [House of Commons]. 1996. *The Right to Work/Workfare*. Second Report, HC 82. London: HMSO.

Employment Department Group/Department of Social Security. 1994. *Jobseeker's Allowance*. Command 2687. London: HMSO.

Employment Policy Institute. 1996. *Employment Audit* 1. London: Employment Policy Institute.

Epstein, W. M. 1997. *Welfare in America: How Social Science Fails the Poor*. Madison: University of Wisconsin Press.

ERGO. 1992. *Phase One Final Report*. Brussels: Directorate General for Employment, Industrial Relations and Social Affairs of the Commission of the European Communities.

ES/DfEE [Employment Service/Department for Education and Employment]. 1997. *New Deal: Delivery through Partnerships*. London: ES/DfEE.

Esping-Andersen, G. 1990. *The Three Worlds of Welfare Capitalism*. Cambridge, UK: Polity Press.

————. (Ed.). 1996. *Welfare States in Transition: National Adaptations in Global Economies*. London: Sage.

Evans, P. M. 1995. Linking welfare to jobs: Workfare, Canadian style. In *Work-

*fare: Does It Work? Is It Fair?*, ed. A. Sayeed, pp. 75–104. Montreal: Institute for Research on Public Policy.

Field, F. 1990. Britain's underclass: Countering the growth. In *The Emerging British Underclass*, IEA Health and Welfare Unit, pp. 37–41. London: Institute of Economic Affairs.

———. 1995. *Making Welfare Work: Reconstructing Welfare for the Millennium.* London: Institute of Community Studies.

———. 1996. Making welfare work: The underlying principles. In *Stakeholder Welfare*, IEA Health and Welfare Unit, pp. 7–44. London: Institute of Economic Affairs.

———. 1997. Give them the tools. *Guardian* August 12: 13.

Finn, D. 1987. *Training without Jobs: New Deals and Broken Promises.* Basingstoke, UK: Macmillan.

———. 1995a. The Job Seekers' Allowance—Workfare and the stricter benefit regime. *Capital and Class*: 57: 7–11.

———. 1995b. Uncompelling evidence: The Job Seeker's Allowance won't help the unemployed. *New Economy*: 3: 60–65.

———. 1996. *Making Benefits Work: Employment Programmes and Job Creation Measures.* Manchester, UK: Centre for Local Economic Strategies.

———. 1997. *Working Nation: Welfare Reform and the Australian Job Compact for the Long-Term Unemployed.* London: Unemployment Unit.

Fleming, S. 1997. Welfare to where? *New Statesman* August 1: 18–19.

Fletcher, D. R. 1997. Evaluating special measures for the unemployed: Some reflections on recent UK experience. *Policy and Politics* 25: 173–184.

Fox, L. 1996. A conversation with Maryland's Lynda Fox. *Public Welfare* 54: 24–30.

Fraser, D. 1976. Introduction. In *The New Poor Law in the Nineteenth Century*, ed. D. Fraser, pp. 1–24. London: Macmillan.

———. 1984. *The Evolution of the British Welfare State.* Second edition. London: Macmillan.

Fraser, N. 1993. Clintonism, welfare, and the antisocial wage: The emergence of a neoliberal political imaginary. *Rethinking Marxism* 6: 9–23.

Fraser, N., and Gordon, L. 1994. A genealogy of *dependency*: Tracing a keyword of the U.S. welfare state. *Signs* 19: 309–336.

Freedman, S., and Friedlander, D. 1995. *The JOBS Evaluation: Early Findings on Program Impacts in Three Sites.* Washington, DC: Office of the Assistant Secretary for Planning and Evaluation, U.S. Department of Health and Human Services.

Friedlander, D., Hoetz, G., Quint, J., and Riccio, J. 1985. *Arkansas: Final Report on the WORK Program.* New York: Manpower Demonstration Research Corporation.

Fund, J. H. 1995. Learning from Canada's Reagan. *Wall Street Journal* February 23: A14.

Funiciello, T. 1993. *Tyranny of Kindness: Dismantling the Welfare System to End Poverty in America.* New York: Atlantic Monthly Press.

GAIN Advisory Council. 1994. *Recommended Strategies for Improving the GAIN Program.* Sacramento: California Department of Social Services.

GAO [General Accounting Office]. 1987. *Work and Welfare*. Washington, DC: U.S. Government Printing Office.

Gardiner, K. 1997. *Bridges from Benefit to Work: A Review*. York, UK: York Publishing Services.

Geddes, J 1995. Defining liberalism for the next century. *Financial Post* July 8: 19.

Giddens, A. 1981. *The Class Structure of the Advanced Societies*. Second edition. London: Hutchinson.

———. 1998. *The Third Way: The Renewal of Social Democracy*. Cambridge, UK: Polity Press.

Gilder, G. 1981. *Wealth and Poverty*. New York: Basic Books.

———. 1987. Welfare's "new consensus": The collapse of the American family. *Public Interest* 89: 20–25.

———. 1993. *Wealth and Poverty*. Second edition. San Francisco: ICS Press.

———. 1995. End welfare reform as we know it. *American Spectator* June: 24–27.

Gilens, M. 1996. "Race coding" and white opposition to welfare. *American Political Science Review* 90: 593–604.

Gillespie, E., and Schellhas, B. (Eds.). 1994. *Contract with America: The Bold Plan by Rep. Newt Gingrich, Rep. Dick Armey, and the House Republicans to Change the Nation*. New York: Random House.

Gingrich, N. 1984. *Window of Opportunity: A Blueprint for the Future*. New York: Tom Doherty.

———. 1994. Washington Research Group Symposium, November 11, 1994. In *Contract with America: The Bold Plan by Rep. Newt Gingrich, Rep. Dick Armey, and the House Republicans to Change the Nation*, eds. E. Gillespie and B. Schellhas, pp. 181–196. New York: Random House.

———. 1995. *To Renew America*. New York: HarperCollins.

Glynn, S. 1994. Welfare, work and politics. In *Social Policy towards 2000: Squaring the Welfare Circle*, eds. V. George and S. Miller, pp. 64–88. London: Routledge.

Goldstein, L. 1999. Workfare still works for Harris. *Ottawa Sun* September 7: 15.

Goodwin, L. 1983. *Causes and Cures of Welfare: New Evidence on the Social Psychology of the Poor*. Lexington, MA: D. C. Heath.

Gordon, D. M. 1977. Class struggle and the stages of urban development. In *The Rise of the Sunbelt Cities*, eds. D. Perry and A. Watkins, pp. 55–82. Beverley Hills, CA: Sage.

———. 1996. *Fat and Mean*. New York: Free Press.

Gordon, D. M., Edwards, R. C., and Reich, M. 1982. *Segmented Work, Divided Workers: The Historical Transformation of Labor in the US*. Cambridge, UK: Cambridge University Press.

Gordon, L. 1988. What does welfare regulate? *Social Research* 55: 609–630.

Gough, I. 1979. *The Political Economy of the Welfare State*. London: Macmillan.

Government of Quebec. 1996. *Income Security Reform: The Road to Labour Market Entry, Training and Employment*. Quebec: Ministère de la sécurité du revenu.

Gray, J. 1998. A strained rebirth of liberal Britain. *New Statesman* August 21: 28–29.

Greenberg, D., and Wiseman, M. 1992. What did the OBRA demonstrations do? In *Evaluating Welfare and Training Programs*, eds. C. F. Manski and I. Garfinkel, pp. 25–75. Cambridge, MA: Harvard University Press.

Greenberg, M. 1993. *The Devil Is in the Details: Key Questions in the Effort to "End Welfare as We Know It."* Washington, DC: Center for Law and Social Policy.

———. 1994. *Understanding the Clinton Welfare Bill: Two Years and Work.* Washington, DC: Center for Law and Social Policy.

———. 1995. Fixing welfare waiver policy. *Public Welfare* 53: 10–17.

———. 1996. *Limits on Limits: State and Federal Policies on Welfare Time Limits.* Washington, DC: Center for Law and Social Policy.

Gregg, P. 1997. *Jobs, Wages and Poverty: Patterns of Persistence and Mobility in the New Flexible Labour Market.* London: Centre for Economic Performance, London School of Economics.

Grieve Smith, J. 1997. *Full Employment: A Pledge Betrayed.* Basingstoke, UK: Macmillan.

Grimes, A. 1996. *Unemployment: A Modest Proposal.* Economic Report #10(6). London: Employment Policy Institute.

Grove, M. 1995. *Michael Portillo: The Future of the Right.* London: Fourth Estate.

Grubb, W. N., Badway, N., Bell, D., Chi, B., King, C., Herr, J., Prince, H., Kazis, R., Hicks, L., and Taylor, J. C. 1999. *Toward Order from Chaos: State Efforts to Reform Workforce Development Systems.* MDS-1249. Berkeley: National Center for Research in Vocational Education, University of California.

Gueron, J. M. 1987. *Reforming Welfare with Work.* New York: Ford Foundation.

———. 1996. A research context for welfare reform. *Journal of Policy Analysis and Management* 15: 547–561.

Gueron, J. M., and Pauly, E. 1991. *From Welfare to Work.* New York: Russell Sage Foundation.

Hamilton, G., Brock, T., and Farkas, J. 1994. *The JOBS Evaluation: Early Lessons from Seven Sites.* Washington, DC: U.S. Department of Health and Human Services and U.S. Department of Education.

Hamnett, C. 1996. Social polarisation, economic restructuring and welfare state regimes. *Urban Studies* 33: 1407–1430.

Handler, J. F. 1995. *The Poverty of Welfare Reform.* New Haven, CT: Yale University Press.

Handler, J. F., and Hasenfeld, Y. 1991. *The Moral Construction of Poverty: Welfare Reform in America.* Newbury Park, CA: Sage.

———. 1997. *We the Poor People: Work, Poverty, and Welfare.* New Haven, CT: Yale University Press.

Harrington, M. 1984. *The New American Poverty.* New York: Holt, Rinehart, and Winston.

Harrison, B. 1972. *Education, Training, and the Urban Ghetto.* Baltimore: Johns Hopkins University Press.

Harrison, B., and Bluestone, B. 1988. *The Great U-Turn: Corporate Restructuring and the Polarizing of America.* New York: Basic Books.

Harvey, D. 1989. *The Condition of Post-modernity: An Enquiry into the Origins of Cultural Change.* Oxford, UK: Blackwell.

Haskins, R. 1991. Congress writes a law: Research and welfare reform. *Journal of Policy Analysis and Management* 10: 616–632.

Haughton, G., Peck, J., Jones, M., Tickell, A., and While, A. 2000. Labour market policy as flexible welfare: Prototype employment zones and the new workfarism. *Regional Studies* 34: 669–680.

Haveman, R., and Wolfe, B. 2000. Welfare to work in the US: A model for other developed nations? *International Tax and Public Finance* 7: 95–114.

Havemann, J., and Vobejda, B. 1997. After getting responsibility for welfare, states may pass it down. *Washington Post* January 28: A1.

Hayes, C. E. 1984. *Welfare to Wages? Women in the WIN Program.* Washington, DC: Wider Opportunities for Women.

Heclo, H. 1994. Poverty politics. In *Confronting Poverty: Prescriptions for Change*, eds. S. H. Danziger, G. D. Sandefur, and D. H. Weinberg, pp. 396–437. Cambridge, MA, and New York: Harvard University Press and Russell Sage Foundation.

Herod, A. (Ed.). 1998. *Organizing the Landscape: Geographical Perspectives on Labor Unionism.* Minneapolis: University of Minnesota Press.

Herr, T., Wagner, S., and Halpern, R. 1996. *Making the Shoe Fit: Creating a Work-Prep System for a Large and Diverse Welfare Population.* Chicago: Erikson Institute.

Heseltine, M. 1990. *Where There's a Will.* London: Arrow Books.

Hirsch, D. 1998. *A Note on US Welfare to Work Policy: The Current State of Play and Issues Raised for the UK.* York, UK: Joseph Rowntree Foundation.

HM Treasury. 2000. *Budget: March 2000.* HC 346. London: HMSO.

Hogan, L. A. 1996. *Work First: A Progressive Strategy to Replace Welfare with a Competitive Employment System.* Washington, DC: Democratic Leadership Council.

Holcomb, P. A., Pavetti, L., Ratcliffe, C., and Riedinger, S. 1998. *Building an Employment Focused Welfare System: Work First and Other Work-Oriented Strategies in Five States.* Washington, DC: Urban Institute Press.

Holmes, J., and Rusonik, A. 1991. The break-up of an international labour union: Uneven development in the North American auto industry and the schism in the UAW. *Environment and Planning A* 23: 9–36.

Holtham, G., Ingram, P., and Mayhew, K. 1998. The long term unemployed: What more can be done? In *Welfare in Working Order*, eds. J. McCormick and C. Oppenheim, pp. 123–137. London: Institute for Public Policy Research.

House of Commons. 1995. *Right to Work.* Bill 158. London: HMSO.

House of Commons, Social Security Committee. (1998). *Social Security Reforms: Lessons from the United States of America.* HC 552. London: HMSO.

HRD Canada [Human Resources Development Canada]. 1994a. *Improving Social Security in Canada: A Discussion Paper.* Hull, Quebec: HRD Canada.

———. 1994b. *Unemployment Insurance Developmental Use Programs.* Hull, Quebec: HRD Canada.

Hum, D. 1983. *Federalism and the Poor: A Review of the Canada Assistance Plan.* Toronto: Ontario Economic Council.

Hutton, W. 1995. *The State We're In.* London: Jonathan Cape.

———. 1996. Churning in and out of poverty in Tory Britain. *Observer* October 20: 24.

ILO [International Labour Office]. 1999. *World Employment Report 1998–99: Employability in the Global Economy*. Geneva: ILO.

Isaac, L., and Kelly, W. R. 1981. Racial insurgency, the state and welfare expansion: Local and national level evidence from the postwar United States. *American Journal of Sociology* 86: 1348–1386.

Izumi, L. 1992. Doleful stories: What's behind the welfare boom? *National Review* September 14: NWR1.

Jacobs, L. A. 1995. What are the normative foundations of workfare? In *Workfare: Does It Work? Is It Fair?*, ed. A. Sayeed, pp. 13–38. Montreal: Institute for Research on Public Policy.

Jacoby, S. 1997. *Modern Manors: Welfare Capitalism since the New Deal*. Princeton, NJ: Princeton University Press.

Jenson, J. 1989. "Different" but not "exceptional": Canada's permeable Fordism. *Canadian Review of Sociology and Anthropology* 26: 69–94.

———. 1990. Representations in crisis: The roots of Canada's permeable Fordism. *Canadian Journal of Political Science* 23: 653–683.

Jenson, J., and Mahon, R. 1993. Legacies for Canadian labour of two decades of crisis. In *The Challenge of Restructuring: North American Labor Movements Respond*, eds. J. Jenson and R. Mahon, pp. 72–92. Philadelphia: Temple University Press.

Jérôme-Forget, M. 1995. Foreword. In *Workfare: Does It Work? Is It Fair?*, ed. A. Sayeed, pp. 3–4. Montreal: Institute for Research on Public Policy.

Jessop, B. 1990. *State Theory: Putting Capitalist States in Their Place*. Cambridge, UK: Polity Press.

———. 1992. Fordism and post-Fordism: A critical reformulation. In *Pathways to Industrialization and Regional Development*, eds. M. Storper and A. J. Scott, pp. 46–69. London: Routledge.

———. 1993. Towards a Schumpeterian workfare state? Preliminary remarks on post-Fordist political economy. *Studies in Political Economy* 40: 7–39.

———. 1994. Post-Fordism and the state. In *Post-Fordism: A Reader*, ed. A. Amin, pp. 251–279. Oxford, UK: Blackwell.

———. 1995a. *The Future of the National State in Europe: Erosion or Reorganization?* Lancaster Regionalism Group Working Paper #51. Lancaster, UK: Department of Sociology, University of Lancaster.

———. 1995b. Towards a Schumpeterian workfare regime in Britain? Reflections on regulation, governance and the welfare state. *Environment and Planning A* 27: 1613–1626.

———. 1999. The changing governance of welfare: Recent trends in its primary functions, scale, and modes of coordination. *Social Policy and Administration* 33: 348–359.

Jessop, B., and Peck, J. 2000. *Fast policy/local discipline: The politics of scale and the neoliberal workfare offensive*. Mimeo. Lancaster, UK: Department of Sociology, University of Lancaster.

Johnson, A. F., McBride, S., and Smith, P. J. 1994. Introduction. In *Continuities and Discontinuities: The Political Economy of Social Welfare and Labour Market Policy in Canada*, eds. A. F. Johnson, S. McBride, and P. J. Smith, pp. 3–21. Toronto: University of Toronto Press.

Johnson, A. S. 1995. States aren't waiting for federal welfare reform. *Public Welfare* 53: 18–20.

Jonas, A. E. G. 1996. Local labour control regimes: Uneven development and the social regulation of production. *Regional Studies* 30: 323–338.

———. 1997. Reregulating suburban politics: Institutional capacities and territorial reorganization in Southern California. In *Reconstructing Urban Regime Theory: Regulating Urban Politics in a Global Economy*, ed. M. Lauria, pp. 206–229. London: Sage.

Jonas, A. E. G., and Wilson, D. (Eds.). 1999. *The Urban Growth Machine: Critical Perspectives Two Decades Later.* Albany: State University of New York Press.

Jones, J. P., and Kodras, J. E. 1990. The state, social policy, and geography. In *Geographic Dimensions of United States Social Policy*, eds. J. E. Kodras and J. P. Jones, pp. 17–36. London: Edward Arnold.

Jones, M. 1996. Full steam ahead to a workfare state? Analysing the UK Employment Department's abolition. *Policy and Politics* 24: 137–157.

———. 1997. The degradation of labour market programmes. *Critical Social Policy* 52: 91–104.

———. 1999. *New Institutional Spaces: Training and Enterprise Councils and the Remaking of Economic Governance*. London: Jessica Kingsley and Regional Studies Association.

Katz, B., and Carnevale, K. 1998. *The State of Welfare Caseloads in America's Cities*. Washington, DC: Center on Urban and Metropolitan Policy, Brookings Institution.

Katz, J. 1996a. GOP prepares to act on governors' plan. *Congressional Quarterly Weekly Report* February 17: 394–395.

———. 1996b. Shalala: Governors' proposals give states too much power. *Congressional Quarterly Weekly Report* March 2: 558–560.

Katz, M. B. 1986. *In the Shadow of the Poorhouse: A Social History of Welfare in America*. New York: Basic Books.

———. 1989. *The Undeserving Poor: From the War on Poverty to the War on Welfare*. New York: Pantheon Books.

Kaus, M. 1986. The work ethic state. *New Republic* July 7: 22–33.

———. 1992. *The End of Equality*. New York: Basic Books.

———. 1996. Workfare wimp-out. In *The New Republic Guide to the Issues: The '96 campaign*, New Republic, pp. 245–247. New York: Basic Books.

Kay, J. 1998. Evolutionary politics. *Prospect* July: 31–35.

Kelso, R. W. 1922. *The History of Public Poor Relief in Massachusetts, 1620–1920*. Montclair, NJ: Patterson Smith.

Kerans, P. 1990. Government inquiries and the issue of unemployment: The struggle for people's imagination. In *Unemployment and Welfare: Social Policy and the Work of Social Work*, eds. D. Riches and G. Ternowetsky, pp. 47–64. Toronto: Garamond Press.

Kilborn, P. T. 1996. With welfare overhaul now law, states grapple with the consequences. *New York Times* August 23: A10.

King, D. S. 1993. The Conservatives and training policy, 1979–1992: From a tripartite to a neoliberal regime. *Political Studies* 41: 214–235.

———. 1995. *Actively Seeking Work? The Politics of Unemployment and Welfare*

*Policy in the United States and Great Britain.* Chicago: University of Chicago Press.

King, D. S., and Wickham-Jones, M. 1999. From Clinton to Blair: The Democratic (Party) origins of welfare to work. *Political Quarterly* 70: 62–74.

Kirkbride, J. 1995. Compulsory work plan for dole blackspots. *Daily Telegraph* April 3: 1.

Kleppner, P., and Theodore, N. 1997. *Work after Welfare: Is the Midwest's Booming Economy Creating Enough Jobs?* DeKalb, IL: Office for Social Policy Research.

Kodras, J. E. 1997. The changing map of American poverty in an era of economic restructuring and political realignment. *Economic Geography* 73:67–93.

Kotz, D. M., McDonough, T., and Reich, M. (Eds.). 1994. *Social Structures of Accumulation: The Political Economy of Growth and Crisis.* Cambridge, UK: Cambridge University Press.

Kreckel, R. 1980. Unequal opportunity structure and labour market segmentation. *Sociology* 14: 525–549.

Kreklewich, R. 1993. North American integration and industrial relations: Neoconservatism and neo-Fordism? In *The Political Economy of North American Free Trade*, eds. R. Grinspun and M. A. Cameron, pp. 261–270. New York: St. Martin's Press.

Labour Party. 1996a. *Getting Welfare to Work: A New Vision for Social Security.* London: Labour Party.

———. 1996b. *New Labour, New Life for Britain.* London: Labour Party.

———. 1997. *New Labour: Because Britain Deserves Better.* London: Labour Party.

Labour Studies Group. 1985. Economic, social and political factors in the operation of the labour market. In *New Approaches to Economic Life: Restructuring, Unemployment and the Social Division of Labour*, eds. B. Roberts, R. Finnegan, and D. Gallie, pp. 105–123. Manchester, UK: Manchester University Press.

Laslett, P. 1971. *The World We Have Lost: England before the Industrial Age.* New York: Scribner.

Layard, R. 1997. Preventing long-term unemployment. In *Working for Full Employment*, ed. J. Philpott, pp. 190–203. London: Routledge.

———. 1998. Getting people back to work. *CentrePiece* Autumn: 24–27.

Leborgne, D., and Lipietz, A. 1992. Conceptual fallacies and open questions on post-Fordism. In *Pathways to Industrialization and Regional Development*, eds. M. Storper and A. J. Scott, pp. 332–348. London: Routledge.

Legislative Assembly of Ontario. 1998. *Bill 22: An Act to Prevent Unionization with Respect to Community Participation under the Ontario Works Act, 1997.* Toronto: Legislative Assembly of Ontario.

Lerman, R. I., Loprest, P., and Ratcliffe, C. 1999. *How Well Can Urban Labor Markets Absorb Welfare Recipients?* Washington, DC: Urban Institute Press.

Liberal Democratic Party. 1997. *Make the Difference.* London: Liberal Democratic Party.

Lieberman, R. C. 1998. *Shifting the Color Line: Race and the American Welfare State.* Cambridge, MA: Harvard University Press.

Lightman, E. S. 1991. Work incentives across Canada. *Journal of Canadian Studies* 26: 120–137.

———. 1995. You can lead a horse to water, but . . . : The case against workfare in Canada. In *Helping the Poor: A Qualified Case for "Workfare,"* J. Richards, A. Vining, D. M. Brown, M. Krashinsky, W. J. Milne, E. S. Lightman, and S. Hoy, pp. 151–183. Toronto: C. D. Howe Institute.

Lilley, P. 1995. *Winning the Welfare Debate.* London: Social Market Foundation.

Lilley, P., and Portillo, M. 1994. Foreword. In *Jobseeker's Allowance,* Command 2687, Employment Department Group/Department of Social Security, p. 2. London: HMSO.

Lipietz, A. 1987. *Mirages and Miracles: The Crises of Global Fordism.* London: New Left Books.

———. 1992. *Towards a New Economic Order: Postfordism, Ecology and Democracy.* Cambridge, UK: Polity Press.

Lister, R. 1997. From fractured Britain to one nation? The policy options for welfare reform. *Renewal* 5: 11–23.

Little, D. L. 1999. Independent workers, dependable mothers: Discourse, resistance, and AFDC workfare programs. *Social Politics* 6: 161–202.

Lloyd, J. 1997. A plan to abolish the underclass. *New Statesman* August 29: 14–16.

Loprest, P. 1999. *Families Who Left Welfare: Who Are They and How Are They Doing?* Washington, DC: Urban Institute Press.

Mahon, R. 1991. Post-Fordism: Some issues for labour. In *The New Era of Global Competition: State Policy and Market Power,* eds. D. Drache and M. S. Gertler, pp. 316–334. Kingston and Montreal: McGill-Queen's University Press.

Mandell, B. R., and Withorn, A. 1993. Keep on keeping on: Organizing for welfare rights in Massachusetts. In *Mobilizing the Community: Local Politics in the Era of the Global City,* eds. R. Fisher and J. Kling, pp. 128–148. Newbury Park, CA: Sage.

Mandelson, P. 1997. A lifeline for youth. *Guardian* August 15: 17.

Mandelson, P., and Liddle, R. 1996. *The Blair Revolution: Can New Labour Deliver?* London: Faber & Faber.

Marquand, D. 1998. The Blair paradox. *Prospect* May: 19–24.

Maraniss, D., and Weisskopf, M. 1996. *Tell Newt to Shut Up.* New York: Touchstone.

Marshall, J. 1996. Little room for welfare variances. *San Francisco Chronicle* August 5: B1–B3.

Martin, R. 1994. Economic theory and human geography. In *Human Geography: Society, Space and Social Science,* eds. D. Gregory, R. Martin, and G. Smith, pp. 21–53. London: Macmillan.

———. 2000. Local labour markets: Their nature, performance and regulation. In *A Handbook of Economic Geography,* eds. G. Clark, M. Gertler, and M. Feldman, pp. 455–476. Oxford, UK: Oxford University Press.

Martin, R., Nativel, C., and Sunley, P. 2000. *The local impact of the New Deal: Does geography make a difference?* Paper presented at the Royal Geographical Society/Institute of British Geographers annual conference, University of Sussex, Brighton, January 4–7.

Martini, A., and Wiseman, M. 1997. *Explaining the Recent Decline in Welfare Caseloads: Is the Council of Economic Advisers Right?* Washington, DC: Urban Institute Press.

Massey, D. 1995. *Spatial Divisions of Labour: Social Structures and the Geography of Production.* Second edition. Basingstoke, UK: Macmillan.

Mather, G. 1993. The way of the workfarer. *Guardian* February 5: 21.

Matthews, M., and Becker, K. A. 1998. *Making Welfare Work: Lessons from America.* London: Adam Smith Institute.

McBride, S. 1992. *Not Working: State, Unemployment and Neo-conservatism in Canada.* Toronto: University of Toronto Press.

———. 1994. The political economy of Ontario's labour market policy. In *Continuities and Discontinuities: The Political Economy of Social Welfare and Labour Market Policy in Canada*, eds. A. F. Johnson, S. McBride, and P. J. Smith, pp. 268–290. Toronto: University of Toronto Press.

———. 1996. The continuing crisis of social democracy: Ontario's social contract in perspective. *Studies in Political Economy* 50: 65–93.

McSmith, A. 1997. *Faces of Labour.* London: Verso.

McWilliams, D. 1999. US economy is close to a miracle. *Observer* August 29: B7.

MDRC [Manpower Demonstration Research Corporation]. 1999. *Big Cities and Welfare Reform: Early Implementation and Ethnographic Findings from the Project on Devolution and Urban Change.* New York: MDRC.

Mead, L. 1986. *Beyond Entitlement: The Social Obligations of Citizenship.* New York: Free Press.

———. 1989. The logic of workfare: The underclass and work policy. *Annals of the American Academy of Political and Social Science* 501: 156–169.

———. 1992a. The new paternalism: How should Congress respond? *Public Welfare* 50: 14–17.

———. 1992b. *The New Politics of Poverty: The Nonworking Poor in America.* New York: Basic Books.

———. 1996a. Memorandum submitted by Lawrence Mead. In *The Right to Work/Workfare*, Employment Committee [House of Commons], pp. 29–30. Second Report, HC 82. London: HMSO.

———. 1996b. Welfare policy: The administrative frontier. *Journal of Policy Analysis and Management* 15: 587–600.

———. 1997a. From welfare to work: Lessons from America. In *From Welfare to Work: Lessons from America*, Choice in Welfare #39, ed. A. Deacon, pp. 1–55. London: Institute of Economic Affairs.

———. 1997b. Welfare employment. In *The New Paternalism*, ed. L. M. Mead, pp. 39–88. Washington, DC: Brookings Institution Press.

Meager, N. 1997. Active and passive labour market policies in the United Kingdom. *Employment Observatory Trends* 28: 69–75.

Merrett, C. D. 1996. *Free Trade: Neither Free nor About Trade.* Montreal: Black Rose Books.

Milne, S. 1996. Benefits cut-off will squeeze Middle England. *Guardian* January 17: 17.

Ministry of Community and Social Services, Ontario. 1998. 1998–1999 Business Plan. In *Ontario Government Business Plans 1998–1999*, Ontario Government, pp. 1–20. Toronto: Queen's Printer for Ontario.

————. 1999. *Steady job growth in Ontario as welfare caseloads decline*. News release, September 10. Toronto: Government of Ontario.

————. 2000. *Making Welfare Work: Report to Taxpayers on Welfare Reform*. Toronto: Government of Ontario.

————. Nd. *Welfare Reform: Making Welfare Work*. Toronto: Ministry of Community and Social Services.

Mink, G. 1998. *Welfare's End*. Ithaca, NY: Cornell University Press.

————. 1999a. Aren't poor single mothers women? Feminists, welfare reform, and welfare justice. In *Whose Welfare?*, ed. G. Mink, pp. 171–188. Ithaca, NY: Cornell University Press.

————. (Ed.). 1999b. *Whose Welfare?* Ithaca, NY: Cornell University Press.

Mishel, L., and Schmitt, J. 1995. *Cutting Wages by Cutting Welfare: The Impact of Reform on the Low-Wage Labor Market*. Briefing Paper #58. Washington, DC: Economic Policy Institute.

Mishra, R. 1990. *The Welfare State in Capitalist Society: Policies of Retrenchment and Maintenance in Europe, North America and Australia*. New York: Harvester Wheatsheaf.

————. 1996. The welfare of nations. In *States against Markets: The Limits of Globalization*, eds. R. Boyer and D. Drache, pp. 316–333. London: Routledge.

Mitchell, A. 1996. Lone parents need jobs, not training. [London] *Times* June 22: 18.

Mitchell, M. 1990. *Evidence of the Emerging Consensus in Labour Market Policy Reports*. Victoria: British Columbia Task Force on Education and Training.

Mizen, P. 1995. *The State, Young People and Youth Training: In and against the Training State*. London: Mansell.

Moffitt, R. 1992. Incentive effects of the U.S. welfare system: A review. *Journal of Economic Literature* 30: 1–61.

Moore, S. 1995. *Restoring the Dream: A Bold New Plan by House Republicans*. New York: Random House.

Morrison, I. 1997. Rights and the right: Ending social citizenship in Tory Ontario. In *Open for Business, Closed to People: Mike Harris's Ontario*, eds. D. Ralph, A. Régimbald, and N. St-Amand, pp. 68–78. Halifax, Nova Scotia: Fernwood.

Moulaert, F. 1987. An institutional revisit to the Storper–Walker theory of labour. *International Journal of Urban and Regional Research* 11: 309–330.

Moynihan, D. P. 1965. *The Negro Family: The Case for National Action*. Washington, DC: U.S. Department of Labor.

————. 1989. Toward a postindustrial social policy. *Public Interest* 96: 16–27.

MSC [Manpower Services Commission]. 1976. *Towards a Comprehensive Manpower Policy*. London: MSC.

Mullaly, R. 1997. The politics of workfare: NB works. In *Workfare: Ideology for a New Underclass*, ed. E. Shragge, pp. 35–57. Toronto: Garamond Press.

Murphy, J. 1997. Alberta and the workfare myth. In *Workfare: Ideology for a New Underclass*, ed. E. Shragge, pp. 109–129. Toronto: Garamond Press.

Murray, C. 1984. *Losing Ground: American Social Policy, 1950–1980*. New York: Basic Books.

————. 1985. Have the poor been losing ground? *Political Science Quarterly* 100: 427–445.

————. Rejoinder. In *The Emerging British Underclass*, IEA Health and Welfare Unit, pp. 67–82. London: Institute of Economic Affairs.

Murray, I. 1995. *Desperately Seeking . . . a Job: A Critical Guide to the Jobseeker's Allowance*. London: Unemployment Unit.

————. 1996. Compulsion is not working. *Working Brief* February: 17–21.

Muszynski, L. 1985. The politics of labour market policy. In *The Politics of Economic Policy*, ed. G. B. Doern, pp. 251–305. Toronto: University of Toronto Press.

Myles, J., and Pierson, P. 1997. Friedman's revenge: The reform of "liberal" welfare states in Canada and the United States. *Politics and Society* 25: 443–472.

Naples, N. A. 1999. From maximum feasible participation to disenfranchisement. In *Whose Welfare?*, ed. G. Mink, pp. 56–80. Ithaca, NY: Cornell University Press.

NAPO [National Anti-Poverty Organization]. 1989. *You Call It a Molehill, I'll Call It a Mountain*. Ottawa: NAPO.

————. 1995. *NAPO's Response to the Federal Discussion Paper "Improving Social Security in Canada."* Ottawa: NAPO.

Nathan, R. P. 1986. *The Administrative Presidency*. New York: Macmillan.

————. 1988. Workfare in Britain and America: A personal view. *Economic Affairs* April–May: 16–17.

————. 1993. *Turning Promises into Performance: The Management Challenge of Implementing Workfare*. New York: Columbia University Press.

National Council of Welfare. 1995. *The 1995 Budget and Block Funding*. Ottawa: National Council of Welfare.

NCW [National Council for Welfare]. 1997. *Another Look at Welfare Reform*. Ottawa: Minister of Public Works and Government Services Canada.

————. 1998. *Profiles of Welfare: Myths and Realities*. Ottawa: Minister of Public Works and Government Services Canada.

NGA [National Governors' Association]. 1987. *Making America Work*. Washington, DC: NGA.

————. 1994. *The National Governors' Association Survey of State Welfare Reforms*. Washington, DC: NGA.

Nightingale, D. S., and Haveman, R. H. (Eds.). 1995. *The Work Alternative: Welfare Reform and the Realities of the Job Market*. Washington, DC: Urban Institute Press.

Noël, A. 1995. The politics of workfare. In *Workfare: Does It Work? Is It Fair?*, ed. A. Sayeed, pp. 39–74. Montreal: Institute for Research on Public Policy.

Norris, D. F., and Thompson, L. 1995. Findings and lessons from the politics of welfare reform. In *The Politics of Welfare Reform*, eds. D. F. Norris and L. Thompson, pp. 215–238. Thousand Oaks, CA: Sage.

Novak, T. 1997. Hounding delinquents. *Critical Social Policy* 50: 99–109.

Nye, R. 1996. *Welfare to Work: The "America Works" Experience*. London: Social Market Foundation.

OCAP [Ontario Coalition Against Poverty]. 1997. *The Fight for Work not Workfare in Ontario*. Toronto: OCAP.

O'Connor, J. 1989. Welfare expenditure and policy orientation in Canada in comparative perspective. *Canadian Review of Sociology and Anthropology* 26: 127–150.

O'Connor, J., Orloff, A. S., and Shaver, S. (Eds.). 1999. *States, Markets, Families: Gender, Liberalism and Social Policy in Australia, Canada, Great Britain and the United States*. Cambridge, UK: Cambridge University Press.

OECD [Organisation for Economic Co-operation and Development]. 1990. *Labour Market Policies for the 1990s*. Paris: OECD.

———. 1999. *The Battle against Exclusion, Volume 3: Social Assistance in Canada and Switzerland*. Paris: OECD.

Offe, C. 1984. *Contradictions of the Welfare State*. London: Hutchinson.

———. 1985. *Disorganized Capitalism: Contemporary Transformations of Work and Politics*. Cambridge, UK: Polity Press.

Olasky, M. 1992. *The Tragedy of American Compassion*. Washington, DC: Regnery.

Oliker, S. J. 1994. Does workfare work? Evaluation research and workfare policy. *Social Problems* 41: 195–213.

O'Neill, J. 1990. *Work and Welfare in Massachusetts: An Evaluation of the ET Program*. Boston: Pioneer Institute for Public Policy Research.

O'Neill, P. M. 1997. Bringing the qualitative state into economic geography. In *Geographies of Economies*, eds. R. Lee and J. Wills, pp. 290–301. London: Arnold.

Ontario. 1996. *A Summary of the Ontario Works Program*. Toronto: Queen's Printer for Ontario.

Ontario Progressive Conservative Party. 1995. *The Common Sense Revolution*. Toronto: Ontario Progressive Conservative Party.

Orloff, A. S. 1996. Gender in the welfare state. *Annual Review of Sociology* 22: 51–70.

———. 1999a. Ending the entitlement of poor mothers, expanding the claims of poor employed parents: Gender, race, class in contemporary US social policy. *European University Institute Working Paper* #99(3). Florence, Italy: European University Institute.

———. 1999b. Gender in the liberal welfare states: Australia, Canada, the United Kingdom and the United States. In *State/Culture* ed. G. Steinmetz, pp. 321–354. Ithaca, NY: Cornell University Press.

Osborne, D. S. 1998. *Laboratories of Democracy*. Boston: Harvard Business School Press.

Pal, L. A. 1983. The fall and rise of developmental use of UI funds. *Canadian Public Policy* 9: 81–93.

———. 1988a. Sense and sensibility: Comments on Forget. *Canadian Public Policy* 14: 7–14.

———. 1988b. *State, Class and Bureaucracy: Canadian Unemployment Insurance and Public Policy*. Kingston and Montreal: McGill-Queen's University Press.

Pear, R. 1983. Anecdotes and the impact they've had on policy. *New York Times* December 27: B6.

Peck, J. 1990. The Youth Training Scheme: Regional policy in reverse? *Policy and Politics* 18: 135–143.

————. 1994. From corporatism to localism, from MSC to TECs: Developing neoliberal labour regulation in Britain. *Economies et Sociétés* 17: 99–119.

————. 1996. *Work-Place: The Social Regulation of Labor Markets*. New York: Guilford Press.

————. 1998. Geographies of governance: TECs and the neo-liberalisation of "local interests." *Space and Polity* 2: 5–31.

————. 1999. New labourers? Making a New Deal for the "workless class." *Environment and Planning C* 17: 345–372.

————. 2000a. Job alert! Shifts, spins and statistics in welfare-to-work policy. *Benefits* forthcoming.

————. 2000b. Workfare *versus* the cities. *Urban Geography* forthcoming.

Peck, J., and Haughton, G. 1991. Youth training and the local reconstruction of skill: Evidence from the engineering industry of North West England, 1981–88. *Environment and Planning A* 23: 813–832.

————. 1996. Editorial introduction: Geographies of labour market governance. *Regional Studies* 30: 319–321.

Peck, J., and Jones, M. 1995. Training and Enterprise Councils: Schumpeterian workfare state, or what? *Environment and Planning A* 27: 1361–1396.

Peck, J., and Rutherford, T. 1997. Tools for the job? Decentralization, partnership and market forces in British and Canadian labour market policy. In *Social Partnerships for Training: Canada's Experiment with Labour Force Development Boards*, eds. A. Sharpe and R. Haddow, pp. 251–287. Ottawa and Kingston: Centre for the Study of Living Standards, Caledon Institute of Social Policy, and School of Policy Studies, Queen's University.

Peck, J., and Theodore, N. 1998. Welfare to work in America: A comparison of labour force attachment and human capital development models. In *Pathways into Work for Lone Parents*. Seventh report, session 1997–98. Command 646. House of Commons Education and Employment Committee, pp. 81–88. London: HMSO.

————. 1999. *Dull Compulsion: Political Economies of Workfare*. Working Paper #30. Manchester, UK: International Centre for Labour Studies.

————. 2000a. Beyond "employability." *Cambridge Journal of Economics* 24: 729–749.

————. 2000b Work first: Workfare and the regulation of contingent labour markets. *Cambridge Journal of Economics* 24: 119–138.

————. 2001. Exporting workfare/importing welfare-to-work: Exploring the politics of Third Way policy transfer. *Political Geography* forthcoming.

Peck, J., and Tickell, A. 1994. Searching for a new institutional fix: The *after* Fordist crisis and global–local disorder. In *Post-Fordism: A Reader*, ed. A. Amin, pp. 280–316. Oxford, UK: Blackwell.

————. 1997. *Manchester's Jobs Gap*. Manchester, UK: Manchester Economy Group, University of Manchester.

Peterson, P. E., and Rom, M. C. 1990. *Welfare Magnets: A New Case for a National Standard*. Washington, DC: Brookings Institution Press.

Philp, M. 1994. Consensus growing on need for social-policy reform. *Globe and Mail* January 25: A1, A4.

Philpott, J. 1997. Workfare and Labour's New Deal. In *From Welfare to Work: Les-*

*sons from America*, Choice in Welfare #39, ed. A. Deacon, pp. 65–79. London: Institute of Economic Affairs.

Piachaud, D. 1999a. Progress on poverty. *New Economy* 6: 154–160.

———. 1999b. Wealth by stealth. *Guardian* September 1: S1–3, 9.

Pierson, P. 1994. *Dismantling the Welfare State*. Cambridge, UK: Cambridge University Press.

Piore, M. J. 1970. Jobs and training. In *The State and the Poor*, eds. S. H. Beer and R. E. Barringer, pp. 53–83. Cambridge, UK: Winthrop.

Piven, F. F. 1995. Is it global economics or neo-laissez-faire? *New Left Review* 213: 107–114.

———. 1999. Welfare and work. In *Whose Welfare?*, ed. G. Mink, pp. 83–99. Ithaca, NY: Cornell University Press.

Piven, F. F., and Cloward, R. A. 1971. *Regulating the Poor: The Functions of Public Welfare*. New York: Vintage Books.

———. 1985. *The New Class War: Reagan's Attack on the Welfare State and Its Consequences*. Revised edition. New York: Pantheon Books.

———. 1987a. The contemporary relief debate. In *The Mean Season: The Attack on the Welfare State*, F. Block, R. A. Cloward, B. Ehrenreich, and F. F. Piven, pp. 45–108. New York: Random House.

———. 1987b. The historical sources of the contemporary relief debate. In *The Mean Season: The Attack on the Welfare State*, F. Block, R. A. Cloward, B. Ehrenreich, and F. F. Piven, pp. 3–44. New York: Random House.

———. 1988. Welfare doesn't shore up traditional family roles: A reply to Linda Gordon. *Social Research* 55: 631–647.

———. 1993. *Regulating the Poor: The Functions of Public Welfare*. Second edition. New York: Vintage Books.

Polanyi, K. 1944. *The Great Transformation: The Political and Economic Origins of Our Time*. Boston: Beacon Press.

Porter, K. 1990. *Making JOBS Work: What the Research Says about Effective Employment Programs for AFDC Recipients*. Washington, DC: Center on Budget and Policy Priorities.

Premier's Council. 1990. *People and Skills in the New Global Economy*. Toronto: Queen's Printer for Ontario.

Prince's Trust. 1996. Memorandum submitted by the Prince's Trust. In *The Right to Work/Workfare*, Second Report, HC 82, Employment Committee [House of Commons], p. 32. London: HMSO.

Prince's Trust Volunteers. 1996. Memorandum submitted by the Prince's Trust Volunteers. In *The Right to Work/Workfare*, Employment Committee [House of Commons], p. 32. Second Report, HC 82. London: HMSO.

Pulkingham, J., and Ternowetsky, G. 1998. *A State of the Art Review of Income Security Reform in Canada*. Ottawa: International Development Research Centre.

Quadagno, J. 1984. Welfare capitalism and the Social Security Act of 1935. *American Sociological Review* 49: 623–647.

———. 1988. *The Transformation of Old Age Security: Class and Politics in the American Welfare State*. Chicago: University of Chicago Press.

———. 1994. *The Color of Welfare: How Racism Undermined the War on Poverty*. New York: Oxford University Press.

Ralph, D., Régimbald, A., and St-Amand, N. (Eds.). 1997. *Open for Business, Closed to People: Mike Harris's Ontario.* Halifax, Nova Scotia: Fernwood.

Raspberry, W. 1996. Welfare reform, Wisconsin style. *Washington Post* July 15: A19.

Ravallion, M. 1998. *Appraising Workfare Programs.* Research Report #1955. Washington, DC: World Bank.

Rea, K. J. 1985. *The Prosperous Years: The Economic History of Ontario, 1939–75.* Toronto: University of Toronto Press.

Rector, R. E., and Butterfield, P. 1987. *Reforming Welfare: The Promises and Limits of Workfare.* Backgrounder #585. Washington, DC: Heritage Foundation.

Rector, R. E., and Youssef, S. E. 1999. *The Determinants of Welfare Caseload Decline.* Heritage Center for Data Analysis Paper #99–04. Washington, DC: Heritage Foundation.

Reese, M. 1982. Life below the poverty line. *Newsweek* April 5: 20–28.

Régimbald, A. 1997. The Ontario branch of American conservatism. In *Open for Business, Closed to People: Mike Harris's Ontario,* eds. D. Ralph, A. Régimbald, and N. St-Amand, pp. 45–53. Halifax, Nova Scotia: Fernwood.

Regional Policy Commission. 1996. *Renewing the Regions: Strategies for Regional Economic Development.* Sheffield, UK: Sheffield Hallam University.

Reich, R. B. 1992. *The Work of Nations: Preparing Ourselves for 21st-Century Capitalism.* New York: Vintage Books.

———. 1999. We are all Third Wayers now. *American Prospect* March–April: 46–51.

Reischauer, R. D. 1989. The welfare form legislation: Directions for the future. In *Welfare Policy for the 1990s,* eds. P. H. Cottingham and D. T. Ellwood, pp. 10–40. Cambridge, MA: Harvard University Press.

Rentoul, J. 1995. Eighteen months to go. . . . *Independent* November 18: 9–10.

Reynolds, E. B. 1995. Subsidized employment programs and welfare reform: The Quebec experience. In *Workfare: Does It Work? Is It Fair?,* ed. A. Sayeed, pp. 105–141. Montreal: Institute for Research on Public Policy.

Riccio, J., and Friedlander, D. 1992. *GAIN: Program Strategies, Participation Patterns, and First Year Impacts in Six Counties.* New York: Manpower Demonstration Research Corporation.

Riccio, J., Friedlander, D., and Freedman, S. 1994a. *Executive Summary: GAIN: Benefits, Costs, and Three-Year Impacts of a Welfare-to-Work Program.* New York: Manpower Demonstration Research Corporation.

———. 1994b. *GAIN: Benefits, Costs, and Three-Year Impacts of a Welfare-to-Work Program.* New York: Manpower Demonstration Research Corporation.

Rice, J. J. 1985. Politics of income security: Historical developments and limits to future change. In *The Politics of Economic Policy,* ed. D. B. Doern, pp. 221–250. Toronto: University of Toronto Press.

Richards, J., and Vining, A. 1995. Welfare reform: What can we learn from the Americans? In *Helping the Poor: A Qualified Case for "Workfare,"* J. Richards, A. Vining, D. M. Brown, M. Krashinsky, W. J. Milne, E. S. Lightman, and S. Hoy, pp. 1–36. Toronto: C. D. Howe Institute.

Richards, J., Vining, A., Brown, D. M., Krashinsky, M., Milne, W. J., Lightman, E. S., and Hoy, S. 1995. *Helping the Poor: A Qualified Case for "Workfare."* Toronto: C. D. Howe Institute.

Rimlinger, G. V. 1971. *Welfare Policy and Industrialization in Europe, America and Russia.* New York: Wiley.

Riverside County DPSS [Department of Public Social Services]. 1994. *Transferability Package for High Output Job Placement Results.* Riverside, CA: Riverside County DPSS.

Robertson, D. B. 1986. Mrs. Thatcher's employment prescription: An active neoliberal labour market policy. *Journal of Public Policy* 6: 275–296.

Rodkey, G. 1995. *NEWTisms: The Wit and Wisdom of New Gingrich.* New York: Pocket Books.

Rogers, H. R. 2000. *American Poverty in a New Era of Reform.* Armonk, NY: Sharpe.

Rogers, J. J. 1997. Making welfare work. *New Statesman* August 29: 17–20.

Rose, M. E. 1971. *The English Poor Law, 1780–1930.* Newton Abbot, UK: David & Charles.

———. 1976. Settlement, removal and the New Poor Law. In *The New Poor Law in the Nineteenth Century,* ed. D. Fraser, pp. 25–44. London: Macmillan.

Rose, N. E. 1989. Work relief in the 1930s and the origins of the Social Security Act. *Social Service Review* 63: 63–91.

———. 1995. *Workfare or Fair Work: Women, Welfare, and Government Work Programs.* New Brunswick, NJ: Rutgers University Press.

Rossiter, C. 1955. *Conservatism in America.* New York: Knopf.

Rueschemeyer, D. 1986. *Power and the Division of Labor.* Stanford, CA: Stanford University Press.

Rusk, J. 1995. Tory "workfare" plan alters consensus. *Globe and Mail* May 20: A3.

Rutherford, T. 1996a. The local solution? The Schumpeterian workfare state, labour market governance and local boards for training in Kitchener, Ontario. *Regional Studies* 30: 413–428.

———. 1996b. Socio-spatial restructuring of Canadian labour markets. In *Canada and the Global Economy: The Geography of Structural and Technological Change,* ed. J. N. H. Britton, pp. 407–432. Kingston and Montreal: McGill-Queen's University Press.

Sabatini, E. 1996. *Welfare—No Fair: A Critical Analysis of Ontario's Welfare System (1985–1994).* Vancouver: Fraser Institute.

Safire, W. 1982. Reagan's anecdotage. *New York Times* March 8: A19.

———. 1988. Coiners' corner. *New York Times Magazine* July 17: 8, 10.

———. 1993. *Safire's New Political Dictionary: The Definitive Guide to the New Language of Politics.* New York: Random House.

———. 1994. Newtonomics is powering up for launch. *Denver Post* November 20: F4.

Sainsbury, D (Ed.). 1999. *Gender and Welfare State Regimes.* Oxford, UK: Oxford University Press.

Savner, S., Williams, L., and Halas, M. 1986. The Massachusetts Employment and Training Program. *Clearinghouse Review* 20: 123–131.

Sayeed, A. (Ed.). 1995. *Workfare: Does It Work? Is It Fair?* Montreal: Institute for Research on Public Policy.

Schott, L., Greenstein, B., and Primus, W. 1999. *The Determinants of Welfare*

*Caseload Decline: A Brief Rejoinder.* Washington, DC: Center on Budget and Policy Priorities.

Schottland, C. I. 1970. Public assistance. In *The State and the Poor*, eds. S. H. Beer and R. E. Barringer, pp. 84–105. Cambridge, MA: Winthrop.

Schram, S. F. 1995. *Words of Welfare: The Poverty of Social Science and the Social Science of Poverty.* Minneapolis: University of Minnesota Press.

SEU [Social Exclusion Unit]. 1998. *New Deal for Communities.* London: SEU.

Sennett, R. 1998. *The Corrosion of Character: The Personal Consequences of Work in the New Capitalism.* New York: Norton.

Shafritz, J. M. 1988. *The Dorsey Dictionary of American Government and Politics.* Chicago: Dorsey Press.

Shankman, K. 1995. *Jobs That Pay: Are Enough Good Jobs Available in Metropolitan Chicago?* Chicago: Chicago Urban League; Latino Institute; Northern Illinois State University.

Sharpe, A., and Haddow, R. (Eds.). 1997. *Social Partnerships for Training: Canada's Experiment with Labour Force Development Boards.* Ottawa and Kingston: Centre for the Study of Living Standards, Caledon Institute of Social Policy, and School of Policy Studies, Queen's University.

Shaw, A., Walker, R., Ashworth, K., Jenkins, S., and Middleton, S. 1996. *Moving Off Income Support: Barriers and Bridges.* Department of Social Security Research Report #53. London: HMSO.

Sheldrick, R. M. 1998. Welfare reform under Ontario's NDP: Social democracy and social group representation. *Studies in Political Economy* 55: 37–63.

Shragge, E. 1997a. Introduction. In *Workfare: Ideology for a New Underclass*, ed. E. Shragge, pp. 13–16. Toronto: Garamond Press.

———. 1997b. Workfare: An overview. In *Workfare: Ideology for a New Underclass*, ed. E. Shragge, pp. 17–34. Toronto: Garamond Press.

———. (Ed.). 1997c. *Workfare: Ideology for a New Underclass.* Toronto: Garamond Press.

Shragge, E., and Deniger, M-A. 1997. Workfare in Quebec. In *Workfare: Ideology for a New Underclass*, ed. E. Shragge, pp. 59–83. Toronto: Garamond Press.

Simeon, R., and Robinson, I. 1990. *State, Society, and the Development of Canadian Federalism.* Toronto: University of Toronto Press.

Simmonds, D., and Emmerich, M. 1996. *Regeneration through Work: Creating Jobs in the Social Economy.* Manchester, UK: Centre for Local Economic Strategies.

Simpson, J. 1995. With welfare reform, Ontario's politicians promise puzzling solutions. *Globe and Mail* May 21: A20.

Skocpol, T. 1995. *Social Policy in the United States: Future Possibilities in Historical Perspective.* Princeton, NJ: Princeton University Press.

Snower, D. 1997. Three diseases that could kill the Welfare to Work initiative. *Guardian* August 11: 17.

Solow, R. M. 1998. *Work and Welfare.* Princeton, NJ: Princeton University Press.

SPCMT [Social Planning Council of Metropolitan Toronto]. 1996a. The political economy of workfare. *Social Infopac* 14(5): 1–12.

———. 1996b. Workfare for whom? Social assistance recipients and labour force participation. *Social Infopac* 14(3): 1–11.

———. 1996c. Workfare: What we know. *Social Infopac* 14(4): 1–16.

Standing, G. 1990. The road to workfare: Alternative to welfare or threat to occupation? *International Labour Review* 129: 677–691.

———. 1992. Alternative routes to labor flexibility. In *Pathways to Industrialization and Regional Development*, eds. M. Storper and A. J. Scott, pp. 255–275. London: Routledge.

Stephens, P. 1995. A change in the weather. *Financial Times* October 6: 18.

Streeck, W. 1992. National diversity, regime competition, and institutional deadlock: Problems in forming a European industrial relations system. *Journal of Public Policy* 12: 301–330.

Swift, J. 1995. *Wheel of Fortune: Work and Life in an Age of Falling Expectations*. Toronto: Between the Lines.

Szanton, P. L. 1991. The remarkable "quango": Knowledge, politics, and welfare reform. *Journal of Policy Analysis and Management* 10: 590–602.

Tanner, M. 1995. *Ending Welfare as We Know It*. Policy Analysis #212. Washington, DC: CATO Institute.

———. 1996. *The End of Welfare: Fighting Poverty in the Civil Society*. Washington, DC: CATO Institute.

Tarling, R. (Ed.). 1987. *Flexibility in the Labour Market*. London: Academic Press.

Taylor, F. 1995. Working for the welfare dollar. *Globe and Mail* June 3: D2.

Taylor, J. H. 1987. Sources of political conflict in the Thirties: Welfare policy and the geography of need. In *The "Benevolent State": The Growth of Welfare in Canada*, eds. A. Muscovitch and J. Albert, pp. 144–154. Toronto: Garamond Press.

Teeple, G. 1995. *Globalization and the Decline of Social Reform*. Toronto: Garamond Press.

Teles, S. 1997. Beware the Clinton welfare trap. *New Statesman* June 6: 22–23.

TEN [Training and Employment Network]. 1997. *Making the "New Deal" Work*. London: TEN.

Theodore, N. 1995. *When the Job Doesn't Pay: Contingent Workers in the Chicago Metropolitan Area*. Chicago: Chicago Urban League; Latino Institute; Northern Illinois State University.

———. 1998. *On parallel paths: The Clinton/Blair agenda and the new geopolitics of workfare*. Paper presented at the Royal Geographical Society/Institute of British Geographers annual conference, Guildford, UK, January 5–8.

Theodore, N., and Peck, J. 1999. Welfare-to-work: National problems, local solutions? *Critical Social Policy* 61: 485–510.

Théret, B. 1999. Regionalism and federalism: A comparative analysis of the regulation of economic tensions between regions by Canadian and American federal intergovernmental transfer programmes. *International Journal of Urban and Regional Research* 23: 479–512.

Thomas, R. 1997. Freeing young jobless from welfare "hammock." *Guardian* May 15: 8.

Thompson, E. P. 1968. *The Making of the English Working Class*. London: Penguin Books.

Thompson, T. Nd. *Building a Stronger America: A Blueprint for the States . . ., and the Next Century*. Washington, DC: National Governors' Association.

Thrift, N. J. 1989. New times and new spaces? The perils of transition models. *Environment and Planning D: Society and Space* 7: 127–129.

Tickell, A., and Peck, J. 1995. Social regulation *after* Fordism: Regulation theory, neo-liberalism and the global–local nexus. *Economy and Society* 24: 357–386.

———. 1996. The return of the Manchester Men: Men's words and men's deeds in the remaking of the local state. *Transactions of the Institute of British Geographers* 21: 595–616.

Tilly, C. 1996. *Workfare's Impact on the New York City Labor Market: Lower Wages and Worker Displacement*. Working Paper #92. New York: Russell Sage Foundation.

Torjman, S. 1996. *Workfare: A Poor Law.* Ottawa: Caledon Institute of Social Policy.

———. 1997. *Disentanglement or Disengagement?* Ottawa: Caledon Institute of Social Policy.

———. 1998. *Welfare Reform through Tailor-Made Training.* Ottawa: Caledon Institute of Social Policy.

Toulin, A. 1994. Social safety net overhaul possible by yearend. *Financial Post* February 17: 17.

Towns, E. 1995. Necessary flexibility or ad hoc decision-making? *Public Welfare* 53: 6.

Trattner, W. I. 1984. *From Poor Law to Welfare State: A History of Social Welfare in America.* New York: Free Press.

Treasury. 1984. Helping markets work better. *Economic Progress Report* 173: 1–5.

TUC [Trades Union Congress]. 1988. *Report of the 120th Annual Trades Union Congress.* London: TUC.

———. 1994a. *Jobs not JSA: JSA and Workfare.* London: TUC.

———. 1994b. *Why Workfare Won't Work and Isn't Fair.* London: TUC.

———. 1995. *Workfare: A TUC Briefing.* London: TUC.

Turk, J. 1992. If "training" is the answer, what is the question? In *Training for What? Labour Perspectives on Job Training*, ed. N. Jackson, pp. 1–7. Toronto: Our Schools/Our Selves Education Foundation.

Turok, I., and Edge, N. 1999. *The Jobs Gap in Britain's Cities: Employment Loss and Labour Market Consequences.* Bristol, UK: Policy Press.

Turok, I., and Webster, D. 1998. The New Deal: Jeopardised by the geography of unemployment? *Local Economy* 13: 309–328.

Unemployment Unit. 1996. Memorandum submitted by the Unemployment Unit. In *The Right to Work/Workfare*, Second Report, HC 82, Employment Committee [House of Commons], pp. 12–27. London: HMSO.

Urban Institute. 1990. *Evaluation of the Massachusetts Employment and Training (ET) Choices Program.* Washington, DC: Urban Institute Press.

Valpy, M. 1995. The question is, how will workfare work. *Globe and Mail* October 17: A19.

Vartanian, T. P. 1999. Locational effects on AFDC exits: Examining local labor markets. *Journal of Socio-Economics* 28: 607–631.

Vosko, L. F. 1998. *Workfare temporaries: The rise of the temporary employment relationship, the decline of the standard employment relationship and the feminization of employment in Canada.* Mimeo. Toronto: Women's Studies Programme, York University.

Walker, J. 1995. Quebec's six-year experiment with workfare hasn't paid off. *Financial Post* July 1: 15.

Walker, R. 1991. *Thinking about Workfare: Evidence from the USA*. London: HMSO.

———. 1998. The Americanization of British welfare: A case study of policy transfer. *Focus* 19: 32–40.

Walters, J. 1999. Beyond the welfare clock. *Governing* April: 21–26.

Walters, W. 1996. The demise of unemployment? *Politics and Society* 24: 197–219.

Weaver, D. 2000. Organizational technology as institutionalised ideology: Case management practices in welfare-to-work programs. *Administration in Social Work* 24: 1–19.

Webb, S., and Webb, B. 1963. *English Poor Law History: Part I, The Old Poor Law*. Hamden, CT: Archon Books.

Weinroth, M. 1997. Deficitism and neo-conservatism in Ontario. In *Open for Business, Closed to People: Mike Harris's Ontario*, eds. D. Ralph, A. Régimbald, and N. St-Amand, pp. 54–67. Halifax, Nova Scotia: Fernwood.

Weir, M. 1992. *Politics and Jobs: The Boundaries of Employment Policy in the United States*. Princeton, NJ: Princeton University Press.

———. 1998. Big cities confront the new federalism. In *Big Cities in the Welfare Transition*, eds. A. J. Kahn and S. B. Kamerman, pp. 8–35. New York: School of Social Work, Columbia University.

White, M., and Forth, J. 1998. *Pathways through Unemployment: The Effects of a Flexible Labour Market*. York, UK: York Publishing Services.

White, M., and Lakey, J. 1992. *The Restart Effect: Does Active Labour Market Policy Reduce Unemployment?* London: Policy Studies Institute.

Willetts, D. 1998. *Welfare to Work*. London: Social Market Foundation.

Williams, K. 1981. *From Pauperism to Poverty*. London: Routledge & Kegan Paul.

Williams, L. A. 1994. The abuse of Section 1115 waivers: Welfare reform in search of a standard. *Yale Law and Policy Review* 12: 8–37.

Williams, R. 1983. *Keywords: A Vocabulary of Culture and Society*. Revised edition. New York: Oxford University Press.

Williamson, L. 1999. Some workfare plans actually work: Ontario's checking out Wisconsin. *London Free Press* September 9: 13.

Wilson, W. J. 1987. *The Truly Disadvantaged: The Inner City, the Underclass, and Public Policy*. Chicago: University of Chicago Press.

Wintour, P. 1995. Labour battle over benefits. *Guardian* November 10: 1.

Wiseman, M. 1987. How workfare really works. *Public Interest* 89: 36–47.

———. 1989. Workfare and welfare reform. In *Beyond Welfare: New Approaches to the Problem of Poverty in America*, ed. H. R. Rodgers, pp. 14–38. Armonk, NY: Sharpe.

———. 1993. Welfare reform in the States: The Bush legacy. *Focus* 15: 18–36.

———. 1995. Fixing welfare waiver policy. *Public Welfare* 53: 10–16.

Wolfe, D. 1989. The Canadian state in comparative perspective. *Canadian Review of Sociology and Anthropology* 26: 95–126.

———. 1996. Institutional limits to labour market reform in Ontario: The short life and rapid demise of the Ontario Training and Adjustment Board. In *So-

*cial Partnerships for Training: Canada's Experiment with Labour Force Development Boards*, eds. A. Sharpe and R. Haddow, pp. 155–188. Ottawa and Kingston: Centre for the Study of Living Standards and Caledon Institute of Social Policy.

Wood, L. 1995. Workfare: No easy option. *Financial Times* October 12: 17.

Woodcock, C. 1999. Did Harris just fall off the turnip truck? *Toronto Sun* September 4: 13.

Woodward, B. 1994. *The Agenda: Inside the Clinton White House.* New York: Simon & Schuster.

Workfare Watch. 1996a. From the steering committee. *Workfare Watch Bulletin* 1(2): 1.

———. 1996b. Is New York Ontario's future? *Workfare Watch Bulletin* 1(1): 1–2.

———. 1997. Workfare and downloading: Two strategies for cutting welfare. *Workfare Watch Bulletin* 1(4): 1–2.

———. 1998a. Unmasking the Wisconsin welfare "miracle." *Workfare Watch Bulletin* 3(6): 1–2.

———. 1998b. Workfare in the private sector. *Workfare Watch Bulletin* 3(7): 1–2.

———. 1999a. *Broken Promises: Welfare Reform in Ontario.* Toronto: Social Planning Council of Metropolitan Toronto.

———. 1999b. Workfare: Symbolic purposes at the expense of substantive benefits. *Workfare Watch Bulletin* 1(9): 1–12.

Yalnizyan, A. 1994. Securing society: Creating Canadian social policy. In *Shifting Time: Social Policy and the Future of Work*, eds. A. Yalnizyan, T. Ran Ide, and A. Cordell, pp. 17–72. Toronto: Between the Lines.

York, G. 1994. Reality, not red book, sets Grit course. *Globe and Mail* January 25: A4.

Ziliak, J. P., Figlio, D. N., Davis, E. E., and Connolly, L. S. 1997. *Accounting for the Decline in AFDC Caseloads: Welfare Reform or Economic Growth?* IRP Discussion Paper #1151–97. Madison: Institute for Research on Poverty, University of Wisconsin.

# Index

Adam Smith Institute, 344
Advanced-welfare-state countries, transition to workfare in, 73–77
AFDC (*See* Aid to Families with Dependent Children)
Aid to Families with Dependent Children (AFDC), 72, 91, 122n.7, 134, 157
Alberta, Canada, 218, 219, 235–236, 257
Albo, G., 239
Altvater, E., 351
Amdur, R. S., 249
Anderson, Eloise, 192
Anti-welfare sentiments, 53–54
Anti-workfare politics (*See* Oppositional politics)
Axworthy, Lloyd, 230

**B**

Baird, John, 247
Baltimore, Maryland, 365
Banting, K. G., 226–227
Barclay, Peter, 266
Bardach, E., 198
Barnett, A., 325
Baum, Erica, 97
Becker, K. A., 344
Benefit fraud, 326–327
   British programs addressing, 334–335n.21
Benefits hot-line, 283, 334–335n.21

Bentham, Jeremy, 40–41
Beveridgean welfare state, 274, 292
Beveridge Report, 310
Bevins, Anthony, 333–334n.12
Blair, Tony, 278, 333n.3
   Jobseeker's Allowance, 290, 291
   New Deal program, 302, 306, 316, 325–326, 328
   and politics of "disentitlementarianism," 120
   and welfare reform, 4, 261–263, 299, 300, 301, 328
   and workfare, 5, 306–307
   Working Families Tax Credit, 324
Blank, R. M., 345–346
Block grants, 70, 71, 152, 153, 156, 158, 163
Blunkett, David, 306, 314
Boundary institutions, 52, 63
Braverman, H., 62
Briscoe, Simon, 283
"Britain Works" scheme, 298–299
British Columbia, Canada, 218–219, 257–258n.5
British welfare reform (*See also* New Deal program)
   and Tony Blair, 4, 261–263, 299, 300, 301, 328
   Blair-Clinton alliance, 262–263
   Commission on Social Justice, 275–278
   human capitalism, 277–278
   Jobseeker's Allowance, 282–292

British welfare reform (*cont.*)
  and Labour, 261–262, 275–281,
    299–301, 329
  and notions of welfare state, 329–330
  and time limits, 354
  and U.S. policy influence, 262–263,
    318–324
  and welfare dependency, 329
British workfare, 3–4, 26 (*See also*
    New Deal program)
  and benefit fraud, 326–327
  Commission on Social Justice on,
    276–277
  deterrent function, 298
  and economic cycles, 332
  emergence, 264
    in labor-market policies, 268–273
  Employment Committee definition,
    293
  Employment Committee
    investigation, 293–296
  as interinstitutional phenomenon,
    272
  job-search and training programs,
    269, 273
  and Jobseeker's Allowance, 282–292
  mandatory participation principle,
    279, 281
  origins of and paths to, 326–333
  political consensus around, 330–331
  politics of, 274–275, 292–299
  rhetoric of, 273, 329
  Third Way policy, 324–326
  and U.S. policy influence, 4, 5, 263,
    271, 318–324
  and welfare dependency, 4, 329
  and welfare policy modernization,
    275–282
Brodkin, E. Z., 134, 190, 359
Brown, Gordon, 278–279, 281, 291,
    301–302, 302, 310, 336n.39,
    336n.44, 342–343
Bush, George, 98–99, 102, 124n.15
Bush, George W., 206
Butterfield, P., 84–85, 91, 140


C

California, 187
Canada (*See also* Canadian welfare
    reform; Canadian workfarism;
    Canadian work-welfare regime)
  permeable Fordism in, 222–224

Canada Assistance Plan (CAP), 220,
    223, 228, 233, 254
Canada Health and Social Transfer
    (CHST), 220, 233
Canadian Auto Workers, 254–255
Canadian welfare reform, 213–214
    (*See also* Canadian work-
    welfare regime)
  and federal-provincial political
    dynamics, 230–232
  provincial workfare experiments,
    216–219
  restructuring of work-welfare
    regime, 253–257
  themes in, 215–216
  and time limits, 354
  U.S. policy influence, 214, 215
Canadian workfarism, 25–26, 214
  and cost control, 234–235
  and defederalization, 226–228, 233
  and "deficitist" politics, 233–234
  deployment of local policy
    knowledge, 232–233
  and federal-provincial political
    dynamics, 230–232
  federal support and policies, 219–
    222
  and mutually referential policy
    development, 6
  opposition to, 254–255
  provincial experiments, 216–219,
    228–229, 232
  regional labor markets and
    implementation, 235–236
  restructuring of work-welfare
    regime, 254–257
  supply-sidism in, 229
  U.S. policy influence, 5
  *See also* Ontario, Canada, workfare
    in; Ontario Works program
Canadian work-welfare regime
  Canada Assistance Plan, 223
  defederalization, 226–228
  depression era crisis and
    federalization, 224–225
  dynamics of federal-provincial
    relations, 223, 230–232
  restructuring of, 253–257
  workfarist experiments, 228–229
CAP (*See* Canada Assistance Plan)
Cardinal, Mike, 218, 219
Castle, Stephen, 278
CATO Institute, 107, 125n.28

Centralization, in welfare regime, 64–68
Charles, Prince of Wales, 298
*Charter Against Workfare,* 303, 306
Chicago, Illinois, 63–64
Childcare
    and Ontario Works program, 251
    and U.K.'s New Deal program, 303
CHST (*See* Canada Health and Social Transfer)
Civilian Conservation Corps, 65
Civil Works Administration, 65
Clarke, Kenneth, 283
Clinton, Bill, 142
    and British welfare reform, 262–263
    and entitlements, 117
    and National Governors' Association, 140
    and welfare reform, 10, 97–98, 99–100, 102–103, 110, 113–114, 115–116, 131, 143, 149, 152–153, 165
        passage of Personal Responsibility and Work Reconciliation Act, 116–117
        rhetoric of, 87–88, 119, 124n.17, 124–125n.18, 125n.19
Cloward, R. A., 31, 35, 39, 44, 53–54, 58, 140, 182, 188–189, 342
Commission on Social Justice (U.K.), 275–278, 300, 306
*Common Sense Revolution,* 5, 236, 240–247, 330
Community Action (U.K.), 293
Community Programme (U.K.), 265
Community sector model of workfare, 78(table)
Community Work Experience Program (CWEP), 91, 122nn.5&6
Compulsion
    in British workfare, 279
        New Deal program, 280–281, 302–303, 306–307
        and U.S. policy influences, 321
    in labor-market participation, 188–190, 342, 352, 353, 354, 356
    and Riverside GAIN program, 174–175, 176, 183–184, 188–190
Conservative Party (U.K.)
    and benefit fraud, 327
    and Jobseeker's Allowance, 290, 291–292
    labor-market programs, 265, 267–268

    and Ontario's *Common Sense Revolution,* 5, 330
    U.S. policy influence, 321
    and welfare localization, 291–292
    and welfare reform, 330
    and workfare, 264, 272, 281–282, 290, 292–293, 297–299, 327
Contingent employment
    and Riverside program, 184–186
    and workfare, 353–356, 357–358
Contingent workforce (*See also* Secondary workers; Welfare population; Working poor)
    economic marginality, 43
    labor market inclusion and exclusion, 51–52
    qualitative reorganization of, 52
    and Riverside program, 184–186
    social distribution of waged work, 41–42
    and workfare, 22, 350, 353–356, 357–358
"Contract for Work" (U.K.), 297
*Contract with America,* 70–71, 87, 103–104, 110, 118
Convery, Paul, 295
Cope, M., 73
Corbyn, Jeremy, 292
Corporatist welfare states
    transition to workfare in, 74, 75–76(table)
    welfare regime in, 75(table)
Cost-neutrality principle of welfare reform, 100–101
Council of Economic Advisers, 344
Crétien, Jean, 219
"Culture of opportunity," 107–110
Curtis, Dean, 179–180, 191
Curtis & Associates, 179

**D**

D'Amato, Alfonse, 105, 110–111
Darling, Alistair, 313, 324, 339n.79
Davis, Peter, 336n.40
Deacon, A., 299, 331
Dean, H., 271
Decentralization
    and welfare, 70–73, 163, 164, 165
    and workfare, 71–72, 362
        in Canada, 226–228, 233
        U.K.'s New Deal program, 312–313

Defederalization, and Canadian
    workfarism, 226–228, 233
Dehli, K., 89, 232–233, 240
Democratic Party (U.S.), 66
Denis, C., 219
Department of Transitional Assistance
    (Massachusetts), 143, 146–147,
    158–159, 160, 161
Dependency
    industrial, 47
    and Massachusetts welfare reform,
        157
    postindustrial, 57
    See also Welfare dependency
Deregistration effects, 343–344, 345–
    347
Deterrent effects of workfare, 298,
    348–349
Detroit, Michigan, 198
Deukmejian, G., 190–191
Devolution, and workfare, 360–361
Dewar, Donald, 274
Dickson, N., 331
Dionne, E. J., Jr., 107
Disentitlementarianism, 117–122
Dole, Bob, 107, 111, 116
Dolowitz, D. P., 272
Downey, Thomas, 96
Drache, D., 253
Drew, E., 105
Dukakis, Michael, 135, 138, 165–
    166n.6

E

Ecker, Janet, 242
Economic inequalities, and regimes of
    regulation, 48–49
Economic Policy Institute, 185
Economistic-therapeutic-managerial
    (ETM) discourse, 93–95, 119
Ellwood, David, 101
Employment and Training Choices
    (ET) program, 97, 135, 138–
    139, 161
    politics of, 139–143
Employment Committee (U.K.), 293–
    296
Employment Insurance (Canada), 221,
    231
Employment Policy Institute, 283
Employment Service (U.K.), 286, 296

Employment Training Program (U.K.),
    267–268
Entitlements, politics of
    "disentitlementarianism," 117–
    122
Epstein, W. M., 93, 200, 202
ET program (See Employment and
    Training Choices program)
European Union, 311, 338n.63
Evaluation
    economistic-therapeutic-managerial
        discourse, 93–95
    under MDRC, 91, 92–93, 94–95,
        96
    and waiver system, 101
Evans, P. M., 215
Evers, James Charles, 90

F

Family Assistance Plan, 90
Family Support Act (FSA), 92, 95, 96,
    97, 98, 99, 124–125n.18, 140–
    141
Federal Emergency Relief
    Administration, 65
Federalization
    in Canadian work-welfare regime,
        224–225
    and New Deal, 64–66
    in U.S. welfare policy, 66–68
Field, Frank, 293, 296–297, 299–300,
    312, 313, 324, 327, 331,
    336n.38, 338n.64, 340n.94
Finn, Dan, 334n.18
Fletcher, D. R., 269
Fogden, Mike, 282
Fordism, in Canada, 222–224
Forget Commission (Canada), 226
Forth, Eric, 335n.33, 337n.54
Fraser, D., 62
Fraser, N., 68
FSA (See Family Support Act)

G

GAIN program (See Greater Avenues
    for Independence program;
    Riverside GAIN program)
Gender
    and welfare regimes, 47–48
    and workfare regimes, 22–23

General Assistance (Massachusetts), 133, 145, 146, 161
Geographies of relief, 60–61 (*See also* Spaces of regulation)
spatial images of welfare dependency and workfare success, 95–96, 112–113
workhouse regime, 61–64
Geopolitics
of workfare, 358–367
of workfare discourse, 88–89
*Getting Welfare to Work,* 291
Ghettos, and welfare dependency, 68–69
Giddens, Anthony, 319
Gilder, George, 88, 106, 125n.26
Gingrich, Newt, 86–87, 104, 105–106, 107–111, 116, 118, 152
Ginsberg, Mitchell, 69
GOPAC, 85–86
Gordon, L., 68
Gore, Albert, 206
Gray, John, 313
Great Depression
in Canada, 224–225
extent of, 64
negative symbolism of relief, 53
New Deal, 64–66
Greater Avenues for Independence (GAIN) program, 72, 169, 173, 207–208n.18 (*See also* Riverside GAIN program)
Greenberg, Mark, 114–115, 186
Grimes, Alistair, 306
Gueron, Judith, 111, 172–173, 181, 192, 203–204

**H**

Hague, William, 330
Handler, J. F., 58–59, 149, 164
Harcourt, Mike, 218
Harman, Harriet, 303, 313, 324
Harrington, Michael, 60
Harris, Mike, 5, 242, 248, 249, 251, 252, 259nn.32&33
Hasenfeld, Y., 58–59, 149, 164
Health and Human Services Department (U.S.), 149, 152
Heclo, H., 99
Heritage Foundation, 105, 139–140
Heseltine, Michael, 281–282

Hewitt, Patricia, 336n.39
"Hollowing out," 163, 364
Howell, Sir Ralph, 292, 293
Human capital, (re)investment in, 76
Human capital development models, 78(table), 90, 119
abandonment of, 196
in Canada, 234, 235
cost issues, 235
evaluations of, 186, 191
Lawrence Mead's rejection of, 193
in urban areas, 201
Human capitalism, 277–278

**I**

Illinois, entry-level jobs, 208n.33
Illinois Job Gap Study, 185
*Improving Social Security in Canada,* 254
Income protection, and workfare, 40
Industrial dependency, 47
Industrial workers, 63
Institute of Directors, 303
Institutionalization, 36
Intermediate labor market models, 306

**J**

Jenson, J., 222, 223, 224
Jérôme-Forget, Monique, 219
Jessop, B., 80–81
Job availability, 158–159
Job competition, and workfare, 40
Job development, in Riverside program, 177–181
Job Opportunities and Basic Skills (JOBS) program, 97, 140, 141, 142, 144
Job searches, in Riverside program, 179
Jobseeker's Agreement, 284–285, 287–289(figure)
Jobseeker's Allowance (JSA), 297, 307, 331
methodology, 284–290
piloting powers, 335n.29
political consensus around, 290–292
restructuring of benefits regime, 282–284
Jobseeker's Direction, 285–286

JOBS program (*See* Job Opportunities
    and Basic Skills program)
Jones, M., 268
JSA (*See* Jobseeker's Allowance)

**K**

Katz, Michael, 33, 64
Kaufman, A., 134, 359
Kaus, Mickey, 348–349
Kay, John, 262
Kelso, R. W., 350
Kennedy, Edward, 116
Kerans, P., 226
Keynesianism, in Canada, 223, 225
King, Edward J., 135
Kinnock, Neil, 268
Klein, Ralph, 218
Knight, Angela, 281
Kreklewich, R., 215

**L**

Labor-force attachment, 76, 90, 119,
    157 (*See also* Riverside GAIN
    program; Work-first workfare)
  applying to urban areas, issues in, 201
  in Canada, 234–235
  cost issues, 235
  evaluations of, 186, 191
  and labor-market regulation, 188–
    190
  and labor-market segmentation, 180
  Charles Murray on, 180–181
  and Ontario Works program, 243–
    244
Labor-market inequalities, and
    workfare, 355
Labor-market policy
  deregulation and workfare, 55
  in U.K., 265–266
    dismantling of labor-market
      corporatism, 267–268
    and New Deal program, 310–312
    Stricter Benefit Regime, 266–267,
      269
    workfarist trends, 268–273
Labor-market reintegration, 74
Labor markets (*See also* Contingent
    employment; Contingent
    workforce)
  boundary institutions, 52
  and Canadian workfarism, 235–236

"churning" in, 13, 14, 354
  deregulation, 55
  power relationships in, 42–43
  primary and secondary employment
    in, 42
  social distribution of waged work,
    41–42
  social regulation, 34–35
  and U.K.'s New Deal program, 309–
    310, 313–314
  and welfare decentralization, 72
  and workfare, 22, 55, 353–358
Labor-market segmentation, and labor-
    force attachment, 180
Labor regulation
  institutionalization in, 36
  and Massachusetts welfare reform,
    160–161
  modes of inclusion and exclusion,
    51–52
  and Ontario Works program, 244–
    245, 246
  regimes of, 45–50, 56–58
  and relief systems, 35–40
    in crisis and change, 52–56
    politics and the labor market, 40–
      45
  and shifting labor-market
    boundaries, 50–52
  social, 34–35
  spaces of, 58–77
  and welfare reform, 34
  and workfare, 6–7, 12, 14, 21–24,
    39–40, 55–56, 182–190, 349–
    350, 352–358
  *See also* Regimes of regulation;
    Regulatory crises
Labour Market System, 286
Labour Party (U.K.) (*See also* New
    Deal program)
  Commission on Social Justice, 275–
    278
  Jobseeker's Allowance, 290–291
  and politics of
    "disentitlementarianism," 120
  and U.S. policy influence, 322
  and welfare reform, 261–262, 275–
    281, 299–301
  and workfare, 3–4, 264, 278–281,
    327–330, 332–333
Lamont, Norman, 272
*Language: A Key Mechanism of Control*
    (Gingrich), 86

Layard, Richard, 356–357
Levin, Sander, 96
Liberal welfare states
    welfare regime in, 75(table)
    workfare in, 75–76(table), 76
Lightman, E. S., 227, 233
Lilley, Peter, 274, 291–292, 335n.30
Lister, Ruth, 290, 300
Local administration, in relief cycles,
    58–59
Local labor markets
    effects of relief arrangements in, 59–
        60
    and local administration of
        workhouse regime, 62–63
    and urbanization, 63–64
Local welfare administration
    and British welfare, 291–292
    and decentralization, 72, 73
    and reform, 143–144
Local workfare, 71–72, 77, 163, 361
    coupling of economic and social
        policy, 363–364
    and metagovernance, 364
    and micromanagement, 362
    and oppositional politics, 363, 364,
        365–366
    spatial unevenness, 362–363
    state model of, 78(table)
    and U.K.'s New Deal program, 318,
        322–323
Local workhouse regime, 61–64
Lott, Trent, 106, 116
Low-wage labor (See also Contingent
        employment; Contingent
        workforce)
    regulation by relief systems, 39
    and workfare, 40

**M**

Macdonald Commission (Canada), 226
Mahon, R., 240
Major, John, 274, 297, 334n.13
"Manchester Rules," 59
Mandelson, Peter, 279–280, 311–312
Manpower Demonstration Research
        Corporation (MDRC), 91, 92–
        93, 123nn.9&10
    applying labor-force attachment
        model in urban areas, 201
    and Employment and Training
        Choices program, 140, 141, 142

promotion of work-first programs,
    194–195
Riverside program evaluation, 169,
    170, 186, 190, 191, 195, 202–
    203
Manpower Services Commission, 265,
    268
Market forces, 45
Market model of workfare, 78(table)
Market relations, 44–45
Marshall, Will, 204
Massachusetts welfare reform, 133–
    134
    Employment and Training Choices
        program, 135, 138–143
    and induced low-wage dependency,
        160–161
    and job availability, 158–159
    liability to failure, 162
    long-term effects, 156–157
    off-the-peg policies, 148
    politics of implementation, 159–161
    summary of, 150–151(table)
    themes and trends in, 131–133
    under William Weld, 130–131, 142–
        143, 145–149, 152, 156–157,
        158–159
    Work Training Program, 135
Massachusetts welfare system, 129–130
Mather, Graham, 275
Matthews, M., 344
Maude, Francis, 290
Maxwell, Judith, 230
McGuinty, Dalton, 249
McKenna, Frank, 229
McLoughlin, Patrick, 333n.11
McWilliams, D., 343
MDRC (See Manpower Demonstration
        Research Corporation)
Meacher, Michael, 290
Mead, Lawrence, 57–58, 68–69, 91,
    95, 111, 143–144, 164–165,
    193, 194, 326, 327, 328, 330,
    332, 337n.55, 341, 348, 350,
    352
Migration, welfare-induced, 102
Moore, Stephen, 107
Morris, Bill, 334n.18
Moseley-Braun, Carol, 116
Mott, Charles, 41
Moynihan, Daniel Patrick, 88, 96, 97
Mulgan, Geoff, 312, 313, 338n.66
Murphy, J., 257

Murray, Charles, 180–181, 300, 335n.29
Murray, I., 285, 286

**N**

Nathan, Richard, 94, 138, 159, 207n.16, 331
National Governors' Association (NGA), 98, 113, 115, 140, 144, 152
National Institute for Economic and Social Research (U.K.), 307–308
National states, "hollowing out" of, 163, 364
National Welfare Rights Organization, 66
National welfarism, 360–361
NB Works, 230
Neoliberal governments, mutually referential policy development, 6
New Brunswick, Canada, 229–230
New Deal program (U.K.), 4, 280–281
    central control and shortened policy cycles, 315–318
    compulsion regime in, 302–303, 306–307
    and decentralization, 312–313
    and declining youth unemployment, 345
    delivery challenges, 332
    and economic recession, 313–315
    and "full employability," 343
    gender dimension, 22–23
    implementation issues, 307–308, 317, 331–332, 337–338n.58
    introduction of, 301–302
    and labor-market growth, 309–310, 313–314
    and labor-market policy, 310–312
    and local economic conditions, 315
    local partnership arrangements, 318, 322–323
    main elements of, 302, 304–305(figure)
    and New Labour leadership, 313
    politics of, 328–329
    quality control issues, 331
    risks of exaggerating, 325–326
    and social exclusion, 311–312, 323
    and U.S. policy influence, 318–324
    and weak labor markets, 325
New Deal (U.S.), 53, 64–66
New Democratic Party (Canada), 236, 237–240
"New Federalism" (U.S.), 70
New Labour (U.K.) (See also Labour Party)
    leadership, 313
    task forces, 301, 336n.40
    welfare reform, 261–262, 329
    and workfare, 3–4, 5, 279–280, 327–330, 332–333
New Poor Law (England), 62
New Right (U.S.), workfare rhetoric, 85–87
New York City, 365
NGA (See National Governors' Association)
Nixon, Richard, 70, 90
Noël, A., 222
Norris, D. F., 148
North American Free Trade Agreement, 215
Novak, T., 286, 290

**O**

OBRA (See Omnibus Budget Reconciliation Act)
Offe, C., 50
Off-the-peg policies, 148
Old Labour (U.K.), 281
Oliker, S. J., 93
Omnibus Budget Reconciliation Act (OBRA), 91
    demonstration projects, 134–138, 161
Ontario, Canada, 5
    federal welfare expenditures in, 225
    and mutually referential policy development, 6
    "welfare problem" in, 236–237
    welfare reform in, 236–237
        and New Democrats, 237–240
    workfare in, 216–217, 347 (see also Ontario Works program)
    Common Sense Revolution, 5, 236, 240–247, 330
        and New Democrats, 238–240
        political dynamics of, 247–251
        workfare discourse, 251–253

Ontario Coalition Against Poverty, 242
Ontario Progressive Conservative
    Party, 236, 237, 240–241, 243,
    247–248, 249–250, 252–253
Ontario Training and Adjustment
    Board, 239–240, 258n.18
Ontario Works program, 217, 358
    and Bill 22, 252–253
    and childcare shortages, 251
    cost issues, 244
    delivery issues, 243
    impact on welfare caseload
        structure, 245–246
    and labor-market regulation, 244–
        245, 246
    number of workfare assignments in,
        248
    opposition to, 241–242, 248, 249–
        250, 251–252
    and political dynamics in Ontario,
        247–251
    in Toronto, 242, 243
    and welfare dismantling, 250–251
    and workfare discourse, 251–253
    work-first approach in, 243–244
"Opportunity society," 107–110
Oppositional politics, 20–21, 363, 364,
        365–366
    in Canada, 254–255
    toward Ontario Works program,
        241–242, 248, 249–250, 251–
        252

P

Pearson administration (Canada), 231
People and Skills in the New Global
        Economy, 239, 240
Permeable Fordism, 222–224
Personal Responsibility Act (PRA), 87,
        104
Personal Responsibility and Work
        Reconciliation Act (PRWORA),
        18, 71, 101, 116–117, 153,
        163, 195, 204, 364
    and caseload reductions, 344
    deterrent effect, 348
    and expenditure limits, 157–158
    and labor market problems, 185
    and Massachusetts welfare reform,
        131
    significance of, 360

Philp, M., 220
Philpott, John, 319
Piachaud, D., 325
Piore, M. M., 42
Piven, Frances Fox, 21, 31, 35, 39, 44,
        53–54, 58, 140, 182, 188–189,
        342
Polanyi, K., 44
Policy transfers, 4–5, 15–16, 360, 361–
        362 (See also United States,
        policy influence)
    incremental, 321
    selective, 320
    U.S. influence on British policies,
        318–324
Poor (See also Contingent workforce;
        Working poor)
    urbanization of, 70, 123n.11
    and workfare regulation, 120–121,
        364
Poor Laws (England), 59, 62
Portillo, Michael, 267, 282, 290, 302
Postindustrial dependency, 57
Poverty
    and Riverside program, 203–204
    urbanization of, 70, 123n.11
    and workfare, 120
PRA (See Personal Responsibility Act)
Primary employment, 42
Progressive Policy Institute, 204
Project Work program, 295–296, 297,
        298
PRWORA (See Personal Responsibility
        and Work Reconciliation Act)

Q

Quadagno, J., 36, 79
Quayle, Dan, 88
Quebec, Canada, 218, 235

R

Race, and welfare regimes, 47–48
Reagan, Ronald, 98
    anti-welfare initiatives, 53–54
    anti-welfare language of, 95–96,
        123–124n.12
    defederalization of welfare, 70
    and entitlements, 117
    "New Federalism," 70
    and welfare reform, 91–93, 120, 161

Reagan, Ronald (*cont.*)
workfare experiments, 68, 91–93
and workfare rhetoric, 84
Rector, R. E., 84–85, 91, 140
Regimes of regulation, 36–37
deepening of social and economic
inequalities, 48–49
race and gender realtions, 47–48
and relief cycles, 45–46
and shifting labor-market
boundaries, 50–52
and social regulation, 49–50
spatial structures and relations, 60–
61
workhouse regime, 61–64
workfare as, 54–55, 56–58
workhouse regime, 46–47
Regulation (*See* Labor regulation;
Regimes of regulation;
Regulatory crises; Social
regulation; Spaces of
regulation)
Regulatory crises
principle of less eligibility, 40–41
social distribution of waged work,
41–42
Relief cycles, 31–32
analytical challenges, 38–39
and regimes of regulation, 45–46
and spatial aspects of regulation,
58–59
and workfare, 37–38
Relief systems (*See also* Welfare;
Workfare; Workhouse system)
crisis and change in, 52–56
geographies of, 60–61
institutionalization in, 36
and labor-market regulation, 35–39,
39
labor market power relationships,
42–43
politics of, 40–45
negative symbolism, 52–53
rise of workfare, 54–56
uneven access to, 43
Rentoul, John, 302
Republican Party (U.S.)
Contract with America, 70–71, 87,
103–104, 110, 118
and federal welfare reform, 152–
153
Personal Responsibility Act, 104

politics of "disentitlementarianism,"
117–122
welfare reform and workfare
rhetoric of, 85–87, 103–111
Resocialization, under workfare, 57–58
Restart program, 266
*Restoring the Dream,* 107–108
Richards, J., 216
Riverside, California, 98
local conditions affecting GAIN
program, 199–201
low-skilled workforce in, 210n.62
Riverside GAIN program, 25, 317,
358
applying to cities, issues in, 197–
199, 201
case management in, 177, 207n.16
and cost cutting, 173–174, 186–188
destabilizing welfare, 181–182
dissemination of, 195–197
dress code, 176(figure)
dropouts, 184
impact on welfare reform, 201–206
influence and significance of, 190–
191
job-club/job-search function, 174–175
and job development, 177–181
job-search component, 179
and labor-market segmentation, 180
and labor regulation, 182–190
MDRC evaluation, 169, 170, 186,
190, 191, 195, 202–203
methodology, 173–176
overview of, 169–172
performance-contracts regime in,
177, 206n.8
and poverty, 203–204
reproduction of contingent work
and contingent workforce, 184–
186
sanctions for noncompliance, 175
shaping client behavior, 174–176,
183–184
success of, 180
role of local conditions in, 199–
201
and transferable generic practices,
191–195
unit costs, 173
and work ethics, 168, 170, 171
work-first philosophy, 169, 170–
173, 180–181, 182–190

"Riversidization," 195–197
Robinson, Ian, 336n.40
Rodgers, H. R., 360
Roosevelt, Franklin D., 64, 92
Rose, Nancy, 23
Rowell-Sirois Commission, 225
Royal Commission on Dominion-
    Provincial Relations (Canada),
    225
Rutherford, T., 228


S

Safire, William, 90, 117, 121–122
Schram, S. F., 89, 93–94
Schumpeterian workfare regime, 80
Secondary workers (*See also*
    Contingent workforce)
  social distribution of waged work,
    41–42
Shalala, Donna, 115
Sheldrick, R. M., 238, 240
Sheppard, Gillian, 298
Sinclair, Alan, 307
Single mothers
  paid-work model of relief, 49
  and welfare reform, 34
Smith, Andrew, 309, 328
Smith, John, 278
Snower, Dennis, 308–309
Social democratic welfare states
  welfare regime in, 75(table)
  workfare in, 74, 75–76(table), 76
Social exclusion, 311–312, 323
Social inequalities, and regimes of
    regulation, 48–49
Social regulation
  of labor markets, 34–35
  and welfare reform, 49–50
Social Security Act (U.K.), 266
Social Security Act (U.S.), 65, 98
Solow, R. M., 39–40
Spaces of regulation, 58–77
  crisis of welfare and workfare's
    emergence, 68–73
  decentralization of welfare, 70–73
  effects of relief arrangements in local
    labor markets, 59–60
  and Great Depression, 64
  local jurisdictional responsibility,
    59
  in relief cycles, 58–59

transition to workfare in advanced-
    welfare-state countries, 73–77
welfare dependency in ghettos, 68–
    69
in workhouse regime, 61–64
Standing, Guy, 84
State welfare reform, 112–114
  interplay between federal and state
    levels, 131–132, 133, 161, 162,
    163
  off-the-peg policies, 148
  overview of, 155(table)
  and Personal Responsibility and
    Work Reconciliation Act, 153
  state responsibility in, 165
  themes in, 143–144
  time-limit provisions in, 149, 152
  *See also* Massachusetts welfare
    reform
Stricter Benefit Regime (U.K.), 266–
    267, 269
Supported Work Demonstrations
    (SWD), 90–91, 122n.5
Swanson, Jean, 235
SWD (*See* Supported Work
    Demonstrations)
Swift, Jamie, 182


T

Talmadge, Herman, 68, 90
Talmadge Amendments, 90
TANF (*See* Temporary Assistance for
    Needy Families)
Taylor, Martin, 336n.40
Taylor-Gooby, P., 271
Temporary Assistance for Needy
    Families (TANF), 48, 157
Théret, B., 222
Third Way policy, 324–326
Thompson, L., 148
Thompson, Tommy, 6, 125–126n.29
Time-limits, 101, 102–103, 149, 152,
    359
Todd, Ron, 268
Torjman, Sherri, 214
Toronto, Canada, 216, 242, 243, 347,
    365
Townsend, Lawrence E., Jr., 170, 182–
    183, 187
Trades Union Congress (U.K.), 268,
    290, 310

Training and Enterprise Councils
(TECs), 268, 269, 296, 320
Training Commission (U.K.), 268
Transport and General Workers Union
(U.K.), 268, 334n.18
Trattner, W. I., 62
Tsubouchi, David, 241
"Two-track" welfare system, 47

**U**

Unemployment, in U.K., 264–265,
268
Unemployment benefits (U.K.)
benefit fraud and programs
addressing, 326–327, 334–
335n.21
conditions attached to, 294–
295(figure)
restructuring under the Jobseeker's
Allowance, 282–284
Stricter Benefit Regime, 266–267,
269
See also Benefit fraud; Labor-market
policy
Unemployment Insurance (Canada),
221, 226, 227, 230, 231
United Kingdom (See also British
welfare reform; British
workfare; Conservative Party;
Labour Party; New Deal
program)
Jobseeker's Allowance, 282–292
labor-market policy, 265–273
Third Way policy to workfare, 324–
326
unemployment in, 264–265, 283
and U.S. policy influence, 318–324
welfare policy modernization, 275–
282
United States
geographies of relief in, 60–61
New Deal, 53, 64–66
policy influence
on British welfare reform, 262–
263, 318–324
on British workfare, 4, 5, 263,
271, 318–324
on Canadian welfare reform, 214,
215
on Canadian workfarism, 5
"two-track" welfare system, 47

urbanization of poverty, 70
welfare regime in, 64–68
crisis in, 68–73
Urban areas
anti-workfare politics, 365–366
implementing workfare in, 197–199,
201, 347
Urbanization
and local labor markets, 63–64
of poverty, 70, 123n.11
Utah, 133

**V**

Vining, A., 216
Voinivich, George, 158

**W**

Wages, downward pressure and
workfare, 354, 357
Waiver system of welfare reform, 98,
99, 100–102, 113–116, 143,
153, 161–162
Walker, Robert, 262–263, 271, 273
Walters, William, 277–278, 309, 346,
348
Webb, S. and B., 44
Weekly, Ernest, 89
Weld, William, 130–131, 142–143,
145–149, 152, 156–157
"Weldfare," 131 (See also
Massachusetts welfare reform)
Welfare (See also Canadian work-
welfare regime; Welfare crises;
Welfare dependency; Welfare
reform; Welfare regimes;
Welfare state)
advocacy, and Massachusetts welfare
reform, 146, 147–148
America's New Deal, 64–66
centralization in, 64–68
contrasting with workfare, 13–
14(table)
and decentralization, 70–73, 163,
164, 165
destabilizing, in Riverside program,
181–182
etymology, 89
geographies of, 60–61
"Great Relief Hoax," 39
internal dynamics of regulation in, 79

and labor-market regulation, 39
Piven and Cloward's analysis of, 31–
    32
qualitative reorganization of
    workers, 52
and shifting labor-market
    boundaries, 50–52
and social regulation, 49
structured toward race and gender,
    47–48
transition to workfare, 14, 73–77
Welfare caseloads
and Ontario Works program, 245–
    246
and workfare deregistration effects,
    343–344, 345–347
Welfare crises
in Canada, 224–225
decentralization of welfare, 70–73
discourse on the meaning of welfare
    and workfare, 81–82
transition to workfare, 73–77
and welfare dependency, 68–69
and working poor, 69–70
Welfare dependency, 68–69
and British workfare/welfare reform,
    4, 329
spatial images of, 95–96, 112–113
and welfare reform rhetoric, 88, 119
"Welfare magnets," 102
Welfare population (See also
    Contingent workforce; Single
    mothers; Working poor)
and Riverside GAIN program, 174–
    176, 183–184
and sorting by workfare, 347
Welfare recipients, and workfare
    regulation, 120–121, 364
Welfare reform
and block-grants, 152, 153, 156,
    158, 163
and George Bush, 98–99, 124n.15
and Bill Clinton, 10, 97–98, 99–100,
    102–103, 110, 113–114, 115–117,
    131, 143, 149, 152–153, 165
and decentralization, 70–73, 163,
    164, 165
deepening of social and economic
    inequalities, 48–49
deregistration effect, 345–347
and "disentitlementarianism," 117–
    122

federal bills, 116–117, 126n.30,
    152–153, 154(table)
ideological presuppositions in, 52
impact of Riverside program on,
    201–206
implementing in cities, 347
interplay between federal and state
    levels in, 131–132, 133, 161,
    162, 163
intrinsic spatiality of, 132
and labor-market regulation, 34, 35–
    36, 70
at local level, themes in, 143–144
overview of key processes in, 161–
    163
politics of, 32–33
and presidential election of 2000,
    206
and Ronald Reagan, 91–93, 120, 161
and Republicans, 152–153
and social regulation, 49–50
spatial images of, 95–96, 112–113
    reconfigurations and qualitative
        restructuring, 163–165
structural contexts, 36, 37
supply-side flaws in, 158
waiver system, 98, 99, 100–102,
    113–116, 143, 153, 161–162
and workfare, 10, 32, 33–34, 95–96,
    112–113
and working poor, 69–70
See also British welfare reform;
    Canadian welfare reform;
    Massachusetts welfare reform;
    State welfare reform; Welfare
    reform rhetoric
Welfare Reform Group, 336n.40
Welfare reform rhetoric
anti-welfare language of Reagan, 95–
    96, 123–124n.12
of Bill Clinton, 87–88, 119, 124n.17,
    124–125n.18, 125n.19
language of, 83, 88
of Republican right, 86–87, 103–111
and welfare dependency, 88, 119
Welfare regimes
American, 64–68
    crisis in, 68–73
    race and gender in, 47–48
in social democratic welfare states,
    75(table)
"Welfare shopping," 102

"Workfare consensus," 88
"Workfare funnel," 348
Workfare regimes (*See also* Canadian work-welfare regime)
  gender dimension, 22–23
  of regulation, 54–55, 56–58
  Schumpeterian, 80
Workfare rhetoric
  and Bill Clinton, 87–88
  geopolitics of, 88–89
  and language of reform, 83–84, 121–122
  origins and development of, 84–85
  and politics of "disentitlementarianism," 118–122
  of Republican right, 85–87, 104–107
  in U.K., 273, 329
Workfare Watch, 241–242, 246, 375
Workfarist equilibrium, 350
Work-first workfare (*See also* Labor-force attachment; Riverside GAIN program)
  applying to cities, issues in, 197–199, 201
  dissemination of Riverside approach, 195–197
  labor-market effects, 353–358
  and labor regulation, 182–190, 352–358
  MDRC's promotion of, 194–195

  and Ontario Works program, 243–244
  supply- and demand-side constraints, 205
Workhouse system
  internal dynamics of regulation in, 79
  and labor-market regulation, 50
  principle of less eligibility, 40–41
  regulatory regime in, 46–47
  spatial structures and relations, 61–64
Work Incentive (WIN) program, 90–91, 133
Working class (*See also* Working poor)
  positive effects of welfare, 43
Working Families Tax Credit (U.K.), 324
Working poor (*See also* Contingent workforce; Welfare population)
  effects of workfare on, 69–70
  resocialization under workfare, 57–58
Works Progress Administration, 64
Workstart (U.K.), 293, 296

**Y**

Youth Opportunities Program (U.K.), 265
Youth Training Scheme (U.K.), 266–267, 302
Youth Training (U.K.), 268

# About the Author

Jamie Peck is Professor of Geography at the University of Wisconsin–Madison, having previously worked for more than ten years at the University of Manchester, England. Author of Work-Place: *The Social Regulation of Labor Markets* (Guilford Press, 1996), he has published widely on issues relating to economic restructuring, employment policy, urban political economy, and theories of regulation and governance. Since the early 1980s, he has also been involved in policy research and advocacy in the areas of job-training strategies, local economic development, and measures to combat unemployment. His future plans include work on contingent labor and the restructuring of low-wage labor markets in U.S. cities.